J.F.K.

THE MAN

AND

THE MYTH

THE MAN
J.F.K. AND
THE MYTH

Victor Lasky

THE MACMILLAN COMPANY, NEW YORK

To My Wife

PATRICIA PRATT LASKY

Eleventh Printing, 1963

The Macmillan Company, New York
Collier-Macmillan Canada Ltd., Toronto, Ontario

Library of Congress catalog card number: 63-16367
Printed in the United States of America

DESIGNED BY ANDOR BRAUN

Contents

"For the greatest enemy of the truth is very often not the lie—deliberate, contrived and dishonest—but the myth—persistent, persuasive and unrealistic."

—JOHN FITZGERALD KENNEDY

Yale University
June 11, 1962

President

1

There is nothing more difficult to carry out, nor more doubtful of success, nor more dangerous to handle, than to initiate a new order of things.

—Machiavelli

The Presidency needs someone creative and dynamic. The President alone must make the decisions. The President cannot share his power, cannot delegate. He alone is the chief of state.

—Senator John F. Kennedy
June 19, 1960

There's no reason why we should do everything.

—President John F. Kennedy
November 1961

On a warm April day, just three months after his inauguration as the 35th President of the United States, John F. Kennedy rose from his desk to greet a former Senate colleague who had been invited to drop by the White House for a chat.

"What a lousy, fouled-up job this has turned out to be," he said.

Senator Barry Goldwater could hardly believe his ears. Was this the same young man who had so passionately—and, at times, so ruthlessly—fought for the Presidency? Was this the same Kennedy who as a candidate for the highest elective office in the free world had confidently assured the nation that he knew all the answers?

"It wasn't the Kennedy I used to know," Goldwater said later.

That the President was deeply anguished over the turn of events in Cuba—probably the greatest United States disaster since Pearl Harbor—was apparent to other visitors. Richard Nixon, for example, expressed astonishment at the physical changes in the man who had narrowly bested him for the Presidency only a few months before.

"There was a lot more gray in Jack's hair," said Nixon.

But why was Kennedy so anguished? Was it about the 1,200 anti-Castro invaders who had met death or capture in the Bay of Pigs? Or was it about the enormous damage done to the carefully cultivated Kennedy image as a knowing, sure-footed young leader? Or was it a combination of both?

Until Cuba, it had seemed that Kennedy could do no wrong. He had moved into the White House with the same exuberant energy he had displayed during the campaign. His rhetoric was consistently peremptory: We Must, I Shall, We Shall. The image was one of hope, exhilaration, afflatus, and resolution.

"We can do anything," he seemed to be saying.

A few weeks before he took the Oath of Office Kennedy had talked with *Time-Life*'s John Steele in the drawing room of his Georgetown home. Supremely confident, the President-elect discussed the problems he expected to face as Chief Executive. A low wood fire sputtered in the grate. Mrs. Jacqueline Kennedy had just left for her first complete tour of the White House. Outside, Secret Service agents were patrolling the area.

"Sure, it's a big job," said Kennedy. "But I don't know anybody who can do it any better than I can. I'm going to be in it for four years."

Nor did the President-elect's father have any doubts about his son's capacity to handle the job. Joseph P. Kennedy told a newsman that the confident decisiveness and the wide factual knowledge which Jack had displayed during the televised debates were the main requisites of the Presidency.

"I've seen the President's job from the inside and I know what it requires," said the Ambassador. "You need a man in the White House with two things—wide factual knowledge and the ability to make decisions, and to make them stick."

The campaign charge that Kennedy was inexperienced continued to infuriate his father, who pointed out that his son, at the age of twenty-three, had written a highly regarded book on Great Britain's lack of preparedness for World War II. "The year before that, in 1939, when the war started, Jack was working for me in the Embassy in London. When the Germans sunk the British ship *Athenia,* which had a lot of Americans aboard, I sent Jack up to Glasgow to handle the whole job of investigating the sinking and taking care of all the American survivors. He was only a boy in college at the time. If that isn't experience, I don't know what is."

The euphoria of the New Frontier was infectious. The Washington press corps, by and large, was caught up in the excitement. One reason, of course, was Kennedy's own flair for press-agentry. Rarely had any politician devoted so much time to cultivating the friendship of newsmen. "That could be developed into a good Sunday backgrounder," Kennedy was overheard telling Pierre Salinger during the campaign. Not only was he adept in the use of journalistic argot—having, briefly, once been a newspaperman himself—but Kennedy has a dramatic flair which makes good copy. His absolute candor in off-the-record briefings won him many friends in the press corps. These otherwise sophisticated newsmen developed a sense of personal identification with Kennedy which came through in their campaign dispatches. Perhaps it was because Kennedy did them the great honor of reading what they had written. He was always quick to respond with plaudits and "well dones" to astonished newsmen.

Immediately after his election, Kennedy became the most accessible President since Theodore Roosevelt. "It is a long time since a President has enjoyed such a mixture of liking and respect from the majority of American reporters; Mr. Kennedy's recent activities—from playing golf with Mr. W. H. Lawrence of the *New York Times* to banging on Mr. Joe Alsop's door in the small hours—seem designed to enhance this feeling," reported the London *Economist*'s man in Washington. Dozens of writers were granted exclusive interviews. Publishers from all over the country were invited to lunch at the White House to hear about the problems he faced. Photographers and TV cameras penetrated the inner rooms of the White House. The payoff was tremendous. Rarely had any President obtained the kind of friendly—sometimes almost ecstatic—coverage as did Kennedy. And rarely had so many writers discovered, almost overnight, so many hitherto unknown facets of the new President's character.

Typical was the feature story of Kennedy's first sixteen days published in the *Washington Post*. "The fact is," wrote Chalmers Roberts on February 5, 1961, "that the President came to office well prepared, probably better prepared than any man in history, to run the United States Government. . . . The President quite obviously has immediately taken a firm hold on his office; he expects his word to be law. There is a firmness in his language which no one can mistake, yet it lacks both bombast and barb. . . . He is using every means of communicating with the public. . . . He has made the White House once again the center of national life. Yet, especially in the foreign policy field, it may take some crisis to focus the Nation's attention the way Mr. Kennedy wishes. . . ."

Kennedy got his crisis soon enough; but it was hardly the kind of crisis Kennedy wanted. If anything, it revived campaign allegations that Kennedy was immature and ill prepared to guide the ship of state through troubled international waters. And disillusionment unavoidably set in among the newsmen. Chalmers Roberts, who had expected so much from the New Frontier, wrote on November 12, 1961, that Kennedy's main problem "is that he has still to find that sense of direction, to embody it in a grand design and to use his undoubted eloquence to work for that design and to convince the American people and the rest of the free world that he is headed in the right direction."

The fact that Kennedy did not appear to know where he was going—or what he was doing—shocked many of his staunchest supporters. "The realization dawns in Washington that the President isn't always the cold-blooded operator he seemed to be while directing his Presidential campaign," wrote *Newsweek*'s Kenneth Crawford. "The discovery that he's fallible, after all, comes as quite a jolt to some of his admirers."

Why this should have surprised some of the nation's keenest newspaper observers was, in itself, surprising. But it told a great deal about the press corps which, in large measure, had helped propel a charming—but thoroughly unprepared—young man into the most important job in the world.

For one thing, many Washington correspondents are Democrats—a fact of life with which Republicans have had to contend ever since the days of the New Deal. Even so, most of them have tried to remain objective in their coverage of political events. A good example is James Reston of the *New York Times,* one of the better of the Washington pundits. Reston, a Liberal, was usually fair with the opposition. And he had never previously demonstrated any excessive regard for Kennedy. In fact, he appeared to be disturbed by some of the methods Kennedy employed in seeking power—particularly his Machiavellian use of the religious issue. Yet, in the closing weeks of the campaign, when a Nixon supporter complained about his coverage of the Vice President's activities, Reston replied: "I'm afraid we differ about Korea, Radford, Nixon, Knowland, Bridges, etc. You like their policy, and I don't."

Reston may not have liked their "policy," but at least it was a policy. But what was Kennedy's policy? What did he stand for? The truth was that he had never outlined any specific program, or even any very specific catalogue of faults. Kennedy had squeaked through to victory on the strength of personality and tactic. Newsmen had been fascinated by the determined manner with which Kennedy had seized the nomination as well as by the incredible power of the Kennedy bandwagon organization as it coursed across the land. As a result, many correspondents felt Kennedy could do almost anything. And Kennedy thought so too.

Rarely has there been a candidate in American history who said so much that meant so little. "I have—let me confess it—an overwhelming personal predilection for John F. Kennedy," Murray Kempton wrote in the *New York Post* during the campaign. "I have never known a politician who seemed to me quite so privately engaging. . . . He has character, firmness, intelligence and arrogance. . . ."

"Kennedy says he will be a stronger President than Nixon," the *Post* columnist continued. "So far Kennedy has said nothing which indicates he would apply his strength to any relevant purpose. During the debate he was asked about the internal menace of Communism and he answered so firmly that you could almost see the poor old ladies being herded on the boats. I suppose such ceremonies are only possible with a strong President, and that is one reason to doubt the value of a strong President."

Westbrook Pegler, who had known and for a time admired Kennedy even before Kempton had heard of him, had also viewed the televised debate but had concluded that Kennedy was "fronting" for Communist-appeasing elements. And "Peg" had another beef: "Kennedy, in the supercilious arrogance which Harvard inculcates in lace-curtain Irish, doggedly mispronounced ordinary words. . . . This was the true Rooseveltian contempt for the common man. He seems afraid to be taken for a valid American."

On one thing Pegler and Kempton—and, for that matter, Dwight Eisenhower—had agreed. They agreed that John F. Kennedy was "arrogant."

It was an arrogance that somehow appealed to certain intellectuals.

"Well, there's your first hipster," someone told Norman Mailer at the Los Angeles Convention. "Sergius O'Shaughnessy born rich."

Having observed Kennedy at a press conference, Mailer wrote in *Esquire* that "there was an elusive detachment to everything he did. One did not have the feeling of a man present in the room with all his weight and all his mind."

"Kennedy had a dozen faces," Mailer continued. "Although they were not at all similar as people, the quality was reminiscent of someone like Brando whose expression rarely changes, but whose appearance seems to shift from one person into another as the minutes go by, and one bothers with this comparison because, like Brando, Kennedy's most characteristic quality is the remote and private air of a man who has traversed some lonely terrain of experience, of loss and gain, of nearness to death, which leaves him isolated from the mass of others."

To the American people, however, Kennedy came through as a somewhat paradoxical figure who radiated extreme confidence while talking of grave troubles ahead. To a nation winding up eight fairly comfortable years under a most popular President, Kennedy kept dinning home a message of unease, of things left undone. To a nation powerful enough to flex its muscles from Lebanon to the Formosa Straits, to fly U-2 spy planes across the Soviet land for four years, Kennedy talked of declining military power and prestige. And to a people sharing the highest level of prosperity in history, Kennedy campaigned with Depression-like fervor for new and bigger welfare programs.

His single theme, single-mindedly propelled with little subtlety of approach, was: Elect me and I will start the United States moving again. But he was remarkably vague. On foreign policy, he called for new diplomatic "initiatives," "imagination," and "vigor"—whatever that meant. He did specifically call for disengagement from Quemoy-Matsu and for aiding the Cuban rebels, which gave the impression of being both soft and hard toward Communism—the double image. His welfare programs were not new—they called only for more spending. Though aimed at satisfying human needs, they carried the threat of unbalanced budgets and more inflation. True, he had suggested that the extra burdens were to be carried by expanded national growth, but just how he intended to accomplish this he never quite made clear. His solution to the multibillion-dollar farm scandal—90 per cent price supports—was so complex that even Kennedy's Harvard advisers couldn't understand it.

Kennedy managed to etch a picture of himself as a driving personality, endowed with the same *charisma* that his predecessor had in abundance. And, like Eisenhower, Kennedy projects a kind of sincerity and conviction even while talking of ordinary things in an ordinary way.

"In an age where thought is painful and decision-making unthinkable," commented *National Review,* "the polling booth becomes a registrar of popularity. We have retreated back to our school days, and Jack Armstrong Kennedy will chair the dance committee."

After the campaign, Joseph P. Kennedy said he was at a loss to explain his son's voting appeal. People just seem to like Jack, Joe said. "He'll put on a pair of old dungarees and go out and talk to the gardener or anybody. . . . He looks just like some hayseed from Kansas."

The Ambassador obviously did not mean to offend the Sunflower State. "Nevertheless," the *El Dorado* (Kansas) *Times* complained, "it indicates clearly the superior feeling an ultra-rich man from Massachusetts has about this prairie domain in the center of the country. In additional degree, it bespoke the snobbish attitude embodied by the phrase, the 'unconscious arrogance of conscious wealth.' "

There is about Kennedy, too, the appeal of Hollywood. But it isn't just smile and profile. For there is also the aura of royalty—the ineffable quality of *noblesse*—about Kennedy. All this, and American, too. Wherever he goes, they ask for his autograph more than his credo. Who could ever forget the "jumpers," those shoals of ecstatic young ladies—some not so young—whose leaping and screaming delighted reporters during the campaign? "I *see* him, I *see* him," excited girls had screamed everywhere. "Oh," their friends invariably responded, "I could die!" (Kennedy hired a crowd psychologist to analyze what such behavior meant in political terms.)

The Presidency can bequeath a man such an aura, but Kennedy already had it; and, even more than he, his wife had it.

"There is something very eighteenth century about this young man," commented Prime Minister Macmillan after his second meeting with President Kennedy in the spring of 1961. Macmillan was commenting on the ease with which Kennedy was able to switch, at the end of the day, from the grave affairs of State to the gay sociability of a dinner party. "He is always on his toes during our discussions," said Macmillan. "But in the evening there will be music and wine and pretty women."

A year later, James Reston was writing about how Kennedy was developing a distinctive "American style" in diplomacy. Following another visit by Macmillan to the United States, Reston wrote: "In the past the visit of a British Prime Minister to Washington was usually a solemn procession, full of hands-across-the-sea clichés, formal meetings and dinners, and vapid communiqués. Harold Macmillan's visit here this time, in contrast, was like a house party and at times almost like a spree."

Early in the Kennedy reign, a distinguished Latin American official, attending a diplomatic function, found himself momentarily isolated in a corner of the room with the President. He seized the opportunity to alert Kennedy to the desperate political situation in his homeland, where Communist agitators were successfully whipping up pro-Castro movements. After a minute, President Kennedy blandly observed, "I like that dress your wife is wearing."

History may well record that the most serious thing that could be said about Kennedy is that he is the product of an age in which men felt they could achieve special distinction by the techniques of super-press-agentry rather than by the espousal of serious ideas. What fascinated him, he once said, were "not so much the ideas of politics [but] the mechanics of the whole process." And Kennedy's politics, essentially, are to be for Kennedy with complete faith that Kennedy will be good for whatever cause he chooses to lead.

"The political world is stimulating," he told a *Time* man shortly before his nomination. "It's the most interesting thing you can do. It beats following the dollar. It allows the full use of your powers. First, there is the great chess game—the battle, the competition. There's the strategy and which piece you move, and all that. And then in government you can do something about what you think."

But what exactly did Kennedy think? When he talked to the *Time* man he was preparing to endorse without reservation the most far-out, radical platform ever devised by a major political party—a platform that veteran Socialist Norman Thomas considered so "utopian" as to be impractical. But when the last hurrah was sounded, Kennedy told his defeated rival that he didn't believe in all that left-wing nonsense. He had endorsed the platform in order to get the nomination.

Kennedy's election was one of the weirdest in American history. For with a preponderant Democratic registration and the built-in advantages of the South and the Catholic vote, Kennedy triumphed by only a photo-finish. London's *Economist* was most unhappy about the "exquisite narrowness" of Kennedy's victory because it meant that the American people "had not rallied wholeheartedly and convincingly to his appeal for new exertions" in the challenging days ahead. And "the composition of Mr. Kennedy's majority is the second cause for disappointment. He has won . . . not on the basis of broadly distributed support, but mainly as the result of an uncomfortable alliance between a few big cities in the Northeast and the stubbornly and unexpectedly loyal South."

In other words, Kennedy's victory could be credited to such remarkable bedfellows as John McClellan and Walter Reuther, and Herman Talmadge cheek-by-jowl with Martin Luther King. The Voice of the People, calling for John F. Kennedy, bore in part a Southern accent. And he would not be allowed to forget it.

Despite the narrowness of the victory Walter Lippmann, with typical perspicacity, said it provided a "clear mandate" for enactment of Kennedy's hundreds of campaign promises. Lippmann said that "a narrow win by Nixon would have inaugurated an era of severe political, economic and sectarian bitterness." However, "Kennedy's win promises to bring on a period of effective government," what with the new Administration forming "effective majorities over and above the Democratic reactionaries and obstructionists."

" 'Clear mandate,' forsooth," commented Scripps-Howard columnist Richard Starnes. "It all reminds me of a line from a song in 'Pal Joey,' which goes 'Walter Lippmann wasn't being *brill-i-ant* today,' and it's a little sad when you think about it."

The *Wall Street Journal* claimed that "the voters made one thing quite clear in this election. They have given a mandate to nobody."

And so, for weeks, the commentators and editorialists argued with each other on just what the election signified. Kennedy read the commentaries, as he does all his press notices, and still couldn't make up his mind. He besought the advice of Arthur Schlesinger Jr. What Schlesinger advised Kennedy was never disclosed. But it could perhaps be deduced from what the bow-tied historian subsequently said on CBS–TV's "Face the Nation." Asked whether Kennedy's narrow margin of victory might not force the new President to follow a more conservative course, Schlesinger replied:

"It need not do so. I think to a degree the Presidency generates its own mandates. One can recall a number of Presidents who came in as minority Presidents—Woodrow Wilson was one, Abraham Lincoln was another, James K. Polk another—who nonetheless were not deterred from carrying out quite bold and clear-cut policies. My guess is that John Kennedy will be in this tradition."

It was a bad guess.

On the same program, Schlesinger also spoke of the "instinct for the future" which distinguished great Presidents. It was, said he, "some vision, some image in their minds of what the United States ought to be like, of the direction the world is moving, the direction they want the United States to move. . . ." And he left no doubt that he believed John F. Kennedy possessed the necessary instinct, vision, and image.

There could be no doubt that Kennedy reciprocated the admiration which Schlesinger had frequently voiced for him. The question arose as to what Schlesinger could do on the New Frontier. He did not want an ambassadorship. He wanted to be close to "the center of things." Nor was he keen on an assistant secretaryship of state for cultural affairs. He had no desire to become a "cultural bureaucrat," he said.

Finally, Bobby Kennedy—with whom Schlesinger had established extraordinary rapport—came up with a simply "t'riffic" suggestion to which Arthur reacted favorably. He was to be a Special Assistant to the President, handling big problems. What big problems? Any that cropped up—foreign or domestic. Though Schlesinger accepted the job early in January, the President-elect held up the announcement until Chester Bowles was confirmed as Under Secretary of State. Kennedy apparently wanted to forestall any right-wing outcry that he was loading the New Frontier with ADA-niks.

The appointment predictably drew the fire of the *New York Daily News:* "Junior is an egghead to end all eggheads, so we shudder to think of the tripe he may sneak into Kennedy's speeches unless the President watches him like a hawk. On the other hand, Junior is a cartoonist's dream and a natural figure of fun for columnists and editorial writers. For that reason, we're glad he landed this job; and we can hardly wait, folks, we can hardly wait. . . ."

The *News* didn't have to wait long. Schlesinger was sworn in on January 30, and that night he found himself in hot water. What happened was that, in debating William F. Buckley Jr. on "Freedom and the Welfare State," he was quoted in the press as having said that the "best defense" against Communism was an American welfare state. This instantly aroused the fallen-but-not-quite-vanquished coalition of Republicans and Southern Democrats to a fury that shook the Kennedy honeymoon cottage at 1600 Pennsylvania Avenue.

The *New York Daily News,* needless to say, went to town in an editorial titled: SCHLESINGER GOOFS. The irreverent organ of New York's masses claimed that "welfare statism" had begun in Germany under Bismarck and "in the fullness of time gave way to the totalitarianism of Adolf Hitler."

Reeling from the assaults, Schlesinger addressed a letter to Senator Mike Mansfield (perhaps because he didn't want to reply directly to Dixiecrat Strom Thurmond who had attacked him) in which he defended his controversial assertion. He defined a welfare state simply as one that assures all its citizens the minimum necessities of life. And he quoted statements by Winston Churchill and the late Robert A. Taft, which, Schlesinger said, set forth the same goals.

This, of course, was "quotemanship," an ancient sport along the New Frontier—the technique of quoting something someone in the opposition was supposed to have said in order to bolster your own argument. But, as Raymond Moley noted, the Churchill and Taft quotations were fragments—hardly "to be considered the life philosophy of either man."

That was the last to be seen of Schlesinger—publicly, that is—for some months. He next turned up as a participant in the extraordinary events leading to the Bay of Pigs. If the results had not been so tragic, the spectacle of Arthur Schlesinger Jr. garbed in cloak and dagger would truly have been funny. But such is life along the New Frontier.

The night after the election President-elect and Mrs. Kennedy dined with three close friends at Hyannis Port. They were artist William Walton, and Mr. and Mrs. Benjamin Bradlee of *Newsweek*. And they discussed politics and personalities with the new President. In the happy, relaxed conversation, one of the men said, "There is just one thing I want you to do—fire J. Edgar Hoover!"

"No," the second said, "much more important than that, get Allen Dulles out of the CIA *immediately.*" The night after the U-2 episode, he said, he had heard Dulles declare at a dinner party that the flight was "a triumph of American foreign policy." "Dulles," Kennedy's guest warned, "would be trying to carry on his dead brother's policies in your Administration."[1]

The next day, at a press conference, the President-elect announced that as his first appointive acts he had requested the Directors of the Federal Bureau of Investigation and the Central Intelligence Agency to remain on the job.

The announcement was not exactly greeted with joy by Kennedy's ultra-Liberal supporters, but the President-elect—still stunned by the closeness of his victory—was most anxious to win national acceptance of his leadership. And regardless of what the *New York Post* might think, J. Edgar Hoover was admired by most Americans, regardless of party. Allen Dulles was something else again.

In the days that followed until the Inauguration, Kennedy tried to fill 80 top echelon, policy-making posts, 40 other secondary posts involving policy decisions, and over 4,000 other important jobs. By the time Jack took the oath of office, only 84 appointments—including the 80 top jobs—had been filled. So many Harvard faculty members were called to serve that James Reston wrote: "There's nothing left at Harvard except Radcliffe."

But there was a danger in raiding the universities for men to staff the various Government agencies. "The great majority of them are new to power," Richard Rovere pointed out in the *New Yorker*, "and their education has included little in the way of training in the uses of power. It is a most radical experiment—a gamble that has never been tried even in the European democracies, which over the years have made far greater use of the intellectuals than we have."

"To be sure," commented Max Ascoli in the *Reporter*, "a few of the members of Mr. Kennedy's official family have proved to be successful coiners of slogans. . . . The wide circulation of such phrases as 'take-off stage of economic development' or 'affluent society' simply proves that Madison Avenue has no corner on the production and merchandising of clichés."

Kennedy's appointments generally were well received. There was, as expected, a predominant representation of Liberal ideologues (Bowles, Ken-

---

[1] The Hyannis Port episode, sans names of Kennedy's guests, is described in Helen Fuller's *Year of Trial: Kennedy's Crucial Decisions* (New York, Harcourt Brace & World, 1962).

nan, Stevenson, Galbraith, Schlesinger, and Murrow) with a judicious sprin-
kling of capable bureaucratic technicians from the foundations, educational
and managerial strata (Rusk, Bundy, Dillon, and McNamara). Most of the
appointees were a disciplined lot with a clear insight into who was boss. For
John F. Kennedy has no patience with mavericks, a fact which Chester
Bowles was soon to discover. What the President sought in an associate were
the self-effacing qualities possessed by Dean Rusk. (The Secretary of State
was to become known as the Hugh Downs of the Kennedy Administration.)

One potential maverick, John Kenneth Galbraith, 'was exiled to New
Delhi. Galbraith, who had hoped to remold America into a society more
affluently to his liking, found himself, as United States Ambassador to India,
giving unwanted advice to Nehru and Company on how they should run
their country. Before too long Pandit Nehru had a belly full of Galbraithisms
and Galbraith of Nehruisms, and in 1963 Professor Galbraith was on his way
back to Harvard.

But, at the beginning, all was well in the new administration. Walter
Lippmann, from his oracular heights, pronounced Kennedy's appointments—
with à few exceptions—as giving "solid grounds for confidence." And Lippmann said, "It is not an Administration led by corporation executives." Happy,
happy day. As his first piece of advice to Kennedy, Lippmann suggested putting the military men, who went around making anti-Communist speeches, in
their places. "Once the civilian appointees have the self-confidence to exercise
civilian supremacy," wrote Lippmann, "they can and should impose a strict
civilian discipline on the statements and speeches issued by the chiefs of staff
and by local commanders throughout the world."

By far the most controversial appointment was the Attorney General
designate, the President-elect's thirty-five-year-old brother Bobby, who had
managed his election campaign. Even Kennedy supporters said (though not
loudly) that Bobby was too young, too inexperienced (he had never tried a
case in court), and too partisan. About which the President-elect quipped,
"I can't see that it's wrong to give him a little legal experience before he goes
out to practice law."

Inauguration week was one that Washington will not soon forget. It set
the tone of the incoming New Frontier. It had everything—even Frank Sinatra. Its pitch was global, shunning controversial domestic gags about pork
chops in West Virginia and schools in Segregalia. It soberly sounded a double
theme—peace and sacrifice. However, after a display of top hats and Cad-
illacs, bouffant hairdos and beaded gowns, mink and music, the celebrants
relaxed, each feeling that peace was for him and sacrifice was for the other guy.

"The inauguration of President Kennedy proclaims a new era for Washington, the nation and the world," proclaimed Cholly Knickerbocker in his
Smart Set column.[2] "But his ascension to power is more than just a change-

2 Cholly Knickerbocker is actually Igor Cassini, whose brother, Oleg, is dress designer to the First Lady.

over of administration and a party victory; it is the proclamation of a new American dynasty—the Kennedys."

And overnight, the nation's capital felt the impact. The Kennedys, all of them, had taken over. Including in-laws, they numbered over a hundred. The only Kennedy kin missing were the President-elect's aged grandmother, widow of the fabled Honey Fitz, who was not well enough to make the trip, and Kennedy's two young children. At the various parties there were almost as many Kennedys as there were other guests.

Then there were Kennedy's friends—"all those wondrously wealthy people," as the *New York Mirror*'s Suzy described them, "riding around in limousines, wearing glittering jewels and ball gowns and, well, just looking rich. That's why this Inauguration and the festivities that go along with it have taken on the glamor, the opulence, the razzle-dazzle quality that only money —a lot of money—can give."

Fulton Lewis Jr., however, "found the tone and style of the Kennedy inauguration disturbing in some striking aspects. For one thing, there was an unmistakable aura of pseudo-monarchial dynasty. The invitation to Robert Frost for a special Inaugural poem somehow smacked of a Poet Laureate in the British royal tradition. This mood was sustained by President Kennedy's mother wearing the precise gown in which she was presented at the British Court in 1938."

The other side of the Inaugural picture was bizarre and in sharp contrast. According to Fulton Lewis, there was "something deeply shocking in the spectacle of Frank Sinatra and his Rat Pack running the show on the entertainment end. Sinatra's associations and connections are scarcely in accord with the historic dignity of the occasion." Lewis said that "Kennedy's bounding boyishly in the small hours up the steps to a private party in Georgetown" was unseemly. "Now that he holds the nation's highest office, Kennedy's playboy proclivities afford a painful spectacle." (On Inauguration night, he dropped Jackie at the White House and went on to a late party at the home of Joseph Alsop.)

Even Inez Robb, a confirmed Democrat, couldn't take the Inaugural poetry about "Ladybird the Angel" and "Jackie, you are so sweet, we will worship at your feet." And nobody in authority would tell inquisitive newsmen the cost of those striking Oleg Cassini creations worn by Mrs. Kennedy, perhaps because public disclosure might have depressed all those people in all those depressed areas.

For a time, it looked as if Frank Sinatra would get almost as much publicity from the Inauguration as John F. Kennedy. The Rat Pack, of which he was The Leader, had a brocade-vested interest in the election because of Peter Lawford's marriage to Kennedy's sister Pat. Clansman Dean Martin put out the story that President-elect Kennedy was going to appoint him "Secretary of Liquor."

Sammy Davis Jr., a convert to Judaism, had other ambitions. "Sinatra will be Ambassador to Italy," he said. "I'm hoping for Jerusalem, but I'll be lucky if I get Kenya."

The Rat Pack's antics were not approved by all Hollywoodians. Dore Schary, a loyal Democrat, said, "I don't know who can stave off this rush of professional showmen into politics, but somebody had better do it right away." Others agreed with Republican Dick Powell, "I think these people hurt Kennedy by their cheap publicity." And Mercedes McCambridge, a Stevensonian who had labored dutifully for Kennedy during the campaign, sounded off bitterly, "I'm tired of democracy. We should have a monarchy, with Tuesday Weld as one of the princesses and a nice couple from Armpit, Nevada, to reign. I have a *Citizen Kane* feeling about Daddy Kennedy sitting out here directing the show behind the scenes from Marion Davies' house."

Equally displeased was Lady Lawford, Peter's mother, who had been earning a living doing bit-parts in movies and television.

"But now that Peter has joined the royal family," she complained, "they don't want me to act."

Lady Lawford, the *New York Times* reported, denied that she had been making disparaging remarks about President-elect Kennedy. "He is one of the family," she observed. "Of course, it is true I would have voted for Nixon if I could have voted. I think Nixon is so much more mature, you know."

Lady Lawford had not seen Peter or Pat, whom she spoke of as "Miss Kennedy," for nearly a year. "We would have liked Peter to pick a bride from court circles," she complained. She charged that the Rat Pack (Petah included) had tried to get her out of the country during the campaign by offering her an expense-paid tour abroad.

"They're very age-conscious, those Kennedys," she explained. "They don't want me around because I don't look enough like Whistler's mother."

Only hours after he arrived in Washington to stage a Hollywood-style Gala for the Inaugural—which, he predicted, would make a mint—Frank Sinatra was warring with newsmen. For one thing, questions had been raised as to why Sammy Davis Jr. had been omitted from the star-studded bill—an omission which, according to Dorothy Kilgallen, was "generally regarded as a gesture of appeasement to the segregationists." However, Sinatra made a point of escorting Mrs. Nat King Cole to a bash tendered by the Stephen Smiths (she's Jack's sister, Jean), and when a correspondent asked the name of his date, Frankie shot back, "Where you from? Bulgaria?"

Every pet and pout of The Leader was flashed to a waiting world. For example, he got sore when fashion designer Don Loper, of Hollywood, announced that Sinatra had called on him to design eight outfits to wear during the Washington ceremonies. The wardrobe included an Inverness cape, black patent leather pumps, silk top hat, and an ebony walking stick with a silver crook. "Frank will be the most elegantly dressed man in Washington," Loper predicted. "I've always designed feminine attire, but Frank especially requested I outfit him for the Inauguration."

"All the materials for Frank's wardrobe were brought over here from London's famous Savile Row," Loper continued. "Everything I've made for Frank is terribly small, elegantly tailored and terribly chic. To me he is one of the most elegant men in the world."

The most elegant man blew a gasket when he read Loper's comments in the press. Comedian Joe E. Lewis had wired him: "May I have the first dance?" Frankie doesn't like to be laughed at. And he stamped his foot and announced he wouldn't wear a stitch of Loper's clothes. An associate in the Rat Pack described Sinatra as "mad, mad, mad." The *Chicago Tribune* noted: "With that refinement of sentiment for which he is renowned, Mr. Sinatra is said to have felt that this represented an attempt to capitalize on his friendship with what he calls 'the family,' meaning the Clan Kennedy. A more reasonable interpretation, perhaps, is that the pique arises because Mr. Loper disclosed that he had made two of everything 'in case Frankie spills anything on himself.' The very hint that The Leader would be capable of ladling soup into the lap and dripping the bubbly down the shirtfront is indelicate, offensive, and probably unconstitutional under the charter of 'the clan.' "

Somehow, Sinatra got over his pout and got on with his show. Wearing Loper's exquisite clothes, Sinatra exclaimed to show business historian Earl Wilson, "I am a thing of beauty."

And when the pre-Inaugural show was over, Sinatra heard some unusual praise from the President-elect. ". . . I'm proud to be a Democrat, because since the time of Thomas Jefferson, the Democratic Party has been identified with the pursuit of excellence," said Kennedy. "And we saw excellence tonight. The happy relationship between the arts and politics which has characterized our long history I think reached culmination tonight. I know we're all indebted to a great friend, Frank Sinatra. Long before he could sing, he used to poll a Democratic precinct back in New Jersey. That precinct has grown to cover a country. . . ."

Sinatra beamed. "I only wish my kids could have heard it," he said.

Sinatra notwithstanding, the most ogled celebrity that incredible week was, of course, the President-elect. And he carried his new role off magnificently. His was "more a triumph of manner," wrote the normally anti-monarchist Murray Kempton. "He has managed, by mere gesture, to make us all feel entitled to consider ourselves Americans again. Or better, subjects of the Crown. In the same way, I have known Englishmen who felt alienated from England, but who carried a residual affection for the Royal Family."

It all depends on where you sit. For example, the social arbiter of Washington, Mrs. Carolyn Hagner Shaw, would probably not have agreed with Kempton. Mrs. Shaw, whose "The Social List of Washington, D.C.," the so-called "Green Book," remains a boon to harassed hostesses, had this to say to *Newsweek:*

"Kennedy is one of the rudest, most thoughtless men I've ever seen. I think it's deplorable. At the Inauguration he was crawling over seats to see friends, leaving Jackie to sit by herself. He is always walking 10 feet or so ahead of his wife. Truman and Eisenhower never did that.

"And Kennedy and the movie actors—this, that, and the other thing." Mrs. Shaw, pausing a moment, drew a gentle hand over her brow. "Frank Sinatra," she said, finally. It was hard for her to pronounce the name.

"As for the five Inaugural balls," Marya Mannes wrote in the *Reporter,* "you in your living rooms were far better off than I with my tickets, for incredible traffic snarls kept me from reaching the Armory, and one late look at the Statler ball aroused such undemocratic emotions that I took my leave. From what my many informants told me, it seemed clear that style, elegance, and dignity were notably lacking in all these events, that there was little dancing anywhere, and that at the Armory the packed thousands merely stood and stared at the President and his wife like mesmerized cattle. . . .

"But I suspect that the real Democratic jubilees took place in private houses. The theme of one amiable rout, a costume party on the Potomac above Chain Bridge, was New Frontiers," and guests "adorned themselves with signs, gags and symbols, or simply wore rugged pioneer clothes highly suitable to the outside weather. One couple, chained together, were identified as Old Age Care and Social Security." Senator Albert Gore of Tennessee came as a "Texas egghead," in a ten-gallon hat, cowboy boots, and the academic hood of a university degree around his neck. "From Austin to Boston," he explained, echoing Lyndon Johnson's favorite campaign line. Senator and Mrs. Eugene McCarthy represented our frontier states—the Senator in an Alaskan fur jacket; his wife in a muumuu with leis of Hawaiian orchids around her neck.

Arthur Schlesinger Jr. came dressed as himself. Averell Harriman wore a velvet vestment with knee breeches. Kennedy's choice for Ambassador to India, John Kenneth Galbraith, was draped in kilts. Harris Wofford was in a Confederate uniform representing civil rights, which was his area during the campaign. ABC commentator Ed Morgan arrived as "depressed areas," with a flat tire over his shoulder. Drew Pearson was dressed like the proverbial Irishman, entirely in green from high hat on down; while Mrs. Pearson, with a gold drain on her head and gold coins in her purse, represented gold depletion. Senator "Scoop" Jackson wore an Uncle Sam cap. Douglass Cater, of the *Reporter,* in a Russian shirt and fur hat, wore a sign on his back: "Never fear to negotiate." His wife was entirely hidden under an Arab-style garb, veil and all, with a sign pinned on her back reading, "Uncommitted."

"There was real gaiety here," wrote Miss Mannes, "a sense of release after protracted effort, a feeling that this might constitute the last real foolish fun for quite a while." At least until the summer when Teddy Kennedy, fully dressed, began jumping into swimming pools.

Probably the most charming memoir of that incredible week was penned for the *Nation* by Lincoln Kirstein, general director of the New York City

Ballet. It seems that on Monday, January 16, 1961, Kirstein was awakened at dawn to receive the following telegram:

DURING OUR FORTHCOMING ADMINISTRATION WE HOPE TO EFFECT A PRODUCTIVE RELATIONSHIP WITH OUR WRITERS, ARTISTS, COMPOSERS, PHILOSOPHERS, SCIENTISTS AND HEADS OF CULTURAL INSTITUTIONS. AS A BEGINNING, IN RECOGNITION OF THEIR IMPORTANCE, MAY WE EXTEND YOU OUR MOST CORDIAL INVITATION TO ATTEND THE INAUGURATION CEREMONIES IN WASHINGTON ON JANUARY 19 AND 20. RESERVATIONS FOR INAUGURAL CONCERT, PARADE, BALL ARE HELD FOR YOU. ROOM ACCOMMODATIONS AND HOSPITALITY WILL BE ARRANGED FOR YOU BY A SPECIAL SUBCOMMITTEE. RSVP WHICH EVENTS DESIRED AND WHAT ACCOMMODATIONS NEEDED BY TELEGRAPHING K. HALLE, 3001 DENT PLACE, N.W., WASHINGTON.

SINCERELY

PRESIDENT-ELECT AND MRS. KENNEDY

Among the 155 other artists, musicians, writers, scientists, educators, and theologians to whom the command had been delivered were Igor Stravinsky, Arthur Miller, Edith Hamilton, Roger Sessions, Linus Pauling, Samuel Barber, Mark Rothko, Franz Kline, Tennessee Williams, Paul Tillich, Reinhold Niebuhr, John Steinbeck, and W. H. Auden.[3]

Kirstein, who knew that snow had been promised by the *Farmer's Almanac* and that there was a possibility of a railroad strike, thought it a most unpromising adventure, but W. H. Auden insisted that they go since, he observed, "this was not an invitation but a command."

The "command" had been ordered, according to the *Washington Post,* "to offset, cynics suspected, the sour publicity emanating from Sinatra's Rat Pack" carryings-on.

One of the more grateful recipients of the command—snow or no snow —was Arthur Miller, who saw in the invitation to intellectuals a rosy harbinger of things to come. Before a Book and Author luncheon, the playwright said, "It seems we will now be looking at, or at least glancing towards, our poets, writers, men-of-the-mind for more than a laugh." Actually, it appears, Miller was not on the list for the original invitation. Presumably he was kept off by some Red-baiting witch hunter whose kind could still be found at the Democratic National Committee. An invitation was finally wangled for Miller through the intervention of photographer Henri Cartier-Bresson.

Kirstein's first discovery was that the beginning of what had been an-

---

[3] Those who didn't show included William Faulkner, Ernest Hemingway, and Thornton Wilder. Shortly before his death, Faulkner was invited to a White House soiree. "Why should I go?" responded Faulkner. "I don't know any of those people."

nounced as the New Administration's "productive relations with our artists" involved them in purchasing $50 Inaugural Concert seats. John Hersey looked a bit dashed when he picked up the tickets, but fortunately he had the fifty bucks on him.

Another Kirstein discovery was that President-elect Kennedy was a good friend of William Walton. When he and Auden arrived in Washington, they headed for Georgetown, but "the street where we were going was cut off by television trucks and cops." It seems "Mr. Kennedy was visiting a friend, Mr. William Walton, a young painter. . . ." And later, at the Inaugural Concert, Walton showed up with the Kennedys—Mrs. Kennedy "appearing a princess in a magnificent white dress (Oleg Cassini) with long sleeves."

"And *who* is William Walton?" asked W. H. Auden during the intermission. "Any relation to Willie?" Sir William (Willie) Walton had written the march *Crown Imperial* for the coronation of Elizabeth II. Kirstein explained there was no relation; that Walton, a young painter, had "some years earlier quit as a foreign correspondent for *Time* from chagrin at the editing of his copy."

But that wasn't the whole story. *Time*'s foreign editor at the time of the incident had been Whittaker Chambers. As Chambers told the story in his monumental book *Witness,* here is what happened: "Among *Time*'s war correspondents was a young man named William Walton, who was once pointed out to me, but whom I do not recall ever having met. I knew only that he was personable and well thought of. Everyone spoke highly of his courage in parachuting into Normandy on or around D-Day.

"After the collapse of Germany, Walton, for some reason, got to Prague. From there, he filed a ten- or twelve-page cable describing how, under Soviet occupation, 'a middle-class revolution' or a 'white-collar revolution' had taken place in Czechoslovakia.

"I read the long cable over several times with astonishment. I had no first-hand facts about the situation in Prague. But I knew something about how Communists could be expected to mask their control there. Above all, I knew that, in a country as intensely middle class as Czechoslovakia, a 'middle-class revolution' is a contradiction in terms. Whatever Walton thought that he had seen, it could not be a 'middle-class revolution.' I concluded (quite correctly, we now know) that Walton's 'middle-class revolution' meant that the Communists had moved into controlling positions in the Czech Government. If I ran the cable, as I was urged to do, a million Americans would gain a completely mistaken notion of the balance of political forces in the country of which Bismarck had said: 'Who controls Bohemia controls Europe.' I refused to run the cable or any part of it.

"The ensuing storm swept from the editorial to the executive floors of *Time*. Clearly, I was behaving like a despot. Part of an editor's business, I pointed out, is to be a brute. But it was felt that I was questioning the integrity of a correspondent.

"I was not questioning Walton's integrity at all, of course. I was questioning the political discernment of a war correspondent. I thought that Walton was an inexperienced young American who had been sold a bill of goods, and that is what I said. There was never any question of firing Walton. I believe it was two or three years later that he subsequently left *Time* entirely under his own steam.

"Testifying in public session before the House Committee on Un-American Activities, on August 25, 1948, Alger Hiss said that a newspaperman had told him that a man on *Time* had told him that Whittaker Chambers was mentally unstable. Hiss was reluctant to name his ultimate *Time* source, but under pressure he did so. The source was William Walton."

Walton was also Deputy Grand Marshal of the Inaugural Parade and Marya Mannes exulted at the sight of "a painter, writer and friend in that exalted position, watching him doff his silk hat from his prize fighter's head with all the elegance of an old political hand. It was a big day for the arts."

But, according to Kirstein, it was not a big day for music. In fact, he found the overture commissioned for the Inaugural Concert "a piece of alarming mediocrity. . . ." In the intermission, Auden observed, "The least they could have done was to ask Stravinsky to write a twelve-tone Fanfare; his late pieces are so nice and short."

At a cocktail party tendered by the Walter Lippmanns for all those artists, musicians, writers, scientists, educators, and theologians ("nobody below the rank of a Nobel prizewinner"), there was considerable talk about how the conjunction of the snow and Inauguration was demoralizing Washington. "Mrs. John Steinbeck said she was going to *everything;* to hell with the snow," Kirstein reported. "Steinbeck looked sleek and purring. Arthur Miller towered benignly over all." Miller talked about the weather. "When *All My Sons* opened in Boston, it had snowed two days before," he said. "I wasn't known then. On the opening night, the theater was about a quarter full. But the box office guys told me we were in." The analogy may have been farfetched; but intellectuals are always looking for symbols and omens.

And as he watched the Inaugural parade across from the White House, Kirstein reflected on all that had occurred those few incredible days. Sure, the concert hadn't been much good; but, he asked himself, "What would we have gotten from Pat and Dick?"

"Listen," he told himself, "we wouldn't have been there."

But those who weren't there and who watched the Inaugural ceremony on television had, according to Kirstein, "a much clearer idea of what went on than most of us in the crowd in front of the National Capitol. They saw the Diplomatic Corps form in the rotunda, the Justices gather, and Mr. Kennedy scratch Ike's back when he couldn't reach where it itched. . . . But standing in the crowd, what one did see was intensely impressive; what one heard was mightily moving. The dignity of the event was on the level of its importance to the world. . . . Mr. Kennedy has the public magic of inbred but detached authority; when was it last seen in America on such a scale of physical attraction? Not since the Duke of Windsor was Prince of Wales. . . ."

"What did we share, you on television and we at the scene?" wrote Marya Mannes. "We both saw the grace of Mr. Eisenhower, the overabundance of Kennedy women with all that hair, teeth, and energy. . . . And we must have dwelt long on the face of the President's young wife, not only because of its beauty but because of a touching inwardness, a quality of serene removal that reminded me of archaic Greek or Khmer heads; a smile that had nothing public about it, that spoke of things withheld and guarded. . . . The lack of communication between the President and his wife was noted by all. It may have been the reserve of two people who are unwilling to reveal their feelings in public, but nothing, however slight, seemed to pass between them during those long public hours together. . . ."

The transition from Dwight David Eisenhower to John Fitzgerald Kennedy was unmarred by the personal feudism of the Hoover-Roosevelt and Truman-Eisenhower change-overs. Eisenhower and Kennedy had met for three hours in early December. The day before the Inauguration, when they conferred again, Eisenhower pledged he would not second-guess his successor from the sidelines; but, he said, he would not hesitate to speak out publicly in opposition if the Kennedy Administration sought to change United States policy toward Communist China. (Nixon, too, had emphasized to Kennedy at Key Biscayne the importance of maintaining a policy of nonrecognition. "I did so because Senator Smathers had told me that Chester Bowles and some of Kennedy's other foreign policy advisers were urging him to reappraise our position on that issue," said Nixon. "Kennedy said he was opposed to recognition. . . . He indicated, however, that strong arguments had been presented to him in favor of the so-called 'two Chinas policy.' ")

Eisenhower also demonstrated to Kennedy the procedure for evacuating the White House in case of emergency. Ike lifted the phone and spoke a few words. Five minutes later, an Army helicopter hovered over the White House lawn. Kennedy was suitably impressed by the helicopter; so much so, in fact, that he was to make full use of this Eisenhower "inheritance."

Then they met with Cabinet officers of the old and new administrations in what a joint communiqué described as a "full discussion of the world situation." Leaving the White House, Kennedy said of Eisenhower and his associates, "I don't think we've asked for anything that they haven't done."

Out on the portico, a reporter asked, "Are you excited?" Kennedy turned to his questioner and answered reflectively, "Interested."

The next day—Inauguration Day—the Kennedys showed up at the White House earlier than the official time in order to have coffee with the Eisenhowers. During the next few hours, until John F. Kennedy took the Oath, he discussed with his predecessor a book on D-Day he was reading—Cornelius

J. Ryan's *The Longest Day*. Ike had liked the book and Kennedy said it had taught him a lot he hadn't known about the European war.

Over in the Capitol plaza, shorn of snow, the Inaugural platform filled slowly with the great figures of Washington and the nation: the Justices of the Supreme Court, the members of the Senate and House of Representatives, the diplomatic corps, the new Cabinet officers, the Joint Chiefs of Staff—and, of course, the Kennedy family and friends.

The sun glared in the clear blue sky and Senator John McClellan asked, "Is that Father Joe over there?" The man from Arkansas shielded his eyes with his hand. "Why," he said, "I do believe it is."

And it was.

Beaming and laughing, Joseph P. Kennedy was telling friends, "This is what I've been looking forward to for a long time. It's a great day."

The wind was sharp as the ceremonies began. Essentially, it was a religious affair with the representatives of the various faiths praying in behalf of the first Catholic President in United States history. As Boston's Cardinal Cushing delivered his long invocation, smoke began to waft from the lectern. The tall, gray-haired prelate did not appear to be ruffled as men rushed up with water and fire extinguishers. Finally, the trouble was located; a plug was pulled and the smoke drifted away.

The only other trouble came when Robert Frost, his white hair fluttering in the wind, tried to read a newly written dedication to his famed poem, "The Gift Outright." Senator John Sparkman, Chairman of the Inaugural Committee, had introduced the eighty-six-year-old New Englander as a distinguished American poet "who will recite an original composition," an introduction which, to some of the invited intellectuals, smacked of a high school exercise.

The bright sun blinded the poet and the wind whipped the paper in his hands. "I am not having good light here at all," he said. Lyndon Johnson tried to shade Frost's paper with his hat, but it did no good. At length, Frost turned boldly to the microphones and his voice rang clear in the iambic pentameter of the poem Kennedy had requested. There was something strangely symbolic about the entire episode. Kennedy had asked Frost to change the last line of "The Gift Outright" in order to remind listeners of the New Frontier. "It is not a change which a man with an instinct for poetry, as distinct from propaganda, would have asked for," commented the *Economist's* man in Washington. "The episode seems to illustrate the chilliness and calculation which some people detect in Kennedy. Perhaps the President-elect, like the pioneers of whom Frost writes in the poem, will reflect on two of its lines: 'Something we were withholding left us weak. Until we found out it was ourselves.'"

At last came the moment Joseph P. Kennedy had awaited so long and had worked so tirelessly to bring into reality. The Chief Justice of the United States, Earl Warren, stepped forward, and John F. Kennedy rose, slipping out of his topcoat. And over a closed, family Douay Bible, Kennedy repeated the

Oath of Office in a clear, crisp voice. Whatever lay ahead of him, this would most certainly remain the high moment of John F. Kennedy's life.[4]

Kennedy's Inaugural Address was not without a certain attempt at grandeur in an otherwise haphazard occasion, what with a blizzard threatening to turn the event into a farce. "The delivery of his message had ringing Rooseveltian overtones," commented William V. Shannon in the *New York Post*. "Certainly, he intends to capture if he can F.D.R.'s mastery of the public scene and the popular imagination."

The Inaugural Address left plenty to the imagination. The language sounded forthright. The delivery was vigorous. But the speech had its share of those banal antitheses which ghost writers have been composing ever since F.D.R.'s memorable line that we have nothing to fear except fear itself.

"Let us never negotiate out of fear," said Kennedy. "But let us never fear to negotiate."

Actually there was more of Abe Lincoln than F.D.R. in Kennedy's address. Where Lincoln was approaching "the irrepressible conflict," Kennedy saw himself entering "a long twilight struggle." Kennedy's borrowings from Lincoln included the words: "In your hands, my fellow citizens, will rest the final success or failure of our course." Lincoln had put it: "In your hands, my dissatisfied fellow countrymen, and not in mine, is the momentous issue of civil war."

Lincoln said: "America is the last great hope of earth." President Kennedy made it ". . . the United Nations, our best hope. . . ." In his second Inaugural, Lincoln said, ". . . with malice toward none and charity for all. . . ." In concluding his address, Kennedy said, ". . . with a good conscience our only sure reward, with history the final judge of our deeds. . . ." Lincoln went on, "let us strive on to finish the work we are in" and Kennedy said, "let us go forth to lead the land we love."

There were echoes of other brilliant writings in the Kennedy speech. George Pope Morris, the poet of the Civil War period, coined the phrase, "United we stand, divided we fall." In Kennedy's speech, this came out, "United, there is little we cannot do, divided, there is little we can do. . . ."

Perhaps the best remembered line in the Kennedy Address was the repetition of his campaign call for sacrifice: "My fellow Americans, ask not what your country can do for you—ask what you can do for your country."

This, as the *Chicago Tribune*'s Walter Trohan pointed out, was "a fortuitous blending of Grover Cleveland's insistence that it was not for the govern-

---

[4] In one of his last campaign speeches—the one at the New York Coliseum on November 5, 1960—Kennedy had administered the Oath to himself. He said: "And if I am successful on Tuesday, it is my intention to be, in the fullest measure of the word and office, the next President of the United States—and I shall, without hesitation or reservation take a solemn oath on the 20th of January 1961 to 'solemnly swear that I will faithfully execute the office of President of the United States, and will to the best of my ability preserve, protect, and defend the Constitution * * * So help me God.'"

ment to support the people but for the people to support the government and similar campaign injunctions of Richard M. Nixon. . . ."

It was a speech that knocked them dead from Syracuse to Paris. Partisans of diverse opinion were struck mute at the sweep of historical perspective and at the ethos of guileless moral rectitude asserted in a style not heard since Winston Churchill was preparing to hurl empty Guinness bottles at the invading Nazi hordes.

Almost everyone loved it—Democrats and Republicans, liberals and conservatives, the Free and Slave Worlds—all found a basis for hope in Kennedy's first 1,355 words as President.

"What Mr. Kennedy spoke yesterday was for the most part not new in concept, although the rhetoric was beautiful," commented the *Washington Post*. "Thus the real import of Mr. Kennedy's words will lie in the measures and methods he proposes by which to call forth the effort and sacrifice of his countrymen and the confidence of people elsewhere. He has supplied a necessary and stirring preamble to creative leadership."

Generally the criticism was mild. Commented the *Los Angeles Times:* "He is wrong in implying that the beginning comes with him, but he is right in suggesting that the perfecting of mankind is tedious and unpredictable."

In the South, newspapers expressed relief that Kennedy had made no references to civil rights; while Negro leaders, expecting the millennium, were disappointed.

Morrie Ryskind, however, couldn't believe that it was the same Kennedy he had heard during the campaign. "In fact, when Earl Warren rose to swear him in, I was so certain that our new President was going to dramatically open the New Frontier by refusing to take the loyalty oath that I had given 8 to 5 on it. When he double-crossed me by reciting it word for word, I thought the Liberals who had elected him would at least try to tear him limb from limb. Instead, they applauded like mad. . . .

"And, a few minutes later, when he blithely threw the Los Angeles platform, which presented a past-due bill for what the government owed its people, into the discard and handed us a bill for what we owe our government, the applause was even wilder. . . .

"Such talk hasn't been heard from the Democratic side of the house since Grover Cleveland . . . and for a moment I got the impression that Harry Byrd had ghost-written the speech. I am assured, however, on impeccable authority that the President wrote it himself, and I accept the statement at face value. . . . But, though every word and phrase of the final draft be the President's, I am prepared to maintain that it shows the strong influence of another Kennedy, Joe. This is said in no spirit of criticism. There's nothing wrong in a son being influenced by his father, is there?"

Holmes Alexander thought "Kennedy gave us one of the great speeches, and one of the great personal performances, of American history." He felt the President had reached "the zenith of wisdom and maturity" in this passage: "All this will not be finished the first Hundred Days. Nor will it be finished in the first thousand days, nor in the life of this Administration, nor even perhaps in our lifetime on this planet.

"But let us begin!"

Joe

2

The story of the son is not wholly separable from the story of the father. For John Quincy Adams was, as Samuel Eliot Morison has described him, "above all an Adams"; and his heartwarming devotion to his father and the latter's steadfast loyalty to his son regardless of political embarrassment offer a single ray of warmth in that otherwise hard, cold existence.

—John F. Kennedy in *Profiles in Courage*

And it can also be faithfully recorded that the story of John Fitzgerald Kennedy is not wholly separable from the story of the father.

For though many a doting parent has envisioned his son as growing up one day to become President of the United States, few have gone about realizing that dream with more drive and determination than Joseph P. Kennedy, of Hyannis Port, Palm Beach, Park Avenue, and Cap d'Antibes.

That today his son is indeed President is a fact about which there was little of luck or happenstance. It was well planned—every step of the way.

"There are no accidents in politics," Joseph P. Kennedy said following his son's election as President.

The Kennedy bandwagon didn't just happen. It was the direct result of perhaps the most effective campaign organization in recent political history. And it provided a testament to the drawing power of the chameleon in United States politics. Basically, however, it boils down to a family crusade—the Kennedy clan against the field. The clan—three generations of it—went to bat with money, sweat, and occasional tears to win the White House for a Kennedy.

The story of John F. Kennedy, therefore, is also the story of a remarkable, close-knit and, in the President's words, "tremendously mutually supporting" family. This is not merely obvious; the Kennedys are aggressive about it.

Asked what single person had the greatest impact on his political thinking, President Kennedy once replied, "the family atmosphere . . . my mother and father. . . ."

Within "the family atmosphere," however, Joseph P. Kennedy was the dominant personality. This was underscored in December 1961 when the head of the clan was felled by a stroke in Palm Beach. As columnist Marquis Childs noted at the time: "The fact that one of the sons who rushed to his bedside is President of the United States and another Attorney General owes more to the fierce, driving ambition of the senior Kennedy than will perhaps ever be clearly understood."

Mrs. Rose Fitzgerald Kennedy, the President's mother, was in many ways the opposite of her husband. She played a more subordinate role in family affairs. "She was terribly religious," Jack Kennedy observed. "She was a little removed and still is, which I think is the only way to survive when you have nine children."

Shortly after her husband was stricken, Rose Kennedy entered a Boston hospital for a minor operation. Except for her youngest son, Ted, none of her copious brood visited her. "They have more important things to do," she explained.

There can be little doubt that Joseph P. Kennedy was a *paterfamilias* in the grand tradition. Possessed of fierce energy and ambition, he was a proud, domineering father. He ran his family like a tribal chieftain.

"Long before it ever became a slogan," he once said, "my family and I had togetherness."

But it was a "togetherness" based on doing what Joe wanted. Quite often, he could be dictatorial. According to a family friend, investment banker Charles F. Spalding, being late for lunch could be fatal when the elder Kennedy was "in one of his Emperor Augustus moods."

Once, at Palm Beach, when daughter-in-law Jacqueline Kennedy arrived late, her father-in-law began to give her what-for. Her anger flashed. She mocked him, "You ought to write a series of grandfather stories for children like 'The Duck with Moxie' and 'The Donkey Who Couldn't Fight His Way Out of a Telephone Booth.' "

The family was stunned by the outburst. Joe Kennedy was mute. His face turned white. Then, he let out a bellow of laughter and the silence was broken.

Joe Kennedy reared his children in his own image—in a family where competition is almost a way of life. Nothing mattered but winning.

"I don't think much of people who have it in them to be first, but who finish second," he explained. "If you've got a second choice, then you haven't got a first choice."

Jacqueline Kennedy's first look at the family's competitive spirit came when she saw a five-year-old Kennedy push over a four-year-old Kennedy who, in turn, immediately shoved a three-year-old Kennedy.

A Washington reporter once summed up the Kennedys with a line from a pep talk he overheard Robert F. Kennedy giving to one of his seven small children, "Let's swing higher and try for a new record. A Kennedy shouldn't be scared."

Out of this heritage came Jack Kennedy's own controlled competitiveness, his determination to succeed at all costs, and his matter-of-fact faith (at times shaken since he took office) that he is as well equipped as anyone in the country to be President. In anyone else, this might have been called arrogance. Among the Kennedys, it was to be expected.

Before he was stricken, Joe Kennedy was asked by a reporter what problems his youngest son, Ted, could expect if he ran for United States Senator. "None," he said unhesitatingly. In the Kennedy clan nothing is impossible.

Soon after reaching his thirtieth birthday in early 1962, Edward Moore (Ted) Kennedy announced his willingness to represent the people of Massachusetts in the Senate seat forsaken by John F. when he went to the White House. True, his tender years and almost total lack of qualifications were bound to evoke considerable criticism. "Ted wants a Senate seat the way other young men want a Jaguar," an opponent asserted. Logic, however, loses its power to persuade when it runs counter to the ambition of a Kennedy. Not only do the Kennedys make their own rules, but they generally get away with it.

"What are my qualifications?" asked Ted, somewhat annoyed at the question. "What were Jack's when he got started?"

Though it is difficult to try to sum up any human being, columnist Richard Starnes made a stab at it. "I'd say that Ted Kennedy wants very, very badly to reach the Senate, not so much in response to some Kennedy fetish for power but in answer to the very personal stimulus of a younger man who grew up under the spell of a father, and who now finds himself in the shadow of two brothers who are among the most influential men in the world."

Whatever the motivation, there was nothing funny about Ted Kennedy's desire to win public office. He seems to subscribe, without humor, to Mr. Dooley's dictum, "Politics ain't bean bag." If he had any doubts, he kept them to himself, relying on his ability to play the game that was born and bred into him.

"Play to win," his father used to tell his sons. And, to the Kennedys, politics is the grandest game of all.

It was Joseph P. Kennedy who insisted that Teddy be permitted to run for Senator. The President, at first, was said to be opposed. He had enough problems without having Teddy's youthful ambitions hurled at him. Anyway, he argued, Teddy's young; he could wait a couple of years.

"But," Joe Kennedy reportedly replied, *"I* can't wait."

Joseph P. Kennedy had once entertained White House ambitions for himself. When they were thwarted, he groomed his oldest son, Joe Jr., to carry out this driving ambition. Young Joe died during the war—a hero's death—and the father decided that his second-born son should go into politics.

"I got Jack into politics," Joseph P. Kennedy said in 1957. "I was the one. I told him Joe was dead and therefore it was his responsibility to run for Congress. He didn't want to. He felt he didn't have the ability and he still feels that way. But I told him he had to."

Winning the White House for Jack became *the* family project. As Joseph Dinneen, in his admiring study of the Kennedy clan, put it in 1959: "In the course of time, it has become an organization dedicated to one purpose—the election of John F. Kennedy to the Presidency of the United States."[1]

In recent years, efforts had been made to minimize the role played by Joseph P. Kennedy as the ranking clansman. In January 1961, Irwin Ross told of a conversation he had with Robert F. Kennedy, in which the Attorney General "was at pains to minimize his father's guidance of his sons."

Joe Kennedy's role as the top clansman had to be minimized for a very good reason—he had become one of the nation's most controversial figures. He was particularly upsetting to those Democrats whose hearts belonged to Adlai. Harry S Truman didn't like him either. It wasn't the Pope he was worried about, Harry once said—it was Pop.

But his presence was felt. The enormous fortune he had amassed over forty incredible years was being put to good use. When it came to realizing his life dream—a Kennedy in the White House—Father Joe spared no expense.

In early 1960, *Newsweek* quoted Adlai Stevenson as saying that "the amount of money being spent" by the Kennedys "is phenomenal, probably the highest amount spent on a campaign in history." Stevenson was also quoted as describing Jack Kennedy as "somewhat arrogant." Called upon by Kennedy to explain these remarks, Stevenson said he had been misquoted.

Rarely had any one man made so many enemies—both political and personal as had Joseph P. Kennedy. Liberals disliked him because he was a friend and outspoken admirer of the late Senator Joseph R. McCarthy. And during World War II he was an ardent isolationist who sincerely believed Hitler would win the war. Also, he had broken with Franklin D. Roosevelt (whom he had supported for three terms) and New Dealers regarded his

[1] *The Kennedy Family,* by Joseph F. Dinneen. Boston, Little, Brown, 1959.

views as reactionary, if not worse. In the postwar period he had dubbed the United Nations "a hopeless instrumentality" and had condemned "lavish spending" to aid foreign nations. In many ways he was a premature Birchite.

Joe Kennedy was also disliked because of his penchant for using vulgar ethnic tags for minority groups. This contributed to the widespread impression that he was violently anti-Semitic. He has always denied the charge. He insisted that he was always on the best of terms with Jews, that as a lad in East Boston he used to earn a few pennies on the Sabbath by lighting fires in Jewish homes. He boasted about being "the only Christian member" of the Jewish golf club in Palm Beach. Why did he join? "Because it's near my home and I like to play golf there." Besides, some of his best friends were Jews.

Finally, he was unpopular because of his utter ruthlessness in his business dealings. A tough and tight-fisted operator, he had made bitter enemies in his buccaneering days on Wall Street, in Hollywood, and in liquor and real estate. Many of his embittered ex-associates refuse to speak of their ventures with Joe Kennedy, or to him.

Like many men of wealth, Joseph Kennedy is a study in contrasts. He could coldly demand a business associate's life insurance as security for a $150,000 loan. Yet, when the Ziegfeld Theater was up for sale, he withdrew from the bidding at the request of impresario Billy Rose, then a total stranger. Rose told Kennedy that to him owning the Ziegfeld was a matter of sentiment; to Kennedy, merely a matter of business.

Then, after son Teddy was expelled from Harvard for sending a proxy to take an examination, Joe Kennedy quietly aided thirty-one West Point cadets who were expelled in the cribbing scandal of 1951. Through the Joseph P. Kennedy Jr. Foundation, set up in memory of his oldest son, the senior Kennedy arranged for the ex-cadets to enter other colleges, and paid their tuition fees.

Joseph Kennedy was also an unforgiving man. Back in 1940, the *Boston Globe* published an interview that forced his resignation as United States Ambassador to Great Britain. Among other undiplomatic things, Kennedy was quoted as saying that democracy was doomed in Britain. Kennedy angrily demanded a retraction. The *Globe* stood by its embattled reporter. Kennedy decided to teach the paper a lesson. He withdrew the advertising controlled by a liquor firm he controlled. The *Globe* refused to be intimidated and remained cut off from the lucrative advertising revenues until 1946 when Kennedy sold the firm. ("Twenty years after the famous interview," Irwin Ross reported in the *New York Post,* "Kennedy is unembarrassed as he tells a visitor about that vain effort to browbeat an honest newspaper.")

Kennedy's vengeful nature was again demonstrated following publication of Winston Churchill's first volume of wartime memoirs, *The Gathering Storm.* As the United States Ambassador in London in the late thirties,

Kennedy had aroused Churchill's hostility as an "appeaser." Their personal dislike for each other was monumental.

On September 26, 1948, the *New York Times* published a letter from Kennedy declaring that the Churchill memoirs were so "replete with serious inaccuracies" that "they should be handled with care." He said that Churchill's "misquotations" from public documents "make it difficult for one to rely on his quotations from documents that are not generally available. Other facts not yet made public may further bring into question Mr. Churchill's position as a raconteur of history. They will not, of course, derogate from the vividness of his style."

Because of stories such as these, Joseph P. Kennedy became a legend in his time. Derogatory anecdotes, however, cannot erase the fact that he had a vision of sorts. Back in 1952, when he was plugging for his son Jack to take Henry Cabot Lodge's Senate seat, Kennedy wore a deep blue tie with the silver inscription, "Kennedy for President." It was a gift from friends, but to Joseph P. Kennedy it was no joke.

Aside from unlimited cash and plenty of influence in the right political circles, Joe Kennedy's major weapon was the monolithic solidarity of his family, the fierce loyalty of the clan to each of its members, and the undisputed supremacy in that hierarchy of Joe Sr.

However, the subtle rules of the game called for the ranking clansman to remain on the sidelines. In 1952, recognizing that he had become a political liability to his son, Joe Kennedy tried to sever the cords of political inheritance. He announced he was "in complete disagreement" with his son on foreign policy. "I couldn't possibly have a worse argument with anyone about foreign policy than I have had with my son," he said.

The extent to which Jack Kennedy was his father's son was brought home in December 1961 when the President dropped the nation's business to fly to his stricken father in Palm Beach. The quick gathering of the clan at the patriarch's hospital bedside helped focus attention on a family situation more important than a mere display of love and affection. The episode dramatized what some observers had dubbed the "Kennedy dynasty."

This, of course, was no new development. Back in March 1959, the Gridiron dinner in Washington had Joe Kennedy singing:

> All of us
> Why not take all of us?
> Fabulous—
> You can't live without us.
> My son Jack
> Heads the procession.
> Then comes Bob,
> Groomed for succession.

At these press affairs, many a truth is sung in jest. But with the Kennedys, the grooming of Robert F. to succeed John F. is no laughing matter. The succession is already taken for granted by those on the inside. The build-up already is under way. In June 1962, at a convention of the powerful Hatters' Union, Bobby heard himself proposed for the Presidential nomination in 1968. The proposal was made by Alex Rose, leader of New York's influential Liberal party and a maker of political policy in the highest echelons of Labor.

Another tip-off was provided by Robert W. Richards of the Copley Newspapers in July 1962. He reported a conversation beside a swimming pool in which Mrs. Eunice Kennedy Shriver, sister of the President and wife of the Commander in Chief of the Peace Corps, talked to a friendly newspaperman.

Mrs. Shriver asked the newsman what he thought of a "Kennedy-Kennedy ticket in 1964," meaning, of course, brothers John, the President, and Bobby, the Attorney General.

"You wouldn't dare!" the astonished newsman exclaimed.

"What's wrong with that?" Mrs. Shriver challenged. "Nothing that I can think of."

This was not spoken in jest; no Kennedy ever jokes about political matters involving the family.[2]

In many ways, Joseph P. Kennedy is a far more fascinating study than any of his sons. His is a story so unbelievable in certain respects that even Hollywood would consider it too fantastic for filming. As a former movie producer himself, Joe Kennedy would probably have rejected it.

Arnold Toynbee's historical theory of challenge and response is perfectly illustrated in the Kennedy story. Set down in conservative, traditionalist Boston where every taboo worked against the Irish, Kennedy was spurred on to tireless endeavor to amass a huge fortune.

Joseph Kennedy appears to have been deeply influenced by his heritage as an Irish-American reared in a city dominated by an aloof Brahmin minority. His story is one of frustrations and slights, fancied or otherwise. Part of the legend is the remark he was supposed to have made when a Boston newspaper referred to him as an Irish-American:

"How long do you have to live in this country before you become an American? We've been here for two generations. Isn't that enough?"

But it was no rags-to-riches story. Joe's parents were well-to-do; and any work he did either as a candy butcher or a "sabbath goy" was because, even as a youth, he liked money. Nevertheless, his incredible ability to dig a dollar out of every opportunity—even during the worst of the Great Depression—was the sort of thing that often prompted hyperbole.

[2] Where did this leave Lyndon Johnson? "It is no great secret in Washington," wrote Walter Trohan in the *Chicago Tribune* of July 28, 1962, "that Johnson will probably not be asked to run again for the Vice Presidency, because he is not as strong in the South as he was." For the Kennedys, Johnson had evidently served his purpose.

His grandparents had arrived in Boston shortly after the devastating Irish potato famine of 1848. The atmosphere was not exactly hospitable. Mayor Theodore Lyman Jr. referred to the Irish newcomers, then swelling the city's population too quickly to be readily assimilated, as "a race that will never be infused into our own but on the contrary will always remain distinct and hostile."

To native Bostonians, the beaten survivors of the Great Hunger seemed scarcely more than beasts. Drunken and obstreperous, belligerent when aroused and hard to handle, they were too illiterate even to read the "Protestants Only" factory signs. So long as they confined themselves to the most menial of tasks they were endured and exploited—at a distance.

In Joe Kennedy's youth, the phrase "Irish Need Not Apply" was still an echo if not an actual phrase for hired help in New England newspapers. No group was more determined to maintain a wall between the Irish and itself than the Boston Brahmins.

It was a world which Joe Kennedy grew to despise with all his heart and soul.

It was a world from which Joe Kennedy fled at the first opportunity.

It was a world which he would make sure his children would never know.

This was the world into which he was born in September 1888, the only son of Patrick and Mary Kennedy. His father Patrick J. Kennedy owned a popular workingman's saloon in East Boston. Tall, blue-eyed, and possessed of a handle-bar mustache, P.J. cut a handsome figure. And like any wise saloonkeeper, he rarely sampled his wares. Instead, he entered politics, rising quickly in Democratic ranks. He was elected to the State Senate and, as his power in the ward increased, he became a member of the unofficial Board of Strategy, a coalition of party bosses who picked the candidates and ran the city pretty much as it wanted.

Those were the days when Boston was obtaining national attention, in the words of the muckrakers, as "a horrible example of graft and corruption."

On the strategy board, P.J. came to know John F. Fitzgerald, the "Honey Fitz" whose daughter would one day marry his son Joe. Though they found themselves political allies more times than not, P.J. and Honey Fitz did not like each other personally. At the turn of the century they probably would have shuddered at the thought that they would one day have grandchildren in common.

They were as dissimilar as any two men could be. Where P.J. was the backstage oligarch, Honey Fitz was the frock-coated ham who could weep at will at a stranger's wake. It was said he was the only man who could sing "Sweet Adeline"—his political theme song—cold sober and get away with it. And he made a triple threat of the "Irish switch" in a reception line. Usually attired in top hat and morning coat, he could pump one person's hand, chat with another, and gaze fondly at a third.

Both P.J. and Honey Fitz had married girls from families—Irish, to be sure—on a higher social plane than their own. Where they had been "shanty Irish," their wives were "lace curtain Irish." (In *The Remarkable Kennedys,* author Joe McCarthy wittily describes "lace curtain Irish" as "a family that has fruit in the house when nobody is sick.") Their common enemy—James Michael Curley, he of *The Last Hurrah*—began referring to P.J. and Honey Fitz as the "F.I.F.'s"—the First Irish Families.

Years later, the F.I.F.'s were to obtain their revenge for all the insults suffered at Curley's hands. This occurred when a young, downy-cheeked Congressman named John F. Kennedy refused to join with other politicians in seeking a presidential pardon for Curley following his conviction on a mail fraud charge.

The Kennedys rarely forgive or forget—even ancient slights.

The episode has often been cited as an example of Jack Kennedy's independence and political courage.

However, in 1952, when Jack Kennedy was seeking Henry Cabot Lodge's Senate seat, "the former's father, Joseph P. Kennedy," Curley later wrote in his autobiography, "paid me a visit and asked me to speak on the radio in behalf of his son's candidacy. When I refused . . . he asked if I would agree not to speak against him. I assented, but when Henry Cabot Lodge also came to call during that campaign, my wife Gertrude said: 'I want you to know that I am not voting against Jack Kennedy. But I also want you to know that I am going to vote for Henry Cabot Lodge.' "[3]

It is noteworthy that one of President Kennedy's first official acts was to name the Presidential yacht *Honey Fitz,* in honor of his maternal grandfather who died in 1950. The President has recalled that he first learned about politics from Grandfather Fitzgerald, almost as soon as he learned to spoon up his Pablum by himself. As a tot, he toured the wards with Honey Fitz—then engaged in a tough fight for Governor. (In the vernacular of Boston politics, a campaign is always a "fight.") Honey Fitz had been Mayor of Boston, but he had been beaten for re-election by Curley.

With the exception of Curley, Honey Fitz had no political enemies. This was because he had no strong political convictions. He was famous for his smile, his dapper appearance, his air of insouciance, and his florid speeches. One of his favorite themes was how the future of New England industry depended on encouraging every American to wear long woolen underwear.

In his race for Governor in 1922, Honey Fitz told the people of the state that he would foster establishment of new industries in the Commonwealth. But he left unspecified the means by which he would accomplish this. He spent considerable time denouncing the trend toward federal centralization, belaboring "paternalism" on both state and national levels, citing as

[3] *I'd Do It Again,* by James Michael Curley. Englewood Cliffs, N.J., Prentice-Hall, 1957.

examples Prohibition and the pending proposals for federal education and maternity aid.

"Unless we make a start and correct the situation," Honey Fitz declared, "the time will come when we will no longer determine what kind of life we are going to lead, but our lives will be determined for us by men and women on the Government payroll."

In the end, Honey Fitz and his fellow Democrats offered little more than to outdo the Republicans in the realm of economy and sound administration. A Democratic newspaper, the *Berkshire Evening Eagle,* in fact, endorsed Fitzgerald because he promised "he will put a stop to state extravagance." The Republicans' own zeal in this regard and Honey Fitz's own past profligacies limited the effectiveness of such campaign tactics. And Honey Fitz went down to defeat.

"My grandfather had a way with him," President Kennedy recalled many years later. "When campaigning in the Irish wards, he exuded enough blarney to charm the shamrocks off a glen in Dunmore. It wasn't too difficult, of course, with a name like Fitzgerald.

"However, he used another technique at Italian-American rallies, where his Irish ancestry wasn't exactly an asset. At such meetings, campaign helpers spread the word that his real name was Geraldini, or perhaps Gardini, and that he sprang from one of the great families of Venice."

Honey Fitz became an internationally renowned character. In 1911, he toured Europe with a delegation from the Boston Chamber of Commerce. As Mayor, he was spokesman for the delegation. On July 25th of that year, the *Chicago Tribune* published a brief editorial entitled "Honey Fitz and Geography," which read as follows:

We wonder how much abashed Boston will be on hearing of the speech of its brilliant mayor, the celebrated "Honey Fitz," at Düsseldorf when he visited that city. "We are glad to come to Düsselberg," said Honey Fitz at a dinner given to the visitors, "and we look forward with pleasure to our visit to the capitol. From thence we will visit those other German cities, Vienna and Budapest."

We expect that the Boston Latin school, where Fitz got his education, is rent from cellar to dome. But what will happen to him when he reaches Budapest?

Though Honey Fitz was wont to describe himself as "the last honest Mayor of Boston"—a slap, of course, at the redoubtable Jim Curley—it later developed that during the Fitzgerald Administration the city of Boston indulged in the habit of paying for each side of a paving block.

"According to the quixotically honest City Clerk Wilfred Doyle," wrote Francis Russell, a chronicler of Boston's tribal affairs, "in Honey's day everybody in City Hall from department head to scrubwoman had to kick back. Honey Fitz, the host of the old Woodcock Hotel, was brazen. Elderly politicians in the city can still today repeat limericks about his blond friend, 'Toodles' Ryan."

The name of "Toodles" was brought into the political wars by Mayor Curley in 1917. What happened was that Curley had granted permission to the Socialists to stage an anti-war parade and rally. He was promptly rebuked by Honey Fitz for giving aid and comfort to subversion. And he made it clear he would oppose Curley for Mayor.

Curley then issued this statement:

"The only individual anxious to suppress the truth or to restrict free speech is the one whose acts, public or private, will not permit thorough scrutiny or exposure to the world. . . . I am preparing three addresses which, if necessary, I shall deliver in the fall and which, if a certain individual had the right to restrict free speech, I would not be permitted to deliver.

"One of these addresses is entitled: 'Graft, Ancient and Modern,' another, 'Great Lovers from Cleopatra to Toodles,' and last, but not least interesting, 'Libertines: From Henry VIII to the Present Day.' "

That day, Honey Fitz dropped out of the Mayoralty race.

Honey Fitz was, like some politicians of today, his own greatest admirer. He invariably claimed credit for any accomplishment—whether he had a hand in it or not—while he was in public office. Thus, at a banquet tendered in his honor, the toastmaster observed, "Fitzie discovered Niagara Falls, conceived the High School of Commerce, built City Hall Annex, put an end to the Spanish and First World Wars, planned the Chamber of Commerce, freed Ireland and invented the Ku Klux Klan to save the Irish from being bored in America."

The Ku Klux Klan was always useful as a whipping-boy. Honey Fitz and Jim Curley would vie with each other in ranting about the KKK, an organization that never amounted to anything in Massachusetts. Curley, particularly, would make a major issue of supposed anti-Catholic discrimination against him. On several occasions when he spoke, a cross would begin to burn on a nearby hillside, and Curley would say, "There it burns, the cross of hatred and not the cross of love, upon which Our Lord Jesus Christ was crucified, the cross of human avarice and hate and not the cross of Christian charity."

Some people charged at the time that the incendiary performances were staged by Curley's henchmen, but no one could prove it. Years later, in his autobiography, Curley with devastating candor admitted that they were "stage props" arranged in his behalf, and went so far as to name two of his "fire-lighters."

In contrast to Curley and Fitzgerald, P. J. Kennedy—President Kennedy's other grandfather—operated quietly, but effectively, behind the scenes. He made enough money to buy a few more saloons, invest in a coal business, and become a large stockholder in the Columbia Trust Company. And he moved his family into a fine house on Jeffries Point, East Boston's equivalent of Back Bay.

P.J. was doing so well, in fact, that he could afford to send young Joe off in style to Boston's Latin School, so beloved of Boston's Brahmins, and then to Harvard, not so beloved of the Boston Irish of the day. At Harvard, Joe excelled at sports but was mediocre in his studies. Few of his classmates viewed him as a man who early in life would make a fortune in high finance. His later deftness with a balance sheet was not demonstrated at Cambridge. Ironically, he did poorly in such subjects as banking and finance.

During the summers he demonstrated a characteristic that would dominate his entire career—an uncanny ability to make a fast buck. But how he made it was most instructive. The oft-publicized story is that he and a friend ran a sightseeing bus to historic Lexington, netting $5,000 on the venture. (Those were the days when a dollar was worth a dollar.)

"The real story," reported Drew Pearson, "comes to me in documented detail from the bookkeeper of the Colonial Auto-Sightseeing Company, which suddenly found its license fee upped from $2 to $3,000 a year."

The fee had been upped by Mayor John F. Fitzgerald. Once a month, according to Pearson, a dapper Harvard student would come around to pick up a company check. The bookkeeper paid under protest.

"Here's your filthy lucre," he once said angrily.

"Friend, it may be filthy lucre," replied the nattily dressed student. "But you'll note I take the filthy lucre and put it in my pocket. Good day to you, sir."

According to Pearson, the Harvard student was Joseph P. Kennedy.

Even as a youth, Joe Kennedy knew the value of the right connections. On graduating from Harvard in 1912, he had no problem in landing a job as a state bank examiner. The pay wasn't much ($125 a month) but the experience was invaluable.

In later years, Kennedy would delight in telling how, at twenty-five, he became the youngest bank president in the nation when the directors of the Columbia Trust Company asked him to take the job. This was a simplification of what really occurred.

Actually, in his post as examiner, Kennedy had prior access to important financial intelligence. Thus he learned that Columbia was about to be merged with a larger institution. By borrowing $45,000 from relatives and friends, and with the help of his family, he won control of the bank.

By this time, Joe was courting Rose Fitzgerald, the lovely dark-haired slip of a daughter of Honey Fitz Fitzgerald. One of six children, Rose was the apple of her father's eye. And, frankly, he couldn't see her marrying the son of P. J. Kennedy. He thought his Rose could do better. He tried to interest her in a wealthy contractor, but she would have none of him. Later, Honey Fitz would boast that Rose had turned down the marriage offer of that tea-makin', sail-boatin' Englishman, Sir Thomas Lipton.

And so, on October 7, 1914, Rose and Joe were married. The Fitzgerald and Kennedy clans were linked at a nuptial Mass performed by William Cardinal O'Connell in his private chapel. The following year, Joe

Jr. was born. John F. came into the world in 1917. Then, during the twenties, in rapid succession, were born five girls and a son—Rosemary, Kathleen, Eunice, Patricia, Jean, and Robert F. Finally, in 1932, Edward was born.

The story goes that Kennedy had vowed to become a millionaire by the time he was thirty-five. This he accomplished many times over. But he wanted something else. He wanted social acceptance. It had always galled him at Harvard that, though he was popular as an athlete, he could never make the "best" clubs—the so-called "final clubs" such as Porcellian and A.D. And he took little consolation in the fact that other illustrious graduates of that ancient institution had not been picked for these elite groups. In his own class of 1912, for example, humorist Robert Benchley and author Frederick Lewis Allen had been passed by.

Even when he began to amass great wealth, he found the "best" clubs in conservative Boston still closed to him. These were the places where the Yankees could still hold out against rising immigrant pressures. In fact, they were the last places.

When he finally packed his growing family off to New York, Kennedy made no bones about the fact that he wanted to live where he could be accepted as an American and not as an Irishman.

"I felt Boston was no place to bring up Catholic children," he later explained. "I didn't want them to go through what I went through when I was growing up there. They tell me it's better now, but at that time the social and economic discrimination was shocking. I know so many Irish guys in Boston with real talent and ability that never got to first base only because of their race and religion."

So to strike a blow against racial and religious discrimination, he and his family wound up living in Bronxville, a super-select, largely white Protestant community in Westchester County known for its restrictive covenants.

For a summer residence Joe Kennedy bought a rambling ten-bedroom house at Hyannis Port, overlooking Nantucket Sound, where the neighbors, mostly Pittsburgh millionaires, sniffed at the Kennedys as "moneyed Boston Irish."

For winter vacations the clan selected Palm Beach, probably the nation's most segregated town where, in the well-chosen words of Robert Lewis Taylor, "at sundown, Negroes quietly retreat from the sidewalks to disappear into some murky, Kennedy-supported black Ghetto across Lake Worth."[4]

---

[4] In his brilliant analysis of the "Palm Beach Frontier," appearing in *National Review* of April 10, 1962, *New Yorker* writer Taylor noted that the Palm Beach police "are quick to act at the sight of a misplaced dark face; here Negroes function as low-paid servants, and any attempt to enhance their status, even at the point of a window-shopping stroll, is certain to end in trouble. *No Negro is permitted to own a home in the President's winter town.* . . . At the railroad and bus depots . . . Negroes sit in small, special waiting rooms, have separate restrooms, and drink from non-white water fountains. Several employees, questioned, have never heard a Kennedy protest any of these colored facilities. The movies—a favorite recreation of the Presidential group—are kept rigidly separate."

In the person of his son Jack, Joe Kennedy achieved the ultimate in social status. With Honey Fitz's grandson, the wheel seems to have come full circle. In President Kennedy can be seen the final product of the gradual transition from shanty to lace curtain to cut glass Irish. One of his grandfathers may have owned a saloon, but Jack Kennedy has style, money, charm, and high connections.

Born to wealth and wedded to beauty and high social status, his is not the America of the big metropolis or of middle-class suburbia. His is the America of Palm Beach and Hyannis Port, of Choate and Harvard, of El Morocco and Le Pavillon. His is a world of dazzling women, sophisticated parties, sun worshiping, and long weekends in the country. He entered the race of life with that serenity, that security from abrasive money worries, that self-confidence that only inherited wealth could provide.

"For him," the *Reporter*'s Douglass Cater has written, "the fairy-tale version of life in America is, like the two best-selling books he has written, strictly non-fiction."

Both in his person and in his family, Kennedy represents the flowering of a new class. He may well be described as our first melting-pot aristocrat.

"After the American Revolution," as Francis Russell has observed, "the provincial squirearchy of Massachusetts, the Brattles and the Vassals and the Hutchinsons, were succeeded by the money-grubbing mercantilism of the Lowells and the Cabots and the Lawrences. These latter families flourished briefly in one generation in the so-called golden age and took two more to fade."

With the rise of the Kennedys the pattern was repeated.

In the old days, Honey Fitz could always move his proletarian audiences to derisive cries with a scornful reference to Harvard as "that place across the river." His grandson, however, would be elected an overseer at "that place," indistinguishable in look and manner from his Yankee predecessors. The identification with the Yankees became so close that in 1954 the then Senator Kennedy refused to endorse the candidacy of Italian-American Foster Furcolo against his Republican colleague and fellow Harvardian, the blue-blooded Senator Leverett Saltonstall.[5]

As a third-generation aristocrat, President Kennedy fits into the *noblesse oblige* tradition of F.D.R. and Adlai Stevenson as the leader of the Democratic party—the section of the party composed of minorities and urban workers. Not once, during the 1960 campaign, did Kennedy ever apologize for his wealth as he flew around the country in the family-owned, two-engine Convair, making political mileage out of the chic, flair, and good looks of his assorted clansmen and women.

[5] In his book *Who Killed Society?* (New York, Harper, 1960), Cleveland Amory said that any listing of Bostonian "name" families, such as the Adamses and Lodges, "is perhaps incomplete without the recent accomplishments of John Fitzgerald Kennedy, of Boston's illustrious Kennedys." "Indeed," wrote Amory, "this family is almost a text-book example of the progression from celebrity (Grandfather Fitzgerald) to society (Joseph P. Kennedy) to aristocracy (the present generation)."

"Do I resent criticism about the Kennedy family being wealthy?" his sister Eunice once asked. "Not at all. Speaking for myself, I've found that being wealthy can be very pleasant."

"Never before," wrote Robert Lewis Taylor, "have lamentations about the Common Man been raised to such heights of absurdity by a family wallowing in luxury. The mansion in Palm Beach, the baronial compound on Cape Cod, the French chateau, the town house in Boston, the Virginia plantation, the other *pied-à-terres,* assuredly give clues to the Kennedys' natural fondness for the simple life. Without question, they favor it for others, though not necessarily for their social coterie; the owners of large houses usually prefer to exchange visits with other owners of large houses. . . . Sun-drenched, charming, palace-studded, dripping with gems and mink, bumper-to-bumper with Rolls Royces, uniquely rife with class distinction, Palm Beach may not indeed be the ideal place for President Kennedy to plan his spineless Socialist heaven."

Only religion links Kennedy with the Irish politicians of old. And even here there are subtle differences for a young man who refers to his Catholicism as his "religious affiliation." As President, he shuns being photographed in the company of Catholic prelates; but he summons the photographers whenever a Billy Graham or some other Protestant churchman comes a'calling.

In June 1959, the then Senator Kennedy was present when Harvard University awarded an honorary degree to Richard Cardinal Cushing. Though a number of devout Catholics gathered beforehand to kiss His Eminence's ring, observers noted with interest that the Senator merely shook hands. Kennedy was present at the ceremony as an overseer of Harvard, though the Cardinal was an old friend of the family.[6]

Shortly afterward, his father proudly boasted, "A few years ago, Jack was elected to the Board of Overseers at Harvard, which would have been unheard of in my day. It seems to me that if a Catholic can be elected to the Board of Overseers at Harvard, he can be elected to anything."

He could even be elected President of the United States.

And, as Joseph Dinneen observed in his friendly 1959 book, Father Joe, "one of the richest men in the country, if not in the world, is prepared to spend his last dime to achieve that end if it appears that his son has a fighting chance."

Though he did not need to spend his last dime to achieve that ambition, Joseph Kennedy spent plenty. Probably no one will ever know how many millions he poured into winning the White House for his son. About all

---

[6] The President's youngest brother Teddy, however, didn't object to using a photograph of Cardinal Cushing and himself in his 1962 campaign. His Democratic opponent for the nomination, Edward McCormack, made the point that he was often photographed with the Cardinal but that he did not think such photographs should be used in a political contest.

that can be said is that without his father's enormous fortune behind him it is highly doubtful that Jack Kennedy could ever have become President of the United States.

Back in 1937, *Fortune* magazine took a good, hard look at the man behind this fortune: "The legend of Joe Kennedy made him at once a hero of a Frank Merriwell captain-of-the-nine adventure, a Horatio Alger success story, and E. Phillips Oppenheim tale of intrigue and a John Dos Passos disillusioning report on the search for the big money. The truth makes him the central character of a picaresque novel of a sort not yet written."

The Kennedy fortune rates well ahead of the individual Rockefellers, the Henry Fords, the Pews, the Harrimans, and the Whitneys. In 1957, *Fortune* listed Kennedy twelfth among America's ruling families with wealth estimated at between $200 and $400 million.

Joe Kennedy told a reporter that *Fortune* was wrong. Which way he wouldn't say. Asked to give the correct figure, he snapped, "It's none of your business."

Having read about their wealth in the papers, Rose Kennedy asked her husband, "Why didn't you tell me you had all that money?"

"How could I tell you?" he replied. "I didn't know it myself."

And, in all probability, he really had no idea of what he had salted away in investments and holdings around the world.

Significantly, money was never discussed at the family table. How Dad made his millions was not considered a fit topic for comment. The talk was largely about politics. Father Joe also inculcated an irreverence for the old barons of finance. He was not a member of their "Establishment"; he was often a loner; and he did not view the titular rulers of commerce and industry as infallible. Perhaps it was this instinct J.F.K. was reflecting when, as President, he exploded following the steel price rise in the Spring of 1962.

"Big businessmen are the most over-rated people in the country," Joe would tell his sons. "Here I am, a boy from East Boston and *I* took 'em. So don't be impressed."

The result was that the Kennedy boys grew up to be active, able, enthusiastic politicians. And though they had plenty, they learned nothing about money, at least not in its relationship to economic policy and principle. Only recently has President Kennedy been getting an economic education— the hard way.

Making money, however, was only part of the Joseph P. Kennedy saga. It was what could be done with it that counted. Money represented power and eventual social acceptance. Thus he used money to rise high in national-level politics. It was his contribution to Franklin Roosevelt's 1932 campaign that levered him into a position among horrified New Dealers in Washington, and that led eventually to the ambassadorship to the Court of St. James's, the social pinnacle representing assured position for him and his family.

At one time, Joe Kennedy even had White House aspirations for himself. When those dreams were dashed, he turned to furthering his sons' careers. And money was able to open many doors in their strivings for the ultimate.

As his tribe and fortune increased, Joe Kennedy moved out of Boston into the big time of Wall Street, then on to other bold ventures in Hollywood, Texas, Florida, and Chicago. Most of the details of his financial killings have been lost to the chronicler, simply because he has never wanted to discuss them.

"I hate reminiscing about business affairs," he once explained.

During the frenzied twenties, Wall Street considered him a man of mystery. He never appeared on the market. He always operated through others. "He moved in the intense, secretive circles of operators in the wildest stock market in history," *Fortune* recalled in 1937, "with routine plots and pools, inside information and wild guesses."

As a Wall Street plunger, he specialized in setting up pools (along with such partners as Harry Sinclair and "Sell 'Em Ben" Smith), inflating cheap stocks through rumors and erratic—but well publicized—buying and selling. The "action" was calculated to impress the suckers. When the price of the stock was inflated sufficiently, the pool would sell short for huge profits.

The suckers would be left holding the bag—stocks which invariably took a plunge.

All Kennedy had done, he once said, was to "advertise the stocks." Today, such advertising is outlawed.

In 1933, Joe Kennedy made such a financial killing on a deal which he had master-minded for the Libby-Owens-Ford Glass Company that the Senate Banking and Currency Committee investigated the transaction.

Prohibition was being repealed and the word somehow got around, according to the Senate Committee, that the glass company "was engaged in manufacturing bottles for the liquor industry"—which, in fact, it wasn't.

However, the Senate Committee could find nothing illegal in the fact that a few "insiders," including Joe Kennedy, had cashed in heavily at the expense of numerous investors. (As one of Joe's favorite comedians, W. C. Fields, would say, "Never give a sucker an even break.")

By the late twenties, Kennedy had made a profitable detour into show business. He flourished as a board chairman, special adviser or reorganizer of five film, vaudeville and radio companies (Paramount, Pathé, First National, Keith-Albee-Orpheum, and RCA). Whether Kennedy actually strengthened the film companies—or milked them—is still a subject of debate among Hollywood old-timers. One top executive insists, "Joe came in when the industry was in distress and left a shell." The implication was that Joe got the nut meats.

"How come you're in the movie business?" Marcus Loew once asked Kennedy. "You were never a furrier."

Furrier or not, Joe Kennedy enjoyed Hollywood. He liked the company of glamorous stars. He liked the excitement of producing films on his own. They may not have been art, but they made plenty of money. Westerns were his favorites. They were cheap to make; and they appeared to satisfy the entrepreneurs of the vast wasteland constituting the movie business of the day.

Once, his father recalled, Jack Kennedy participated in the making of a screen star. Unable to decide whether to put football star Red Grange under contract for a series of college pictures, Joe Kennedy asked his young sons Joe and Jack what they thought. Their enthusiastic approval decided the issue.

Kennedy also produced several films in partnership with and starring Gloria Swanson, whom he much admired. In turn, Miss Swanson greatly admired Kennedy. So much so, in fact, she named an adopted son, Joseph, in his honor.

In Joseph Kennedy, Miss Swanson "found a friend, patron saint, and bank roll all in one and the same person," chronicled Hollywood historian Hedda Hopper.[7] "Soon after this lucky meeting Gloria accompanied Mr. and Mrs. Kennedy to Europe. It must have been a mighty trying trip for Mrs. Kennedy. I often wondered how she weathered it."

One of the Joseph P. Kennedy productions, starring Miss Swanson, was never completed. Originally written and directed by the eccentric Erich von Stroheim, the film, *Queen Kelly,* developed into a story about a convent-bred girl who, after being seduced by a Prussian officer, inherits a string of bawdy houses in Africa.

Just the thought of his imprimatur on the vividly portrayed film made Kennedy—father of a model Catholic family, husband of a deeply pious woman, and a heavy contributor to church undertakings—sweat. He fired von Stroheim and hired another director to rework the controversial scenes. But to no avail. Some $200,000 later, Kennedy finally shelved the production, writing off the losses to the tune of $950,000.

The episode may also have led to the sudden termination of Kennedy's meteoric career in Hollywood. For one thing, his wife was complaining of his long absences from his children. As Hedda Hopper tells the story: "Joe Kennedy's father-in-law, the legendary Honey Fitz, ordered Joe to wind up his film affairs and get out of Hollywood by a given date or certain secrets —still secret except to a few—would burst out into the open. Joe always was a lucky Irishman. He sold out his Hollywood holdings at the peak, took a profit of six million dollars, and wound up as our Ambassador to Great Britain during F.D.R.'s first term."

Though the "certain secrets" have remained secret to this day, Joseph P. Kennedy has long been gossip-prone. And he never appeared to be unduly concerned about the rumors which surrounded his incredible rise in the

---

[7] *From Under My Hat,* by Hedda Hopper. Garden City, N.Y., Doubleday, 1952.

worlds of show business, high finance, and politics. Only later, when the White House appeared a definite certainty for his son, did he begin remonstrating about unfair stories circulating about him.

Joseph P. Kennedy never liked his father-in-law Honey Fitz Fitzgerald. He would bridle when introduced as the "Mayor's son-in-law." There was the time, too, when Honey Fitz burst in on his son-in-law unannounced and uninvited. This occurred in the mid-forties when the Ambassador was entertaining in a private dining room in New York's Toots Shor's restaurant. His guests were legislators and newsmen from Massachusetts. The occasion was a campaign which Kennedy then headed to promote industrial redevelopment in the Commonwealth.

Joe was about to make a speech when Honey Fitz burst into the room. "Hello boys," he beamed. "Nice to see you all from the good old Bay State."

"Give us a song, Fitzie," someone shouted.

And out poured a rendering of "Sweet Adeline." An angry Joe Kennedy, meanwhile, departed. He never did make his speech. And he didn't talk to his father-in-law for months.

Toward the end, Kennedy was forced to help out his father-in-law financially. Honey Fitz was never able to hold on long to his City Hall–gotten gains. As a former associate observed, "Joe never had respect for somebody he had to do something for."

After leaving Hollywood, Joseph Kennedy made a splendidly defiant gesture in moving his family from Brookline. He hired a private railroad car to take his wife, children, servants, and belongings to New York.

"In Boston," he said later, "they wouldn't have asked my daughters to join their exclusive clubs."

Resuming his stock manipulation in New York, Kennedy became more and more involved in more and more deals. It was a dangerous business because Wall Street was populated almost entirely by wolves eager to gobble up the Bostonian.

"But," as John Galvin, managing director of Boston's World Trade Center put it, "Joe licked a lot of those Meadow Brook polo players at their own game."

A lot of those polo players were ruined in the Great Crash of 1929. But not Joe. Not only did he escape the consequences of the Black Day but, as one journalist observed, "he rode the market down and grew rich out of the depression."

Joseph P. Kennedy always did well when things were tough for others. He was an expert at buying at distress prices. He enlarged his holdings in blue-chip stocks after they hit rock bottom during the depression. When nobody else did, he always seemed to have cash.

Even his homes came cheaply. Talking to Bob Considine once, down at Palm Beach, Joe Kennedy pointed to his sixteen-room winter residence on Millionaires Row and proudly observed that he had purchased it for a mere $15,000, though he had since put more than $150,000 into it. Then, pointing to the ocean retaining wall, he said, "It cost me more than $15,000 just to put in the wall."

Joe Kennedy was a farsighted speculator. One reason he supported Franklin Roosevelt in 1932 was because of his opposition to Prohibition. Anticipating the repeal of the Volstead Act, he organized a liquor importing company, Somerset Importers, Ltd. Then, accompanied by the President's oldest son, James Roosevelt, Kennedy took a quick trip to England where he cornered the United States franchise for Scotch whiskies (Haig & Haig, King William, and John Dewar) and gin (Gordon's) for a reported $118,000. Then he somehow wangled Government permits to import big quantities of Scotch and gin for "medical purposes." When the bars were legally opened, the Kennedy warehouses were bulging and ready to flow.

Five years later, when Joe Kennedy was Ambassador to the Court of St. James's, the *Saturday Evening Post* published an article by Alva Johnston which asserted that James Roosevelt had not only helped arrange the diplomatic post for him but had been instrumental in opening doors for him among British distillers.

Kennedy, in New York at the time, indignantly denied the charges. With his twenty-one-year-old son Jack by his side—they were sailing for England aboard the French liner *Normandie*—the Ambassador declared, "Kennedy was doing all right by himself before he ever met Jimmy Roosevelt."

Which no one—not even Alva Johnston—was disputing.

"I admit I am the Ambassador," Kennedy continued, "but I deny that I am the premier Scotch whisky salesman in this country. I do like to be the best in everything."

Though Kennedy denied he ever had business relations with Roosevelt, Jimmy thought he did. Jimmy had been under the impression that he was in for twenty-five per cent of the Somerset action. After all, one wonders if he didn't feel if it hadn't been for his—or, more precisely, his father's—influence, the deal with the British distillers could not have so easily been arranged.

What James Roosevelt discovered, as have others, was that Joseph Kennedy did not like to have partners. Many years later, one of Kennedy's friends, speculating on Eleanor Roosevelt's outspoken hostility to his son's presidential aspirations, said (according to author Joe McCarthy), "I suspect it may go back to that time when Jimmy Roosevelt helped Joe with that Scotch deal. Maybe Jimmy thought he and Joe were going to be partners. If so, he soon found out that when Joe Kennedy is starting a business he doesn't have partners."

In the liquor business as in everything else Joe Kennedy was a ruthless competitor. His rivals insist he took unfair advantage of his Ambassadorial post in London to practically corner the Scotch market. Anticipating World War II, Ambassador Kennedy amassed something like half a million cases.

"And then," a former competitor complained, "Joe dropped the price $4 a case on us, driving three big distributors out of business."

(During the 1960 campaign, Jack Kennedy—after being introduced at a New York banquet by a liquor magnate who had purchased his business from Joe Kennedy—declared, "I was amazed to hear such warm praise from anyone who has done business with my father!")

As with his myriad other ventures, it is often difficult to come by the precise truth in allegations made about the elder Kennedy's behind-the-scenes operations. Thus, for years he was called the world's richest bootlegger. This hardly seems possible. For one thing, he could scarcely have had the time during the Prohibition era to devote to that illicit pursuit, no matter how profitable it was.

Curiously, Kennedy never seemed to make any conscientious effort to reply to charges growing out of his lengthy association with the liquor business. Perhaps it was because whisky had always been good to the Kennedy family. He was brought up in an atmosphere of saloons. During the depression, liquor provided him with a lot of ready cash.

"I'd rather have whisky than money," he used to tell his associates.

Joe's real secret weapon, however, was getting the right people to work for him. "He had the ability of a football coach," a former associate explained. "Not only did he get the right people but he got them all enthused. And they often lost sight of the fact that there was very little reward for their enthusiasm or desire for his approval."

Thus, in 1946, after thirteen years of dizzy profits, Kennedy sold the Somerset Company for $4,500,000—paying off the top executives who had run the show with a piddling $37,500 each.

"Joe never gives anything away, without the world knowing about it," the former associate added. "That's why he could be so generous on one hand giving $3 million to a Catholic church, and be so niggardly on the other hand. The one gift is well publicized, as is every gift he makes, but the other, within his own organization, would never get any publicity, and so he isn't very interested."

Joseph Kennedy's lengthy career is studded with ex-friends. "Few, if any of the people who started with him, remained with him. He made huge profits himself, but didn't cut in any of the executives who helped make them possible. He paid them a salary and, as far as he was concerned, that was enough.

"He was very good at forgetting promises, particularly if they were to cost him any money."

About the stories of Joe Kennedy's alleged anti-Semitism, this former associate who knew him intimately for many years insists that there was no streak of it in the financier's makeup. He was just a salty, outspoken individual and like a lot of Boston Irishmen was always referring to Jews as "sheenies," Italians as "wops," and Irishmen as "micks" or "harps."

"Joe was too ruthless, and too interested in making use of people with know-how, to care about a man's religion or race. All that really mattered with Joe was whether the individual involved could do him some good."

Once a prominent magazine editor, disturbed about Joe's reported anti-Semitism, asked a mutual friend, a noted Boston newspaperman, to arrange for him to see Joe Kennedy. Kennedy didn't want to dignify the subject, but finally he agreed.

"Okay," he said, "bring the sheeny in then."

The session lasted two hours. Kennedy pointed out that many of his top advisers were Jews, that he had promoted Jews in his organization on many levels. He brought out documents and named names.

The editor was impressed in spite of himself. Later, he said, "I don't think Kennedy likes Jews, but I also don't think he's anti-Semitic."

The mutual friend added this postscript, "I don't think Joe liked *him.*"

As the years passed, and the tales of Kennedy's exploits, both social and financial, became more and more outlandish, one close friend began to worry.

"Joe," he told Kennedy, "now that the kids are growing up and noticing things, what are you going to tell them if they begin to ask you embarrassing questions?"

"They won't ask me," Kennedy said complacently.

"But, suppose they do."

Joe Kennedy's eyes grew cold. "Well," he snarled, "if they do, I'll tell them to mind their own Goddamn business."

F.D.R.

3

The Wall Street Crash of 1929, though it made him even richer, completely unnerved Joseph P. Kennedy. "I am not afraid to record," he wrote in 1936, "that in those days I felt and said I would be willing to part with half of what I had if I could be sure of keeping, under law and order, the other half."[1]

Joseph Kennedy had been afraid that the Great Depression would generate pressures that could explode into violent social revolution. Such a catastrophe would, of course, wipe out his fortune and everything he had worked for.

In his view, the Hoover Administration "appeared blind to the necessity of a new social approach to economic problems." What America needed was a man of action; one able to get things done; a leader who could give orders and obtain his authority afterward.

Such a man was Franklin Delano Roosevelt. Only he could save the capitalist system in its moment of dire peril. Only he could save Joseph P. Kennedy's fortune.

Thus, as Kennedy put it, he became "the first person with more than $12 in his pocket to come out for Mr. Roosevelt." They had first met in 1917. At the time, Kennedy was an executive at the Bethlehem Shipyards at Quincy and F.D.R. was an Assistant Secretary of Navy. Legend has it that they hit it off together.

[1] *I'm for Roosevelt*, by Joseph P. Kennedy. New York, Reynal & Hitchcock, 1936.

At any rate, long before the 1932 Democratic convention Joe Kennedy hopped on F.D.R.'s bandwagon. Four years later, he still was in F.D.R.'s corner, explaining why in a small book called *I'm for Roosevelt*. (Ironically, in listing the accomplishments of the New Deal, Kennedy failed to note the repeal of Prohibition—one Rooseveltian measure that further helped assure the economic security of the Clan Kennedy.)

In a more recent explanation of why he had backed F.D.R., Kennedy told author Joe McCarthy, "long before the stock market crash, back at the peak of the boom, when Jack was nine or ten years old, I had established million dollar trust funds for each of our children. After the Crash, I began to wonder if those trust funds were going to be worth a damn. I was really worried. I knew that big, drastic changes had to be made in our economic system and I felt that Roosevelt was the one who could make those changes. I wanted him in the White House for my own security, and for the security of our kids, and I was ready to do anything to help elect him."

Some cynics have suggested that a more cogent reason for his support was that he knew F.D.R. would win. Nevertheless, his various explanations were revealing—all he appeared concerned about was "my own security . . . the security of our kids. . . ." Other people's security was apparently an afterthought.

In 1932 Kennedy gave his time, his tireless energy, and an undetermined amount of money to help put his favorite man of action in the White House. Though the precise extent of his services to Roosevelt cannot be accurately determined, the fact is that he rode the campaign train with F.D.R. and served as a financial adviser.

Kennedy claimed he played a pivotal role "by bringing William Randolph Hearst around for Roosevelt." Subsequently, a convention deadlock between Roosevelt and Al Smith for the nomination was broken when California, under the prodding of the newspaper publisher, switched her forty-four votes from John Nance Garner to F.D.R. As part of the deal, Garner obtained the vice-presidency.

"But you won't find the episode mentioned in the history books," said Kennedy. "Hearst even sent his contribution to Roosevelt through me."

Since some people figured Kennedy as a man who never put up a nickel without getting something in return, his friends figured him for a Cabinet post.

Originally, Kennedy wanted to be named Secretary of the Treasury. But he was bitterly opposed by F.D.R.'s closest political adviser and confidant, Louis McHenry Howe, who—according to his biographer—"didn't care for Mr. Kennedy for reasons known only to himself."[2]

Howe did point out, at the time, that F.D.R. had run a campaign aimed at driving the money-changers out of the temple; and to have a money-

[2] *The Man Behind Roosevelt, The Story of Louis McHenry Howe,* by Lela Stiles. New York, World, 1954.

changer around the White House would prove embarrassing to the New Deal.

Kennedy was hurt, deeply hurt. He was the only major Roosevelt backer who did not immediately obtain a top job in the new Administration. But, thanks to Raymond Moley, he wasn't left out of the political arena too long. The Securities Exchange Act had been passed and F.D.R. needed a chairman for the watchdog commission it created. Moley, then a leading brain-truster, suggested Joe Kennedy.

F.D.R. thought it an amusing idea. The SEC was designed to prevent exactly the kind of Wall Street wheeling-and-dealing in which Kennedy himself had been engaged. Moley also felt that the appointment would reassure the nation's financial community that the New Deal was not out to strangle investment activity.

When the news of the prospective appointment leaked out in June 1934, the Liberals literally gasped in disbelief. Their comments included such words as "incredible," "grotesque," "shocking," and "appalling." Men around F.D.R., including SEC commissioners James Landis, Ferdinand Pecora, and Benjamin Cohen, were outraged. Only the previous February Kennedy's name had been spread large on the record of the Senate inquiry into the Libby-Owens-Ford pool.

"I say it isn't true," wrote John T. Flynn, then a Liberal columnist. "It is impossible. It could not happen."

But happen it did—after a dramatic scene in the White House, when in Roosevelt's presence Ray Moley put it straight to Kennedy: "Joe, I know darned well you want this job. But if anything in your career could injure the President, this is the time to spill it. Let's forget the general criticism that you've made money in Wall Street."

As Moley recalled the scene in his authoritative account of the early New Deal period, "With a burst of profanity [Kennedy] defied anyone to point to a single shady act in his whole life. The President did not need to worry about that, he said. What was more, he would give his critics—and here again the profanity flowed freely—an administration of the SEC that would be a credit to the country, the President, himself, and his family— clear down to the ninth child."[3]

To the surprise of the Liberals and the anguish of the market manipulators (who, after all, considered Joe one of their own), Kennedy proceeded to administer the SEC with a strong, unwavering hand. He proved a spectacular success. He made the SEC the New Deal's most successful and popular agency. He received acclaim from all sides. And, for the first time in his career, Joseph P. Kennedy truly became a national figure.[4]

For one thing, unlike most New Dealers, Joe Kennedy got things done. Never much of a philosopher, he liked direct action, the shortest way. He

---

[3] *After Seven Years,* by Raymond Moley. New York, Harper, 1939.

[4] Even such doubters as James Landis were won over by Kennedy's performance as SEC chief. Landis later went on the Kennedy payroll as a legal troubleshooter.

once said that one of the penalties we have to pay for living in a democracy is that we don't know exactly what we want and another is that we cannot agree upon procedures to get it. No theorist, no follower of any dogma, Joseph P. Kennedy could not see the need for any antagonism in the world. All we needed was a "leader who will lead" and get things done. He was, he said, "very pragmatic."

When the SEC was well launched, Kennedy returned to private life. But he had made arrangements for the President to obtain—regularly—the finest products Scotland could produce. And F.D.R. was most appreciative. After one delivery of Scotch, F.D.R. wrote to Kennedy "how much I am enjoying the contents of the two trunks. I am saving some for you."

In 1936, Joe Kennedy formed a businessman's organization to back F.D.R. for a second term. He also wrote *I'm for Roosevelt,* in which he castigated "irresponsible wealth" for its "unreasoning, fanatical, blind, irrational prejudice against President Roosevelt" and his "courageous, clearheaded, inspiring leadership." Not only did Kennedy defend various New Deal policies, but he argued eloquently for a "planned economy" to prevent depressions and save the capitalist system.

"The more complex the society the greater the demand for planning," he wrote. "Otherwise there results a haphazard and inefficient method of social control, and in the absence of planning the law of the jungle prevails."

The fact that a wealthy speculator could be so outspoken against fellow millionaires was widely noted; but in fairness to Kennedy it must be remembered that he had not yet been fully accepted in traditionally conservative business circles. In such circles Kennedy was viewed as a plunger who profited on the misfortunes of others.

That Kennedy passed on his antagonisms to his sons was revealed in April 1962 when Big Steel proposed to raise prices. Angered over what he considered an industry double-cross, President Kennedy was quoted by the *New York Times,* "My father always told me that all businessmen were sons-of-bitches but I never believed it till now!"[5]

President Kennedy's lack of concern about businessmen and their problems was obvious long before the steel dispute. Some Liberal intellectuals loved it. Wrote Alfred Kazin in the *American Scholar,* "When one adviser, submitting a memorandum on Latin American problems, noted that certain recommendations could be highly irritating to American business, Kennedy waved the hypothetical objection aside. This elasticity makes him exciting to work for, and to pass from so detached a mind to the endless analysis of itself that Washington goes in for might well make an intellectual in Washington feel that 'brain power' is at the center of things again, that the few have again the chance to do well by the many."

Thus, to one certified intellectual at least, it is a sign of "elasticity" for a

---

[5] "President Kennedy ought to know what he's talking about," commented a Midwestern publisher. "His father is a business man."

President to reject out of hand any consideration of possible business complaints toward a course of Governmental action.

Once, when a Senator, Kennedy was asked about the industrialists who were invited to President Eisenhower's stag dinners and often played golf with him. "My God," said Kennedy, "how does he stand them? They're such awful bores."

Recently the *New Republic*'s "T.R.B." analyzed the makeup of the White House stag dinners, "at which Eisenhower tried to pick the brains of those attending." About half of the guests were businessmen. "Compare that with Kennedy!" T.R.B. exulted. "At a recent reception there were all the U.S. winners of Nobel prizes and not a businessman in the lot!" Happy, happy day!

"Many businessmen now charge that President Kennedy is anti-business," commented *Time*. "He is not against business; the problem is one of understanding. In both his public and private talk, and even when he is trying to be most conciliatory, he tends to refer to business as 'them'—as though 'they' were some strange entity. When he crushed Big Steel, he surely did not anticipate that he was triggering a crisis of confidence in the business community. He did not seem to realize that intervening bluntly in the U.S. economic system is something like slapping a lady: no one can really tell what will happen, but the results will almost surely be dramatic."

John F. Kennedy, of course, never had to work for a living. Everything had been handed to him. In 1930, as a lad of thirteen away at boarding school, he wrote to his father confessing puzzlement: his classmates had told him there was a Depression. What was a Depression? Jack had not heard about it at home.

In 1937, Joe Kennedy had hardly re-established himself in New York when F.D.R. put in an SOS asking him to head up the new Maritime Commission, designed to revive the United States Merchant Marine.

Kennedy tried to argue his way out of the assignment. "But, Mr. President," he said he told F.D.R., "I've just finished my tour of duty as chairman of the Securities and Exchange Commission, and it has cost me about $100,000 a year personally, because I couldn't trade on the stock exchange. If it's all the same to you, let some other patriot take it on the chin for a while. I'm fed up. I'd like to enjoy, for a change, the companionship of my wife and nine children. And there's a lot of money to be made on the market. I'd like to skim off my share of the profits."

Somehow F.D.R. prevailed upon Kennedy to forego his profits. The Maritime post, however, proved tough and frustrating. Before long Kennedy was at war with the unions. For one thing, he insisted that the Merchant Marine, like the Armed Forces, should be immune from unionization. What with the labor movement in the ascendant, however, Joe Kennedy became a decided embarrassment to the New Deal. Finally, F.D.R. pulled him out and sent him to London as the United States Ambassador.

Some of the circumstances surrounding the London appointment were never properly explained. According to James Roosevelt, Kennedy had ardently sought the ambassadorship which, he added, by political tradition he richly deserved. Moreover, the idea of a red-haired Boston Irishman representing the United States in the Court of St. James's had tickled F.D.R.'s funny bone.

But according to the self-styled Presidential agent, Cornelius Vanderbilt Jr., F.D.R. appointed Kennedy with little enthusiasm. "It was partly to please Jimmy Roosevelt, a business associate of Joe Kennedy's. Certainly the English raised a terrific hue and cry over the appointment. And in private F.D.R. did not hesitate to mention Catholic connections as a bar to political trust. . . ."[6]

By this time, James Roosevelt had emerged as a power in the New Deal. And Liberals didn't like it. For one thing, they complained, he was too close to Joe Kennedy. (How times have changed! In 1962, Congressman Roosevelt came under bitter Conservative attack for the "Leftist" views expressed in a book he edited, *Liberal Papers.*)

"Jimmy has his father's ear at all times," Secretary of the Interior Harold L. Ickes noted in his diaries. ". . . Jimmy has no political ideals, he is not a liberal. . . . Joe Kennedy's influence has been bad too. It was Kennedy who dissuaded the President from appointing Lowell Mellett as Kennedy's successor on the Maritime Commission. Kennedy was afraid that Mellett would settle the labor difficulty which he had not been able to settle, and so he persuaded the President to appoint a stooge of his own."[7]

The backbiting inside the New Deal was conducted on a truly grand style.

About the only thing that could be said in favor of the ambassadorial appointment was that Joe Kennedy spoke the language. Many Boston Brahmins were shocked at the spectacle. The son of an Irish saloonkeeper as the envoy to the Court of St. James's? What was the world coming to?

The thought of P. J. Kennedy's boy, all dressed up in satin knickers and bowing and scraping before British royalty, was likewise discomfiting to Boston's Irish. They could not decide whether to be indignant or flattered.

Joe Kennedy was flattered. This was the most prized of diplomatic posts, one that placed him at the very peak of the social world of two continents. For his children it meant social preferment. And he savored the reports of the dismay his ambassadorship had caused among the Back Bay aristocrats who had kept him out of their exclusive clubs. As far as he was concerned, they knew where they could go.

Kennedy, however, brought smiles to the faces of Boston's Irish when he

[6] *Man of the World,* by Cornelius Vanderbilt, Jr., New York, Crown, 1959.
[7] *The Secret Diary of Harold L. Ickes,* New York, Simon & Schuster, 1954.

refused to don knee breeches for the royal court. (According to Westbrook Pegler, this resulted in a controversy over whether the Ambassador was "bandy-legged or knock-kneed . . . but reference back to pictures of the Harvard baseball team gave strength to the bandy faction.")

At the outset, Kennedy proved to be an eminently popular Ambassador. London greeted the colorful new envoy, his charming wife, and their nine children with delight. At his first press conference, the Ambassador shocked British newsmen when he planted his feet on the desk. "You can't expect me to develop into a statesman overnight," he said.

One of his first moves was to do away with the custom of presenting at court the daughters of socially ambitious American families visiting in London. He explained he considered "undemocratic" the practice previous Ambassadors had followed of selecting annually a "small number of young ladies from a long list, very few, if any, of whom, he has ever seen." The job, he said, was "distasteful." Accordingly, Kennedy confined presentations to the families of United States officials in England and to members of the American colony.

Some London newspapers saw in this unprecedented action "a bitter blow to United States social climbers."

At the first Royal Court of the 1938 season, the Kennedys presented seven American girls to the King and Queen. Two of them were their daughters, Rosemary and Kathleen.

Addressing the Pilgrims Club in London, Kennedy compared himself to a Pilgrim father who had so many children he couldn't get them all into the *Mayflower*. While it was possible to find a steamship large enough to transport his family across the Atlantic, Kennedy said that because of school and other complications it was necessary for them to go over "in installments."

Not all Englishmen were amused by Kennedy's antics, however. In his diaries, Ickes noted a conversation he had with Colonel Josiah Wedgwood, an outstanding Liberal member of Parliament: "Apparently he doesn't think much of Kennedy. On the contrary, at a time when we should be sending the best that we have to Great Britain, we have not done so. We have sent a rich man, untrained in diplomacy, unlearned in history and politics, who is a great publicity seeker and who is apparently ambitious to be the first Catholic President of the United States."

The increasing frequency with which Joe Kennedy was being mentioned as a possible successor to Roosevelt in 1940 began to trouble the White House. Kennedy, nearing fifty years of age, was reported as acceptable to conservative Democrats. As for his Catholicism, the *Chicago Tribune* said that "Kennedy's conservativism as compared with other Roosevelt followers will offset religious prejudice in the South."

But there was one hitch to Kennedy's reported ambitions. It was becoming increasingly obvious that F.D.R. was considering the possibility of becoming the first man in the nation's history to occupy the Presidency for three terms.

It was also obvious that relations between Kennedy and Roosevelt had grown chilly. In June 1938 when Kennedy returned to the United States to attend the Harvard graduation of his number one son, Joe Jr., the Ambassador was called to Hyde Park to meet with the President.

Citing the usual unimpeachable sources, the *Chicago Tribune* reported that "the conversation was carried on in a frigid atmosphere because Mr. Roosevelt has received positive evidence that Kennedy hopes to use the Court of St. James's as a steppingstone to the White House."

The "evidence" consisted of memoranda which Kennedy had been sending to selected Washington correspondents from Grosvenor Square. They contained inside information about his ambassadorial labors and other newsy tidbits that had not yet been reported to the State Department.

Kennedy returned to his ambassadorial post to nurse his bruised ego and to participate in behind-the-scenes efforts to bolster Prime Minister Neville Chamberlain's efforts to reach an accommodation with Hitler. These efforts culminated in the September 1938 agreement reached at Munich.

Kennedy was outspoken in his defense of the Prime Minister. At a Trafalgar Day dinner—one month after "peace for our time" was supposedly obtained at Munich—the United States Ambassador declared that Chamberlain's "all but superhuman efforts in behalf of peace should command the respect of us all." Then Kennedy presented his own—and quite startling— formula for peace:

"It has long been a theory of mine that it is unproductive for both the democratic and dictator countries to widen the division now existing between them by emphasizing their differences. . . . Instead of hammering away at what are regarded as irreconcilables, they could advantageously bend their energies toward solving their common problems by an attempt to reestablish good relations. . . . There is simply no sense, common or otherwise, in letting these differences grow into unrelenting antagonisms. After all, we have to live together in the same world, whether we like it or not."

Kennedy called upon the quarreling nations to curb the armaments race which he said was hurtling the world toward catastrophe.

From Cambridge, Massachusetts, where his number two son was attending Harvard, Jack Kennedy wrote his father that his Trafalgar Day speech "while it seemed to be unpopular with the Jews etc., was considered to be very good by everyone who wasn't bitterly anti-fascist. . . ."

The *New York Post* angrily observed: "If this precious specimen of diplomatic expediency had been written in the British Foreign Office it could not have served better to bolster the propaganda of Prime Minister Chamberlain." And anti-Chamberlain leaders in Britain, led by Winston Churchill, charged that the Ambassador had come close to interfering in Britain's internal affairs.

Nettled by these attacks, Kennedy reminded United States interviewers that "there was no official criticism, because the speech was read in Washington before I delivered it."

Many years later, Kennedy was to add a fascinating footnote to this grim period. He said that following the signing of the Munich Pact, President Roosevelt cabled him a congratulatory message to pass on to Chamberlain.

"I went over to Number 10 Downing Street the day I received the cable," Kennedy recalled. "But instead of handing the cable to Chamberlain, as is customary, I read it to him. I had a feeling that cable would haunt Roosevelt some day, so I kept it."

Apparently the proper occasion never arose for Kennedy to use it against F.D.R.

In November 1938, in an effort to soften criticism, Ambassador Kennedy offered a plan whereby Germany's 600,000 Jews would be resettled in sparsely inhabited parts of the world. The proposal was hailed by *Life* magazine: "If the 'Kennedy plan' succeeds, it will add new luster to a reputation which may well carry Joseph Patrick Kennedy into the White House."

But the "Kennedy plan" did not succeed. It was never attempted. Both F.D.R. and Secretary of State Cordell Hull dashed cold water on it. "Hull came as near to being tart as he ever does in his comments on Kennedy's activities," one dispatch reported. And then came the White House announcement that Myron C. Taylor would henceforth speak for the United States on all matters concerning European refugees—an indirect rebuke to Ambassador Kennedy.

The chilling shadow of 1940 had fallen on whatever friendship had existed between Kennedy and Roosevelt. And the Ambassador was making no secret of his annoyance with the President.

Harold Ickes faithfully recorded in his diaries a conversation he had with John Cudahy, our Ambassador to Ireland. According to Cudahy, wrote Ickes, "Kennedy does some pretty loud and inappropriate talking about the President. He does this before English servants, who are likely to spread the news. According to John, Kennedy is vulgar, coarse and highly critical in what he says about the President. And when John cautioned him on one occasion, Joe said he didn't give a damn. John did say that if Joe couldn't be loyal to the President, he ought to resign. . . ."

On June 13, 1938, the German Ambassador in London, Herbert von Dirksen, reported to Berlin on several talks he had had with Ambassador Kennedy.

Von Dirksen reported that Kennedy had expressed sympathy for Nazi Germany: "Although he did not know Germany, he had learned from the most varied sources that the present government had done great things for Germany and that the Germans were satisfied and enjoyed good living conditions."

A little while later in the dispatch: "The Ambassador then touched upon the Jewish question and stated that it was naturally of great importance to German-American relations. In this connection it was not so much the fact that we wanted to get rid of the Jews that was so harmful to us, but rather the loud clamor with which we accompanied this purpose. He himself understood our Jewish policy completely; he was from Boston and there, in one golf club, and in other clubs, no Jews had been admitted for the past fifty years. His father had not been elected Mayor because he was a Catholic; in the U.S., therefore, such pronounced attitudes were quite common, but people avoided making so much outward fuss about it."

In a subsequent dispatch, von Dirksen reported: "Today, too, as during former conversations, Kennedy mentioned that very strong anti-Semitic tendencies existed in the United States and that a large portion of the population had an understanding of the German attitude toward the Jews. . . . From his [Kennedy's] whole personality I believe that he would get on well with the Führer."

When these memoranda were published in 1949, in a State Department collection of captured Nazi documents, Kennedy termed the references to him "complete poppycock." He maintained he could recall no such conversations. He said von Dirksen "must have been trying very hard to set himself right in Germany by telling the German Foreign Office the things he thought they'd like to hear."

Following Jack Kennedy's Presidential nomination, the *New York Times* reported that excerpts from the von Dirksen dispatches were being used in a whispering campaign against him. "Anticipating this," the *Times* said, "James M. Landis, former dean of the Harvard Law School and a supporter of Mr. Kennedy, has been going through the former Ambassador's records, hoping to find Mr. Kennedy's version of the talks."

However, if Landis did come up with something, he failed to make it public.

Kennedy has always insisted that his widely publicized isolationist views about World War II were animated solely by his concern over United States interests and not by any admiration for Germany.

The Soviet-Nazi non-aggression pact of August 1939, which touched off World War II, shocked Kennedy. H. V. Kaltenborn visited the Ambassador in London at the time. The veteran broadcaster found Kennedy pacing the room in his shirtsleeves in a "dramatic" mood.

"You have come to me in one of the most important moments in world history!" he exclaimed. "We are engaged in a fight for time!"

Though now pessimistic about the possibility of working out any lasting settlement with Hitler, Kennedy told Kaltenborn, "Anything that keeps Britain at peace is in the interest of the United States. . . . Chamberlain feels he cannot make too many concessions. Yet gaining time is the most important thing we can do at this point."

Britain was at war with Germany within a few days. Several months later, the Chamberlain Government gave way to one headed by Winston Churchill. For Joseph P. Kennedy, this was a bitter blow.

As Hitler's blitz hardened Britain's resistance, Kennedy became even more isolationist. He had no faith that the tight little isle could resist a Nazi invasion. He even reported that Churchill would not last long as Prime Minister. And when the British began their desperate efforts to evacuate their troops from Dunkirk, Kennedy cabled: "Only a miracle can save the British expeditionary force from being wiped out." (The "miracle," of course, occurred.) The fall of France only deepened his fears. "It seems to me," he cabled F.D.R., "that if we had to protect our lives, we would do better fighting in our own backyard."

On another occasion Kennedy cabled Washington an implicit warning that Britain might manufacture an incident to draw America into the war. "This morning an American correspondent of an English paper mentions that all it needs is an 'incident' to bring the United States in. If that were all that were needed, desperate people will do desperate things. A course of action that involves us in any respect, that presupposes the Allies have much to fight with except courage is, as far as England goes, I think, fallacious."

In private conversation Kennedy was consistently defeatist and pessimistic about the war's outcome. To one United States newsman he confessed his inability "to make head or tail out of what this war's all about. If you can find out why the British are standing up against the Nazis you are a better man than I am." His defeatist views were well known in Berlin. Several of his cables had been leaked to German officials in Washington, who immediately dispatched them to their Foreign Office.[8]

In March 1940 the Ambassador returned to Washington to provide F.D.R. with a personal report. An episode then occurred at the State Department office of Ambassador William C. Bullitt, of which Harold Ickes made note. Bullitt was being interviewed by Joseph M. Patterson, publisher of the *New York Daily News,* and Doris Fleeson, then the *News'* Washington correspondent. In walked Kennedy.

"Before long," wrote Ickes, "Kennedy was saying that Germany would win, that everything in France and England would go to hell, and that his one interest was in saving his money for his children."

Bullitt took issue when Kennedy began to criticize the President very sharply. "The altercation became so violent that Patterson remarked he suspected he was intruding, and he and Doris Fleeson left," Ickes continued.

". . . Bill told him he had no right to say what he had before Patterson

---

[8] The source of these leaks to the German Embassy in Washington was never identified. Presumably, since this was the period of the Soviet-Nazi Pact, a Communist agent planted in the State Department may have been the source.

and Fleeson. Joe said that he would say what he Goddamned pleased before whom he Goddamned pleased—or words to that effect. Joe's language is very lurid when it is unrestrained. Bill told him he was abysmally ignorant on foreign affairs and hadn't any basis for expressing any opinion. He emphasized that so long as Joe was a member of the Administration he ought to be loyal—or at least keep his mouth shut. They parted in anger."

Kennedy never forgave Bullitt. In fact, Kennedy later virtually pinned the blame for World War II on Bullitt. He did this in a conversation with James Forrestal in 1945.

In his diary, Forrestal noted that Kennedy's view was "that Hitler would have fought Russia without any later conflict with England if it had not been for Bullitt's urging on Roosevelt in the summer of 1939 that the Germans must be faced down about Poland; neither the French nor the British would have made Poland a cause of war if it had not been for the constant needling from Washington. Bullitt, he said, kept telling Roosevelt that the Germans wouldn't fight, Kennedy that they would, and that they would overrun Europe.

"Chamberlain, he says, stated that America and the world Jews had forced England into the war. . . . In the summer of 1939, the President kept telling him to put some iron up Chamberlain's backside. Kennedy's response was that putting iron up his backside did no good unless the British had some iron with which to fight, and they did not. . . ."

Why didn't F.D.R. recall his controversial Ambassador?

One reason, suggested in their newspaper column by Joseph Alsop and Robert Kintner, was that F.D.R. believed that Kennedy was likely to do less harm in London than in New York. If relieved of his diplomatic duties, Kennedy would most certainly express his opinions the moment he got through customs. "The President is represented as fearing he will reduce large numbers of leaders of opinion to such a state of hopeless funk that our foreign policy will be half-mobilized by fear," the columning team wrote.

There was, perhaps, another reason. Having decided to run for a third term, F.D.R. wanted to immobilize any potential opposition.

Kennedy's Presidential ambitions had one last gasp. Early in 1940, his name was put forth as a possible Democratic candidate, by a group of admirers who announced that a slate of delegates pledged to the Ambassador would be entered in the Massachusetts primary. Kennedy, however, declined the honor. He declared that his job as Ambassador "involves matters so precious to the American people" that his energies could not be diverted.

In October 1940, a few weeks before the election, Joe Kennedy returned to the United States. It was understood that he intended to combat F.D.R.'s third-term aspirations. But before he could say anything, he was whisked off for a confidential chat with Roosevelt. Emerging from the White House, he endorsed F.D.R. for a third term.

"The reason for the switch was simple," Stewart Alsop was to report in the *Saturday Evening Post* many years later. "Roosevelt offered Kennedy—or so Kennedy firmly believed—the Presidential nomination in 1944. When instead Roosevelt ran for a fourth term, Joe Kennedy was understandably bitter."

As part of his deal with F.D.R. Kennedy purchased some $20,000 in air time to deliver an unusually strong plea for F.D.R.'s re-election. He conceded he had had some sharp differences with the President. "However, these are times which clamor for national unity—times when national teamwork is vital." On the basic issues, he said, he could find little on which to disagree with the President. It was, according to *Life,* the most effective vote-getting speech of the 1940 campaign.

The next night, in Kennedy's home town, Franklin Roosevelt told an election crowd that he had been happy to welcome back "to the shores of America that Boston boy, beloved by all of Boston and a lot of other places, my Ambassador to the Court of St. James's, Joe Kennedy." (This was the speech in which F.D.R. also said, "And while I am talking to you mothers and fathers, I give you one more assurance. . . . Your boys are not going to be sent into any foreign wars.")

Following the election, Joe Kennedy was in an expansive mood. In Boston, he talked freely to Louis Lyons, of the *Boston Globe,* thinking—he said later—that his comments were off-the-record. According to Lyons, this is what the Ambassador said:

"I'm willing to spend all I've got to keep us out of the war. There's no sense in our getting in. We'd only be holding the bag. What would we get out of it?

"I know more about Europe than anybody else in this country. . . . Democracy is finished in England. It isn't that she's fighting for democracy. That's the bunk. She's fighting for self-preservation. . . ."

The Ambassador also referred to Winston Churchill's fondness for brandy; King George's speech impediment; and the fact that the Queen looked more housewifely than regal in her clothes.

Perhaps his biggest indiscretion—politically speaking—was in discussing Eleanor Roosevelt. "She bothered us more on our jobs in Washington to take care of the poor little nobodies than all the rest of the people down there put together. She's always sending me a note to have some little Susie Glotz to tea at the Embassy."

After the interview was published, Joseph Dinneen, then with the *Globe,* telephoned Kennedy at his home in Bronxville, New York, and read him the story. The Ambassador did not deny his statements but said he thought the interview had been off-the-record. "There is nothing left for me now but to resign," he told Dinneen.

The next day, Kennedy repudiated the interview publicly. He said he had been misquoted and that his confidence had been betrayed. But there was no retrieving his words. Within days, Joseph Kennedy offered his resignation as Ambassador. It was quickly accepted by the White House. The very directness and candor that had always spiced his conversation had led to his downfall. His political career had been virtually destroyed. And he knew it.

Early

4

One reason President Kennedy may not have wanted his youngest brother, Teddy, to enter the political wars in Massachusetts was that he knew one of the skeletons in the family closet might be exposed to view. That had to do with Teddy's expulsion from Harvard in 1951 after university officials learned he had persuaded or employed a friend to take a Spanish examination for him which he feared he couldn't pass.

Teddy was only eighteen years old when he was caught cheating by proxy. Evidently he was forgiven because of his youth. Allowed to return, Edward Moore Kennedy was graduated from Harvard in 1956. Other colleges may have more stringent codes on cheating, but other academic delinquents do not have fabulously wealthy fathers who may be tapped for endowments.

In March 1962, Ted Kennedy manfully confessed to his youthful indiscretion. "What I did was wrong," he told a friendly newsman who broke the story. But there seemed to be more regret over "the unhappiness I caused my family and friends" than over his offense.

Robert Ruark, the Swahili-speaking columnist, was really glad that Teddy had confessed all: "A man can build a staunch reputation for honesty by admitting he was in error, especially when he gets caught at it." Tongue in cheek, Harvard's Young Republicans suggested a title for a campaign biography: "How to Succeed at Harvard Without Really Trying."

At any rate, Ted Kennedy eventually learned enough Spanish to do his bit in 1961 to advance the New Frontier along the highways and byways of South America. He was going great in Brazil until someone told him the language was Portuguese. His unorthodox approach was further revealed when, addressing a group of ragged peasants in poverty-stricken Northeast Brazil, Ted declared, "President Kennedy is personally concerned with your welfare and as proof of this has sent me, his own brother, to talk to you as an equal."

The Kennedys had come to consider one of the two Massachusetts seats in the Senate as family property, and what the Kennedys want they go after. Attorney General Robert F. Kennedy quipped while receiving an honorary Doctor of Laws degree from Manhattan College: "To those of you who have or have not received such degrees, I suggest that you get your brother elected President and there is no telling where you may go."

Teddy turned thirty, the Constitutional minimum for a Senator, in February 1962. A month later he announced his candidacy. All the Kennedy resources, including the womenfolk and their luncheons for wives of delegates to the Massachusetts Democratic Convention, went into operation.

The Senate seat had been kept warm for Teddy until he came of age. A pliant family friend, Benjamin A. Smith II, who had been one of J.F.K.'s roommates at Harvard, somewhat reluctantly announced he would step down. Political opponents alleged that Teddy's political proxy in the Massachusetts race was really big brother.

In defeating State Attorney General Edward J. McCormack Jr. in the first round of their contest for the Senate, Ted Kennedy showed he had energy, aggressiveness, and one of the best smiles in the business. Nevertheless, the most powerful presence at the June 1962 state Democratic Convention in Springfield was that of the President himself. Teddy's slogan was that, if elected, he would "speak with a voice that will be heard"—presumably by his two brothers already in the Government.

"Ted Kennedy's style," reported John L. Saltonstall Jr. in the *New Republic,* "is strongly reminiscent of his brother's in 1952, 1958 and 1960: the same sort of earnest, clean-cut young men and crisply pretty girls handling their assignments with unruffled efficiency; the rather menacing if-you're-not-with-us-watch-out air; the professional experts on hand but kept well in the background; the obvious indications of plenty of money in the campaign till; the same spirit of ruthless pragmatism which seems to suggest that every problem can be solved by careful analysis and vigorous action."

Ed McCormack, who was not free of a touch of nepotism himself (he is the favorite nephew of Speaker of the House John W. McCormack), didn't stand a chance, even though he had a clear majority in liberal-academic backing. Just prior to the convention Professor Mark de Wolfe Howe of Harvard Law School (and a former adviser to then Senator Kennedy) wrote a letter to some 4,000 academicians across the state seeking support for McCormack. He said the choice was "between a bumptious newcomer and an experienced and gifted public servant," and called young Kennedy's candidacy "both preposterous and insulting."

Most Massachusetts Democrats agreed. A few brave souls, in fact, turned up at the convention with one arm in a sling and the other bearing a sign that read: "Don't let them twist your arm." Others carried signs with the legend: "Mommie, can I run for the Senate?" Another exasperated delegate cried out, "I'm too old to get a post office, so I cast my vote for McCormack."

The lure of a postmastership was only one of the pressures on the 1,719 delegates. Before the convention, it was made known that from now on, win or lose, Teddy would be in charge of state patronage for the Kennedy Administration.

There were other pressures. It was alleged that one McCormack delegate was being investigated for income-tax irregularities; that another was facing deportation charges against his family. "It's pressure, pressure, pressure, post office, post office, post office," bellowed McCormack's father, "Knocko." In addition, Stephen Smith, a Kennedy brother-in-law who had recently left the State Department, was in charge of keeping track of the delegates. Another Kennedy relative, Joseph Gargan, had also resigned as an Assistant U.S. Attorney to help Teddy's campaign.

The effect of all this, with Big Brother watching, was summed up by one delegate just after conferring with Ted: "Teddy's been an assistant district attorney for a year or so. He's completely unqualified and inexperienced. He's an arrogant member of an arrogant family." Then he smiled, and said, "And I'm going to be with him."

Another delegate explained: "If Teddy weren't the President's brother, he wouldn't get 100 votes in the convention. . . . But the Kennedys will be around for a long time, and they have memories like elephants. What am I supposed to do, cut my throat?"

McCormack himself contended that "if it had been a secret ballot, I would have won two to one." He said it was his "patriotic duty" to oppose Teddy in the primary, since a Kennedy victory would "give the Republicans their greatest national domestic issue in 1964, the charge of a Kennedy dynasty."

The dynasty theory, which started off as a joke, was now being taken more seriously by professional politicians. After Jack has been in the White House for eight years, the theory goes, Bobby will be on hand to take over in 1968. Then, in 1976, Teddy will be available.

Then it will be 1984.

By that time, according to some sardonic Massachusetts "pols," a regency will be set up to keep the Presidency available for the Kennedy's now-infant son.

Another skeleton in the Kennedy closet has to do with the maternal grandfather John F. Fitzgerald, after whom the President was named.

During the 1960 campaign the President's mother, Rose, spoke fondly of her father at the teas and *kaffeeklatsches* she threw across the country. Invariably she told her guests that both Jack and Bobby learned their politics on Honey Fitz's knee. James MacGregor Burns, in his semi-official biography of J.F.K., devoted much space to Honey Fitz and his influence on Grandson Jack. He described Honey Fitz as impeccably honest, one who would never do what another Boston politician, James Michael Curley, once did—take a Civil Service examination for a friend who could not pass it.[1]

Most Kennedy biographies assert that after he lost the Boston Mayoralty to Curley in 1914, Honey Fitz was never again elected to public office. This doesn't exactly conform with the facts as stated in the *Biographical Directory of the American Congress 1774–1949*.

This official U.S. Government publication states that Honey Fitz was elected to the House of Representatives in 1918 after defeating the incumbent Democrat, Peter Francis Tague, by 238 votes out of the 15,293 cast.

Tague contested the election, charging that the balloting had been rigged by Honey Fitz and a local ward leader by the name of Martin M. Lomasney. Pending an investigation by the House Elections Committee, Honey Fitz was seated in Congress on March 4, 1919. His term ended abruptly the following October 23 when the House Committee expelled Honey Fitz on the grounds that his election was "fraudulent." Peter Tague was ordered seated in his place.

There are old-timers in Boston who, despite such shenanigans (common in his day), remember Honey Fitz as a grand old man, a prince of a fellow, loyal to his pals. Nor should we be too hard on J.F.K.'s campaign biographers for failing to unlock this particular closet.

But for the grandson, as President, to name the Presidential yacht *Honey Fitz* seems to indicate a clannish loyalty so strong as to flaunt a historical fact of no real credit to the family.

But it could be argued that Honey Fitz's grandson Jack also cut corners when he first ran for office. To put it more bluntly, he launched his political career on the basis of a misrepresentation. The episode occurred in 1946 when Kennedy, then twenty-nine years old, decided to run for the Congressional seat vacated by James Michael Curley.

To enter a Massachusetts primary, a candidate is required to submit the names of 250 party supporters. On April 2, 1946, John F. Kennedy presented such a list to the Office of the Registrars of Voters and Election Commissioners of the Commonwealth.

There was one thing wrong, however. John Kennedy himself was not

---

[1] *John Kennedy: A Political Profile,* by James MacGregor Burns. New York, Harcourt, Brace, 1960. Even though an election-year biography, this is a valuable work. Professor Burns, though a Kennedy partisan, is also a distinguished historian, a fact which shows in this better-than-usual book.

an enrolled Democrat. The law clearly provided that while a serviceman could register to vote by mail, he must appear in person to enroll as a member of a political party. Jack Kennedy had not done so.

The last filing day was April 30. To be eligible to file, a candidate would have had to be a certified party member for not less than thirty days before that date.

Kennedy's oversight was discovered on April 2. The following day—twenty-seven days before the filing day—he quietly slipped into City Hall where he registered as a Democrat. He did this despite the fact that the law permitted no exceptions.

A small, inconsequential technicality? Perhaps. Yet, as a friendly book put it so delicately, it was "an embarrassing moment that would have been fatal to anyone whose name wasn't Kennedy."[2]

Joseph Kennedy had originally envisioned his eldest son Joe Jr., as the politician in the family. Tall, handsome, outgoing, and robust, Young Joe—the photographs show—was his father to the life. They were also alike ideologically. At Harvard Law School he helped organize a keep-America-out-of-war group and made speeches decrying United States intervention in "foreign wars." In one speech he declared the United States would be better off dealing with a Nazi-occupied Europe on a barter system than engaging in total war on the side of Great Britain.

Young Joe had long known what he wanted. His teacher at the London School of Economics, Harold Laski, later recalled how he "often sat in my study and submitted with that smile that was pure magic to relentless teasing about his determination to be nothing less than President of the United States."

Young Joe launched his political career in 1940 as an anti-Roosevelt delegate at the Democratic National Convention, pledged to support James A. Farley for President. Despite the pressures of the third-termers (including John W. McCormack)—one even called his Ambassador father in London to intervene—Young Joe stuck to his guns. When the Massachusetts delegation was polled, his resolute young voice could be heard calling out, "James A. Farley." The episode provided another chip of ice in the cool expanse that eventually divided the Kennedy and Roosevelt families.

Four years later, Joseph Kennedy Jr. died a hero's death in the European war. And it was foreordained that, as the next in line, John F. Kennedy would take his place and carry on for the family.

"I thought everybody knew about that," Father Joe once said to author Joe McCarthy. "Jack went into politics because Young Joe died. Young Joe was going to be the politician in the family. When he died, Jack took his

---

[2] The book, *Front Runner, Dark Horse,* by Ralph G. Martin and Ed Plaut (New York, Doubleday, 1960), provides an extraordinary insight into the forces and events that have shaped recent Democratic party history.

place. Joe used to talk about being President some day, and a lot of smart people thought he would make it."

In carrying on for Young Joe, however, as author McCarthy noted, Jack Kennedy "may be less consciously carrying on for his father."

Unlike his gregarious, robust brother Joe, Jack Kennedy was a sickly child, suffering from various ailments that required recurrent periods of convalescence. He was more bookish, preferring "Billy Whiskers" and James Fenimore Cooper to the family calisthenics. ("I wasn't a terribly good athlete," he later said, "but I participated.")

According to his father, "Joe was altogether different from Jack, more dynamic, more sociable and easy going. Jack was rather shy, withdrawn and quiet. His mother and I couldn't picture him as a politician. We were sure he'd be a teacher or a writer."

Joseph Kennedy was long unable to talk about his dead son without choking up. In 1957 Bob Considine asked him whether he would comment on Joe Jr. "One of the top financiers of the age," Considine reported, "a man known in many fields as cool beyond calculation under fire, suddenly and terribly burst into tears at the luncheon table and for five full minutes was racked with grief that cannot be described."

The same effect was produced when he discussed the problem of aiding retarded children, an enterprise to which the Kennedy Foundation has contributed millions. Joseph Kennedy was himself touched by the tragedy; his eldest daughter Rosemary, who was born handicapped, lives in a Wisconsin nursing home.

Four years after Joe Jr. was killed, Kathleen, the next-to-the-oldest daughter, died in a plane crash in France. Widow of the Marquis of Hartington, the son of the Duke of Devonshire, who himself had been killed leading his Coldstream Guards in battle, Kathleen had survived the London blitz as an American Red Cross worker.

The untimely passing of two of the best and brightest of the Kennedys may help account for the tremendous drives, the ambition to excel at any cost, that mark the surviving Kennedys.

"The boys," a family friend told the *Saturday Evening Post* in 1957, "are trying to live up to the image of Joe as they remember him. They are trying to do the things he might have done if he had lived. The girls feel the same obligation to emulate Kathleen."

Whatever their motives, the fact remains that Joe Kennedy ran his family like a tribal chieftain. When he gave an order he expected it to be unhesitatingly obeyed. The children had to be at the meal table five minutes early, and they often heard their father's reminder that Lord Nelson had attributed *his* success to the fact he was always fifteen minutes ahead of time.

"I remember that we always kept a tight ship," Ted Kennedy recently reminisced. "We had a clear idea of what we could do and what we could not do. You could ride your bike on the property, but not off. You had to be in the house when the lights went on. We had to pick up our clothes."

A close family friend told *McCall's* Eleanor Harris, "Every single kid was raised to think, first, What shall I do about this problem?; second, What will Dad say about my solution?"

Yet, while his children were growing up, he was often absent on deals, devoting himself to the gathering of the green with a zeal that put Daddy Warbucks in the shade.

Once, in 1924, Joe Sr. spent seven straight weeks in a New York hotel room juggling stock. While there his daughter Patricia was born in Boston. He did not see his new baby until a month later.

But he justified this feverish money-making as a means of guaranteeing his children's security.

"Making money is not important to me," he said recently. "In the beginning I had no alternative in order to provide security for myself and my children. But I was far more interested in public service at which I spent twenty-five years of my life."

The trust funds he established for each of his children, he said, were aimed at freeing his brood from mundane labors so that it could devote itself to public service.

"I fixed it so that any of my children could look me in the eye and tell me to go to hell," he claimed.

Jack Kennedy, however, has a different view.

"That was in 1929 and Dad was speculating," he said. "It was a very risky business. He was speculating pretty hard and his health was not too good at the time, and that was the reason he did it. There was no other reason for it."

For those seeking to trace President Kennedy's political development in his formative years, much remains a mystery. Jack was fifteen when Franklin Roosevelt took office. "In a recent interview," the *Reporter's* Douglass Cater noted in 1959, "he was entirely prepared to admit that the coming of the New Deal had little intellectual or emotional impact on him." For one thing, he could not remember that it was the subject of much discussion around the family table. Most of 1932, moreover, Jack was away at an exclusive boys' boarding school.

"Those discussions at dinner were never a formal thing," Joseph P. Kennedy said. "Never organized debates. They were more a discussion of personalities rather than politics. It's a natural thing to do, to talk about the people you know and the people you read about—but don't forget that I was away a great deal of the time. Their mother had a lot to do with their education. She spoke to them on different subjects."

Jack Kennedy's memory is somewhat different: "At first, they were mostly monologues by my father . . . well, not exactly monologues. But we didn't have opinions in those days. Later, the discussions included us more, but mostly about personalities, not debates on issues and things. I never had any particular interest in political subjects in those days."

For many years Joe Jr. alone of all the children was permitted to talk at mealtimes with his father. And when the father was away, it was Joe Jr. who ruled the roost. Like his father, he was driving, domineering, hot-tempered, and demanding of absolute obedience from his younger brothers and sisters.

"I don't think I can ever remember seeing him sit back in a chair and relax," Jack Kennedy has written of his older brother. "Even when still, there was always a sense of motion forcibly restrained. And yet, this continuous motion did not have its roots in restlessness or nervousness but rather came from his intense enthusiasm for everything he did and his exceptional stamina."

What kind of child was President Kennedy? "By and large," his mother said, "he wasn't any different from any other little boy in the neighborhood. He liked to play, and he had a terrible way of misplacing things like items of clothes. Sometimes he disobeyed, and then he was spanked."

But she also recalled that, even as a little boy, Jack Kennedy had a way with people, occasionally raising havoc with her discipline. "Sometimes I'd punish him by sending him off to bed with only bread and water. Then he'd slip downstairs and charm the cook into feeding him."

Jack Kennedy's earliest memories are not of the baronial splendors to which he later became accustomed. They are of his early childhood years in Brookline, the Boston suburb where he was born on May 29, 1917. In those days the Kennedys lived on a comparatively modest scale.

"At that stage," recalled Rose Fitzgerald Kennedy, "we were happy to pile our growing family into a model-T Ford every Sunday and Joe would drive ten miles to Winthrop to visit his parents. . . ."

What with her husband away a good deal of the time, it was not easy for Mrs. Kennedy.

"I don't think I know anyone who has more courage than my wife," Joe Kennedy said recently. "In all the forty-six years that we have been married, I have never heard her complain. Never. Not even once. I know that she has been sick, because other people have told me. But she never has. This courage is a quality that children are quick to see."

Though Mrs. Kennedy had the actual job of rearing the children, it was her husband who directed the rearing. Father Joe taught his children to be tough; winning the game was the big thing. He charged them with his own competitive energy. Once he ordered Joe and Jack from the table when he learned that, in fooling around, they had lost a sailing race. Tennis and touch football were played with the same intensity. If you were a Kennedy, you had to win.

Their competitive spirit in what might laughingly be called a sporting match was rough indeed. Shortly after she was married, Jacqueline Kennedy broke an ankle playing touch football with the Kennedys. And that was the last time she ever engaged in intramural sports with them.

"Even when we were six or seven years old," Jack's sister Eunice recalled, "Daddy always entered us in public swimming races. If we won, he got terribly enthusiastic. Daddy was always very, very competitive. The thing he always kept telling us was that coming in second was just no good. The important thing was to win—don't come in second or third, that doesn't count, but win, win, win."

There was a ceaseless sense of urgency about the whole family. "They never relax even when they're relaxing," Jacqueline Kennedy told Eleanor Harris in 1957. "After dinner they all play guessing games like Categories or charades or Twenty Questions—you're doing mental somersaults all the time."

The parlor game of Monopoly was a great favorite of the Kennedys (a fact a psychiatrist probably would find most intriguing) and they played it almost every night. When Jacqueline would get too bored, she would deliberately make a couple of mistakes to end the game.

"Does Jack mind?" she was asked.

"Not if I'm on the other side," she replied.

As sister Eunice has observed, "Jack hates to lose. He learned how to play golf, and he hates to lose at that. He hates to lose at anything. That's the only thing Jack gets really emotional about—when he loses. Sometimes, he even gets cross."

One of the most realistic accounts of life with the pre-White House Kennedys was written by David Hackett, a weary weekend visitor. Excerpts from *Rules for Visiting the Kennedys:* "Anticipate that each Kennedy will ask what you think of another Kennedy's (a) dress, (b) hairdo, (c) backhand, (d) latest public achievement. Be sure to answer 'terrific.' This should get you through dinner. Now for the football field. It's 'touch,' but it's murder. If you don't want to play, don't come. If you do come, play, or you'll be fed in the kitchen and no one will speak to you. Don't let the girls fool you. Even pregnant, they can make you look silly. Above all, don't suggest any plays, even if you played quarterback at school. The Kennedys have the signal-calling department sewed up, and all of them have A-pluses in leadership. Run madly on every play, and make a lot of noise. Don't appear to be having too much fun, though. They'll accuse you of not taking the game seriously enough. Don't criticize the other team, either. It's bound to be full of Kennedys too, and the Kennedys don't like that sort of thing. . . . To be really popular, you must show raw guts. To show raw guts, fall on your face now and then. Smash into the house once in a while going for a pass. Laugh off a twisted ankle or a big hole torn in your best suit. They like this. It shows you take the game seriously as they do.

"But remember. Don't be too good. Let Jack run around you now and then. He's their boy. . . ."

There is a great deal of veiled truth in this mildly sardonic essay. The Kennedys practiced the gentle art of *One-upmanship* long before that subtle process of maneuvering for advantage ever became a new word in the language.

"We soon learned that competition in the family was a kind of dry run for the world outside," Jack Kennedy has observed.

Thus, Joseph Kennedy's children grew into an exceptionally close-knit family. Less admiring acquaintances have suggested that their insular solidarity made them extremely self-centered. Hard-driving, success-bent and closed-ranks, the Clan Kennedy always knew what it was going after, and invariably got it.

Why a devout family like the Kennedys (Jack was married by Cardinal Cushing; Bobby and Teddy by Cardinal Spellman) would insist on secular educations for the boys may have puzzled some of the folks in East Boston. But Joe Kennedy's motives were the same as his own father's in sending him to Harvard—if you're going to take over from the enemy, you have to know their ways before you lick 'em.

"Their mother insisted that the girls go to Catholic schools," Joe Kennedy once said. "I had other ideas for the boys' schooling. There is nothing wrong with Catholic schools. They're fine. But I figured the boys could get all the religion they needed in church, and that it would be broadening for them to attend Protestant schools. On the other hand, I think it would be good for a Protestant boy to attend a Catholic school for a year. That kind of thing, I think, does away with narrow viewpoints."

It is part of the family legend that when Joseph Sr. was Ambassador and the family was living in London, Bobby was sent to a Protestant boarding school where chapel was compulsory. For several weeks Bobby was ordered to attend. Knowing the tenets of his church forbade it, Bobby refused to go. Finally, of his own accord, he packed up and left the school.

The most curious of the elder Kennedy's actions appeared to be his sending Joe Jr. and Jack to the London School of Economics to study under Socialist Harold Laski.

Perhaps, in retrospect, the action was not so curious. Laski, a close friend of F.D.R., had enormous influence among top New Dealers. And Joe Kennedy had begun to develop large political ambitions for himself.

Nevertheless, the London School was a funny place for "a former knight-errant of the speculative art"—as Harold Laski would one day describe Joe Kennedy—to send his kids. LSE was a mecca for domestic Socialists and revolutionaries from all parts of the Empire. Many a stratagem against British Imperialism was hatched over cups of tea in the cafeteria and many a Tory denounced the school as "a hotbed of Bolshevism." One prominent Laski alumnus was India's controversial V. K. Krishna Menon.

Into this unlikely setting arrived eighteen-year-old Jack Kennedy, fresh out of Choate.

"My father wanted me to see both sides of the street," he later explained.

But unlike his brother who the year before had won the Marxist theoretician's praise for his quick comprehension of economic principles, Jack Kennedy did not get much out of Laski's dialectics. Young Jack fell ill with jaundice and was forced to return home.[3]

As a child, Jack was constantly plagued by bad health. In those years he had to stay in bed, first after scarlet fever and later with what he described as "some blood infection that left me lacking in white corpuscles." He never complained when he was sick; he had already developed a stoical attitude toward pain. In 1957 his father told Eleanor Harris, "I can tell Jack's sick by looking at him but not by listening to him."

In this attitude, as in others, Jack copied his older brother. According to their father, Joe would never complain if he were ill. "And whatever Joe did, Jack did. Joe won all the championships at sailing, then Jack did. Then they became a team and won all the championships together."

Jack was thirteen years old when in 1930 he first left home to begin his college preparatory studies at Canterbury School. This was the only Catholic school he ever attended. At best he was an average student. In some subjects, notably Latin, he was less than satisfactory. "He can do better than this," his Latin teacher wrote to his parents.

Nor was Jack proficient in spelling. Long after he left Canterbury, spelling was to prove difficult for him. In a letter to his parents he reported he had learned to play "baggamon" and in another he told his devout mother that "we have chapel every morning and evening and I will be quite pius I guess when I get home."

At Easter he was laid low by an appendicitis attack and was unable to finish the spring semester at Canterbury. The next fall he shifted to Choate, in Wallingford, Connecticut, a rather select private school with a strong Episcopal flavor, of which—according to experts on society—"it is of incalculable benefit to a young man to attend." Prominent alumni include Adlai Stevenson and Chester Bowles.

Joe Jr. was there, making a name for himself as an athlete. Jack, lighter and smaller, found himself unable to compete with his brother on the varsity level. Indeed, Joe won the Harvard trophy, given each year to the Choate boy who best combined sportsmanship and scholarship.

Jack could boast of neither. And Father Joe was not at all pleased. From Washington he wrote crisp things about Jack's grades and his failure to apply himself to his studies as had his brother. "Now, Jack, I don't want to give the impression that I am a nagger, for goodness knows I think that is the worst

---

[3] However, LSE still remembers Jack. His 1960 election as President was described in a school publication under the heading, "Old Student's Success."

thing any parent can be. . . . I definitely know you have the goods and you can go a long way. Now, aren't you foolish not to get all you can out of what God has given you? . . . After all, I would be lacking even as a friend if I did not urge you to take advantage of the qualities you have. It is very difficult to make up fundamentals that you have neglected when you were very young and that is why I am always urging you to do the best you can."

Jack, then in his mid-teens, was slightly built, not overly strong, but he desperately tried to live up to his father's expectations of him. "I hope my marks go up," he wrote to his father, "because that is the best way to say thanks for the trip. I really do realize how important it is that I do a good job this year, if I want to go to England. . . . I really feel, now that I think it over that I have been bluffing myself about how much real work I have been doing."

And to his mother, Jack wrote, "Maybe Dad thinks I am alibiing but I am not. . . . I have also been worrying about my studies."

When he did get good grades, Jack was rewarded substantially. Once it was a trip to England. Another time it was a pony. Then there was a sail-boat he named *Victura,* which he explained was Latin "meaning something about winning."

Jack was growing up. He was beginning to take on the so-called Choate "look." The dancing lessons he had taken so reluctantly were beginning to come in handy as he began to attend dances with young ladies. He had dis-covered girls and he liked what he discovered. In this he aped his father who also appreciated feminine charm. One winter, one of Jack's sisters tattled on him in a letter to their father: "Jack was a very naughty boy when he was home. He kissed Betty Young under the mistletoe down in the front hall. He had a temperature of 102 degrees one night, too, and Miss Cahill couldn't make him mind."

According to his Choate roommate Lemoyne Billings (today a vice president of the Lennen & Newell advertising agency in New York), "Ken"— as Kennedy was known at the time—was very busy socially. The scrapbooks of Billings, who is a frequent weekend guest of President Kennedy, are packed with telegrams from the mid-thirties, summoning him to a party at Hyannis Port, a dance in Boston, or a weekend in New York, often informing him what young ladies would be available as dates.

The golden days of boyhood were about over. Jack was eighteen and a senior at Choate. But his grades hadn't improved much. He had trouble with languages. Biology and chemistry bored him. He did somewhat better in English and history. "He only applied himself with average effort so he only got average grades," a teacher recalled. "He'd promise to do better, but the results were not forthcoming." A classmate said, "He didn't work too hard."

But Lem Billings summed it up this way, "The difference between Jack then and today is that today, if he found he was weak in some particular field, he'd work at it to better himself."

In June 1935, Jack was graduated from Choate, sixty-fourth in a class of 112.

It is one of the ironies of Jack Kennedy's life that though he has become so identified with Harvard University he never wanted to go there in the first place.

Instead, fresh out of Choate and a visit to the London School of Economics eighteen-year-old Jack entered Princeton. The reason for this is not quite clear. He has since stated he decided on Old Nassau because his best friend from Choate, Lem Billings, was going there. More probably he wanted to break away from the shadow of his brother Joe, who was already at Harvard.

Whatever the reason, his career at Princeton was cut short by what has been described as either a recurrence of jaundice or a bad case of hepatitis. After recuperating from his illness he decided in September 1936 to enter Harvard as a freshman and thus keep his family's Harvard ties alive. Of such little shifts are careers fashioned: as a Princetonian, even a Kennedy would have had difficulties coping with the tribal requirements of Massachusetts politics—or with Harvard-style economics.

At Harvard, Jack is remembered by his professors as a bright but—at least until his senior year—not overly industrious student. His undergraduate years gave little portent of greatness. Few, if any, of his classmates regarded him as a future President.[4]

All that Stanley Geller, a classmate, who is now a New York Reform Democratic leader, can remember about the President on the campus is "that he was a nice-looking, bushy-haired young man who was on the swimming team."

Not only did he mature slowly at college, but the furious drive that characterized his political career was then channeled into unrealized attempts at campus prominence.

Ironically, the future President of the United States was not conspicuously successful in campus politics. He made his first fling at politics as a freshman. One of thirty-five candidates for class president, he wound up far back in the pack. As a sophomore he failed to muster enough votes to win a place on the Student Council. In his last months at Harvard he finally won an election. He put his name up for the Permanent Class Committee. Six were to be elected and, when the votes were counted, he squeaked in fifth.

"He was a pleasant, interesting guy," says author Cleveland Amory, then editor of the Harvard *Crimson,* the undergraduate newspaper. "But the legend that we considered him destined for the Presidency is pure hogwash."

---

[4] "Musing, no doubt, about this singular lack of prophetic indications," the *Washington Post* reported on February 27, 1961, "today's undergraduates at Winthrop House, where young Jack lived, have posted a sign at the portals: 'Be Kind to Your Roommate.' "

He was two years behind his brother Joe, who already was the best-known member of his class.

"Jack was bound to play second fiddle," says Eric Cutler, a Harvard contemporary, more recently Dean of Admissions.

The spirit of fierce competition, instilled in them by their father, was not dimmed by campus life. "Everything became a contest," says Jack's former roommate, Benjamin Smith, "whether a swim in the pool or a race to the breakfast table."

But the pace set by Joe was too difficult for Jack to follow. Joe was an above-average student, a leading campus politician (on the Student Council his first three years, he became chairman in his senior year), and a varsity football player.

Jack tried to compete in athletics. He desperately sought to make the varsity football team, but was limited by his weight which hovered around 160. He had to settle for the junior varsity, and in the process he seriously injured his back.

And in endeavoring to live up to his father's expectations young Jack further injured his health, by trying to win a place in the backstroke for the swimming team's all-important meet with Yale. A week before the race he was laid up at the infirmary with the flu. Fearing his light diet would weaken him, Jack had his roommate smuggle in steaks and malted milks. Then, he'd sneak out to the pool and practice when no one was around.

But it didn't work. He was edged out in the trials by Richard Tregaskis, who later won fame as the author of *Guadalcanal Diary*.

Even his most ardent admirers will concede that as a student Jack showed little of the drive and diligence that later characterized his campaign for the Presidency. In his first two years he took the "gentleman's C" in most subjects, and a C average was just enough to keep him out of trouble with the Dean's office.

The most charitable description of those years is probably that of Professor Ronald Ferry, then head of Winthrop House; he said that Jack was "reasonably inconspicuous."

Dr. Payson Sibly Wild, Kennedy's tutor and professor of government, recalls his most famous student "as very shy and very determined."

"I'd had his brother Joe, too," said Dr. Wild, more recently at Northwestern University, "and I remember Jack saying that he had to work hard for his grades, unlike Joe who could cram all one night and get good marks. Jack didn't get the best marks at first, but he was always punctual for our sessions, and he always had his assignments completed."

One reason his assignments were always completed was given by a classmate who recalled that "whenever Good Old Jack needed a helping hand, some of us would pitch in and help him write his papers."

Kennedy's extraordinary shyness in this period was also commented upon by Harold Ulen, retired Harvard swimming coach.

"I had Jack on my teams for three years and I remember him very vividly," Ulen recalls. "He was more of a team man than an individualist and, in fact, was so modest that he used to hide when news photographers would come around to take pictures of the team."

In the rigid social hierarchy at Harvard, Jack began to enjoy status, but not too much of it. "After all," as a classmate later put it, "Jack made the Spee Club, but not the Porcellian."

At least this was a step up for the Kennedy family. The Spee Club, consisting of students whose families were socially prominent, had denied membership to Joseph P. Kennedy, It was a social triumph of sorts.

Jack also became a member of St. Paul's Catholic Club, Hasty Pudding (known for its annual musical revues), and was a successful chairman of the Freshman Smoker Committee.

The Smoker Committee was a peculiar Harvard institution (abolished in 1956 for not being consistent with the college's tradition) that allowed first-year men a chance to blow off steam which might otherwise be directed into riots in Harvard Square. A good smoker was a stag party in which chorines, comedians and other entertainers would hold forth before the whole freshman class—each one of whom had been given a corn cob pipe to smoke.

After a brief tryout period Jack was named to the business staff of the *Crimson*. But Jack did not devote as much time or effort to the newspaper as did a predecessor, Franklin D. Roosevelt, class of 1904, who was *Crimson* Chairman.

A brief glimpse into the workings of Kennedy's mind at the time has been provided by Blair Clark, then Chairman of the *Crimson*. Clark, more recently a CBS correspondent, recalls a hot argument he had with Jack over the question of labor's right to organize. Clark says that Kennedy took what he considered to be an ultra-conservative position by arguing that something had to be done about curbing labor's excesses. At the time, Jack's father was Chairman of the Maritime Commission and had come under terrific attack by the labor movement.

Generally, however, Kennedy avoided discussions of this type. For one thing, he did not see politics in his future. "I recall that I was a Freshman at Harvard when Henry Cabot Lodge was elected to the U.S. Senate," he once wrote. "I don't suppose I ever thought in those days I would some day defeat him for the Senate." Kennedy was as apolitical as any student could be in those days. He avoided forums such as the Young Democrats and the Liberal Union. To him, these groups consisted of doctrinaire young men who, he said later, espoused their causes with a certitude which he could never quite understand.

This was a passionate, frenzied period on the campus. The civil war in Spain, the growing menace of Nazi Germany, and the possibility of United States entrance into war abroad had divided the student body between isolationist and interventionist forces.

Brother Joe, in fact, was a leading spirit in the Harvard movement to keep America out of foreign wars.

But Jack managed to remain aloof from the bitter controversy. "He had no interest in causes," says his former professor, Arthur Holcombe. "His approach was that of a young scientist in a laboratory."

The truth is that no one was really interested in what Jack thought about worldly issues.

"Joe was the only Kennedy you heard of at Harvard then," a classmate has recalled. "He was a handsome, back-slapping, driving man, a born politician."

"I can still remember Joe," says Mrs. George de Pinto—"Mrs. Dee" to the thousands of boys she has served in Harvard dining rooms since 1928. But to the Kennedy boys she was "Deedee."

"Joe," she said, "was a real diplomat. He always had a twinkle in his eye, and he'd always know just the right thing to say. One day, he was kidding around, like he always did, and he came up to me and said, 'Deedee, you shouldn't have to work here. When I become President, I'll take you up to the White House with me.' "

The story Deedee likes to tell the most concerned the Kennedy boys and their father. Joseph Sr. had been invited to give a talk at Winthrop House one night, but the boys got there late, after everybody started eating.

"They came in and started to go up to their father; they stopped as if feeling it was too late. Then the housemaster said, 'Go on, boys, say hello to your father.' They went up to him and both boys kissed him."

According to Deedee, she will never forget the affection the boys showed their father. "It's as clear now as it was then," she added.

Unlike his brother, Jack Kennedy had gained a reputation for being inordinately reserved.

"You'd always see Joe in his convertible, the top down, and the prettiest girl in town beside him," a friend admiringly recalls. "But Jack never even went steady until late in his senior year."

Who the girl was no one outside the family seems to recall. Whoever she was, however, she apparently had made a big impression on Jack. For as his mother wrote to her husband, following Jack's graduation from Harvard, "Jack seems a little depressed that he let his girl get away. He says she is the only one he really enjoyed going out with. And yet he admits that he did not want to get married."

When Joe was graduated and then entered Harvard Law School, Jack began to come into his own. He inherited Joe's "gentleman's gentleman," George Taylor, and roomed with Harvard's football hero of that period, Torbert Macdonald, today a Congressman from Massachusetts. Later, they shared a four-man suite with Benjamin Smith, who recently filled Kennedy's unexpired term as Senator from Massachusetts, and Charles G. Houghton Jr., today an executive vice president of a Milwaukee corporation.

Jack's roommates had early learned not to mix in Kennedy family arguments.

"Once Joe Jr. came up to us after football practice and offered some unsolicited advice," recalls Macdonald. " 'Jack,' he said, 'if you want my opinion, you'd be better off forgetting about football. You just don't weigh enough and you're going to get yourself banged up.' "

Macdonald watched Jack's face closely as his brother was talking. "I saw his face flush with anger. But he held his fire. So I decided to put in my two-cents' worth."

" 'Come off it, Joe,' I said—or something like that—'you're making too much out of nothing. Jack doesn't need any looking after.'

"I soon saw how right I was. Jack whirled on me and told *me* off in no uncertain terms for butting into a family affair. I never did it again."

In the summer of 1937, before beginning his sophomore year, Jack Kennedy, accompanied by his Choate roommate Lem Billings, visited France, Spain, and Italy. Jack, then twenty years old, had a ball. He climbed the smoldering heights of Vesuvius, watched a bullfight, and won a small sum at Monte Carlo. (The woman next to him "was quite upset by my winning $1.20 while she lost about $500," he reported triumphantly to his father.) He also had an audience with the Pope and he visited with Cardinal Pacelli, whom Jack described as "quite a fellow." (The Cardinal, later to become Pope Pius XII, had visited the Kennedy home in Bronxville in 1936.)

In a letter from Rome, Jack Kennedy advised his father he couldn't help admiring the way in which the Fascist corporate system operated. For one thing, it was tidy; and, he added, "everyone seemed to like it in Italy." (Other, more sophisticated observers, were led to utter now-embarrassing words of praise for the Mussolini regime because, among other things, the trains ran on time.)

From Madrid, Jack wrote of his impressions of the new Franco regime. He spoke of "the almost complete ignorance 95% of the people in the U.S. have about situations as a whole here. For example, most people in the U.S. are for Franco, and while I felt that perhaps it would be far better for Spain if Franco should win—as he would strengthen and unite Spain—yet at the beginning the government was in the right morally speaking as its program was similar to the New Deal. . . . Their attitude towards the Church *was* just a reaction to the strength of the Jesuits who had become much too powerful—the affiliation between church and state being much too close."[5]

The following year, his father—by now United States Ambassador in London—suggested that Jack tour Europe. "It's not just to be a holiday for

---

[5] Jack Kennedy was obviously misled by his own lack of political knowledge. Far from being a popular figure with "most people in the U.S." at the time, Francisco Franco was a hated name, particularly among Liberals. Apparently, young Kennedy's sweeping judgment was based on opinions expressed within the limited circles in which he then was moving.

John," his mother told newsmen in Paris. "The idea is to see whether he wants a career in the diplomatic service."

On a semester's leave from Harvard, Jack spent six weeks in Paris, nearly a month in Warsaw, and did a grand tour of Germany, Latvia, the Balkans, the Soviet Union (Leningrad, Moscow, the Crimea), Turkey, and Palestine.

In Moscow, he stayed with the United States Embassy's Second Secretary, Charles (Chip) Bohlen. The Soviet Union, he decided, was a "crude, backward, hopelessly bureaucratic country." On leaving Jerusalem, he wrote to his father that he believed British policies toward the Palestine problem were eminently fair, but what was needed was a solution acceptable to both the Jews and the Arabs. (As President, Kennedy soon discovered that such solutions are not as easy to devise as he had thought.)

On plunging into a hard-working senior year in the fall of 1939 (to recover the lost semester, he said, "I had to work like hell"), he undertook his first piece of disciplined intellectual work. To graduate with honors in political science he had to do a thesis. He chose for his subject "Appeasement at Munich."

According to biographer Burns, the thesis "was a typical undergraduate effort—solemn and pedantic in tone, bristling with statistics and footnotes, a little weak in spelling and sentence structure." An arresting quality of the thesis was Kennedy's emotional detachment from the crisis he described. "He criticized people for being too emotional over Munich. He was no alarmist, he insisted, as though being an alarmist in the spring of 1940 were a sin."

Another arresting quality was the echoing of Joseph P. Kennedy's contention that Neville Chamberlain and Stanley Baldwin were not responsible for Munich. Rather, Jack Kennedy stressed the role of the pacifists, the economizers, the concern of both labor and business with immediate self-interest, the fear of regimentation.

In Jack Kennedy's view, the Munich Pact was inevitable and even desirable. It was inevitable because Britain had delayed her rearming; and it was desirable because it bought time to rearm.

"Most of the critics have been firing at the wrong target," he wrote. "The Munich Pact itself should not be the object of criticism but rather the underlying factors, such as the state of British opinion and the condition of Britain's armaments which made 'surrender' inevitable."

Far from sharing young Kennedy's belief that Munich was a shrewd play for time, Neville Chamberlain actually seemed convinced that it was a great, enduring master-stroke that, as he then boasted, would assure "peace with honour, peace for our time." Moreover, young Kennedy soft-pedaled Chamberlain's naïveté and glossed over his smugness, such as his unfeeling verdict on Hitler's dismemberment of Czechoslovakia: "A quarrel in a far-away country between people of whom we know nothing."

This, of course, reflected Joseph P. Kennedy's own smugness toward the Nazi onslaught in Europe. Though he shared his father's isolationist views at the time, young Kennedy did not go to the extreme of opposing aid to the Allies. As he then wrote to his father, "I of course don't want to take sides too much."

Though it may have been a "typical undergraduate effort," the thesis was completely out of line with Kennedy's previously far-from-brilliant academic efforts. It won for Jack a *magna cum laude*. And he informed his father that he was graduating *cum laude* in political science. Back came a cable: "TWO THINGS I ALWAYS KNEW ABOUT YOU ONE THAT YOU ARE SMART TWO THAT YOU ARE A SWELL GUY LOVE DAD."

And to a friend in New York, the Ambassador cabled a request that Walter Winchell be informed that Jack was graduating from Harvard *cum laude.* (In those days, the columnist and the Ambassador were good friends.)

Somehow "the typical undergraduate effort" was converted into a best-selling book, *Why England Slept.* And Ambassador Kennedy was not loath to take credit for his son's first literary effort. In August 1940 he told a British correspondent that, "When I was in the states with Jack and heard some professors talking about Munich, I realized they knew nothing about it. I said to Jack, 'You get down to it and tell them all about it.' "[6]

From London, Jack received a steady stream of advice on rewriting, editing, and publishing contacts.

By now it was the gray spring of 1940. Most of Europe had fallen to Hitler's legions. Winston Churchill had become Prime Minister of a beleaguered England. And Ambassador Kennedy had a change of mind about who to blame for the British predicament. Now Father Joe thought that Jack had gone too far in acquitting Baldwin and Chamberlain of responsibility. He suggested that Jack blame both the people and their leaders.

Agreeing, Jack replied: "Will stop whitewashing Baldwin."

Curiously, a month before, the Ambassador had been quoted as having said, "I have always thought and felt that the British people ought to put up a bust for Chamberlain, in honor of Munich."

Joseph P. Kennedy's contacts proved useful to his son. The family's good friend, Arthur Krock, then Washington bureau chief of the *New York Times,* recommended the title *Why England Slept,* playing deliberately on Churchill's earlier *While England Slept.* It was Krock who found an agent and arranged for publication of the book. Another of the Ambassador's friends, *Time-Life* publisher Henry R. Luce, agreed to do the foreword. Selection by the Book-of-the-Month Club followed.

According to Burns, the facts and views in the book were little changed from the thesis, except for "a surprisingly rhetorical ending" that expressed doubt whether a democracy can face the challenge of a dictatorship and sur-

---

[6] *Diary of a Diplomatic Correspondent,* by George Bilainkin. London, George Allen & Unwin, 1942.

vive as such. "Actually, these and a few other sentences of exhortation he had taken almost verbatim from a letter from his father."

In his book Kennedy argued that England only "woke up" with Munich. "Until that time, business was unwilling to give up its special interests, labor was unwilling to give up its interests, the people as a whole were unwilling to cooperate for fear of sacrificing some of the things which they considered their democratic rights. I do not believe that in fighting a Fascist country, you have to set up Fascism, but I do believe that certain aspects of democracy and capitalist economy must go when a nation is at war with a totalitarian nation."

The book, published during the blitz in England, proved an immediate best seller. Book reviewers were properly astonished that a 23-year-old could have marshaled his material so skillfully, make such temperate judgments, and reach his conclusions in such effective language. The *New York Times* called it "a book of such painstaking scholarship, such mature understanding and fair-mindedness, such penetrating and timely conclusions that it is a notable textbook for our times." The *Herald Tribune* described it as "This electrifying diagnosis . . . an extraordinarily able achievement." The *London Times Literary Supplement* said that though it was "a young man's book," it "contains much wisdom for older men."

The volume was remarkable "for having been written by one so young," Henry Luce said in his foreword. "I cannot recall a single man of my college generation who could have written such an adult book on such a vitally important subject during his senior year at college. In recent months there has been a certain amount of alarm concerning the attitude of the younger generation. If John Kennedy is characteristic of this young generation, and I believe he is, many of us would be happy to have the destiny of this Republic handed over to this generation at once. . . ."

In London, Ambassador Kennedy could hardly contain himself for joy. Proudly, he sent copies of *Why England Slept* to Harold Laski, Winston Churchill, and Queen Elizabeth.

And he airmailed a letter to his son.

"You would be surprised," the Ambassador wrote to Jack Kennedy, "how a book that really makes the grade with high-class people stands you in good stead for years to come."

It was a lesson which Jack Kennedy would not forget.

Pol

5

John Fitzgerald Kennedy became President of the United States first because of an accident—a tragic accident—and subsequently by design as inexorable as the denouement of a Grecian drama.

The accident occurred in 1944 when a B-17 Flying Fortress, headed for *Festung Europa,* suddenly exploded over the English coast. Aboard was Joseph Kennedy Jr. Lieutenant Kennedy, a naval officer who had volunteered for the mission, was twenty-nine years old.

President Kennedy has often wondered what career he might now be pursuing had his brother Joe remained alive. He feels certain he would not have entered politics.

"I'm sure I would have gone to law school after the war," he said recently. "Beyond that, I can't say. I was at loose ends. I was interested in ideas, and I might have gone into journalism. The exchange of ideas that goes with teaching attracted me, but scholarship requires a special kind of discipline; it wouldn't be my strength."

Following his graduation from Harvard in June 1940, Jack Kennedy spent a somewhat aimless year. He considered enrolling in law school—at Yale, not Harvard (he wanted no direct competition with brother Joe). Instead, he entered Stanford's Graduate School of Business for the fall term. But after six months he decided a business career was not for him and, according to his biographers, he went off on a long, leisurely trip through Latin America.

For some reason Kennedy has never been particularly loquacious about his south-of-the-border trip. His office once reported that he visited Argentina, Brazil, and Chile. His companions, if any, were not disclosed. All that could be said about this period, generally, was that Kennedy—like others of his generation—was restless. He could not decide on a career; and the war in Europe threatened to engulf the United States.

Meanwhile, his father had launched a one-man crusade to keep America out of war. Joseph P. Kennedy felt he had good personal reason to oppose F.D.R.'s warlike maneuvers. Indeed, one friend recalls a conversation from their SEC days when Kennedy mentioned the possibility of another European war. "I have four boys," he said, "and I don't want them to be killed in a foreign war." As he spoke, the friend said, Kennedy's eyes began to cloud.

Kennedy himself later denied any such consideration. He felt, he said, that World War I had solved nothing and that a second would be equally tragic and useless.

Within a month of resigning as United States Ambassador, Joseph Kennedy took to the air waves to argue that United States aid to Britain "should not and must not go to the point where war becomes inevitable." Accordingly, he bitterly opposed the Lend-Lease bill which, he said, would confer on the President "authority unheard of in our history."

"This is not our war," he said. "We were not consulted when it began. We have no veto power over its continuance."

In a Spring commencement speech at Oglethorpe University the former Ambassador argued that the United States should not become a belligerent "just because we hate Hitler and love Churchill. We cannot divert the tides of mighty revolution now sweeping Asia and Europe. Any attempt to do so would end in failure and disgrace abroad, in disillusionment and bankruptcy at home."

In his autobiography Ben Hecht reported that Kennedy "had spoken to fifty of Hollywood's leading Jewish movie makers in a secret meeting at one of their homes. He told them sternly that they must not protest (against Nazi atrocities) as Jews. . . . Any Jewish outcries, Kennedy explained, would impede victory over the Germans. It would make the world feel that a 'Jewish War' was going on. . . ."[1]

But for some reason Kennedy did not put up the all-out fight against Lend-Lease that he had promised. "He got throat trouble, as the ball-players say, and choked up," chronicled his former friend, Westbrook Pegler.

"During this episode, Burton K. Wheeler, then an antiwar Senator from Montana, got, so he thought, a promise from Kennedy to fight Lend-Lease in the hearings in the Senate. Therefore when Kennedy's course was otherwise, Wheeler called on him in considerable pique and high temper at the Carlton Hotel to straighten things out. He rang the bell and banged on the door. There was no answer.

[1] *A Child of the Century,* by Ben Hecht. New York, Simon & Schuster, 1954.

"So Wheeler called a maid and explained that he was a friend of Ambassador Kennedy who had left his overcoat inside. Would she open the door with her passkey? Sure she would, Senator. So Wheeler flung open the door and there, by his own word, was Ambassador Joe Kennedy. I have no verbatim, but Wheeler is an emphatic man."

It was obvious that Joseph Kennedy had begun pulling his punches in his antiwar crusade. Why? According to Pegler, it was because the Internal Revenue Service had suddenly manifested interest in Old Joe's income tax returns.

"Four years ago," wrote Pegler in April 1960, "Joe Kennedy angrily denied that he had been in trouble over his tax problems. But the late Reverend James M. Gillis, the great Paulist missionary, had been my first authority for this, and later I made a number of personal calls at a secret office which Joe maintained at great expense in a suite of the old Marguery Hotel on Park Avenue, now vanished in favor of a typical ice-cube edifice. There I discovered a staff of numerous lawyers and accountants working on Joe's books.

"The chief was James M. Landis, former secretary to Justice Brandeis, former member and secretary of the Securities Exchange Commission, and former Dean of Harvard Law. This was manpower! Kennedy insisted that this mass of subtle knowledge was performing only routine chores. But their chores went on and on through the Truman regime and the office was terminated only when the wreckers knocked the structure away from around them."

In these years Joe Kennedy's "attitude toward Franklin D. and Mrs. Roosevelt smacked more of blunt South Boston scurrility than the twittering reverence of his mood today." The Ambassador, Pegler wrote, invariably praised "my dogged attacks on the avarice and corruption in the Roosevelt regime and household. Nowadays, I find myself drawing comparisons between the Kennedys and the Roosevelts to the moral detriment of neither."

All through the war years Joseph Kennedy was beset by what he angrily decried as "libelous and actionable" accusations made against him in the public prints. He was accused of being almost everything—a Nazi sympathizer, an isolationist, a reactionary, a turncoat, a Roosevelt-hater.

Some particularly cruel stories were spread about the Ambassador by Liberal sources. Questions had been raised about his courage in London during the Nazi air raids. *PM*, for example, in an April 21, 1942, story from its Washington bureau then headed by James Wechsler, actually asked why the Ambassador had "found it convenient—to put it in its best light—to remain in the country, away from the Embassy, during most of the London blitz."

Victor Bienstock, London correspondent of the Overseas News Agency, had previously reported that Ambassador Kennedy was known to American correspondents as "Jittery Joe."

"He certainly did not distinguish himself by any personal courage when the raids on London began," said Bienstock. "When a bomb fell near the estate he had taken comfortably outside London, the British Press Association reported that he had a narrow escape. A correspondent phoned him to check up.

" 'How far did it fall from the house?' he asked.

" 'Three hundred yards—I measured it myself,' the Ambassador replied excitedly.

" 'Coming or going?' was the retort."

"Who are they who say these things," Joe Kennedy angrily asked a newspaperman-friend in 1944, "and how do they get that way? They are said or written first by irresponsible columnists and commentators who pretend to have inside information. . . . They can't name the informant because there is none and then the reliable commentators call me for verification and the denial never catches up with the falsehood.

"Sometimes it is libelous and actionable, but not to such a degree that a victim feels compelled to do something about it. It is better judgment to ignore it than to make an issue of it and focus further public attention upon it."

What made the Ambassador particularly bitter was the fact that two of his sons were in the service. "Jack is back in this country after having a motor torpedo boat shot out from under him," he observed. "I never wanted this war. I don't think anybody in the United States wanted it. I opposed it with all the vigor I could command. I was bombed in the Battle of Britain. A bomb with my initials fell in my back yard. I was in an automobile that was blown up on the sidewalk. I reported honestly to the President what I heard and saw and I urged that we keep out of this war."

Both his sons had volunteered for service before Pearl Harbor. After completing his second year at Harvard Law, Joe Jr. had joined the Navy as an aviation cadet in June 1941, winning his commission and wings the following May. Jack, rather than compete with his brother, had tried for the Army. But he was rejected because of his old back injury. However, after a series of treatments and exercises to strengthen his back he was accepted by the Navy.

At first he had to content himself with a desk job in Washington, preparing a daily news summary for the Navy Chief of Staff—work he found dull and routine. He then was transferred to Charleston, South Carolina, to work on a project dealing with the protection of defense plants against enemy attack. He found this boring too. Lem Billings, his buddy from Choate, recalls a 1941 scene when Kennedy, then a fledgling naval officer, delivered a detailed lecture on bombs to factory workers, relying heavily on the Navy's textbooks. Kennedy, he said, was momentarily stumped when a worker asked him how to disarm an incendiary bomb.

"I'm glad you asked that question," Kennedy replied. "I'll have a bomb specialist come down next week and explain it."

Fearing he might be stuck with a desk job for the rest of the war, Jack Kennedy once again relied on his father to pull some strings to insure he would get some sea duty. Father Joe contacted his old friend, Under Secretary of the Navy James V. Forrestal, and the right strings were pulled. Eventually, Jack was transferred to the more informal and strongly Ivy League atmosphere of the torpedo boat training station at Melville, Rhode Island. There he joined such old college chums as Torbert Macdonald in learning how to handle the speedy, highly maneuverable PT boats that had already won acclaim for such feats as rescuing General MacArthur from Corregidor. Early in 1943 Lieutenant (j.g.) John F. Kennedy shipped out from San Francisco for unknown adventures.[2]

By now the story of how Jack Kennedy became a hero in the South Pacific is an old one. Told and retold in the magazines (and by John Hersey in the *New Yorker*), three books, television shows, and in a full-length Hollywood production, the story bids fare to take its place in the nation's folklore. Though the story has assumed a Made-on-Madison-Avenue look, it must be stated that it was indeed the real thing. The significance, frequently overlooked, however, is that Kennedy was only one of many who—without dramatics or posturing—rose to greatness in World War II, one of a great band of heroes.

"Everything else dates from that adventure," wrote Robert T. Hartmann in the *Los Angeles Times* in February 1960, "and Kennedy's superabundant charm is never more engaging than when he leaps back to wartime reminiscence with a receptive ex-veteran of the Solomons campaign.

"That was, perhaps, the only time Kennedy ever was wholly on his own, where the $1 million his father gave him wouldn't buy one cup of water."

But it must also be stated there were those Navy skeptics who wondered how it was possible for Jack, as the skipper of PT 109, to have gotten such a small maneuverable craft into position to be slashed in two by the bow of a Japanese destroyer—and this in Allied-controlled waters. No other motor torpedo boat was reported to have suffered such singular misfortune in any of the oceans in World War II.[3]

Back on duty, Jack became ill with malaria and dropped to 120 pounds. His old back injury, aggravated by the PT boat disaster, began to trouble

---

[2] By now Jack Kennedy was nicknamed by fellow officers "Shafty." The origin of the nickname, however, is unclear. One version is that it had to do with Kennedy's being so skinny. Kennedy himself once told a newsman it was because once, annoyed by an assignment, he let loose with a bit of Naval slang, "Boy, did I ever get shafted." And added Kennedy, "The fellows all laughed at the way I said 'shahfted,' and they started to call me 'shahfty.'" Fortunately for Kennedy, the nickname never stuck.

[3] On July 10, 1960, Drew Pearson quoted General Douglas MacArthur as having asserted that Kennedy "should have been court-martialed" for letting "a Japanese destroyer mow him down. When I heard about it, I talked to his superior officer." However, the former Pacific Commander-in-Chief promptly denied having made any such statement.

him. "I feel like hell," he told shipmates. In December 1943, rotated home on leave, he headed for Palm Beach where his parents were wintering.

"As soon as he dropped his bags and said hello to us," family friend Chuck Spalding recalled, "he wanted to go right away to a night club and live it up. I guess when he was hanging onto that wrecked half of PT boat in the South Pacific, Jack thought he would never see a pretty girl or hear dance music again."

When his leave was over Kennedy was assigned to PT duty in Miami. Several fellow PT skippers from the Solomons were there too. Their job was to come up with ideas on improving PT teamwork, which had been criticized by the high command in the South Pacific.

Once they threw a bad scare into the civilian population. This came during a simulated Army-Navy invasion of the city. The PT boats, with Lieutenant Kennedy at the helm of one, moved in first. Approaching the shore, they began laying smoke. Unfortunately the wind blew the fumes inland.

A goodly throng was present at the dog track, watching the greyhounds chase the mechanical rabbit. A cloud of ugly, dark smoke came pouring in from the bay. Though relatively harmless the fumes had an acrid smell. Someone shouted, "Poison gas," and there was panic. Some spectators actually thought the Germans had landed. Despite the rush for the exits no one was seriously injured.

And that is how Jack Kennedy helped bring the reality of war to fun-loving Miami.

In the late Spring of 1944 Jack had a bad fall aboard ship while on a practice cruise. His back trouble flared again and he was ordered to Chelsea Naval Hospital, near Boston, for treatment. At the hospital he was received with a small ceremony at which he was awarded the Navy and Marine Corps Medal. It was as good a way as any to prepare for the agonizing months ahead of him.

But it was small comfort, indeed, when he learned from his anguished father one August weekend at Hyannis Port that Joe Jr. had been reported missing in action off the Normandy coast. Only later was it learned that after two complete tours over enemy waters Joe Jr. had passed up home leave to volunteer as a pilot of a highly secret "drone" plane, aimed at a Nazi V-2 launching site. The idea was for Joe and his co-pilot to parachute to safety while the radio-guided plane headed for its target. Just before their scheduled jump the explosives-laden plane exploded. The bodies were never found.

Just three months earlier young Joe had been present at the London civil ceremony at which his sister Kathleen—known to the family as "Kick"—was married to William Cavendish, the Marquess of Hartington, heir of the Duke of Devonshire. A lively, pretty girl, Kathleen had met Billy, as the young nobleman's friends called him, during her debutante days in London. After a stint as a writer on the *Washington Times-Herald* she returned to wartime

London as a Red Cross worker and began seeing the marquess again. It was a poignant, Montague-Capulet romance—both the Catholic Kennedys and the Protestant Cavendishes were dismayed. As *Time* wrote about the prospective union, "One of England's oldest and loftiest family trees swayed perceptibly."

In this emotional crisis Kick was able to turn to only one member of her family, Joe Jr., who was stationed in England as a Navy pilot. "Never did anyone have such a pillar of strength as I had in Joe in those difficult days before my marriage," she later wrote. ". . . In every way he was the perfect brother, doing, according to his own light, the best for his sister with the hope that in the end it would be the best for the family."

And so, on May 6, 1944, she was married in a civil ceremony at the Chelsea Registry Office. Her brother Joe was there to give her away. In the United States, the Kennedy family maintained an icy silence. Rose Kennedy, taking it harder than anyone else, was in the Cardinal O'Connell House of St. Elizabeth's Hospital at Boston. She was decidedly unimpressed by the fact that her daughter, as the Duchess of Devonshire, would one day be first lady in waiting to the Queen of England. All she knew was that her beloved Kick was marrying outside the church. In reply to reporters asking for comment, Rose Kennedy sent word that she was "too sick to discuss the marriage."

The Marquess and Marchioness were able to live together a little more than a month when he went into combat in France with his Coldstream Guards regiment. When Kathleen learned of Joe Jr.'s tragic death, she flew to the States to comfort her parents at their time of grief. Less than a month after she arrived at Hyannis Port, she received word that her husband had died in action. And then Kathleen herself was killed in a plane crash on a vacation trip to the Riviera four years later.

Years later, Joseph Kennedy noted that had Kathleen and her husband lived, she would have become not only first lady in waiting to the Queen, but a niece by marriage of Prime Minister Harold Macmillan. Moreover, her husband would have probably become grand master of the craft of Freemasons, along with his ducal rank, and—boasted Joe Kennedy—"I'd be father-in-law of the head of all the Masons in the world."

Following a disc operation on his back, Jack Kennedy was released from the Navy in January 1945. A few months later he became a special correspondent for the newspaper chain owned by his father's good friend William Randolph Hearst. Before going off on a series of reportorial assignments, however, he spent a week in February drafting a short thesis in rebuttal to Harry Hopkins' plea for rearmament published in the *American Magazine.*

The Kennedy piece, which was never published, was entitled "Let's Try an Experiment in Peace." Kennedy later recalled that he wrote it "more as a kind of exercise for my own satisfaction than as a serious effort," because, he said, he was outraged at Hopkins' judgment that "we did everything possible to prevent war—except prepare for it." (This was truly a remarkable position for the author of *Why England Slept.*)

Distressed that some people were saying, "Let America be the strongest nation in the world and no one will attack her," Kennedy exclaimed that "this is a plan for superarmament!" A postwar arms race would mean heavy taxes and hence the stifling of private enterprise and full employment. Instead, Kennedy proposed an agreement among the postwar Big Three—Britain, Russia, and the United States—for limiting postwar rearmament plans. How was this to be achieved? Here, Kennedy was vague. "There will, of course, have to be a strong growth of mutual trust between these countries before any comprehensive plan can be worked out."

But he warned, "there are people in this country, for example, who feel that Russia's unilateral settlement of the problems of eastern Europe precludes any workable postwar agreements being worked out with the Soviet. . . . These people have much evidence on which to base their suspicions, and there will have to be a radical change in the Soviet attitude before the people in this country would agree to work out arms limitations . . . with the Russians.

"Likewise, we will have to demonstrate to the Soviet our own willingness to try to work out European problems on equitable lines before the Russians will put any real confidence in our protestations of friendship. The Russian memory is long, and many of the leaders of the present government remember the years after the last war when they fought in the Red Armies against the invading troops of many nations, including Britain's and the United States'."[4]

Jack Kennedy was to see at first hand how elusive unity with the Soviets would be when, as a Hearst correspondent, he covered the founding convention of the United Nations in San Francisco. Billed as a "PT boat hero" who was expressing "the GI viewpoint," he reported every detail of Vyacheslav Molotov's "belligerent" performance.

Spelling out his own speculations on why the Russians were behaving so badly, Kennedy wrote on April 30, 1945, "Most important there is a heritage of twenty-five years of distrust between Russia and the rest of the world that cannot be overcome completely for a good many more years. . . ." The stormy sessions of the first week led him to conclude that it would be a long time before Russia would entrust her safety to any organization other than the Red Army. "The Russians may have forgiven, but they haven't forgotten, and they remember very clearly those years before the war when Russia was only looking in the kitchen window. Hence, any organization drawn up here

---

[4] A more realistic assessment of the role played by Allied troops in the Siberian intervention of World War I is provided by one of President Kennedy's favorite diplomats, George Kennan, in *Russia and the West* (Boston, Atlantic-Little, Brown, 1961): "Soviet historiography portrays the intervention as a major deliberate military effort by the Western governments, mustering all the force they could, to overthrow the Soviet government. Nothing could be further from the truth. . . . Never did the intervention occupy anything like a central place in Allied purposes. . . ."

will be merely a skeleton. Its powers will be limited. It will reflect the fact that there are deep disagreements among its members."

As the parley continued, Kennedy's pessimism deepened. "The world organization," he wrote, "that will come out of San Francisco will be the product of the same passions and selfishness that produced the Treaty of Versailles." But then, he added, humanity could not afford another war. However, he soon was reporting "talk of fighting the Russians in the next ten or fifteen years." And when the U.N. conference ended, he wrote approvingly of the new U.N., provided it would not interfere with the Monroe Doctrine.

John Mahanna, of the *Berkshire Evening Eagle,* who had happened to be in San Francisco at the time of the U.N. meeting, later commented that Kennedy had one thing going for him as a reporter that very few of his colleagues had—entree. "On the strength of his father's contacts," he said admiringly, "Jack could call top officials, United States and foreign, from the hotel lobby and go right up for interviews."

Covering the British elections in June 1945, Kennedy warned that Prime Minister Churchill might be defeated. "This may come as a surprise to most Americans, who feel Churchill is as indomitable at the polls as he was in war," he cabled. "However, Churchill is fighting a tide that is surging through Europe, washing away monarchies and conservative governments everywhere, and that tide flows powerfully in England. England is moving towards some form of socialism. . . ."

After the Labor upset, Kennedy wrote on July 27 that "people are already saying, 'I told you so,' which they may have done, but if they did, I do not remember it. Professor Laski himself told me he had only anticipated a Labor majority of fifty seats."

He attributed the Socialist victory to "time-for-a-change" sentiment and "above all, the fact that living conditions in England have always been difficult for the working-man." The Socialists "pulled out all the stops on the 'campaign oratory' and it was 'happy days are here again for everyone.'" But Churchill, as in 1940, offered the people nothing but "toil and sweat," saying the Tories would make no glib promises they could not keep. "Unfortunately, for the Conservatives, the people of this island have been on a diet of toil and sweat for the past five years."

But Kennedy did not stick it out for long as a newspaperman. He has since said that he didn't like daily journalism because it was too passive. "Instead of doing things," he said, "you were writing about people who did things." And he wanted to do things. Actually, journalism was simply not his vocation. He failed to create any excitement in the newspaper world. And the Hearst people reluctantly concluded he would never become another Bob Considine.

Joseph P. Kennedy had spent the war being unhappy and making money. Middle age found him tall, square-shouldered, with a ruddy freckled face. His manners, except for swift flashes of anger, were Park Avenue. His English was Boston Back Bay. "He was so good-looking in his fifties when I began to know him," wrote Westbrook Pegler, "that I believe he must have been the very devil in Harvard."

Following Pearl Harbor, Kennedy had wired Roosevelt offering his service: "NAME THE BATTLEFRONT. I'M YOURS TO COMMAND." But the President failed to respond.

More embittered than ever, Joe Kennedy decided to write a book exposing Roosevelt's "follies" that led the United States into war. In fact, he had completed most of the manuscript when Roosevelt called him to the White House. F.D.R. argued that the book would play into the hands of Axis propagandists. Kennedy finally agreed to hold up publication. And it was understood that the Ambassador would be appointed to some high-ranking civilian job in the war effort.

The possibility of Kennedy's return, reportedly as coordinator of the nation's shipping program, met with opposition. Liberal spokesmen did not buy the argument put forward, for example, by Arthur Krock that the appointment would advance national unity. In Washington dispatches presumably approved by James Wechsler, *PM* argued "that such a man as a shipping czar could hardly add to the morale of U.S. seamen, who are daily running greater risks in submarine-infested waters." Also, *PM* held Kennedy "largely responsible for the nation's hands-off policy that enabled Franco to subdue Republican Spain. As Ambassador, Kennedy was in frequent consultation with Franco representatives and said Franco was trying only to save the country from Communism."

The upshot was that Roosevelt, in Joe Kennedy's elegantly phrased words, "chickened out on the appointment."

In 1944, there were published reports that Ambassador Kennedy would lace into F.D.R.'s fourth-term ambitions. In fact, Kennedy was said to have reserved radio time for that purpose. Again he was called to the White House for a confidential chat with the President. What the chat was all about was never disclosed. Kennedy said nothing when he left the White House. But he did cancel his radio time.

Meanwhile, Kennedy was making money hand over fist in real estate. And it happened almost by accident. He had asked a leading New York realtor whom he had met through the then Archbishop Spellman to sell his Bronxville home for him. The realtor, John J. Reynolds, arranged a trade for a business building in White Plains. Kennedy was so pleased that, at lunch one day, he casually asked Reynolds, "If I give you a couple of million dollars, do you think you can make any money for me in real estate?"

"We both could," replied Reynolds.

One deal involved the Siegel-Cooper Building on Sixth Avenue, between 18th and 19th Streets. Kennedy bought the building in 1944, in the midst of war, and immediately doubled all tenants' rents, demanded ten-year leases, and six-month security payments. Complaints reached a New York

State legislative committee headed by John Lamula, then investigating the need for commercial and business rent controls to prevent wartime profiteering.

An investigation unearthed the fact that Ambassador Kennedy owned the building. When Lamula, a Republican, brought this intelligence to the attention of Thomas E. Dewey, the Governor exploded in a rare show of anger. "That's just like the New Dealers. They're always yelling about how they're for the little people. But, brother, give them the opportunity and they'll gouge the little people to death."

Largely because of this episode, the Legislature finally froze commercial and business rents. "Anyhow, Kennedy got away with it," says Lamula. "In 1945 he sold the building, for which he had put down $200,000 in cash, to the J. C. Penney Company for a million dollar profit."

And that's how Kennedy made another fortune in the midst of a war. Later, Reynolds estimated that in New York real estate alone, Kennedy made over $100 million.

But Kennedy's greatest coup, which still staggers the imagination, was achieved in Chicago in 1945 with the purchase of the Merchandise Mart, twenty-four stories and over two million feet of rentable floor space. Kennedy bought the building, then a spectacular money-loser, for $12.5 million, putting up only $800,000 in cash. Two years later he mortgaged it for $17.5 million, realizing an immediate cash profit of $5 million. The building today is worth from $75 to $100 million, and produces in annual rents more than its original purchase price. (In 1947, Kennedy transferred principal ownership of the building to his wife and children.)

When the war ended, Kennedy lost his enthusiasm for real estate and began to concentrate on a political career for son Jack. The truth is that after Young Joe's tragic death, Jack did not step instinctively into his brother's shoes. It took plenty of persuasion on the father's part to convince him of the necessity of turning politician. A less likely-looking politician would have been difficult to imagine at this point. Tall and gangling, Jack was still suffering from the grim consequences of his South Pacific adventure. And there was a grave possibility he might never again enjoy really robust health. But his father refused to take "no" for an answer. Young Joe was dead, and he had no alternative but to carry on for his brother.

"Just as I went into politics because Joe died," Jack Kennedy said later, "if anything happened to me tomorrow, my brother Bobby would run for my seat in the Senate. And if Bobby died, Teddy would take over for him."[5]

Evidently the process of growing up did not start early with Jack Kennedy. "By the age of twenty-eight," wrote biographer Burns, "he had earned

---

[5] "When the Kennedys are described as a dynasty," wrote author McCarthy, "the word is not used in a loose figurative sense." Thus it should be comforting to the nation to know there will be no problem about a succession in the royal line what with Bobby, as heir apparent, learning the ropes as Attorney General and with Teddy starting at the top as a United States Senator.

a B.A. degree, learned how to swim and sail and to golf; he had written a successful book, traveled extensively and learned courage and endurance in the years of the war. But the man and the political leader of a dozen years later was unformed; his political views and his personality were still in the making."

Gradually, Jack got used to the idea of entering politics. There were several problems, however. One was political geography. He had lived in Bronxville, Cambridge (as a student), Hyannis Port, London, and Palm Beach. Where was Jack's home? He could hardly call himself a Boston boy. Then there was the question of what political office Jack should run for.

All these problems were resolved by, of all people, James Michael Curley, the family's despised enemy. Curley, who had been in Congress since 1942, was sick of Washington and wanted to be Mayor of Boston again. This meant that his Congressional seat would be vacant.

In the Kennedy family war councils it was decided that Jack would make his political debut in the race for Curley's seat in the Eleventh District of Massachusetts—a Democratic citadel which, though it includes Cambridge and Harvard, is made up largely of slums and the Irish and Italian wards of East Boston. This was the district in which the family had deep roots. Here was where Jack's grandfathers had their political strongholds and the names of *Kennedy* and *Fitzgerald* were still magic.

On hearing that John Fitzgerald Kennedy was seeking to supplant him as Congressman, Jim Curley declared, "Kennedy! How can he lose? He's got a double-barreled name. . . . He doesn't even need to campaign. He can go to Washington now and forget the primary and election."

It wasn't that simple, however.

At the outset of the campaign the voters wondered who this handsome, seemingly shy outsider was. He didn't live in Boston and was a newcomer to politics. True, his parents were born in the District and his grandfather had controlled its votes. But he had grown up elsewhere, and he knew little about the area he wanted to represent in Congress. Later he observed that the only person whom he really knew there at the time was his grandfather Honey Fitz, then eighty-three and living in retirement at the Hotel Bellevue, a political hangout adjacent to the State House on Beacon Hill.

But in politics, money atones for many deficiencies.

The problem of a legal residence was quickly solved. A suite was rented for Jack at the Bellevue Hotel, and in filing his papers as a candidate for office he used it as his official address. Actually, until then, his legal residence was Palm Beach, the home of his father. Later he acquired as his official residence a three room apartment at 122 Bowdoin Street, across from the State House on top of Beacon Hill.[6]

[6] "He's the first carpetbagger voter to get to the White House," a Boston politician was to complain. "The least he could have done for appearances' sake was to have bought a house here." Bobby and Teddy, along with their wives, have also used the Bowdoin Street apartment as their legal address. The truth is none of them ever used

At first Kennedy appeared ill at ease and pathetically self-conscious as he made the rounds of the tough tenement neighborhoods that largely made up the District. It was a district in which Republicans are as scarce as they are in Mississippi. The big objective was to win the Democratic nomination in the all-important primary fight. The November election was a mere formality.

The skinny, crew-cut Harvard graduate, yellow with atabrine and racked with pain from his unhealed spinal surgery, launched his campaign apologizing to all concerned.

"If Joe were alive today," he would say, as though trying to justify himself, "I wouldn't be in this. I'm only trying to fill his shoes."

One of his associates, attorney John Droney, recalled how Jack convinced him to join his campaign team. "I had no intention of going into politics," Droney said. "I told Jack how I felt and he said he had the same feeling, but that his brother Joe had been killed in the war and his family seemed to feel he was best fitted to carry on."

"Sometimes," Droney recalls Jack telling him, "we all have to do things we don't like to do."

It was in the 1946 campaign that Jack Kennedy first employed the techniques that were to bring him electoral success after success. First, he had gotten off to an early start. Long before his rivals bestirred themselves, he was campaigning. Then he began building his own personal organization composed of college chums, wartime shipmates, and Ivy Leaguers. Some were Republicans, and most were uncommitted ideologically. But all pitched in to help out Good Old Jack. There were, for example, Lem Billings, Jack's roommate from Choate, in from Baltimore; and Red Fay who, having served with "Shafty" in the PT squadron, flew in from San Francisco. Then there was Timothy (Ted) Reardon, one of Joe Jr.'s buddies, who was to be part of the Kennedy entourage all the way to the White House.

But Joseph P. Kennedy was taking no chances with the likes of these. He brought in a phalanx of seasoned ward heelers. The Ambassador had the final word on who was to be put on the payroll. "For the amateur and the pro," as Martin and Plaut observed, "the contempt was mutual. But always in the hovering background was the smell of Kennedy money, even when it

---

the apartment for any length of time. The apartment serves one purpose only: to give the Kennedy brothers a political residence. Protests have been made about what is technically a violation of the law, but nothing was ever done about it. In March 1960 some Massachusetts Democrats moved to bar Bobby from going to Los Angeles as a convention delegate on the grounds he was not a Bay State resident. Bobby, it was then pointed out, lived on a palatial Virginia estate, and at one time considered making the Old Dominion his political base. Objections, too, were raised as to brother Jack's status as a Boston resident. The then Senator's residence was a luxurious Georgetown house in Washington's highest-priced residential neighborhood. The only time in recent years he used the Boston flat was for an Ed Murrow "Person to Person" TV appearance with his wife.

wasn't there; the sense of Kennedy power, even when it wasn't used; the hope of Kennedy reward, even when it wasn't promised."

The Ambassador brought in Francis X. Morrissey, once secretary to Governor Maurice Tobin, as campaign manager. But everyone knew he was Old Joe's eyes and ears. The Ivy Leaguers around Jack, in fact, scornfully referred to him as "an odd-job man" and "a fixer." (By 1961, Morrissey—a municipal court judge, thanks to Jack Kennedy—was shepherding Ted Kennedy around the state, getting him to meet the right folks, just as he had done with Jack in 1946. And the word went out that Frank was slated for a federal judgeship, despite the fact it had taken him twelve years to become a lawyer and he had never practiced law. One of his strongest attributes appeared to be his foresight in having once called Joseph P. Kennedy "one of the great personalities of our time.")

To teach Jack politics, the Ambassador brought in his first cousin Joe Kane, a forty-year veteran of the Bay State's political wars. The fact that Kane was a bitter foe of Honey Fitz was of no importance. What was important was that he impart to young Jack some of the tough, cynical shrewdness so vital to a politician anxious to succeed in the Boston version of politics.

Possessed of a caustic tongue, Kane provided young Jack with an insight into the mechanics of political infighting. "In politics," he drummed into his protégé's head, "you have no friends, only co-conspirators."

The tutoring took time. It wasn't easy for young Jack to turn backslapper overnight. "I wish Joe was around," he would say. "Joe would have been Governor by now."

During one of these tutoring sessions Honey Fitz Fitzgerald—happier than ever now that his grandson was in politics—ambled into the room. Taking one look at his ancient political foe, Joe Kane shouted, "Get that sonofabitch out of here!"

Jack Kennedy looked dumbfounded. "Who?" he asked, *"Grandpa?"*

"Yes," Kane kept shouting, "that no-good louse. Get him out of here!"

But Kane's tutelage paid off. One night Joseph Kennedy drove down to Maverick Square, a gathering place for Italian-Americans. He watched with amazement as his son moved among an unfriendly crowd, shaking hands and making small talk. "I never thought Jack had it in him," he said.

As the campaign progressed, however, Joe Kane found himself being shoved to the side. The "amateurs"—his description of the volunteers clustering around Jack—were taking over. But before he disappeared he left them with the key slogan for the Kennedy campaign: "The New Generation Offers a Leader."

Kane also suggested that Kennedy avoid announcing for office until almost the last minute. The idea was to keep political opportunists from jumping into the primary—an old Boston custom—hoping for payoffs to remove themselves as candidates. Also, there was some question as to whether

Jack should run for Congress. Governor Tobin flew to Palm Beach to ask the Ambassador to run Jack for Lieutenant Governor. Besides being an impressive title, the post was a good steppingstone to the governorship itself. And, as Jack said later, in those days he would not have minded being Governor.

But finally, on April 22, 1946, eight days before the filing deadline, Jack Kennedy formally announced his candidacy for the Democratic nomination for United States Representative from the Eleventh Massachusetts District.

"The temper of the times imposes an obligation upon every thinking citizen to work diligently in peace, as we served tirelessly in war," he declared.

The statement was calculated to sound good but to say as little as possible. What did Jack Kennedy stand for? Specifically, he would not say.

During the course of the campaign a troubled Radcliffe miss arose at a Harvard Liberal Union meeting to ask the speaker, former Congressman Thomas H. Eliot, whether he felt that Jack Kennedy would make "the kind of progressive representative we're working for."

Eliot, the Proper Bostonian grandson of President Charles Eliot of Harvard University and, as James Michael Curley was wont to note, the son of a distinguished Unitarian minister, took his time in replying.[7]

Measuring his words carefully, Eliot finally said, "I spoke with Jack for about three hours the other afternoon on many of the issues facing this country—and I don't really think I'm qualified to answer your question."

This story was told in the *New Republic* of June 27, 1960, in an illuminating article on what makes Kennedy tick by Selig S. Harrison, managing editor of that journal. Continued Harrison: "It would be difficult to forget the irritation which Kennedy displayed when this reporter, then at Harvard on the *Crimson,* peppered him with questions in an interview during his 1946 campaign. Kennedy at twenty-nine gave the same impression he does today of an earnest and engaging personality. But he was clearly determined to avoid specific commitments."

Actually, Kennedy was running on his heroic war record. According to the private polls financed by his father, this is what the people were interested in—the story of how he won the Navy and Marine Corps Medal in the South Pacific. And Kennedy, with appropriate modesty, would tell and retell the story before campaign audiences, usually referring to himself in the third person. ("The commanding officer of the PT 109, believing it to be a Japanese destroyer, turned the bow of his PT to make a torpedo attack. . . .")

Then he would describe the death struggle that lay ahead between col-

---

[7] Curley, whose colorful likes will probably never again be seen in Boston politics, once described the Unitarians as "a curious sect who seem to believe that Our Lord Jesus was a young man with whiskers who went around in His underwear." Curley also had little use for Harvard intellectuals.

lectivism and capitalism, winding up with this stock exhortation: "We in this country must be willing to battle for the old ideas which have proved their value, with the same enthusiasm that people do for new ideas and creeds."

One critic noted it sounded more like Joseph Patrick Kennedy than like Franklin Delano Roosevelt.

As the campaign progressed, Kennedy's Ivy League advisers proposed changing the tenor of the speech. While there was nothing wrong with patriotism as a gimmick, they pointed out that the Eleventh District had some serious bread-and-butter problems. A new speech was evolved by a sort of brain-storming, one that discussed such issues as price and rent controls, more and better housing, higher minimum wages, jobs, etc.

The new speech sounded more like F.D.R. than like Joe Kennedy.

The big question was: in which speech did Jack Kennedy really believe?

"I'm not doctrinaire," Kennedy told Selig Harrison at the time. "I'll vote them the way I see them," he said. And if it was necessary to tag him politically, he added, "make it 'Massachusetts Democrat.' "

During the interview Kennedy spoke in vague terms of "the struggle between capitalism and collectivism, internally and externally." However, he said he was most definitely not in favor of *laissez-faire;* that, in his view, business needed regulation by Government "to eliminate the trends of overproduction and low purchasing power which periodically throw the economic structure out of kilter."

Just what the Government should do specifically about regulating business, the youthful candidate would not say. However, Harrison's conclusion in the *Crimson* was this: "Kennedy seems to feel honestly that he is not hedging . . . by refusing to offer a positive specific platform. He feigns an ignorance of much in the affairs of government and tells you to look at his record in two years to see what he stands for."

Kennedy's rivals in the primary included Michael F. (Mike) Neville, then Mayor of Cambridge; John F. Cotter, secretary to James M. Curley; Joseph Lee, a patrician Yankee who liked to run in Catholic districts; two men with the same name, Joseph Russo; and lawyer Catherine Falvey, a former WAC major who liked to show up at rallies in her gleaming white dress uniform.

At first the rest of the candidates laughed Kennedy off. Then, as the campaign progressed, the taunts changed to outraged indignation. Charges were voiced that Old Joe Kennedy was trying to buy the election for his carpetbagger son—charges that were to ring in Jack's ears throughout his political career.

Once Mike Neville walked into the State House press room with a $10 bill hanging out of his breast pocket.

"That's a Kennedy campaign button," he said.

On another occasion, while strolling through the State House (where he had once been a member of the Legislature), he spotted a crap game in progress. Turning to a companion, he said, "The only way I'll get my name in the newspapers is if I join that game and get pinched by the cops."

Patsy Mulhern, an Irishman who, according to Martin and Plaut, "always looked drunk but never touched liquor," gave this eyewitness report of Kennedy in action:

"Kennedy covered every street in da district. Every street, for chrissakes. I musta introduced him t'two million people. Cheesus, more people. Shook hands wit more people than I ever knowed in a campaign. People wouldn't go for him at first. Then he caught on. . . .

"He kept going. Never ate much. Great frappe drinker. Frappes, frappes, frappes [a Boston concoction consisting of ice cream whipped up in flavored milk, like a New York milk shake] . . . Cheesus, he could drink frappes. He had the biggest rallies ever held in the North End; rallies, house parties, dances, every girl there was gonna be Mrs. Kennedy, for chrissakes. There was a storekeeper told me, 'I let out more gowns this week than in a whole year before. I wish he'd run forever.'

"But Jack didn't like for nothing to go wrong. At a rally, if there wasn't a good crowd, he'd say, 'Something went wrong and it won't happen again. Didn't they know I was comin'? They expected me, didn't they?'

"I'd say, 'Had nothin' t'do with it, John, it's all up t'the big guys around.' The pols called him the Miami candidate and we hadda sell him t'the Curley mob."

Curley himself, as much as he opposed any and all Kennedys, took no position regarding Jack's candidacy. In a shrewd maneuver Honey Fitz—his ancient rival—had assured Curley's neutrality by announcing his support of the "Purple Shamrock" for Mayor.

Meanwhile, flying in from everywhere were other Kennedys—thus setting a pattern that was to be repeated in future elections. (In later elections, however, they were to be supplemented by wives and husbands and were to be regarded by many Bostonians as foreigners. "As soon as the last vote is counted," one newsman said, "the Kennedys and their wives and husbands are hurrying to the airport to catch the next plane out of town. They don't even wait until the tents are taken down.")

Brother Bobby was assigned to East Cambridge where Mike Neville had considerable strength. Bobby had spent the closing months of the war, as a Second Class Seaman, aboard the newly commissioned destroyer *Joseph P. Kennedy Jr.*, named after his hero brother. His naval service consisted of six dismal months in the Caribbean, spent mostly scraping paint, with no sign of the enemy. Recalled a Milton Academy classmate, "It was much tougher in school for him than the others—socially, in football, with studies." But he compensated with a grim determination to succeed.

Other Kennedys swarmed into the wards, going from house to house, ringing doorbells, cradling babies, and telling thousands of voters what a wonderful brother Jack was. His sisters helped organize neighborhood house parties. Kennedy sometimes went to half a dozen of them in a single evening. The Kennedy organization supplied everything—coffee, cookies, china, silverware, flowers. At campaign headquarters a careful record was kept of everyone who attended the parties. Later, they were asked to talk to their neighbors about Jack.

Jack's back still hurt. Sometimes he used crutches or dragged a leg when the round of political rallies ran late. Invariably his appearance on crutches evoked considerable sympathy—for unlike any of his rivals he was truly a war hero who nearly died for his country.

The big social event of the campaign was the formal tea and reception at the Hotel Commander in Cambridge, at which the numerous Kennedys, including the candidate, stood on the receiving line. It was quite a sight too. For the Ambassador was there, resplendent in a white tie and tails in what turned out to be his first and only public appearance in any of Jack's campaigns. Though it had been one of the hottest days of the year, the crowd was tremendous. The "pols" couldn't figure it at all. But, as Martin and Plaut have suggested so perceptively, it demonstrated Jack Kennedy's double appeal: while the hyphenated Americans could claim him as one of their own, there was also a unique snob appeal in the Kennedys—"the first of the Irish Brahmins."

"They expect the vote of every son of Erin," wrote Paul F. Healy in the *Saturday Evening Post* in 1953, "but they are still mildly irked to find themselves still being socially stratified as Irish-Americans. 'How long do we have to be here before we lose the hyphen?' they want to know."

Joseph Kennedy had poured money into the 1946 campaign as if it were a drive for the White House itself. But the display of the enormous Kennedy resources almost became a liability; some of the other candidates—Catherine Falvey, for one—dubbed Kennedy "the poor little rich boy," doing his father's bidding.

"According to one story," Burns reported, "the old man claimed that with the money he was spending he could elect his chauffeur to Congress."

Joe Kennedy was also master-minding the publicity and advertising campaigns. An advertising agency, in which the Ambassador had put some money, was brought in to help. Nothing was left to chance. Soon the entire Eleventh District was plastered with Kennedy billboards, posters and stickers. Trolley cars passing through the area each carried three or four Kennedy placards. The radio was saturated with Kennedy "spots." A *Reader's Digest* condensation of John Hersey's *New Yorker* article on Kennedy's heroism in the South Pacific was widely distributed. Political advertisements touting Kennedy flooded the newspapers which, in turn, devoted considerable non-commercial space to the handsome war hero running for his first public office.

Still, as primary day neared, Jack Kennedy hungered for even more publicity. Once, driving to a meeting in East Cambridge, a friend advised

Jack to expect trouble since the neighborhood was a pretty tough one. "Good," said Jack, "if we get beat up, then we'll really get some publicity." As it developed, the meeting was orderly.

"Jack was all over," an associate said later, "on the streets, on the radio, on the billboards, in the newspapers . . . the people saw Kennedy, heard Kennedy, ate Kennedy, drank Kennedy, slept Kennedy, and Kennedy talked and we talked Kennedy all day long. His old man spent so much, you couldn't guess how much. . . ."

How much was spent? Only Joe Kennedy could possibly have known. His first cousin Joe Kane said later it was "a staggering sum." But Kane contended most of it was unnecessary: "Jack could have gone to Congress like everyone else for ten cents."

Then why did his father spend so much?

Because, said Kane, he was taking no chances on any possible slip-up. "Everything his father got, he bought and paid for," he added. "And politics is like war. It takes three things to win. The first is money and the second is money and the third is money."

Primary day—June 18, 1946—finally rolled around. This was the day that counted. The victor in the primary would be the next Congressman. Election day in November would be a mere formality; in years to come, people would find it difficult to remember the name of the Republican candidate (Lester W. Bowen). But even in the closing hours of primary day, Joseph P. Kennedy was leaving nothing to chance. Every car for hire and available cab in town was put into service transporting Kennedy voters to the polls. The polls were well-guarded by Kennedy watchers; Joseph Kennedy, of course, being strongly opposed to any hanky-panky at the polls that might be hurtful to his son. (One of the Ambassador's earliest memories, in fact, was hearing two men report to his father, "Pat, we voted 128 times today.")

And to no one's great surprise, when the votes were counted, Jack Kennedy's name led all the rest. He received 22,183 votes, almost double that obtained by his closest rival Mike Neville.

It was for the Clan Kennedy a sweet victory, indeed. For Old Honey Fitz, it was proof positive of the political virility of Grandson Jack. So stirred was Grandfather Fitzgerald that he climbed on to a table at campaign headquarters that night and danced a stiff-legged Irish jig and sang in a cracked voice "Sweet Adeline." It was the swan song of the old, colorful and rascally breed of Boston Irish politics. A new breed of politician was about to take over.

Congress

6

As even his most ardent admirers have conceded, John F. Kennedy's six years as a member of the House of Representatives were hardly marked by initiative, diligence, or courage. On the whole, his legislative performance was listless and uninspired. From his votes, as the *New Republic*'s Selig Harrison has observed, "it would have been hard to classify him as a 'liberal' or a 'conservative' among House Democrats."

Kennedy himself has acknowledged that his record as a Congressman was not the most distinguished. He had worked hard for a job he really had not wanted; and he found himself voting on issues about which he couldn't care less.

"After all," he later told Ralph Martin, "I wasn't equipped for the job. I didn't plan to get into it, and when I started out as a Congressman, there were lots of things I didn't know, a lot of mistakes I made, maybe some votes that should have been different."

There were speeches, too, which he wished he hadn't made; like those bitterly assailing Franklin D. Roosevelt as an appeaser of Communism. In June 1948, for example, he had addressed the Massachusetts Association of Polish-American Citizens Clubs in Roxbury. The next morning's *Boston Herald* carried this headline:

KENNEDY SAYS
ROOSEVELT SOLD
POLAND TO REDS

Roosevelt had done this terrible thing, said the young Congressman, "because he did not understand the Russian mind."

Further evidence of Kennedy's animus toward Franklin Delano Roosevelt was provided in a Salem, Massachusetts, speech on January 30, 1949, when he declared:

"At the Yalta Conference in 1945 a sick Roosevelt, with the advice of General Marshall and other Chiefs of Staff, gave the Kurile Islands as well as the control of various strategic Chinese ports, such as Port Arthur and Dairen, to the Soviet Union."[1]

Kennedy then quoted approvingly former Ambassador William Bullitt as having declared: "Whatever share of the responsibility was Roosevelt's and whatever share was Marshall's the vital interest of the United States in the independent integrity of China was sacrificed, and the foundation was laid for the present tragic situation in the Far East."[2]

In view of Kennedy's later ambitions, one of his first votes as a fledgling Congressman was somewhat surprising. That was his vote in favor of the Twenty-second Amendment limiting the occupancy of the White House to two terms. New Dealers considered the amendment a retroactive slap at F.D.R., who in 1940 had defied historic tradition by running for an unprecedented third term.

Kennedy later denied that any anti-Roosevelt bias had influenced his vote. He said he had had a talk with Dr. Frank Lahey of Boston's Lahey Clinic.[3] Dr. Lahey, one of several physicians who had examined Roosevelt before the 1944 campaign, "felt that the President should not have run again and the doctors should have told him not to. Two months later Roosevelt was dead."

However, as the Eisenhower case demonstrates, a two-term limit does not provide against Presidential illness. And it is biographer Burns' judgment that Kennedy voted for the anti-F.D.R. gesture because he "shared the conservatives' belief in maintaining the traditional balance between Congressional and Presidential power."

Moreover, it is conceivable that young Kennedy—perhaps subconsciously—was again fighting his father's battles, this time against a dead President.

Generally, Kennedy's six years as a Congressman were those of a "Massachusetts Democrat," doing precisely those things which his working-

[1] The recently published State Department documents on Teheran disclose that Roosevelt's concessions to Stalin, at the expense of China, were originally made at Teheran on November 30, 1943. The Yalta agreements merely confirmed, elaborated, and formalized the Teheran concessions. Roosevelt, in November of 1943, was healthy and in full possession of his faculties.

[2] The complete text of Kennedy's Salem speech can be found in Appendix A.

[3] According to Westbrook Pegler, Jack Kennedy frequently sojourned at the Lahey Clinic, registering under the name "Mr. Kay."

class constituents expected him to do. On labor, social security, public housing, price and rent controls, he voted down the line with what was then the Fair Deal. On most House roll calls, only a Harvard accent, a boyish face, and a slightly bookish air distinguished him from scores of Democrats from the big city machines of the North.

Young Kennedy had a clear, frank attitude toward his legislative responsibilities. "No one should represent a workingman's district who is not in sympathy with what the workingmen want," he told a Harvard seminar in 1950. But he added this qualifying—and revealing—phrase, "A person from a wealthy district, like Representative Christian Herter's Back Bay, would be equally justified in opposing social legislation."

In foreign affairs, too, Kennedy was saying things his largely anti-Communist constituents wanted to hear. He would occasionally shake up members of the House Liberal bloc by challenging President Truman's foreign policies. And just to make sure he was being heard at the White House, he wrote complaints directly to the President. Apparently Truman didn't forget, as witness the former President's "is the country ready for you?" remark to Kennedy prior to the 1960 Democratic Convention.

Kennedy's career as a Congressman had begun fairly inauspiciously. On February 6, 1947, a month after he was sworn in, the *Washington Times-Herald* published a short profile of the new Congressman. The interviewer, Elizabeth Oldfield, had remarked that "it was nice to meet Kathleen's brother."

"Oh yes," Kennedy replied. "I remember she did the column for several months, so, of course, I am familiar with it. For a long time I was Joseph P. Kennedy's son, then I was Kathleen's brother, then Eunice's brother. Some day I hope to be able to stand on my own feet."

In his first week on the Hill, a veteran Congressman snapped his fingers at him and demanded a copy of a bill. Kennedy, who was wearing a dark suit similar to those worn by page boys, smiled and asked, "Where do I get it?"

"How long have you been a page?" the old-timer bellowed.

"Hell, I'm a Congressman," Kennedy informed his nonplused colleague.

As a result of such episodes there was some talk of requiring Congressional pages to wear knickerbockers so they could be distinguished from some of the more youthful-looking lawmakers.

At hearings of the House Labor Committee, to which he was assigned, Kennedy had to listen to one witness repeatedly address him as "laddie." Crusty old Edward A. O'Neal, a veteran farm lobbyist, meant no disrespect; it just seemed the natural thing to say to someone who looked more like a college student than a member of Congress.

It was difficult for other old-timers on the Hill to take young Kennedy seriously. Reminiscing some months before he died, Speaker Sam Rayburn observed, "When Kennedy came to the House, he had a swarthy, dark-yellowish complexion. It looked as if he had had that Pacific fever. And he looked so spare. I had no idea how tall he is. He is a pretty tall man; I looked upon him as a little fellow.

"He went to the Senate in 1952, and someone asked me a while back if at that time I felt that Kennedy would ever be President. I said, 'No,' thinking about him as I had seen him in the House."

But Elizabeth Oldfield had seen Kennedy somewhat differently. "Young Kennedy looks like Charles Lindbergh did when the latter made his flight to Paris," she reported at the time. "Six feet tall, broad-shouldered, and weighing 140 pounds (malaria contracted in the South Pacific pulled his weight down), he has frank blue eyes, a shock of straight blond hair, perfect teeth, and freckles. His socks slip college-boy fashion, for he wears no garters. He's so clean-cut, so typically American, you find yourself wishing Hitler could have seen this production of American youth."

During this period Kennedy suffered occasional attacks of malaria; and his face had a yellowish tinge. His back hurt too, but he refused to curb the strenuous life to which the Kennedys are addicted. He sailed, swam, and played touch football. Evenings he went to the movies, dating various girls around town. One of his closest friends was George A. Smathers of Florida, also a bachelor then, who had entered Congress the same time as Kennedy. Kennedy and Smathers (now a Senator) are still the closest of friends, even though the Floridian does not go along with many New Frontier legislative proposals. In 1961, for example, he supported Kennedy only forty-seven per cent of the time.

"I don't subscribe to all of the President's political beliefs, but he doesn't expect me to be with him on everything," Smathers explained recently. "He understands." (President Kennedy has not been so understanding with everyone who fails to go along with him.) "We see each other a lot," Smathers added, "and sometimes we argue and he gives me hell. But we understand each other. We have a lot of fun over it."

Kennedy has long had fun with Smathers who, as a raconteur, has few peers in the halls of Congress. To this happy facility, he adds a drawl that, particularly when he travels in his beloved Sunshine State, sounds as if he had been weaned on a Dixie cup.

In 1950, supported by John F. Kennedy, he entered the Florida primary seeking to smather Senator Claude Pepper, then under bitter attack as "Stalin's mouthpiece in the Senate." Smathers hit hard on Pepper's affinity for Left wing causes, including an alleged palship with the late Soviet dictator whom he visited at the end of the war. The bitter campaign produced a truly remarkable political speech—one in which Smathers informed an audience of backwoods Floridians about the character of his opponent:

"Are you aware that Claude Pepper is known all over Washington as a shameless extrovert? Not only that, but this man is reliably reported to practice nepotism with his sister-in-law, and he has a sister who was once a Thespian in Greenwich Village. Worst of all, it is an established fact that Mr. Pepper, before his marriage, practiced celibacy."

Jack Kennedy has long considered this speech a political classic—a superb demonstration of the *One-upmanship* in which the Kennedys revel. True, Smathers had done his level best to make Claude Pepper a pervert by assonance; but what really mattered, after all, was winning. And Smathers won.[4]

Kennedy, meanwhile, had settled down in a rented Georgetown house on Thirty-first Street with his sister Eunice, who was then working at the Justice Department. Joseph P. Kennedy had assigned as housekeeper and general factotum his cherished cook Margaret Ambrose who, as the Ambassador was wont to observe, had "prepared feasts for royalty." George Thomas, a Negro valet previously employed by Arthur Krock, was hired as Jack's gentleman's gentleman. Frequently, Mother Rose would pop in to make a personal inspection of the domestic arrangements. Father Joe, a less frequent visitor, preferred to keep in touch with Jack on the long distance phone.

As Kennedy now recalls this period, life was pleasant enough. But hardly what one would call exciting. There were the usual parties. One of the first Jack (along with sister Eunice) attended was in honor of a young Senator from Wisconsin who had performed the incredible feat of besting Bob La Follette with the slogan, "Congress Needs a Tail Gunner." In those days, however, Senator Joe McCarthy was considered a Liberal Republican, devoting considerable of his copious energies to the fruitless task of electing Harold E. Stassen President of the United States.

McCarthy became quite friendly with the Kennedy family. In fact, sister Eunice and the man whom she would marry in 1953, R. Sargent Shriver, considered Joe more than a good friend. In 1960, reporters noticed that the Shrivers possessed a silver cigarette box on which was inscribed: "To Eunice and Bob, from one who lost, Joe McCarthy."[5]

Congressman Kennedy was a hostess's dream as an extra man. Unmarried, handsome, and witty, he was usually available for the better dinner parties. Perle Mesta, the "hostess with the mostest," once seated Kennedy next to Margaret Truman ("I was always trying to make a match for Margaret," Mrs. Mesta explained) at a dinner party she tendered in honor of President and Mrs. Truman in April 1949.

[4] Ironically, in 1962 President Kennedy found himself endorsing Claude Pepper who was attempting a political comeback by running for the House from the new Miami Congressional District. "During your many years in Congress," the President wrote the ex-Senator, "the people had an outstanding and valiant fighter on behalf of the public interest." Forgotten was Pepper's Left wing record that had once so appalled Jack Kennedy.

[5] Today Sargent Shriver heads the Peace Corps.

However, as Mrs. Mesta has since written, "I wasn't prepared for Jack Kennedy to be wearing brown loafers with his tuxedo!"[6]

Ted Reardon, then his administrative assistant, recalled still another episode when the Congressman set out for a Washington dinner party clad in a blue serge jacket and a pair of Navy chinos. Reardon expressed his horror at this sartorial outrage, but Kennedy refused to be budged.

Until he married Jacqueline, Jack was a notoriously sloppy dresser. He owned no more than four winter suits that fit. Not that he had any reluctance to purchase more; his wardrobe was kept down to a minimum because he was notoriously absent-minded. He had an unhappy habit of leaving a suit behind when he checked out of a hotel. When he would wipe his spectacles, he would pull out a shirt tail, occasionally forgetting to replace it. Once he delivered a speech on the House floor with his shirt tail hanging out. Such eccentricities were of a sort, however, that helped create a genial legend.

In his first month in office, Congressman Kennedy was named by the Junior Chamber of Commerce, along with Arthur Schlesinger Jr. and others, one of the outstanding young men of the year 1947.

By coincidence, several months later Schlesinger wrote an article for *Partisan Review* in which he bitterly assailed the Congressman's father, Joseph P. Kennedy, as representing "cowardice rationalized in terms of high morality."

This, of course, was long before the precocious Harvard professor ever thought of Jack Kennedy as made of Presidential stuff or of himself as a future White House adviser. Wrote Schlesinger: "Even in America, the capitalist fatherland, the death-wish of the business community appears to go beyond the normal limits of political incompetence. . . . The foreign policy of the business community is characteristically one of cowardice rationalized in terms of high morality. The great refusal to take on the Russians today is perfectly typical. That *doyen* of American capitalists, Joseph P. Kennedy, recently argued that the United States should not seek to resist the spread of Communism. Indeed, it should 'permit Communism to have its trial outside the Soviet Union if that shall be the fate or the will of certain peoples. . . .' On this ground Kennedy has opposed all foreign loans from the British loan on."

To contain Communism abroad, Schlesinger proposed that the United States not only initiate "vast programs of economic reconstruction" abroad but give active backing to European "parties of the non-Communist left." Schlesinger conceded this would be a "risky" business. Apart from ideological pitfalls, "its proponents must combat the death-wish of the capitalists, as exemplified by Mr. Kennedy, and the befuddlement of the fellow travelers, as exemplified by [Henry] Wallace, both of whom unite in opposing a policy of resistance to Soviet expansion. The triumph of either the Kennedy or the

---

[6] Which may have been one of the reasons why Mrs. Mesta, a life-long Democrat, refused to support Kennedy for President in 1960. The story of the dinner party is told in Mrs. Mesta's autobiography, *Perle,* published in New York by McGraw-Hill in 1960.

Wallace views, if there is much difference between them, would . . . remove all present obstacles to the Soviet conquest of Europe." ·

Joseph Kennedy's theory was that the Communists would inevitably fall because of an inability to keep promises or to match the accomplishments of "the American way of life." Joseph Kennedy was consistent. He was still expressing Fortress America views.

Schlesinger contended, however, that a parliamentary Socialism that respected civil liberties and due process of law could effectively combat Communism. "There seems no inherent obstacle to the gradual advance of Socialism in the United States through a series of New Deals," Schlesinger added. (Asked recently by columnist Henry Taylor how he felt about his 1947 views, the Presidential adviser replied by quoting Sir Winston Churchill in his famous remark, "I neither withdraw nor apologize. . . .")

Beginning in 1945 Joseph Kennedy made several widely publicized speeches in which he viewed with alarm the "unmistakable drift toward statism" and tax burdens "sufficient to destroy all initiative." In one speech before Chicago's Economics Club, he addressed himself particularly to a proposal by Harold Laski that the United States should trade in its free economy for some brand of Socialism. Said Kennedy:

"How can Laski have the gall to assert that Capitalism is dead when the British Empire has been saved twice in thirty years by the capitalistic United States? I know Laski and he is an arrogant apostle of anarchy. . . ."

The Ambassador warned that the United States was in danger of stumbling into some form of Socialism. "Whether we keep our free economy or trade it for something about which we know very little," he said, "is the big political issue ahead.

"It is up to businessmen to sell our economic system to the public. They must do as good a job on that as they do on their own products. Unless the advantages of our system over others are brought home to everyone, there is no reason to believe that the trend toward more and more government will be checked. . . . It is the last chance for those who believe in our system of constitutional Government. We must win now or the cause is lost."

Only uninformed people, he added, were ready to believe the smear charges against businessmen. Nowhere did he refer to businessmen as "sons-of-bitches."

John F. Kennedy also sounded the alarm over the increasing power of centralized Government to meddle in the affairs of private citizens. In 1950 he told the Italian-American Charity Fund Appeal in Boston, "The scarlet thread running through the thoughts and actions of people all over the world is the delegation of great problems to the all-absorbing Leviathan—the State."[7]

---

[7] In January 1962, the *New York Post* defended President Kennedy's high-priced budget proposals by referring disparagingly to "the right-wing nonsense being spoken about the bugaboo of 'the Leviathan state.' "

According to young Kennedy, charity was a priceless ingredient of modern civilization and, as such, was a direct responsibility of a free society.

"I suppose," he added, "it would be easier for us if we requested that the Government assume the responsibility for the money we are seeking to raise [for charity]. Yet only by doing the work ourselves, by giving generously out of our own pockets, can we hope to maintain the authority of the people over the State, to insure that the people remain the masters and the State the servant.

"Every time that we try to lift a problem from our own shoulders and shift that problem to the Government, to the same extent are we sacrificing the liberties of the people."

At the University of Notre Dame where he received an honorary doctor of laws degree, Kennedy asserted there was a great need—"more than ever before"—for educated Catholics in Government. Noting the tendency to hand over major problems to "the great Leviathan, the state," Kennedy warned that "it is therefore vital that we become concerned with maintaining the authority of the people, of the individual, over the state."

Needless to say, John Kennedy was to discard the jargon of the Hayeks and the Von Mises to adopt the whole Galbraithian gospel calling for "public supervision" over the economy, bigger government, more revenues to support the "public sector," and changes in the economic system to foster a "welfare society."

As a result, it takes a long reach of memory to recall that in his Congressional years John F. Kennedy frequently sided with the House economy bloc in efforts to curtail excessive Fair Deal spending.

In 1950, for example, Kennedy departed from the Democratic leadership to support a proposal by Congressman John Taber, the Grand Old Party's Watchdog of the Treasury, for a $600 million across-the-board cut in federal spending.

"How long," Jack then demanded of the House, "can we continue deficit financing on such a large scale with a national debt of over $285 billions?"

So opposed was Kennedy to what he termed "wasteful spending" that he voted against a bill that would have provided federal assistance to local libraries. In 1950, he voted against doubling hospital construction grants under the Public Health Service. In 1951, he was one of only twenty-six Democrats in the House who voted to sustain President Truman's veto of a veterans' pension bill.

"Today the dollar is a strategic material and its use for non-defense purposes must be stopped," he said on May 15, 1951, during a House debate on his amendment to slash a flood-control appropriation for the Department of Agriculture from $8 million to $2.5 million. "My amendment would save $5.5 million and, like all other non-defense projects, the work laid out for this year's program could be postponed without affecting our defense efforts." (The Kennedy amendment was defeated, 118 to 110.)

No one took Kennedy very seriously in those days. Not even Kennedy himself, according to Arthur Schlesinger Jr. Most of his colleagues considered him a pleasant young man merely voicing his father's views.

"Sometimes we didn't have the pleasure of Jack's company for months at a time," recalls a fellow member of the House Labor and Education Committee. "We used to tease him a good deal about his frequent absences; but, frankly, we were not as much critical as envious."

His colleagues on the Committee—particularly the younger ones—were envious for another reason. Jack was obtaining considerable publicity as one of the nation's most eligible bachelors; the society columns often linked him in print with attractive society belles. On January 20, 1947, for example, the *New York World-Telegram*'s Charles Ventura reported that "Palm Beach's cottage colony wants to give the son of Joseph P. Kennedy its annual Oscar for achievement in the field of romance.

"The committee says that young Mr. Kennedy splashed through a sea of flaming early season divorces to rescue its sinking faith in the romantic powers of Florida, The Moon and You.

"Worried dowagers were voicing the fear that the divorce court bench had taken the place of the love seat in Palm Beach when Jack saved the situation by giving Durie Malcolm Desloge the season's outstanding rush. . . .

"Only the fact that duty called him to Washington . . . kept Jack from staying around to receive his Oscar in person, so it may be awarded to Durie. The two were inseparable at all social functions and sports events. They even drove down to Miami to hold hands at football games and wager on the horses.

"Durie is the daughter of the George H. Malcolms of Palm Beach and Chicago. She is beautiful and intelligent. Tiny obstacle to orange blossoms is that the Kennedy clan frowns upon divorce. Durie has said 'Good Morning Judge' with F. John Bersbach. A similar salutation in St. Louis with Firmin V. Desloge 4th makes it two."

In 1957 there was a curious, still-unexplained development. The Association of Blauvelt Descendants, of East Orange, New Jersey, published an expensively bound genealogy tracing the family tree back to 1638. The tome was largely the work of Louis Blauvelt, a professional genealogist who carried on research for the book for thirty years and who has since died. *The Blauvelt Family Genealogy* was published in 1957.[8]

One of the notations concerns a Durie Malcolm: "We have no birth date. She was born Kerr, but took the name of her stepfather. She first married Firmin Desloge, IV. They were divorced. Durie then married F. John Bersbach. They were divorced, and she married, third, John F. Kennedy,

[8] *The Blauvelt Family Genealogy*, compiled by Louis L. Blauvelt. Hillsdale, New Jersey, The Association of Blauvelt Descendants, 1957 (U.S. Library of Congress Catalog Card No. 56–10936).

son of Joseph P. Kennedy, one time Ambassador to England. There were no children of the second or third marriages."

Checking into this notation, a reporter discovered that on July 11, 1947, Durie Malcolm Desloge was married to a Thomas H. Shevlin in Fort Lee, New Jersey, at the residence of Magistrate J. William Aronsohn, who performed the civil ceremony. Mrs. Shevlin was located at her summer home in Newport, Rhode Island. She denied marriage to John F. Kennedy. "Why everyone knows the President has been married only once," she said.

The White House was then called. "Absolutely false," Press Secretary Pierre Salinger exclaimed. "And we have an affidavit from the Blauvelt Family Association in New Jersey saying there is no material in their files about the President marrying Miss Malcolm."

"But there must have been some material, right or wrong, at some time, in those files," the reporter persisted. "That notation was no figment of the genealogist's imagination."

"Wouldn't know about that," said Salinger. "But it's just not true."

At first, the White House tried to ignore the rumor that President Kennedy was once secretly married. But the rumor would not die. Instead, it obtained even wider circulation. Various persons and groups throughout the country distributed copies of the page of the Blauvelt Genealogy alleging there had been such a marriage. To individuals who wrote the White House asking about the rumor, a simple reply went out:

"The President has been married only once—to his wife Jacqueline Kennedy."

On September 17, 1962, the *Washington Post* brought the whole matter out into the open. It published an advance article from *Newsweek* magazine, which it owns. The article branded the rumor as groundless and false. The *Post* said that it had reached the conclusion that "recent revival of the rumor has brought it to public attention and made notice of it seem advisable."

Other news media, thereupon, reported that they had tried to establish the facts but had reached the same conclusion. There was no record of any such marriage that reporters were able to find.

However, still unanswered was this question: What basis did Louis Blauvelt, who died in 1958 at the age of seventy-nine, have for publishing his statement?

Newsweek suggested that the basis appeared to be an old clipping from a Miami gossip column, reporting that Durie Malcolm and young Jack Kennedy had been "seen" together in a Miami restaurant right after World War II. *Newsweek* quoted a "Blauvelt in-law" as saying the whole thing was a "colossal mistake." The in-law added: "It was likely that the old man formed the idea in his head, seeing that clipping and the family hadn't had anyone that famous for a long time."

But the *New York Times* quoted James N. Blauvelt, president of the Association of Blauvelt Descendants, as saying, "I am sure that Louis

Blauvelt could not have put it in his book unless he were sure of his facts. Where he got his information I would not know."

And thus was born one of the Capital's biggest mysteries.

As a young Congressman, Jack Kennedy never appeared to take himself or his duties too seriously. And according to a former colleague, "He took our kidding good-naturedly."

Once, however, when teased unmercifully about his absentee record, Jack let loose. "What's the point in hanging around Washington at the beginning of the session when I can be in Florida? Nothing important is going on anyway. Besides Ted can handle things in the office."

Ted, of course, was Timothy Reardon who, after working for Jack in the 1946 campaign, had agreed to go to Washington as the new Congressman's chief assistant.

On one occasion Kennedy's absence from Washington did visibly exasperate a fellow solon—and an important one, to boot. This occurred when a group of Congressmen sat down to discuss a housing bill. John W. McCormack, the powerful House Majority Leader, looked around for his fellow Bostonian. Then, holding aloft a Boston newspaper headlining a Kennedy demand for action on the housing front, McCormack loudly demanded:

"Where's Johnny? Where's Johnny?"

Where "Johnny" was that day no one ever did find out. Not that, in itself, his whereabouts was of any great importance. What was important in retrospect, however, was whether Kennedy—in the words of another former colleague—"really gave a damn about housing or anything else for that matter."

For Jack Kennedy had been sounding off a great deal on the need for more low-cost public housing. He supported a comprehensive housing bill co-sponsored by Senators Robert A. Taft, Allen J. Ellender, and Robert F. Wagner—the "TEW" bill. And he assailed the American Legion for opposing TEW, quoting *America,* the Jesuit weekly, as describing the Legion's housing committee as a "legislative drummer boy for the real estate lobby."

One day, in arguing against a Legion-backed veterans' pension bill, Kennedy blurted out, "The leadership of the American Legion has not had a constructive thought for the benefit of this country since 1918!"[9]

Once he said it, however, Kennedy was sorry. Fully recognizing the political hazards involved in assailing a supposedly sacrosanct veterans' organization, he told Reardon, "Well, Ted, I guess we're gone."

Faced with the specter of unemployment, Reardon asked whether Kennedy had attacked just the leadership as being bereft of ideas or the Legion in general. Kennedy could not remember. It had been one of those rash, impulsive statements. Checking the transcript, Reardon was relieved to discover the word "leadership" in his boss's remarks.

[9] The American Legion was founded in 1919.

Nothing of consequence occurred. The Legion, which had previously dismissed Kennedy as an "embryo" Congressman, just ignored him. At any rate, he was not the main foe of the pension bill. John A. Carroll, a Colorado Democrat who had served in both wars, had organized the opposition. Also Glenn R. Davis, a Wisconsin Republican (then thirty-four years old, nine battle stars and a Presidential citation), had told the House: "The problem of veterans' pensions cannot be solved by floods of emotionalism." Eventually, the bill was defeated.

However, with the passage of time the episode began to assume heroic proportions. Kennedy's hard-put supporters began to cite it as an example of his great political courage.

According to Burns, Kennedy had obtained membership on the Labor Committee—one of the choicer assignments for a novice Congressman—"without trying very hard or thinking much about it, and without knowing much about the subject." Later, when asked how he had become a member, Kennedy said he could not remember.

Another member of the Committee was a Republican newcomer from California, Richard M. Nixon, also a Navy veteran of the Solomons. Both Kennedy and Nixon, in fact, took their oaths of office the same day. They first met, according to Ted Reardon, on January 3, 1947, when they appeared on a radio program with other freshmen Congressmen.

Apparently Kennedy was impressed by the Californian. Attorney Mark Dalton, who was helping Jack with some legislative chores, recalls Kennedy pointing to Nixon at a hearing and whispering, "You never heard of this guy, but he's going to be a big man down here."

In the Spring of 1947 Kennedy journeyed to McKeesport, Pennsylvania, to debate the merits of the Taft-Hartley Labor bill with Nixon. "I doubt if either of us," Nixon wrote later, "or those who were in the audience of 150 to 200 that night will recall much of what was said. . . . I was for the bill. Kennedy was against it. . . . After the meeting, we rode a sleeper from Pittsburgh back to the capital. I remember that our discussions during the long, rocky ride related primarily to foreign affairs and the handling of the Communist threat at home and abroad, rather than the Taft-Hartley Act. I do not recall the details of our talk but of one thing I am absolutely sure: neither he nor I had even the vaguest notion that either of us would be a candidate for President thirteen years later."[10]

Kennedy first discovered the joys of Red-baiting as a freshman member of the House Labor Committee. One of his first "victims" was Harold Christoffel, a Milwaukee official of the United Auto Workers (CIO). According to Louis Budenz, a former top Communist who had broken with the party, Christoffel had engineered a wartime strike at the Allis-Chalmers plant aimed at crippling weapons production earmarked for Nazi-threatened

[10] *Six Crises*, by Richard M. Nixon. New York, Doubleday, 1962.

Britain. This was in 1941, during the Soviet-Nazi Pact when the Reds were assisting Hitler in his war against British "imperialism."

Budenz, whom Kennedy later described as "one of the ablest experts on Communism," had testified that Christoffel was acting as a party member, under Communist instructions, in fomenting the harmful labor dispute.

Called before the House Committee in 1947, Christoffel denied he was a Communist. According to his attorney, O. John Rogge, several Congressmen including "Nixon of California and Kennedy of Massachusetts badgered Chris, grilled him, bullied him."[11]

Kennedy demanded that Christoffel be indicted for having denied party membership. Though civil libertarians considered his call for an indictment rather hasty, Kennedy was vindicated when Christoffel was convicted.

The Supreme Court, on an obscure legal point, came to the labor leader's rescue. So infuriated was Kennedy that he and a Republican colleague issued a statement denouncing the decision as a "travesty on justice." The joint statement, in part, declared:

"Not only does the decision give a witness an opportunity to go free after falsely denying he was a Communist, but also the decision will have far-reaching effect on the operations of congressional committees and the many subcommittees, and will retard the working of the committees, which in turn will affect the legislative processes. . . . What a travesty on justice, that a Communist witness testifies untruthfully before a recognized committee of the House and then escapes the consequences of perjury by a technical claim. . . ."

Though Christoffel was subsequently retried, convicted, and imprisoned, the statement disturbed those who view the courts as the last bulwark against violations of due process.

Others saw it differently. "As an effective anti-Communist liberal," wrote Paul Healy in the *Sign* in July 1950, "Kennedy is more hated by Commies than if he were a reactionary."

Another "victim" of Kennedy's "witch-hunting" tactics, as the Left wing press described them at the time, was Robert Buse, also of the Allis-Chalmers UAW Local 248. Kennedy grilled him as to whether several associates were Communists. In each case, Buse said "no." An extract from the official hearings follows:

KENNEDY: Lennis Lindberg, he is not a party-liner?

BUSE: He is not.

KENNEDY: He signed the 1938 Communist Party nomination of Fred Blair.

BUSE: I would not know.

[11] *Our Vanishing Civil Liberties,* by O. John Rogge. New York, Gare Assoc. Inc., 1949.

KENNEDY: Of the Wisconsin Communist Party?

BUSE: I do not know.

KENNEDY: Do you know that he made a statement, and I quote him: "The free enterprise system by itself either is not able or will not plan in terms that guarantee full-scale operations in our economy."

BUSE: I would not know.

KENNEDY: Would you agree with that statement?

BUSE: Wait a minute. I did not get it entirely.

KENNEDY (reading):
"The free enterprise system by itself either is not able or will not plan in terms that guarantee full-scale operations in our economy."
Do you agree with that statement?
You do not have to answer that if you do not want to. It may be difficult to understand.

BUSE: I would like to say, Congressman, that Lindberg is here.

KENNEDY: I want to know because you were the one that said that it was not Communist-dominated.

BUSE: I will tell you.

KENNEDY: Do you know whether the courses at the Abraham Lincoln School were presented to the local 248 education classes?

BUSE: They were.

KENNEDY: Do you believe that the Abraham Lincoln School teaches courses that are, if not in sympathy with Russia, at least hew to the party line?

BUSE: The courses that were taught in local 248 were not Communist in any way, shape, or manner.

KENNEDY: No sympathy with Communists?

BUSE: Had nothing to do with Communism.

KENNEDY: Why did a reader of the *Daily Worker* write to the *Daily Worker* requesting a series of articles on the same line of the Abraham Lincoln School lectures? Do you know the reason for that?

BUSE: I would not know.

Still another "victim," ironically, was named Nixon—Russ Nixon, the legislative representative of the Communist-led United Electrical Workers (UE) who, as an economics instructor at Harvard, had taught Kennedy. The confrontation, which provided Boston newspapers with good copy about Kennedy as a "Commie-fighter," began mildly enough:

KENNEDY: As a former pupil of yours I have been impressed by the dexterity with which you have answered the questions today.

RUSS NIXON: I had to set a model for a pupil, you know, Mr. Kennedy.

*   *   *

KENNEDY: . . . Do you think that Communism is a threat to the economic and political system of the United States?

RUSS NIXON: I do not think it is a threat. I think what is a threat is our failure to meet some of the basic economic problems of the people in a democratic way, our failure year after year to expand the basic civil rights of our people.

These are not new problems for us. The problems of the Negro people, the limitations of suffrage in the South, the many other issues of civil rights need to be expanded. I think we have no room for fear of democracy in this country, and if we really do not have fear for it, we will expand and wipe out the limitations . . . this is the framework in which we expect to move ahead to solve all of the problems that arise in our country in the future.

KENNEDY: Mr. Nixon, I agree with a great deal that you said. . . .

* * *

KENNEDY: Do you know what a fellow traveler is?

RUSS NIXON: Well, that is a little more difficult, Mr. Kennedy. I do not think I do know. I think that is a kind of a word that means one thing to one group of persons and another thing to another group of persons.

KENNEDY: Do you know what the National Federation for Constitutional Liberty is?

RUSS NIXON: I do not think it exists any more. I knew what it was.

KENNEDY: Was that a Communist-front organization?

RUSS NIXON: Well, I just indicated to you I do not know exactly what the terms mean, so it is very difficult for me to answer your question.

KENNEDY: According to the Attorney General, Mr. Biddle, that organization was a "part of [what] Lenin called the solar system of organization, ostensibly having no connection with the Communist Party, by which Communists attempt to create sympathizers and supporters of their program."

Were you a member of that organization?

RUSS NIXON: I am not sure that I was. I spoke at it. . . . I think that organization was a prewar organization.

* * *

KENNEDY: If it can be shown that the acts of your union were in accordance with, on every step, the foreign policy of the *Daily Worker,* would you not say that it indicated that the leadership of your union was Communist inspired or guided?

RUSS NIXON: No; I would not draw that conclusion. . . .

KENNEDY: I will quote you from Lenin on Left Wing Communism: "We must be able to withstand all of this, to agree to any sacrifice, and even if need be to resort to all sorts of artifices, evasion, subterfuges, only so as to get into the trade unions and remain in them and to carrry on Communist work in them, at all costs."

RUSS NIXON: I did not teach you that at Harvard, did I?

KENNEDY: No; you did not. . . .

* * *

KENNEDY: Do you know of any Communists or former Communists of your union?

RUSS NIXON: Oh, yes.

KENNEDY: Could you tell me whether Julius Emspak (treasurer of the United Electrical Workers) is a Communist?

RUSS NIXON: You do not need to rely upon me to tell you that. He testified before the Senate Labor Committee and was asked that specifically, and said he was not.

KENNEDY: Was he ever a Communist?

RUSS NIXON: He was not asked that question. I do not think he ever was.

KENNEDY: You do not think he was a Communist?

RUSS NIXON: No; I have no information that would lead me to believe that he ever was.

KENNEDY: For your information, he was a Communist, and documentary proof can be provided.
Who is the other leader of your union besides Mr. Fitzgerald?

RUSS NIXON: You mean the other elected officers?

KENNEDY: Matles. Was he ever a Communist or is he a Communist?

RUSS NIXON: Really you should not be asking me these questions.

KENNEDY: You are representing the union.

RUSS NIXON: Yes; I am.

KENNEDY: You should know, should you not, whether they were Communists?

RUSS NIXON: About that?

KENNEDY: Yes.

RUSS NIXON: Well, not necessarily, but I can tell you that he, too, was asked in the Senate Labor Committee hearing whether or not he was a Communist and he said he was not.

CHAIRMAN LANDIS: Your time is up.

KENNEDY: Could I go on just for a few more minutes? You know the picture called *Deadline for Action?*

RUSS NIXON: I know it very well.

KENNEDY: Who made that?

RUSS NIXON: Union Films, Inc.

KENNEDY: Did you ever hear of Earl Oliver Mosani?[12]

RUSS NIXON: Oh, yes . . . he was the prime factor in the production of that film.

[12] Actually, Carl Marzani.

KENNEDY: Did you know that he was formerly of the State Department and was indicted for denying he was a Communist and now awaiting trial in the United States District Court?

RUSS NIXON: Yes; I know that.

*   *   *

KENNEDY: Do you know that one of the policies of the Communist Party is to attack "big business" and by its attack bring its prestige and the prestige of capitalism down in the eyes of the worker.

RUSS NIXON: I do not know whether that is the purpose.

KENNEDY: Here is a quotation from that film which I saw this morning and——

RUSS NIXON: Of course this was the UF film and not a Communist film.

KENNEDY: It was a UF film?

RUSS NIXON: Yes.

KENNEDY (reading): "Big business is international. Its name is imperialism, and it leads to war as Hitler's story shows. He called his dream the New Order. Germany's big business was weakened during the war, and today American big business is the strongest, and they have a dream, too, to dominate the world. They call their dream the American Century, which means the century of big business, instead of the century of the common people."

*   *   *

KENNEDY: Do you know the party line in regard to China?

RUSS NIXON: The what?

KENNEDY: Do you know that line, Communist Party line in regard to China, was to get American troops out? Did you know that that was a part of the Communist line?

RUSS NIXON: I am not very well acquainted with that. It may well be. I do not know.

*   *   *

KENNEDY: Do you know whether the UE has ever taken a stand against or criticized Soviet Russia, to your knowledge?

RUSS NIXON: I think we have never taken a stand one way or the other.

KENNEDY: Have you ever criticized Soviet Russia?

RUSS NIXON: We have never criticized or praised.

KENNEDY: You have criticized Great Britain, China, Spain, Greece, and the foreign policy of the United States, and have done so in several cases. You have attacked British imperialism. Did you ever attack Russian actions in Poland?

RUSS NIXON: Mr. Kennedy, our position on foreign policy which you can read in our convention proceedings was adopted unanimously at our last convention. It was agreed to by Mr. [James] Carey, who was a member of the subcommittee of the resolutions committee which drafted that resolution.

I think you should be careful about going into that.

KENNEDY: My question still stands. Has the UE leadership in any statement at any place ever attacked the aggression of the Soviet Russia? Just answer that "Yes" or "No."

RUSS NIXON: That is easy; "No."

KENNEDY: That is all. Thank you.

Yet, curiously, when questioned by Congressman Wingate Lucas of Texas, Russ Nixon listed Kennedy along with Adam Clayton Powell as Congressmen "whom we consider friends on this committee." The other committee members were dubbed "unfriendly to labor."

A month later, Kennedy did his bit for the labor movement by signing the minority report (this was the Republican Eightieth Congress) filed by his Democratic colleagues on the Committee that branded Taft-Hartley as near-slavery and concluded ringingly if not very originally: "We at least will have no part in pressing down the crown of thorns upon the brow of labor."

The 29-year-old Kennedy, however, had his own views on how labor problems should be handled. To assist him in preparing his own statement, Kennedy called in one of his father's old associates, Joseph Healy, a Boston attorney. Healy worked with Jack at the latter's home in Georgetown, and he recalled that the Congressman provided background music. A phonograph kept playing over and over, "Younger Than Springtime."

His "supplemental" report called down a plague on all three parties to the controversy. "The simple truth is that management, labor and government . . . have failed their responsibilities," he said.

In some respects, his own recommendations went even further toward regulating unions than Taft-Hartley. For example, he proposed permanent, rather than limited-time, anti-strike injunctions in disputes imperiling the public health and safety. His solution: Let the Supreme Court take up such injunctions directly and rule on them without a time limit and under its broad equity powers.

"Management has been selfish," he observed. "Labor has been selfish."

And he warned that enactment of "repressive and vindictive labor legislation" would result in "a tide of left wing reaction which may well destroy our existing business system. At the same time, if labor continues to insist on special privileges and unfair advantage in its relations with management, I have grave doubts as to the future of the trade union movement."

Taft-Hartley became law, and despite its restrictive provisions there was to be no clanking of chains. In fact, the labor movement grew stronger. And instead of the "tide of left wing reaction" which Kennedy had predicted, Taft-Hartley helped set into motion forces that enabled organized labor to cleanse its house of the Communist infiltrators whose presence had so alarmed the youthful legislator.

The truth is that no one paid much attention to Kennedy's views in the supercharged Washington atmosphere. As Kennedy himself later noted, there were 435 other members of the House at the time. "We were just worms over in the House—nobody paid much attention to us nationally," he said.

On January 25, 1949, Congressman Kennedy attracted some attention. Just as the invocation was completed, he arose to request unanimous consent to address the House for one minute. Speaker Rayburn nodded his approval and a somewhat nervous young Kennedy began to read from a sheet of paper:

"Mr. Speaker, over this weekend we have learned the extent of the disaster that has befallen China and the United States. The responsibility for the failure of our foreign policy in the Far East rests squarely with the White House and the Department of State.

"The continued insistence that aid would not be forthcoming, unless a coalition government with the Communists were formed, was a crippling blow to the National Government.

"So concerned were our diplomats and their advisers, the Lattimores and the Fairbanks, with the imperfection of the democratic system in China after twenty years of war and the tales of corruption in high places that they lost sight of our tremendous stake in a non-Communist China.

"Our policy, in the words of the Premier of the National Government, Sun Fo, of vacillation, uncertainty, and confusion has reaped the whirlwind.

"This House must now assume the responsibility of preventing the onrushing tide of communism from engulfing all of Asia."

At this crucial point in history the picture was, indeed, grim. Free China was being engulfed by the Yenan Communists, who were backed by Soviet Russia and munitioned by the military stores captured from the Japanese and the vast stocks of hardware furnished to the Soviet Far Eastern Armies by the United States in the closing months of World War II.

General George C. Marshall, moreover, had embargoed arms to Chiang Kai-shek's forces for eighteen months. Our policy toward the Republic of China was equivocal if not downright hostile. There was high indignation in the United States over the sorry prospect in China. Anti-Communists raised a hue and cry. "Who lost China?" they asked. "Who, in high places, were responsible?" they demanded.

And Congressman Kennedy echoed their demands. In his speech at Salem, Massachusetts, on January 30, 1949, he declared that those diplomats and their advisers who were responsible for the China debacle should be searched out and spotlighted. And he concluded: "This is the tragic story of China, whose freedom we once fought to preserve. What our strong men had saved, our diplomats and our President have frittered away."[13]

Kennedy's friends, who speculated about his motives in challenging his President and party leader (along with General Marshall), suspected the hand of Joseph P. Kennedy, by then a bitter foe of the Fair Deal and all its works.

---

[13] The text of this speech is published in Appendix A.

According to Westbrook Pegler, it was the Ambassador who had supplied him with "the text of the dirty letter which Harry Truman had written to Bernard Baruch in the 1948 campaign." This was the letter in which Truman had upbraided the elder statesman for not taking a post on the Finance Committee, reminding him that politics was not a one-way street. Its disclosure proved enormously embarrassing to Truman and Baruch.

"With Joe sitting by," wrote Pegler, "I phoned Baruch in New York and needled him until he was hopping mad at Truman. He not only confirmed the gist and some phrases of the Truman letter, but added in an angry voice that Truman was a 'rude, uncouth, ignorant man.' But his courage oozed away overnight and next day he accused me of breaking confidence. I said 'you are a damned liar' and that was the last between us."

What is most revealing about this story is that Joe Kennedy and Bernard Baruch had been friends for years. Why the Ambassador should seek to embarrass him has always puzzled Baruch.[14] At any rate, according to Pegler, it constituted one of those "amusing hours" which he enjoyed in Joseph Kennedy's company.

However, Jack Kennedy's personal revolt against the Truman Administration—going full blast in his third term in Congress—may also have been inspired by higher political ambitions. Kennedy was well aware (thanks in part to the findings of the pollsters financed by his father) that President Truman's policies, particularly in the foreign sphere, were becoming increasingly unpopular in Massachusetts. And his political ambitions called for total disassociation from Harry S Truman.

"I never had the feeling I needed Truman," Kennedy said later.

Consequently, Kennedy opposed many Truman programs and made no secret of his virtual contempt for the man in the White House. In February 1949, he opposed a three-year extension of the Trade Agreements Act. (When recommittal failed, he reversed himself and voted for final passage.) But his original opposition was an attack on one of the programs most sacred to the Democratic Party—the reciprocal trade policies launched under the New Deal.

Party loyalty meant nothing to him when it conflicted with his political ambitions.

"I'm certainly worried by the revelations of corruption in the Executive Department," he told a "Meet the Press" panel in 1951. "I don't think the Democratic party should win an election unless it does clean up. And if it doesn't do it, then I don't think we deserve to win the election."

During the Korean war, Kennedy took one of the strongest positions in Congress for a balanced budget, advocating even higher excise taxes and increased levies on personal and corporate incomes. He repeatedly took Presi-

[14] As one of his many ex-friends has remarked, "When you have Joe Kennedy for a friend, you don't need any enemies."

dent Truman to task for failing to head off what Kennedy dubbed "a gallop-
ing inflation." His strong advocacy of economic austerity placed him at odds
with many groups seeking exemptions from the anti-inflation program. "At
one time or another," biographer Burns noted, "he took on real-estate interests, oil interests, processors of farm commodities, airlines (in a hard fight for
separation of airlines' subsidies from airmail payments), and various agricultural and other producer interests." He opposed an RFC loan to the bank-
rupt Waltham Watch Company, arguing: "It's a question of how far government can go in propping up a private business that can't keep going on its
own."

However, there was one special-interest group which Kennedy failed to
take on in his crusade for economic austerity; and that was organized labor.
The *CIO News* box score showed that, in fifty-seven votes on issues affecting
labor, Kennedy went "wrong"—in the CIO's view—just twice in his six years
in Congress.

In his call for a balanced budget and an end to deficit financing, Kennedy was even willing to slash appropriations for the State Department. In
the *Congressional Record* of April 20, 1950, there appeared this colloquy
between the Bay Stater and John J. Rooney of Brooklyn:

KENNEDY: I would like to ask the gentleman whether or not he feels that it is
more dangerous to carry a deficit of $6,000,000,000 in a prosperous year like
today, or cut some of these appropriations by ten percent? I do not see how we
can go on carrying a deficit every year. I should think it would be much more
preferable to cut some of these appropriations by that figure.

ROONEY: I do not believe in further cutting this appropriation, which is for a
vital service, in one of our most important departments, the Department of State.

KENNEDY: How are we going to bring that deficit of $6,000,000,000 down to
a reasonable figure unless we make some of these cuts? . . . Does not the gentleman think that a very important item in the cold war is the economic stability of
our country so that we will have resources in case of war?

All through this period, Congressman Kennedy was opposed to various
federal aid programs on the premise that most of them were doing New
England much more harm than good and that they invariably favored other
sections of the country.[15]

Thus he voted regularly against federal appropriations for various flood
control, navigation, and atomic power projects around the country. His most
significant vote—in view of his later ambitions—was one in 1952 in favor
of slashing $14 million from appropriations for the Tennessee Valley Au-
thority. "We are in danger of losing two basic industries, textiles and shoes,
to the South," he explained to the House. "There are three reasons for this:

[15] However, in 1949, Congressman Kennedy proposed that federal aid to education
be limited to the thirteen Southern states where he said help was needed most.

First, lower wages; Second, lack of unionization; and Third, cheap power. Now we do not blame the South for trying to build their industrial position. I think we, in New England, have been backward not to develop water power in our own area. But if the South attempts to extract our industries, they cannot expect us to contribute to our own demise as we are doing."

A clash resulted when Kennedy reminded his fellow lawmakers that Representative (now Senator) Albert Gore of Tennessee had opposed a Government effort to assist New England "by permitting certain defense contracts to be given to distress areas, even if they may not be the lowest bidder."[16]

"Gore cannot expect us to contribute our taxes to increase unemployment in our state," Kennedy added.

In replying, Gore charged that the Kennedy-backed amendment would knock out two units of the Shawnee steam plant "supplying electricity to the atomic energy plant" at Paducah, Kentucky, "upon which the security of this country may depend."

Other Tennesseans joined the fray. Congressman Pat Sutton referred to Kennedy's arguments as "the same old platinum-plated bull"; and Congressman Joe L. Evins asked: "Will the time never come when the private power lobbyists, the paid snipers and underminers of TVA will cease their despicable work of attempting to cripple the TVA and do injury to our country?"

On another occasion, Kennedy argued against appropriations for flood-control projects on the grounds that New England wasn't getting very much from the half-billion dollar "pork barrel" bill. "Five out of the six New England states will receive no money in this bill for any project," he declared.

Representative Louis C. Rabaut, the Michigan Democrat handling this bill, denounced Kennedy for his "strictly parochial" arguments. "All the gentleman has talked about since he has been here is New England," Rabaut observed.

"Does the gentleman object to that?" countered Kennedy.

"No," replied Rabaut, "I do not object to it, but this is not a parochial bill; this is a bill for the benefit of the United States of America."

Kennedy's various views in this period cannot be easily labeled. At times he voted like a conservative; other times like a liberal. But, always, he thought in terms of the needs of his constituents.

A perceptive article in the *New Republic* of October 13, 1952, reported that "Kennedy himself claims with truth that he reflects the views of his constituents, who want 'more done' about Communism; it is difficult to condemn him for supporting the McCarran Anti-Communist bill when almost every other Democrat and Republican in the country also did so. It ls generally true in Massachusetts that Democrats, most of them Catholic, are more strongly anti-Communist than Republicans; at present the Republican *Boston Herald*

---

[16] This was one of Congressman Kennedy's pet schemes.

condemns McCarthy while the 'Democratic' *Post* calls the Wisconsin Senator 'one of our greatest Americans,' and will likely endorse both [Governor] Dever and Kennedy while implying that Adlai Stevenson is a dangerous radical."

"On foreign policy, Kennedy's position is more difficult to defend," the *New Republic* article continued. "He talks more isolationist than he votes; again, he has admitted that this is related to his constituents, poor men with a deep suspicion that 'someone' on the top levels of government is betraying them and sending them off to die."

Nevertheless, Kennedy was "internationalist" enough to demonstrate great interest in those countries whose sons and daughters had emigrated to the Bay State. For example, he demanded the admission of former Polish soldiers to the United States as atonement for the "betrayal" of Poland at Yalta. On November 20, 1947, he called for interim aid to Italy.

"Mr. Speaker," he declared in the House, "I rise to speak on the need and wisdom of aiding Italy immediately. As we talk here today, riots and strikes are now ravaging the Italian Peninsula. If Italy is to be saved, we must act immediately. If we do not act immediately, Italy may soon fall before the onslaught of the Communist minority. . . . Italy can become a bastion of democracy in Europe. Italy must receive assistance from the United States. I most strongly endorse Secretary Marshall's request for aid to Italy."

Three years later, after Italy (and, for that matter, most of Western Europe) was saved, Congressman Kennedy not only voted to slash economic assistance abroad, but he spoke up firmly against the whole concept of foreign aid as "utopian." Reporting on an "inspection trip" he had made to Asia, Kennedy told the Boston Chamber of Commerce on November 19, 1951:

"We cannot reform the world. . . . Uncle Sugar is as dangerous a role for us to play as Uncle Shylock. . . . The thirty billions of dollars we are spending in Europe have yet to prove that they have made for self-defense in that area; but whatever is true there, to repeat such a procedure in Asia or the South Pacific is impossible. . . .

"We cannot abolish the poverty and want that for centuries has characterized this area. There is just not enough money in the world to relieve the poverty of all the millions of this world who may be threatened by Communism. We should not attempt to buy their freedom from this threat. All we can do is help them achieve that freedom if they really wish to do so.

"Our resources are not limitless. We must make no broad, unlimited grant to any government. Aid and help in the matter of techniques is a different thing. But as some of our recent experiences demonstrate, mere grants of money are debilitating and wasteful. Moreover, we ought to know that mere expenditures bring no lasting results—people who are with us merely because of the things they get from us are weak reeds to lean upon.

"The vision of a bottle of milk for every Hottentot is a nice one, but it not only is beyond our grasp, but is beyond our reach. Because of a naive belief that the export of dollars would solve the world's ills, the United States has failed to realize the possibilities that lie in encouraging the export of techniques."[17]

While traveling in Asia and the Near East, Kennedy was not overly impressed with the caliber of United States diplomats whom he encountered. "With some notable exceptions who are doing a real job for us under difficult circumstances," he said, "our representatives abroad seem to be a breed of their own, moving mainly in their own limited circles, not knowing too much of the people to whom they are accredited, unconscious of the fact that their role is not tennis and cocktails. . . ."[18]

In his final term as a Congressman, Kennedy proposed a commission to study the Truman Administration's foreign spending activities which, he claimed, were "extravagant and wasteful." Because of the "shocking" waste in administrative expenditures, he charged that Marshall funds were "not getting down to the people of Western Europe." And he supported the recommendations of the Hoover Commission, of which his father was a key member. Herbert Hoover, with whom the Ambassador was by now on the best of terms, later called Joe Kennedy "the greatest member" of his commission on the reorganization of the Government.

Speaking on behalf of the Massachusetts Committee for the Hoover Report, Congressman Kennedy declared: "In spite of the fact that we have poured out billions of dollars in economic aid to the nations of Western Europe, we have neither strengthened nor raised the standard of living of the ordinary citizens and workers of those countries."

Kennedy then said that Congress was unable to prevent the "mushrooming" of the number of United States employees abroad because, he

[17] The reference to "a bottle of milk for every Hottentot" recalled a famous speech made by Henry Wallace in May 1942. "The object of this war is to make sure that everybody has the privilege of drinking a quart of milk a day," the then Vice President said. For this humanitarian idea Wallace was lambasted unmercifully. His words were distorted into an interpretation that he wanted to give a bottle of milk a day to the Hottentots. He never said that. "Today," wrote NEA columnist Peter Edson in January 1962, "the conservatism of Mr. Wallace's 1942 words would possibly entitle him to honorary membership in the John Birch society. For the New Frontiersmen have cooked up a plan 'to establish school lunch programs involving at least 500 million children within five years.' "

[18] Unaware, perhaps, of this speech which, for some reason, was not made part of Strategy for Peace, a collection of Kennedy's pre-Presidential utterances, White House aides Maxwell Taylor and Walt Rostow permitted themselves to be photographed in tennis shorts at a Saigon tennis club in October 1961 while on a fact-finding mission for President Kennedy in South Vietnam. On June 15, 1962—in the New Frontier's second year—Senator Hubert H. Humphrey told a group of State Department and foreign aid officials they could do a more effective job abroad if they attended fewer cocktail parties and black-tie dinners, and spent more time learning about the countries where they were stationed.

charged, "it has been virtually impossible for members of Congress to obtain accurate, current figures on the number of ECA employees across the world, specifically the number of foreigners on contract work."

However, he did have some figures. As of October 1951, he disclosed, United States employees overseas included 1,300 in the Veterans Administration; 7,000 in the Interior Department; 4,000 in the Commerce Department; and 200 in ECA—the Economic Cooperation Administration.

In all, according to Kennedy, some 12,500 employees were living high on the hog at United States expense abroad—truly, an alarming state of affairs.[19]

Prior to Korea, Kennedy repeatedly assailed the Truman Administration for its economy program in the defense establishment. For example, he inserted into the *Congressional Record* a February 13, 1950, column by Joseph and Stewart Alsop as a warning of the "effect that economies are having in our defense structure." The column, entitled "Mr. Johnson's Untruths," accused the then Defense Secretary, Louis A. Johnson, of failing to tell the American people the truth about the state of national unpreparedness.

Yet, curiously enough (in view of his stand on China), Kennedy showed a remarkable lack of enthusiasm for President Truman's vigorous position on Korea following Communist aggression there. In fact, he even told a Harvard group that he could see no reason why the United States was in Korea.

This, of course, reflected his father's views. The man who had lost his oldest son and his first son-in-law, who had nearly lost Jack, could see no reason for the Korean war. And he did not hesitate to say so, though a fellow Democrat was in the White House. Speaking before the University of Virginia Law School in December 1950, during the retreat of General MacArthur's forces, Ambassador Kennedy called the Truman-Acheson foreign policies "suicidal" and urged that we pull out of Korea "and any other place in Asia where we cannot hope to hold our defenses." He would have pulled out of Berlin too. He urged that we spend our defense budget fortifying Canada and Latin America.

Congressman Kennedy, meanwhile, warned against redeploying United States troops to the Far East from areas he considered of more vital importance. "I think that we are heading for a major disaster in Western Europe," he said in August 1950, a statement hardly qualifying him as a prophet. Yet, a year later, he told the House: "Many of us feel that the United States has concentrated its attention too much on Western Europe."

At the same time, however, Kennedy demanded that Truman unleash Chiang Kai-shek's troops against the Red Chinese forces who had entered the war in Korea. And he proposed a rigid embargo by the United States and her allies on the shipment of any goods to Red China that could conceivably be

---

[19] Today, an estimated 166,000 United States employees are working abroad, and the number appears to be increasing. Foreign nationals employed by United States agencies abroad number 180,000.

useful to the Communist war effort. On May 9, 1951, he introduced a bill that would put an end to such "trade in blood." In seeking to clamp trade restrictions on nations other than the United States, Kennedy's bill would have prohibited "American economic or financial assistance . . . to any foreign country which exports or permits to be exported such materials to China or Hong Kong."

Following a five-week trip through Europe, Kennedy delivered a radio report in February 1951 which declared that the most important task facing the United States "during the next few months would be the question of our relationship to Western Europe in the face of the growing threat of Soviet expansion."

The very survival of the nation depended on a correct solution of that problem.

"That program from this country's standpoint cannot be the product of one man's thought or that of a small group," he insisted. "It is this nation acting through the Congress and the Executive that must fashion that program and coordinate it with our own defense."

"It is important that Western Europe be saved," Kennedy added, "but we cannot do so ourselves or pay a price that will endanger our own survival. We cannot link our whole fate to what is presently a desperate gamble. We can and will survive without Europe, but with her it will be that much easier."

As he then saw it, Congressman Kennedy thought it absolutely imperative for the peoples of Western Europe to concentrate—no matter the sacrifices—on arming to the teeth in the face of Soviet threats.

"The plain and brutal fact today is that Europe is not making these sacrifices," he insisted.

He found, for example, that in Germany "skepticism toward the rearmament effort was rife." Most Germans wanted no part of militarism. Then Kennedy came to the heart of the quandary: "We had been preaching the evils of militarism, destroyed their war industries and are still doing so, when at the same time we seem to be urging their rearmament. As a popular German joke goes, two Americans leave on a plane from New York, one has a mission to disarm Germany, the other's mission is to urge Germany to rearm.

"Obviously," Kennedy observed, "Germany cannot do both."

Kennedy called upon the Truman Administration to exert every effort to bring West Germany into what was then called the Atlantic Pact system. "Her geographical location in the heart of Europe and her industrial potential make her essential," he said.

Kennedy also argued that Spain would have to be involved in any plans for the common defense of Western Europe, even though he had found "considerable distrust and distaste" for the Franco regime in Britain and France. But, Kennedy argued, Spain with "an army willing to fight and as a base of operations, as a source of power, and because of its strategic position straddling the Mediterranean can no longer be ignored."

Joseph P. Kennedy, however, came to somewhat different conclusions following his May 1951 trip to Europe. The Ambassador told INS's Kingsbury Smith in Paris that Europeans felt the United States was pushing them to rearm too hard and too fast; that they feared their economies would be wrecked by costly rearmament programs.

Subsequently, Jack Kennedy had a change of heart. In voting for a $350 million slash in mutual aid funds for Europe, he said that "this program of rearmament of Western Europe as we are now doing it is the best way to bring on a world war with Russia."

In October 1951, on a visit to SHAPE headquarters near Paris, Kennedy asked General Eisenhower whether there was not a great danger of the Russians being frightened by our armament program and attacking the West. General Eisenhower replied he did not believe the Russians could be frightened into aggressive war by the limited forces we were building up.

Meanwhile, Kennedy had again ruffled the President's feelings by lining up with anti-Truman forces on the question of sending United States troops to Europe. One of 1951's more explosive Congressional issues, it arose as a result of a Presidential decision to integrate United States armed units within a NATO military force with Eisenhower as the Supreme Commander.

A sharp debate arose and Senator Kenneth Wherry introduced a resolution that would have barred the President from sending troops abroad in peacetime without Congressional approval. Truman bluntly declared he could do that without such approval. This led to protracted hearings before the Joint Foreign Relations and Armed Services Committees.

One of the witnesses was Congressman Kennedy, recently returned from Europe. Without commenting on the Wherry Resolution, Kennedy proposed an alternative program also in sharp contrast to the Administration's position. He called for the adoption of a ratio system under which the Europeans would be required to provide six troop divisions for every one sent from the United States. And he proposed close Congressional supervision of this ratio system, implying the Truman Administration might seek to sabotage it.[20]

Senator Wayne Morse asked whether the Kennedy proposal might not indicate "that we lack confidence in the Executive to administer our obligations under the North Atlantic Pact in accordance with the best national interests."

Kennedy replied, "No, but I think there is a Congressional responsibility in this matter, and there is no reason why we should not participate in this decision. . . ."

"Do you think," continued Morse, "it actually involves Congressional participation in the actual deployment of troops, which in times past has been assumed to be reserved to the Executive as the Commander-in-Chief?"

[20] By a vote of 69 to 21, the Senate finally voted a compromise—approving the dispatch of four additional United State divisions to Europe, but requesting the President to advise Congress before sending any more.

"I think that is a constitutional question, perhaps, Senator, which you could probably answer."

"I wish I could."

"I think," said Kennedy, "perhaps we can do it through our appropriation power or in other ways that might be worked out."

Senator Morse said he rather doubted it.

Then Senator Walter George, the courtly Democratic elder, took over the questioning. Looking over his spectacles, he said, "I want to commend you for what I think is a very clear statement of your point of view. The question I am going to ask you—I want to assure you in advance—is an impersonal one. I mean it not as personal.

"You come from a very distinguished American family that exercises a great influence on American public opinion. I want to ask you very impersonally, whether you remember the able speech of your father in December 1950?"

To refresh young Kennedy's recollection, Senator George painstakingly quoted from Joseph P. Kennedy's speech delivered two months before at the University of Virginia Law School Forum.[21]

This was the speech in which the Ambassador had urged the United States to "get out" of Korea and Berlin, adding—with surprising equanimity—that he could see no way to prevent the Soviets from overruning Europe; one could merely hope to keep the Reds on the other side of the Atlantic.

"Today it is idle talk of being able to hold the line at the Elbe or the line at the Rhine," the Ambassador had stated. "Is it not best to get out now? The truth is that our only real hope is to keep Russia, if she chooses to march, on the other side of the Atlantic. It may be that Europe for a decade or a generation or more, will turn communistic."

What Senator George wanted to know was whether the son differed—or agreed—with the father.

Jack Kennedy's reply was diplomatic. From his observations on his trip to Europe, he said, he knew the difficulties involved in quickly creating a powerful military force in Western Europe—"and I think it partly explains my father's position. . . . To him and to a lot of other Americans it looks like an almost hopeless job and that we are committing troops to be lost."

"But," he continued, "after adding up all of these factors and considering them as cold-bloodedly as I can, I still feel that we should take the risk to save Western Europe. . . ."

"That is my position," he concluded. "I think you should ask my father directly as to his position."

In the fall of 1951, Jack Kennedy made a round-the-world trip accompanied by sister Patricia and brother Bobby. The trip included "study

[21] So highly regarded were Joseph Kennedy's views in Moscow at this time that *Pravda*—official organ of the Soviet Government—paid the Ambassador the high, and unusual, honor of reprinting the full text of this speech.

stops" in the Middle East, Pakistan, India, Indochina, Malaya, and Korea. The stopover in Indochina was to have a particular importance for Kennedy because, when elected to the Senate, that Communist-menaced area became "his" issue.

In his ten days in Saigon, young Kennedy managed to annoy the United States Minister, Donald R. Heath, as well as the Commander-in-Chief of the French forces, General Jean Marie de Lattre de Tassigny. Heath, a veteran French-speaking career officer, had only recently been assigned to Saigon, an explosive and dangerous assignment not made any easier by a visiting Congressman wearing an anti-colonial bias on his sleeve. Neither was the Minister's difficult position eased by Kennedy's penchant for dealing with subordinates critical of the French.

One of those subordinates was Edmund A. Gullion who, according to the *New Republic*'s Selig Harrison, "felt so strongly about the disastrous implications of pro-French U.S. policy in Indo-China (and Heath's cover-up cables to Secretary Acheson) that he held nothing back when Kennedy asked for his views. This did not endear him to powerful old-liners in the Department and when, during the period of Gullion's subsequent (1952–54) tenure on the Policy Planning Staff, Kennedy spoke out on Indo-China, there were those who assumed that he was the evil genius (actually, the speech was Kennedy's own work, though Gullion saw a draft)."

How Kennedy felt about Gullion could be seen from this pre-election pledge made to Harrison in early 1960: "Ed Gullion would be one of the first people I would turn to next year. He is one of our best men." And this was one pledge Kennedy kept—Gullion was named Ambassador to the troubled Congo in 1961.

On his 1951 visit to Saigon, Kennedy also managed to so ruffle the feelings of General de Lattre de Tassigny (thirty years Kennedy's senior) that the French Commander—whose only son had been killed in the Indochinese fighting the previous May—complained bitterly of the young Congressman's impertinence. His letters to Washington friends began, "I am far from overestimating Mr. Kennedy, but . . ."

By coincidence, another visitor to Saigon about this time was Thomas E. Dewey, who managed to get along with both Heath and De Lattre. Dewey found Heath to be an able foreign officer whose "long training in treading lightly where political land mines were plentiful has stood him in good stead in his delicate task." As for De Lattre, Dewey described the French Commander as "a consecrated man who believed the soul of France was being revived by her noble struggle against Communism in Indochina."

According to Dewey, De Lattre recalled his son's death and said: "The American mother weeps for her boy in Korea. The French mother weeps in the same way for her boy in Indochina. The Americans want nothing from Korea but to halt aggression and leave that poor country in peace. We French have pledged ourselves to withdraw from Indochina when there is peace."

This, then, was the old, heroic soldier whom Congressman Kennedy had heckled.

In a radio broadcast following his return, Kennedy assailed United States policy in Indochina "where we have allied ourselves to the desperate effort of a French regime to hang onto the remnants of empire."

In the same speech, Kennedy took a swipe at "our intervention in behalf of England's oil investments in Iran, directed more at the preservation of interests outside Iran than at Iran's own development." He also criticized "our avowed willingness to assume an almost imperial responsibility for the safety of Suez. . . . these are things that have failed to sit well with Arab desires and make empty the promises of the Voice of America."

Communism, he said, could not be stopped "by merely the force of arms," a statement echoing perhaps the hour-long talk he had had in New Delhi with Nehru which the Indian Prime Minister later was unable to recall.

Throughout the Middle and Far East, Kennedy had found enormous resentment toward the United States because of "our close alliance with the French and the British."

"Our prestige was high at one time due to the liberation of the Philippines and to the large part we played in the liberation of Indonesia," he said. "However, matters have gone steadily down hill since then. We've lost that prestige."

Conversely, he said sorrowfully, Russia has made friends in this part of the world.

As an example of hostility toward the Western world, Kennedy cited the fact that he and his party had to travel under armed guard as soon as they left the capital city of Malaya. The young Congressman forgot to note however that the "hostility" was being expressed by Communist guerrillas then conducting a vicious subversive war in the then British colony, of a sort that in years to come would confront President Kennedy in South Vietnam.

Subsequently, Jack Kennedy had a change of heart about supporting foreign aid programs.

"He told me with a rather sour grimace," Ralph Blagden wrote in the *Reporter* in September 1952, "that we are now so deeply extended in Europe that we might as well continue our present policy. British and French colonialism worry Kennedy considerably. Yet his vigorous support of Franco's Spain raises the question of whether he is concerned so much about the enslaved as over the identity of the enslaver.

"Somehow," continued Blagden, "such retreats and advances, such reservations and contradictions suggest that Kennedy has not yet achieved very solid convictions. Is he a parvenu in world thinking who will find sure footing, or will he develop into a 'reservationist,' whose reservations could represent the margin of failure?"

These questions were to be raised again and again as Jack Kennedy moved up the political ladder. They are even being raised today.

Lodge

7

"On November 10, 1950," began a *New Republic* article published nearly two years later, "a young Massachusetts Congressman told an informal gathering of Harvard University students and professors—of which this writer was a member—that (a) he could see no reason why we were fighting in Korea; (b) he thought that sooner or later we would 'have to get all these foreigners off our backs' in Europe; (c) he supported the McCarran Act and felt that not enough had been done about Communists in government; (d) that he rather respected Joe McCarthy and thought he 'knew Joe pretty well, and he may have something'; (e) that he had no great respect for Dean Acheson or indeed almost any member of the Fair Deal Administration; (f) that he personally was very happy that Helen Gahagan Douglas had just been defeated in California by Richard Nixon."

The young Congressman was, of course, John F. Kennedy. The article was authored by John P. Mallan, then a Harvard teaching fellow and more recently a professor at Smith College.

Kennedy's Harvard auditors were appalled by what they heard. "Their feelings were not exactly assuaged when it was brought out in later conversation with the disarmingly frank and charming Mr. Kennedy that his reasons for these views were in many cases not so much ideological as a matter of casual intuitive feeling. His liking for McCarthy seemed to be on a personal basis, as was his feeling that Mrs. Douglas was 'not the sort of person I like working with on committees.' While he opposed what he considered to be

Communist influence at home, he refused to become emotionally aroused even on this issue."

But so aroused emotionally was young Kennedy against Helen Gahagan Douglas that he made what could well have been a disastrous slip in terms of his later ambitions. In 1950, John F. Kennedy made a personal contribution to Richard M. Nixon in his Senate campaign against the California Congresswoman.

"The check, of course, is of record," according to Robert W. Richards, chief of the *San Diego Union*'s Washington Bureau. Like any other contribution it was turned over to the Nixon Senate Campaign Committee in California.

Fortunately for Kennedy, the Richards dispatch published on July 20, 1960, soon after his nomination for President, did not obtain wider circulation. At any rate, as Richards told the story:

"The new Democrat standard-bearer's pop, Joe, who master-minded son Jack's climb up the money tree to the party's presidential nomination, also liked Nixon as a warrior against Communism. But the check which Jack Kennedy, then in the House, brought in person into the Nixon office—the vice president also was serving his second term in Congress—was signed not by his father, but by himself and drawn against his own account."

There had been published reports that Joseph P. Kennedy had contributed liberally to the Nixon campaign because he considered Mrs. Douglas "too far to the left." But the Richards dispatch was the first to disclose that Jack Kennedy had personally helped Nixon out with a four-figure contribution.

All this happened during the bruising Nixon-Douglas contest, the repercussions of which were still being felt a decade later during the 1960 presidential campaign. Ironically, anti-Nixon sentiments nurtured in 1950 were to be capitalized upon by the Kennedy forces. As Richards wrote of the 1950 episode:

"Shock-haired Kennedy strode into the Nixon House offices to ask if the Congressman was available. He was informed that Nixon was out. Jack then suggested that he'd like to see Nixon's confidential secretary privately and was turned over to William Arnold. Pulling the check for $1,000 from his pocket the Boston House member said he wanted to offer it to help out Nixon's campaign against Representative Douglas.

"He didn't need to spell out to the then Nixon aide that it might be embarrassing if a Democrat member of Congress was known to be giving cash to the campaign of a Republican senatorial candidate.

"Nor has Nixon ever betrayed the Kennedy campaign gift to this day."

Richards' "unimpeachable source," who, he said, was neither Nixon nor any of his staff, had revealed the story only because Kennedy, in his speech accepting the Presidential nomination, had struck some "low blows" against his Republican rival.

For one thing, Kennedy had asserted that before Nixon deals, "someone had better cut the cards."

Such statements, according to Richards' informant, "were paradoxical in view of what had happened only a decade ago" when Kennedy sought the defeat of Mrs. Douglas.

"Perhaps," observed Richards, "it is one of those swings of the pendulum that politics imposes on the ambitious."

How the pendulum swung for Kennedy, in terms of his Senate ambitions, was described by the Mallan article. It was in the fall of 1951, during another Harvard appearance, when Congressman Kennedy disclosed his intention to seek election to the Senate the following year. And, without characterizing his remarks as off-the-record, he outlined the kind of campaign he intended to wage against the Republican incumbent Henry Cabot Lodge Jr., promulgating what could be termed the theory of the "visual contrast." (This, of course, was before the term "image" had entered the language.) Dr. Mallan continued, "Lodge, said Kennedy, is young, as I am. He is a veteran of World War II, as I am. (He might have added that both men were decorated for bravery.) I cannot disagree with him on foreign policy. There is no way, in short, that I can create a 'visual contrast' between myself as a young reformer bringing change and Lodge as a crusty representative of the Old Guard. One thing remains: I must attack Lodge on domestic issues. I must attack his record on housing, on price control, on labor, on the St. Lawrence Seaway and economic aid for New England. I must, in brief—Kennedy might have added—become a New Dealer."

According to Mallan, Kennedy's Harvard appearances illustrated the irony of Massachusetts politics. "Again and again, Democratic leaders whose personal beliefs seem to indicate a deep-dyed conservatism become 'liberals' when forced to deal with politics on the national scene. The regular Democrats fall easily into a New Deal position when it is necessary to do so. One Democratic National Committeeman from New England put it this way, 'I can't stand this New Deal Socialism—except at election time.' "

Massachusetts Liberals, however, had some specific complaints about Kennedy.

For one thing, they held him largely responsible for the death of several federal aid to education bills.

What happened was this: in 1949 the Senate, by a 58 to 15 vote, passed an aid to education bill (sponsored by Robert Taft, among others) that would have permitted states to allocate part of federal funds to parochial and other private schools for textbooks and school bus services.

When this bill was referred to a House Labor and Education Subcommittee, Chairman Graham A. Barden of North Carolina came up with his own bill which differed from the Senate version chiefly by restricting the use of federal funds to "tax-supported schools." The intent obviously was aimed at barring the use of federal funds to assist parochial schools.

Subsequently, Francis Cardinal Spellman, speaking at Fordham University, attacked Barden as a "new apostle of bigotry" and charged him with "conducting a craven crusade of religious prejudice against Catholic children and their inalienable rights."

This brought Mrs. Eleanor Roosevelt into the fray. In her newspaper column, she defended Chairman Barden against the charge of "bigotry." This led to a sensation-causing exchange of letters between the former First Lady and the Cardinal. The resulting public uproar, with charges and counter-charges from various pulpits, constituted the nation's most acrimonious religious quarrel since 1928.

Acrimony flared within the subcommittee as well. Chairman Barden accused Kennedy to his face of having "leaked out" confidential matters to certain "interested parties." Kennedy also found himself in a bitter dispute with a fellow Catholic, Congressman Andrew Jacobs of Indiana, who was opposed to federal aid to private schools. Their bitterness was to have a repercussion at the 1956 Democratic Convention when Jacobs prevented the stampeding of the Hoosier delegation into voting for Kennedy for Vice President.

The public controversy dealt a death blow to federal aid to education. Kennedy voted against the Barden bill.

In July 1950, the *Sign,* a respected Catholic monthly, published Kennedy's version of the controversy: "Boston's boyish Congressman was in the thick of the adroit intra-committee maneuvering waged over the boiling hot federal aid to education issue. Much credit is due him for the fact that neither the Barden bill, which would have prevented federal aid to parochial school children, nor the Truman-backed, Senate-passed measure, which would have left the matter up to the states, was reported out.

"Kennedy carried the ball from the position taken by the National Catholic Welfare Conference. This position—which Kennedy says was badly misunderstood by the public—was that if federal money is to be spent for education, parochial school children (as distinct from parochial schools) should benefit at least to the extent of obtaining federal aid in meeting the expenses for such personal services as bus transportation. Kennedy's amendment was also defeated in committee and no federal aid to education was reported out."

The Kennedy amendment would have allowed the use of federal funds for parochial, as well as public, school bus transportation. Its introduction touched off another acrimonious debate with Chairman Barden assailing Cardinal Spellman, and Eleanor Roosevelt denouncing the amendment. The next day, the amendment was killed in committee.

Kennedy had voted against the 1950 aid to education bill. His was the deciding vote; the bill was killed 13 to 12.

Whereupon Boston's archdiocesan weekly, the *Pilot,* dubbed Kennedy "a White Knight" for his efforts. "This gentleman of youthful appearance but extremely mature intelligence fought valiantly in the interests of large groups of citizens who are merely asking for their just share. . . ."

Years later, in discussing his amendment, Kennedy observed: "The issue of the separation of church and state was never really present here. It was purely a question of providing funds to aid all children—no matter what school they went to. Direct aid to the parochial schools themselves would, of course, have been unconstitutional."

There was nothing original in Kennedy's explanation of his stand—the only time, he later claimed, when he was on record as favoring a traditional Catholic position in public affairs.

In this period, Kennedy was a strong advocate of religious education. Though himself the product of secular schooling, he told a TV panel in 1952, "Religious education is very important. The trend against religious education in this country has been growing." He did not agree with Harvard University President James B. Conant, whom he described as favoring separation of religion from education.

He did agree, however, with a statement released by the Roman Catholic Bishops of the United States in which they expressed concern over a movement to divorce religion from education in the public schools.

"We don't want a uniform education system or a uniform anything else in this country," Kennedy said, adding that religious education is "a strengthening influence."

The Mallan article, entitled "Massachusetts: Liberal and Corrupt," hit the Bay State like a bombshell. Kennedy's protectors moved in quickly to deflect criticism. They claimed his remarks had been quoted out of context and that even if he had made the remarks, Kennedy had surely resorted to exaggeration in order "to arouse his academic audience. . . ."

A further criticism came from Professor Arthur N. Holcombe who, in a letter to the *New Republic,* said he had invited Kennedy to speak at Harvard "to a strictly academic audience and with the reasonable expectation that anything he might say . . . would not be used against him in a subsequent political campaign."

Kennedy himself, though annoyed by the article, never took public issue with it. And biographer Burns conceded there was "enough truth . . . in the report to put liberals even further on guard. . . ."

A political scientist who had heard Kennedy described his "pitch" as "not philosophical but mainly practical—he was out to serve his district and to get re-elected on the basis of his record of service. He did not preclude the possibility that the constituency interest could be and should be reconciled with some conception of a broader national interest. Yet there was very little beyond 'district' which he appeared to have found attractive.

"There was, in fact, little of what he said which could be used to identify him as a partisan Democrat. He appeared to be not very interested in the party as a vehicle through which broader political values could be realized; rather the party was a label which was the most expedient to run under in his district. . . ."

Kennedy's refusal to be categorized as a Liberal and his dislike of those who claimed the label were notorious. Once (as reported by the *Washington Star*'s Mary McGrory), Congressman Kennedy diverted reporters, after dismissing a band of earnest reformers, by saying, "Those goofs are really obnoxious." However, he went on to display that collectedness which was to become his hallmark by adding immediately, "for the record, we're doing everything we can."

At Harvard in 1950, Kennedy had asserted his unwillingness to follow any "liberal line." Doctrinaire people of any type made him uneasy. Once, in exasperation, he demanded, "Just what is a liberal?"

It was a good question.

What, precisely, is a Liberal?

The term is not easy to define. Its meaning has changed considerably with the passage of time. Liberalism, as we now know it, undoubtedly had its origins in the New Deal. Yet, it has generally been forgotten that the original foreign-policy inclinations of the New Deal were nationalist and isolationist; and that Roosevelt's scuttling of the London Economic Conference in 1933 was then hailed in Liberal circles as a healthy move away from Herbert Hoover's "internationalism."

The young men who had burst on the Washington scene in the early New Deal days came from different places with differing mental attitudes. Some, like Ray Moley, were academic types, precise, analytical, and, above all, possessed of extraordinary honesty. Some came out of the labor movement. Some, like Harold Ickes, were originally conservationists. Others were reformers blooded in the battle against big city political machines. Still others were products of those machines. Like Averell Harriman, a few were born to wealth and, having developed guilt complexes, wished to atone in public service. Others, like Lee Pressman and Alger Hiss, were Communists.

"Franklin Roosevelt picked their brains, selecting and discarding as suited his purpose of the moment," Joseph C. Harsch noted in a brilliant *Reporter* article in September 1952. "But in subsequent years the clamorous disunity of the early New Dealers gave way to a new dogmatism. The word 'liberal' as used by the New Dealers about themselves began to take on specific meaning. At first it meant only the search for the answers to the problems of economic depression. Later it came to involve loyalty to the aspirations of organized labor and racial minority groups. In order to qualify as an American Liberal a man had to favor compulsory FEPC, regard Taft-Hartley as completely evil, believe in the total wickedness of Generalissimo Chiang Kai-shek, take his political economics from John Maynard Keynes, and look to Washington for the answers to all problems."

As the movement became more cohesive, it gave itself an organizational form in Americans for Democratic Action—the ADA. "It evolved not only its theology but also its hierarchy of saints and devils. A political movement born of the depression had become a political religion."

And Jack Kennedy, as yet, didn't have religion. He did not regard Taft-

Hartley as completely evil, or Chiang Kai-shek as totally wicked. Neither—or so he said—did he look to Washington for the answers to all problems.

Only later would he "get" religion.

But before that profound event was to occur, John F. Kennedy demonstrated an intense dislike of the ADA. He made his feelings abundantly clear in 1953 when interviewed by Paul F. Healy for the *Saturday Evening Post.* Noting his resistance to being tagged with any ideological label and his annoyance with letters chiding him for not being a "true liberal," Healy quoted Kennedy as saying:

"I'd be very happy to tell them I'm not a liberal at all. I never joined the Americans for Democratic Action or the American Veterans Committee. I'm not comfortable with those people."

The resultant Liberal clamor was so intense that Kennedy tried to make amends by questioning the accuracy of the quotation attributed to him. But, as Burns observed, "I am satisfied from other evidence that Healy quoted Kennedy accurately."

Writing to an American Veterans Committee leader, Kennedy said he could not recall having made any comment about that Liberal veterans' group. The reason he had never joined AVC, he said, was that he felt that progressive-minded World War II veterans would have more influence by joining established groups like The American Legion and Veterans of Foreign Wars.

But Kennedy missed the point in the Liberal protests. It was clearly—and indignantly—phrased by an irate ADA housewife living in a Boston suburb.

"You don't have to join ADA or the AVC," she wrote to Kennedy, "but why do you express your discomfort about associations which you not only accept, but which you court when they can do you any good?

"I don't know whether you will ever develop a 'political philosophy'; however, it would seem to be a good idea for a United States Senator to renounce opportunism for a certain degree of consistency. As one of the people with whom you 'are not comfortable' may I say that I have talked to many people who are uncomfortable about you."

Thanking the indignant lady for her "frankness," Kennedy replied that he hoped the ADA would not base its attitude toward him on a statement which a magazine attributed to him. "We both have known that my record was not in accordance with the program of ADA on all occasions, but I never did believe that uniformity of opinion was what that organization required."

If Kennedy was not a Liberal, then what was he? The question continued to agitate many Massachusetts Liberals. John Mallan had tried to answer it by, first, observing that like most regular Democrats, Kennedy's "record on labor and welfare legislation is far better than that of Lodge. . . ."

But this, he added, had "little to do with any ideological concern for labor or liberalism as such. Such a man can oppose 'the Socialist trend' in general, while voting for almost every specific bill to aid the aged, the work-ingman or the minority group. Here Kennedy is in tune with the Democratic city boss now fading in importance—such a boss as his own grandfather, 'Pea Jacket' Kennedy of tough East Boston. . . .

"His position cannot exactly be called 'liberalism'; it might be referred to as 'popularism'—a willingness to give the people what they want in specific situations, while shunning the generalities of a liberal ideology."

"Kennedy readily acknowledges that this might be the case," Paul Healy noted. "In any event his political philosophy is still developing. Meanwhile, he disagrees amiably on most major issues with his father, who stands polit-ically a little to the right of Senator Taft, and expects his son to grow more conservative with the years."

"Was there, then, no pattern to the man?" James MacGregor Burns asked in almost plaintive tones. "Was he completely outside the ordinary definitions of American politics? Certainly if Kennedy had had his choice, the answer would have been 'yes.' "

Kennedy, of course, was a politician—buffeted by pressures both from within and without. As Burns has suggested, "it was somewhat similar to the problem of the 'inner-directed' versus the 'outer-directed' man which David Riesman has described."

And Kennedy was an ideal example of the "outer-directed" man in politics. Unlike the "inner-directed" man who feels guilty when he violates his inner ideals, the "outer-directed" man rarely has inner ideals to violate. "A speech of Kennedy's, or a conversation with him, reveals him to be a man of conviction—but of little passionate conviction," wrote the *New York Post's* Irwin Ross in July 1956. "He concedes the point, though arguing that his beliefs are no less steadfast." Kennedy offered this explanation: he came to his Liberal views largely through the force of circumstances; he was elected to office in a working-class district.

Lacking interior conviction and purpose, Kennedy's most noticeable quality lay not in adherence to a coherent view of things but in a remarkable ability to acquire whatever happened to be the political fashion of the mo-ment. In these terms, much about Kennedy that has confused even his loyal admirers becomes clear. Thus, though he has invariably resisted identification with issues, he has, indeed, been responsive to national moods. "Kennedy was committed only to noncommitment," was the way James Burns put it. Neither Liberal nor Conservative, Kennedy's peculiar strength lay not in the posses-sion of any particular ideological viewpoint, but rather in its absence. As he himself informed a "Meet the Press" panel in December 1951:

"I think that's the difficulty in politics; you are always bound to lose supporters once you take a stand on an issue."

And John F. Kennedy was not addicted to losing supporters.

Tied to no public policy or philosophy, Kennedy found it possible in 1952 to solicit—and obtain—the backing, at one and the same time, of

Liberals and anti-Liberals; of Laborites and anti-Laborites; of McCarthyites and anti-McCarthyites; as well as such organizations as the ADA and the far-right Constitution party. The latter group, headed by a former broadcaster, Upton Close, described itself as opposed to the "international conspirators" among whom, incidentally, it listed the ADA.

Kennedy had been running for higher office even before his first term as Congressman was over. This was one of the reasons why his record of absenteeism in the Congress was the worst of any of the fourteen-member Massachusetts delegation. "Indeed," wrote the *Reporter*'s Ralph Blagden, "Kennedy's on-the-record percentage for the entire Eighty-second Congress was fifty-seven, placing him among the bottom four members in the whole chamber."

On his statewide speaking engagements Kennedy rarely touched on controversial subjects. He was not seeking to stir anybody up. What he sought was to make his name known throughout the state.

But what was he running for?

At first he did not know. "I didn't know whether I would run for the Senate or for Governor," he said later. "I would have liked to have run for Governor in 1948, and then run against [Senator Leverett] Saltonstall four years later."

In 1950 Kennedy gave Paul Healy this reason for wanting to become a Senator: "You can do a lot of independent thinking and the level of your colleagues is a lot higher than the public generally gives it credit for."

In 1953 Paul Healy observed in the *Saturday Evening Post:* "Kennedy made no great record in the House as an effective legislator. He was away most of the time, traveling abroad, campaigning for the Senate in Massachusetts or flat on his back with recurrences of the malaria he picked up in the Pacific."

Only an insurmountable technicality prevented Kennedy from seeking the governorship in 1948. One of the qualifications for that high office, as set forth in the State Constitution, was that the Governor have seven years' residence in the Commonwealth. And for all intents and purposes, Kennedy had been an inhabitant of Florida. Not only had he enlisted from that state but he had filed his income tax returns, claiming Palm Beach as his home.

There was no possible way of circumventing this rigid residential requirement. "It is not an election regulation that may be waived," explained the *Boston Herald*'s political columnist, W. E. Mullins, on February 4, 1948. "It is a hard and fast part of the Constitution that permits of no loophole or short cut."

In other words, there was no way of putting in the "fix."

Thus Kennedy began campaigning long before he knew what he was campaigning for. Certain, however, that an early start would be a great asset, he sought speaking engagements before almost every club and organization in almost every community in the state.

"Back there in 1948," recalled John Galvin (in whose advertising firm Joe Kennedy had invested), "Jack had me driving on dark winter nights over those steep, icy roads in the Berkshires to meetings of the Eagles and the Loyal Order of the Moose in places like North Adams and Pittsfield."

"The pros wait too long to start," Kennedy said in explaining his 1952 strategy. "I began running four and a half years ahead of time. My opponent, Henry Cabot Lodge Jr., didn't go into action until two months before Election Day."

Actually, Kennedy did not know for sure who his opponent would be until April 1952 when Governor Paul Dever finally decided not to oppose Senator Lodge. Dever, a good friend of the Kennedys, was the most important Democratic politician in the state. He was the logical candidate to run for the Senate.

"I was prepared to defer to the Governor," Kennedy said later. "Dever finally decided to run for a third term because he considered Lodge unbeatable. He was afraid to take on Lodge."

Kennedy did not hold with the prevalent theory that Lodge was invincible. His intelligence reports from throughout the state (paid for by his father) indicated increasing disaffection with the handsome Republican.

For one thing, Lodge's role in promoting Eisenhower for the Presidency had not endeared him to the conservative Republicans who favored Robert A. Taft. And, as Joseph P. Kennedy said at the time, "this may be the key to the election."

In a friendly, but revealing, *McCall's* article, Eleanor Harris reported five years later that much of the 1952 campaign had been planned well ahead of time in Joseph Kennedy's New York offices at 230 Park Avenue (one of the Ambassador's more lucrative real estate holdings).

"The plans were both audacious and effective," reported Miss Harris, "although father's and son's statements differ as to Mr. Kennedy's role in the campaign. Jack Kennedy says, 'The rest of the family was in Boston helping me, but my father stayed up at the Cape the whole time.'

"Says his father, 'I was in Boston throughout.' "

Though Jack Kennedy has since minimized his father's role in the 1952 campaign, the fact was—as the *Reporter*'s Ralph Blagden reported at the time—"there is much evidence that the former Ambassador's part is a big one."

But for the most part, Joseph P. Kennedy remained out of public view. The last time he had hit the headlines was in December 1951 when, addressing Chicago's Economic Club, he dubbed the Truman-Acheson foreign policies "a total failure" and urged the United States to end its "far-flung" foreign aid commitments in order to concentrate on building a Fortress America.

It was a speech that was gleefully reported in the Soviet press as "one more confirmation of the deep crisis in United States foreign policy." But it was to be the Ambassador's last major speech. He decided not to speak again in public, lest he embarrass his son's political prospects. And from now on, those prospects were to be the elder Kennedy's major concern in life.

"The elder Kennedy is very much alive," reported Ralph Blagden. "From the State House on Beacon Hill to the ramshackle City Hall in Boston I heard reports of the former Ambassador's meetings at the Ritz-Carlton with the political powers of Massachusetts Democracy. Lodge told me that Joe Kennedy was in fact his son's campaign manager, and I picked up the former Ambassador's tracks everywhere I went."

Operating behind the scenes, Joe Kennedy had built an organization, the likes of which was never before seen in the Commonwealth. Nothing was left to chance. All bases were touched. The operation reeked of money; more money than the pols had ever before seen lavished on a statewide campaign. "You could live the rest of your life on the billboard budget alone," a labor leader told John Mallan.

"The father was a tremendous factor in the campaign," a Boston attorney told Ralph Martin. "He remained out of public view. He didn't run things; but they happened according to his plans. He cast the die. He anticipated problems and brought in people to handle them."

The attorney didn't "want his name in print because he plans to stay in Boston." The Kennedys, he indicated, could be unforgiving.

"Sometimes you couldn't get anybody to make a decision," another Kennedy worker declared. "You'd have to call the old man. Then you'd get a decision."

The Ambassador brought in high-priced talent from all over the country. James Landis, the former Harvard Law dean who had served on the SEC, was put to work as a speech writer. Assigned to devising issues for the candidate was Ralph Coghlan, whose prewar isolationist editorials for the *St. Louis Post-Dispatch* had won the Ambassador's approval. Lynn Johnson, an attorney employed in the Ambassador's New York offices, was placed in overall command of the campaign organization. A young man named Sargent Shriver, who had previously worked for *Newsweek,* was brought in as part of the brain trust.

"There would often be conferences in the morning in the father's apartment," a participant recalled. "The father was always very much in the background, away from public view. I don't know how much direct influence he had on Jack. I remember the terrible anguish of the father about the anti-Semitism thing. Another time, I remember Joe Kennedy bawling Jack out for hurting himself. You don't argue with Joe Kennedy."

The result of all this, according to Martin and Plaut, was "the most methodical, the most scientific, the most thoroughly detailed, the most intricate, the most disciplined and smoothly-working statewide campaign in Massachusetts history—and possibly anywhere else."

While all this was going on, Henry Cabot Lodge wasn't even there. After devoting most of his time to getting General Eisenhower nominated for

President, he took a much-needed vacation. Meanwhile, he sent a message to Joseph P. Kennedy.

"Do you know what he said?" asked the Ambassador. "He told Arthur Krock to 'tell Joe not to waste his money on Jack because he can't win. I'm going to win by 300,000 votes.' That's what he told Krock, to warn me to save my money because Jack couldn't win."

Joe Kennedy never had any doubts that his son would win.

"The Ambassador worked around the clock," recalled one of the $1,000-a-week speech writers he had brought in. "He was always consulting people, getting reports, looking into problems. Should Jack go on TV with this issue? He'd call in experts, get opinions, have ideas worked up. . . ."

Henry Cabot Lodge never knew what hit him.

The basic strategy of the Kennedy campaign was to outflank Lodge from both the Left and the Right. Not only was he seeking to create a "visual contrast" between himself as a "young reformer bringing change" and Lodge "as a crusty representative of the Old Guard," but Kennedy assiduously sought the support of the Old Guard.

Primarily, however, obtaining this support was Joe Kennedy's department.

Gardner "Pat" Jackson, an old-line New Dealer, was brought in to handle the Liberals, who were not responding to young Kennedy with any great show of enthusiasm.

"The first thing [Jack] wanted me to do was to get the support of the ADA," Jackson later recalled. "I went to see Papa Schlesinger (Professor Arthur Schlesinger Sr.) first. He has been one of my great friends since the Sacco-Vanzetti fight. It took some doing to get his support, and then we worked on the others, and the ADA finally supported him openly. Then I went to various labor leaders and persuaded them; and that wasn't always easy because Cabot Lodge had been a friend of labor."

The *Reporter*'s Ralph Blagden put it this way: "It is difficult to see how Lodge deserves retirement from the Senate. Massachusetts and the nation have a fourteen-year investment in his career. He has developed steadily toward maximum usefulness. His position on world problems is firm and predictable. He is a bridge between the parties in the construction of responsible and continuing foreign policy. . . . His domestic record is moderate and modern. It is highly questionable what could be gained by substituting a Freshman Democratic Senator for Lodge."

Some Liberals were concerned about Kennedy's "failure to address himself to the menace of McCarthyism." So Pat Jackson prepared a high-level pronouncement citing Senator Margaret Chase Smith's "Declaration of Conscience," and a manifesto "on the twin evils of McCarthyism and Communism" signed by ninety-nine Notre Dame faculty members.

Kennedy was willing to sign the statement provided House Leader John

McCormack would do likewise. McCormack agreed. The idea was to publish it as a newspaper advertisement.

"So I took the statement up to Jack's apartment the next morning," said Jackson. "The place was a hubbub of activity. Jack had his coat on and went dashing out just as I arrived."

Sitting at a card table in the center of the room were Joseph P. Kennedy; Frank Morrissey; and three Kennedy ghost writers—James Landis, John Harriman [Averell's cousin, and a *Globe* financial writer] and Joseph Healy, "another old comrade-in-arms from the Sacco-Vanzetti fight."

"I read them the ad at Jack's request," continued Jackson, "and I hadn't gone two sentences when Joe jumped to his feet with such force that he tilted the table against the others."

Storming over to Jackson, he shouted at the top of his voice, "You and your sheeny friends are trying to destroy my son!" Not only was he not opposed to Joe McCarthy, but, he thundered, he had contributed to Joe's campaign. Again and again he charged that the Liberals, the labor people and the Jews were out to destroy his son. Moreover, he stormed, his son had gone too much down the labor union line to suit him. He shouted obscenity after obscenity.

"And what's more," he yelled, "this statement will never be published." As, in fact, it wasn't.

"I can't estimate how long he poured it out on me," Jackson later recalled. "It was just a stream of stuff—always referring to 'you and your sheeny friends.' No one has ever shouted at me that way in my life."

Jackson went into the back room where he kept his typewriter. Joe Healy came in and said, "Don't worry about him, his bark is worse than his bite." Jim Landis added, "But I still think it would have been a mistake to try to do anything about McCarthy."

The next morning Jackson returned to the candidate's apartment. Kennedy tried to soothe his Liberal adviser's feelings. "I hear my father really gave you a bad time," he said.

"How do you explain your father, Jack?" Jackson asked.

Kennedy thought for a few minutes. "I guess," he said, "there isn't a motive in it which I think you'd respect, except love of family." Then, pausing, he added, ". . . although sometimes I think it's pride."

Joseph Kennedy has since denied the incident ever occurred.

"Oh," he told Irwin Ross, "Pat Jackson has been living off that story for years."

But then, according to Ross, he went on to argue that Jackson was quite wrong in urging his son to attack McCarthy since that would have meant suicide in the 1952 campaign.

The McCarthy problem was a particularly thorny one for a candidate seeking the votes of both militant supporters and militant foes of the controversial Wisconsin Senator. The great fear in the Kennedy camp was that McCarthy might come to Massachusetts and endorse Lodge.

Joseph Kennedy managed to solve the problem in familiar style. He contributed $3,000 to McCarthy's re-election campaign and the story circulated he did so in order to keep the Wisconsinite out of the Bay State.

"Baloney," said the Ambassador later. "I gave Joe McCarthy a small contribution, a couple of thousand dollars, but not to keep out of Massachusetts. I gave it to him because a mutual friend, Westbrook Pegler, asked me to. As a matter of fact, McCarthy told my son Bobby, at the time, that as much as he disliked Lodge he would have to campaign for him in Massachusetts if the Republican National Committee asked him. He didn't do it because Lodge didn't want him."

But this version of the facts differs markedly from that provided by Westbrook Pegler. According to Pegler:

"My statement is that I did not ask Kennedy to give any money to McCarthy.

"Joe McCarthy had gone through dangerous surgery and was unable to go barnstorming. Joe Kennedy had professed friendship for Joe and sympathy for his fight against the Communists in the State Department, Fort Monmouth, and elsewhere.

"We were discussing McCarthy's illness and his busted condition. . . . And Joe Kennedy volunteered to send McCarthy $3,000 in currency and asked me to transmit the money myself. I took counsel of a wiser head who warned me not to touch the money or have anything to do with the deal. Therefore I kept hands off and I was told later in New York that an intimate friend of the Kennedys and an old friend of mine arranged to deliver the money to McCarthy. But I did not 'ask' Joe Kennedy to do anything for McCarthy, although by this time he may believe my mention of Joe's financial problem amounted to a request. . . .

"I did not then suspect that Joe's motive in contributing to McCarthy was to keep McCarthy out of Massachusetts. But soon afterward a wise and cynical head in New York who had known Joe Kennedy of old said, 'Joe will be around to collect from McCarthy.' He was dead right. Those Kennedys are cold-blooded and long-headed but it takes experience and disillusionment to learn them.

"In the fall, Joe Kennedy asked me to persuade McCarthy to keep out of Massachusetts. So my New York sage had been right. This was to be the payoff.

"Still, I didn't mind. I told McCarthy to let Lodge croak and foolishly ventured that Jack Kennedy, though a Democrat, was at heart a fine American. He would be a better Red-baiter than Lodge had been. . . .

"A day or so later, McCarthy phoned again. The 'pressure' was on him to go help Lodge.

"I said: Go on out there to Indiana and help Bill Jenner. He is having a hard time and he will be a real Republican and a good Red-baiter.

"Joe McCarthy lit out for Indiana and Joe Kennedy later admitted freely to me that his abstention from the fight in Massachusetts had been helpful—possibly he said decisive—in young Jack's victory over Lodge."

Throughout the 1952 campaign Jack Kennedy managed to avoid the McCarthy issue like the plague. Once, however, he did criticize the Senator's record on some economic issues. ("That's like being against Khrushchev because of his farm program," commented "Pat" Jackson.) This was at a rally staged by the Jewish Committee for Jack Kennedy.

Kennedy had good reasons to organize a Jewish Committee. His father's occasional anti-Semitic outbursts were no secret within the Jewish community. Moreover, Lodge had a strong pro-Zionist record; while Jack Kennedy had once introduced a foreign-aid amendment hurtful to Israel.

This was an amendment that would have slashed economic assistance to Africa and the Middle East from $175 to $140 million. Kennedy fought vigorously for the cuts even though then Congressmen Abraham Ribicoff and Jacob Javits tried patiently to explain to their youthful confrere that his amendment's across-the-board features would hurt Israel. Kennedy disagreed, insisting his proposed cuts would apply only to those areas for which he specifically disapproved aid. Though, as Martin and Plaut noted, "his defeated amendment was construed as an anti-Israel amendment, the general acceptance is that Kennedy misunderstood the language of the original bill. . . ." (If Kennedy had misunderstood, indeed a startling observation, he has never so confessed publicly.)

On the other hand, as his critics then noted, Kennedy had introduced an amendment to provide Spain with $75 million in military assistance. "There should be only one qualification before a country becomes eligible for military assistance," he had argued on July 19, 1950, "and that is: Are they guilty of aggression against other countries? Spain is not."

Aware that the vital Jewish vote was in danger, Joseph P. Kennedy appealed to Congressman John W McCormack for help. Though sometimes referred to as the "Bishop of Boston," McCormack had great influence among the city's Jews. McCormack arranged a rally in the heavily Jewish Fourteenth Ward. He announced that it was he who had written the "anti-Israel" amendment "and I gave it to Congressman Kennedy to offer in his name" to stave off another Congressman's plan to slash even more funds.

McCormack's wily ploy had been cut out of whole cloth. There had been no other amendment, nor was one being prepared. "The old pro from Dorchester," *Newsweek* later conjectured, "may have changed the course of history that day."

Toward the close of the campaign, leaflets telling of Joseph Kennedy's alleged anti-Semitism were widely distributed in Jewish districts. One leaflet bore the heading: "GERMAN DOCUMENTS ALLEGE KENNEDY HELD ANTI-SEMITIC VIEWS." This, of course, was a reference to the captured Nazi documents published by the State Department.

The Kennedy forces countered with their own leaflet declaring: "SHAME

ON YOU, MR. LODGE! Lodge endorses McCarthy in Wisconsin and Lodge Supporters Use McCarthy Tactics Here. . . ." Distribution of the leaflet was confined to the same Jewish districts—to minimize the use of the McCarthy name.

Once the name was raised to an embarrassed silence. This was the occasion when, according to Murray Kempton, Harry Truman came to Boston "to address a wondrous wake of Irish professionals and fairly spat the names of Jenner and McCarthy." Kennedy had preceded the President on the rostrum with "a delicately-carpentered speech built around alliterations about 'the Capeharts and the Cains,' which could outrage no one within line of sight." It was a speech in which Kennedy warned that a GOP victory would give Senate Committee chairmanships "to the Brickers, Capeharts and Cains, truly a murderers' row of reactionism." But the candidate uttered nary a word about the Liberals' principal *bête noire* of the season—Joe McCarthy.

In seeking to outflank Lodge from the Right, Kennedy appealed for votes from conservative Republicans with the argument that he was far closer on foreign policy to Senator Robert A. Taft—Mr. Republican himself—than was his distinguished opponent.

"Kennedy has been an outspoken critic of many elements of the Truman Administration's Foreign Policy," began a study circulated by Kennedy's campaign headquarters. "In this respect, he has been much closer to the position of Taft than has Lodge. Indeed, the latter has been riding at the head of the so-called foreign policy parade since 1947. . . ."

The study—a forty-page affair prepared by Ted Reardon, presumably with the candidate's approval—was also remarkable in its efforts to demonstrate that Henry Cabot Lodge was soft on Communism. For example, Lodge was accused of "straddling on the big issue of the guilt or innocence of Owen Lattimore, John Service and Philip Jessup. . . . Of Jessup, he said that he was willing to accept General Eisenhower's word that he was 'a splendid American.' "

"The outstanding question, of course, in [Lodge's] case as well as the Administration's," the document concluded, "is why there has not been more of an awareness for a strong anti-Communist policy in the Far East."

The strategy also called for capitalizing on the bitterness among conservative Republicans toward the role played by Lodge—as Eisenhower's campaign manager—in engineering the defeat of Robert Taft for the presidential nomination.

"So strong was this feeling that Lodge, running in the fall for re-election in Massachusetts, was openly set upon by large groups of influential Taft men—a circumstance that materially contributed to the victory of his Democratic opponent, John F. Kennedy, but a circumstance for which Lodge himself rightly never blamed Taft personally," noted Taft's biographer, William S. White.[1]

[1] *The Taft Story,* by William S. White. New York, Harper, 1954.

Trading on his friendship with Taft, Joseph P. Kennedy moved in quickly to win conservative support for his son's candidacy. As Burns noted, the strategy was obvious: "attack Lodge as a Republican who had deserted his party, a political adventurer clinging to Eisenhower's coattails, an internationalist who had repudiated his own grandfather."

In fact, just as soon as the GOP convention ended in Chicago, the Taft headquarters in Boston's Sheraton Plaza Hotel became the headquarters for "Independents for Kennedy." The director, T. Walter Taylor, had been a lieutenant in the Taft movement.

"When I talked with Taylor," reported Ralph M. Blagden, "he said that the organization had been established to provide the Bay State supporters of Senator Taft with a place to go. He pretended to see no incongruity in a movement that called upon the devotees of 'Mr. Republican' to transfer their allegiance to a New Deal–Fair Deal Democrat like Jack Kennedy. Taylor denied with vehement piety that the organization was aimed against Senator Lodge or that it had any financial support except from its prospective members."

But in Blagden's pocket at the time of the interview was a letter that had been sent to a Taft volunteer. In part, it read:

". . . You, being a delegate for Senator Taft, I feel sure will be interested to know that something is being done to assume Senator Lodge's defeat.

"After what he did to Senator Taft, we feel that he has forfeited all rights to expect right-thinking people to support him this fall in returning to office.

"Ambassador Kennedy, who by the way is a very close friend of Senator Taft's, has supported the Senator during the campaign and has spent a large amount of time with the Senator during his campaign, requested me to open and direct a headquarters for his son whom you know is seeking election to the Senate.

"Our work is to reach the Independents and Taft people in behalf of Kennedy so we have opened the Headquarters for Kennedy Independents in the Sheraton Plaza Hotel, in Parlor B, and are very happy at the privilege of bringing the Kennedy message to the people. . . ."

The letter was signed by T. Walter Taylor.

And if the letter reflected the facts, it would thus appear that Joseph P. Kennedy found it possible in the year 1952 to support the Presidential aspirations of both Robert A. Taft and Adlai Stevenson.

Meanwhile, Senator Taft had written to a Bay State supporter urging Lodge's return to the Senate for the good of the party. In Taft's view, biographer White reported, *"any* Republican was . . . better than *any* Democrat."

This was not enough to mollify more conservative Republicans, who viewed Lodge as the Brutus of an anti-Taft plot. Basil Brewer, the publisher of the *New Bedford Standard-Times,* for one, assailed Lodge as a "Truman socialistic New Dealer" and endorsed Kennedy's candidacy. (The importance of the endorsement can be seen by the fact that Kennedy carried New Bedford by some 21,000 votes while Dever, his gubernatorial running mate, squeezed by with 328.)

The *Chicago Tribune* also lambasted Lodge as a "follower of the Truman-Acheson-Lattimore foreign policy. . . . It happens that Representative Kennedy is a good deal more critical of Secretary Acheson's foreign policy than Senator Lodge has ever been."

The *Tribune* dubbed Kennedy "a fighting Conservative."

Two weeks before Election Day, the *Boston Post,* which had been expected to declare for Lodge, unaccountably endorsed John F. Kennedy. It editorially urged its readers to vote for Eisenhower and then switch over to Kennedy because, it said, he had a much better record of fighting Communism than had Lodge.

Because of its influence among Senator McCarthy's many supporters in Massachusetts, the *Post* was generally credited with having—in a year when Eisenhower toppled Democrats everywhere—swung Kennedy's election with a 70,000 vote plurality.

Six years later, a curious story came out of the Congressional investigation into the tangled affairs of textile magnate Bernard Goldfine. John Fox, publisher of the *Boston Post,* who had blown the whistle on Goldfine, was asked if he had ever had business dealings with Joe Kennedy. Fox said that shortly before the 1952 election he had obtained a $500,000 loan for his money-losing newspaper from the elder Kennedy. But he insisted that the loan was made after he had decided to endorse Jack Kennedy.

Following this embarrassing testimony Joseph Kennedy's office in New York issued a statement saying the loan had been a straight business arrangement with no strings attached. Moreover, the loan had been repaid in sixty days with full interest and, added the statement, it was "simply one of many commercial transactions in which this office has participated."

Other politicians familiar with the erratic John Fox, under whom the *Post* went into bankruptcy, were inclined to be skeptical about the loan story. For one thing, other testimony disclosed that Fox had supported other Democrats on the state ticket after obtaining, with the help of then Governor Dever, another loan of $300,000. Then an aide recalled how Fox once paid a visit to then Governor Furcolo's office: "Fox was carrying the galleys of two front-page editorials—one praising Furcolo, the other bitterly denouncing him. We were to choose."

John Mallan's controversial *New Republic* article concluded with this observation:

"It now appears very likely that Massachusetts and the nation will soon see an irregular Republican replaced with an irregular Democrat. One can only hope that the educational experiences of service in the United States Senate—plus probable ambitions for even higher office—will lead John F. Kennedy, like others before him, along the road to more enlightened service."

This was probably the first published reference to John F. Kennedy's ultimate ambitions.

Senate

8

Actually, the 1952 contest between John Fitzgerald Kennedy and Henry Cabot Lodge Jr. was not fought on any great issues. Asked what he thought he could do in the Senate that Lodge could not do as well or better, Kennedy—according to the *Reporter*'s Ralph Blagden—"replied that he could, at least, help a Democratic President organize the Senate."

Since only the most starry-eyed of Adlai Stevenson's supporters could really have expected the 1952 Democratic Presidential candidate to win—and Jack Kennedy was far from being starry-eyed—one must assume that, in seeking to respond to Blagden's query, he was grasping for straws.

Or as Blagden himself deduced, ". . . one is forced to the conclusion that the basic motive for Kennedy's entry is personal and family ambition."

Or, perhaps, both. For Kennedy had long wearied of the House of Representatives where he felt he was going nowhere fast and where "we were just worms. . . ." And his family was not adverse to pushing him onward and upward.

The candidates were well-matched; their assets—a particularly appropriate word—were similar. Both were wealthy, good-looking, and war veterans; both were *cum laude* graduates of Harvard; and both had family backgrounds in politics.

Essentially, the 1952 campaign came down to a question of personalities. And money.

The biggest laugh of the campaign was over a begging letter from Kennedy headquarters that began, "Believe it or not, Jack Kennedy needs money. . . ." No one had any doubt that the Kennedy campaign was more than adequately financed.

Senator Lodge had money; but not *that* kind of money. He began to complain he was in a "battle to buy the senatorship." Ultimately the six Kennedy committees reported a total expenditure of nearly $350,000, a new high for on-the-record spending for political purposes in the Commonwealth. What was spent off the record was another matter. Following the election, Kennedy told the *Saturday Evening Post* he would never have been able to compete without the family bank roll.

Essentially, the campaign was between a truly Proper Bostonian and a Lace Curtain Irishman.

"Kennedy's special importance derives from one fact," Doris Fleeson reported at the time. "He is Irish Catholic to the core. His people have shown signs of slipping from their Democratic moorings. . . . In Kennedy, Massachusetts Catholics have a candidate of special appeal. . . . While they have had their Al Smiths, they have tended to produce politicians long on political instinct, warmth and compassion, but a trifle short on ethics. Kennedy is, so to speak, a case of all this and heaven too. . . ."

"While the liberal may have reservations about Kennedy," John Mallan had written, "the average Democrat seems to have none; when the altogether handsome and charming Kennedy—still a bachelor—makes an appearance anywhere in Massachusetts, the effect is overwhelming. Kennedy is, for one thing, an Irishman of family—and breeding—rare in a state where almost all Democratic leaders are self-made, one-generation and often crude in manner and appearance. He is wealthy enough to be honest without question, in a state where many vote Democratic but feel a little guilty about it. . . . His family has long been active in Catholic charities, and has been officially decorated by the Pope; this again, plus Kennedy's appearances over the years at Communion breakfasts across the state, brings him a kind of personal support which few of the more 'secular' Irish politicians could hope to equal."

Kennedy had another—more elusive—quality. He made people—particularly on the distaff side—want to do something for him. "Every woman either wants to mother him or marry him," someone said. At first glance, he did look a little lonesome, and in need of a square meal if not a haircut. "Something in his appearance," Mary McGrory observed, "suggests to the suggestible that he is lost, stolen or strayed—a prince in exile, perhaps, or a very wealthy orphan."

But whatever he had, it was pure gold. And it was evident from the earliest days. Congressman Thomas P. ("Tip") O'Neill, then a state legislator, was making his usual rounds among the North Cambridge Irish and receiving his usual cordial welcome. He remembers that many conversations would end this way:

"Ah, Tip," the lady of the house would say, "of course, you are not running against that Kennedy boy."

O'Neill would assure the lady he would never think of it.

"Thanks be to God," the lady would reply. "For I could not bring myself to vote against that nice boy."

Another of Kennedy's special appeals was noticeable in this campaign.

"There's something about Jack—and I don't know quite what it is—that makes people want to believe in him," said Robert Capeless, former Pittsfield mayor, in discussing 1952. "Conservatives and liberals both tell you that he's with them, because they want to believe that he is, and they want to be with him. They want to identify their views with him."

Kennedy always said the right things. "Private enterprise cannot be completely private," he told Liberal groups. "Government has got to play a measurable part." At the same time, so persuasive were his calls for more economy and efficiency in Government that he attracted Conservatives. And his father's name and connections didn't do him any harm with this element. "Kennedy is received by small-town Republican businessmen with an enthusiasm no other Democrat could attain," James Mallan reported during the campaign.

Before labor groups, Kennedy would point with pride to his opposition to Taft-Hartley and his espousal of strong rent and price controls. He had also worked hard for the Italian-Americans, so numerous in his district, and opposed the restrictive features of the McCarran Immigration Act; his campaign literature emphasized he was the only Congressman ever decorated by the Italian Government "for his constant assistance to Americans of Italian descent."

There was a good reason why Kennedy was the only Congressman so honored. Senator Lodge had also been tendered the same Italian decoration but he had been unable to accept it, he explained, without special legislation being enacted by the Congress. The Constitution of the United States of America was quite explicit on the subject: "And no person holding any office or trust under [the United States] shall, without the consent of the Congress, accept any present, emolument, office, or title of any kind whatever, from any king, prince or foreign state."

The Constitution allowed no exceptions, no leniency, no elasticity. As far as Kennedy was concerned, however, it was another one of those small, inconsequential technicalities. And yet?

Though between Kennedy and Lodge there was only half a generation difference in years, there was half a century in political techniques. Lodge found himself running not just against Jack Kennedy but a host of frantically active Kennedys. The organizational gifts of the Clan Kennedy were apparent from the beginning. "Coffee with the Kennedys" was a television program that demonstrated the change that had come in campaign methods. Lodge had nothing to match these bold experiments.

"Poor old Lodge never had a chance," a family friend has since said. "The Kennedys were like a panzer division moving down the state."

Complained a Lodge lieutenant: "When Archbishop [now Cardinal] Cushing baptized the baby of Bobby and Ethel in a special weekday ceremony just before the election, that cut our hearts out."

Brother Bobby, recently graduated from the University of Virginia Law School and twenty-seven years old, supposedly managed the campaign; but the elder Kennedy, ensconced in a suite at the Ritz-Carlton, called the signals, hired the experts, and paid the bills.

One Kennedy worker said: "In a lot of matters, I preferred to deal with the father rather than with Jack. He was a businessman and he could evaluate matters. He was also a shrewd judge of people and of talent."

An unabashed effort was made to win the female vote. "We concentrated on women because they do the work in a campaign," said Bobby Kennedy. "Men just talk." Mrs. Joseph P. Kennedy, a small, modish woman looking more like one of her daughters, flew home from Paris to do her bit. An object of feminine fascination, both as the wife of a former Ambassador to Great Britain and as a Papal Countess, Rose Kennedy was everywhere—on television, at women's meetings across the state, and at the now famous teas.

Joe Kennedy, at first, had frowned on the idea of having his wife brought into the campaign. "But she's a grandmother," he had protested to John Powers, who was directing the Kennedy campaign in the Boston area.

"She's also a Gold Star mother," Powers replied, "the mother of a war hero, the beautiful wife of Ambassador Kennedy, and the daughter of John F. Fitzgerald—which means that she's hot stuff in Boston."

Rose Kennedy toured the city with Powers. A *New York Times* correspondent reported that she would change her garb to fit the kind of gathering. Seated in the back of her limousine, she would remove the jewels and furs with which she had delighted suburban matrons to change to a more simple dress when meeting with less pretentious ladies in the poorer wards. She was not the daughter of Honey Fitz Fitzgerald for nothing.

As for wanting to dislodge Lodge, there was a family reason. Back in 1916 Honey Fitz had tried to unseat Lodge's grandfather Henry Cabot Lodge, The First, and lost by 33,000 votes.

Jack's sisters Eunice, Patricia, and Jean also plunged into the campaign. From the Berkshires to South Boston, housewives, stenographers, factory workers, debutantes, and other assorted females received invitations to tea to meet Mrs. Joseph P. Kennedy, her famous daughters and, last but not least, John F. Kennedy himself. In all, 60,000 ladies turned out, and it was not unusual for doting mothers to trot out their eligible daughters to meet young, presumably eligible Jack.

"What is there about Jack Kennedy," asked one Republican leader, "that makes every Catholic girl in Boston think it's a holy crusade to get him elected?"

In town after town the tea parties became the greatest social event in years and received appropriate publicity in the local society columns. And in town after town Jack Kennedy would give the assembled ladies the same brief pitch:

"In the first place, for some strange reason, there are more women than men in Massachusetts, and they live longer. Secondly, my grandfather, the late John F. Fitzgerald, ran for the United States Senate thirty-six years ago against my opponent's grandfather Henry Cabot Lodge, and he lost by only 30,000 votes in an election where women were not allowed to vote. I hope that by impressing the female electorate that I can more than make up the slack."

While the tea parties attracted a lot of attention for the Kennedy campaign, his opponent was plugging away in more orthodox fashion. In nearly every encounter with a group of constituents Senator Lodge disposed of the tea party tactic by observing, "I am told they are quite pleasant little affairs, and I'm sure they are non-fattening."

Other observers, however, couldn't have been more contemptuous. "Kennedy's career is a curious reversal of the law of the long cabin," a veteran reporter told Ralph Martin. "Trappings of power and wealth were in evidence everywhere in that campaign. That family behaved like royalty at their rallies. Whoever heard of reception lines in politics, as though to meet the King and Queen. They fancy themselves in that role, and it was all they could do to keep those old gals who came to the affairs from curtsying. They had every tendency to drop one knee."

So active were the Kennedys that one rally produced what could well be the shortest political speech in history. Bobby showed up alone. "My brother Jack," he told the crowd, "regrets very much he's unable to be with you. My sister Eunice regrets she can't be here. My sister Patricia is sorry she can't be with you. If my brother Jack were here, he would tell you that Lodge has a very poor voting record."

End of speech.

"In the 1952 campaign," Alistair Cooke was to write in the *Manchester Guardian,* "Kennedy was the Frank Sinatra of the Democratic party, bringing to the platforms of bigger men who don't forget a boyish pompadour crowning a handsome grin, a gift of appropriate sweet-talk, which is the political equivalent of perfect pitch in a crooner."

And that's the kind of campaign it was. The chief Kennedy slogan was: "Kennedy Will Do *More* for Massachusetts." Lodge's writers went into a huddle and then countered with: "Lodge *Has* Done—and *Will* Do—the *Most* for Massachusetts." Besides the fact that both candidates were *for* Massachusetts, their voting records were not strikingly different, though Kennedy's record veered more to the left.[1]

---

[1] In 1962, Ted Kennedy also trotted out his brother's 1952 slogan: "Kennedy Will Do *More* for Massachusetts." After all, it worked once.

Kennedy launched his Senate campaign with a claim "there is a crisis here at home in Massachusetts," and he intended to do something about it. "The state's two Senators were demonstrating too much concern about world problems," he said. It was time for Massachusetts to have a Senator who also worried about domestic crises.

"Our competitive industrial position with other states has been weakened," he added. "Our jobs and industries are disappearing."

Meanwhile, Governor Dever—the Democratic standard-bearer—was working the other side of the street. "Business is flourishing," he said, "with 120,000 more jobs than four years ago."

The *Boston Herald* took this position: True, the state's competitive position was bad, but whose fault was that? Kennedy was ignoring the fact that the Democrats had been in control of the White House for twenty years; and that Kennedy himself had been a Congressman for six years "and surely could have helped save Massachusetts industry—if federal charity had been the method of saving the Bay State."

Hard pressed for issues, Kennedy repeatedly assailed Lodge for having voted for Taft-Hartley.

"Your industrial future is tied to trade unionism," he declared in a radio address, "and the Taft-Hartley act dealt it a serious blow. . . . Only when wage scales in textiles and shoes are set nationally, shall we be protected from the cut-throat competition of low wages and non-union mills in the South and West. The Congress must write new legislation affecting labor, which will no longer be treated as a commodity, subject to the inhuman workings of the law of supply and demand."

Kennedy accused Lodge of lacking "integrity and sincerity" for having switched his position on Taft-Hartley. He charged that Lodge's pledge to vote for repeal of the law was motivated by "political reasons—solely to get votes."

"It shows," he added, "the Senator to be as he has been all along—all things to all men."

Kennedy's own "integrity and sincerity" vis-à-vis Labor also came into question. He was caught in the act of using non-union labor and phoney union labels on his political signs. But that wasn't all. The man who promised to "Do *More* for Massachusetts" had sent his printing business out of the state.

What made this situation all the more embarrassing was the fact that Lodge had used only union labor in Massachusetts for his posters.

Kennedy's lame excuse, offered when the AFL's Sign, Pictorial and Display Union threatened to picket his headquarters, was that his people had not been aware they had been dealing with non-union personnel and that, honest to Sam Gompers, they would not do it again.

"But even if we are to believe that the Kennedy people didn't know they were using non-union shops," the *Boston Traveler* quoted a labor official, "they know it now—they have been informed in writing—and still they won't take the phoney union labels off those signs. I still think they should do so, even if we have to picket. Lodge went to the trouble to find out whether his sign painters were unionized. Why should Kennedy get away with a deal like this?"

But Kennedy did get away with it. The "fix" was arranged. And the incident—one that would have plagued the political careers of other would-be benefactors of mankind—was soon forgotten.

The campaign finally got down to a question of who had the less embarrassing absentee record. Lodge, it turned out, could not take full advantage of his opponent's extraordinary absentee rate simply because, as the chief promoter of Eisenhower for President, he himself had been absent from the Senate a good deal.

In a case of the pot calling the kettle black, Kennedy charged that Massachusetts was being "represented in the Senate by phantoms." He said that Lodge had the "second worst absenteeism record among Republican Senators."

"Obviously," he added, "this shows a complete disregard for the welfare of his constituents in Massachusetts. If he had been thinking about the average men and women and their families, it seems to me he would have been in the Senate fighting for price controls."

Lodge also found it difficult to get his opponent within his sights on the basis of "the mess in Washington" and "it's time for a change," because Kennedy himself sounded as if he were running against the Truman Administration.

In fact, Kennedy pinned the Truman label on Lodge. He said that although his worthy opponent claimed to be a Republican, he had "the number one record of support" of Truman's "disastrous" foreign policies. He quoted Lodge as having declared in 1949: "I am not one of those who is critical of our China policy." Then Kennedy added: "I happen to have been among those who in 1949 were critical of our China policy. I believed then and have said since that our diplomats were frittering away victories that your young men won for us."

And he concluded a TV analysis of the Lodge record by declaring: "It is a record that contradicts itself on every turn."

And he won. When the votes were counted, Kennedy was the only Bay State Democrat to survive the 1952 Republican landslide. While Eisenhower carried the state by some 210,000 votes, Kennedy managed to beat the tide and defeat Lodge by 70,000 votes.

"It was those damned tea parties," exclaimed Henry Cabot Lodge by way of explanation. A friend offered this consolation, "Don't take it too hard. You only lost by 9,500,000 cups of tea!"

On January 3, 1953, after taking the oath of office as a United States Senator, John F. Kennedy took his seat in the very last row behind the Democratic contingent.

Six weeks later he began to complain.

"There is nothing lower in Washington than a young member of the minority party in the Senate," he said.

The fact that he had scored a truly sensational victory over one of Eisenhower's staunchest lieutenants in the face of a Republican landslide was clouded by charges that his father had "bought" him the Senate seat.

Years later, Martin and Plaut quoted Kennedy as saying, "People say, 'Kennedy bought the election. Kennedy could never have been elected if his father hadn't been a millionaire.' Well, it wasn't the Kennedy name and the Kennedy money that won the election. I beat Lodge because I hustled for three years. I worked for what I got. I worked for it."

"But," as Martin and Plaut observed, "it's still true that the base of his race was Money. . . .

"Money couldn't pay for the intense loyalty of close friends, but money gave the Kennedy name a glamour that pulled in volunteers by the thousands. Money gave the Kennedy name a political power so that a Kennedy suggestion was translated into an absolute must. . . .

"Why should anybody who has the money not use it? Why should any millionaire father hesitate about flowing out the funds to help his son?

"But there is a small, sticking point. . . .

"If Jack Kennedy, without the fame of his name, without the power of his money, without the strength of his family—if Jack Kennedy were Jack Armstrong, a young Congressman pitted against the prestige of Senator Henry Cabot Lodge, close friend of hero General Eisenhower . . . could Jack Armstrong have won in 1952 by 70,000 votes, no matter how hard he campaigned?

"The answer is: No.

"Could he have won at all?

"Looking back into the upset history of politics, knowing that the driving force of an appealing candidate can penetrate a people, turn a tide, the answer is: Maybe."

In his first statement following his election, Senator-elect Kennedy pledged a continued fight against Communism both at home and abroad. In addition, he praised President-elect Eisenhower's decision to visit Korea—a decision which during the campaign Kennedy had faulted as a propaganda stunt. In fact, he had said that Republican promises to end the Korean war would inevitably lead to a Communist attack on Alaska and World War III.

Now, Kennedy said he was "glad" Eisenhower was going to Korea because, after a first-hand study, the new President could decide on "the desirability of using Chinese Nationalist troops" and perhaps even Japanese forces against the Communist forces. (In Paris, several weeks later, Kennedy urged the United States to take "the risk of permitting Japanese rearmament.") Terming Korea the chief problem facing the incoming Administration, the Senator-elect added:

"I have been in Korea. Anyone in a position of responsibility can benefit themselves and their country by going there. It is admirable that General Eisenhower now can join military and civil responsibility."

This was a period in which Kennedy repeatedly and publicly sympathized with Eisenhower in the numerous problems the new President had inherited from the Truman Administration. Moreover, he took the line that the Eisenhower landslide was inevitable what with the Democrats having been in power for twenty years.

"However partisan you are," he told a Baltimore Democratic dinner in March 1953, "you cannot deny that it had to come to the Democrats." He said the political complexion of the nation had changed markedly since F.D.R. took over the reins of Government in 1932. The reason the country had moved sharply to the right, he said, was ironic: thanks to the munificences of the Democrats, "more people now have a greater stake in the country" and consequently had turned conservative.

In the same speech, Kennedy pleaded with Democrats of all factions— Left wing and Right wing, Northern and Southern—to tone down their differences. If the Democrats permitted their party to become either a Labor party or States Rights party, they would consign themselves permanently to a minority status. Instead, he urged the Democrats to steer a middle-of-the-road course.

"We are a national party," Kennedy said. "Therefore, there are groups within the party which are mutually antipathetic. But they all believe enough in the basic principles to sink their differences."

Invited to address the Kansas Democratic Club at Harry S Truman's invitation, Kennedy couldn't find the time. "I have felt being new to the job that I should confine myself completely to it," he wrote to Truman. And Truman replied he understood. But still, some people thought, a new Senator should not have been so peremptory about rejecting an invitation from a former President of the United States.

It was another of those little things which Harry Truman would not forget when Jack Kennedy came calling for help in obtaining the Presidential nomination.

At the same time, Kennedy went out of his way to pay tribute to Senator Robert A. Taft. At a Boston communion breakfast, for instance, he eulogized the Senate Republican Leader as "a credit to the Senate and the United States." Following Taft's death, Kennedy proposed that the Ohioan be named Man of the Year. On a TV program entitled *"Time's* Man of the Year Revue," Kennedy declared:

"My nominee for the Man of the Year in 1953 is the late Senator Robert A. Taft of Ohio. Sometimes a nation's illustrious dead remain among its most influential men. Their character and personality are sometimes so strong and all-pervading that their influence continues to endure after death."

This was the period when "moderation" and "compromise" were the key words in Kennedy's lexicon. And he desperately sought to avoid controversy.

Thus he shied away from any involvement in the verbal battles surrounding Senator McCarthy's anti-Communist crusade. Significantly, when assigned to the Government Operations Committee, he refused membership on the McCarthy subcommittee even though his brother Bobby had by then joined its staff. Instead, he chose Senator Margaret Chase Smith's relatively cloistered Government Reorganization Subcommittee that dealt with recommendations on federal economies proposed by the Hoover Commission.

For some reason, Kennedy went out of his way to seek the defeat of Senator Margaret Chase Smith in her 1954 campaign for re-election from the state of Maine. And there was talk at the time that he had done so because of Mrs. Smith's opposition to Senator McCarthy.

Mrs. Smith doesn't believe that this was the motivation.

"However," she says, "the factual situation is that when all other Democratic Senators refused to come to Maine to campaign against me and urge my defeat, John F. Kennedy was the only Democratic Senator who did agree to do so and did come into Maine and went on television and urged that I be defeated.

"In the very same year, John F. Kennedy refused to campaign for the election of the Democratic nominee for Senator in his own home state of Massachusetts.

"The two contrasts are interesting—that he was the only Democratic Senator agreeing to campaign against me—and at the same time that he refused to campaign for the Democratic Senatorial nominee in his own home state.

"However, I would doubt very much that his motivation was because of my . . . difference with Senator McCarthy."

Eventually, Kennedy took over as Subcommittee Chairman. In this role he frequently paid tribute to Herbert Hoover's pioneering efforts in seeking reforms in the federal structure. In 1955 Kennedy received a letter from Mr. Hoover commending the Senator "on the way you have been carrying the ball" on governmental reforms.

"We may not always agree on secondary matters but that you are keeping the necessity of reform and economy before Congress and the public is the main thing," the former President wrote. (Joseph P. Kennedy proudly sent photostats of the letter to various conservative friends.)

In the course of a 1954 "Meet the Press" interview, Kennedy came to Mr. Hoover's defense. Reminded that the Democrats had for years "run against Hoover" by blaming him for the 1929 economic crash, Kennedy conceded an "injustice" had been done the former President. However, Kennedy disagreed with Republican contentions that the Democrats were trying "to push the nation into a depression." He did not believe, he said, that "if enough responsible people talk about the dangers of recession" it could conceivably lead to one. "If the basic underlying foundation is sound, however, of course, it can't. As after World War II, they thought there was going to be a depression, and there wasn't. If there are causes of legitimate concern and then people talk about it, I think people become more conservative about their spending—savings have risen in the last few months—and I think it does have a hardening effect, and I think it is unfortunate. On the other hand, you can't ignore it. What you want to do is not just talk about recession; you want to propose alternatives to meet the problem."

The verbal outpouring only served to confuse the panel.

"The Republicans aren't talking about recession or depression," said Lawrence Spivak. "They're talking about prosperity. The only people who are talking about depression are some of the labor people and a great number of Democrats. Your advice to your own party then is they better stop lest they start up a depression."

"No," replied Kennedy, "that isn't my advice. I think there is room for genuine concern. There have been indications of slowdown in economic activity. . . ."

"Are you saying those Democrats who are warning against depression are talking not through their hats, but are talking facts?"

"Provided in their warnings they propose alternative policies, then I believe they should be listened to. Just to warn against depression without offering an alternative is irresponsible and makes no contribution and does cause people concern which does have an effect upon our economy."

Lawrence Spivak then changed the subject.

But it was not all work for the tall, tanned, and handsome lawmaker—at thirty-five, one of the youngest elected to the august Senate. What with his numerous—though casual—dates, the gossip-hungry society columnists were having a field day speculating on the identity of the future Mrs. Kennedy. "Many women have hopefully concluded that Kennedy needs looking after," according to an article in the *Saturday Evening Post*. "In their opinion, he is, as a young millionaire Senator, just about the most eligible bachelor in the United States—and the least justifiable one."

However, the "gay young bachelor," as the *Post* dubbed him, was already courting his future wife. Actually, Kennedy had first met Jacqueline Lee Bouvier at a Long Island wedding in 1948. But things only got serious when they were invited to dinner at the home of Charles Bartlett, Washington correspondent for the *Chattanooga Times*. This was in 1951 and the courtship—what with Jack running for the Senate and all that—was, in Jacqueline's words, "very spasmodic."

The cameo-faced beauty was born July 28, 1929, in Long Island's Southampton Hospital—a fact duly noted in New York's society columns. Her father John Bouvier III was a darkly handsome stockbroker who cut a dashing figure around New York and, because of his year-round suntan, was known variously as "Black Jack," "The Black Orchid," and "The Sheik."

The Bouviers were rich, Catholic, socially impeccable, and so Republican that Jacqueline Kennedy once confessed that all through her childhood she confused Franklin D. Roosevelt with the devil. From birth to young womanhood, Jackie and her younger sister Lee (now married to her second husband, Prince Stanislas Radziwill, a Polish nobleman turned London businessman) lived according to the prescribed pattern of girls whose family is in *The Social Register*.

In 1939, the assured, secure pattern of the Bouvier girls was shattered when their parents called them in to tell them, sadly, that they had decided to separate. The following year they were divorced. Two years later, Janet Bouvier married Hugh D. Auchincloss, a Washington broker. (Auchincloss's second wife had been Mrs. Nina Gore Vidal, whose son by a previous marriage, Gore Vidal, writes titillating things for Broadway and the magazines.) "Black Jack," who died in 1957, never remarried. "He was a most devastating figure," says Jacqueline Kennedy.

Jacqueline Bouvier was practically immersed in education and culture. She attended Miss Porter's School in Farmington, Connecticut, Holton-Arms in Washington, Vassar, the Sorbonne, and George Washington University. At eighteen, she was presented to society in a glittering affair at Newport and she received the ultimate accolade in Cholly Knickerbocker's society column: "This year, for the first time since our predecessor selected Brenda Frazier as the Queen of Glamor, we are ready to name the No. 1 Deb of the Year. . . . Queen Deb of the Year is Jacqueline Bouvier, a regal debutante who has classic features and the daintiness of Dresden porcelain. She has poise, is softspoken and intelligent, everything the leading debutante should be. Her background is strictly 'Old Guard.' . . ."

There was a brief engagement to John G. W. Husted Jr., a socially registered Manhattan broker. The *Washington Times-Herald* on January 21, 1952, had carried the announcement. "The wedding will take place in June," the story said.

But the wedding did not take place in June. Why the engagement was terminated was not disclosed.

Meanwhile, Jacqueline had gone to work for the *Washington Times-Herald* as the "Inquiring Camera Girl" at $42.50 a week. She scored some scoops with intimate glimpses of the family life of the Eisenhowers (as described by their young nieces) and of the Richard M. Nixons (as described by their daughter Tricia).

And then, fresh from his Senatorial victory, Kennedy resumed his courtship with vigor. For six months Jack campaigned tirelessly for Jacqueline's hand, in and out of dinner parties, art theaters and movie houses, and at hunt breakfasts up and down the East Coast.

Their engagement was announced in June 1953. "Black Jack" and his prospective son-in-law got along famously. "They were very much alike," Jacqueline recalled. "We three had dinner before we were engaged, and they talked about politics and sports and girls—what all red-blooded men like to talk about."

Other Bouviers had other reactions. Jacqueline's aunt Maude Davis recalled that her niece telephoned her the news, "but she said, 'You can't say anything about it because the *Saturday Evening Post* is about to come out with an article on Jack called, "The Senate's Gay Young Bachelor," and this would spoil it.' "

Another aunt Mrs. Michelle Bouvier Putnam was quoted by *Time*, "The whole Kennedy clan is unperturbed by publicity. We feel differently about it. Their clan is totally united; ours is not."

On September 12, 1953, John Fitzgerald Kennedy and Jacqueline Lee Bouvier were married by Boston's Cardinal (then Archbishop) Cushing in a picture-book extravaganza in Newport that, thanks to the society columnists in attendance, was well publicized as the Social Event of The Year. There were seven hundred guests at the nuptial Mass, ranging from Marion Davies to Alfred Gwynne Vanderbilt, and nine hundred at the reception. All of Kennedy's colleagues in the Senate had been invited. Jack's pal from Congressional bachelor days, Senator George Smathers, was an usher. The wedding had presented a curious problem for Smathers: could his appearance at St. Mary's Roman Catholic Church have dire repercussions among his Baptist constituents? After checking around with other Southern solons, Smathers decided it would not. Thus the religious issue was put to rest temporarily.

Life with Jack was not all orange blossoms. Naturally enough, Kennedy was utterly absorbed by politics. He ate politics, drank politics, and slept politics. And he was always traveling.

"I was alone almost every weekend while Jack traveled the country making speeches," she once recalled. "It was all wrong."

Politics bored Jacqueline Kennedy.

"Politics was sort of my enemy as far as seeing Jack was concerned," she confessed. "It was like being married to a whirlwind. Life was so disorganized. We never had a home for five years."

Politicians bored Jacqueline Kennedy.

Encountering an old friend on the Hyannis Port golf links shortly after her husband was nominated for President, she gasped, "Oh God, why didn't you tell me you were here? When I think of all those awful politicians!"

Then there were the Kennedys themselves. She had had a taste of life with the Clan in the period before her marriage. There was touch football at Hyannis Port; loud pronunciamentos from Joseph P. Kennedy; and blissful sails on Jack's sloop *Victura* with her fiancé—accompanied by a *Life* photographer.

An old friend, Washington columnist George Dixon, having seen the *Life* cover story, commented that Jackie must be quite a sailing enthusiast.

"No, my husband is," she responded. "They just shoved me into that boat long enough to take the picture."

The family "togetherness" intensified after the wedding. She and her husband would spend their summers at Hyannis Port with the other Kennedys.

On one weekend she estimated over a hundred kinsmen visiting the compound—brothers, sisters, nephews, nieces, uncles, aunts, cousins, second cousins, etc.

"Just watching them wore me out," she once remarked.

The gulf between Jacqueline Kennedy and her in-laws was indicated by a 1960 yachting party: Jacqueline, Prince and Princess Radziwill—and Jack —sat in the stern partaking of *oeufs en gelée avec vin rosé;* while assorted Kennedys sprawled in the bow, munching on peanut butter sandwiches and cokes.

Arthur Krock, who has known Jacqueline since her girlhood, once described her as a "Victorian wife, not the chic Long Island Piping Rock variety, a Beaux Arts type of girl, merry, arch, satirical, terribly democratic and, yes, brilliant."

"An egghead," another close friend once called her, "though not of the Arthur Schlesinger variety, thank God."

Jacqueline was crazy about the arts. Jack, however, never could dig all that cultural jazz. His wife's arty friends annoyed him; and he made no secret of his annoyance. On one occasion, so bored was he with all the discussion of the lively arts, that he left his own dinner table and retired early. The evenings really got rough when Jacqueline and her guests would converse in some foreign language; and Jack was unable to understand a word of what was being said. In entertainment, Jack's tastes ran to big, gaudy musicals and horse operas; Jacqueline preferred Ingmar Bergman and arty little features from Italy that, Jack once complained, "must have been filmed in the dark."

There were other areas of incompatibility. Jack was strictly a meat-and-potato man, while Jacqueline favored the *haute cuisine* of France.

Jacqueline nearly lost her husband in the first year of their marriage. Kennedy's back had begun to hurt more and more. "That metal plate they put into his spine after the war had never healed over," a close friend said. "You could look into an open hole in his back and see it." In the final months of the 1954 session, he hobbled around on crutches. "The last day of the session he was in tremendous pain," his secretary, Mrs. Evelyn Lincoln recalled. "As soon as the Senate adjourned, he went to the airport, where a private plane was waiting to take him to Hyannis to his family's house. He hoped the rest there would cure him."

Instead, his back became increasingly worse. Finally he agreed to two very delicate operations. He knew his chances of survival were slim. "That was the only time he ever mentioned pain to me," said Frank Morrissey. "He told me he'd take the chance of dying—he couldn't stand any more pain."

In October 1954, the Senator entered Manhattan's Hospital for Special Surgery, where Dr. Philip Wilson headed a medical team that performed a double-fusion on his spine. A second operation—the details of which were never officially made public—was performed near a kidney. Twice his entire family was summoned to his bedside because it was feared he was near death; twice he rallied. Just before Christmas he was flown—flat on his back—to his father's home in Palm Beach. In mid-February 1955, he was back in the hospital for another operation. Again he received the last rites of the Catholic Church, and again members of his family prayed for him outside the operating room. This time, the plate was removed successfully.

According to Paul Martin, Washington Bureau Chief of the Gannett newspapers, the Kennedy case at the time was described in the AMA Archives of Surgery, Volume 71, 1955, in an article called "Management of Adrenocortical Insufficiency During Surgery." Written by four New York doctors, including Dr. Wilson who performed the surgical operations, the article reported:

"A man 37 years of age had Addison's Disease for seven years. He had been managed fairly successfully for several years on a program of desoxycorticosterone acetate pellets of 150 mg. implanted every three months and cortisone in doses of 25 mg. daily orally.

"Owing to a back injury, he had a great deal of pain which interfered with his daily routine. Orthopedic consultation suggested that he might be helped by a lumbo-sacral fusion together with a sacroiliac fusion.

"Because of the severe degree of trauma involved in these operations, and because of the patient's adrenocortical insufficiency due to Addison's Disease, it was deemed dangerous to proceed with these operations."

A team of doctors versed in endocrinology and surgical physiology was assembled to help in management of the patient before, during, and after the operation. The AMA report concluded:

"This case is noteworthy because desoxycorticosterone provided a check rein on the tendency to develop salt loss and arterial hypertension. Desoxycorticosterone, it will be recalled, is an adrenocortical-like steroid that permits reabsorption of salt in the kidneys so that urinary salt loss is minimized.

"Though this patient had marked adrenocortical insufficiency, though the magnitude of his surgery was great, and though complications ensued postoperatively, this patient had a smooth postoperative course insofar as no Addisonian crisis ever developed."

This was the blackest period in Kennedy's life. As he lay flat on his back, not knowing whether he would ever walk again, Jacqueline did her best to cheer him up. She was forever bringing fresh surprises—from balloons which he could shoot down with a popgun to Grace Kelly herself, in person. On February 25, 1955, he left the hospital to fly back to Florida. His convalescence was slow, painful, and marked by intermittent depression. His mental state began to worry his aides and family.

"I was feeling glum," he later wrote in the *American Weekly*. "It looked as if corrective surgery for a wartime injury would keep me frustrated and idle in the hospital for several months. Others, I thought, as I lay on my back gazing at the ceiling, restless to return to the Senate and to Massachusetts, had luck, and I didn't.

"Then, one day the letter came. It was from a 90-year-old lady who had always lived in a small Cape Cod village. She, too, was bedridden, she wrote, perhaps for the rest of her life, but she was full of hope and good humor.

" 'Never voted for a Democrat in my life, Mr. Kennedy,' she started right out. 'But I want to vote for at least one before I die—might stand me in good stead up above. So I want you to be up to running in 1958. Don't waste away feeling sorry for yourself, young man. Keep busy. Do all the things you've never had time to do. . . .'

" 'Ninety years old,' I thought, 'and telling me to keep busy, just as she must be keeping busy.' It was a tonic for my spirits. I think if I hadn't received that letter I'd never have got around to writing my book, *Profiles in Courage.*

"After reading the letter, I realized there were a lot of things I wanted to do for which time had never been available. If I couldn't get back to the Senate for a while, I could do the research on courageous Senators of the past that I had long wanted to do (ever since I had read some years ago of John Quincy Adams's brave stand for Jefferson's embargo against the British despite its unpopularity in his home state of Massachusetts). I decided I'd do it.

"The Library of Congress kept a steady stream of .books flowing to my room during all the months of my convalescence. Finally . . . I felt I knew the stories of eight Senators who had put their nation and their conscience ahead of their political careers and their popularity. When my manuscript was accepted by Harper & Brothers, I was actually grateful in a sense for all the hours I had been forced to spend away from Washington—and I recalled with a smile the words of my 90-year-old friend from Cape Cod."

And that's how a Pulitzer prize-winning best seller was born. Kennedy, however, had considerable help. Several historians, including Professors Arthur Schlesinger Jr. and Jules David, pitched in with memoranda and advice. "The greatest debt is owed to my research associate, Theodore C. Sorensen, for his invaluable assistance in the assembly and preparation of the material upon which this book is based," Kennedy noted in his preface.[2]

Nebraska-born Sorensen had joined Kennedy's staff in 1953. And today he is one of the most important men in the New Frontier—and the least publicized. For that's the way Sorensen wants it. Though "he is not loath to have his influence recognized—discreetly," Irwin Ross observed during the 1960 campaign, ". . . he plainly fears that excessive attention might annoy [Kennedy]. Members of an entourage are always safer in the shadows."

A studious young man, replete with horn-rimmed spectacles and Phi Beta Kappa key, Sorensen has also been described as "the most ideologically intense member of the Kennedy staff."

In some ways the Kennedy-Sorensen association is an odd one, for the

[2] *Profiles in Courage,* by John F. Kennedy. New York, Harper, 1956.

two men are poles apart in background and personal style. For Sorensen was reared in the Liberal faith since childhood. He was attending ADA meetings while Kennedy was chasing around Washington and Palm Beach. And while Kennedy enjoyed good living and could always, of course, afford to indulge himself, Sorensen was a puritan—"through rearing and instinct rather than through financial necessity," as Irwin Ross put it. "He has an odd moralist's pride about not smoking or drinking coffee or frequenting fine restaurants. . . ."

Sorensen's credentials as a Liberal activist are of the highest order. Born in Nebraska in 1928, he appeared at his father's side on a political platform before he was out of knee breeches. A crusading attorney, C. A. Sorensen had sailed to Europe on Henry Ford's peace ship; was counsel to the women's suffrage movement; and was one of the leaders in the insurgent movement in the Republican party. Eventually, he became Senator George Norris' campaign manager.

According to Walter Trohan of the *Chicago Tribune,* "Sorensen's mother was an able and dedicated feminist who was accused of pacifist and radical sympathies in World War I. In 1921 she married the attorney who defended her against these charges."

Apparently the pacifist sentiments expressed at home influenced Ted Sorensen to register with the Nebraska draft board as a conscientious objector available for noncombatant military service only. During the Korean war, he was called for a physical examination and was reclassified 4-F, physically unfit. This was after a tumor was removed from behind his ear.

As a student at the University of Nebraska, he found time for politics, worked in local campaigns, and while still a law student served as chief lobbyist before the state legislature in behalf of an FEPC law. When graduated from the University of Nebraska Law School in 1951, he headed for Washington. Twenty-three years old, completely unknown and lacking any important connections, he worked for a while for the Federal Security Agency and the Department of Health, Education and Welfare. Later—through a lawyer whom he met at an ADA convention—he landed a job with a Senate subcommittee studying the railroad retirement system.

When this assignment ended, Senator Paul Douglas recommended him to the newly elected junior Senator from Massachusetts. Kennedy, needing a legislative assistant, hired Sorensen on the basis of two five-minute interviews conducted a day or two apart. In the first session, Kennedy questioned Sorensen; and in the second, the interrogation was reversed. Kennedy had outlined the job as follows: he had been elected on a slogan that he would do *more* for Massachusetts and he needed somebody to create a program.

"I felt I could have had the job right then and there if I wanted it," said Sorensen. "But I also felt that if I was going to throw in with him, then there were things I wanted to know. I didn't want us to be too far apart on basic policy, and so we had another interview and this time I asked the questions— about his father, Joe McCarthy, the Catholic Church. He must have thought

I was an odd duck and I don't remember exactly what I asked or exactly what he said, but I knew we satisfied each other. I do remember him saying, '. . . but on the other hand, I do think Owen Lattimore was guilty of inaiscretion. . . .' "

Satisfied with Kennedy's responses, Sorensen went to work the next day.

Over the years Sorensen has played a key role in Kennedy's political education. He acted as a kind of guide to the unfamiliar world of the committed Liberal. But in Sorensen's opinion both he and Kennedy are practical Liberals, more susceptible to intellectual than emotional persuasion.

"I am personally convinced," he once said, "that the liberal who is rationally committed is more reliable than the liberal who is emotionally committed."

Sorensen's dedication to Kennedy is total. He has been known to become quite irate at suggestions that his boss's behavior is opportunistic. One has to understand, he once argued, "that his father is not a liberal, the pressures of his family background are not liberal," and therefore Kennedy did not show any crusading zeal when he first showed up in Washington. Only later, as he read and traveled and was personally exposed to the backwaters of poverty in an otherwise affluent society, did Kennedy's convictions grow.

Only in one area has Kennedy shown a blind spot, according to Sorensen. "That was his inability to see the dimensions of the McCarthy issue," he said.

In his first year with Kennedy, Sorensen was largely concerned with New England problems. Beginning in May 1953 Kennedy delivered three major speeches on the subject in the Senate. They were pretty much what he had said as a Congressman—only this time, with Sorensen's help, he presented more facts and figures.

"Why do industries move South?" he asked. He conceded that much of the migration was due to "the South's natural advantages"—lots of fresh, pure water, a milder climate, plenty of elbow room and "the hospitality shown new industries. . . ."

"Another major reason has been the influence of Federal programs," he said. "The best example of this is the cost of electric power. The man who wants to start a moderate-size industry . . . would pay an annual electric bill in Boston of $26,800, but in Chattanooga only $11,000." This, of course, was because of the federally subsidized TVA.

Another reason was that federal law permitted practices in the South that were "unfair or substandard by any criterion." He blamed Taft-Hartley, for example, for halting unionization of Southern plants—a point subject to argument since unionization in Dixie had lagged even under the pro-labor Wagner Act. He called for new legislation "to prevent the use of substandard wages, anti-union policies and inadequate social benefits as lures to industrial migration." And he took particular umbrage with Senator J. William Fulbright's amendment, claiming it would prevent the establishment of higher minimum wages in Southern textile mills.

In addition to a minimum-wage increase Kennedy wanted social security equalized and union privileges guaranteed. He called for the closing of tax loopholes and "equal consideration given to all areas in . . . tax write-offs, transportation rates and Government contracts and projects." He also called for federal aid in achieving "the expansion and diversification of industry in our older areas," federal loans to new industries and tax amortization benefits.

It was quite a program but one that had little chance of fulfillment. For Congress was not even buying President Eisenhower's more moderate proposals to assist economically distressed areas. The President had circulated a memorandum to the principal defense-procurement agencies endorsing stepped-up spending in blighted regions.

"This is nothing but creeping Socialism," said Arkansas Senator Fulbright who, in more recent years, has been cautioning against the extravagant talk of "right-wing extremists."

Kennedy himself came under bitter attack in newspapers from Greenville, North Carolina, to San Antonio, Texas. The youthful Senator was accused of "blatantly asking for special and unusual consideration . . . attempting punitive legislation against the South . . . seeking federal interference to help New England and hurt the South . . . Mr. Kennedy's statement can be dismissed merely as the irresponsible words of a new Senator who wants to gain favor with his constituents."

"I find it difficult to believe that any man can be so reckless in his statements," declared Governor James F. Byrnes of South Carolina. "I can understand his being alert for his own state, but I think it is remarkable that [he] would recommend that the Government should help unionize workers in another state."

Kennedy tried to pull back. He said he was misunderstood. It was not his "intention to absolve New England from all responsibility for its economic ills, or to make the South a whipping-boy. . . ." What was sorely needed, he said, was inter-regional co-operation, not political antagonisms.

Kennedy even appeared to be changing his once antagonistic attitude toward the TVA. And he was asked about it by Marquis Childs on "Meet the Press" in February 1954: "You made a series of speeches on how industry was attracted away from New England, and yet when you went down to Tennessee and made a speech about the Tennessee Valley Authority, you said you thought that TVA was a good thing for the region. So you think that the federal government should give a TVA or something like it to New England?"

"I think the federal government should," Kennedy replied.

Despite all the work that had gone into the speeches (later summarized in the *Atlantic Monthly*), they failed to provide the "springboard to national attention" which, according to Burns, Kennedy then was seeking. The repercussions were largely contained in the South. The *New York Times* completely ignored Kennedy. Other opinion-makers viewed the whole business as "just another push in the endless scuffle for local or regional advantage . . .

the dressing up of all these positions in the garments of regional advantage left Kennedy more in the posture of a delegate from New England than that of a spokesman for American liberalism."

Just how deeply committed was Jack Kennedy in his New England crusade?

One labor official had reason to wonder. The background was this: in 1952, Arthur G. McDowell was named chairman of the AFL's Legislative Council Subcommittee on Subsidized Migration of Industry. The idea was to combat "local municipal tax exempt bond subsidy schemes to provide migrating manufacturers with their capital needs." According to McDowell, several bills to disallow tax exemption of these bonds were introduced in Congress. One of them, which passed the House, was killed in the Senate Finance Committee by Senator Russell Long. The situation looked bleak for the Labor-indorsed legislation.

"Then Kennedy came out in the *Atlantic Monthly* with an article on the evils of the subsidized migration—obviously an inferior bowdlerization of our Subcommittee's more scholarly study of 1952," recalled McDowell. "We of the AFL Subcommittee went to Kennedy in great enthusiasm, though his staff (strangely one of the lowest paid and least competent on the Hill) seemed unimpressive on the issue. Already, Sorensen seemed a bit cold."

Shortly after the meeting McDowell received a letter from Kennedy pledging an "all-out fight" for the Labor-backed proposal in the Senate.

"A few weeks later, on my way to Washington, I read a *Wall Street Journal* story to the effect that Kennedy had decided to surrender," McDowell continued. "I asked Sorensen for an explanation. Instead, he asked me not to disturb his boss since it was he, Sorensen, who had persuaded him to drop the fight. I told Sorensen I was not interested in talking to any Senator whose staff could so easily persuade him to break a written commitment.

"The Kennedy surrender was a fatal blow to our cause."

In 1955, Kennedy co-sponsored a bill to curtail right-to-work legislation enacted mainly in Southern states. And he sounded pretty militant about it.

"I object to any suggestion that the states be given the last word on the 'right to work' law," he thundered. "If the Southern states can outlaw the closed shop and the union shop while the New England states accept them, we in the North are going to be under a handicap."

Such talk, needless to say, pleased the Labor people.

"But," as columnist Holmes Alexander later reported, "Kennedy told more than one conservative colleague in both parties that he did not intend to push the bill"—all he wanted was credit for sponsoring it.

At this point, Kennedy's defeat of Lodge was still the high point of his political career—a fact discovered by a Johns Hopkins University political scientist, Steve Hess, who sought to sell an article dealing with the young Senator. The magazines just were not interested. In fact, the *Reporter* returned the manuscript with the observation that its editors could not ascertain any general interest in Kennedy, but to resubmit the piece should the Senator get back "in the news."

The unpublished manuscript is of interest because of its description of Kennedy's voting record in his first two Senate years. Though he ducked two controversial votes—one on the censure of Senator McCarthy and the other on the Status of Forces Treaty—he had no objections about being seen and counted with Virginia's Harry F. Byrd, leader of the Senate's economy bloc. Here is the record of Kennedy's votes on appropriations bills in the Eighty-third Congress as compared with those of Byrd and Hubert Humphrey, a leading Senate Liberal.

	Kennedy	Byrd	Humphrey
1. To increase by $600,000 funds for housing research program	No	No	Yes
2. To reduce by 5 per cent all amounts in First Independent Offices Appropriation for 1954, except that for compensation of President	Yes	Yes	No
3. To increase by $5.9 million funds for Public Buildings Service of General Service Administration	No	No	No
4. To reduce by $4 million funds for repair and maintenance of federally owned buildings outside of District of Columbia	Yes	Yes	No
5. To increase by $15 million funds for hospital construction	Yes	No	Yes
6. To provide $9.4 million for a census of business and manufactures	No	No	Yes
7. To increase funds for the federal-aid airport program to $30 million	No	No	No
8. To increase funds for the Agriculture Conservation Program from $195 to $225 million	No	No	Yes
9. To reduce funds for the Agriculture Conservation Program from $195 to $145 million	Yes	Yes	No
10. To increase by $1.5 million funds for certain payments to state agricultural experiment stations for research	Announced against	No	Yes
11. To increase from $100 to $135 million the loan authorizations for rural electrification	No	No	Yes

	Kennedy	Byrd	Humphrey
12. To add $10 million to the school-lunch program and permit $10 million to be used for non-food assistance to the school-lunch program	Yes	No	Yes
13. To increase from $35 to $70 million additional funds that may be loaned to REA	No	No	Yes
14. To reduce by $2 million funds for general navigation and flood control construction	Yes	Yes	No
15. To reduce by $3.7 million funds for general maintenance and operation of navigation and flood control projects	Yes	Announced for	No

Keeping Kennedy's future voting record in mind, his voting pattern in these earlier years becomes most significant—even amusing. Not only did he reject two appropriations bills to aid the farmers, but he opposed increasing the loan authorization for that Liberal holy of holies—the Rural Electrification Administration. Moreover, he turned thumbs down on additional funds for a housing research program.

In all, Kennedy voted with Senator Byrd and the "economy bloc" thirteen out of fifteen times. The two votes (3 and 7) on which all three Senators agreed were in line with economy bloc thinking. Kennedy differed with Byrd twice (numbers 5 and 12). The extent to which the Bay Stater then was attracted to the golden calf called "economy in government" could be seen from his yes vote (number 15) on a bill to reduce appropriations for navigation and flood control projects—traditionally a prime example of Senatorial pork barreling. Here Kennedy found himself on the short end of an 81 to 4 vote. With Byrd not voting, though announced for it, this left only Senators Barry Goldwater, John J. Williams, Paul Douglas, and Jack Kennedy to champion the economy move.

Just what was Kennedy at this time—Liberal or Conservative? The question continued to perplex observers. *Time* magazine came up with a compromise answer, describing the "mophaired" freshman Senator as "a curious blend of Boston conservatism and New Deal liberalism." And the *Boston Herald*'s political columnist, W. E. Mullins, observed:

"He is a Democrat and a liberal without any touches of Marxism or even the less rabid left wing philosophies. His voting record might qualify him as an independent. . . . He is one of the few members of the Congress who isn't angry at anyone."

Generally, Kennedy went along with much of what the Republican Administration was recommending. In fact, in a personal note from the hospital

Kennedy wrote to Eisenhower how well he thought the President was doing. Publicly, Kennedy described himself as only in "moderate opposition" to the White House.

According to Kennedy, one campaign promise that had returned to haunt the Eisenhower Administration had to do with farm problems. Not that the Junior Senator had any specific proposals of his own. Aptly describing himself as a "city Senator," he freely conceded he knew next to nothing about rural affairs. Only later, in seeking farm support for his Presidential bid, did he begin to pick up "manure on my shoes." Actually, until he saw the light— some time after being bitten by the White House bug—Kennedy was a consistent supporter of the flexible price supports advocated by Secretary of Agriculture Ezra Taft Benson.

Kennedy's later switch from support of Eisenhower's farm policies to almost-vindictive attacks on "Bensonism" need not now be labored. But brief quotations from speeches Kennedy made in 1955–56 indicate how his thinking once ran: "I am opposed to any farm program returning to high price supports fixed at 90 per cent of parity, until such time as the flexible support program has had a sufficient opportunity to prove itself. . . . I am delighted by the fact that, whatever your problems, you have not expected the federal government to solve them for you through subsidies and controls . . . high price supports . . . will not solve that problem [of overproduction] . . . price supports at a lower or flexible level will not solve it either—but at least they will not accentuate it so badly. . . . I have long doubted whether there is any such thing as a 'farm vote' . . . there are more mythical rules, mistaken assumptions and fictional reports about the so-called 'farm vote' than practically any other political phenomenon. . . . No farm platform should be calculated to aid one section of the country at the expense of another. . . ."

Spoken "like a statesman," observed the *Washington Star* which in an editorial—"A Clear Voice Speaks"—praised Kennedy for "the bluntness of his analysis of the political demagoguery generally associated with the farm program."

Just how significant—ideologically—were Kennedy's lapses from the so-called Liberal line? Did they, in fact, reveal a conservative streak in the Junior Senator? Or were they merely gestures to meet the political requirements of a particular time?

The truth is that Kennedy's deviations were usually in areas where, as the *New York Post*'s Irwin Ross then noted, "the interests of the constituents were not apparent." Consider, for example, Kennedy's votes against high farm price supports and flood control projects. These, in truth, were the predictable votes of a New England legislator.

Only once did Kennedy cast a significant vote for a measure which many New Englanders—rightly or wrongly—considered inimical to their area's interests. This was in behalf of the St. Lawrence Seaway.

As part of his 1952 campaign to do *More* for Massachusetts, Kennedy had pledged unalterable opposition to the project.

Why his change in attitude?

No one knew for sure, but Kennedy's argument was this: "Canada will build the seaway . . . regardless of the action taken in the United States Senate" and, that being the case, the United States ought to share in the general benefits—an attitude which he had vociferously castigated while running against Henry Cabot Lodge.

Following his surprise shift on the issue, some New England newspapers assailed Kennedy as the "Suicide Senator." In 1958, the issue was brought up by Vincent Celeste, Kennedy's Republican opponent in the Senatorial campaign. Celeste accused the Senator of voting to bring the Atlantic Ocean conveniently closer to his father's Merchandise Mart in Chicago. "Look how my opponent voted for the St. Lawrence Seaway—it starts right at the front door of the Merchandise Mart, which is owned by old Joe Kennedy." The Senator's father, Celeste added, was calling all the signals.

In 1960 Kennedy was asked the most difficult decision he ever made. Kennedy said it was the vote on the Seaway bill. "I suppose getting married may always be a difficult matter, but I would say speaking seriously that probably the vote on the St. Lawrence Seaway was the most difficult one politically. . . . It was a difficult decision."

As it turned out, the vote did Kennedy little harm. In fact, it did him much good: it enabled his supporters to claim that by voting against regional interests Kennedy had indeed shown a modicum of courage. "It was," said Ted Sorensen, "the turning point between Jack as a Massachusetts Senator and a national statesman."

Perhaps the chief reason Kennedy had escaped relatively unscathed was that when it came to guarding other local interests, few Senators surpassed him in his zeal. For one thing, he was strong on tariffs, asking in one session alone for higher duties for the watch, fishing, and textile industries in order to meet foreign competition. Typically, though, he tried to carry water on both shoulders. In 1954 he was the only Senator from tariff-conscious New England to vote for a more liberalized international trade program.

In early 1956 the *Boston Herald,* which in 1952 had opposed Kennedy because he was too Liberal, paid tribute to Kennedy's "independence," which "seems to be paying off in popularity and vote-getting ability, thereby confounding the old pros." In an editorial, the Republican-leaning journal noted Kennedy's support of the St. Lawrence Seaway, liberalized trade, flexible farm price supports and his espousal of the Hoover Reports.

"And what has happened?" the *Herald* asked. "Has this conservatively brash (or should we say brashly conservative?) young Senator gotten into trouble with people and party? Are there mutterings about being 'sold down the river'? Are his lack of conformity to regional interest (or what others claim is regional interest), and political independence getting him into trouble?

"Not at all. . . . Democrats at home are for him. . . . And so are many Republicans."

And, the *Herald* happily reported, John F. Kennedy was being widely discussed as a possible candidate for Vice President on the Democratic ticket.

Veep

9

Only in America could it have happened.

"After all," as Rowland Evans Jr. wrote later in the *New York Herald Tribune,* "in 1956 his achievements were modest. He had been in the House of Representatives for only six years and in the Senate only four. He had accomplished nothing particularly noteworthy in either place when he arrived in Chicago for the Democratic convention." Yet, despite his lack of major achievements, John F. Kennedy came within a whisker of walking off with the Democratic nomination for Vice President.

As it turned out, however, his narrow defeat in the wildest second-place brawl ever staged by the Democrats was the best thing that could have happened to him politically—except, of course, being born into the House of Kennedy. Had he been nominated over Estes Kefauver, he would have been carried to defeat with Adlai Stevenson in that year of Democratic disaster.

"And they would have pinned the blame on Jack because he is a Catholic," his father, Joseph P. Kennedy, said. "That would have made it much more difficult for another Catholic in years to come."

Actually, Jack's major attraction for the number two spot was precisely because of the fact that he was a Roman Catholic. For once, a candidate's strongest asset to his ticket was his religion. The Democrats were desperately seeking to recapture the Catholic voters who had defected to Dwight David Eisenhower in 1952. "At this moment in history," as the *New York Post's* Irwin Ross then observed, "the accident of birth represents Kennedy's principal claim to national consideration."

The youthful Senator had something else in his favor. He had glamor. The "matinee idol" of the United States Senate, he had few political rivals in the good-looks department. Six feet tall, tanned, and handsome, he had an engaging smile and a shock of unruly brown hair that had become his trademark.[1]

Thanks to the exertions of his multi-millionaire father, he was also independently wealthy. And he was a war hero, to boot—his South Pacific exploits already taking on the aura of a folktale. A Kennedy broadside circulated at the Democratic convention was found to contain such glittering appeals in his behalf as: ". . . 'most videogenic personality of our times,' says the *New York Times* . . . lovely wife; famous colorful family . . . tireless, sparkling campaigner. . . ."

In the new age of television, these were attributes not to be scoffed at in a potential candidate. Kennedy's "videogenic personality" was, indeed, a factor in Vice Presidential calculations. A CBS television producer, who, incidentally, did not happen to like Kennedy politically, had advised top-rung Democrats that the youthful Senator was the only second-place aspirant who could command full television coverage.

"Because Kennedy has box office," the TV producer said.

Adlai Stevenson, for one, was definitely impressed. He told Kennedy's brother-in-law, R. Sargent Shriver, that the Senator's clean "All-American boy" appearance would make an effective contrast on television to Dick Nixon's dark, heavy looks.

Also going for Kennedy in the Vice Presidential sweepstakes was the fact he was on good terms with the party leadership. He hadn't an enemy in the Senate. "In the phrase which Arthur Miller applied to the salesman," wrote Irwin Ross, "he is 'well-liked.' " He was even "well-liked" by the Southerners who had come to recognize his New England economic program for what it was—primarily a vote-getting gimmick. Dixie's solons, particularly, were aware of the necessity for occasionally sounding off for the benefit of the folks back home. On the ever-touchy issue of civil rights, as a *Christian Science Monitor* correspondent reported from the South, "So far, Kennedy hasn't given anyone cause to start waving the Confederate flag."

At first, Kennedy affected a casual indifference toward the Vice Presidency. That was part of the game. Nobody ever runs for the number two spot. Traditionally, the Presidential candidate picks his own running-mate. The idea is to help him pick the right one. Thus, as Kennedy's Harvard roommate, Massachusetts Representative Torbert Macdonald, explained, "Far ahead of the convention, I'd worked on delegates to write to Adlai Stevenson, suggesting that Jack be appointed as his running-mate."

---

[1] In a contest to pick "the handsomest member of the House," three hundred Washington correspondents in 1952 chose John F. Kennedy. Runner-up in the contest (staged in connection with the première of the Dore Schary film *Washington Story*) was Congressman Franklin D. Roosevelt Jr.

The Vice Presidency had become worth fighting for. No longer could it be said in jest that the party leaders merely grabbed the last man out of the convention hall for the job. Eisenhower's heart attack and the major role Richard Nixon was playing in policy-making had given the Vice Presidency an importance it rarely had before.

The Kennedy boom had been launched soon after the Senator, then thirty-eight years old, had returned to Washington following an eight-month leave of absence necessitated by several serious operations nearly costing him his life. And it was almost a hero's welcome that greeted him when he limped into the Senate chamber on May 24, 1955.

"We are glad to have you back, Jack," said Democratic Leader Lyndon B. Johnson. Speaking for the Republicans, Senator Knowland added, "Those of us who have gotten to know him have for him a very warm and high place in our affections." In his office, Room 362 of the Senate Office Building, a large basket of fruit awaited Kennedy. "Welcome home," the tag read. It was signed "Dick Nixon."

Hardly had Kennedy gotten back to work before items began to appear that he was being increasingly discussed in high places as a possible running-mate for Adlai Stevenson. One of the first was published in the Periscope column of *Newsweek,* which is devoted to political and global gossip. Typically, Kennedy telephoned Periscope editor Debs Myers to ask who was doing all the discussing. "Me," replied Myers.

In August 1955—one year before the Convention—the *Boston Post's* Jim Colbert reported "that party leaders in the South have already been sounded out about him and have declared that the Junior Senator from Massachusetts would be acceptable to them. Many Massachusetts Democrats who are not enthusiastic about Stevenson would be forced to revise their views if Kennedy were his running-mate. . . . Stevenson and Kennedy are far closer than is generally realized."

Apparently Stevenson himself had a hand in encouraging these reports. For "sources close to Adlai" were frequently being quoted as asserting that not only would Kennedy be eminently satisfactory as his running-mate, but, in fact, he was first choice. In December 1955 Kennedy lunched with Stevenson at the latter's Libertyville home. The meeting was followed by still more speculation. "When supporters of Adlai Stevenson discuss a possible running-mate for their candidate," a page one dispatch in the *Des Moines Register* reported, "they seldom fail to mention young Jack Kennedy of Massachusetts."

In recalling this period, Stevenson later denied having discussed the Vice Presidency with Kennedy. "But his father came to see me several times—he had contributed to my campaigns—and we talked about Jack in a general way," Stevenson said. "I have a personal fondness for Jack and I admired him, and I told his father that. Then, of course, Jack's sister Eunice and her husband, Sarge Shriver, are good friends of mine. There was also our concern for the Catholic vote, which we had lost in 1952. Yes, we had thought seriously about Jack as a vice-presidential candidate."

On March 8, 1956, Kennedy announced in Washington he would support Stevenson for the Presidency. Not only was Stevenson the best qualified of all the Democratic aspirants, but—said Kennedy—he was "beholden to no group or section" and he belonged "neither to a left wing nor a right wing."

Kennedy's announcement failed to impress the leaders of Massachusetts Democracy. The "pols" back home wanted no part of Stevenson and for a very realistic reason: they felt he didn't stand a chance against Eisenhower. Moreover, they wanted no part of Kennedy. To them he was a "green blood," getting too big for his breeches. Organization Democrats viewed him as a lone wolf who preferred to play the Republican side of the street. Not forgotten—nor forgiven—was his refusal to support the Democratic Senatorial candidate in 1954, Foster Furcolo.

Furcolo, whose differences with Kennedy went back to the days when they both served in Congress, was contesting the seat held by Republican Senator Leverett Saltonstall, a blue-blooded Yankee with whom Kennedy got along amiably. It soon became obvious that Kennedy did not intend to lift a finger in Furcolo's behalf. But even worse: as the campaign picked up speed it even appeared Kennedy was deliberately aiding Saltonstall.

Furcolo had denounced Saltonstall for not doing enough for the Great State of Massachusetts—the very same tack taken by Kennedy against Cabot Lodge two years previously. Soon afterward, Kennedy issued a joint communiqué with Saltonstall listing the numerous achievements flowing from their bipartisan co-operation. Thus, the first three items expressed their joint pride in the "Kennedy-Saltonstall Fishing Research and Market Development Bill," "Kennedy-Saltonstall Fish Stocks Tariff Bill," and "Kennedy-Saltonstall et al. Fishing Boating Protection Bill."

The crowning indignity was yet to come.

It came at a television studio where Kennedy had shown up for a belated campaign appearance with Furcolo. On reading Kennedy's lukewarm endorsement Furcolo—shortly before air time—asked for a stronger statement.

Kennedy exploded. "You have a hell of a nerve coming in here and asking for last-minute changes," he shouted.

Kennedy stalked off to the men's room, returning before the cameras only after the Democratic gubernatorial candidate Robert Murphy pleaded frantically with him. The atmosphere was icy. And in his closing statement Kennedy endorsed the Democratic slate, but pointedly refrained from mentioning Furcolo by name.

A few days later, details of the backstage row leaked to the press. A grim Furcolo refused to comment. In confirming the row, a Kennedy spokesman said the Senator "definitely will not give Furcolo a personal endorsement." GOP leaders were joyful. This was the "one big push" they needed to put Saltonstall over the top.

So close was the balloting that a shift of 15,000 votes would have meant a Furcolo victory. All Furcolo would say was that he had been "knifed" at the polls. An examination of the vote did indicate he had indeed been "knifed" in areas where Kennedy could have exerted a strong influence. "Voters of Italian ancestry," reported the *Boston Herald*'s W. E. Mullins, "are convinced that their man was done in by voters of Irish ancestry. . . ." The mutual suspicion between the Irish and the Italians was further demonstrated by the fact that the defeated Democratic candidate for Governor had been bypassed in areas where Furcolo had demonstrated substantial strength.

Also unforgotten—and unforgiven—by Organization Democrats was Kennedy's refusal, as a downy-cheeked Congressman, to sign a petition seeking a Presidential pardon for James Michael Curley, then in prison for mail fraud. The picturesque Curley had been so dedicated to his job as Boston's mayor that he stuck to it even while serving time. But Kennedy failed to be moved by pleas in his behalf. Curley had been a bitter foe of his grandfather Honey Fitz Fitzgerald, and therefore was anathema to the unforgiving Kennedy clan.

The petition had been circulated for signature within the Massachusetts delegation by House Democratic Leader John McCormack, to whom loyalty to friends was a cardinal principle. An old-fashioned, bread-and-butter Liberal, McCormack could never quite cotton to young Kennedy whom he considered a "playboy" whose Congressional attendance was usually determined by the length of the winter season at Palm Beach.

"He's had it too easy," McCormack once complained.

So when Kennedy decided that the Bay State delegation should support Stevenson, the State Organization—dominated by McCormack, Curley, and William H. ("Onions") Burke—had other ideas. The Organization staged a write-in campaign for McCormack as the state's favorite-son candidate, and he won handily in the April primary, leaving the delegation free to maneuver against Stevenson at the Convention.

For Kennedy, it was a stinging defeat. Since he could not deliver his own state to Stevenson, his own hopes for the Vice Presidency were considerably dampened.

Then Burke went too far. Unable to contain his joy over clobbering the Stevenson forces, the State Chairman suggested that "they ought to be in Princeton listening to Alger Hiss" who was then making his first public appearance following his release from the penitentiary at that university.

Burke's remark caused a storm. The cry of McCarthyism was heard throughout the Commonwealth. It couldn't have been better timed for Kennedy had he planned it himself. It gave the Senator the long-awaited opportunity to demonstrate on home grounds his newly found aversion to McCarthyism—without the necessity, of course, of directly facing up to the issue on which he maintained a grim silence.

Denouncing Burke as "unfit," Kennedy demanded his ouster as State

Chairman. The showdown was scheduled for May 19 when eighty state committeemen would meet in Boston to elect a chairman. What with McCormack announcing he was "1,000 per cent" behind Burke, his re-election seemed assured. Against him, the Kennedy forces put up John M. Lynch, a former Mayor of Somerville.

Though he had characterized Burke as "unfit," Kennedy nevertheless met with him privately. Thereafter, they disagreed as to what had been said. Kennedy claimed he had asked Burke to resign. But Burke said that, in return, Kennedy had promised to see that he would replace James Michael Curley as Democratic National Committeeman from Massachusetts. Burke claimed he had indignantly rejected the proposal.

Curley, thereupon, called in newsmen to announce that Kennedy had tried to bribe him to quit the National Committee to make room for Burke.

"Well," he said, in a remark that could have come from Skeffington in *The Last Hurrah,* "Kennedy hasn't got enough money to buy me at any time. I never took any money from him or his whole family and I never will."

Kennedy, though infuriated, said nothing. Instead, he concentrated on touring the entire state, visiting each of the eighty committeemen personally. His approach was unprecedented. But it paid off.

The four-hour state committee meeting was one of the stormiest in its history. When the votes were finally counted, they showed that Kennedy's man, John Lynch, had won 47 to 31. Burke had only one answer for his surprising defeat. He accused Kennedy of having "bought" his votes. Quivering with rage, he told newsmen that he would never forgive Kennedy and that he intended to contest the Senator's re-election in the primary two years hence.

The new leader of Massachusetts Democracy, John F. Kennedy, was magnanimous in victory. He denied that the struggle for party control had been aimed at curbing the power and prestige of the revered and respected dean of the Massachusetts Congressional delegation, the Honorable John William McCormack.

Hilarious as it may have been in retrospect, the episode is of some importance historically, for it brought into focus for the first time some of the qualities that went into the making of a future President of the United States. A Boston newspaperman who had then observed Kennedy in action said later, "Jack is hard as nails; he is mean and tough. Nobody—short of the voters— is going to stop him from getting what he wants."

Kennedy had gotten what he wanted. It was he—and not the respected John McCormack—who was to go to Chicago as head of the Massachusetts delegation. Thus, not only did his hard fought victory prepare the way for delivering the majority of the state to Stevenson but it considerably brightened his own chances for the Vice-Presidential nomination.

The Kennedy bandwagon began to roll. Leading Democrats around the country received autographed copies of *Profiles in Courage.* (For a time, Kennedy's aides even considered distributing *Profiles in Courage* campaign buttons, but the idea was dismissed as premature.) Convention delegates and alternates also received letters urging them not to miss the dramatization of the Senator's heroic exploits as a PT-boat commander on the television program "Navy Log." And newsmen found the Senator always available for an interview. Having once been a newspaperman himself, though briefly, he knew what made good, readable copy. His public-relations sense even then was superb.

"Kennedy appears to be two personalities," wrote the *Des Moines Register*'s Fletcher Knebel. "One is the sandy-haired, boyish politician with the blue eyes and the easy informality with all comers. The other is the politician who stands aside, studies the politician and tries to decide what makes him tick.

"He is, in fact, a kind of junior edition of Adlai Stevenson."

Which, of course, was the image Kennedy was then seeking to project. In his own words, he considered himself a "moderate liberal," a kind of "second-drawer liberal," not as aggressive as, say, Hubert Humphrey or Herbert Lehman, but just as "forward-looking."

In a Presidential campaign, Kennedy said he would find it easy to tune in on Stevenson's wave length. "The differences between the parties are narrow," he added. "I don't see any point in going to the left to artificially build a distinction."

But in the final analysis, Kennedy's biggest asset as a potential Vice-Presidential candidate was the fact that his "religious affiliation," as he invariably put it, was Catholicism.

As a memorandum prepared in his behalf declared:

"The voter surveys . . . all indicate that there is, or can be, such a thing as a 'Catholic vote,' whereby a high proportion of Catholics of all ages, residences, occupations and economic status vote for a well-known Catholic candidate or a ticket with special Catholic appeal."

The memorandum was written by Kennedy's chief aide Theodore Sorensen. Because Connecticut's Democratic boss John Bailey was mailing it around the country to principal party figures, it became known as the "Bailey Report."*

Historically, the Bailey Report is of enormous significance since it presaged what was to become a major strategy for winning the Presidency for John F. Kennedy. An extraordinary document, it had some surprising things to say:

"But the Catholic vote is far more important than its numbers—about 1 out of every 4 voters who turn out—because of its concentration in the key States and cities of the North. These are the pivotal States with large electoral votes, which vary as to their party support and several of which are inevitably necessary for a victory in the Electoral College. And the strength of the Catholic vote within these States is considerably increased by the findings of Gallup,

* The complete version of the Bailey Report can be found in Appendix B.

Campbell of the University of Michigan [*The Voter Decides*] and others that Catholics consistently turn out to vote in greater proportions than non-Catholics. . . . In short, even a Catholic nominee for President would be judged by most people on his qualifications for the office—and it is apparent that a Democratic Catholic vice-presidential nominee, though admittedly prejudice would be stirred, would lose no electoral votes for the ticket simply because a handful of Southerners or Republicans would not support him."

A chart listed "14 pivotal Catholic states . . . where elections are won or lost." These states accounted for 261 electoral votes, 5 less than the number needed to win the Presidency. The states: Rhode Island (60% Catholic), Massachusetts (50%), Connecticut (49%), New Jersey (39%), New York (32%), Wisconsin (32%), Illinois (30%), Pennsylvania (29%), Michigan (24%), Minnesota (24%), California (22%), Montana (22%), Maryland (21%), and Ohio (20%).

Then came this pointed reminder: "Of these 14 pivotal Catholic states with their 261 electoral votes:

—In 1940, 13 of these States with 240 electoral votes went Democratic, *without which the Democrats would have lost the election.*

—In 1944, 12 of these States with 221 electoral votes went Democratic, *without which the Democrats would have lost the election.*

—In 1948, 8 of these States with 125 electoral votes went Democratic, *without which the Democrats would have lost the election.*

—In 1952, none of these States went Democratic, all 261 of their electoral votes went to Eisenhower, thus making possible the first Republican victory in 24 years."

According to the Bailey Report 30 per cent of the national Catholic vote —normally Democratic—had shifted to Eisenhower, making up 7 per cent of his total vote in 1952. Without that vote, Ike would have lost.

And a Catholic—any Catholic apparently—could get them to return to the fold. "I just want a Catholic on the ticket," said Bailey.

Soon other Catholic politicians were mentioned as possible Presidential running-mates, Montana's Senator Mike Mansfield and New York's Mayor Robert F. Wagner among them.

"It's a myth," said Wagner, "that a Catholic would hurt a Presidential ticket."

Another myth challenged by the Bailey Report was the so-called "Al Smith myth," the contention that the 1928 Democratic candidate lost the Presidency largely because of anti-Catholic bigotry. Not true, said the Bailey Report, which added:

"The year 1928 was a Republican year, regardless of who was on either ticket. It was the year for 'drys' like Hoover, not 'wets' like Smith. . . . Moreover, studies showed midwestern and Southern voters opposing Al Smith as a Tammany product from the streets of New York—a portly, cigar-smoking stereotype of the immigrant-based political boss."

According to portly, cigar-smoking Bailey, Kennedy would be ideal to shoo away the lingering shadow of Tammany's Al Smith. Not everyone bought the Bailey arguments, however. Some political scientists discredited the statistical data; others observed that no ethnic distinctions had been made among Catholics—for example, would an Italian Catholic necessarily vote for an Irish Catholic? And Senator Hubert Humphrey, already an announced candidate for the Vice Presidency, countered with his own memorandum arguing, in effect, that there was no such animal as a "Catholic vote," that "Catholics do not vote as Catholics."

The Humphrey memorandum, prepared by Louis Bean (whose statistical juggling invariably favored Left-wing Democrats), also contended that a Stevenson-Kennedy ticket would "put two dinner jackets" before the voters in November.

According to the memorandum, Kennedy's major handicap was his unacceptability to farmers because of his opposition to rigid 90 per cent price supports, then almost a Wassermann test for Democratic party virtue. Counterattacking, Kennedy's aides noted there were more Catholics than farmers; and that, anyway, a good number of farmers were Catholics.

Kennedy, however, conceded the Midwest was unhappy about his farm record, though he felt it was "sound." As for the religious issue, he told the *New York Herald Tribune*'s David Wise:

"I would hope that no one would vote for or against a man because he was a Catholic."

This, of course, was a prime example of a politician trying to have it both ways.

The various claims and counterclaims of the opposing camps were, of course, designed to influence Adlai Stevenson. Among his law partners he could find no unanimity: Newton Minow, for example, was strongly for Kennedy; Willard Wirtz for Humphrey; while William Blair was torn between.

But Stevenson had other—more pressing—problems with which to contend. He was being vigorously contested for the Presidential nomination by Senator Estes Kefauver. In fact, the Tennessean had won a key primary in Minnesota. Stevenson made a remarkable comeback by taking the crucial primary in California. Two weeks before the convention Kefauver threw in the towel. On July 31, 1956, he announced his support of the Man from Libertyville.

This was followed by rumors of a deal whereby Kefauver would get the Vice Presidency. But those who knew Stevenson rather doubted it; Adlai had never made any bones about his intense dislike of the Senator from Tennessee. Kefauver himself has since recalled, "Many of our people thought Adlai would pick up Kennedy because of the close connections between the Kennedy family and some of the Stevenson staff, and because of their need for the Catholic vote."

One thing, however, was becoming obvious: the closer Stevenson got to the convention, the more difficult it was becoming for him to decide on a running-mate.

Though he had originally been greatly impressed by the Bailey Report, he now began to express doubts about its conclusions. At best, as he told Sargent Shriver, they constituted an "educated guess."

Moreover, he said, he was concerned about Kennedy's health. Various confidential whispers had reached him regarding the several operations which Jack had undergone. The successive bulletins coming from the Kennedy bedside had not been reassuring: his condition at first was described as "excellent," then as "reasonably good," and finally as "fairly satisfactory." To scotch "unfounded and disturbing rumors being circulated especially in Washington," Joseph P. Kennedy was finally forced to issue an optimistic statement regarding his son's condition. But the rumors persisted.

In a year when Presidential health had become a vital political issue, Kennedy himself was concerned that his recovery might not be thoroughly understood. In mid-July he announced he had recently undergone a physical examination and that the doctors said he was in good shape. Happily for him, Kennedy was not yet in a position where newsmen could have demanded a press conference with his medical advisers, as they had done in President Eisenhower's case.

Assured by Shriver that Kennedy was in tiptop physical condition, Stevenson then said, "In the final analysis, it is not the political advantage of the Vice-Presidential choice that is crucial but the needs of the United States—who could best perform the duties and responsibilities of the job."

Shriver pricked up his ears when Stevenson added, "I hope the Convention will give a good deal of deliberation to the Vice-Presidential nomination."

Flabbergasted, Shriver asked Stevenson whether, if he were nominated, he would not select his own running mate. Of course he would, Stevenson said hesitantly, but he had begun to wonder whether Hubert Humphrey might not be better at "giving Nixon hell" than Kennedy.

Shriver, then managing Chicago's vastly profitable Merchandise Mart for his father-in-law, immediately dispatched a memorandum on the conversation to Joseph P. Kennedy.

Other alarming reports disturbed the Stevenson camp. The Stevenson people had heard that Kennedy had made a substantial contribution to Nixon's 1950 Senatorial campaign against Helen Gahagan Douglas—which, in fact, he had. Was it true? A ruffled Ted Sorensen hastily denied the report, explaining it may have been the father, but definitely not the son, who had contributed to Nixon.

Meanwhile, the Kennedy mimeograph machines churned out another memorandum, this one purporting to analyze the various Vice-Presidential aspirants in terms of certain tests: availability, compatibility with Stevenson, geographical background, and marital and veteran's status. The ideal candidate should be a good vote-getter; have a "moderate philosophy like Stevenson's; a warm, sincere appeal on the hustings; and access to plenty of money."

Typical was the memorandum's dissection of Hubert Humphrey: "Strongly pro-Stevenson; married; young and healthy; not a veteran; state adjacent to Stevenson's (11 electoral votes); eight years' experience in Congress; good vote getter; nationally known; considered active ADA-er to Stevenson left; 'right' on farm issue and Taft-Hartley; good speaker and personality; not wealthy."

Thus, with seeming objectivity, these points were made: in an age of "moderation," Humphrey was no "moderate." Moreover, he was not a war veteran which, while "not necessarily essential," was "strongly desirable." And, of course, Humphrey was "not wealthy."

After similarly examining the attributes of other potential candidates, the not altogether surprising conclusion was reached that the ideal candidate would be John F. Kennedy. "It would appear that the best of a good group is Senator Kennedy—young but not as young as [Tennessee Governor Frank] Clement and nearly as old as Teddy Roosevelt when he was nominated Vice President; now fully recovered from his spinal operation; holder of a brilliantly heroic combat record; married to a lovely wife; from the right kind of state in terms of size, location, and political tendencies; with more experience in Congress than Humphrey, Wagner, or Clement; author of a highly-praised best-seller; widely known and popular; a proven vote-getter against big odds; a moderate Stevensonian philosophy; friendly with party leaders in all sections; 'right' on Taft-Hartley and acceptable on the farm issue; with a winning charm, particularly on TV; an able speaker; and independently wealthy, with close contacts with other contribution sources."

The memorandum did concede that Kennedy was not as "experienced" as Senator Clinton Anderson, or as "oratorical" as Governor Clement, or as "pro-farmer" as Hubert Humphrey.

The latter reference reflected the growing awareness that Kennedy faced trouble on the farm issue. As against this, however, Kennedy's "moderate" views were posited as considerably preferable to the thinking of certain "pro-farmers" whose ADA-type views were anathema in the South.

This was the pitch made in June 1956 by one of Kennedy's earliest supporters, Abraham Ribicoff, at the Governors Conference in Atlantic City. "Kennedy would have a wide appeal because he is a middle-of-the-roader," said the then Governor of Connecticut. "Southerners would like his position on most matters."

What those matters were Ribicoff did not specify.

But a hint was provided in a friendly *New Republic* article based on an interview with Kennedy. The main point made by writer Donald Malcolm was that, as a self-styled "Stevensonian liberal," Kennedy "shares the feeling that moderation is in the spirit of the times." In terms of 1956 Democratic politics, however, "moderation" meant chiefly a reluctance to push the South into an all-or-nothing position on school segregation.

"The issue is a judicial problem," the article quoted Kennedy, "not a legislative one, and it is for the Federal District Courts to interpret 'deliberate speed' as they see fit."

Kennedy was therefore opposed to the idea of a *Northern Manifesto* as a reply to the *Southern Manifesto* that, signed by most Dixie Senators and Congressmen, had pledged eternal vigilance against further desegregation efforts.

"No useful purpose," Kennedy argued, "would be served by matching signature against signature [since] time, the law and right are all on the liberal's side. . . ."

According to Malcolm, Kennedy was "highly regarded by a number of Southern Senators, several of whom have been foremost in suggesting his nomination. One of them, Senator Albert Gore of Tennessee, represents the relatively enlightened South. Another, Senator George Smathers of Florida, is popular with the tribal chieftains of darkest Dixie. Between them, they could build up a considerable head of steam below the Mason-Dixon line for Kennedy's nomination."

Nevertheless, there were arguments against Kennedy's nomination. After all, the South would have in Stevenson "as moderate a candidate as it can hope for in 1956." The voters to be wooed, therefore, were not the Southerners but the Negro, farm and labor blocs.

"In this light," continued Malcolm, "Kennedy's prospects shine more dimly. His deviation from the party position of rigid high price supports would prove a handicap in the farm states (Kennedy explains that his vote was in the best interest of the poultry and dairy farmers of his region, who suffer from high feed costs under 90 per cent price-supports). . . . And a 'blue-collar' militant in the second place might make Stevenson's 'white-collar' liberalism more attractive to labor than such a man as Kennedy could."

Kennedy bore still other political burdens. He had aroused the displeasure of Liberal Democrats because of his refusal to take a stand on McCarthyism. Having been in the hospital at the time of the Senate censure of McCarthy, he had been unable to vote. Afterward, he said the issue had been settled and he saw no reason to resurrect it.

But this did not satisfy people like Eleanor Roosevelt. In fact, it only infuriated them.

Another problem was somewhat easier to solve: his controversial father, Joseph P. Kennedy, in a rare display of self-effacement, simply exiled himself to the South of France—out of sight and, hopefully, out of mind. (The elder Kennedy has since stated he was opposed to his son's trying for the Vice Presidency, arguing that Stevenson was bound to lose to Eisenhower. Jack's aides, however, had argued that even if Stevenson lost, the nomination would make Kennedy a nationally known figure and place him on the national scene for possibly bigger things.)

It was in a mood of anticipation and excitement that Jack Kennedy prepared to leave for Chicago. The day before, he spent the afternoon being photographed at the New York studio of Arnold Newman, who recalls finding it difficult to take many statesmanlike pictures because Kennedy spent most of his time answering long distance calls.

"I also remember that he was wearing socks that didn't match," said Newman.

Chicago was—if that was possible—hotter than usual. A searing wind blew in from the prairies like blasts from a furnace. The sickening stench of the stockyards hung like a pall over the city. For Jacqueline Kennedy, who had accompanied her husband, Chicago was an unpleasant experience. Well along in her pregnancy, she wasn't feeling well. But she wanted to be there just in case Jack was nominated.

On Monday, August 13, 1956, the Convention opened in the huge International Amphitheater with the usual band music, circus atmosphere, and oratorical blasts.

The big story, however, was going on behind the scenes. As usual, at a Democratic Convention, it was about civil rights. Reports from behind closed doors indicated a row had been precipitated by Northern Liberals who insisted on a strong plank.

On Tuesday, August 14, Jack Kennedy came in for a moment of glory as the narrator of a campaign film, "Pursuit of Happiness," which extolled the virtues of the Democrats and detailed the failures of the Republicans. The film was considered so partisan that CBS refused to televise it as part of its Convention coverage, and Democratic Chairman Butler criticized the network for its refusal. Frank Stanton, the network president, replied tersely: "Those who make the news cannot, in a free society, dictate to broadcasters, as part of a free press, to what extent, where and how they shall cover the news."

At 1:00 P.M., Wednesday, August 15, Kennedy was summoned into Stevenson's presence. Stevenson said he might want to have the Senator make the nominating speech for him the following afternoon. It all depended on the outcome of the civil rights fight. If the South were humbled, then Stevenson said he would be forced to call upon a Southerner to nominate him in the interests of party unity.

It was a stunning blow for Kennedy. Was he being tossed a bone as a consolation prize for not being selected as Stevenson's running-mate?

"When the Governor told me that," Kennedy said later, "I asked him if that meant I was being disqualified for the nomination and he said, no."

But Kennedy was not satisfied with the reply.

"So when Arthur [Schlesinger Jr.] came to see me, I told him I felt I should know whether or not I was being eliminated before I made the nominating speech."

Schlesinger, then Harvard's major contribution to Adlai's speech-writing fraternity, assured Kennedy the Governor had not yet made up his mind on a running mate.

At 2:00 A.M., Thursday, Stevenson aide Bill Blair called to say a compromise on civil rights had finally been worked out after a week-long battle. While it did not satisfy the Northern Liberals, what really counted was that it did not touch off a Southern revolt.

"You're it," he told Kennedy. "Go to it."

At 11:30 A.M., after working through most of the night with Sorensen on a nominating speech, Kennedy hopped a cab to the Convention hall. With him was the *Boston Globe*'s Tom Winship who observed Kennedy rehearse his speech during the cab ride. Clenching his fist, Kennedy kept whispering to himself, "Go! Go! Go!" Such self-commands, of course, were not unusual with the Kennedys, all of whom had been trained since childhood to do nothing half-heartedly. Besides, the Senator had had only a few hours' sleep.

The speech was well received. The biggest applause-getting line—one that had been provided by Arthur Schlesinger—was an attack on Nixon: "Our candidates will be up against two of the most skilled campaigners in history—one who takes the high road and one who takes the low road." (Needless to say, few of the wildly cheering delegates could have known that Jack Kennedy had once helped finance Nixon's travels along the so-called "low road.")

Another Kennedy line was this: "The grand alliance of the West, that chain from freedom forged by Truman and Marshall and the rest, is cracking, and its unity deteriorating and its strength dissipating. . . ." Thus, amid the Convention hooplah Jack Kennedy had turned a full circle from his former vociferous opposition to Truman-Marshall policies. But no one seemed to notice.

As expected, Stevenson was nominated that evening without any trouble. Unexpected, however, was his refusal to anoint a running mate. He had decided, he told party leaders, to throw the nomination up for grabs, to permit the Convention to select his fellow-victim.

"It's the damnedest fool thing I ever heard of," shouted Convention Chairman Sam Rayburn.

"Forget this foolishness," pleaded Lyndon Johnson.

Other leaders voiced their disapproval, often in discourteous terms. To no avail.

Stevenson argued that an open Convention would furnish a dramatic contrast with the cut-and-dried way in which Nixon was expected to be renominated in San Francisco. Moreover, he said, it would emphasize Eisenhower's disability.

Rayburn scoffed at the argument. He attributed the unprecedented ploy to Stevenson's "congenital indecisiveness."

Jack Kennedy, on hearing of the turn of events, was infuriated. "I remember," said Newton Minow, "Jack coming in and telling Stevenson, 'It's a fixed Convention. You've set it against me.' " (Four years later, the tables were to be turned with Stevenson supporters claiming that Kennedy had "fixed" the 1960 Convention against the Man from Libertyville.)

The night that followed was one of the most frenzied in recent campaign history. Senators Kennedy, Kefauver, Gore, and Humphrey, as well as Mayor Wagner, stumbled into each other as they shuttled bleary-eyed between the various delegations in downtown hotels seeking support. "At 5:00 A.M.," reported the AP's veteran correspondent Jack Bell, "I came across Kefauver doing a television recording in a corridor of the Conrad Hilton Hotel. Kennedy, rushing to another meeting, tripped over the power wires and almost fell into his rival."

Other Kennedys—brothers, sisters, and in-laws—were scurrying around Chicago too, dealing, pleading, and cajoling. Faraway members of the Kennedy clan were busy also. In France, Joseph P. Kennedy was on the trans-Atlantic phone all through the night, talking persuasively with some of his powerful political friends. Jack's brother-in-law, Peter Lawford, who had remained in Santa Monica to be with his *enceinte* wife, Pat, was also on the phone. Recalled Wilbur Clark, his friend from Las Vegas' Desert Inn and chairman of the Nevada delegation: "Peter tracked me down by phone at three o'clock in the morning to make sure Nevada went for Jack." And Nevada did, too, overwhelmingly.

Of all the candidates, as *Newsweek* then reported, the "most skillful" was Kennedy. With New England pretty much committed to him and New York and Illinois promised for the second ballot, he labored doggedly through the night for Southern support. "Amazingly (for a Roman Catholic) he got it," *Newsweek* added. "The arguments: (1) he was a civil-rights moderate, and (2) he was concerned over foreign textile competition."

There was an even more persuasive argument. Kennedy people hit delegation after delegation, chanting the same theme: "It's either Kefauver or Kennedy; and you don't want Kefauver, do you?" The argument hit home; many Southerners didn't want Kefauver because of his Liberalism, while some Northerners didn't want him because his anti-crime investigations had uncovered too many links between racketeers and big city Democratic machines.

Sometime during that incredible night someone announced that a man, name unknown, had been patiently waiting outside to see Kennedy. It turned out to be New York's Tammany Leader Carmine DeSapio with some 98 big delegate votes in his hip pocket.

"We didn't talk too long," DeSapio said later. "I made no promises and he didn't ask for any. But he knew I wanted a Catholic on the ticket because it would help us in New York."

New York, of course, was committed to its favorite son, Mayor Wagner, on the first ballot.

Later that night, Kennedy called on Wagner. The Mayor listened politely to a strong selling speech on the Bay Stater's qualifications.

"You know," Wagner finally interrupted, "that I'm a candidate myself."

Probably the most important hurdle Kennedy had to overcome lay in his own Massachusetts delegation—the *sub rosa* opposition to his ambitions of the veteran John McCormack from whom he had wrested control of the State Organization. After considerable pressure McCormack reluctantly agreed to second his young colleague's nomination for the Vice Presidency. But there were those who claimed that McCormack practically had to be shoved onto the platform to perform the distasteful chore.

And if Governor Ribicoff's nominating speech had "John Kennedy" in every sentence, McCormack's effort mentioned his candidate's name but once —and that in the final sentence. McCormack's strongest statement was, "It is time to go East for a Vice-Presidential candidate."

This followed the more fervent—if not eloquent—nominating speech of Governor Ribicoff: "John Kennedy of Massachusetts is a great Democrat. John Kennedy of Massachusetts is a successful campaigner and a successful candidate every time he has run for public office. John Kennedy is something new. John Kennedy brings the vigor and youth and fresh breeze that blows through this great nation of ours. John Kennedy has a voice and personality that appeal to independent voters. John Kennedy has a personality that will appeal to the many Democrats and his record shows that he is unusually successful in making converts in the Republican ranks, too."

The balloting for the Vice Presidency began with Senator Kefauver a solid favorite. Before long it became apparent that the battle was between Kefauver and Kennedy. At first, it seemed so transparently unfair, so unevenly matched. It was the Coonskin Cap against the Boyish Mop. A young man with no national campaigning experience had challenged the "old warrior" himself—the "Keef" who had demonstrated his grass-roots strength by challenging Stevenson in the primaries, the crime-fighter, the tireless hand-shaker, the Democratic hero of a thousand crossroads.

Yet, it almost happened. And it almost happened because of an extraordinary number of diverse factors. Who would have expected, for example, that Georgia would declare itself for Kennedy? "We all knew how anti-Catholic they were in Georgia," said Sargent Shriver, "and Jack said, just like that, 'Gee, if Georgia went for me, then I may really have a chance.' "

Significantly, the religious issue proved to be of minor consequence.

"I got it mostly from liberal individuals," recalled Representative Frank Smith of Mississippi. "One man from Wisconsin said Kennedy would lose everything in the state outside of Milwaukee because he was a Catholic. . . . There was some feeling and talk in the Texas delegation about it, but it was a question of Kennedy and Kefauver, and they sure didn't want Kefauver."

And they sure didn't want Kefauver because many Southerners felt the Tennessean had "betrayed" the South on civil rights. As Jack's pal, Florida Senator George Smathers, later observed: "The South is always more apt to go for a Northerner who doesn't know any better than for a Southerner who should know better, but doesn't."

Looking back on the roll calls of that Friday afternoon, it was such votes as Louisiana's 24 and Georgia's 32 on the first ballot that gave shape to the surprising news that Kennedy, and not Hubert Humphrey, was Kefauver's leading opponent. "It was then that the strong hand of Lyndon B. Johnson showed itself for Kennedy," reported Jack Bell. "We who had watched the Texan perform some near-miracles in lining up Senate votes knew immediately this operation ran deep and it could spell real trouble for Kefauver."

As the second ballot began, Hubert Humphrey, weary and stunned at the surprise turn of events, sat with some close friends in Sam Rayburn's private room in back of the Convention platform. Michigan's Governor G. Mennen [Soapy] Williams, along with his state chairman Neil Stabler, were there pleading with Humphrey—almost on bended knees—to throw his support behind Kefauver in a stop-Kennedy move. Their argument was that Hubert's friend Orville Freeman would most certainly fail of re-election as Minnesota's Governor if Kennedy were on the ticket, since the Bay Stater's record would not be popular with labor and the farmers.

"Even while they talked," as a participant later recounted the scene to Martin and Plaut, "Kennedy kept gaining and Soapy and Neil were just begging Hubert and somebody else was saying, 'Stick it out, Hubert . . . we can make it on the third ballot, stick it out, we can get Texas and Rhode Island. . . .' Eugenie Anderson was there, too, shouting at all of them, 'Leave Hubert alone. . . . He's got to make his own decision, so leave him alone. . . .' And everyone was crying. Eugenie was crying and I was crying and the tears were just pouring out of Stabler. . . ."

About the only thing TV commentator Martin Agronsky can still vividly recall of the 1956 Convention is that lacrymal scene: "Hubert was crying, really sobbing, and so were some of his friends." When Kefauver entered the tear-sogged room, Agronsky quickly got on the air to report exclusively that Minnesota would now throw its support behind Kefauver and that might mean the ball game. The report, however, was somewhat premature.

Kefauver had to do considerable pleading before it happened. "Hubert," he said, "you've just got to help me . . . you've GOT to help me. . . . Please. . . ." Now Kefauver had begun to cry. "In fact," a witness said, "everyone was crying, grown men all crying. . . . I'll never forget the water gushing in that room."

Jack Kennedy, however, wasn't crying. Sprawled on a bed in his shorts in Room 104 of the Stock Yard Inn, he was watching the television coverage of the dramatic second-place race. According to the *Globe*'s Winship, who faithfully recorded the afternoon's events, Kennedy smiled when the cameras caught brother Bobby moving about from delegation to delegation on the Convention floor.

The first ballot showed Kefauver with 483½, Kennedy 304, Gore 178, Wagner 162¼, and Humphrey 134½. Needed to win were 686½ votes.

Then came the report that Kefauver was on his way to see Humphrey.

"Well," said Kennedy, massaging his ankles, a favorite gesture, "I'd like to talk to Humphrey too."

Ted Sorensen was sent to look for the Minnesota Senator. Under the Convention platform, he ran into Humphrey's floor manager, Representative [now Senator] Eugene McCarthy.

"Jack wants Hubert to come over to see him," Sorensen said.

"Not a chance," McCarthy said wryly. "Up in Minnesota we're Protestants and farmers." McCarthy, a Catholic and a city boy, was thus alluding to Kennedy's two alleged major handicaps—his religion and his "poor" farm record.

"Later," according to Sorensen, "McCarthy told people that Kennedy had sent a boy to see him. But, according to McCarthy, sending Sorensen to get Humphrey "was an incredible boner and somebody should have pointed it out to Jack."

"Now," continued McCarthy, "suppose you were Humphrey, running hard for Vice President . . . and you had this little room in back of the stands, watching the balloting on TV, and watching the chances go down the drain and feeling real lousy about it, and in comes this young man with the announcement that Senator Kennedy would like Senator Humphrey to come across to the Stock Yard Inn to see him, almost as though you were being offered an audience with Kennedy. And suppose, minutes later, Estes Kefauver himself comes running up those two flights of stairs and says, 'Hubert can you help me?' Now suppose you were Hubert Humphrey—which one would you help?' "

Looking back at that wild afternoon, it might have made the difference.

On the second go-round, the first important break came when Arkansas' Orval Faubus declared his state for Kennedy. (Faubus had been personally won over by Kennedy during the night.) Then New Jersey declared for Kennedy. The clerk droned on, calling the names of the states. Mississippi and South Carolina fell into the Kennedy column. It was clear now that Kennedy's strength was coming from New England and the South. Lying on his bed in his underwear, Kennedy watched as his good friend Lyndon Johnson took the microphone.

"Mistah Chairman," Lyndon boomed, "Texas proudly casts its votes for the fighting sailor who wears the scars of battle and the next Vice President of the United States, Senator Kennedy of Massachusetts."

At that moment, Sarge Shriver poked his head in the door to say that, in view of the turn of events, the manager thought it advisable that Jack move to a larger, air-conditioned suite. Protected by a solid squad of Chicago police, Kennedy dashed down the hall in his shorts to await the Call.

There seemed no stopping Kennedy. His total kept moving up to 600, 610, 630. Adlai Stevenson Jr. came over to congratulate him on his all-but-official victory. He also suggested that Kennedy get ready to cross the street to accept the nomination. Kennedy thought so too. He took a quick shower. As he dried himself, the third ballot had begun.

There was one dramatic moment when Kennedy was so close to the nomination that the shift of a single delegation might have turned the trick. At that moment, Lyndon Johnson dispatched an emissary to attempt to convince Oklahoma Governor Raymond Gary to give Kennedy the necessary votes to go over the top.

"No," said Gary, "we're not going to do it. Kennedy voted against the farm bill. We need a man in Oklahoma who is for the farmers and Kefauver is our man."

Oklahoma thus led the farm-state swing to Kefauver.

But could the other states be held? As the excitement in the jam-packed Amphitheater mounted, Bobby Kennedy was doing his darnedest to prevent a rout.

"I'll never forget Bobby Kennedy during the balloting," said North Dakota's Quentin Burdick. "Standing in front of our delegation with tears in his eyes, he pleaded for our support. It didn't do any good. Jack had voted for sliding-scale supports and they don't like sliding-scale supports in our country. He stood there trying to explain his brother's voting position but we said we were sorry and the delegation wouldn't listen to him."

Still another Kennedy chicken came home to roost. Indiana Representative Andrew Jacobs refused to permit his state to be stampeded into switching to Kennedy. Jacobs, who had feuded with Kennedy when both were members of the House Labor and Education Committee, demanded the delegation be polled. "You are not going to switch my vote to Kennedy," he told the State Chairman. By that time, however, the Kennedy upsurge had subsided. Indiana stuck with Kefauver.[2]

The devastating Kefauver comeback continued. Like a surging tide it could not be contained. The hall was in sheer bedlam as various delegations waved their banners for recognition. Chairman Rayburn, for reasons he never explained, recognized Missouri. Chairman Tom Hennings announced for Kefauver. And that did it. Kefauver had gone over the top.[3]

Turning away from the television set, Kennedy said, "That's it—let's go."

Ten minutes later, waving and smiling, Kennedy stood on the Convention platform. The spontaneous demonstration that greeted him was extraordinary even by Convention standards. It had been a hard fought, nerve-racking, suspenseful battle; and the delegates roared their appreciation.

"Ladies and gentlemen of this Convention," Kennedy began. "I want to take this opportunity to express my appreciation to Democrats from all parts

---

[2] A Roman Catholic, Jacobs in 1949 had tangled in committee with Kennedy over the question of Federal aid to church-related schools. Kennedy, at that time, favored such aid. Jacobs opposed it on constitutional grounds.

[3] Still being argued in Boston is whether John McCormack, in retaliation for his loss of state leadership, had not prevailed on his good friend Sam Rayburn to recognize Missouri. McCormack, at the time, was reported standing next to Missouri Chairman Tom Hennings, yelling at the top of his voice, "Sam! Sam! Missouri! Missouri!" McCormack has vehemently denied the story reported in *Time*. He says he wanted Rayburn to recognize Kentucky, a state that wanted to switch to Kennedy.

of the country, North and South, East and West, who have been so kind to me this afternoon. I think it proves, as nothing else could prove, what a strong and united party the Democratic party is."

Still smiling, he leaned on the rostrum and, with tones of good will, he asked that the Kefauver nomination be made unanimous. The delegates roared and cheered.

The Convention was over.

To the strains of "The Tennessee Waltz," the delegates streamed out of the huge Amphitheater where, four years hence, the Republicans were to nominate Richard M. Nixon as their candidate for President. But Kennedy was not then thinking of 1960. Along with his wife and good friend Senator Smathers, he repaired to his suite at the Conrad Hilton. There, he immediately called his father in France.

"We did our best," he told Dad. "I had fun and I didn't make a fool of myself."

Out on the Convention floor, Bobby Kennedy was observed in a boiling rage. "We'll show them," he muttered darkly to no one in particular. (Flying back to Boston the next day, Bobby was still angry. "I sat next to Bobby and he was bitter," said David Talbot, a Massachusetts delegate. "He said they should have won and that somebody had pulled something fishy and he wanted to know who did it.")

"I've never been to an Irish wake before," Smathers said later, "but I guess maybe this was it. The three of us just sat around the hotel room, glum, none of us saying very much. We were there about an hour and a half and all Jack could think of were all the different things he might have done that might have made the difference. He was hurt, deeply hurt. The thing is, he came so close."

It had been Kennedy's first major political defeat; and he took it hard. Exhausted, tense, and depressed, he flew off the next day to France to be with his father. Jacqueline Kennedy, also exhausted, tense, and depressed, flew to Newport to be with her parents in her final weeks of pregnancy.

At Val-sur-Mer on the French Riviera, Clare Boothe Luce, United States Ambassador to Italy, had been visiting the Joseph P. Kennedys. The Wiley Buchanans—he was then protocol chief of the State Department—were there too, and they recall Mrs. Luce remarking to the senior Kennedy, "You must be very proud that Jack came so close to getting the Vice Presidency."

The Buchanans nearly fell off their beach chairs when Kennedy replied, "Yes, I was, but it would have pleased me a lot more if he had run on the Republican ticket."

Only in America could it have happened.

Sight

10

Just when did John F. Kennedy first raise his sights to the White House? The exact time is difficult to pinpoint. For so well-ordered were his ambitions that even close friends disagree on just when the Presidential bug bit.

That he long had his eyes set on the Presidency had been suspected by some colleagues. But he invariably scoffed at the suggestion. "He disclaims any aspiration to be America's first Catholic President," Irwin Ross reported two weeks before the 1956 Convention, "though the story is inevitably heard that this is his fondest desire."

That he may have been thinking about it, however, was indicated by a remark he let drop while discussing his political aspirations with Fletcher Knebel of the *Des Moines Register* earlier that year. "I suppose anybody in politics would like to be President," he said, matter-of-factly.

In retrospect, it was a significant slip of the tongue. But it went unnoticed largely because Kennedy then sought the Vice Presidency which, in itself, would have been a considerable achievement. No one at the time was seriously thinking of Kennedy in Presidential terms.

Except, possibly, Kennedy himself. For it is Arthur Schlesinger Jr.'s contention that Kennedy first heard the Call of Destiny when, following a "private crisis of identity," he decided he could be President of the United States. Then thirty-eight years old, he had just pulled through several near-fatal operations. And since Schlesinger has known Kennedy for many years, it is conceivable that the Harvard professor knew what he was writing about.

Schlesinger's historic revelations can be found in a little book written during the 1960 campaign. Forsaking his academic role, Schlesinger had thrown himself into shilling disturbed intellectuals unable to warm up to Kennedy as the embodiment of their Liberal aspirations. His book, one of the real curios of the Presidential campaign, was entitled *Kennedy or Nixon: Does It Make Any Difference?*[1] As it turned out, it certainly made a difference for Schlesinger: he became the Court Historian of the New Frontier.

The 1956 Democratic Convention had set the stage for the transformation of John F. Kennedy from the status of questionable Vice-Presidential timber to sudden eminence as a Presidential front-runner.

Even Bobby Kennedy, who had darkly vowed to "get" his brother's enemies following Estes Kefauver's nomination by a razor-thin margin, began to refer to the Convention as the time "when Jack was saved from the Vice Presidency." For had "my brother, the Senator," been nominated, he said, a good share of the blame for Stevenson's defeat might well have been assigned to the fortuitous circumstance that Kennedy had been born a Roman Catholic. And this most certainly would have killed Jack's chances for 1960.

Jack himself quickly recovered from the doldrums. The Democratic debacle in November made it easier for him to jest about his Convention defeat. Kennedy put it this way to Bob Considine:

"Joe was the star of our family. He did everything better than the rest of us. If he had lived he would have gone on in politics and he would have been elected to the House and the Senate as I was. And, like me, he would have gone for the Vice-Presidential nomination at the 1956 Convention but, unlike me, he wouldn't have been beaten. Joe would have won the nomination."

Kennedy smiled and added: "And then he and Stevenson would have been beaten by Eisenhower, and today Joe's political career would be in shambles and he would be trying to pick up the pieces."

Kennedy's career, of course, was intact; he did not need to pick up the pieces.

True, it hadn't appeared that way in the grim hours following the Convention. Then, he had not realized how fortunate he was in not beating Kefauver. And, as usual, in times of trouble he had turned to his father for solace.

Jack was out sailing on the Mediterranean when his father received word that Jacqueline had suffered a miscarriage. It took several days before word could be gotten to the Senator. In those several days, Jacqueline's life hung in the balance. By the time her husband reached her bedside the danger was past.

The fact that Kennedy had not been with his wife in her time of crisis

[1] New York, Macmillan, 1960.

provided ammunition for gossip columnists perennially seeking juicy tidbits about the difficulties of the celebrated. There were even published reports that their marriage was on the rocks. As usual, Drew Pearson added to the speculation. According to *Time,* one widely circulated story was that Joe Kennedy had made a million-dollar deal with Jacqueline at New York's River House to keep her from leaving his son.

On July 21, 1957, David Barnett, Washington bureau chief of North American Newspaper Alliance, filed this dispatch:

"A vital element has been added to the well-planned and generously financed campaign to make Senator Jack Kennedy President of the United States.

"The Kennedys, according to excited word on Capitol Hill, are 'expecting.'

"A child will put an end to some of the recurring rumors that the youthful Mr. Kennedy and his beautiful wife are not getting along so well."

By 1958 the rumors had gotten so out of hand that a major propaganda item in his Senate re-election campaign was a TV film emphasizing his home life with Jacqueline. However, by that time little Caroline had come into the world and the rumors had begun to diminish.

According to Kennedy, the 1956 campaign had made him "more a national figure than just merely a Massachusetts figure." In all he made one hundred and forty public appearances in twenty-six states, in behalf of the Stevenson-Kefauver ticket. Wherever he went he found himself a celebrity, with most people recalling the thrill-packed TV drama of the Vice-Presidential race and his graceful concession of defeat.

Some Stevenson partisans, however, wondered whether Kennedy was doing all he could for Adlai. "They feel that if you get out and work hard, Massachusetts may be swung to Stevenson," he was told on "Meet the Press." "Do you think so?"

"I've been working as hard as I can," Kennedy replied. "The chances look good in Massachusetts."

As it turned out, Stevenson took an even bigger beating in the Bay State than he had in 1952. But, as Kennedy observed, it was an Eisenhower year and there was little anyone could have done about it. Moreover, Stevenson's campaign had lacked the fire it had in 1952. He had tried hard to gain public attention by calling for the cessation of nuclear tests. But people weren't listening.

They were listening, however, to Kennedy. Or, at least looking. At one campaign appearance in Louisville, there was a near-riot when girl students at Ursuline College shouted, squealed, blocked his car and yelled, "We love you on TV" and "You're better than Elvis Presley."

The incident failed to ruffle Kennedy. But it was a portent of things to come.

However, there were still some Americans who, while they remembered his face, couldn't quite remember his name. At a Knights of Columbus dinner in Pittsburgh in October 1956, an official referred to him as "Senator Wagner of New York."

Then came the turn of Mayor (later Governor) David Lawrence. With a big smile, Lawrence introduced Kennedy as "Senator John Fitzgerald."

This brought down the house. Hurriedly, Lawrence explained he had been thinking of the Senator's grandfather Honey Fitz Fitzgerald.

All in all, as Kennedy declared in the midst of the campaign, stumping for Stevenson was turning out to be a "strange safari."

Even stranger was the above-the-battle posture Kennedy affected. He took almost a plague-on-both-your-houses attitude toward both political parties.

For example, he told a Rhode Island audience that both the Democrats and the Republicans were making such fantastic claims of virtue that the voters were finding it difficult to understand what the real issues were.

"Which is why," he added, "I don't think too much of electioneering."

He repeatedly decried the campaign emphasis on what he termed "bread-basket" or "pocketbook" issues. In Los Angeles, he called for a foreign policy debate free from "partisan distortion, exaggeration or oversimplification." He said it was oversimplifying things to view foreign affairs simply in terms of anti-Communism. Thus, he insisted that "the East-West struggle" was in no way—"directly or indirectly"—involved in the crisis over Suez then beginning to boil.

The Kremlin thought otherwise. A few weeks later Moscow threatened to launch nuclear rockets if the Israeli-French-British forces failed to halt their "imperialist invasion" of Egypt. Upon United States pressure, the invading forces pulled back.

But Kennedy went beyond mere approval of the Eisenhower Administration's Suez policy.

"Since 1945," he told a communion breakfast of telephone workers in Boston, "we have been tremendously hampered by diplomatic ties with Britain and France who wish to preserve their colonial ties. We have taken a definite moral stand against colonialism for the first time since 1945." He made no reference to Israel, having once been burned for urging a slash in United States aid to the new Jewish state.

Only once during the 1956 campaign did he evidence any embarrassment. That was in Vermont when he urged that Republican farm policies "be given a chance, before they are scrapped."

"Anyway," he said, "it was originally a Democratic plan."

Informed that the local Democrats had been making much of the fact that Senator George Aiken, then seeking re-election, was the ranking Republican on the Senate Agriculture Committee, Kennedy hastily told newsmen:

"I didn't say that I support the entire Republican farm program."

Kennedy also appeared flustered when asked to comment on remarks attributed to Harry S Truman. The former President had been quoted as saying he did not believe that Alger Hiss was a Communist spy and that, anyway, the Congressional probe in the Hiss case was, indeed, a "red-herring."

"I personally don't agree with him," said Kennedy. The Trumanisms, he said, "certainly were no asset to the Democrats." Then, as an afterthought, he added, "It wasn't good politically."

A week before the election Kennedy was asked on "Meet the Press" why Americans, in view of the peace and prosperity they were enjoying, should vote for Stevenson.

Kennedy was hard put for a reply.

"Well," he said, "I think that the Democratic party, the leaders, that is, in Congress, in the various states, Presidential candidates—I think that they are better equipped to lead the country through the next eight years than is the Republican party."

It was not the sort of reply calculated to set off a pro-Stevenson stampede.

Kennedy then was asked about a campaign speech in which he had stated that "when Mr. Eisenhower talks about the party of the future, he is talking about the party of Richard Nixon."

"Suppose he is," asked Lawrence Spivak. "What's wrong with that?"

"The point I was making, Mr. Spivak, on the one hand, the Democrats had a dozen young Senators and Congressmen who I thought represented a very strong hope for the future. The Republicans did not have any young men in a position of leadership except Richard Nixon . . . and therefore the party of the future is really the Democratic party because the only young man of leadership in the Republican party is Nixon."

"Now, you were with him in Congress from I think 1946 to 1950."

"That is correct."

"Do you think that some of the extreme things being said about Nixon by the Democratic orators are justified?"

"Well," replied Kennedy, "I haven't said anything extreme about him except to say he's the leading young man in the Republican party, so if that's an extreme or insult—"

"Now, you are saying—"

"I'm not criticizing Nixon except I am saying he's a conservative, that the conservative members of the Republican party are supporting him, and if he became President, we could expect the Republican policy would switch to the right, and I confine myself to that."

The issue of Eisenhower's health also arose. Stevenson had been questioning the President's capacity to serve out a second term; he said, in fact, that a GOP victory "would mean that Richard Nixon would probably be President of this country within the next four years."

"What about it?" asked Spivak.

"I think it's an important issue," said Kennedy. "And it should be. People should take it into consideration, deciding what they want to do for the future and, after saying that, I think it's up to the American people."

Ironically, the health issue was to arise during Kennedy's own climb to the Presidency; but whenever it came up his managers were to cry foul.

Stevenson's last-ditch efforts to capitalize on his opponent's heart attack, needless to say, proved unavailing. Once again, the Man from Libertyville went down to defeat.

And amid the debris of Stevenson's electoral disaster John Kennedy launched his own drive for the Presidency. He had good reason to lift his eyes, as he put it, "from the VP to the P." For when the Senate convened in January 1957, he returned as one of the nation's better-known political figures.

Yet he held no title in the party; nor did he serve on any of the Senate's high-prestige committees. Despite his eleven years in both houses of Congress, he had never been given any of the assignments he sought in the Senate. Now, he felt, the party was in his debt.

Or so he informed Senate Majority Leader Lyndon Johnson in a memorandum requesting assignment to the Foreign Relations Committee. He also pointed out that he was the only Democrat who came into the Senate in 1953 who had not improved his committee assignments. And, in effect, he asked whether he was not being made the Senate's whipping boy.

By all rights the Foreign Relations plum should have gone to Senator Kefauver. But in what the Associated Press described as a "major surprise," the Democratic Steering Committee—headed by Lyndon Johnson—awarded the highly coveted post to Jack Kennedy.

Kefauver, naturally, was disappointed. "Of course," he said, "I do not blame Senator Kennedy for trying to better his position. But I am interested to learn that apparently seniority is a rule that may or may not be applied by the Senate leadership in deciding the rights of Senators."

According to James MacGregor Burns, the fact that the Democratic insiders had ignored the Tennessean's seniority was a sign of Kennedy's popularity and Kefauver's unpopularity with the conservatives and moderates in the Senate's "inner club." Kennedy was, indeed, getting along with all factions in the Senate; whereas Kefauver was constantly roiling the conservative Democrats.

Moreover, unlike Kefauver, Kennedy had kept in the good graces of Lyndon Johnson. In fact, he had demonstratively rushed to Johnson's defense when the Texan's leadership came under bitter attack by Northern Liberals. The ADA went so far as to accuse Johnson of "betraying" the cause of civil rights, thus helping lose Negro votes in the big cities.

At first, Kennedy had appeared to agree with Johnson's detractors. Two days after the stunning Eisenhower victory he told a Worcester, Massachusetts, audience that in trying "to compromise on the civil rights issue," the

Democratic leadership "had lost a substantial percentage of the Negro vote." And he predicted mounting bitterness between the Northern Liberals and Southern Conservatives in the new Congress.

A month later, Kennedy unaccountably changed his tune. In response to what he claimed were press inquiries concerning his position on "alleged controversies" over party leadership, he issued a statement praising Johnson's "uniquely effective leadership," calling on fellow Democrats to lay aside "party dissension" and "futile debates." As for Johnson's lack of enthusiasm on civil rights, Kennedy said it was useless to pin the blame "on any one policy or man" for the loss of "some groups of voters." Any such effort ignored "the irrefutable facts of the Eisenhower tide."

Assignment on the Foreign Affairs Committee followed. Though, in and of itself, such membership does not automatically confer statesmanlike qualities on its recipient, it did give Kennedy the opportunity to sound off with a measure of authority on subjects that did not violently exercise his constituents.

However, his first major venture into foreign affairs—a militant call for Algerian "independence" in July 1957—was to have profound international repercussions and result in increased French bitterness toward the United States.

Kennedy denied that he had raised the Algerian issue for base political motives. And he denied having any Presidential ambitions.

"I'm not thinking about 1960," he said in November 1957. "I'm tremendously interested in my Senate job and want to stay there."

Actually, by now, it was one of Washington's least-kept secrets that he was running for the Presidency as hard as good taste permitted. Skeptics wondered why, if he really were that "tremendously interested" in the Senate, he was so frequently absent from its deliberations. Moreover, Kennedy was flying off to places so far removed from his bailiwick that he was getting to know the insides of almost every airport in the country.

"When you see a Senator doing much speaking outside his own state," the *Saturday Evening Post* quoted a colleague as saying in September 1957, "it means one of two things. He needs the money or he's got his eye on higher office."

One thing was certain: Kennedy did not need the money. Also, he did not particularly like to make speeches. "Those guys who can make the rafters ring with hokum—well, I guess that's okay, but it keeps me from being an effective political speaker," he said in December 1957. Instead, as *Time* then noted, Kennedy "imparts a remarkable quality of shy, sense-making sincerity."

But what he was being sincere or making sense about was another matter.

In November 1957 the Kennedy-for-President boom received a significant home-town blessing from a gathering of the Italo-American Citizens Committee. An inordinate amount of fence-mending, preceded the meeting at which the Senator was endorsed for 1960 by two Governors, the Mayor of Boston, and an important labor leader.

One of the Governors was Massachusetts' Foster Furcolo.

At best, the mutual esteem between Furcolo and Kennedy was on-again-off-again, with some Bostonians attributing their relationship to the theory that "Gaelic and garlic don't mix."

But now Furcolo declared he would be "walking hand in hand with Senator Kennedy in 1958 and 1960."

The reference to 1958 was to the upcoming Senatorial contest in which Kennedy was widely regarded as a shoo-in for re-election. A landslide victory, however, would improve Kennedy's standing as a Presidential aspirant. Thus, though 1960 was still three years away, Kennedy was running—and running hard.

In 1957 Kennedy made some one hundred and fifty appearances throughout the country. And he was spending a good deal of time in the South where his close Convention loss to Estes Kefauver had made him a hero. Overnight, the Bay State Catholic paradoxically had become a symbol of Southern opposition to a native Southerner identified with Yankee Liberals.

Before the year was out Kennedy had become known as "Dixie's favorite Yankee."

"Southerners were damn nice to me at the Convention," Kennedy told Bob Considine. "And before that and ever since. I couldn't ask to meet finer, higher-minded people than I met speaking recently in Virginia, Georgia and Louisiana."

But Kennedy wasn't just interested in meeting "finer, higher-minded people." He had a larger—more urgent—purpose in mind. Some of his associates were voicing doubts about the chances of a Democratic victory in 1960 because of a potential party split over civil rights. They wanted Kennedy to aim his sights at a subsequent election. But the Senator was in a hurry. For him, it was 1960 or never.

It was Kennedy's hope that, as a "moderate," he could bridge the chasm in his party between North and South. Little Rock, however, provided a test for "moderation." The Democratic Advisory Council, reflecting Northern sentiment, took the tack that the time for appeasing the South was over. And such prominent spokesmen as Chester Bowles, Mennen Williams, and Averell Harriman argued that, rather than continue to be embarrassed on civil rights, the party would be better off without the Southern wing.

Kennedy, however, was not willing to write off the South. In October 1957 the *Washington Post*'s Carroll Kilpatrick reported that Kennedy "believes that a united party is worth fighting for and that it can be achieved if a 'moderate' like himself is nominated instead of an 'extremist' like Harriman or Mennen Williams. . . . As far as 1960 is concerned, Kennedy says it is too early for anyone to say that 'moderation' is dead or alive. . . . But Little Rock or not, Kennedy is not burning his bridges in the South yet. . . ."

It was almost as if Kennedy had laid out his guide lines in his highly successful *Profiles in Courage*. In discussing the Presidential ambitions of another illustrious Senator from Massachuetts, Kennedy quoted Allan Nevins' words about Daniel Webster being aware, over a century ago, that "the first precaution of any aspirant for the Presidency is to make sure of his own state and section."

"Moreover," Kennedy added, "Webster was sufficiently acute politically to know that a divided party such as his would turn away from politically controversial figures and move to an uncommitted neutral individual."

That, the Senator noted, was "a principle consistently applied to this day."

Kennedy, needless to say, was quite "sure of his own state and section." His home-state strength was such that, on the eve of his 1958 re-election campaign, a prominent Republican was quoted as saying, "Jack couldn't lose if he went out and shot the Pope." Nevertheless, he approached the Massachusetts election as if his life depended on it. For he knew that a huge, headline-catching win over respectable GOP opposition would impress the delegates at the 1960 convention.

Furthermore, he intended to do everything he could to insure that the party would not be split irrevocably along sectional lines in 1960. And he would do nothing—or say nothing—that would play into the hands of "extremists" in both North and South on the civil rights question. Meanwhile, he intended to cement alliances with the powerful Southern leaders who, in 1956, had been so impressed with his "moderation."

There was no doubt, by the summer of 1957, that the South had accepted Kennedy as one of its own. "Georgia loves him," remarked the political editor of the *Atlanta Constitution*. And Kennedy loved Georgia, a state where other Northern Democrats were not particularly popular.

In a two-day visit to the Peach State, the Junior Senator was tendered a reception that attracted both political and social leaders throughout the state; he addressed an important trade meeting of peanut growers; he spoke at commencement exercises at the University of Georgia; and he appeared on a television program with Senators Richard B. Russell and Herman E. Talmadge.

On the TV show, Kennedy praised Russell as "a Senator's Senator," which indeed he was. He also paid tribute to "Hummon" Talmadge for having amassed "a remarkable record" in his short time in the Senate—a record which, Kennedy had failed to note, included die-hard opposition to any and all attempts at desegregation. As for his own views on the hotly controversial civil rights bill then before the Senate, Kennedy preferred not to comment.

Kennedy had become so popular below the Mason-Dixon line that in December 1957 the *Christian Science Monitor*'s Bicknell Eubanks was able to report "a growing feeling throughout the region that the Bay Stater may be the one to head a third party in Dixieland."

Talk of a third party—composed of segregationists in the South and, possibly, conservatives in the North—had increased greatly following the Little Rock episode. The spectacle of federal troops being used in the Arkansas capital to quell turmoil occasioned by school desegregation efforts had deeply shocked the South.

"This is where Senator Kennedy comes into the picture," Eubanks wrote. "Because he is from a New England state, Southerners don't expect him to be an ardent segregationist. Nor are they particularly concerned that he supports integration, just as long as he doesn't wear his feelings on his sleeve."

"His handling of the civil rights issue has been deft," Eubanks continued. "He has handled the touchy topic in a simple, but most effective way. He has combined traditional Southern suspicion of Republicanism with the reaction against the Administration for using federal troops in Little Rock."

Then this significant observation: "Almost unnoticed is the fact that Senator Kennedy hasn't put himself squarely on the touchy issue while he has been in the South."

Though Kennedy criticized Eisenhower's role in Little Rock, not once did he suggest how he personally would have handled that explosive situation.

Only when pressed would he uphold—"without applauding," as the AP put it—the Supreme Court decision on school desegregation.

"Whether we favor the decision or oppose it," he said in November 1957, "it is going to be carried out. It is the law of the land; there is no appeal from it."

Aside from its noticeable restraint, the statement was not entirely accurate. The fact was—law of the land or not—the decision, in its specific applications, was being appealed.

However, Kennedy did run into trouble once in his travels in the South. And he turned it to his advantage. On the eve of his arrival to address a Democratic dinner in Jackson, Mississippi, the Republican State Chairman challenged Kennedy to state how he felt about Little Rock.

The next night, Kennedy found fifteen hundred pairs of eyes staring at him expectantly. At first, he repeated the ancient cliché about how it was always possible for good Democrats to disagree with one another. The silence grew heavy. Finally, he referred to the GOP challenge.

"I have no hesitancy," he said, "in telling the Republican State Chairman the same thing I have said in my own city of Boston—that I accept the Supreme Court decision as the supreme law of the land. I know we do not all agree on that issue—but I think most of us do agree on the necessity to uphold law and order in every part of the land."

Still no response from the audience.

Then Kennedy attacked: "And now I challenge the Republican Chairman to tell us where he stands on Eisenhower and Nixon."

The remark, probably the *non-sequitur* of the year, brought down the house. And his audience let loose with rebel yells when Kennedy observed that the then GOP National Chairman Meade Alcorn bore the same name as one of Mississippi's more unpopular Reconstruction Governors. For this remarkable display of erudition, Kennedy then and there won the Presidential blessings of Governor James Coleman.

In 1958 Governor Coleman again endorsed Kennedy for the Presidency. "The South likes Kennedy," he declared at the Southern Governors' Conference.

And judging from what others were saying about Kennedy at the Conference, the Associated Press reported: "You would think that he was Dixie-born, a descendant of Robert E. Lee, and a man who eats hominy grits and corn pone three times a day."

On one of his by-now regular appearances on "Meet the Press," Kennedy was asked how it was possible to "be for civil rights and integration and yet win the support of Governor Coleman."

"I think you would have to ask Governor Coleman that—if he said that," Kennedy replied. "I hope that what is meant is that he feels I am a responsible member of the Senate and meet my responsibilities. How he squares it, I think you would have to ask him."

But May Craig would not settle for that answer. She reminded Kennedy that Coleman had specifically endorsed him as his personal choice for President. "That is what he said," she insisted.

"If he said that—there is no doubt what I said," Kennedy declared, hesitantly. "I appreciate Governor Coleman saying that."

Even before the year was out, Democratic strategists were taking a good, hard look at Kennedy as a candidate who might relieve them of the headache of a possible Southern walkout in 1960 and the loss of some of the 128 electoral votes toward which they hold a proprietary feeling.

Moreover, there was a growing belief in party circles that Kennedy's religion could be a plus factor in luring back to the fold many of the big city Catholics who had defected to Eisenhower. The *Washington Star*'s David Koonce reported at the time: "Many Democrats feel that the late Senator McCarthy appealed to many Roman Catholics in such a way as to transfer great numbers of them to the Republican party. With a Boston Catholic heading the Democratic ticket, it is reasoned that these voters will return to the Democratic fold."

Not all Democrats were happy about the enormous and seemingly organized publicity Kennedy was then obtaining. The Senator's aides claimed the Senator had no need for any organized publicity efforts. They said the magazines were falling all over themselves seeking exclusive stories by and about Kennedy.

"What am I supposed to do when the magazines come to me for stories —drive them away?" Kennedy asked a friend. *Look* magazine had just published a Kennedy profile which reported "an old habit of taking five or six baths daily makes him perhaps Washington's cleanest legislator."

Kennedy was likewise "hot" on television, with panel shows constantly seeking him as a guest. And scarcely a day went by without some columnist devoting precious newsprint to speculation about the Senator and 1960.

Many a "dope" story was published about a possible Kennedy-Nixon "battle of youth" for the White House, particularly after Kennedy himself assessed the then Vice President as "a tough, skillful, shrewd opponent," one who—as the probable 1960 GOP nominee—would be "far from being the pushover as many Democrats smugly expect."

In a March 1957 *Life* article, Kennedy wrote that he would not propose any names of possible Democrats to oppose Nixon. "Their identity," he said, "is less important than their capacity for wise, progressive, responsible leadership." Thus he identified himself with attributes which few men in public life, of whatever political persuasion, would hesitate to claim for themselves.

Kennedy's nationwide exposure was also being aided by televised proceedings of the Senate Rackets Investigating Committee, of which he was a member and brother Bobby chief counsel.

Working as a "brother act," they cashed in on the enormous publicity accruing from the probings into labor union skullduggery. A host of labor statesmen, including Dave Beck and James Hoffa, were paraded before the klieg lights. They were invariably treated with snarling contempt by Bobby while Jack, from time to time, would voice appropriate comments regarding the wages of sin.

The Kennedy brothers were thus creating for themselves the image of young crusaders courageously combating evil.

And behind the "brother act," operating quietly but effectively, was Joseph P. Kennedy with his unlimited resources.

The objective of the unprecedented publicity build-up for Jack Kennedy, as his father explained to Thomas G. [Tommy the Cork] Corcoran, was to make his son "known to everybody in the country." So that, he added, by the time of the 1960 Convention "there won't be a place in America where he isn't familiar."

An old hand in the motion picture business, the Ambassador had great faith in the uses of press-agentry. In fact, he fancied himself as quite an expert in the field of influencing public opinion with ballyhoo. After all, as he often told friends, he had had considerable experience in "bamboozling" moviegoers into viewing many a "turkey" which he himself had produced.

So pleased was Joseph Kennedy by the publicity efforts in behalf of his son that in 1959 he was able to assure Martin and Plaut that "Jack is the greatest attraction in the country today."

"I'll tell you how to sell more 'books,'" he continued. "Just put Jack's picture on a magazine cover. Why is it that when his picture is on the cover of *Life* or *Redbook* that they will sell a record number of copies?"

The old showman knew what he was talking about. Jack Kennedy had, indeed, become the subject of more magazine articles than all his rivals in both parties combined.

Moreover, a promised appearance of the Senator anywhere almost always guaranteed a sell-out crowd. And he was speaking almost everywhere.

Billed to address the Social Science Foundation of the University of Denver, he discovered that the meeting had to be switched to larger halls twice. Finally, an enthusiastic throng of eight thousand (considerably more than had turned out for Stevenson in 1956) jammed Denver's City Auditorium.

"I don't think the crowds are listening to what he's saying," a Capitol Hill observer said. "But they all go wild over him."

The soundness of this observation was clear to anyone who had watched the reactions of a Kennedy audience or had noted the gleam in the eyes of coeds, bobby-soxers, or waitresses as they patiently waited for the Senator's autograph.

"The effect he has on women voters is almost naughty," was the way James Reston sagely commented on the phenomenon in the *New York Times*.

This was not entirely lost on Kennedy, who would freqently note that "there are two million more women than men eligible to vote in this country" —a statistic no ambitious politician could possibly ignore.

For sheer endurance, Kennedy's explorations through the grass roots must have set some sort of record. Clearly he was seeking to exploit a situation in which no Democratic aspirant had a clear advantage, and he was trying to do it early. If the polls were any indication, he was indeed profiting from a lack of major competition.

Accompanying Kennedy on one of his trips in October 1958, James Reston reported from Parkersburg, West Virginia, as follows: "He looked a little self-conscious today riding down the main street of Parkersburg in a scarlet Cadillac convertible with his attractive young wife. Somehow he seemed out of place in a parade with a Democratic donkey and the Parkersburg High School band, especially since few people on main street seemed to know who he was or what the noise was all about."

Less indifferent, however, were the Democratic workers who turned out en masse, to hear a young man being billed as the fastest runner in the party stable.

Not that Kennedy told them anything particularly new or arresting. "He remembered all the names of the state and local candidates on the platform," Reston reported, "and concentrated somewhat wistfully on the good old days when, as he saw it, we used to have leadership in the White House. His main target was not President Eisenhower but Vice President Nixon, whom he scorned at every opportunity. . . ."

But this was, primarily, an exercise in exhibiting the Kennedy personality. "He made his points with an assurance he did not have two years ago," Reston noted. "He hits hard on foreign policy and labor, which he knows best, lacing his speech with learned quotations from Shakespeare, Justice Holmes, Woodrow Wilson and the Founding Fathers."

In short, the effect was that of "a serious and personable young man with a fresh personality."

Joseph P. Kennedy put it this way: "You advertise the fact that Jack will be at a dinner and you will break all records for attendance. He can draw more people to a fund-raising dinner than Cary Grant or Jimmy Stewart. Why is that? It's because Jack has more universal appeal. That is why the Democratic party is going to nominate him. The party leaders around the country realize that to win they have to nominate him."

In comparing Jack with the movie stars, Joe Kennedy put his finger on what was probably the most significant aspect of his son's campaigning. He is probably the only candidate who ever sought the Presidency of the United States—the world's highest elective office—not primarily as a political thinker or doer, but as a glamorous celebrity.

Change

11

In the Spring of 1957 John Kennedy invited several officials of the American Farm Bureau Federation to an urgent meeting in his office. Kennedy came to the point quickly.

"I am going to leave you," he said.

And he was going to leave them for a very good reason—he had decided to "go after the farm vote." Much to his regret, he said, he had learned he could not get it by continuing to back the Federation's conservative policies.

"I'm afraid I have no alternative," the Senator added.

When someone later remarked that it all sounded like a burlesque of a politician switching his position, one Federation official disagreed.

"It was not a burlesque," he told *Fortune*'s John Osborne. "It was a ballet. It was that precise."

Needless to say, the ability to change one's position to confront "political realities" is not uncommon among politicians. But what made the episode somewhat ludicrous was that it occurred shortly after the Junior Senator, in his article in *Life*, had warned his fellow Democrats against continuing their traditional practice of making "special appeals—to the farm vote, the Negro vote, the veterans' vote and all the rest."

"There is," Kennedy had written, "something in our platform or legislative record for everyone (no doubt, if we could, we would devise some inducement for the 'suburban vote'—subsidized commuters' cars or tax-exempt lawn mowers).[1]

"We plot Presidential campaigns in the same way, not in terms of national issues and trends but in terms of so many Southern electoral votes, so many farm states, so many labor areas, and so on and on. The temptation to gain power by wooing or misleading each supposed bloc of voters is very great indeed. Example: The secret of one well-known Governor's success, I was recently told, is that 'the poor think he is a friend of the poor—and the rich know he is not.' "

Kennedy's "adaptability" was extraordinary in that inevitably it encompassed the entire legislative horizon. And, not surprisingly, his shifts in voting behavior were to be hailed as signs of "growth" by Liberal pundits ranging from Arthur Schlesinger Jr. to Drew Pearson. Thus Pearson was to write as follows: "If you trace the Kennedy growth line you will find that in the past Jack has wanted to please both sides. He has straddled. This is not unusual in a young politician. It's especially understandable when a young Senator has been pushed forward both as a boy and as a public servant by an aggressive, wealthy father who has become an economic royalist. . . . However, what you have to watch in a young politician is his growth line. And Kennedy's growth line is good. It has become firm and courageous. The vacillations have been ironed out. And it has consistently followed a left-of-center direction."

The assumption that a politician's "growth line" depends on whether it follows a "left-of-center direction" is one which also permeates Arthur Schlesinger's curious little campaign book.

Equally significant was Schlesinger's thesis that before being bitten by the White House bug, Kennedy had not made full use of his intelligence. That's what Schlesinger said; and he said it this way: "For a long time, however, Kennedy's intelligence was underemployed. . . . At Harvard, he seemed a light and agreeable figure; then, toward the end of his college career, he began to come to life intellectually."

After the war came politics, and "as a Kennedy, he had to do better than anyone else. But it all seemed rather a game, in which one tried hard to win but avoided taking it all too seriously."

Why this "slight tinge of unreality," in Schlesinger's words, in Kennedy's early career?

"Perhaps," he wrote, "it was connected with the illnesses that had assailed him since the war; perhaps he felt that his life might be short and he had better enjoy it while he could." (An intriguing passage, indeed, but one which surely raises the question as to just what point in his career John F. Kennedy should be taken seriously.)

---

[1] Ironically, the 1960 Democratic platform, on which Kennedy conducted his Presidential campaign, contained pledges to every conceivable pressure group, including the promise to help "transport suburban commuters to and from their jobs."

Even after entering the Senate, according to Schlesinger, Kennedy was "still rather an unformed man . . . bright and quick, but he had not resolved the problem of his own style, his own identity."

Generally speaking, it could be considered a sign of immaturity when a man in his late thirties has not yet found himself; most men, nearing forty, are fairly well-formed with styles and identities of their own.

Schlesinger then recalled the series of operations which Kennedy had undergone: "From the moment he knew he was sure to live, ambition, I imagine, took over from enjoyment, and he decided that he could be President of the United States. Like Roosevelt's polio, Kennedy's nearly fatal sickness of 1955 no doubt accelerated his private crisis of identity. Like Roosevelt, he emerged more focused, more purposeful, more formidable. He began to convey an impression of personal weight and authority."[2]

Kennedy's "intelligence now had a goal," continued Schlesinger. "For the first time it swung into full action."

The "goal," of course, was the White House. And the Kennedy "intelligence" really began to swing when he began to comprehend—and accept—the inescapable logic, the verity, and the brilliance of the thesis that the nation had become abandoned to shameful public squalor amidst vulgar private opulence.

Thus it was argued that Kennedy began to fully employ his "intelligence" only when he began to accept the notions propounded by Arthur Schlesinger Jr. and John Kenneth Galbraith. As Schlesinger put it: "The convergence of intelligence and ambition gave Kennedy an increasingly coherent political philosophy."

Admittedly, the character of Kennedy's mind "is less scholarly than Wilson's, less bold and adventurous than Franklin Roosevelt's, less rich and reflective than Adlai Stevenson's."

But it nevertheless had qualities of its own. "His intelligence is sharp, analytical, practical and unfettered," insisted Schlesinger. "He thinks constantly in terms of problems and is willing to consider anything that promises a secure solution. This determined his approach to the Presidency."

In the lexicon of more mundane politicians, this would mean that Kennedy was on the lookout for "issues" or "gimmicks" with which to set himself off from others scrambling for the White House.

Finally, Kennedy found a big issue. According to Schlesinger, he decided to hit out at "the discrepancy between our national potential and our national performance—between the amplitude of wealth and talent and

[2] Apparently, in Schlesinger's eyes, "ambition" becomes a crime only in relation to Richard Nixon. Though Schlesinger conceded he did not know Nixon, he freely described the then Vice President as unprincipled, opportunist, and lacking in basic convictions. He refused to concede that Nixon could ever change. In his view, only Kennedy could change—and always for the better.

resources, on the one hand, and our lagging positions in economic growth, defense, education, social welfare, on the other."

And how was this discrepancy to be overcome?

It all goes back "to the question of Presidential leadership." Kennedy had come to believe that what was necessary "was some means of steering more of our national abundance into the things that build the economic and military and moral power of the nation—and that means could only be affirmative government directed by a strong President."

How Kennedy specifically intended to go about doing all this was not disclosed. All Schlesinger would say was that Kennedy would make a "strong President." Exactly what was meant by a "strong President" was not disclosed, either. But it certainly sounded good; which, in political terms, is probably all that really matters.

Schlesinger's revelations about Kennedy's "inner life" boil down to this: First, Kennedy determined he could win the Presidency. And then he decided to espouse the thesis that the United States—and, for that matter, the whole world—needed remaking to suit the esthetic tastes and economic predilections of Professors Schlesinger and Galbraith.

Thus are Liberals made, or—in the case of Jack Kennedy—created.

How accurately did Schlesinger depict the intellectual development of John F. Kennedy? And how "increasingly coherent" was Kennedy's "political philosophy"?

"I don't have an organized philosophy of life," Kennedy told Joan Younger of the Ladies' Home Journal in early 1960. "I just have my family and my work. I subscribe to the Greek idea of the 'full use of your powers along the ideas of excellence,' and I love politics. Other ways of living to me are challenge without substance—the way to function is by doing. Politics has for me what every other work has, and then some: it's interesting, worth-while, useful, a means of doing things of tremendous importance."[3]

It was a candid explanation and one which should have—but hadn't —raised some questions. Failure to have developed some "organized philosophy of life," at the age of forty-three, was a startling admission from a man seeking to become President of the United States. Even his phraseology was questionable: Greek ideals are only remotely applicable to the present and "doing things of tremendous importance" is a goal to intrigue any schoolboy.

After saying, in effect, that he had found in politics, as in no other pursuit, a purely selfish happiness, Kennedy told Miss Younger: "And in politics the center of action is the Presidency. The force of events, our increasing population, our position in the world all make it so. Right now, running for the Presidency demands an exacting course and a great effort; it's a tough, high climb. But, well—"

---

[3] Kennedy had made similar comments in talks with Bob Hartmann of the Los Angeles Times and Douglass Cater of the Reporter.

Kennedy broke off and smiled—"that smile of his," Miss Younger explained, "with its disarming mixture of confidence and modesty." The end of his sentence did not need to be spelled out: Jack Kennedy thought that a chance at the Presidency was worth all the effort he could muster.

Kennedy took the same line when interviewed by Henry Brandon of London's *Sunday Times*.

"First," he said, when asked why he was seeking the Presidency, "there was an open field and, therefore, there was the opportunity. . . . The most important part, of course, is that it's quite obvious that the Presidency has become the key office."

After talking to Senator Kennedy at length, Bob Hartmann put it this way, "Why, at 42, must he scramble so hard and fast to the highest peak of U.S. power and prestige? His reason is really very simple.

"As the mountaineer said of Mt. Everest: 'Because it's there.' "

John F. Kennedy sought the Presidency, therefore, because—having gone as high as he could in the Senate—he was irresistibly impelled to climb the Mt. Everest of politics. He wanted to become President, not because he had things in mind which only the Chief Executive could accomplish (the Schlesinger thesis), but because the Presidency was agreeable for its own sake.

By his own admission the Presidency appeared to be essentially a source of private gratification.

Availability for the Presidency, however, entails much more than a willingness to run. The only requirements laid down by the Constitution are simple and easily met—that the candidate have attained thirty-five years of age and have been born into citizenship. Unwritten rules are much more demanding.

"A fundamental is that the candidate reflect the mood of the times," *Baltimore Sun* columnist Thomas O'Neill observed on Kennedy's fortieth birthday, May 29, 1957, "and here Senator Kennedy appears well qualified. His moderate liberalism and lack of any impassioned urge for change appear to coincide closely with the general popular temper."

When asked in November 1957 whether he considered himself a Liberal or a Conservative, Kennedy replied, "I'll stick to being a Democrat." Then, he added quickly, "I don't think I've ever been identified with the more extreme wing."

A month later, he said, "An independent position is the only place for me. I'm a Northern Democrat who has some sense of restraint."

So restrained was he, in fact, that a *Time* cover story of December 2, 1957, described him as "in many aspects, a conservative." Moreover, Kennedy had indicated his concern that 1960 could bring a rejuvenation of the Liberals in the Democratic party.

"In a militantly liberal Convention," he said quite frankly, "I wouldn't have a ghost of a chance."

This was the period when Kennedy was protesting vigorously at being linked with such fellow Senators as Paul Douglas, Herbert Lehman, Wayne Morse, and Hubert Humphrey. They were much too Liberal for him.

And he particularly squirmed when Americans for Democratic Action gave him a high Liberal rating. The ADA stamp of approval may have been good politics in the North; but in the South it could mean the kiss of death.

This was the time when Kennedy was carrying on a torrid love affair with Dixie or—as the *News and Courier* of Charleston, South Carolina, put it—when "the decidedly junior Senator from Massachusetts was practicing saying you-all while a commencement speaker at Southern universities. . . ."

The newspaper conceded on October 21, 1957, that Kennedy "is refreshing in some ways—at least he doesn't look like a typical big city politician and he isn't a clown like Estes Kefauver. Despite these assets, we can't buy the line that Senator Kennedy is a nice fella who is just crazy about Dixie."

The editorial quoted columnist Raymond Moley as having noted that "in the selection of test votes on which the collectivist Americans for Democratic Action classified members of Congress, Kennedy had voted their way twelve of fourteen times. By way of comparison, Senator Saltonstall, also of Massachusetts, pleased the ADA only four of fourteen times."

"In short," Moley had summed up, "the record indicates that the Senator may qualify as one whom many conservatives will believe to be conservative, but whom 'Liberals' will know to be otherwise.

"A perfect political setting for the great adventure."

Kennedy was particularly concerned about what he insisted were Moley's misinterpretations of "the tenor of my voting record as a whole." His response, as published in the *News and Courier,* is definitely worth quoting:

"I myself was surprised that the ADA rated me so highly and that they approved 12 out of the 14 votes that they had rated all senators on. When I secured a copy of this 'Voting Record,' I found that my high score was not particularly radical, and in fact, I lagged behind Senators Douglas, Humphrey, Lehman, Morse, Neuberger, McNamara, Neely, Hennings, Murray, Pastore, Kefauver, Gore, Jackson and Laird and achieved the same rating as Senate Majority Leader Lyndon Johnson, President Pro Tempore Carl Hayden, and such other senators as Kerr, Symington, Green, O'Mahoney, Mansfield, Magnuson, Monroney, Clements, Wiley and Langer—hardly a group of 'radicals.'

"I would point out that my record on the issues was identical to that of Lyndon Johnson, except on the natural gas and 90 per cent farm price support bills, where we each voted the needs of our respective sections.

"In explaining the reason for so many high marks being received by Democratic senators and some Republicans who are not generally thought of as being in the ADA 'camp' I would suggest that the issues selected are the key. For instance, Sen. Bridges and I voted against a cut in military assistance abroad without knowledge that the ADA would label that a 'right vote,' just as we did on the Soboloff nomination. I voted with Sen. Byrd on the natural gas and atomic energy roll calls, followed the lead of ranking Finance Committee member Walter George on two social security amendments, and agreed with Dick Russell and most members of my party on two power project votes, all of which were cited in this list.

"In short, I cannot find any of my 12 votes approved by the ADA to be in any way radical or inconsistent with the philosophical position I have always tried to occupy—that of a moderate Democrat who seeks on every issue to follow the national interest, as his conscience directs him to see it."

All of which hardly bears out the romanticized Schlesinger legend of a Kennedy—bold and unafraid—seeking "an affirmative government dominated by intelligence and vision and dedicated to abolishing the terrifying discrepancy between the American performance and the American possibility."

A more conscientious effort to stick to the facts—unpalatable as some may have been—was made by James MacGregor Burns, whose balanced assessment of Kennedy's ideological development was not greeted with noticeable enthusiasm in the Kennedy camp. The semi-official biography, in fact, questioned the depth of Kennedy's commitment to what Liberals consider their holy causes.[4]

A major Burns' thesis is that the closer Kennedy got to 1960 the more he swung to Liberal positions espoused by those who wielded the decisive power as far as getting the nomination was concerned: "Scrutiny of Kennedy's positions in the last several years shows that he does stand in the center of the Wilson-Roosevelt-Truman tradition, defined as embracing both economic welfare and civil liberties. Some contended that this was a shift mainly for political expediency as he came nearer to a national campaign. . . . It was significant that by 1958 and 1959 Kennedy was consistently supporting the liberal Democratic position on welfare issues and on civil liberties and civil rights."

Thus Kennedy, who in the early Fifties had been publicly decrying "the all-absorbing hands of the great leviathan—the state," began more and more to advocate statism as the solution for the ills of the nation.

In so doing, however, he suffered no emotional upheaval. It was almost like changing shirts. As Schlesinger put it, Kennedy "is not particularly committed by spontaneous visceral reactions in the usual pattern of American liberals. He is committed rather by intellectual analysis. . . ."

Or as Kennedy himself once explained: "Some people have their liberalism 'made' by the time they reach their late twenties. I didn't. I was caught

---

[4] Schlesinger's change of address in 1961—from Irving Street, Cambridge, Massachusetts, to 1600 Pennsylvania Avenue, Washington, D.C.—would indicate that his campaign efforts were not displeasing to the movers and shakers of the New Frontier. As of this writing, however, Professor Burns is still teaching political science at Williams College.

in crosscurrents and eddies. It was only later that I got into the stream of things."

Having been struck by "the somewhat emotionless quality" of Kennedy's liberalism, the *New York Post's* Irwin Ross once asked the Senator about it. For a reply, Kennedy went back to the start of his political career.

"In 1946," he said, "I really knew nothing about these things. I had no background particularly; in my family we were interested not so much in the ideas of politics as in the mechanics of the whole process. Then I found myself in Congress representing the poorest district in Massachusetts. Naturally, the interests of my constituents led me to take the liberal line; all the pressures converged toward that end."

By his own account, therefore, Kennedy was interested in the mechanics of political power—and how to obtain it—long before he became aware of "the ideas of politics." The record, moreover, would indicate that his later interest in "the ideas of politics," or issues, was largely manipulative.

But while Kennedy was becoming increasingly down-the-line Liberal, he still sought to keep some ties with the Conservatives. He continued to pay frequent homage to the memory of the late Robert A. Taft. And his admiration (if that was what it really was) for "Mister Republican" was spelled out in one of the essays in *Profiles in Courage.*

Conservatives liked Kennedy's style. "As a Republican," wrote an Armonk, New York, man to the *New York Herald Tribune* in March 1957, "I should like to express my admiration and respect for the very able Democratic Senator from Massachusetts, John F. Kennedy. . . . The fact that he is a moderate in his views toward the important issues should in no wise harm his prospects."

Conservatives were also impressed by the fact that a Special Senate Committee, headed by Kennedy, had selected Robert A. Taft as one of the five all-time Senatorial greats whose portraits were to be hung in the Senate reception room.

This was, incidentally, the type of assignment that Kennedy liked best, one which reaped considerable publicity without getting overly embroiled in partisan controversy.

After considerable hoopla, which firmly established Kennedy with historical good works, his committee also selected Henry Clay, Daniel Webster, John C. Calhoun, and Robert M. La Follette.

The naming of Taft did not escape criticism by a few partisan souls who argued that "Mister Republican" had been too Republican. The resultant tempest-in-a-teacup fitted Kennedy's purposes well. A conservative journalist, writing in the *American Mercury,* reported that "Kennedy's open admiration for the great Ohioan came as some sort of a shock to leftists who had been seeking to portray him as a full-fledged Liberal."

Just how sincere was Kennedy's widely publicized admiration of Taft?

One is entitled to ask because of a review Kennedy was to write for the

Washington Post of an anti-McCarthy book. As the *Reporter's* Douglass Cater noted, Kennedy's "main criticism was directed not at McCarthy but at Senator Taft for his cynical strategy in handling the Communist issue."

And how sincere was Kennedy's well publicized espousal of the federal housekeeping reforms recommended by the Hoover Commission?

According to biographer Burns, it was "a political device to keep some ties with the right wing generally and with Southerners in his own party." (After taking office in 1961 President Kennedy, whom Herbert Hoover had once called "my favorite Senator," made it quite clear to his predecessor that he had other, more pressing, things to worry about than following through on the Hoover recommendations.)

In the *American Mercury* of March 1957, Russell Turner compared Kennedy with Richard Nixon: "Nixon probably is basically a moderate conservative but with some liberal tendencies. Kennedy is basically a moderate liberal, but with many conservative leanings. Neither is an extremist in any sense."

In fact, Turner glowingly dubbed Kennedy the "Democratic counterpart" of Nixon.

This, then, was the image which Kennedy was at the time assiduously seeking, with what Turner aptly described as the Senator's "highly cultivated sense of public relations and an ability to get along with newsmen."

Thus, when Kennedy flew to Lincoln, Nebraska, to attend a university convocation and a party dinner in May 1957, the local newspaper observed:

"Nebraskans apparently liked what they saw in the tousle-haired, unassuming young man. This was in spite of some rather natural handicaps he might bring to the conservative Mid-West: he is identified as a 'liberal' and an internationalist; his farm policy views differ from those of Nebraska Democrats; he is a Roman Catholic and he is young."

But the newspaper added: "So it might be deduced that if Kennedy is acceptable in Nebraska, he could be a big hit in most of the rest of the nation."

No wonder then that the title of the *American Mercury* article was: "Senator Kennedy: The Perfect Politician."

Why

12

How did it happen that a comparatively young man with comparatively few achievements had become—overnight—a leading contender for the highest elective office in the free world?

The question intrigued political observers as they watched the "Golden Boy of Back Bay"—as Kennedy was dubbed by one writer—steadily pull out ahead in the Presidential sweepstakes.

There appeared to be no rhyme or reason for the phenomenon. Washington correspondent Fletcher Knebel, for example, termed the whole thing a "mystery."

In the *Nation*, Robert Spivack made note of the not unimportant fact that in all his years in both houses of Congress, Kennedy "had yet to get out front on any big issue." In all those years his name never appeared on any major legislation enacted into law. And he had rarely, if ever, participated in any great debates. His greatest legislative success had been in sparking the fight against Electoral College reforms which would have limited the power of minority groups in Northern big cities. (Had those reforms gone through, Kennedy might not have been elected President.) Though well-liked and respected, as juniors go, Kennedy was never invited into the charmed "inner club" of born-to-the-toga Senators.

All in all, as his critics were wont to observe, there was little in Kennedy's record to qualify him for treatment in *Profiles in Courage*.

Kennedy's good friend, Rowland Evans Jr. of the *New York Herald*

Tribune, also pondered the phenomenon. On August 9, 1959, he wrote as follows: "Name your own private Presidential choice, other than Kennedy, and you can quickly find a logical reason why he *should* be a candidate in the customs and habits of American politics. A Nixon, for example, because he is already Vice President; a Johnson, because he has had a conspicuous success in running the Senate for six years; a Stevenson, because if twice before, why not once more; a Rockefeller, because almost all Governors of New York always are automatically Presidential candidates; a Humphrey, because he wears the cloak of the New and Fair Deal, and a Symington, because none of the powerful satrapies in the Democratic party have any real reason to veto him."

But why Kennedy? Why were the public opinion polls, without exception, showing the Junior Senator from Massachusetts to be the overwhelming favorite of Democratic voters in state after state?

"Kennedy's secret weapon is really no secret at all to anyone who has brushed elbows with him," reported Evans, in a rare emotional outburst. "His personality is simply the most magnetic, the most appealing, of any politician in business today with the single exception of Dwight Eisenhower. And Senator Kennedy's secret weapon is his personality. He exudes charm without half trying and it bathes his audience in a warm glow."

And that's how Presidential candidates are born.

Handsome, charming, magnetic, and appealing John Kennedy most certainly was. In Rowland Evans' almost classic phrase, Kennedy was "the only authentic poll-fed Presidential candidate in history."

Kennedy was something else: he was a TV personality able to project what Madison Avenue calls a "warm image." As analyzed by Harold H. Martin in the *Saturday Evening Post:* "Kennedy's greatest political asset seems to be an intangible, an indefinable charm, a warmth which makes voters feel instinctively that whatever they believe in, he believes in too. He has the same power to project his personality, friends point out, that Roosevelt had, and that Eisenhower has, though the image created is different. Roosevelt was the brave and confident warrior, standing between his people and all the horrors of depression and war. Eisenhower is the wise and kindly father. Kennedy is the clean-cut, smiling American boy, trustworthy, loyal, brave, clean and reverent, boldly facing up to the challenges of the Atomic Age."

But there is also considerable evidence that the Kennedy personality, far from possessing the "warmth" to which Harold Martin alluded, was actually cold, self-interested and, in Max Lerner's word, calculating:

Item: "The bright charm is only skin deep; underneath there is a core of steel—metallic, sometimes cold, sometimes unbending, unusually durable," commented James MacGregor Burns. ". . . Actually he is a serious, driven man—about as casual as a cash register."

Item: "He's beautifully disciplined," a noted newsman was quoted by the *Ladies' Home Journal* of March 1960. "Behind that generous smile is a cool, calculating machine that is constantly saying, 'What's in it for me?' "

Item: "A liberal Senator who has worked closely with John Kennedy, and who is not unsympathetic to him, has described him as a 'pretty cold fish,' " wrote Max Lerner in April 1960. "His boyish winsome smile, which is somewhat disarming, comes not out of warmth but of shyness."

Item: "Kennedy is turning out to be a tough and clever operator," reported the *Washington Post*'s Chalmers Roberts in January 1960. "He seems to have missed no bets thus far. Already some of his supporters are saying that in the honeymoon period of his Presidency he will be as tough as FDR ever was in using patronage and pressure to work his will with Congress."

Thus we have a curious phenomenon in the Age of Television: a candidate who was a "clever operator," a "pretty cold fish," as "casual as a cash register," who nevertheless projected a "warm image" over TV and who, if elected, would be chosen by the voters very largely because they judged him to be a warm personality.

The unemotional nature of Kennedy's makeup was no secret among his colleagues. One prominent Democratic Senator, discussing candidates with the *Reporter*'s Douglass Cater in 1959, praised his younger colleague's "maturity" and "independent judgement." But then, clasping a hand over his heart, he voiced misgivings. "Let me put it this way," the Senator told Cater. "If my dear old mother were to fall and break her leg, Hubert Humphrey would cry, but I'm not so sure about Jack."

The truth is that Kennedy has never been seen—even by his mother—in raging anger or uncontrollable tears. "He does not lose himself in laughter," commented James MacGregor Burns. "He dislikes emotional scenes at home or at work. . . . He has apparently never lost himself in a passionate, unrestrained love affair."

And neither, it could have been added, has he ever lost himself in a passionate, unrestrained political feud—even with Richard Nixon. Asked by Irwin Ross in 1956 what he thought of the then Vice President, Kennedy replied, "I'd rather not say. Of course, if I were running, I'd have to discuss his fitness to hold office. But I don't want to say anything now."

The reason for the reticence was clear to Ross: Kennedy got along very well with Nixon personally, as he strove to do with almost everyone.

"I don't believe in personal feuds," Kennedy added. "In politics there is no percentage in them."

The key to an understanding of John F. Kennedy lies in the much-used word "image"—the impression he has sought to make on the public.

"His clothes and hair-do are a masterpiece of contrived casualness," James Reston observed in October 1958. The operating word here, of course, is "contrived."

"There is a streak of vanity in Kennedy," *Newsweek* reported in July 1960. "He carries a white manicurist's pencil to make his fingernails whiter.

His suits are custom-made, and he wouldn't think of showing up at a night session of the Senate in the same suit he wore during the day."

A serious man, needless to say, would not have been so chronically troubled about his appearance. Repeatedly, in his confidences to friendly newsmen he would observe that his youthfulness was at once his thorn and his triumph.

"Jack is the only guy I know who says, 'I am *almost* forty-three,' " a close friend told Martin and Plaut.

The age matter gave rise to a story that Joseph P. Kennedy was worried about what his son would do after eight years in the White House when he will have attained the age of fifty-one.

Obviously, Kennedy's oedipoid charms did him no harm among the ladies. "Here is Everywoman's son, and perhaps her lover. . . ." wrote James Wechsler in a rare perceptive mood.[1] "His boyishness invites protection and solicitude; it is he who needs Mama, now considered a very important personage at the polls."

"What he says and does evokes far less interest than his unmistakable assets as charm boy," Wechsler added. "Kennedy's mingled intelligence and lack of visceral responses are the important things about him; but they rarely figure in public discussion about him. His hair-do (shall he wear it long or short?) appears to invite more debate than the state of his eggheadness."

A Kennedy haircut had become virtually an affair of state. "Without the wistful forelock dangling over his right eyebrow," the AP reported in 1957, "his appeal to women might suffer."

Kennedy's Capitol Hill barber, David Highley, was well aware of his profession's responsibility in maintaining the best-known forelock in United States politics. Determining just how much to snip from the front ("enough but not too much") had become not only a weekly ritual but a major command decision.

"We've got to give prominence to the Senator's trademark," Highley explained.

The accent on youth cut two ways. If it appealed to younger voters, it definitely troubled older people. Kennedy was aware of the sentiment, "I can't see anyone as young as Kennedy sitting down with Khrushchev at the conference table."

In reply, Kennedy would point out that Theodore Roosevelt had become President at the age of forty-two,[2] that Washington took command of the

---

[1] *Reflections of an Angry Middle-Aged Editor,* by James A. Wechsler. New York, Random House, 1959.

[2] Teddy Roosevelt, as Vice President, succeeded to the Presidency following the assassination of President McKinley. However, no man had been elected to the Presidency at an age younger than Ulysses S. Grant's forty-six—though several younger men had tried.

Continental Army at forty-three, and that Thomas Jefferson drafted the Declaration of Independence when he was thirty-three.

"Sam Rayburn may think I'm young," Kennedy once complained to Georgetown neighbor Charles Bartlett, of the *Chattanooga Times.* "But then most of the population looks young to a man who's 78."

Kennedy, nevertheless, overlooked nothing in his efforts to reduce the age problem.

At one time he seriously considered the suggestion that he wear a vest in order to look older. "He even wonders aloud," reported Martin and Plaut, "whether his wife Jacqueline is really a political asset because she is so young and so lovely."

Rarely, in American history, has there been a political leader so obsessed and self-conscious about the figure he cut in public.

Rarely, too, has there been a figure in American history who pursued the Presidential nomination with such single-minded devotion for nearly four years.

"He's always in a hurry," his wife once gasped in her soft, breathless voice.

But was he in too much of a hurry?

Some of his advisers thought he had gone too far too quickly and that, as a result, his liabilities would inevitably catch up with his assets. They urged him to slow down, observing that front-runners have a habit of wearying in the stretch.

"When you're out front," they said, "everyone is shooting at you."

Kennedy disagreed. He said it was possible to get so far out front his enemies couldn't hit him. He felt he had certain political handicaps that could only be overcome by a fast start and a bold campaign to appeal to the voters themselves.

"To run early and hard is the only way I know," he explained.

This had been the strategy employed in his first Congressional race in 1946; and in his contest against Henry Cabot Lodge six years later.

It was Kennedy's hope that the more publicity he obtained as a front-runner, the more the voters would become accustomed to attributes that otherwise may have been considered drawbacks. In 1958 Adlai Stevenson was quoted as saying Kennedy had three strikes against him for President: "He's young, rich and Roman Catholic." A Kennedy aide explained to the *Wall Street Journal,* "People get to realize that he doesn't think as young as he looks, that he doesn't wear a bishop's hat, that he doesn't have greenbacks sprouting from his ears."

"Finally," wrote Robert Hartmann in the *Los Angeles Times,* "and this compounds his other problems, there is Mrs. Kennedy. She is also too young, too rich and too beautiful—not in a classic way but with the exotic elfin features of a high fashion model. Those who know Jackie Kennedy like her very much. But to strangers she is visibly bored by campaigning, no match at politics for the practiced partners of Johnson, Humphrey, Nixon and Symington. Besides, there is the baby to be looked after in their cozy Georgetown home."

His father's wealth was proving to be a mixed blessing. The feeling was widespread that Jack was the creature of a strong-willed, multi-millionaire father, that he was playing Trilby to Old Joe's Svengali. As a result, he was forever denying his father was an influence.

Before long, stories began circulating that the Senator had long had political differences with his father, that Jack had a mind of his own and that he really was a sort of intellectual idealist whose notions of the nation's welfare were markedly different from those of Joseph P. Kennedy.

Nevertheless, the Kennedy camp continued to have difficulties in allaying doubts. These doubts, according to Selig Harrison's June 27, 1960, piece in the *New Republic,* arose "from the fact that a command post of [Jack's] political operations over the years has been Joe Kennedy's office in the Kennedy owned building at 230 Park Avenue. One can only imagine how many open-dated blank checks have been given to strategically-placed individuals and interests to help Kennedy get where he is. How many of these checks, if any, would call for repayment by Kennedy as President, no one can foretell."

When the Burns biography was published, the story made the rounds that Joseph P. Kennedy had raised Cain with the publishers because of the jacket photo of his son. "The Senator says this is a typical example of how dad gets blamed for everything," reported Chalmers Roberts in the *Washington Post.* "In fact, it was the Senator who objected because the photo was an eight-year-old one. As everyone knows, Kennedy's youth is one of the political hurdles he faces and a man does age in eight years, even between 34 and 42."

Not that Joseph P. Kennedy wasn't also sensitive about his son's youthful appearance.

"I got into hot water with his father who accused me of saying that Jack looked too young on TV," recalled James A. Farley. "I didn't say that. What I said was that I thought that many people might not vote for him because *they* thought he looked too young on TV."

"You can't be too careful about what you say," the former Postmaster General added.

Widespread concern was being expressed about the degree of Kennedy's dependence on his fabulously rich father. "All the Convention delegates money can buy" went one wisecrack.

Since money was never a problem in his life, Kennedy has never had to worry about where it was coming from; it was always there. Consequently, he has had little or no experience in dealing with or handling money. This is no reflection on Kennedy; it is merely a fact.

In the *Ladies' Home Journal* of March 1960, Joan Younger reported this piece of dialogue:

"Could you move that flowering tree, please," Jack Kennedy said to his caretaker. "I'd like to see it easily from the breakfast-room window."

"Well," said the caretaker, "it would cost a mint."

"I didn't ask you what it would cost," replied Jack. "I'd like it moved."

Parade magazine in 1957 reported this story: "Jack was taking a friend to lunch at an ultra-swank New York restaurant. When he went to sign the check, the waiter whispered something in his ear. Shortly Jack told his guest: 'Dad's cut off my signing privileges here. Do you mind taking care of it?' "

Kennedy's vague attitude toward money was something that frequently startled acquaintances. "He takes money so much for granted," Irwin Ross noted in 1956, "that he often forgets to put a few bills in his pocket."

William Sutton, a 1960 Boston campaign aide, vouched for this. "There'd be six or seven of us at a lunchroom," Sutton said, "and even if the bill was only a couple of bucks he wouldn't have it with him. I'll never forget the time he gave the Archbishop a big check—a million dollars or so—for the Joseph P. Kennedy Jr. Foundation. Four of us went over in a cab and we had to throw in seventy-five cents apiece to pay the cabby."

Many was the time in his bachelor days, when Kennedy would take a girl to a swank restaurant, only to confront an empty wallet when the time came to pay the check. If he was not known in the place, either the girl would advance him the money or he would start phoning friends to come to his rescue.

Ted Reardon, a Kennedy aide, told Ross of the time his boss, heading for Detroit, arrived at the Washington airport with an empty wallet. Reardon loaned him his travel card, which Kennedy used to purchase a plane ticket. Later, he used it to rent an automobile in Detroit, signing the bill as "T. J. Reardon, Jr."

"On the way back," wrote Ross, "he had trouble buying his ticket, for an alert ticket agent saw that he was incapable of duplicating Reardon's signature. But Kennedy insisted that he was Reardon, that he worked for a Representative Kennedy, and that they could check on his identity by phoning the Congressman in Washington. He finally got the ticket, and arrived at the Washington airport in a triumphant state."

For Kennedy it had been a minor triumph in *One-upmanship*.

Like all the Kennedy children, Jack had his money problems handled by their father's New York office at 230 Park Avenue. "Having them use this office means that they never have to bother about managing their money," a staff member said in 1957. A team of experts on taxes, investments, and accounting took care of everything for the Kennedys—their taxes, credit cards, even buying their homes.

The headquarters of patriarch Kennedy's vast financial empire also served as a clearing house for the location of family cars, passports, and servants. If a cook would quit in a huff, which happened occasionally, the crisis was duly noted and handled by the office.

The same office was headquarters for the Joseph P. Kennedy Jr. Foundation, set up by the elder Kennedy in 1945 in memory of his eldest son. Many millions of tax-exempt dollars were given away over the years. In the first few years of its existence, Jack Kennedy acted as its president. Most of the money went to Catholic charities, with a percentage for Jewish and Protestant needy. "Some Catholics believe that through the foundation," reported *McCall's* Eleanor Harris, "Joseph Kennedy is their greatest individual American benefactor."

Whether Jack Kennedy's constant dependence on his father's money was accompanied by an emotional dependence was a question raised by such episodes as his flight to see his father following his 1956 Convention defeat. It was no secret that the closeness of their relationship was the subject of considerable speculation among leading Democrats. The feeling was that, what with the Ambassador's controversial past, it could well erupt into an unappetizing campaign issue. And his activities were continuing to cause controversy.

For example, on November 12, 1959, a New York State Supreme Court Justice described one of the Ambassador's real estate deals (conducted in the name of the family) as "greedy." But Justice William C. Hecht Jr. ruled in the Kennedys' favor, conceding that the family was entitled to receive $2.4 million for a building condemned to make way for New York City's Lincoln Center for the Performing Arts—a building which the Kennedys had estimated under oath to be worth only $1.1 million. Though the $1.1 million had not represented true worth, according to Justice Hecht, he held that the court could not deprive the owners of a fair price simply "because they were greedy enough to try to pay less than their fair share of taxes." The $1.3 million windfall, which fell into the Kennedy pockets, was made up by public funds.

"I confess to being skeptical about your father's influence over you," Drew Pearson told Kennedy.

"Well," Kennedy said, "Father wants me to be President all right. He tells everyone that I'm going to be President. But as far as influencing me, I think my voting record in the Senate speaks for itself. He and I have disagreed on foreign policy and domestic issues for many years, but always very amicably."

Such disagreements would presuppose there had been discussions. But not necessarily.

"As a matter of fact," Kennedy told Robert Hartmann of the *Los Angeles Times,* "we never really discuss those kind of questions—I don't remember ever talking with him or arguing about these matters."

This troubled Hartmann so much that he posed this question for his readers: "Well, if not about foreign or domestic policies, what do the Kennedys talk about if Father has the most political influence on his son? It seemed indelicate to ask Kennedy, but the answer must be: How to become President of the United States."

On another occasion, Kennedy was asked whether his father's "pride in a son who might become President" might not be "greater than his desire to see him agree with his own ideas."

"No," Kennedy told Henry Brandon, "I think it's merely that he feels he has a large family, that they should determine their own lives and make their own decisions. His responsibility is not to impose his political views on his children. It makes a much more successful and lasting relationship, I think, when a parent does not."

Which may not have been entirely responsive to the question.

The truth is that Joseph P. Kennedy was devoting most of his waking moments to carrying out his life-long ambition: The Presidency for a Kennedy. The Presidency, to him, was the Holy Grail. Consequently, he was not as much interested in getting conservative ideas across to his son as in getting him elected. Ideas, in themselves, were only of importance if they could help win the White House.

And in pushing Jack along the upward road Joe Kennedy would spare no expense where expense appeared justified.

"Without the benefit of a tremendous fortune," Drew Pearson observed, "Senator Kennedy, with all his charm and all his drive, would not be Democratic front-runner for President today."

True enough. But Kennedy had something else going for him. He had a superb sense of public relations. Thus he managed to convert his book *Profiles in Courage* into a substantial political asset. Though not much more than a collection of *Reader's Digest*-type anecdotes about Senatorial courage, the book was instantaneously successful. Kennedy kept plowing back his royalties into its promotion with the result that just about every major newspaper carried advertisements linking the handsome Senatorial profile with the word "courage."

And through repetitive use of the word "courage" in his speeches, Kennedy also hoped his listeners would get the point. Another gambit was his frequent reference to Abraham Lincoln who, needless to say, possessed great courage. "Abraham Lincoln had courage and the next President of the United States will need courage," said Senator Kennedy. And, of course, everyone knew who had written that book on courage and, therefore, might know something about it.

Just what did all this have to do with assuring "that government of the people, by the people, for the people, shall not perish from the earth?"

Was there ever a figure in American history who opened his campaign for the Presidency by talking about the need to "act in the image of Abraham Lincoln?" How one acts in the "image" of anyone Kennedy did not say; but his use of the word, in itself, was revelatory.

Was there ever any political leader who devoted so much time to worrying about his hair-do or whether his wife was—or was not—a political asset because she was so young and pretty?

Or was there ever anyone who, in seeking the Vice Presidency, would issue a broadside describing himself as "the most videogenic personality of our times, says the *New York Times* . . ."?

Preoccupied with appearances rather than with realities, Jack Kennedy epitomizes mid-century man. Obsessed with how he appears to others, he resists identification with issues, but he is responsive to national states of mind. If it is a McCarthyite period, he is prudently pro-McCarthy; if an anti-McCarthy period comes along, then he is prudently anti-McCarthy.

Roosevelt, Hoover, La Follette, Truman, Eisenhower, or Taft—their names immediately evoke a political philosophy. As for Kennedy, no coherent viewpoint comes to mind.

Compare him with other Democrats of recent vintage—with Adlai Stevenson, Hubert Humphrey, Lyndon Johnson, Thomas Dodd, Stuart Symington, Paul Douglas, James Eastland, and Orval Faubus. These names, for better or worse, call forth distinctive personal attitudes toward national policy. Kennedy's name evokes no substantive position. He has been all things to all men. He was described in the Burns biography as "an ambitious, hard-working politician, acting in terms of the immediate situation rather than on general and deeply rooted principles, and hence operating in a moral vacuum."

In the *New Leader* of March 7, 1960, Konrad Kellen described Kennedy as a "synthetic" man. "I once had the pleasure of meeting him briefly, and I mean pleasure," Kellen wrote. "He has everything. He is as irresistible as Rex Harrison, as poised as George Sanders, as suave as John Barrymore and as tough as George Raft. . . . Can you visualize him issuing instructions to a Henry Stimson, George Marshall, Harold Ickes, or to yourself? I can't. . . . Nixon, however, is a man in his own right. No father, mother, brother or sister finances his campaigns or runs around the country for him; no million-dollar trust fund is ready for him if he gets licked. . . . Of course some rich men have become President, for example F.D.R. But F.D.R. was an entirely different type who, by transcending his origins, made people forget that he was a wealthy aristocrat, which is the last thing Kennedy has done."

According to Burns, Kennedy was aware that one of his main problems was the widespread feeling that he was "a political playboy, bright but superficial, energetic but incapable of following through, a compromiser who avoided the tough issues."

He was even compared with one of his PT-boats, darting around, closing in on a target to unloose a torpedo, zigzagging evasively, and disappearing into the darkness.

As Kennedy himself once told an interviewer, he was "so inhibited by all the pressures" in the Senate that he was "not very much good to anybody." Things, however, were different in the House of Representatives where, he said, he had been "independent" and even "brash."

This was a remarkable piece of self-analysis coming from the author of *Profiles in Courage,* a book about highly individualistic Senators who, refusing to bow to pressures, "spoke and voted their convictions irrespective of the temper of the times."

Significantly, virtually all of Kennedy's heroes had paid the price for their courage: they rose no higher than the Senate and some of them lost whatever offices they held. Robert A. Taft, for example, failed to obtain a Presidential nomination largely because the Ohioan lacked what Kennedy described as "the politician's natural instinct to avoid controversial positions and issues."

It was a natural instinct which Kennedy possessed in abundance.

While courage was to be admired, Kennedy took the line that it had to be tempered with compromise. During the 1957 row over civil rights, Kennedy urged a group of teen-agers to learn to compromise "because it is compromise that holds the union together."[3]

At Harvard University, where he was awarded an honorary degree as a "son of Harvard," "brave officer," and an "able Senator who remains steadfast to principle," Kennedy suggested there are occasions when a politician, in order to stay alive politically, is forced to compromise on principles.

In his speech, he drew a significant distinction between the goals of politics and education: while educators seek the "advancement of knowledge and the dissemination of truth," politicians "are interested, of necessity, in winning popular support—a majority; and only indirectly is truth the object of our controversy."

The politician, he added, "is resentful of the scholar who can, with dexterity, slip from position to position without dragging the anchor of public opinion."

Resentful or envious?

Kennedy began to complain about the problems confronting a Senator with White House ambitions.

"The Senate," he said, "is not a good place to pick a Presidential candidate because a Senator must take a stand on controversial issues."

Only one man, in fact, had gone to the White House from the Senate. And, as Kennedy noted, easy-going Warren G. Harding was never really involved in hotly contested issues.

"No matter how you vote," added Kennedy, "somebody is made happy and somebody unhappy. If you vote against enough people, you are dead politically. If you vote for everybody—in favor of every appropriation but against every tax to pay for it—you might as well be dead politically, because you are useless."

This could help explain the apparent note of envy that crept into Kennedy's article in *Life* when he observed that the probable 1960 GOP Presidential nominee, Richard Nixon, would have "four years in the spotlight without being required as his competitors in both parties will be, to go on record (except in rare cases) on controversial issues."

---

[3] "Flashing a dazzling white smile," according to the *Washington Daily News* of July 2, 1957, Kennedy also told some two thousand boys attending the Key Club International Convention that "many of you seated here today are the Dwight Eisenhowers of the future."

It was almost as if Kennedy were saying it just wasn't fair.

The *Life* article attempted a "penetrating reappraisal" of the Democratic party, outlining what, in Kennedy's opinion, the party needed to do to recapture national supremacy from the Republicans.

Calling for "new ideas, new policies and new faces," Kennedy warned his fellow Democrats against living on the glories of the past. (Of which, the *New York Post* wryly commented: "As Mr. Coolidge once observed, it is also unmistakably clear that the future is ahead of us.")

Decrying "the evasion of controversial issues," Kennedy also called for an end to "straight-from-the-shoulder platitudes" on such subjects as civil rights.

Yet the net effect of the article was one of sheer evasion.

In essence, the article was a call for moderation. Kennedy thus aligned himself with the Democratic leadership in Congress—Senate Majority Leader Lyndon Johnson and House Speaker Sam Rayburn, the usually middle-way Texans. Specifically, he expressed sorrow over the quarrel between Congressional Democrats and the National Committee's establishment of a Democratic Advisory Council. He took the position that while there was no harm in Democratic governors, mayors, state legislators, and elder statesmen advising on legislation, the responsibility for shaping party policy must belong to the Congressional leaders.

But, as one who had joined Johnson and Rayburn in declining to serve on the Advisory Council, Kennedy failed to emphasize one other aspect of the controversy. The principal purpose of the Council was to formulate Liberal legislation on the theory that the future of the party as a national power lay in a sharp swing to the left. It was this concept that Johnson, Rayburn & Company were having no immediate part of.

Basically, what Kennedy sought to achieve in his *Life* article was the elaborate feat of contending that the grave issues dividing his party had to be boldly confronted without giving offense to any Democrat, living or dead. Thus, this single paragraph:

". . . the responsibility for the party's actual record on national issues falls primarily upon the Democrats in Congress under the leadership of Senate Majority Leader Johnson who—though perhaps not always pleasing to all the extremes of left and right—represent the most effective consensus on most issues of our multi-interest, multi-sectional party. It is up to us in Congress, despite the restrictions imposed by the compromises necessary to keep our party intact, and despite the possibility of fighting losing battles, to push forward a progressive program any Democratic candidate can run on with pride and hope."

The *New York Post* lashed into the article as "a drab rhetorical device to call for a forthright program limited only by political expediency." Kennedy was pictured as impersonating "a prematurely elder statesman who wants to grow up to be Lyndon Johnson."

"Such double-talk," the *Post* continued, "if voiced by a Democratic politician in the twilight of his life, might seem understandable. . . . But it sounds pathetically spiritless when voiced by a rising young Democrat who purports to speak for a new generation of Democrats."

Kennedy had noted that the first Democratic reaction to the 1956 defeat "was to search for old scapegoats instead of new leadership." In the even-handed spirit he then was affecting, the Junior Senator reproached those who were blaming the defeat on *either* Senator Eastland or Adam Clayton Powell or on *either* the Dixiecrats or the ADA-ers—"everyone in fact but Dwight D. Eisenhower."

"These false equations," commented the *Post,* "are the ancient refuge of cautious politicians. . . . There is no honorable compromise between Jim Eastland and those who believe in the cause of civil rights, any more than there was an honorable compromise between Joe McCarthy and those who believed in the cause of civil liberties."

Though the *Post* was eventually to change its tune, "personal advance-ment . . . through slick accommodation" was to remain the yardstick by which to judge John Kennedy. In fact, he was to obtain the *Post*'s support for the Presidency precisely because he was willing to accommodate himself —rhetorically, at least—to its Far-Left-of-Center views.

Appeasing the ultra-Liberals was to prove one of Kennedy's most notable achievements on his road to power. For they have managed to develop what, in the final analysis, amounts to a collective veto over any Democratic Presidential aspirant. Without their approval he might just as well have re-mained at Hyannis Port.

With great ingenuity he developed a record that had something in it for everyone. But on the key issues his position was one of carefully contrived contradictions.

On one issue, however, Kennedy failed to satisfy anyone—Liberal or Conservative. That issue was *McCarthyism.*

Mac

13

The trouble with writing a book like *Profiles in Courage* was that it opened up the whole subject of Kennedy's own courage. The Old Testament wish that "mine adversary had written a book" was granted his critics. And it created the quick quip that refused to die: that Kennedy should show less profile and more courage. It was a bon mot widely attributed to, among others, Lyndon Johnson and Eleanor Roosevelt—everyone in fact but Dorothy Parker. And its repetition irritated Kennedy. He began to complain that critics like Mrs. Roosevelt insisted on weighing him on scales they did not apply to others.

The Kennedy book made literary history. A Pulitzer prize topped off glowing reviews. Since reviews generally are written in a vacuum, it was not too surprising that, except for the non-conforming likes of a Murray Kempton, few of the critics commented on its Walter Mitty aspects.

"For," as Kempton noted, "during the period of its conception, poor Jack Kennedy had a moral test and he failed it badly."

The test was over *McCarthyism*. And how Kennedy faced this test demonstrated much about his character, integrity, responsiveness, and—as Eleanor Roosevelt put it—his "convictions," and—as Westbrook Pegler put it—his "moral courage." Or as Arthur Schlesinger Jr. put it, "Kennedy's misfortune was that, by writing the book, he invited particular attention to his own circumspection in the McCarthy period."

But the test was also one for Arthur Schlesinger Jr. and his fellow Liberals. And most of them failed it as badly as did Jack Kennedy.

For among Liberals, the one thing that had long separated the *good guys* from the *bad guys* was the issue posed by the Senator from Wisconsin. To the Schlesingers *et al.* this was the unbridgeable gulf. Anyone who refused to make known his unequivocal hatred of *McCarthyism,* or to speak of the "unspeakable" McCarthy in any terms other than those of total abuse, was automatically declared *persona non grata.*

There could be no exceptions.

Yet an exception was made in the case of Jack Kennedy, even though he refused to utter the ritualistic phrases condemning *McCarthyism.*

And in making the exception, the Liberals brought into question their own principles. For they themselves had made the narrow issue of *McCarthyism* a holy cause, one which divided truth from falsehood, right from wrong, honor from dishonor.

Some of Kennedy's more vocal supporters, with total disregard for the morality implicit in their rules, even composed apologetics in Kennedy's behalf, slinging opprobrium at those benighted souls who dared question the Senator's Liberal credentials.

Arthur Schlesinger Jr., for example, denounced efforts to saddle Kennedy with *McCarthyism* as "a prime example of dirty play."

Yet he himself conceded, "Kennedy's record on McCarthy, as I told him at the time, seemed to be discreditable." Nor was he willing to buy the argument that an aggressive anti-McCarthy policy would have backfired among Kennedy's Roman Catholic constituents.

"John Kennedy was in a uniquely strong position to oppose McCarthy," said Schlesinger.

"When one condemns his silence, however, several other points should be made. For one thing, very few Senators, including very few of the liberal Senators spoke up against McCarthy in 1950–53."

Nevertheless, Kennedy was the Senator who was running for President. And he was the fellow who wrote that book on political courage.

What, therefore, is the explanation for the willingness of so many McCarthy-obsessed Liberals to swallow Kennedy and even to go all-out to put him into the White House?

Perhaps the answer can be found in the historic words uttered by Arthur Schlesinger Jr. in Harvard Yard in March 1960. James Reston had come to inquire why so many of the Cambridge intelligentsia had suddenly decided in their nonconforming way that Adlai Stevenson—their hope for deliverance in two previous campaigns—would make a fine Secretary of State.

"I guess I'm nostalgically for Stevenson, ideologically for Humphrey, and realistically for Kennedy," said Schlesinger, who quickly added that he would gladly work for "any two-legged liberal mammal who might beat Nixon."

And there you have it: the Liberal demonologists sought to exorcise the very evil spirits they had themselves unloosed. The Liberals—or some of them—had come to believe their own myths about Richard Nixon. In other words, they were quite willing to swallow John Kennedy—*McCarthyism* and others of his faults—in the name of realism and of beating Nixon at all costs.

But why were the Liberals so emotionally—and, at times, so irrationally —opposed to Nixon in the first place?

The usual reason given was Nixon's conduct in the 1950 Senate race against Helen Gahagan Douglas in California. It was indeed a rough campaign on both sides; but not as rough as the myth-makers have made it out to be, particularly when compared with Kennedy's tactics against Hubert Humphrey in the 1960 Presidential primaries.[1]

Assuming the most horrendous version of the Nixon-Douglas contest to be true, why did Schlesinger, in his campaign book, so magnanimously concede that *l'affaire* Douglas was perhaps not "germane to whether [Nixon] should be elected President?"

Was it because Jack Kennedy had made a substantial contribution to Nixon in the 1950 campaign?

Or was it because Kennedy had announced at Harvard how "personally happy" he was that Mrs. Douglas had been defeated by Nixon because, as he then put it, she was "not the sort of person I like working with on committees?"

Of course, as Murray Kempton has put it, Kennedy has always been a bit of a "snob." He was always much more at home with "Father's friends at Palm Beach" than with the kind of people who look askance when asked to dress for dinner.

For example, what is one to make of Kennedy's curious attitude toward his favorite whipping-boy James R. Hoffa? As a Senator, he once explained his attitude toward the labor leader: "Anyone who gets that kind of power who has no discrimination or taste or style is a menace." Are we to interpret this as meaning that Hoffa is a "menace" not because of his "power," but because he "has no discrimination or taste or style . . ."? Surely these are esthetic judgments, not ethical ones.

And how are we to interpret Kennedy's cutting remarks about Helen Gahagan Douglas? Not even an esthete from Hyannis Port could have possibly believed that Mrs. Douglas, a vivacious, well-groomed former actress, lacked discrimination, taste or style. Was it because she was too much of a "bleeding heart," too involved in "causes" to suit his taste? This, of course, was the period when Kennedy didn't feel "comfortable" in the presence of ADA people.

Needless to say, the Kennedy forces did exploit the Douglas episode to capitalize on the Nixonphobia deeply imbedded in the Liberal community. As Konrad Kellen had written in the *New Leader,* the Liberal attitude toward Nixon was "actually very similar to the attitude that Republicans had toward F.D.R.: When the subject of Nixon is brought up, they foam at the mouth, stammer, roll their eyes and having nothing really relevant to say." This "toxic and emasculating effect on their opponents" was produced "mainly because

---

[1] A reasonable presentation of the Nixon-Douglas contest can be found in Earl Mazo's biography *Richard Nixon.* New York, Harper, 1959.

their mere existence reduced their opponents to raging political infants" and was "of an entirely different order than that of the ordinary politician."

This was noted at the height of the 1960 Presidential campaign by Harold G. Tipton, who had been Helen Gahagan Douglas' 1950 campaign manager. In a privately published pamphlet,[2] Tipton noted that "Liberal voters, without whom the Democrats can't win, are being enticed into voting for Kennedy by ultra-Liberal Kennedy pronouncements and by the exploitation of their natural and long-standing horror of the idea of Richard Nixon in the White House."

"Where are Kennedy's real sympathies?" Tipton asked.

"I submit that no man who could applaud Nixon's defeat of Mrs. Douglas—as Kennedy publicly did—was a liberal in 1950. I submit that no Congressman whose closest Congressional cronies were, for years, George Smathers, reactionary Southern Democrat, and John Lodge, conservative Connecticut Republican, was a liberal. . . ."

It was Tipton's contention that Kennedy was practicing *McCarthyism* long before Senator McCarthy established his own practice.

As a young Congressman he had flailed the Truman Administration for the "sell-out" of China to the Communists. He had demanded that the White House "search out and spotlight" those responsible for the tragedy, "the diplomats and their advisers." And he himself spotlighted Professors Owen Lattimore and John K. Fairbank.[3] This was a year before Senator McCarthy mentioned the gentlemen's names and also demanded their roles in the China debacle be probed.

Despite Liberal opposition, Kennedy supported without criticism the activities and contempt citations of the much-abused House Un-American Activities Committee. And he voted consistently for all legislation aimed at the Communist conspiracy.

In 1950 he voted against statehood for Hawaii. The chief opposition had come from House members who contended that Hawaii was in the grip of Harry Bridges and the Communists.

In 1950, too, Kennedy voted for the McCarran Internal Security Act which called for the registration of Communist groups, tightened-up espionage and subversive laws, authorized internment of subversives in time of war, etc. Then he voted to override its veto by President Truman who called the bill "a terrible mistake" and "the greatest danger to free speech, press and assembly since the Alien and Sedition Acts of 1798."[4]

[2] *One Liberal's Answer: Nix on Kennedy,* by Harold G. Tipton. Seattle, 1960.

[3] Professor Fairbank of Harvard is related by marriage to Arthur Schlesinger Jr. They married sisters.

[4] Because Kennedy had voted to override Truman's veto, and because Justice Felix Frankfurter finally upheld it, Murray Kempton on February 15, 1962, suggested that "in fairness to all parties, it should henceforth be described as the McCarran-Frankfurter-Kennedy Law."

This was the period, of course, in which John F. Kennedy won minor fame as a Red-baiting witch hunter. In 1952, in fact, he appealed to the pro-McCarthy element in seeking election to the Senate. Senator McCarthy co-operated. By staying out of the Bay State in that race, McCarthy (the recipient of a substantial campaign contribution from Joe Kennedy) undoubtedly helped elect Kennedy. At least, that is what the elder Kennedy told Westbrook Pegler. As Pegler put it later:

"Kennedy found no fault with McCarthy's 'methods' then. Joe stayed out [of Boston] after personal request by Jack's father, so that McCarthy would not pull Irish Catholic votes over to Republican Lodge. But after Kennedy was elected Senator he never opened his trap on McCarthyism until Mrs. F.D.R. twisted his arm in 1959. Then he ratted on McCarthy. How do you like that profile in moral courage?"

Senator McCarthy, a most convivial soul, had been on friendly terms with the entire Kennedy family. He was a frequent visitor to Hyannis Port, where in more recent years Kennedy has entertained such Liberal worthies as Arthur Schlesinger Jr. and John Kenneth Galbraith.

And who could ever forget the spectacle of Senators Kennedy and McCarthy playing croquet on the lawn overlooking the Atlantic?

These days it takes a long reach of memory to recall that Robert F. Kennedy first came to national attention as a lawyer on McCarthy's staff. One can only speculate on what turn history might have taken had Bobby remained one of McCarthy's aides. Fortunately for Kennedy, Bobby resigned from the McCarthy Committee in mid-1953. He resigned not because of any distaste for McCarthy or his methods, but because of an intense personal feud with Chief Counsel Roy Cohn. The Kennedys, of course, are famous for decisions on the basis of personal feuds.

The younger Kennedy, after graduating from the University of Virginia Law School, took a job in 1951 in the Justice Department's criminal division and plunged into the ultimately unsuccessful prosecution of Owen Lattimore. At the Senator's invitation he joined the McCarthy Committee.

His chores included the investigation of homosexuals in the State Department and a somewhat more celebrated probe into relations between foreign shipping firms and the Chinese Communists. The latter investigation led to McCarthy's announcement that he, as Committee Chairman, had "negotiated" an "agreement" with Greek shipping interests to deprive Communist nations of vital goods shipments. The episode led to a well publicized blowup with President Eisenhower.

Refusing to play second fiddle to Roy Cohn, Bobby Kennedy resigned. In a letter accepting the resignation with great regrets, McCarthy told Bobby that he had "been a great credit to the committee and had done a tremendous job."

In 1954, after working several months for the Hoover Commission, Bobby Kennedy returned to the McCarthy Committee as counsel to the

Democratic minority. He was on hand during the televised Army-McCarthy hearings, at which time he had a celebrated run-in with Roy Cohn, almost coming to blows in front of the TV cameras.

Though it is a memory which he now would eagerly efface, the fact is Bobby was an impassioned McCarthyite. So much so that once he walked out of a dinner of the United States Junior Chamber of Commerce rather than listen to Edward R. Murrow deliver the major oration. This was in 1955 when Bobby was named by the Chamber as one of the ten outstanding young Americans of the year. Only after the TV personality concluded did Bobby return to his seat, telling all within earshot he had no use for the blankety-blank Murrow, after what he had done to his good friend Joe McCarthy.

McCarthy's best friend in the family was the head of the clan, Joseph P. Kennedy, to whom—unlike his sons—the claims of friendship invariably took precedence over caution.

"In case there is any question in your mind," he told one interviewer, "I liked Joe McCarthy. I always liked him. I would see him when I went down to Washington, and when he was visiting in Palm Beach he'd come around to my house for a drink. I invited him to Cape Cod."

Why had he liked McCarthy?

"He was always pleasant; he was never a crab," replied the Ambassador. "If somebody was against him, he never tried to cut his heart out. He never said that anybody was a stinker. He was a pleasant fellow. He went out on my boat one day and he almost drowned swimming behind it, but he never complained."

As he began to talk about the final, bleak days of Joe McCarthy and his sudden death, according to the interviewer, the senior Kennedy's eyes "clouded and his voice wavered."

"I thought he'd be a sensation," he said. "He was smart. But he went off the deep end."

Though not as close as those of his father, Jack Kennedy's relations with McCarthy were friendly. In 1950 he had stated at Harvard he "rather respected Joe McCarthy" and thought he "knew Joe pretty well, and he may have something."

A political scientist who heard these remarks later described Kennedy as "an ambitious and likable young politico on the rise," but one who viewed *McCarthyism* with "nonchalance and minimal concern."

"It appeared to me," the political scientist told biographer Burns, "that he quite sincerely thought the problem of rent control was considerably more important [because of his constituency] and more worthy of his attention than was this rather abstruse and philosophical concern which was so exercising us intellectuals."

The fact is that Kennedy, at first, didn't see anything particularly wrong with *McCarthyism*. He couldn't quite understand what the Liberals were screaming about. To him the interminable anti-McCarthy jihad was largely a waste of time. The whole continuing ruction was making a mountain out of what he regarded as a molehill.

To Kennedy, McCarthy was no "menace" to American institutions; rather he had become simply an unpleasant colleague who not only refused to conform to predominant sentiment, but just didn't know how to get along.

Shortly after he entered the Senate, Kennedy was asked what he thought of McCarthy. "Not very much," he replied. "But I get along with him. When I was in the House, I used to get along with [Vito] Marcantonio and with [John] Rankin. As long as they don't step in my way, I don't want to get into personal fights." (Marcantonio, of course, was the loud-mouthed pro-Communist from New York; and Rankin, Mississippi's foul-mouthed racist.)

"You must understand," Kennedy told Irwin Ross in 1956, "that I had never known the sort of people who were called before the McCarthy committee. I agree that many of them were seriously mishandled, but they all represented a different world to me. What I mean is, I did not identify with them, and so I didn't get as worked up as other liberals did."

Accordingly, he did not "identify with" or get "worked up" about James Wechsler when the *New York Post* editor was hauled before McCarthy to be questioned about some books he had written as a young Communist in the Thirties. About the only thing McCarthy accomplished with this ploy was that rather improbable feat: he smeared Wechsler.

Though the forces of Liberal righteousness protested mightily, the voice of John F. Kennedy, as usual, was silent. And his silence, in the minds of many Liberals, including Wechsler, was construed as assent.

As Ronald W. May, co-author of an anti-McCarthy book, was to put it: "The Congressional Record shows that during those years Kennedy sat in the House, later the Senate, and heard attacks on Democrats as the party of treason, on liberals in both parties, on national leaders such as General George Marshall and on constitutional freedoms. But Kennedy was not aroused to defend these men and principles."

By 1954 it was obvious that the McCarthy issue would be put to a test in the Senate. This would mean a test for the Junior Senator from Massachusetts. How would he react?

The folks back home, both pro- and anti-McCarthy, waited with almost bated breath. One morning during this period, Murray Kempton observed Kennedy as he watched "an especially wild flight of McCarthy as investigator." Kennedy's sole comment was "that it was all very interesting." He would say nothing more.

The mail from home had become heavier than usual. His constituents wanted to know just where he stood on *McCarthyism*. The *Boston Post* began raising hell too. The pro-McCarthy daily, which had supported him in 1952, warned Kennedy that he had better continue to play ball with McCarthy or else face political oblivion.

"Cleaning Communists out of Government is not a party matter," the paper declared. "If Senator Kennedy wants to maintain his political viability he ought to consult a few solid and loyal Democrats in Massachusetts who are every bit as determined to clean Communism out of Government as is Senator McCarthy."

Typically, Kennedy sought to straddle the issue. "I appreciate knowing of your support of Senator McCarthy," he wrote to a lady in Fitchburg. "I have always believed that we must be alert to the menace of Communism within our country as well as its advances on the international front. In so doing, however, we must be careful we maintain our traditional concern that in punishing the guilty we protect the innocent."

McCarthy's probe into trade with Red China had served a useful purpose, he informed a Boston newsman, adding that "other inquiries which have been reported in the press would not appear to have produced results of sufficient value to justify the bitter controversies raised by the methods employed."

"It is ironical," he told another newsman, "that one of the major disputes involves the Congressional investigative procedure. We can not inhibit or limit in any way the right of Congress to investigate, but I am willing to concede there have been some evils. We should hem in the procedure to protect the rights of witnesses and to guarantee them fair treatment." (This, of course, was the kind of equivocating statement to which no member of the Senate—not even McCarthy himself—could possibly have taken offense.)

Asked by an irate pro-McCarthy constituent to explain his "inconsistencies," Kennedy replied, almost plaintively, that "the storm that has swirled about Senator McCarthy's head has caused many level-headed individuals to become emotionally upset and violent pro and anti attitudes have been struck. . . ."

During the Army-McCarthy hearings Kennedy took the attitude that while it was important "to get an answer in the dispute," the imbroglio was overshadowing far more important events. He said the only man with no opinion on the controversy was "a mythical man."

But if Kennedy had an opinion he never voiced it.

Meanwhile, he was criticized back home for his small role in a maneuver aimed at embarrassing the Republicans on the Communist issue. This occurred in the closing hours of the Eighty-third Congress when Senator Hubert Humphrey, without warning, introduced legislation to outlaw the Communist party.

"It may be that Senators Humphrey and Kennedy, in promoting the amendment to outlaw the Communist party," editorialized the *Boston Herald,* "persuaded the voters that the Democratic party is not soft on Communism, but they added no luster to their liberalism thereby."

Professor Robert Braucher of Harvard Law School denounced "our own Senator Kennedy" for having joined "some 'Liberal' Democrats, the kind who are always shouting about the 'current hysteria,'" in promoting legislation that, in essence, was based on "an hysterical idea."

The McCarthy issue came to a head in July 1954 when Senator Ralph E. Flanders introduced a motion to censure the Wisconsin Senator for conduct unbecoming a United States Senator. In the ensuing stormy debate, Kennedy spoke only once; and that was to say he didn't think there were "adequate grounds for censure in the Annie Lee Moss case because of the questions" asked by McCarthy. But he did think some of the questions which Roy Cohn had asked the Negro woman (accused of Communist links) were not "adequately based."

The moment of truth came on December 2, 1954. That day the Senate voted to censure McCarthy. But Kennedy did not vote. He was in a New York hospital where he had undergone spinal surgery. The only other Senator unrecorded on the issue was Alexander Wiley, of Wisconsin, who had the excuse of protocol.

Nevertheless, Kennedy could have gone on record either for or against censure by pairing his vote with that of another absent colleague who held an opposite view. Even after returning to the Senate Kennedy refused to make known how he would have voted.

"I was out in the hospital about nine to ten months, and I had a bad year," he explained on TV in mid-1956. "Now, if you can give me back that year, I will be glad to tell you how I would have voted."

On another occasion Kennedy said, "If you are in a hospital, I suggest there are other things on your mind than following what is going on before some committee."

However, the record shows that on January 28, 1955, between operations, Kennedy was recorded as having paired on Senator Lehman's side when the New Yorker fought a losing battle to amend the Formosa Resolution by excluding Quemoy and Matsu.

"But," as Kennedy later told the *New Republic,* "I was following that in the *Times* and Lehman seemed to make sense."

To most Senators, Lehman did not make sense. His amendment was overwhelmingly beaten.

The claim that Kennedy was "unable to 'pair' against McCarthy" because he had been hospitalized was made in a column by Pete Edson.

The column drew the fire of Gardner Jackson, the labor lobbyist who had the celebrated run-in with Joseph Kennedy over *McCarthyism* during the 1952 campaign. In a letter to the *Washington Daily News,* Jackson made this point: "Though Kennedy was suffering a serious illness involving operative procedures, he was not in so grave a condition he could not have let his position be known on so grave a political-social question as censure of fellow-Senator McCarthy.

"It is interesting to note that he began work soon after this on his *Profiles in Courage* during the year of absence to which Mr. Edson refers."

Other critics also wondered why, if Kennedy was able to write a book, he could not have taken the trouble of recording his position on censure.

Drew Pearson went so far as to charge that the book had actually been ghost-written. But Pearson was forced to retract his allegation.

Several of Kennedy's friends, however, saw a connection between the writing of the book and his dilemma over McCarthy. "If he had a crisis of conscience over McCarthy [other friends dispute that he did]," wrote Irwin Ross, "the book may have been his way of resolving it."

In 1956 Kennedy was selected to address the annual ceremonies of the National Book Awards. This led Murray Kempton, then still unimpressed by the charms of "the most attractive young politician in Washington today," to ask why Kennedy was picked to keynote an event "which means nothing if it does not cry out that truth must lift its tiny voice in the clangor of slogans." There was something "obscene" about the spectacle of "having a politician come by to swing a little incense before a group of private citizens gathered to do honor to culture or liberty or any other abstraction of which the politician is a natural enemy."

"We ought to be accustomed by now to heroes whose acts have nothing to do with what they say," Kempton continued. "Our children must look to the dead for the vision of courage; the living cannot be expected to represent it. It is required of a man only that he celebrate the principle; he is not asked to suffer for it."

In a sense Kennedy did suffer because of his palpable unwillingness to come to grips with the McCarthy issue. It haunted him through the long years which, with single-minded determination, he devoted to obtaining the Presidency.

"Senator," he was asked by TV's Chet Huntley at the height of the 1960 campaign, "did you duck the McCarthy issue?"

"No," Kennedy replied, "I was in the hospital for a long time. I had indicated before I went to the hospital that I would support the censure."

But if Kennedy had so indicated *publicly,* the record fails to bear him out.

The record does demonstrate Kennedy's acute awareness of the enormous hold that Senator McCarthy had on many of his Massachusetts constituents.

"What was I supposed to do—commit hara-kiri?" he once asked.

"To understand my situation," he explained to Irwin Ross just before the Chicago Convention in 1956, "you must remember that my father was a friend of Joe's, as was my sister, Eunice, and my brother Bobby worked for him. So I had all those family pressures."

"Then," Kennedy added, "I frankly thought that McCarthy would eventually fade away." (In which case, presumably, Kennedy could have safely criticized McCarthy without fear of hara-kiri at the polls in 1958.)

Senator McCarthy died in May 1957. But as far as Kennedy was concerned, the controversy surrounding him failed to "fade away."

"How many Senators spoke out against McCarthy in states where it would have hurt them?" Kennedy asked.

Kennedy had begun to demonstrate an unseemly touchiness on the subject. Following a November 1957 broadcast he upbraided NBC's Martin Agronsky for having raised the issue. All Agronsky had asked was, "Would you, or would you not, have voted to censure Senator McCarthy?"

Obviously annoyed, Kennedy replied as follows: "I have pointed out on many occasions that I had been away from the Senate for nine months when that came up. I was not then a member of the jury. I would have been perfectly prepared if it came up in the summer of 1954; but it did not come up while I was in the Senate and I was not equipped for it when it did come up. It came up only three or four weeks after I was in the hospital. I have said since then, based on the evidence presented and upon Senator McCarthy's transgressions of the rules of the Senate, that I thought the censure was a reasonable action. I don't know what more I can say about it."

On another occasion Kennedy was rendered almost inarticulate when the subject arose. Kennedy was being interviewed by CBS's Walter Cronkite during the 1960 campaign. This is what the official transcript shows:

CRONKITE: Does the thing that used to come up occasionally about softness towards McCarthyism, does that bother you at all—personally?

KENNEDY: No, because I—[inaudible].

CRONKITE: This one rolls off?

KENNEDY: I've been against nearly every legislative act that came up, so I don't—but these things, they say everything about everybody. I just don't feel that, on the whole, I don't feel that I have been—the people make the judgment, and I have been fairly judged so far.

Kennedy first came to realize the potency of the issue in terms of his political future in 1956 when he sought the support of Eleanor Roosevelt for his Vice-Presidential bid.

Mrs. Roosevelt had advised the Kennedy family attorney James Landis, that the Senator "must stand up and be counted" on the issue. Landis argued vainly that the McCarthy business "is all a thing of the past" and should "have nothing to do with the present situation."

On August 14, 1956, the second day of the Democratic convention, Jack Kennedy called on Mrs. Roosevelt in Chicago. Memories differ on what transpired on that occasion. About the only agreement was that her Blackstone Hotel suite was a madhouse with phones ringing and Roosevelt children and friends all over the place.

"It was," Kennedy said, "like eighteen people in a telephone booth."

"I admit there was a lot of confusion," said Mrs. Roosevelt. "All I did was ask him one question: why he hadn't taken a stand on McCarthyism. And the answer he gave me just wasn't enough of an answer for me. . . ."

The next day, the *Washington Post* reported that "Kennedy found it difficult to placate her with the explanation he would make his position clear when the occasion presented itself. Mrs. Roosevelt suggested that he make the occasion himself and clear up the cloudiness."

A biography of Mrs. Roosevelt contains this dialogue:[5]

MRS. R: "I am concerned about your failure to have taken a position on McCarthy."

KENNEDY: "It was a political necessity in my Senate race not to speak out against him."

MRS. R: "It's been some time since you were elected."

KENNEDY: "Besides, it's a dead issue."

MRS. R: "The greatest Senators are not those who are most effective in getting bills passed, but those who have great convictions—like Herbert Lehman."

Kennedy's recollection was this: "She was giving what I said only half attention. . . . She was giving her views on McCarthy—not listening to what I was saying. My point to her was that, since I had never really been especially vigorous about McCarthy during his life, it would make me out to be a complete political prostitute to be champing and jumping to change, to denounce McCarthy when he was gone politically."

What Eleanor Roosevelt wanted from Kennedy was a public declaration of "the harm that *McCarthyism* did to our country and that he opposes it actively." This Kennedy refused to give. It had been an encounter neither would forget in coming years.

Nevertheless, following McCarthy's demise, Kennedy began to make faint attempts to do what he had told Mrs. Roosevelt he morally could not do.

In 1959 his office disclosed that back in July 1954 Kennedy had been prepared to make a speech discussing censure. His failure to do so was attributed to the fact that the censure resolution had been hurriedly referred to a Select Committee headed by Senator Arthur V. Watkins.

The undelivered speech was calculated to stir a minimum of resentment both in his family and in his state. It stated that "the issue involves neither the motives nor the sincerity of the Junior Senator from Wisconsin. . . . Many times I have voted with Senator McCarthy, for the full appropriation of funds for his Committee, for his amendment to reduce our assistance to nations trading with Communists, and on other matters. I have not sought to end his investigations of Communist subversion, nor is the pending measure related to either the desirability or continuation of those investigations. Nor

[5] *Mrs. R: The Life of Eleanor Roosevelt,* by Alfred Steinberg. New York, Putnam, 1958.

does this motion affect Senator McCarthy's Committee chairmanships or seat in the Senate. . . ."[6]

The undelivered speech sought to eliminate the rather broad charges that had been leveled against Joe McCarthy. Instead, it criticized Roy Cohn for having used abusive language toward Army personnel, and concluded with an expression of "severe disapproval of particular conduct permitted, if not encouraged, by a particular Senator."

This was a form of censure that would not have challenged the right of Kennedy's constituents to remain pro-McCarthy.

"But," as John Chamberlain observed in the *National Review,* "if all this leaves Kennedy personally in the clear as regards his own basic sincerity, he remains willing to accept the votes of both the pro-McCarthy Irish and the anti-McCarthy members of the Harvard University faculty."

Which, of course, is politics.

Kennedy's office also released a mimeographed statement, "Notes on the Record of Senator Kennedy on McCarthyism and Civil Liberties," in 1959. Cited as evidence of Kennedy's anti-McCarthyism were his votes against the confirmation of Scott McLeod and Robert E. Lee, and for the confirmation of Charles E. Bohlen and James B. Conant.

"On the secondary issues connected with McCarthyism," wrote Schlesinger, "Kennedy voted with regularity against the Wisconsin Senator. . . ."

According to Gardner Jackson, the argument was farfetched. "It is scarcely likely," he observed, "that the criteria uppermost in Kennedy's mind on each vote included as the foremost one what position McCarthy was taking on the particular set of issues underlying each case."

Actually, it took very little courage to vote for Charles Bohlen and James B. Conant. Their diplomatic posts were assured—over McCarthy's objections—when Majority Leader Robert A. Taft led the fight for their confirmation.

Ironically, Kennedy claimed to have voted against confirming McLeod and Lee because they were "McCarthy's pals."[7]

But another of "McCarthy's pals" was Robert F. Kennedy.

"I never said I was perfect," Kennedy told Martin and Plaut. "I've made the usual quota of mistakes. The Joe McCarthy thing? I was caught in a bad situation. My brother was working for Joe. I was against it. I didn't want him to work for Joe, but he wanted to. And how could I get up there and denounce Joe McCarthy when my own brother was working for him? So it wasn't so much a thing of political liability as it was a personal problem."

[6] In 1953 the ADA score card gave Kennedy a minus mark for having supported McCarthy's efforts to reduce economic assistance to those nations trading with Red China.

[7] Messrs. McLeod and Lee went on to serve their country with particular distinction—the former as United States Ambassador to Ireland and the latter as a member of the Federal Communications Commission.

In June 1959 the *Washington Post* announced that Kennedy had agreed to review Richard Rovere's antagonistic biography of the late Senator McCarthy. But for those Washingtonians who had expected a breast-baring *mea culpa* the review was decidedly disappointing.

"Once more the name of McCarthy will be on the lips of the cocktail circuit riders—and Senator McCarthy would have liked that," Kennedy began with a note of sarcasm. Though the nation had "recovered its health" from the "McCarthy contagion," Kennedy predicted that Rovere would receive the "usual stream of abusive, venomous letters from the still-vibrant cult of McCarthy admirers."

The incredible thing about the review, however, was that Kennedy directed his main fire not at McCarthy but at, of all people, Robert A. Taft. And he accomplished this feat by cautiously quoting Rovere to the effect that the Ohioan had adopted a cynical strategy in handling the Communist issue.

"In the light of later events," Kennedy wrote, "Taft's strategy . . . must surely be accounted one of the supreme blunders of American public life. The 'fallout' from this decision may continue to affect the atmosphere for the foreseeable future."

Taft, of course, was dead; he was not around to defend himself.

But he was the same Taft whose integrity Kennedy had eulogized in *Profiles in Courage.* In paying tribute to a spokesman of rather opposite views Kennedy quite obviously sought to impress conservatives with his broad-mindedness.

"I will no longer be sucked in by Senator Kennedy," Bazy McCormick Tankersley wrote in the *Chicago Tribune,* "when he praises someone I, too, respect because I will know that another day he may turn on him for a different audience."

Not unexpectedly, Kennedy came under attack by McCarthy sympathizers. But he weasled. "I am sorry that you disagree with my review . . . ," he wrote critics. "I assure you that my comments were directed solely at the merits of the book and the skill of the author. If you will read or reread the review, you will find that it does not make any attempt at any analysis of the complex McCarthy character. This would call for a considerably extended discussion and many expressions of personal opinion about the various aspects of Senator McCarthy's career."

The *Boston Globe* had requested permission to publish the review simultaneously with the *Washington Post.* But Kennedy's office refused, explaining that the review had been written for a Washington and not a Boston audience. How the audiences differed was not explained.

However, the review did appear in Boston. Waiting a day, the *Globe* published it as a front-page news story.

The *Chicago Tribune,* which in 1952 had described Kennedy as a "fighting conservative," now damned him as a "hypocrite." And it dubbed his review "eyewash," tailored to meet the requirements of the "Liberal" gospel. "It ought to satisfy even Mrs. Roosevelt, who once found it 'unforgivable' to think that Alger Hiss and Lauchlin Currie, one of her husband's White House assistants, might be Communists. Senator Jack, after due delay, has found it prudent to be nimble in his response to the demands of the orthodox 'liberal' dogma, but as a 'profile in courage,' he resembles a mess of squash, after it has been put through a sieve."

The editorial was entitled "A Profile in Pusillanimity."

Kennedy, however, was much too irked with Mrs. Roosevelt to try to appease her. That was to come later.

Mrs. Roosevelt had begun to sound the alarm about the dread possibility of Kennedy in the White House.

"White House decisions," she said in 1958, "should not be in the hands of someone who understands what courage is and admires it, but has not quite the independence to have it."

The coolness between them turned to ice when Kennedy pointedly turned his back on her during a Senate hearing on the minimum wage law. Mrs. Roosevelt had testified before a Subcommittee, of which Kennedy was Chairman.

Following her testimony, while other committee members gathered around to pay their respects to the *grande dame* of American Liberalism, Mrs. Roosevelt asked innocently, "And where is Senator Kennedy? I would have liked to say hello to him."

Senator Kennedy was not around. He had stalked out of the hearing room without saying a word.

In 1959 Kennedy was asked in Wisconsin to comment on Mrs. Roosevelt's remark that he had been "soft on *McCarthyism."*

"I am not ready to accept any indictment from you or Mrs. Roosevelt on that score," he snapped back.

Mrs. Roosevelt plainly had gotten under his skin. But, as usual, he evaded the issue.

He still refused to make "the flat denunciation of McCarthy that the liberals demanded," James MacGregor Burns wrote. "Why not? Partly out of sheer pride. . . . Partly out of political expediency. . . . But mainly because the old pressures within him are still operative to some extent. . . ."

What old pressures? Kennedy's biographer did not amplify.

"If one were assessing a Senatorial candidate with a heavily Irish Catholic constituency," wrote the *New Republic*'s Selig Harrison in June 1960, "his record concerning Joseph McCarthy might be discounted. . . . This is not so, however, when one is measuring the size of a potential President. The Kennedy record on McCarthy leaves it an open question whether or not when storms break, he will stand by what his intelligence and best instincts dictate."

The greatest irony of all this is that Kennedy's continuing lack of candor found Westbrook Pegler siding with Eleanor Roosevelt.

In Pegler's case, as he explained, he had "come down with a passing crush on Jack Kennedy because of his conduct as master of a small naval vessel which was sunk in Japanese waters. I accepted Jack's own version as handed to me by his father. I have no evidence to dilute his heroism except a dramatic failure of his moral courage in his repudiation of Joe McCarthy long after Joe was in his grave. Senator Kennedy had written a book in tribute to the moral courage shown by American public men in trying situations and now his betrayal of Joe McCarthy came as the most sordid act of the kind in all experience."

Courage

14

The night the United States Senate refused to confirm his appointment by President Eisenhower as Secretary of Commerce, Admiral Lewis L. Strauss waited in his office for the vote. As he waited, thoughts of a crowded lifetime passed through his mind. It had been a lifetime of notable achievement not only for himself but for his country. Finally his reverie was interrupted. Friends reported the Senate had rejected his appointment by a vote of forty-nine to forty-six.

The Admiral smiled. He opened a book lying on his desk. The flyleaf bore the inscription "To a man of courage and distinction." In this way, Senator John F. Kennedy, author of *Profiles in Courage,* had indicated the high esteem he felt for Admiral Strauss.

On the floor of the Senate, however, Senator Kennedy had voted to reject the "man of courage and distinction."

Several months previously, as chairman of a dinner of the Jewish Theological Seminary of America, Strauss had introduced Senator Kennedy, the principal speaker, as "a young man of great moral stature." He said it was "good to meet in an academic atmosphere where our differences on topical subjects and the cares which invest the day are out of bounds."

In his prepared text Kennedy had specifically criticized the United States for "trying to remain aloof from the Algerian and similar controversies in the United Nations and elsewhere." In speaking, however, he deleted both this and a criticism of "devising high strategy on the brink of war" without a prior attempt at making peace. Kennedy told reporters later he had "decided not to get involved in a particular controversy, as against the whole general question of colonialism."

Voting against Strauss's confirmation had not been easy. Kennedy had known—and presumably had admired—Strauss for years. The Admiral was one of the small band of Herbert Hoover's intimates with which Joseph P. Kennedy was keeping in close touch. The truth is that Kennedy did try to duck the issue. But Majority Leader Johnson advised his younger colleague every vote counted in what somehow had become a matter of high honor between the two parties. And Clinton Anderson, the New Mexico Democrat who had precipitated the row over Strauss, had also warned Kennedy.

"I'm a candidate for President," Kennedy later told the Admiral's friends. "Anderson told me if I didn't vote against Strauss he would fight my nomination. I had no choice."

Consequently, when the chips were down, the author of a book on political courage voted against "a man of courage and distinction." Had he done otherwise, he would also have felt the wrath of those Liberals who— and this was in June of 1959—still viewed his Presidential aspirations with considerable misgivings. By voting against Strauss, Kennedy demonstrated his willingness to stand up on issues the Liberals considered important.

Kennedy's penchant for ducking controversy was demonstrated even before the vote on Senator McCarthy's censure. In 1953 the controversial Status of Forces Treaty came up for Senate approval. The treaty, subjecting United States troops abroad to the vagaries of foreign justice, was highly unpopular in Massachusetts. Most Liberals were for it. Confronted with a dilemma—to vote or not to vote for the treaty—Kennedy solved the problem in his customary forthright manner: he simply failed to show up. Nor did he record an opinion, either by pairing or announcement.

"Hypocrisy may be customary in politics," editorialized the *Chicago Tribune* of the Strauss episode, "but the Massachusetts Democrat seems to be making a career of it. He would rather be President than right, and in his relentless pursuit of his party's nomination, he has been trimming to every breeze."

Nowhere was Kennedy's "trimming" more obvious than in the field of civil rights. And if the McCarthy issue could be airily dismissed by Arthur Schlesinger Jr. as ancient history, the same could hardly have been said about Kennedy's ambivalence on civil rights.

Here, again, on a do-or-die issue for American Liberals, they failed to abide by the morality implicit in their own rules. For when the showdown came, they swung their not inconsiderable weight behind a Presidential candidate whose position on civil rights was, at best, a bundle of carefully contrived contradictions.

There could be no question about Kennedy's ritualistic obeisance toward the goal of ultimate equality for American Negroes. And his voting record in the area did not differ perceptibly from that of most Northern Democrats.

Yet even Schlesinger once conceded that Kennedy was slightly soft on civil rights.

But when the 1960 votes were counted, they showed that the bulk of American Negroes voted for Kennedy; and if it had not been for their vote, he would not have been elected President.

Four years previously, during the 1956 Democratic Convention, civil rights exponents had viewed Kennedy with suspicion because of his passionate love affair with the South. Their suspicions were heightened with the March 1957 publication in *Life* of the young Senator's article on the Democratic party.

"Let it not be said," Kennedy declared, "that we are fearful or incapable of solving with fairness and forthrightness the sensitive, complex issue of race relations. The Democratic party is best equipped to provide responsible leadership in this area: first, because we are a national party, including within our membership both a majority of Negroes and a majority of southerners; and secondly, because we have always, as a party, emphasized human values and human ideals.

"I, for one, do not share the view that Negro voters are leaving the Democratic party for good. A majority is still with us, because it judges the two parties on their records and leadership on a variety of issues rather than on the civil-rights statements of a few prominent figures."

Previously, Kennedy had advised his fellow Democrats to avoid handing out "straight-from-the-shoulder platitudes" on civil rights.

The way of the trimmer, like that of the transgressor, is hard. This Kennedy discovered in the summer of 1957 when he tried to please both North and South on civil rights legislation proposed by the Eisenhower Administration.

"In the highly controversial civil rights issue now before the Senate you can see exposed, more dramatically than usual, the danger inherent in the necessity of Senators' going on record on major issues before the people," commented the late Thomas L. Stokes. "That record can be dug up later, as it usually is.

"The Senate chamber is air-cooled. But you can almost see the beads of perspiration as Senators known to be looking longingly toward 1960's national nominating conventions—and that's a lot of Senators—squirm under the compulsion of making decisions on this or that provision, or this or that amendment, related to the Eisenhower civil rights bill."

The civil rights bill had gotten through the House in fairly good shape. But it ran into a buzz saw in the Senate. The buzz saw was named James Eastland. As Chairman of the all-important Senate Judiciary Committee, the Mississippi Democrat once boasted that he was carrying a civil rights bill around sewed up in his pocket.

In his role as presiding officer of the Senate, Vice President Nixon ruled that the new legislation could be brought directly to the floor of the Senate, bypassing the Eastland Committee and certain death.

Nixon had previously made another important ruling over Rule 22, governing cloture of debate. In January 1957 he had ruled from the chair that "the Senate should not be bound by any provision in these previous rules which denies the membership of the Senate . . . its constitutional right to make its own rules."

The ruling did grave structural damage to the very foundations of Rule 22. It also signified that for the first time in the decade-old struggle the conservative Republicans broke clear of their tacit alliance with the Southern Democrats. Leading the fight for civil rights were Minority Leader William Knowland for the Republicans, and Senator Paul Douglas for the Democrats.

All of which, as Tom Stokes then commented, meant "real trouble" for Jack Kennedy. "You can imagine what sort of a swivet he's in today trying to please both North and South," the columnist wrote. "He has kept out of the fight so far. In the preliminary test-voting he straddled nicely."

Senator Kennedy voted with the South to send the entire civil rights package to the Eastland Committee for consideration. He predicted woeful calamity as a result of any reckless break with Senate tradition. Nothing of the sort, however, developed.

"The most disgusting news I have heard in a long time," a Long Island Negro wrote to Kennedy.

Other letters were even more angrily written. One New Yorker, a civil rights leader, wrote that Kennedy's vote demonstrated the truth in the Republican's 1956 campaign taunt that "a vote for any Democrat is a vote for Eastland."

"Your vote," he added, "plainly and simply confirms the charge of the Republican party and will without question force thousands of loyal Democrats, both Negro and white, into the ranks of the Republican party. . . . Speaking for myself personally, I made the switch as soon as I saw your 'Profile in Cowardice' in my copy of this morning's *New York Times*. Senator, you are a leading candidate for the Democratic presidential nomination in 1960, and even though I abhor Richard Nixon, I must in good conscience inform you that I will do all in my power to see that you lose not only in New York State but in New York City as well."

Kennedy replied that the New Yorker had misjudged his vote which, he said, he had taken "after thorough and conscientious thought." Any advantage to be gained from bypassing the Eastland Committee would be purely temporary and not worth a dangerous precedent that could conceivably return to haunt Liberals. (Kennedy's concern over Senate traditions, at this stage of his career, was indeed remarkable.)

A few days later Kennedy hopped nimbly across the Mason-Dixon line to side with the North. First, he favored an unsuccessful motion to choke off Dixie filibusters. Then he voted for Title III which would have given the Attorney General wide power to move in on racial cases. He explained that the way the debate was going had made the issue a vote either for or against the Supreme Court school decision. "My own endorsement of that decision and its support in the state I have the honor, in part, to represent, has been too clear to permit me to cast a vote that will be interpreted as a repudiation of it." The apologetic tone of his comments annoyed civil rights spokesmen.

Not unexpectedly, Title III failed to pass.

The decisive civil rights struggle was yet to come. And when it came it provided, in effect, still another test-match between Kennedy and Nixon.

It came in the form of a jury-trial amendment tacked onto the civil rights bill. Introduced by Senator Joseph O'Mahoney of Wyoming, it called for jury trials in criminal contempt cases involving voting rights. Until then, the district judges were the chief enforcement agents. Of the amendment, President Eisenhower asserted, "Rarely in our entire legislative history have so many extraneous issues been introduced into the debate."

Also dead set against the O'Mahoney amendment was the vociferous civil rights bloc of labor, NAACP and ADA leaders who felt it would emasculate the Administration bill by making it impossible for a federal court to enforce compliance with a voting rights order.

What Southern jury would convict a fellow citizen for trying to keep elections lily-white?

And what with Southern juries, judges, and prosecuting attorneys, the realistic Southern theory was that some of the heat would be taken out of civil rights controversies.

Both North and South squared off for a showdown. Both North and South counted on Kennedy's support. He found himself under great pressure. A wire from a Southern Governor read, "Still hearing good things about you and your future."

Partisans were watching Kennedy to see which way he would go. That he was then walking the tightrope of Presidential ambition no longer was a secret on Capitol Hill. His was a vote that could have historical repercussions.

Once again Kennedy voted with the South. And the South won the battle, 51 to 42. On the roll call, Kennedy was opposite such Democrats as Douglas, Humphrey, Clark, and Symington; he had voted cheek-by-jowl with Johnson, Byrd, Eastland, Talmadge, and Thurmond.

"This is one of the saddest days in the history of the Senate," Richard Nixon told reporters. It had been, he declared, "a vote against the right to vote."

Kennedy, meanwhile, tried to explain his position. "I consider it a mistake to insist dogmatically on the purity of the original act at peril to its larger objective," he told the Senate.

Then he quoted several Harvard law professors as agreeing with him that the O'Mahoney amendment would not blunt the effectiveness of the civil rights bill in any consequential way. He quoted Professor Paul A. Freund as having observed, ". . . to accept the jury trial for criminal contempt would not in my view constitute a betrayal of principle." And Professor Mark De-Wolfe Howe, also a noted civil libertarian, had advised him that there was "merit" in the jury trial provision.

This was an application of innocence by association which did not go down too well with civil rights exponents. "Certainly," commented London's *Economist*, "Mr. Kennedy is trying hard to accommodate himself to the South." And James Reston noted with sorrow that "the Republican leaders had counted on his support on the O'Mahoney amendment.

"However, it was pointed out to him that the South, which had supported his candidacy for the Vice-Presidential nomination in the early ballots at Chicago last summer, would not take kindly to any Presidential candidate who insisted on rejecting the jury trial principle of the bill.

"It may be, of course, that Mr. Kennedy was merely persuaded by the philosophical and historical arguments about the tradition of jury trial and decided to brave the wrath of those who favored the Administration's policy. But, in any event, his vote eventually went to Mr. Johnson when before it had been confidently expected by Mr. Knowland."

"In the 1957 show-down on civil rights," as Florida's *Sarasota News* was ruefully to recall three years later, "Senator Kennedy clearly identified himself among the party unity compromisers. He voted with Lyndon Johnson, and against the Northern liberal bloc, for the crucial compromise that made that year's civil rights bill so eminently acceptable to the South that a half dozen (of the two dozen) Southern Senators actually voted for it.

"That vote, we must assume, was far enough removed from consideration of the political necessities of a Presidential campaign to fairly reflect Senator Kennedy's true feeling on the matter. Certainly it was the vote by which he came to be regarded—among his Southern friends as elsewhere—as a moderate rather than a militant on civil rights."

"Had Kennedy, then, shown a profile in cowardice?" asked biographer Burns. Because of the Senator's support of Title III, Burns said, "No." He added, "Certainly, however, he showed a profile in caution and moderation. He walked a teetering tightrope; at the same time that he was telling liberals of the effectiveness of a bill that included the O'Mahoney provision, he was assuring worried Southerners that it was a moderate bill that would be enforced by *Southern* courts and *Southern* juries—Kennedy's italics."

"The course of expediency followed by the author of 'Profiles in Courage' is not unusual in politics," wrote Tom Stokes, "and in particular among politicians who aspire to ascend higher than the Senate. In fact, it is quite typical. It requires incessant caution to zig at the right moment and zag at the right moment.

"By keeping himself in the good graces of the Southern leaders in the

Senate, who are powerful there, Kennedy helps himself and his career. But he must be careful not to antagonize leaders and rank and file in the larger section of his party, which is outside the South. The delegates representing that larger section of the country are most numerous in Conventions."

Kennedy's zigzag behavior on civil rights had indeed antagonized powerful Northern forces. His predicament was dramatized when Roy Wilkins, executive secretary of the National Association for the Advancement of Colored People, assailed him in a Boston speech as a "compromiser with evil."

Kennedy became alarmed. Wilkins' bitter attack could not be ignored. The Senator sought to explain his position; but the NAACP leader refused even to acknowledge Kennedy's letters.

Brought onto the Kennedy payroll about this time were Marjorie and Belford Lawson, a man-and-wife team active in Negro affairs. Their job was to straighten out the Kennedy image within the Negro community.

"Certainly I was disappointed on his voting on the civil rights bill," said Mrs. Lawson. "He made a mistake. Everyone can make a mistake. You can't discard a person because of a single mistake."

But was it really a mistake?

"I think he felt he could compromise on this issue as a sop to the South," one of his strongest Negro backers told Ralph Martin. "I think he felt he could convince the South that he is not an unreasonable civil rightist and at the same time avoid antagonizing northerners. He can't have it both ways, but I think he believed he could."

The Lawsons had their work cut out for them. The Roy Wilkins attack continued to have reverberations among Negroes.

"If only Roy would acknowledge receipt of Kennedy's letters, the Senator would make a substantial contribution to the NAACP," Belford Lawson advised Louis Lautier, a Washington correspondent for Negro newspapers. Lawson asked Lautier to intervene with Wilkins in behalf of Kennedy.

"Lawson and I were probably the only Negroes outside of Massachusetts who knew Kennedy," recalled Lautier. "Lawson tried to get me to go on Kennedy's payroll. I didn't see that at all. However, at his urging, I did talk to Kennedy and Ted Sorensen. They were concerned about the misinterpretations being placed on the Senator's jury-trial vote. They claimed that a couple of Harvard professors had assured them that the amendment would not cripple the effectiveness of the civil rights bill which finally passed."

Lautier wrote a column presenting the Kennedy side of the argument. Then Lautier got in touch with Wilkins "and eventually Roy and Kennedy made up."

Kennedy made other fumbling efforts to refurbish his image among Negroes. This was indicated by his desire to appear before Negro audiences. At Lawson's request, Lautier made arrangements for a dinner at the National Press Club at which the Senator would address a Negro YMCA group. The night of the dinner found Kennedy detained in Boston. His brother Bobby read the Senator's speech and announced a one thousand dollar contribution to the work of the "Y."

Kennedy, of course, was following his traditional practice of keeping a foot in each camp. He was still staking his chances for the Presidential nomination on his ability to rally a substantial Southern bloc—as he did for the Vice Presidency in 1956.

Predictably, he drew the fire of the *New York Post,* which tartly observed: "While he dare not desert the anti-filibuster cause lest he be totally repudiated in the North, the other side of his mouth is addressed to the South. The total result, as in his evasion of the McCarthy issue, is a portrait of irresolution."

The *Post's* ire had been aroused by Kennedy's "bland" responses on a "Meet the Press" show following the Senator's re-election victory in November 1958. Asked whether he thought Eisenhower was doing all he could to bring about compliance with Supreme Court decisions, Kennedy replied:

"I think probably looking back since 1954 I would say that he has not done it in perhaps the way other people might have. I think perhaps in recent months that he has done the best he can, yes."

The *Post* could hardly believe these were Kennedy's true sentiments. "Surely he is aware of the record of the President's moral abdication and retreat. Kennedy's response provided a striking exhibit of the timidity that dominates the style of current American politics."

Though "politics is 'the art of the possible,' " the *Post* added, ". . . politics can also involve the ability to speak with passion and conviction . . . and, perhaps, most of all, to understand that the people have a remarkable capacity for detecting double-talk. . . ."

Among Negro leaders, Kennedy's ambivalence had rooted a suspicion of political expediency not easy to erase. Their suspicions erupted into outright hostility in June 1959—thirteen months before the 1960 Convention—when Alabama Governor John Patterson announced he favored Kennedy for the Presidency.

Patterson's endorsement came after he and an associate, Sam Englehardt, a leading light in the White Citizens Councils, had breakfasted with the Senator at the latter's Georgetown home.

Patterson was one of Dixie's more outspoken foes of civil rights. Once he enlivened a gubernatorial race by waving a blown-up photograph of a Negro being pommeled in Little Rock and exclaiming, "This is how I will treat them if you make me your Governor."

In endorsing Kennedy, Patterson paid him a high tribute: "I think he's a friend of the South." Then he added: "I will use all the influence I have to see that he gets the nomination." Which eventually he did.

Kennedy declined to comment on the Patterson endorsement. "I haven't seen it," he said, "so I better let it go."

Patterson kept singing Kennedy's praises. "As far as I know," he said, "he is the only potential candidate for President who has visited all the Southern states in recent months."

And Kennedy hadn't visited all the Southern states to preach the virtues of the Supreme Court decision on school desegregation.

"If elected," Patterson added, "Senator Kennedy will be sympathetic to the problems of the South."

Officials of the NAACP received the Patterson endorsement of Kennedy coolly. "It is very difficult for thoughtful Negro leaders to feel at ease over the endorsement . . . ," said Roy Wilkins.

And on June 29, 1959, Adam Clayton Powell—Harlem's emissary in Congress—called on delegates to the 1960 Convention to "repudiate" Kennedy as a Presidential candidate because of his acceptance of support from "Negro-hating" Alabama officials.

Governor Patterson replied immediately, "I thought that Negro was a Republican. What's he got to do with the Democratic party?" This was a reference to Powell's 1956 endorsement of the Eisenhower candidacy.

Prior to the convention, Kennedy made every effort to avoid committing himself fully on civil rights. He was one of the few Senators who failed to respond to a questionnaire on the subject submitted by the American Veterans Committee.

"He doesn't realize that the closer we get to the Convention," a Negro leader said in September 1959, "the more important this issue looms. It goes to the heart of our greatest problem and he still hopes he can maintain a slightly neutral position and I keep telling him that he cannot, that he must make it clear where he stands."

Meanwhile, Kennedy "discovered" Africa. Though appointed Chairman of a Senate Subcommittee on African Affairs, he never called a meeting. However, he made speeches denouncing white-man's rule in the Dark Continent, demanding the immediate termination of European colonialism. This was a good way to avoid more pressing domestic problems.

On January 2, 1960, in announcing his availability for the Democratic nomination for President, Kennedy said "the real issues of 1960" were: "How to end or alter the burdensome arms race, where Soviet gains already threaten our very existence; how to maintain freedom and order in the newly-emerging nations; how to rebuild the stature of American science and education; how to prevent the collapse of our farm economy and the decay of our cities; how to achieve, without further inflation or unemployment, expanded economic growth benefiting all Americans; and how to give direction to our traditional moral purpose, awakening every American to the dangers and opportunities that confront us."

The fact that Kennedy had failed to list civil rights as one of the major issues did not go unnoticed.

Asked by a newsman how he expected "to retain the support of Southerners like Governor Patterson and win Negro support," Kennedy replied:

"Well, Governor Patterson has announced his support of me, and as far as I know that support still stands. It seems to me the real question here is that if—I think I have made my views quite precise on civil rights. I hope I have. I am delighted to do so at any time in the future. If anyone then decides they want to support me knowing what my views are, it seems to me that is within their rights. That goes for anyone in the Democratic party."

"We know all of those things," a California Negro weekly observed, "what we don't know and what we would like to know is what 'President Kennedy' would recommend to Congress and what he would do to enforce equality before the law in Governor Patterson's state, and in Louisiana, and in Mississippi and in other southern states where he has so many friends and supporters."

During the 1960 Southern filibuster, when most civil rights advocates were stumbling groggily through the pre-dawn hours to answer quorum calls in order to keep the Senate in session, John F. Kennedy was conspicuously absent from the siege.

On March 10, 1960, the *New York Times* reported that Kennedy had failed to appear for a single post-midnight call. By contrast, Senator Lyndon Johnson, whose newly found devotion to the cause was even more suspect, turned out for every call during the graveyard hours of early morning when the going was roughest.

Though Kennedy did align himself with the civil rights bloc during debates on strengthening the 1957 Civil Rights Act, the NAACP regretfully noted he failed to vote or to pair himself (though he did announce his position as favoring) on two key amendments. One was to establish a permanent Commission on Equal Job Opportunity Under Government Contracts; the other was to provide technical assistance to areas desegregating their schools. Both amendments were defeated.

"No sincere proponent of civil rights would have absented himself from these crucial votes," commented an important Negro leader at the time.

Kennedy's sincerity was often a matter of speculation by persons not altogether won over by his charm. As a Presidential candidate, for example, he promised action to break down artificial and arbitrary barriers to employment based on racial discrimination. However, as a Senator, he had voted within the Labor Committee against a motion made by Republican Senator Prouty to create a special subcommittee to study the need for legislation to ban such discrimination.

Also, as a candidate, Kennedy pledged enactment of FEPC legislation. Yet all through the years he headed a Labor Subcommittee with responsibility in this area, no hearings were held, and, consequently, no action was taken on FEPC proposals. Likewise, when President Eisenhower asked passage of a bill to "establish a Commission on Equal Job Opportunity Under Government Contracts," the Kennedy-chaired Subcommittee never brought the bill to a vote.

As the Convention neared, Governor Patterson's endorsement was raised against Kennedy. "It's a millstone around my neck," he complained. The endorsement was recalled by Jackie Robinson, in presenting the anti-Kennedy case in his *New York Post* column.[1] A man of understandably intense convictions on civil rights, the former baseball star had dubbed Kennedy "the fair-haired boy of the Southern segregationists."

Kennedy denied having made any alliances with Messrs. Patterson and Englehardt, as Robinson had alleged. "Although it is true that I once had breakfast with them," he replied to Robinson, "it is equally true that a few days later I had lunch with Mr. Thurgood Marshall. No implications can be drawn from either of these meetings other than my own public statements."

It was, according to Robinson, a typical Kennedy remark—cold, aloof, even arrogant. "If Kennedy thinks he can use a luncheon with the NAACP's Thurgood Marshall to counterbalance his endorsement by Governor Patterson," wrote Robinson, "then his opinion of the intelligence of Negro Americans must be very low indeed."

Robinson said that Thurgood Marshall, in a telephone conversation with him, had "repudiated any attempt to use him in this way." Marshall, moreover, "said he had protested directly to Kennedy over his silent acceptance of Patterson's support. Furthermore, though Patterson announced his political endorsement of Kennedy after eating with him, Thurgood said he very definitely did not and does not."

"As long as he continues to play politics at the expense of 18,000,000 Negro Americans," Robinson wound up, "then I repeat: Senator Kennedy is not fit to be President of the United States."

At a secret meeting with Harlem Democrats on Convention eve, Kennedy described the Patterson endorsement as "the greatest cross I have to bear."

But, if it was, he never repudiated it. Not that anyone really expected him to. The truth is that Kennedy has always regarded civil rights as strictly a political issue. Rarely has he demonstrated any steadfast interest in the subject. He has never felt the kind of moral struggle which many Southerners feel toward the problem. Rather he has blown hot and cold whenever the issue arose. The same is true of Robert F. Kennedy.

"Bob Kennedy has no strong feelings about civil rights," an old friend told Stan Opotowsky.[2] "He is not for the Negroes and he is not against them. His decisions will be entirely political. But once his mind is made up, he'll stick to it. He won't be talked out of anything."

Opotowsky reported this episode at the 1960 Democratic Convention: after the platform committee adopted a tough civil rights plank, fol-

---

[1] The *Post,* long a champion of the cause of freedom of expression, discontinued the column after Robinson endorsed Richard Nixon for President.

[2] *The Kennedy Government,* by Stan Opotowsky. New York, Dutton, 1961.

lowing a bitter fight, one of its architects immediately buttonholed Bobby and said, "You should promise to support this plank to the hilt. You're not getting the Southern delegates anyway and so you have nothing to lose there and plenty to win in the North."

Kennedy said nothing for a moment, then made his decision. "It's a a tough plank, eh? All right, we'll support it."

Asked if he'd care to read it, Kennedy said, "No, we'll support it."

And the next morning, according to Opotowsky, without pausing to learn just what the plank pledged, Bobby Kennedy handed down the line to his brother's caucus: "This plank must be passed without a word changed —not a word." What it said didn't matter as much as the fact it could help propel a Kennedy into the White House.

In the Spring of 1960 Senator Kennedy was addressing an audience that had loudly applauded Hubert Humphrey's suggestion that the Southern lunch-counter strikers represented the America of Lexington and Concord. Kennedy said he was for civil rights everywhere and that included the right of every citizen to drink Coca-Cola—and anywhere he wanted to. According to Murray Kempton's on-the-scene report, "he offered the word 'Coca-Cola' as though it were a flag and a signal for automatic applause; the response was all for the stage. He had reduced the material of epics to a mere physical thirst. Nothing more indicates his peculiar deafness to tones; he can offer any response short of the poetic."

But with that frankness which has been his most engaging characteristic, Kennedy conceded that in these matters he had the disadvantage of his environment; he had never known enough Negroes to know how they think. After all, one does not usually run into them in such sheltered white man's preserves as Palm Beach, Hyannis Port, or even Georgetown—except, of course, as servants. He had, he said, "limited experience" with Negroes.

"I haven't had much opportunity to learn about the Negro," Kennedy told Jackie Robinson.

And Robinson commented: "He has been in Congress fourteen years and he tried to tell me he hadn't had an opportunity to learn about the Negro."

Robinson was also disturbed by the fact that, in several conversations with him, "Kennedy didn't look me in the eye."

"I couldn't support a man like that," Robinson said.[3]

Virtually on the eve of the convention Kennedy faced an incipient revolt by Negro members of the Michigan delegation who had publicly questioned the depth of his devotion to civil rights. Informed of this by Michigan's chief Kennedy booster, Governor G. Mennen ("Soapy") Williams, Kennedy sent his family Convair to Detroit to pick up ten Negro delegates for brunch at his Georgetown home.

---

[3] "Kennedy looks at people through half-shut eyes," wrote former admirer Westbrook Pegler. "If a guy can't look me square in the eye, I don't trust him."

According to Kennedy's guests it was "a real red-carpet welcome." Said one: "We had brunch on the patio, and there was a subtle punch beforehand—I thought there was gin in there, but I heard it was cognac. There was chicken and some fancy kind of eggs, and there were whites and Negroes waiting on us. Afterward, that man must have given away $100 worth of cigars from some foreign country. Mrs. Kennedy was there, too, and later they had the press conference for television and everything. We were all impressed."

"You'd like me to be more like Hubert Humphrey," Kennedy told them at one point, "but Hubert and I have different kinds of glands."

"Kennedy didn't hurt himself any," commented "Soapy" Williams.

A prominent Negro editor reported that though Kennedy "is a friendly person," he isn't "what you would call warm." And P. L. Prattis of the *Pittsburgh Courier* added:

"One gets the impression that Senator Kennedy is always adding or subtracting and that he is tremendously good at figures. Figures may be favorable, but they are not warm."

And it was precisely his ability to count noses that ultimately converted Kennedy—in rhetoric, at least—into a militant civil rights advocate.

Senator Kennedy's unique ability "to talk out of both sides of the face simultaneously" was noted by another Negro editor, Chuck Stone, of the *New York Citizen Call:* ". . . There's one thing money can't buy. And that's a liberal and forthright attitude toward Negroes and their fight for equality.

"Senator Kennedy just does not have this attitude. . . . Senator Kennedy has been equivocating on civil rights so long, he wouldn't know a forthright statement on racial equality if it were dragged across his breakfast table.

"Search his Senate speeches. Has he ever condemned the South's barbaric attitude? Has he ever spoken out against the inequities of housing discrimination or job discrimination? Has he ever shown deep concern about the second-class citizenship of Negroes?

"He once worried aloud about the Algerian problem and said France ought to solve it soon. He never said that about the American Negro-white problem.

"Kennedy is the same man who sat down to breakfast with Governor Patterson, one of the staunchest Negro-haters in America. Kennedy is the same man who went to Mississippi, made a speech and received a standing ovation. What kind of man can be called a friend of the Negro who receives a standing ovation in Mississippi?

"Kennedy has never repudiated the warm endorsement of Governor Patterson. He has never urged the South to hurry and shake off its Neanderthal racial blinders.

"He has never once urged speedy compliance with the Supreme Court school desegregation decision of 1954.

"Where in Senator Kennedy's career can one point to a single aggressively definitive stand on racial integration? What has he ever done before or during his Senate career to actively promote better race relations or desegregation?

"In the present spectrum of Democratic and Republican candidates, Senator Kennedy is unquestionably the worst of the lot for the American Negro and this includes Lyndon Johnson. . . .

"Juxtaposing Senator Kennedy's civil rights record next to these men, it is a political tragedy that this bright young man stands only a few Convention votes away from being able to continue the compromise of the basic rights of 18,000,000 Negroes."

Rarely was there a Presidential candidate less likely to obtain the overwhelming bulk of the Negro vote. Yet, thanks to unlimited funds poured into the right places, tireless press-agentry, exaggerated campaign pledges, and a telephone call to Mrs. Martin Luther King, John F. Kennedy achieved the impossible.

Labor

15

On a veranda overlooking the historic Rhine, columnist Holmes Alexander was lunching with someone whom he described as a non-political American celebrity. The time was the Summer of 1960, shortly after John F. Kennedy had been nominated for President. Naturally, the conversation turned to Kennedy and what made him tick. Finally, his luncheon companion told him:

"I don't know Senator Kennedy—which is strange. For many years I have been testifying before Senate and House committees. Because of my responsibilities and position, people are always saying, 'You ought to have a talk with So and So—he's very influential in Congress.' But nobody has ever said this about Senator Kennedy and I have never talked with him."

The anecdote illustrated something which has been well-known to many Washington correspondents—a fact made painfully evident in the first two years of the New Frontier. As Holmes Alexander explained it shortly after the ill-fated Congressional bobtail session of August 1960:

"Alas, the Democratic candidate for President is no leader. In his fourteen years in House and Senate, he never became an important legislator. He is not a man of whom knowledgeable people would tell an outside financier, diplomat, scientist or statesman, 'You ought to meet him.' The Senator's failure to put over in Congress even a token part of his post-Convention program did not surprise anybody here. The lack of Kennedy legislation has been going on for years."

The lack of Kennedy legislation continues today. For this is still a country where the President proposes and Congress disposes. Hardly a day goes by when the White House is allowed to forget it. And with all the professorial help around the White House, J.F.K. still doesn't know how to compose legislation. It has always been so. It was that way in the Senate when a Kennedy measure of any substance seldom went through in the form in which it came from his office. "One of the mildest men in the Senate, Prouty of Vermont, once took a Kennedy measure on loyalty oaths and reversed its meaning Z to A," reported Alexander.

The sad fact is that the President, although a Pulitzer Prize winner and an able after-dinner speaker, was never able to get his name on a single item of major legislation enacted into law during fourteen years of service in both House and Senate. Most of his colleagues in the House felt he had merely coasted as a Congressman, awaiting some higher office. This was also substantially true of Kennedy's eight years in the Senate.

However, after he had set his sights on the White House, Kennedy desperately sought to get his name on some legislation. Occasionally he persuaded colleagues to drop their claims to authorship and permit his name to appear on labor and depressed-area bills, but none of these measures was enacted into law. Usually he met defeat at the hands of members of his own party in Democratic-controlled Congresses. Once his hopes of getting a law with his name on the books was blighted by an Eisenhower veto.

Young Kennedy's habit of borrowing (if that is the word for it) other solon's legislative proposals was notorious. It occasionally prompted some angry muttering in the back benches.

Senator Wayne Morse, who is easily outraged, was once moved to protest when Kennedy introduced a comprehensive measure to extend the minimum wage law. The Oregon Democrat pointedly observed that the Kennedy bill was substantially based on measures which he himself had introduced and that were already being considered in committee.

Several months later, Kennedy put his name on a bill to liberalize immigration laws. He was obviously hoping to become the darling of what the political committees call the "nationalities."

The only trouble with the Kennedy bill was that it appeared to be a twin of a previous proposal advanced by Senator Everett M. Dirksen. Even Kennedy's "explanation of the bill," which he inserted into the *Congressional Record,* appeared to be an insufficiently edited version of the explanation of the Dirksen bill.

Senator Hubert Humphrey also accused Kennedy of "trying to take credit" for some of his proposals to use farm surpluses to win friends abroad. "I'm the daddy of those programs, blood test and all," Humphrey asserted.

One reason Kennedy was forced to these expedients was he was usually out campaigning. "Mr. Kennedy's record for absenteeism in both branches of Congress was high," the *Chicago Tribune's* Walter Trohan reported on January 10, 1962. "Some of his absences were due to illnesses induced by his war service, but many were due to the fact that he didn't like to listen. He preferred to appear on the floor when he had something to say or when he could advance himself politically, as he did between his Presidential nomination in Los Angeles and the final days of the 86th Congress, when he was unable to put over much the same program he is trying to gain today."

On paper, Kennedy's record—from a Labor viewpoint—looked impressive. The AFL–CIO's Committee on Political Education (COPE) listed him as voting "right," so far as COPE was concerned, on 25 out of 26 issues between 1947 and 1958. Behind this shiny paper record, however, was a dismal performance, one in which he invariably failed to match his words with deeds. Close examination of Kennedy's performance as a Senator shows he consistently placed personal political advantage ahead of progress in legislation designed to aid working men and women.

Item: In July 1956, several weeks before the Democratic Convention opened, the Senate Labor Committee favorably reported out a bill to aid depressed areas. The bill contained protective language that would have prevented its powers and funds from being used to create employment in one area at the expense of another. This was precisely what Kennedy, in his New England program, had been demanding: safeguards to prevent the misuse of area redevelopment programs to encourage industrial migration and thus create new areas of unemployment. However, as floor manager of the bill Kennedy accepted an amendment offered by Senator Fulbright to strike out these safeguards. One Senator, Connecticut's Purtell, protested that the Fulbright amendment had taken the heart out of the bill. Kennedy's ploy, however, did him no harm among the Southern delegations at the Democratic Convention.

Item: The 1960 Democratic platform recognized that when a woman worked side by side with a man on a job, performing with equal efficiency, she should be paid a comparable wage. For five years President Eisenhower had advocated equal pay for women in his Congressional messages, and four Republican Senators introduced legislation to carry out his recommendation. The National Federation of Business and Professional Women's Clubs asked Senator Kennedy to initiate action on the equal pay measure, but his Labor Subcommittee held no hearings, took no action.

Item: Many men working on Government construction projects have to labor fifty-six hours a week before they get any overtime compensation—because of outmoded statutes. The Eisenhower Administration asked Congress to revise unjust, discriminatory provisions in the laws applying to federal and federally assisted projects. Four Senators introduced corrective legislation, but the Labor Subcommittee, headed by Senator Kennedy, held no hearings, took no action on the legislation.

Item: After eighteen months' experience with the Welfare and Pension

Statute, Eisenhower's Secretary of Labor James P. Mitchell found it to be a "shameful illusion," for it provided no effective safeguards for the more than $30 billion invested in employee and welfare pension plans. Bills to safeguard the health and retirement benefits of an estimated eighty-five million working people were introduced. The Labor Subcommittee, headed by Senator Kennedy, held no hearings and took no other action on this legislation.

Item: In 1959 the Subcommittee on the Problems of the Aged and Aging conducted field investigations in seven cities, including Boston. Senator Kennedy, a member, was not present at any of them. Hearings were also held in Washington on eight different days. Kennedy was not present at any of them. In 1960 hearings were held in Washington on six different days, and Kennedy was not present at any of them. This did not prevent the Senator from denouncing the Republicans in this area.

Item: Though Kennedy and the 1960 Democratic platform pledged repeal of the Taft-Hartley law leaving the right-to-work question up to the states, the Labor Subcommittee, headed by Kennedy, had never given any consideration to such legislation through the years.

Item: After making a firm commitment to the building trades unions to put up a strong fight for a common situs picketing bill favorable to labor, Kennedy went off campaigning for the Presidency. Again in March 1960 he told the AFL–CIO Building and Construction Trades Department that the 1960 Congress "shall not adjourn until this measure is brought to a vote." Not only was it not brought to a vote, it never got out of the Senate Labor Committee.

Item: And then there was Senator Joseph Clark's remark of May 11, 1960: "I think the Senate will pass a minimum wage increase if we can just get Sonny Boy back from the cricks and hollers long enough to report it out of his Committee." Sonny Boy, of course, was preparing to campaign against those do-nothing Republicans.

Kennedy's inability to "write" legislation was never more clearly demonstrated, however, than in his efforts to steer a labor reform bill through Congress. He worked hard on the Senate labor-reform bill, but it got ground up in the Congressional mills.

Every Senator likes to equip his career with a "gimmick," a vote-getting issue that could reap a harvest of publicity without doing too much damage with any segment of the electorate. Such a "gimmick" was Kennedy's membership on the McClellan Labor Rackets Committee, of which brother Bobby was the much-televised Chief Counsel.

The investigation into labor racketeering gave Washington its big Kennedy brothers act, with tousle-haired Bobby impaling such labor barons as James Hoffa and Dave Beck on his shrill questions, and Jack coming to his aid when things got rough.

Never before in Senate history has a Junior Senator, with or without a brother, taken over a Senate Committee the way Jack Kennedy took over the McClellan Committee.

"I am sorry for Senator John McClellan," Barry Goldwater, a member of the Committee, later observed. "He is an honest man who lacked knowledge of the power of the union rackets. He could not head off the Kennedys when they took over the investigation with Bobby running the sessions."

And rarely had any Chief Counsel taken such complete charge of a Senate Committee's activities. Incredibly, the Senators found themselves virtually powerless against Robert F. Kennedy. Brother Bobby had so managed events that the Senators on the dais lost their authority.

"Bobby didn't consult us," said Goldwater. "We would arrive for hearings and there we would find witnesses called by the Kennedys without our knowledge."

"I've never served on a committee before where I didn't know what was going on until it happened," the late Senator Irving M. Ives had stated in anger.

Still shrouded in mystery is how the Kennedys managed to seize such control. One thing appears certain: it could not have been done without the blessing of the Majority Leader of the Senate, Lyndon B. Johnson.

Senator Johnson was going out of his way to butter up the Kennedys. As a back-bencher then explained to NANA's David Barnett: "Lyndon hopes to get a Johnson-Kennedy ticket in 1960. He's liable to find out, before he's through, that he's built Kennedy up so that it would be easier to get a Kennedy-Johnson ticket."

The origins of the highly publicized labor probe can be traced back to the 1956 Presidential campaign when Robert F. Kennedy, on leave as Chief Counsel of the Permanent Investigations Subcommittee—the former McCarthy Committee—was working with the Stevenson team. In October 1956, a few weeks before the election, he announced that his subcommittee would begin an investigation of financial abuses in certain unions, particularly the Teamsters and the Carpenters.

The respective leaders of these unions, Dave Beck and Maurice Hutcheson, had announced their support of Eisenhower for re-election.

A few months earlier—at the Chicago Democratic Convention—Senator Kennedy had come within a hair's breadth of winning the Vice-Presidential nomination. He had had the support of the most Conservative delegations at the Convention—mainly the Southerners. It was at this point that a major part of the Kennedy strategy for obtaining the 1960 nomination began to develop.

To retain his Conservative support Kennedy could not appear to be overly pro-Labor. At the same time he could not afford to alienate the absolutely essential Liberal support that surely would be antagonized by anti-Labor activities.

The McClellan Rackets Committee investigation, as it became known, was the device which was used to achieve these apparently incompatible objectives.

Quite early in the hearings, the Kennedy brothers established themselves in the public mind as shining knights dedicated to driving corrupt and venal leaders from the House of Labor. They concentrated on Dave Beck and Jimmy Hoffa.

Both Beck and Hoffa were at constant odds with Walter Reuther, of the United Automobile Workers. And Liberals, both in and out of the Labor movement, were uniformly pro-Reuther in this controversy. Consequently, there were no Liberal squawks when the Kennedys concentrated their fire on the Teamster bosses. In fact, the Teamster probe had Reuther's tacit support.

Thus, Senator Kennedy had the best of both worlds: he retained the friendship and support of Walter Reuther while convincing many Americans he was independent of the labor bosses.

When the time came to write legislation correcting abuses unearthed by the Rackets Committee, the Kennedy brothers cooled off perceptibly. Organized Labor, in the person of AFL–CIO President George Meany, did not take kindly to what was being proposed.

"My only comment, Senator," snapped Meany in March 1958, "is, God save us from our friends."

Quietly, Kennedy replied, "I say that, too, Mr. Meany."

The exchange occurred after Kennedy had offered a labor reform bill.

Yet, two years later George Meany and the general board of the AFL–CIO discovered that Kennedy was just the man to "save" them. They endorsed him for President and, along with him, his running mate Lyndon Johnson whom they credited with a "middle of the road" record on labor legislation. Meany, however, was able to do much better than this modest salute when he turned to Kennedy. Jack's labor record, he said, was "near perfect."

This was probably Jack Kennedy's most spectacular feat on his way to the White House. He obtained the indispensable backing of the Labor barons while, at the same time, wearing the toga of a union-racket-busting Senator.

It wasn't always easy.

As Frederic W. Collins, Washington correspondent of the *Providence Journal,* reported in the *Nation:* ". . . Mr. Kennedy's idea of a good, substantive program is to marry the labor movement in order to reform it. This subtle operation is complicated by the fact that he and his brother Bob . . . have so little trouble in dissembling their love for labor. A sensitive unionist might get the idea that Jack didn't really like him or his cause, and that the Kennedy concept of reform might be fairly equated with bondage.

"Be that as it may, Mr. Kennedy is embarked on a course of introducing at least one item of labor legislation every day. On a rough count, seven pieces of mail bearing Senator Kennedy's frank thud each twenty-four hours onto the desks of Washington's news practitioners, and his zeal may be measured by the fact that now and then they actually come postage paid. His material on strengthening state unemployment-compensation systems cost him personally thirty cents per envelope. It is quite possible, indeed, that his campaign may collapse from sheer exhaustion of stationery. It is a bit puzzling to open a piece of mail sent by Kennedy in an envelope of the Foreign Relations Committee and find inside the draft of a minimum-wage law; but this is balanced by a weighty speech on foreign economic assistance borne in an envelope of the Committee on Labor."

One powerful labor leader didn't think Kennedy's antics were funny. A. J. Hayes, head of the International Association of Machinists, at the annual luncheon of the League for Industrial Democracy, compared Senator Kennedy with Juan Perón, ousted dictator of Argentina. He read a statement made in 1944 by Perón, outlining the dictator's attitude toward Labor. Then he declared:

"Surely, without stretching the imagination, that statement might have been made by one of the so-called liberals of the McClellan Committee or, for that matter, by one of the eminent professors who helped draft the so-called Kennedy bill. It sums up, in honeyed words, the attitude of the 'benevolent' but tyrannical state toward the labor movement: You are free to seek your own best interests, but I will tell you what your best interests are and how you may best achieve them."

The 1958 bill failed to pass. In 1959 Kennedy tried again. This time he sought to steer through the Senate a reform measure that contained some provisions irksome to Organized Labor—the Kennedy-Ervin bill.

Any objective analysis of his handling of the bill makes it apparent that Kennedy tried in every way to restrict the scope of the reform provisions. His aim was obvious: he was trying to capitalize on the public indignation generated by the McClellan Committee's startling exposés, while not offending the labor leaders.

On April 24, 1959, Senator McClellan offered an amendment to include a strong "Bill of Rights" for union members in the Kennedy-Ervin bill. The amendment was considered disastrous by most labor leaders. Senator Kennedy considered it a calamity.

In the ensuing debate McClellan defended his amendment as protecting the rights of the individual worker who, he claimed, "is just as helpless within his union as he was within his industry when the tyranny of the all-powerful corporate employer is replaced by the tyranny of the all-powerful labor boss. The worker loses either way."

In opposing the Bill of Rights, Kennedy suddenly became an impassioned spokesman for states' rights. He denounced the McClellan amendment as constituting a vast intrusion of federal intervention into the sacred precincts reserved for state jurisdiction.

"My objection to the amendment is not that I think that union members should not be provided with these rights," he told his colleagues. "My objection is that I think members of unions are provided these rights more satisfactorily by present state laws than by provisions of the bill and by the Taft-Hartley Act."

This position was a far cry from the one Kennedy had taken as a freshman Congressman in 1947, when in his one-man minority report on Taft-Hartley he had stated the need for a Bill of Rights for Labor: "Equally fundamental is the right of each union member to a square deal from his union. On this score there have been serious abuses in the past. I favor democratizing union election procedures and administration."

Which is what Senator McClellan was seeking in 1959.

The *Baltimore Sun,* meanwhile, took issue with "Senator Kennedy's apparent wish to drown rational debate in a splurge of partisan sentimentalism."

Over Kennedy's protests the Bill of Rights was tied on to the Kennedy-Ervin bill. The vote dismayed Kennedy. In terms of his Presidential ambitions, it was described by the *New York Times* as a "grave defeat."

Kennedy fought back. Realizing his own stake in the controversy, Majority Leader Johnson began to deliver the vote to defeat one tough McClellan proposal after another. At one point Kennedy turned to McClellan and warned him that his Bill of Rights would cripple unions rather than clean out the crooks. "The difference between the Senator from Arkansas and me," he said, "is that every time he sees a union, he sees racketeers."

Finally the Kennedy-Ervin bill—with a watered-down and ineffectual Bill of Rights—passed the Senate 90 to 1. The dissenting vote was cast by Senator Barry Goldwater who characterized the bill as "a flea bite on the back of a bull elephant."

The dissenting vote was a courageous one for the Arizona Republican to have cast. As he later told friends, it was overwhelmingly lonesome sitting in the Senate Chamber, listening to the roll call, and wondering what the voters back home were going to think.

"The measure had been advertised as a cure-all for the evils uncovered by the McClellan Committee investigation," Goldwater later declared. "I opposed it because I felt certain that legislation which pretended to respond to the popular demand for safeguards against union power, but actually did not do so, would preclude the possibility of meaningful legislation for some time to come."

Goldwater's lone-wolf stand was vindicated, however. The House of Representatives was to reject Kennedy-Ervin for the much stiffer Landrum-Griffin bill.[1]

---

[1] Lyndon Johnson also favored a tough reform bill. "Throughout my public life," he wrote to his constituents in August 1959, "I have favored strong, effective regulatory legislation to protect Americans from improper labor practices, having voted for the

Things were going badly for Kennedy. "As a leading Democratic aspirant to the presidency, Senator Kennedy must be judged in part by the record he has written on labor reform legislation," editorialized the *St. Louis Post-Dispatch*. "We find the record disappointing."[2]

According to the *Post-Dispatch:* "Senator Kennedy early identified himself with the labor question by taking a prominent part in the McClellan Committee investigation. . . . The Senator headed the Subcommittee which wrote the Senate's first version of the bill, and took a conspicuous part in the debate. Thus he presented himself to the public as a vigorous champion of legislation to curb excesses of certain union leaders.

"Yet, when the chips were down, Senator Kennedy was found fighting for a weaker bill than the one President Eisenhower recommended. Although there was no occasion for a Senator to mix into the labor controversy in the House, Kennedy took it upon himself to warn that branch against adopting a bill which contained effective curbs on secondary boycotts and blackmail picketing.

"His brother, who had done so much by television appearances to arouse public interest in labor legislation, took the same line. The Kennedys, in short, were strong for a labor bill, but not for a labor bill that offended the union leaders too much. . . ."

The *Post-Dispatch* then raised these questions: "Does Senator Kennedy have convictions on secondary boycotts and blackmail picketing? If so, he ought to make them public—not by vague and fuzzy talk about protecting honest unionism, but by clear and specific discussion of the substantive issues.

"Does he believe unions ought to retain the power to evade the present law's restraints on boycotts? If so, let him say so, and tell why. Does he think unions ought to retain the power to picket indiscriminately where there is no labor dispute? Let him say so if he does, and explain his reasoning. But fighting for the union leaders' position while posing as the author of labor law reform does not recommend him."

For nearly three weeks the fourteen-man Senate-House conference tried to work out an agreement between Landrum-Griffin and the milder Kennedy bill. As sponsor of the original reform legislation Kennedy was in a perilous position.

If he got too rough with the unions, the AFL–CIO's leadership could well veto his Presidential chances. But if he eased up too much on the unions, giving the impression of bending under labor pressure, he could lose the good

---

Vinson bill, the Smith-Connally act, the Taft-Hartley act, and in the last two instances, having voted to override a Democratic president to make these measures law." The letter later was to prove embarrassing in Johnson's drive for the Presidential nomination. It was cited by Kennedy partisans as proof that Johnson was "anti-labor."

[2] A year later, however, the *Post-Dispatch* endorsed Kennedy for President.

will of the general public which he built over two years as a member of the McClellan Committee.

Kennedy thus found himself in the middle. Once again, all eyes were on Kennedy: would he compromise in order to get a labor reform measure out of conference or would he insist on his Senate stand for a milder bill in order to hang on to his labor support?

Kennedy compromised. He made a show of opposing some of the more severe Landrum-Griffin provisions, but then he voted for the measure as a whole.

"Compromises are never happy experiences," Kennedy told newsmen when it was all over. "I think it's the best bill we can get—and get a bill."

But it was a bill for which it was no longer desirable to claim paternity. At Kennedy's request, his name was removed from the legislation. Jimmy Hoffa, however, continued to call it the Kennedy-Landrum-Griffin bill.

Kennedy succeeded in gulling top labor leaders into the belief that he had fought for their interests. George Meany, in fact, named Kennedy—along with Senators Wayne Morse, Pat McNamara, and Jennings Randolph—as one of the liberals who had "worked tirelessly to get rid of some of the more obvious injustices" and were "partially successful."

Senator Morse, for one, disagreed violently on Kennedy's role. The Oregon Democrat called Kennedy the "principal architect" of a "viciously anti-labor bill" and flatly accused him of pushing the law to advance his Presidential ambitions.

Kennedy's habit of tipping his hat to both sides as he erratically walked down the middle of an issue was nowhere better demonstrated than in his handling of the labor bill.

In a form letter to people who wrote to him about the measure, Kennedy described Landrum-Griffin as "sound, effective legislation." He added: "The bill which has been enacted is responsive to each of the recommendations made by the investigating committee. I believe the bill is sound and in the public interest.

"By any standard," he concluded, the bill was "a major legislative accomplishment."

But there was "another" Kennedy—one who did not hesitate to speak of the bill in derogatory terms, as if he had had nothing to do with putting it in the statute book.

This is what Kennedy had to say about the "major legislative accomplishment" on October 12, 1959, when he addressed the United Automobile Workers' convention in Atlantic City:

"I realize that the labor-management act of 1959 is not the bill that you want or the bill that I wanted. It contains many features inserted by the enemies of organized labor."

Nowhere, of course, did he explain how honest labor leaders could be hurt by provisions aimed at corruption and dictatorial tactics—provisions for which, incidentally, he had voted.

But Kennedy could pose safely as an enemy of corruption by attacking the AFL–CIO's enemy, the Teamsters' Hoffa. "Jimmy Hoffa may not approve of me," he told the UAW-ers, "but I do not apologize for having earned his hostility."

It was like homecoming week when Kennedy appeared at the convention in the role of a potential Presidential candidate. He was wildly cheered by the delegates, and he returned the compliment—with calculated modesty—by suggesting that his good friend Walter Reuther, head of the UAW, also "would do very well" as a Presidential candidate.

There could be no doubt of the closeness of relations between Walter Reuther and Jack Kennedy. That relationship has been the cause of considerable conjecture in terms of the investigations of the McClellan Committee into labor racketeering. There were those who argued that the Kennedy brothers' principal contribution to the hearings was, as the *Chicago Tribune* put it, "to protect Walter Reuther's United Automobile Workers against a too searching inquiry into its picket line goon tactics."

Walter Reuther is one of the most powerful figures in the United States. His influence within the Democratic party is so great that his vetoing of any Presidential hopeful could constitute the kiss of death. Which may explain why the McClellan Committee—under Bobby Kennedy's guidance—concentrated its fire almost entirely on the Teamsters and old-line AFL unions for the "labor mess," while steering its muckraking away from Reuther and the CIO unions. Significantly, most of the labor bosses who came under Bobby Kennedy's withering fire had records of supporting the Republican cause.

"Robert Kennedy has ignored continued demands for an investigation of Reuther, GOP members say privately," *Newsweek* reported in July 1957. "And they further emphasize the coincidence that the labor leaders subjected to the committee's sharpest attacks are the ones who have stood in the way of Reuther's domination of American labor."

In private, the Republicans said candidly that the way the investigation was going every labor leader who might block Reuther would be destroyed. "Dave Beck had no use for Reuther and now he's through," one GOP-er told *Newsweek*. "Jimmy Hoffa hates Reuther's guts and look at him now."

"We never got around to investigating Dave Dubinsky and his Garment Workers," Barry Goldwater later recalled. "Their names came up a couple of times."

Perhaps one reason for this lack of interest on the part of the Kennedy brothers was because the ILGWU and President Dubinsky swing a lot of political weight in New York City. Not unnoticed was the fact that Senator Kennedy was the only one of a long list of Democratic hopefuls who had been invited to address the May 1959 convention of the ILGWU in Miami Beach.

And if Messrs. Dubinsky and Kennedy saw no political significance in the occasion, it was clear the one thousand delegates did. The delegates cheered when Dubinsky introduced the Senator with these words:

"There has been considerable talk in informed circles—and I am innocent, I don't know—about the possibilities of his holding the highest post in the nation. But one thing I do know. If this should happen, we will have a better America and better legislation for the working people of America."

As the *New York Times* reported his speech: "Senator Kennedy further endeared himself to the convention when he criticized the recent criminal indictment of a garment union local and a union vice president by the Justice Department on charges of conspiracy to monopolize the blouse industry. Mr. Dubinsky has accused the Eisenhower Administration of political motivation in bringing the case."

Another kind of concern over Bobby Kennedy's activities was being voiced by civil libertarians who, as one of them put it, had "not forgotten his McCarthyite background." Years later, Yale Law Professor Alexander Bickel questioned Robert Kennedy's qualifications in a *New Republic* article entitled "The Case Against Him for Attorney General." In that article Bickel did not raise the common complaints about Bobby's legal inexperience and youth (at thirty-five he became the second youngest Attorney General in United States history), nor what he called "a widespread but rather generalized distrust of Robert F. Kennedy," but rather his "abuses" in the very job which won him national acclaim—chief counsel for the Senate Rackets Committee.

According to Bickel, the Committee "with Mr. Kennedy in the lead . . . embarked on a number of purely punitive expeditions" and engaged in "relentless, vindictive battering" of some witnesses. And the professor filled out his case with several exhibits of Counsel Kennedy in action (Kennedy v. Joseph F. "Joey" Glimco, president of Chicago Teamsters Local 777, often arrested but seldom convicted):

KENNEDY: And you defraud the union?

GLIMCO: I respectfully decline to answer because I honestly believe my answer might tend to incriminate me.

KENNEDY: I would agree with you.

CHAIRMAN: I believe it would.

KENNEDY: You haven't got the guts to [answer], have you, Mr. Glimco?

GLIMCO: I respectfully decline . . .

CHAIRMAN: Morally you are kind of yellow inside, are you not? That is the truth about it?

According to Professor Bickel, this and other episodes from the record show that Kennedy was building up an unfair inference of guilt and abusing the Fifth Amendment as well as the witness.

If some lawyers came away with the impression that Counsel Kennedy was, as one Teamster attorney put it, "a sadistic little monster," others felt the opposite. One of the latter, significantly, was Joseph L. Rauh, who represented Walter Reuther and the UAW before the Committee, and who is a former National Chairman of the ADA.

"He was trying to be a fair investigator," Rauh has stated, "and any abuses were not due to 'vindictiveness,' but to his lack of experience. If it sometimes led to abuse of witnesses, it sometimes led to witnesses like Hoffa getting away with murder. The technique of questioning is an art, and Bobby wasn't experienced at it—he didn't know how to go for the jugular. Far from browbeating Hoffa it was more of a case of Hoffa browbeating *him*."

There can be little doubt that frequently Hoffa made a monkey out of the crusading Committee Counsel. There was the occasion when Bobby asked the Teamsters' boss what he did with a batch of Minifons (tiny tape-recording devices) which he had ordered and received:

HOFFA: What did I do with them? Well, what *did* I do with them?

KENNEDY: What did you do with them?

HOFFA: I am trying to recall.

KENNEDY: You could remember that.

HOFFA: When were they delivered, do you know? That must have been quite a while.

KENNEDY: You know what you did with the Minifons and don't ask me.

HOFFA: What did I do with them?

KENNEDY: What did you do with them?

HOFFA: Mr. Kennedy, I bought some Minifons and there is no question about it, but I cannot recall what became of them. . . .

[After more of the same, came the final "answer."]

HOFFA: Well, I will have to stand on the answers that I have made in regards to my recollection and I cannot answer unless you give me some recollection, other than I have answered.

It must be emphasized that the Republican members of the McClellan Committee did not object to probing into the affairs of Jimmy Hoffa and his retinue. In fact, in a separate report released in February 1960, Senators Goldwater, Mundt, Capehart, and Curtis conceded that the Committee had done a good job in exposing people like Hoffa. They said: "When investigating unions other than those affiliated with the leadership of Walter Reuther, the Chief Counsel worked effectively and cooperatively with all members of the Committee—Democrats and Republicans alike—but whenever investigation touched upon the domain of Walter Reuther, an altogether different procedure was followed."

Goldwater *et al.* then added:

"Not until the Gosser case [in the final days] did Assistant Counsel Manuel have an opportunity to question witnesses at open hearings. And in that hearing Chief Counsel Robert Kennedy attacked those attempting to ascertain the true status instead of aid the investigation. We are convinced that corruption, misappropriation of funds, bribery, extortion and collusion with the underworld have occurred in the UAW."

Richard T. Gosser was senior Vice President of the UAW and, according to the report, "second in power to Reuther, himself." A Toledo local charged Gosser with "corruption." The Reuther executive committee found him not guilty and fired the financial secretary of the local who had made the charge.

"The evidence shows that Richard Thomas Gosser, alias Richard McMullen, Richard Goffer and Richard Goofer, has a police record of arrests and indictments for burglary, auto theft and receiving stolen property," the minority report said. "He was convicted of armed robbery and sentenced to 2½ to 15 years in Michigan State Reformatory."

Gosser owned a residence in Toledo and another in Hollywood, Florida, and a ranching firm with 1,184 acres in Michigan and 1,829 acres in Florida. He also had numerous bank accounts—and all this on a salary of $12,000 a year plus receipts from an informal sideline of slot machines in Toledo.

Yet, no real effort was made to conduct a full-scale inquiry into Gosser's affairs. The investigation really consisted of nothing more than asking Gosser if he was honest and accepting his word that he was.

The GOP report also spoke of a "clear pattern of crime and violence" by the Reuther union, marked by "imported professional hoodlums who, through mass picketing, terroristic tactics, personal threats and intimidation" sought to win such strikes as those against Kohler in Wisconsin and the Perfect Circle Company in Indiana. And despite repeated demands Counsel Kennedy refused to take the intiative in investigating either strike.

The minority report charged that the UAW had enjoyed a benevolent dispensation from the Committee's Democratic Senators in general, and the Chief Counsel in particular. Brother Bobby "refused in more than one instance to probe into areas which would have fixed the responsibility for the career pattern of crime and violence which has characterized UAW strikes. . . . The immunity which the UAW and Walter Reuther appear to enjoy seems to be based upon political intimidation and influence."

The extraordinary lengths to which the Kennedy brothers went in their efforts to protect Walter Reuther and the UAW were demonstrated in the investigation of the Gosser case conducted by Senator Curtis and Minority Counsel Robert Manuel.

When they began taking testimony from Gosser in executive session, Senators Kennedy and Church demanded that the hearings be held in public. When this was done, Kennedy and Church then said open hearings would also be unfair to the UAW and that they should be suspended. Their proposal was rejected by Senator Mundt, who noted: "It is interesting that the two Senators who have complained the most about the witness talking in public were the two who voted originally to have it in public session."

Whereupon the Kennedy brothers—Jack and Bob—took turns ridiculing the GOP inquiry. They said the matters being looked into were old hat.

The UAW, of course, yelled "political witch-hunt."

When a UAW employee testified he had been forced to pay $5 a week —and others as much as $43 a week—to a compulsory "flower fund" kickback, Senator Kennedy showed his annoyance by declaring:

"It seems to me that if you are going to partake of the loaves and the fishes that you have to contribute something to maintaining the organization. . . . It seems to me that if you did not like it you should have worked some place else."

After another witness testified about the compulsory kickbacks, the Senator still could see nothing wrong. Kennedy compared it favorably with the system Hoffa used in taking union dues. Beclouding the issue, Kennedy referred to an investigation which had disclosed that the Du Pont family had contributed $250,000 to political candidates in 1956. The witness replied, "I have been and am against—even though I had to participate in it—the expenditures of the dues dollars of the UAW workingman for any candidate that he does not designate himself." It was an effective point.

After Senator Mundt noted that a few members of Congress had gone to jail for accepting kickbacks, Senator Kennedy insisted there was a difference. The difference was that no *federal* funds were involved in the UAW kickbacks. Moreover, the issue of morality—raised by Mundt—did not disturb him.

But to Mundt, the fund was a "sticky business," particularly since the books had been destroyed. "For employees to kick back to hold their jobs," said the South Dakotan, "smacks of the old indenture system which I thought we eliminated in this country since our old colonial days."

The pattern of action by the Kennedy brothers was clear. They would move heaven and earth to prevent any investigation of charges that might prove embarrassing to the United Auto Workers.

On February 16, 1960, Senator Kennedy declared:

"Why didn't you do to Reuther what you did to Beck and Hoffa, I have been asked. Reuther and the UAW have made mistakes, as I have pointed out. But as a general proposition the UAW is an honest union and Walter Reuther is an honest union official who attempts to run an honest union.

"For some people that is untrue. Any attempt to equate the UAW with the Teamsters, or Reuther with Hoffa, will fail—and in fact, did fail. The sooner this fact of life is accepted in the country, the better off we shall all be."

On June 8, 1960, the *Washington Star* reported that at a news conference in Grand Rapids, Michigan, "Senator Kennedy said he was hopeful of getting backing from United Auto Workers President Walter P. Reuther before the Democratic Convention opens July 11."

Senator Kennedy already had that backing.

Gall

16

In a collection of essays critical of the American way of life, John Kenneth Galbraith once described what he called the "build-up." Galbraith, known in the trade as the Mort Sahl of the Economists, defined the term as the "egregious exaggeration of the public figure" which, he added, means "giving a public figure a character which, in fact, he doesn't have."[1]

According to the professor, there are two types of "build-up," the *contrived* and the *autonomous*.

Best understood is the *contrived* which "consists of synthesizing a public reputation as a matter of deliberate design." And, as Galbraith further explained in *The Liberal Hour,* the *autonomous* build-up "always strikes someone who is already in the public eye . . . for doing an important and difficult job in a restricted area of public endeavor. Or he had made a promising start on such a job. Or, in a common case, he has just assumed public office. . . . Then comes the build-up. He is a man transformed—indeed he is no longer a man but a superman. . . . Where others ponder, he has solutions. . . . It has been the fault of lesser men that they had left the impression that there was a choice only between equally grim alternatives."

In fact, the build-up is most likely to take place at times "when problems are numerous, vexatious and incomprehensible." And, added Galbraith, "Not knowing how to control nuclear energy, disarm, increase needed expenditures, balance the budget, eliminate farm surpluses and come abreast of the Russians

---

[1] *The Liberal Hour,* by John Kenneth Galbraith. Boston, Houghton Mifflin, 1960.

in space exploration, we find it desirable to invent people who can do these things. The press and the networks, sensitive as always to the needs of the customer, assist. Working with whatever material is at hand, they create the master statesman who will see us through."

Unfortunately, the trouble with such synthetic creations is that the manufactured Superman may not be properly equipped to cope with enormous problems should he get into position to do so. Once in power, all the devious arts associated with the build-up cannot produce the tough, hard decisions so vital for the nation's survival. Though it still may be possible to hoax the American people with carefully contrived publicity gimmicks, of one thing there can be little doubt: the men in the Kremlin are not so easily deceived.

Nevertheless, John Kenneth Galbraith—perhaps even deliberately—has provided future historians with an extraordinary, first-hand insight into how almost overnight John F. Kennedy's image was converted from that of a "moderate Democrat" and "Dixie's favorite Yankee" into that of a "master statesman," a "fearless innovator," a "new F.D.R.," and—finally—"The Man of the Sixties."

It was a build-up without parallel in the history of American politics. In retrospect, it was the work of a well oiled political machine, a generally friendly press, power-craving intellectuals and—last but not least—the senior Kennedy who had often remarked that money was no object in furthering his son's White House ambitions.

Then, of course, there was the product behind all the salesmanship— John F. Kennedy, no slouch in the image-making department himself.

When it comes to developing news and cultivating newsmen, John F. Kennedy has few peers. Kennedy's handling of the press, as Stewart Alsop observed, was "consistently brilliant." Favored correspondents—and they were legion—were provided numerous briefings and frequent access to his confidential polls. Nor was he inept at appealing to their vanity. "Jack called me the other day," a noted correspondent proudly announced shortly before the Los Angeles Convention, "and asked me who I thought should be his floor manager. I told him Ribicoff." Rarely had correspondents been so close to a front-running Presidential possibility. And it paid off in reams of friendly copy. In fact, it still is paying off. Kennedy has even been willing to swallow his pride to pay a visit to the Georgetown home of Drew Pearson in order to straighten out certain of the columnist's misconceptions about him. The payoff was several columns, one of which on April 8, 1960, observed:

"In the American political scheme of things, build-ups are necessary. In the last analysis, however, there must be a real product behind the build-up. And Jack Kennedy, despite his youth, has become a product of substance.

"You feel this coming through when you talk to him. There's a quiet determination, a depth of understanding which was not in the same Jack Kennedy a few years ago. . . . And this writer, who has watched many would-be Presidents come and go, is convinced that Senator Kennedy, if he attains the great goal of the White House, would not be politically influenced by either his father or his church."

As part of the build-up, Kennedy was forced to demonstrate complete independence of his church in the realm of public affairs. "He has acted calculatedly to puncture fears that a Catholic President would be beholden in any way to the Church," the *Reporter*'s Douglass Cater observed in December 1959. "He points out that neither his votes nor his closest advisers have been Catholic-oriented."

Significantly, most of the early opposition to Kennedy on religious grounds stemmed from Liberal elements who viewed the Church of Rome as a reactionary power bent on doing away with separation of Church and State.

The fear was so real for New York's Liberal party that it assigned Reinhold Niebuhr to question Senator Kennedy "in depth," and that eminent divine reported back to David Dubinsky and other troubled Seventh Avenue theologians that the would-be Presidential candidate had satisfied his Protestant doubts.

The Niebuhr report was never made public.

Nor was there any report on what Kennedy told the editors of the *New Republic*. However, that journal did report on September 19, 1960, "that the editors have in several private talks with Senator Kennedy found quite telling reason to believe that, as Dr. Bennett puts it, he 'knows his way around in his church' and is hardly overawed by it."

Dr. John C. Bennett, Dean of Union Theological Seminary, had written in *Christianity and Crisis* that a Catholic President who is a Liberal Democrat could, with a clear conscience, offer more effective resistance to pressures from within the hierarchy than many non-Catholic officeholders. "A Catholic who knows his way around in his church," Dr. Bennett argued, "might well be better to handle these pressures . . . because he would be better able to measure the degree of authority behind him."

Some Catholics developed the feeling that Kennedy was going too far to the Left in order to appease the ADA wing of the Democratic party—a group not noted for its pilgrimages to Vatican City. This feeling was put in words by the Reverend Juniper B. Carol, in a widely circulated article published in *Human Events,* entitled: "Kennedy for President? A Catholic Priest Says 'No!' "[2]

As part of his build-up, Kennedy came to the defense of the National

[2] Needless to say, there was nothing anti-Catholic in Father Carol's article. Yet, the article was labeled "hate literature" by Senator Estes Kefauver, among others. In offering the article to editors, *Human Events* declared: "Reprinting *Human Events* articles is forbidden to anti-Catholic publications. An anti-Catholic publication is one which believes that no Catholic has the right to become President of the United States. *Human Events* opposes Senator Kennedy solely because of his political philosophy. *Human Events* regards Adenauer and de Gaulle—BOTH CATHOLICS—as the two greatest European statesmen. If Kennedy had the capacity and wisdom of these men, we would FAVOR, not oppose, his election to the Presidency of the United States."

Council of Churches of Christ in the U.S.A., some of whose leaders had been tabbed as alleged Reds or fellow travelers in an Air Force manual. Kennedy scored publication of the manual as "shocking and distasteful," said the National Council was "as strongly opposed to Communism as any church group in the country," and called upon that Protestant body to express its views "on the major social and economic issues confronting our Nation."

At the same time Kennedy was repeatedly calling for complete separation of Church and State. His statements were interpreted as meaning that if elected to the Presidency, he would stay clear of the influence of his own Church.

In his campaign confrontation with Protestant ministers in Houston, Texas, Kennedy would go so far as to say:

"If the time would ever come . . . when my office would require me to either violate my conscience or violate the national interest then I would resign the office."

It was an extraordinary thing to say. The implication was that his Church could conceivably exert really heavy pressure upon him and, if that would happen, he would resign.

"Is this the sort of man we want for President?" asked author Herbert Asbury. "One who would quit in the face of pressure."

Generally speaking, most Americans agree that a man's religious belief, as such, is a personal matter and not a proper issue in a political campaign. Some Americans, however, argue that when a religious belief has temporal implications it becomes a proper subject for political consideration. The pertinent question involves separation of Church and State.

Senator Kennedy dealt with this issue when he told Fletcher Knebel (*Look,* March 3, 1959):

"Whatever one's religion in his private life may be, for the officeholder, nothing takes precedence over his oath to uphold the Constitution and all its parts—including the First Amendment and the strict separation of Church and State. . . . I believe . . . that the separation of Church and State is fundamental to our American concept and heritage. . . ."

The Jesuit weekly, *America,* replied to the Senator's statement: "Mr. Kennedy doesn't really believe that. No religious man, be he Catholic, Protestant or Jew, holds such an opinion. A man's conscience has a bearing on his public as well as his private life."

And in his column in the *Commonweal,* the liberal Catholic weekly, John Cogley said that "a Catholic President . . . would have to acknowledge that the teachings of the Church are of prime importance to him."

"Strangely enough," commented the Right Reverend James A. Pike, Bishop of the Episcopal Diocese of California, "Senator Kennedy's statement, far from posing the threat of ecclesiastical tyranny, would seem rather to represent the point of view of a thorough-going secularist, who really believes that a man's religion and his decision-making can be kept in two watertight compartments."[3]

This had not always been Kennedy's view. At Notre Dame in January 1950, the then Congressman Kennedy declared:

"You have been taught that each individual has an immortal soul, composed of an intellect which can know the truth and a will which is free. Because of this, every Catholic must believe in the essential dignity of the human personality on which any democracy must rest. Believing this, Catholics can never adhere to any political theory which holds that the state is a separate, distinct organization to which allegiance must be paid rather than a representative institution which derives its powers from the consent of the governed."

On close reading, Kennedy appeared to have said in 1950 pretty much what *America* said in 1959.

Late in 1959 the religious issue was again brought to the fore by the disclosure that Kennedy had withdrawn from a 1950 interfaith meeting at the insistence of Catholic leaders. The story was told by Dr. Daniel A. Poling, editor of the *Christian Herald*.[4]

Dr. Poling had invited representatives of the three faiths to participate in the dedication of the Chapel of the Four Chaplains at Temple University. Dr. Poling's son, the Reverend Clark Poling, was one of the four chaplains who had died in the sinking of the troop transport *Dorchester*. The chaplains, two Protestants, a Rabbi, and a Catholic priest, had given away their life preservers and had gone down with the ship, their arms linked and joined together in prayer.

Senator Herbert H. Lehman spoke as a member of the Jewish faith. Charles P. Taft, then Mayor of Cincinnati and President of the National Council of Churches, was the Protestant. The third speaker was to have been the then Congressman John F. Kennedy.

Two days before the meeting, Kennedy telephoned Dr. Poling he would have to cancel his appearance. "His Eminence, Cardinal Dougherty of Philadelphia, had requested him not to speak," wrote Dr. Poling. "His speech was prepared, he said, and he would gladly forward it to me but, as a loyal son of the Church, he had no alternative but not to come. . . . Unquestionably, he was profoundly embarrassed."

The story had a happy ending. An equally distinguished Catholic layman, the late General William "Wild Bill" Donovan, vice president of the fund-raising committee for the Four Chaplains memorial, appeared on the program with President Truman, who delivered the dedication address.

Dr. Poling's account of the episode appeared in the press on December 5, 1959. On December 7, Senator Kennedy declined to comment. On December

[3] *A Roman Catholic in the White House*, by James A. Pike. New York, Doubleday, 1960.

[4] *Mine Eyes Have Seen*, by Dr. Daniel A. Poling. New York, McGraw-Hill, 1959.

8, the Senator's office issued this terse statement: "Senator Kennedy's office states that the story is inaccurate." Five weeks later, on January 15, 1960, Kennedy issued a more detailed statement in which he admitted that Dr. Poling's facts "were accurate," but that the conclusions drawn from them were not.

"A few days before the event," Kennedy said, "I learned as Dr. Poling described it in his book, that I was to be 'the spokesman for the Catholic faith.' [The exact quotation from the book: 'a spokesman for his Roman Catholic faith.'] . . . I further learned that the memorial was to be located in the sanctuary of a church of a different faith. This is against the precepts of the Catholic Church. . . . I felt I had no credentials to attend in the capacity in which I had been asked. . . . I informed the Rev. Dr. Poling of my difficulty and told him I would have been delighted to have taken part in any joint memorial to which I was invited as a public officer."

Dr. Poling does not have the same recollections. For example, he does not recall Kennedy's offer to take part in the joint memorial as "a public officer."

Kennedy's *Look* interview continued to arouse debate. Robert Hoyt, for example, wrote in the Catholic monthly, *Jubilee:* "It wasn't really necessary for him to stress that his education was almost wholly secular—somebody would have noticed it."

According to Hoyt, Kennedy's approach to the parochial school question "is debatable not because Mr. Kennedy is on the 'wrong side' or disagrees with the 'Catholic position'—no such thing exists—but because he does not argue the question convincingly, if at all.

"It may be, of course, that Mr. Kennedy doesn't argue the case against parochial school aid in detail because it seems to him too self-evident to need argument. . . . It is also conceivable that Mr. Kennedy has tended to close his mind on the issue for reasons of political expediency; if so, he is still in good company."[5]

Senator Kennedy did not appear to be overly concerned with criticism from Catholic sources. But, according to Douglass Cater, he "noted with satisfaction" that his views were "well received by a variety of critics, including Paul Blanshard." Blanshard, who writes books comparing the Vatican to the Kremlin, had announced that his dire warnings about "Catholic power" did not apply to Kennedy.

Actually, Kennedy had not always been as ardently opposed to the appointment of an Ambassador to the Vatican or to federal aid to church schools as he implied to *Look* and other publications.

In 1949 and 1950 he had introduced in the House general federal-aid

[5] Unlike President Kennedy, his brother Teddy—in his Senatorial campaign—championed federal aid to parochial schools. This, of course, was good politics because Irish and Italian Catholics are the backbone of the 900,000 registered Democrats in Massachusetts.

bills authorizing funds for buses, health services, and textbooks for private and parochial schools.

As a Presidential aspirant, however, he changed his mind. On February 4, 1960, when Wayne Morse sought to amend the School Assistance Act to provide a measure of aid for parochial as well as public schools, Kennedy was paired nay in opposition—the only one of twelve Catholic Senators to oppose it. Yet all the Morse amendment would have done was to provide for a $75 million program of low interest loans (loans, not grants) for construction of classrooms in non-profit, private schools.

Kennedy also had a change of heart on the subject of an Ambassador to the Vatican. On April 12, 1954, responding to a Cambridge constituent's query, he wrote that, since both F.D.R. and Truman had favored United States representation at Vatican City, he would vote in favor of an Ambassador should the question arise in the Senate.[6]

"Kennedy is quite prepared to meet the Catholic issue," reported Irwin Ross on the eve of the 1956 Convention. "I asked him how he felt about past proposals for an American Ambassador to the Vatican. He quickly replied that he was against the suggestion. 'I don't think it's worth doing if it will cause a lot of distress to a lot of Americans,' said Kennedy."

The diplomatic touch was not the least of his talents.

"Many of his friends do not even believe him to be religious," continued Ross, "though in response to a reporter's query Kennedy avers that he is— 'though not intense about it.' He adds that other members of his family are more fervent than he."

On the eve of the 1960 Convention, Kennedy told Henry Brandon of the *London Sunday Times* that his religion had made him a "controversial" figure. "But," he added, "I don't know whether it wasn't advantageous— looking at the situation as it was in '57, '58 and '59—to be controversial in one way or another."

Following his Presidential nomination, the *London Observer*'s man in Washington observed: "But the curious fact remains that Senator Kennedy has got so far as he has simply because he is a Catholic. It has been his special 'gimmick.' . . . The one thing that thrust him squarely into the public view, that kept him on the television screen and in the headlines, was his religion.

"He was an endless subject of serious debate. Could a Catholic reconcile the Constitution with his obedience to Rome? Could a Catholic keep the Presidential oath? Could a Catholic be a free man, particularly in the White House? Kennedy's skillful and aggressive answers satisfied many people or at least induced in them the sort of guilt that made it seem squalid to bring these questions up.

[6] Ironically, it was Joseph P. Kennedy who had acted as Franklin D. Roosevelt's emissary to the Vatican on this matter.

"The other curious thing is the nature of his faith. He is a hereditary Catholic, stuck with his religion as a refugee is with his accent. He has never been to a Catholic school. His knowledge of the subtleties and intricacies of his faith is minimal."

And the irreverent Murray Kempton flatly predicted that if elected, John F. Kennedy would become America's "first anti-clerical President."

Meanwhile, Kennedy was sharpshooting every angle in his bid for the nomination. After years of lackadaisical behavior as a legislator Kennedy was attempting to establish some sort of record with which to heighten his prospects for 1960. And he was trying to do it quickly. His budget reform bill, to force federal agencies to account for and justify their special project expenditures on an accrued basis, was so worthy that it was endorsed by practically everybody. And his proposals for changes in the McCarran-Walter Immigration Act were so non-controversial that they were endorsed by that vigilant watchdog of immigration barriers, Congressman Francis E. Walter himself. To the *New Republic,* however, his proposals were farcical and trivial. "Is it not farcical, for example, to amend such a statute by tinkering with its provisions about aliens with symptoms of tuberculosis?" asked that journal of Liberal opinion.

With each new audience, Kennedy seemed to respond more enthusiastically to local problems. Occasionally he talked as if the rest of the nation wasn't listening. Thus, in New Hampshire he hinted broadly that trade protectionism could solve New England's industrial decline—an attitude quite different from the Democratic low tariff position set by F.D.R. "We can protect our textile and shoe industries," Kennedy told a Manchester audience.

Eventually, Kennedy was to offer the nation a Kennedy plan or a Kennedy bill for every conceivable social ill.

Considerable effort was expended in refurbishing the Kennedy image among those Liberals who refused to buy him as an adequate substitute for Adlai Stevenson. For one thing, Kennedy's belated turnabout on McCarthyism was viewed as sheer opportunism. They failed to be overly impressed when he championed repeal of the loyalty oath required of college students who finance their education under the National Defense Education Act. This was viewed as an effort to bolster his prestige among those disappointed by his nonfeasance on the McCarthy issue.

Carl Sandburg—later to emerge as apologist-laureate of the New Frontier —had this to say about Jack Kennedy in March 1960: "Merely a high-powered high-school boy. He's got more money than pleases some of us. Whether he has spent one or more millions to get the nomination would be interesting to know. The money is there for him through the quiet, smooth backing of his father, whose record gives some of us no elation."

Part of the build-up was the publication of a new book, *The Strategy of Peace,* a carefully selected collection of Senator Kennedy's speeches and statements on foreign policy, defense, peace, national security, and related domestic issues.[7]

The Manchester *Guardian* devoted an editorial to the book on its publication in England. "On the whole," it observed, "his criticisms are reassuringly vague and unspecific. The speeches in this volume are full of eloquent denunciations of complacency and drift, bristling with appeals to the patriotism and idealism of his countrymen. But even President Eisenhower would presumably agree that complacency and drift are to be discouraged: and no one in any country willingly disparages patriotism and idealism. The art of democratic leadership consists, above all, in bringing latent conflicts to the surface. The objection to these speeches is that, too often, the really controversial questions are dodged. No one, for example, will quarrel with a call for a more effective defense system. But who is to pay for it? . . . Similarly few people would dispute that the problem of Berlin must one day be solved—but how? . . . On all these points, Senator Kennedy's challenge to conformity turns out to be half-hearted."

The book was edited by the eminent American historian Allan Nevins, who had written the foreword for *Profiles in Courage*. In his introduction, Professor Nevins painted Kennedy in unfamiliar colors. "All are familiar with his interest in the rights of the Negro," he asserted. "He has . . . a special concern for the promotion of culture on a national and international basis."

Then this rather astonishing observation: "[Kennedy's] detestation of McCarthyism and all similar invasions of decency and justice is thorough and well documented here." The book's index fails to note a single reference to either McCarthyism or Senator McCarthy. As usual, Kennedy had avoided the subject like the plague.

Kennedy himself had come under attack for indulging in blanket charges against groups of people. During the labor hearings he and brother Bobby had leveled general accusations of bribery or payola against certain newsmen they did not name. They accused Senator Goldwater and other Republicans of having planted lies about them in newspapers and some news magazines.

Kennedy was accused of "smear tactics" by the president of the American Bar Association after he had unburdened himself of a sharp attack on "crooked labor lawyers."

"Senator Kennedy talks a lot," commented Bar Association head Charles S. Rhyne. "He ought to stop talking and furnish the facts. . . . People like him have an obligation not to smear the legal profession in general. One should and must be specific so that the 99 44/100 per cent of the profession will not be smeared by the occasional black sheep who are members of the profession."

Included in *The Strategy of Peace* are Kennedy's views on Algeria which won for him accolades in the Liberal press. The *Nation,* for example,

---

[7] *The Strategy of Peace,* by John F. Kennedy. New York, Harper, 1960.

called his proposals "timely and sensible." Previously, Kennedy had never shown the slightest interest in the subject. He had never been there and knew little about it.

Suddenly, in seeking an issue—in fact, any issue—with which to call attention to himself, Kennedy latched on to the North African rebellion. And without regard for the diplomatic niceties, he exploded a firecracker in the Senate that not only rattled White House windows but painfully burned an ally some four thousand miles away.

On July 2, 1957—two days before Independence Day—he delivered a lengthy Senate speech that, in effect, excoriated the French for their Algerian policy and the Eisenhower Administration for not lending its weight to the cause of Algerian independence.

His words annoyed the French, embarrassed Washington, and solved nothing. But they did one thing: they introduced Kennedy the Statesman.

"The elegant, rich young man—so good looking that the mothers of America consider him devastating—has not been a notable liberal," wrote Patrick O'Donovan, Washington correspondent of the *London Observer,* "but he has tilted at a safe target: Colonialism. His speech, carefully distributed in advance, achieved gratifying publicity."

The tragedy, however, was that—as the *New York Times* then observed —Kennedy had "added fuel to a raging fire. . . . To be of service in a situation like this requires the most delicate exercise of diplomacy and not a smashing public attack. . . . Neither from the French nor American point of view is the problem as clear or simple as Senator Kennedy tries to make it. Perhaps the strongest criticism of the Senator's efforts is that he has run a strong risk of making the situation worse. . . ."

The Kennedy speech dismayed even those Frenchmen most critical of their Government's Algerian policy. *Le Monde,* the ultra-Liberal daily, called Kennedy "badly informed" and guilty of "injustices and excesses."

"Even those Frenchmen most favorable to Algerian independence see the speech as increasing the trouble rather than lessening it," Volney Hurd cabled the *Christian Science Monitor.* "It is felt his speech could lead to more bloodshed by encouraging the extremist Moslems whose record of assassinations and ruthless bombings of children and women has shocked the majority of Frenchmen. . . . In other words, the present U.S. policy of officially keeping out of the Algerian situation but pressing hard through secret diplomatic channels for a liberal settlement is considered the much more hopeful method of settling the issue.

"Concern lest Kennedy may have upset the careful work done so far is acute here today."

Amidst the uproar, some French commentators speculated as to Kennedy's documentation. Their Gallic curiosity was whetted by the fact that, as *Le Monde* noted, the speech "shows exceptional knowledge of the French political milieu." Not that Senator Kennedy was not "sufficiently brilliant to have written the speech himself"—perish the thought!—"but it would seem he was guided in his task by advisers most *au courant* as to the intricacies of French politics."

Who were these advisers? Gossiping Parisians had a field day trying to identify them. Finally, in what was billed as a semi-official reply to Kennedy, Robert LaCoste, France's Governor-General in Algiers, contended that "the documentation was supplied to the Senator by the son of an important North African political personage"—presumably Habib Bourguiba Jr., the son of the Tunisian Premier, a diplomat in Washington, and a friend of Kennedy.

"Kennedy's speech was the act of a juvenile playing with matches near dynamite," said LaCoste. "It appears to be a characteristic of some American politicians to meddle in other people's troubles for political advantage at home."

Meanwhile, the White House let it be known it was seething over what it regarded as a "brashly political" move by Kennedy to embarrass the Administration's slowly mending relations with France. In fact, President Eisenhower and his top foreign policy advisers met to pool their thinking on the "whys" underlying Kennedy's "damaging fishing in troubled water."

A White House source, according to Ruth Montgomery, said this was the conclusion: Kennedy, the most junior member of the Senate Foreign Relations Committee, was eager to gain stature as a "world-thinking states-man." He selected Algeria, the source said, "because there is no such thing in this country as a 'French' or 'Algerian' vote."

At a press conference, Secretary of State Dulles said he would be "very sorry" to see the Algerian crisis, with its "exceptional difficulty and com-plexity," become a United States problem. And he suggested that if Kennedy's primary interest was in fighting colonialism, the Senator could start where it was at its evil worst—in the Soviet empire.

The next day, President Eisenhower noted that the "best role" the United States could play in Algeria was to "try to be understanding to both sides" while working behind the scenes for solutions. "That means you don't get up and begin to shout about such things, or there will be no effectiveness."[8]

But the unkindest cuts came from Kennedy's fellow Democrats. Adlai Stevenson, following a ten-week tour through Africa, told German newsmen that Algerian independence—as suggested by Kennedy—"at this time would in my opinion be an invitation to chaos." And, he added, "I know that a situation so intricate cannot be solved either by terror within or pressure without."

Congressman Emanuel Celler also charged in. The veteran Brooklyn Democrat said the Kennedy speech "at this time is as immature as it is unfair."

[8] On March 21, 1962, President Kennedy described the Algerian situation as "a very sensitive and difficult matter," and said that the United States should act "to build" there "rather than attempting for political purposes to exploit a situation."

Jolted by the adverse reactions, Senator Kennedy began to wonder whether he had blundered badly. And in time-honored fashion he again turned to his father for advice. The Senator telephoned the senior Kennedy who was then summering in the South of France.

"You lucky mush," the Ambassador told his son. "You don't know it and neither does anyone else, but within a few months everyone is going to know just how right you were on Algeria."

Dean Acheson, for one, didn't think so. The former Secretary of State, whom Kennedy had scathingly chided for the sell-out of China, derided the Senator's Algerian proposals as "the supreme touch of naïveté." Without mentioning Kennedy by name in his book *Power and Diplomacy,* Acheson wrote of France's plight: "The adjustment of a society to loss takes time. It will not help for us to snap impatient fingers at a people who were great before our nation was dreamt of, and tell them to get on with it."

Since then Kennedy has not snapped "impatient fingers" over Algeria. They had gotten burned too badly. In a February 1959 TV interview he was asked why—since his Algerian sortie—he had not again spoken out on the subject.

"I have refrained because I think it is unhelpful for a Westerner to make a comment, an American to make a comment," he replied.

Kennedy, however, confessed to one regret about his call for Algerian independence: "We might have spoken about permitting the Algerians to determine their relationship with France. The use of the word 'independence' may have been unwise. I have never seen an issue which has as much emotion in it as Algeria in France."

An extraordinary statement, it suggests that Kennedy may not have been fully aware of all the implications—and possible repercussions—in the crusade he had quickly launched and, just as quickly, dropped in 1957. Not to have known how emotion-packed the issue was in France was a surprising disclosure coming from a member of the Senate Foreign Relations Committee.

In June 1960 a British correspondent reminded Kennedy that in his Algerian speech he had stated, "The Western house must be swept clean of its own lingering imperialism."

"Well," said Kennedy, "I think an impressive job has been done on that. There are still areas where the Western house isn't clean. . . . But great progress has been made in the last fifteen years in freeing Africa from the remnants of Western imperialism. I don't think there's any doubt at all that Africa is going to be free in another decade."

At least this was a switch in emphasis for the Senator who a year before had gone beyond this usual anti-colonial theme to urge the United States to ignore "our traditional allies" in Europe in order to aid the peoples of Africa to gain their independence. Addressing the American Society of African Culture on June 28, 1959, Kennedy declared:

"It must not be that these people when free will look at the United

States as a country which was indifferent to their efforts to win their recognition. Instead we must hold out the hand of friendship to them now during this vital period, even if on occasion it brings us into disagreement with countries of Western Europe who have been our traditional allies. In doing so we serve the cause of freedom. In this matter we cannot remain neutral."[9]

In effect, Kennedy was proposing unilateral United States intervention in African affairs, even if it should lead to "disagreements" with our European allies.

What makes the Kennedy formula unrealistic is that there is, in fact, no basic contradiction between upholding the Western alliance and pursuing an anti-colonial policy. For the colonial powers had long been granting independence to their overseas possessions.

John F. Kennedy has long held a Europe-is-doomed attitude; the wave of the future, he believes, is with the Afro-Asian powers. In speech after speech, he warned of "total catastrophe" unless the leaders of the West accepted his anti-colonial nostrums.

Yet his sincerity in raising these issues was for a long time questioned. "Senator Kennedy is too shrewd to make a hobby out of Algeria," wrote Alistair Cooke in the Manchester *Guardian*. "It has brilliantly served its purpose of pitching him into center-stage. . . . This is as safe a mode of indignation as any man from Massachusetts could express.

"The choice of Algeria was a careful one. Precisely because it is a country that knows neither friend nor enemy in Massachusetts, it is no liability to his own constituents. But it has nicely suggested to his supporters that the Senator is a statesman, something like Stevenson, of majestic disinterestedness. . . . Ergo, the Senator's shadowy figure is suddenly spotlighted. . . ."

Kennedy denied that his Algerian speech was motivated by political considerations. Rather, he said, it was a natural outgrowth of his earlier concern with French colonialism in Indochina. Though he had never been to Algeria, his youngest brother Teddy had been there in 1956 along with Frederick L. Holborn, a Harvard government instructor. When they urged him to strike a blow for Algerian freedom, he was receptive, he said.

Previously, in 1955, Bobby Kennedy had returned from a Soviet trip singing a different tune. His journey, he said, had convinced him it would be "most enlightening" if the United Nations would "look into Soviet colonialist policies in Soviet Central Asia." While the Reds were wringing their hands over the fate of North African peoples under French "colonialism," Bobby informed a New York communion breakfast, the Kremlin itself was enforcing strict segregation between Russians and Moslems, sternly denying any kind

[9] Significantly, this quotation, which was taken from the *New York Times,* was excised from the text of the speech as published in Kennedy's *The Strategy of Peace.*

of local autonomy and keeping tight control on all jobs in the Asian republics.

Jack Kennedy also pointed out he had been making anti-colonialist speeches ever since his visit to Indochina in 1951. On July 8, 1954, he had warned the Senate that the price the United States was paying for the good will of its European allies was "a heavy price in connection with our relationship with the peoples of the Middle East and Asia." The Senator had not yet discovered the importance of the emerging nations of Africa.

"If we continue to pay this price," he continued, "we are going to be faced with other Indochinas all over the world where colonialism is maintained."

This was the speech in which Kennedy made what apparently was his first public reference to Latin American problems. "The two places in the Western Hemisphere where Communism developed were British Guiana and Guatemala," he noted. "Guatemala has been the victim of economic imperialism for many years in the past."

In retrospect, it was a curious statement. It was made only a few weeks after a Left-wing dictatorship had been toppled in Guatemala with the not-so-covert backing of the Central Intelligence Agency.

The successful CIA operation—a far cry from the bungling that was to take place in Cuba under Kennedy's auspices seven years later—was applauded by other Senate Democrats.

Lyndon Johnson, for example, gave this analysis: "International Communism builds up groups within states which are designated for conquest. . . . When they reach a certain point of strength they are then armed and are turned loose for military conquest. We have reached that point in the Western hemisphere."

In other words, while Johnson viewed the rise of Latin American Communism as the result of outside Soviet intervention, his younger colleague blamed it primarily on United States and British imperialism. In early 1960, according to Selig Harrison of the *New Republic,* "Kennedy was amused when reminded of his transgression in suggesting that the United States could be guilty of imperialism. 'Particularly,' in his words, 'with all those Boston banana kings.' "

Once again, a Kennedy was slashing back at the Boston Brahmins.

In his various speeches and remarks, Kennedy has demonstrated an almost obsessive hostility toward France—a fact which does not augur well for the Western alliance.

"The French bomb is aimed toward Washington rather than Moscow," he said in Palm Beach on December 15, 1959. ". . . This is an odd way to run an alliance."

It was an even odder thing to say. What he apparently meant was that the primary purpose of the French atomic bomb was not to increase French capabilities but to increase French stature in the North Atlantic Alliance.

But it could have led to the conclusion that Kennedy considered France a greater menace than the U.S.S.R. On another occasion, the Senator had stated that should "France, or China, or half a dozen other nations successfully test an atomic bomb, then the security of both Russians and Americans is dangerously weakened."

The genesis of Kennedy's Francophobia is difficult to pinpoint. Some authorities have ascribed it to traditional Irish antipathy toward colonialism. However, Kennedy's identification with the Irish was always minimal; and, moreover, he never demonstrated the same antipathies toward the British.

Kennedy's first anti-French remarks were made following his trip to Indochina in 1951. And once in the Senate, the Indochina war became "his" issue. In April 1953 he introduced an amendment to the foreign aid bill providing that Indochina funds "be administered in such a way as to encourage through all available means the freedom and independence desired by the people of the Associated States. . . ." That the French had already announced such plans was a fact brought to his attention by Democratic elder Walter George, then Chairman of the Foreign Relations Committee. Kennedy, however, refused to withdraw his amendment. As Ted Sorensen later recalled, "All that Walter George and the others could say was 'France is our ally.' "

In the Spring of 1954 when things looked bleak for the French in Indochina, Admiral Arthur Radford, then Chairman of the Joint Chiefs of Staff, recommended United States intervention; and Secretary Dulles declared that the "imposition in Southeast Asia of the political system of Communist Russia and its Chinese Communist ally . . . should be met by united action."

"The 'united action' which is said to be desperately needed for victory in that area," said Kennedy on April 6, 1954, "is likely to end up as unilateral action by our own country. . . . I am frankly of the opinion that no amount of American military assistance can conquer an enemy which is everywhere and at the same time nowhere, 'an enemy of the people, which has the sympathy and covert support of the people."

But what the Junior Senator recommended as a course of action was difficult to fathom. One alternative, he said, was for the United States to involve itself more directly—and militarily—in the conflict. The other was to negotiate a peace "based either upon partition of the area between the forces of the [Communist] Vietminh and the French Union, possibly along the 16th Parallel; or based upon a coalition government in which Ho Chi Minh is represented. Despite any wishful thinking to the contrary, it should be apparent that the popularity of Ho Chi Minh would cause either partition or a coalition government to result in eventual domination by the Communists."

Which alternative did Kennedy favor?

It could be argued that he favored both. "Certainly, I, for one," he told the Senate, "favor a policy of a 'united action' by many nations whenever necessary to achieve a military and political victory for the Free World in that area, realizing full well that it may eventually require some commitment of our manpower." Then came the kicker: "But to pour money, material, and men into the jungles of Indochina without at least a remote prospect of victory would be dangerously futile and self-destructive." And later, Kennedy observed that "if we are considering stepping in—and if we are to get the support of the American people for such a policy—and I believe the policy should be supported—we should insist that the causes of the struggle be clarified. . . ."

This, of course, was *Kennedyese* at its purest, demonstrating the Senator's remarkable ability to shuttle back and forth between positions that would appear to be diametrically opposed—and still sound sincere in doing it.

On April 16, 1954, when the French outpost at Dien Bien Phu was under attack, Vice President Nixon appeared at an off-the-record session of the American Society of Newspaper Editors. He was asked this hypothetical question: Would the United States send troops if the French pulled out?

Nixon replied: "The United States is the leader of the free world and the free world cannot afford in Asia a further retreat to the Communists. . . . Under the circumstances, if in order to avoid further Communist expansion in Asia and particularly in Indochina, if in order to avoid it we must take the risk by putting American boys in, I believe that the Executive branch of the government has to take the politically unpopular position of facing up to it and doing it, and I personally would support such a decision."

The statement "leaked" out. Soon news tickers crackled with garbled bulletins to the effect that the United States had threatened to enter the Indochinese war. In Congress, there were speeches assailing Nixon for "whooping it up for war." In Chicago, Kennedy said that if "Nixon's words are to be taken at their face value, we are about to enter the jungle and do battle with the tiger," adding that "the American people should be told the truth about the situation in the Far East. This has not been done."

On May 28, after the Geneva conference on Indochina was under way, Kennedy warned that there was "a definite possibility that within the next few weeks" Eisenhower would ask Congress to authorize United States military intervention.

It never happened.

What did happen was a negotiated settlement at Geneva, providing for the division of Vietnam at the 17th Parallel.

Some of Kennedy's colleagues—Lyndon Johnson and Stuart Symington, among them—castigated the settlement as "appeasement." Adlai Stevenson claimed "the West suffered its worst disaster since the loss of China." The Republicans, he added, had "successfully identified negotiation with appeasement."

Forgotten was the fact that the Indochina war had been going on for more than five years when the Eisenhower Administration took office. And that once China was lost to Communism, the victory of the Vietminh was practically assured.

Kennedy, however, disputed the "appeasement" characterization. He saw the West salvaging all that could be salvaged in Vietnam.

"I am not in sympathy with those who label every attempt at negotiation as appeasement," he told Hearst correspondent David Sentner. "We are not selling ourselves or our friends down the river even if we agree to compromise, as long as the results are in the interests of our national security and preferable to the continuation of a bloody struggle."

Nevertheless, Kennedy confessed surprise when, instead of taking over all of Indochina, the Communists settled for North Vietnam. Reflecting on the settlement in early 1960, he said, "I don't know why they ever agreed to that. They were on their way there."

Perhaps one reason why the Reds failed to press their advantage was their uncertainty as to whether they might not be pushing the United States too far.

In 1962, in the second year of the New Frontier, the United States at long last entered the jungle to do battle with the tiger. And this time it was the Republicans who demanded that the American people be told the truth about our involvement. Richard Nixon, however, announced general support of President Kennedy's Vietnam policy.

From 1954 to 1957 when he delivered his controversial speech on Algeria, Kennedy made no great splash on foreign policy. As 1960 neared, however, he began taking increasingly Liberal positions on foreign aid, nuclear disarmament, and negotiations with the Russians.

"Kennedy's post-1956 foreign policy ventures were unmistakably inspired to a great extent by dreams of 1960 . . . ," wrote Selig Harrison. "But in each case what he did had roots in what he had said and done earlier. He was fortunate in that his own intellectual flirtations had been leading him in the Stevenson-Bowles direction, a direction that politically speaking would prove helpful."

Kennedy's interest in India was aroused by what he heard at a small dinner party given in October 1957 in honor of Barbara Ward (Lady Jackson). Miss Ward, a former editor of London's *Economist* and a high priestess in the foreign-aid cult, had known Kennedy since 1945; she was a friend of Kennedy's sister Kathleen (the late Marchioness of Hartington) and had taken him around to Socialist rallies when he covered the 1945 British elections for Hearst.

What Kennedy heard from Miss Ward in 1957 was a powerful appeal for an enormous increase in United States aid to India. Indian Democracy, she argued, was in competition with Chinese Communism for the allegiance of countless Asians. India, therefore, must be made to succeed. So impressed was Kennedy with her arguments that the Senator began telling audiences that "when I asked Barbara Ward where the United States should concentrate in Asia, she said, 'India first, India second, India last.' "

"We want India to win that race with Red China," he declared in

November 1959. "We want India to be a free and thriving leader of a free and thriving Asia. But if our interest appears to be purely selfish, anti-Communist, and part of the Cold War—if it appears to the Indian people that our motives are purely political—then we shall play into the hands of Communist and neutralist propagandists, cruelly distort America's image abroad, and undo much of the psychological effect that we expect from our generosity."

The statement demonstrated the extent to which John F. **Kennedy** was employing Liberal jargon. The linking of the words "selfish" and "anti-Communist" was typical. And it may have later come as a surprise to Kennedy that other Asian nations—Pakistan, Burma, and Ceylon among them—actually feared India's "brown Imperialism" almost as much as they did Chinese Communism.

Instead of advocating assimilable types of aid to India, Kennedy took the lead in proposing huge, unrealistic programs designed to encourage Nehru's mania for grandiose five-year plans. As President, however, he began taking a new look at Asian realities. An agonizing reappraisal of aid to India was begun in the second year of the New Frontier.

As Senator, Kennedy also fought hard and successfully for an amendment to the Battle Act to permit United States aid to Communist Poland. The proposal made less of a splash than his Algeria speech, but Senator Knowland labeled it "an effort to get us to pick up the check," when it would have been better to let the Russians do it. "It seems to me," added Knowland, "that Senator Kennedy is now asking the American people to undertake a whole economic plan of bolstering the Communist world."

In a *Foreign Affairs* article in 1957, Kennedy warned against rigidity of policy, against relying on "paper defenses" like SEATO, against irresponsible pledges to "liberate" the satellites, against getting "lashed too tightly" to a single man and party, such as Chancellor Adenauer and his Christian Democrats. And he condemned the use of foreign-policy bipartisanship to stifle dissent, the lack of presidential direction, the "mongrelization of clashing views" from agencies operating in a vacuum that in time lead to central policy-making bodies becoming "mere vendors of compromise."

The essay was stronger on criticism than positive proposals. For example, while upbraiding Secretary Dulles for the "jagged" ups and downs of his Middle Eastern policies, Kennedy offered no significant alternatives. "Still," according to James MacGregor Burns, "it was a signal achievement—meaty, informed, insightful, and candid. Our foreign-policy makers, Kennedy said, must avoid both the utopian moralism of Don Quixote and the doubt and vacillation of Hamlet. It was clear that he proposed, as a possible top foreign-policy maker, to be neither."

No longer was Kennedy talking of how President Truman had "frittered away" victory in China because of bad advice from "the Lattimores and the Fairbanks." (If he had, he might have been accused in his own party of subscribing to the "twenty years of treason" line of criticism.) "How we 'lost' China or why we are in Korea are subjects of gross oversimplification," he now wrote. "Thus is our foreign policy mythology created, chapter by chapter." If they were myths, Jack Kennedy had helped to create them.

Kennedy's new line on China was that while he would keep the Red Chinese out of the United Nations as long as they fail to meet certain standards of behavior, he would let the offshore islands of Quemoy and Matsu go to Mao Tse-tung on the ground that they were "indefensible" and "provide a needless irritant." (He did not realize that with the abandonment of Quemoy and Matsu, Formosa itself would become the new and more dangerous irritant.) He also proposed "bringing the Chinese into the nuclear test ban talks at Geneva"—a policy of indirect recognition of the Peiping regime, opposed by the "China Lobby" of which Jack Kennedy himself was once a fervent spokesman. Moreover, Kennedy was one of the few Senators who refused to endorse the work of the Committee of One Million (in which such Liberal Democrats as Senator Paul Douglas were active), an organization devoted to keeping Red China out of the U.N.

In short, Jack Kennedy—to use the phrase his camp had hurled against Henry Cabot Lodge in the 1952 campaign—had become increasingly "soft on Communism"—the Chinese brand, at least.

Not that anyone was using this McCarthyite terminology against Kennedy. To a great extent he was immune from the kind of attacks he used to level on others. For as John Chamberlain put it in the *National Review* in April 1960: "There is one particularly reassuring thing about Kennedy: as a Catholic he could hardly capitulate to Communism. That *would* be letting his co-religionists down."

"Since the Roman Catholic Church is militantly anti-Communist," *Time* observed, "Kennedy feels that his Catholicism makes him pretty much immune to any suspicion of 'softness' toward Communism. Accordingly, he can take the political risks of declaring himself 'wholly opposed' to any U.S. commitment to defend the Nationalist Islands of Quemoy and Matsu."

Thus was Kennedy able to project a double image—hard and soft toward Communism at one and the same time.

At this time Kennedy began living what appeared to be a full legislative life. He attempted to carve out certain areas where he could be shown to speak with authority and leadership—labor reform, minimum wage extension, pension plan regulation, wider Social Security benefits, and economic aid to foreign nations. His activities in these areas were to counteract the criticism that if he did stand for something, it was for a way of thought too conservative for the standard-bearer of the Democratic party.

Behind this belief was his enormous popularity in the South. The fact that he had been dubbed "Dixie's favorite Yankee" had not been lost on the ADA, the NAACP, and other Liberal groups which can make or break a Democratic Presidential candidate. According to Alan Otten of the *Wall*

Street Journal, Kennedy's aides were now insisting that "the South wasn't for Jack, but against Kefauver at the 1956 Convention."

In fact, in Columbus, Ohio, Kennedy described himself as a "liberal, I hope a vigorous liberal."

"This was," reported the *Cleveland Plain Dealer's* Murray Seeger on July 29, 1959, "just after he asserted the Democrats must nominate a 'vigorous liberal' for President."

" 'Liberal' is hardly the tag most political observers would hang on Kennedy," Seeger added. "Usually he is considered somewhere between the liberal wing of the party in the Senate and the conservative, Southern wing."

"As a candidate," John Osborne reported in *Fortune* during the 1960 campaign, "Kennedy is working hard to prove himself a worthy leader of the liberal Democrats. But his father, the formidable Joseph Kennedy, laughs out loud at the notion that his son Jack is really a liberal. At this writing the Senator has yet to call himself a 'liberal' in the explicit way that Nixon calls himself an 'economic conservative.' "[10]

Though his father may have laughed out loud at the preposterous idea, the fact is that his son's political "growth line"—to use Drew Pearson's term—had veered most sharply in a left-of-center direction. In November 1959 Kennedy finally succumbed and joined the Democratic Advisory Council which consisted of such Liberal luminaries as Adlai Stevenson, Eleanor Roosevelt, Herbert H. Lehman, and G. Mennen Williams.[11] That year, too, Kennedy obtained a perfect voting rating from the ADA, an organization whose members had once made him feel so "uncomfortable."

On the opposite side of the fence the Americans for Constitutional Action reported in 1960 that in the previous five years Kennedy had voted "conservative" on only eleven per cent of the issues that conservative group had selected for analysis.

In February 1960 Senator Humphrey—during primary campaigning in Wisconsin—described Kennedy as "an election-year convert to true liberalism." This was not exactly accurate. The conversion took place in fits and starts over a period of years.

On April 10, 1960, the *Washington Star* published a full-page study of Kennedy's voting record which, according to writer David S. Broder, showed the Senator "has changed in the last four years from the most rugged individualist of the four Democratic hopefuls in the Senate into the biggest conformist. . . ."

The other Senate hopefuls were, of course, Stuart Symington, Lyndon

[10] After one year in office, President Kennedy—so the *New York Times* reported on January 2, 1962—"still refuses . . . to describe himself or his Administration as either liberal or conservative, right or left. Rather, he will commit himself only to what he calls a progressive course."

[11] One of Kennedy's first acts following his election as President was to abolish the Democratic Advisory Council.

Johnson, and Hubert Humphrey. Beginning in 1953, when Kennedy entered the Senate, the four men took positions on 893 roll-call votes. "In every year through 1956 when he missed by a whisker being the party's Vice-Presidential nominee, Senator Kennedy stood alone more often than any of his rivals," reported Broder.

"Since 1956, his lone stands have diminished in frequency each year, until in 1959 he was a 'loner' on only one vote."

Year by year, this was the record:

1953—Of the 68 votes on which the four hopefuls took positions, Senator Kennedy stood alone on 14. Most of these "lone wolf" votes were concerned with slashing federal spending.

1954—Of 145 votes, Kennedy stood alone on 25, half of which stemmed from his support of the Eisenhower farm policies. Not only did he support slashes in public works funds, but he opposed a boost in REA loan authorizations. At the same time, he voted against an amendment that would have authorized the Atomic Energy Commission to produce electric power and give preference to public bodies and co-operatives in distributing that power.

1955—On 8 of 71 roll calls, of which half were on farm matters, Kennedy stood alone. On the others, he voted for economies in foreign aid, against the Colorado River reclamation project, and was the only Senate Democrat to back the Eisenhower Administration's plan to finance construction of the interstate highway system through a bond issue.

1956—On 19 of 120 roll calls, Kennedy stood alone, chiefly on farm bills.

1957—For the first time since 1953, when he entered the Senate, Senator Kennedy was not the leading "lone wolf" of the four presidential aspirants. That role was played by Lyndon Johnson who stood alone on 11 of 102 roll calls, while Kennedy was by himself on only 4, his disagreements dealing with his efforts to reduce spending for the soil bank, public works, and one category of foreign aid.

1958—On 6 of 179 roll calls, fewer than either Humphrey or Johnson, Kennedy stood alone. These, however, were on relatively minor issues, including efforts to freeze or boost dairy price supports which Kennedy opposed.

1959—Senator Kennedy, now the least "different" of the quartet, stood alone on only 1 of 208 roll calls—and this was on an extremely insignificant issue, one on which he voted against making floating drydocks eligible for federal ship mortgage insurance.

In short, Kennedy became a Liberal (the trade name for the coalition of dissident minorities which F.D.R. had first put together) about the time he began to explore the route to the Presidency. He realized that national power, for an aspiring Democrat, depended on that coalition. "Lacking those urgent needs for reform that powered the New Deal with idealism," as *Life* noted in October 1960, "the 'Liberal' coalition today is merely synthetic and opportunistic. No coherent political-economic philosophy unites it (certainly not Jack Kennedy's). The New Frontier is a synthesis of the reasons Harvard professors think the people may have for voting Democratic."

Meanwhile, Kennedy began taking swipes at the Eisenhower Administration on domestic matters. Typical was a June 11, 1958, speech urging West Virginians to elect two Democratic Senators because they will be needed "to take effective measures against a recession, block undesirable Presidential appointments, and override arbitrary Presidential vetoes" during the last two years of the Eisenhower regime.

"These are," the *Morgantown* (West Virginia) *Post* said, "desirable objectives and nobody will find fault with Senator Kennedy for suggesting their importance. But since he is already a Member of the Senate and has made a record there which presumably reflects his honest convictions and his considered actions, Senator Kennedy might have been more convincing if he had told his hearers—

"What effective measures against a recession has the Eisenhower administration failed to take which Senator Kennedy himself favors?

"What undesirable Presidential appointments has Senator Kennedy voted to block?

"What arbitrary Presidential vetoes by President Eisenhower has Senator Kennedy voted to override?

"In a hasty check through the *Congressional Quarterly Almanac* for the years 1953–57, both inclusive, we have been unable to find a single instance in which Senator Kennedy voted to override any of President Eisenhower's 86 vetoes.

"Nor have we been able to run up a single instance in which Senator Kennedy voted to block any of the 20,753 appointments which President Eisenhower made in 1953, any of the 45,017 he made in 1954, any of the 40,686 he made in 1955, or any of the 43,467 he made in 1956.

"Of the 43,114 appointments which President Eisenhower made in 1957, Senator Kennedy is recorded as voting against confirmation of Jerome K. Kuykendall as Chairman of the Federal Power Commission, Dr. Don Paarlberg as Assistant Secretary of Agriculture, and Scott McLeod as Ambassador to Ireland.

"On the record, it appears that the occasions for Senator Kennedy to vote against undesirable Presidential appointments have been few and far between, and in each of the instances where he found himself voting against confirmation, the verdict of the Senate was decidedly in favor of confirmation."

Despite such pinpricks, the Kennedy build-up progressed as if on schedule. His speeches and articles took on a more intellectual flavor. Many, of course, were now being drafted—if not written—by professorial types on whom the Senator had begun to rely for what he termed "new ideas."

The truth is that Kennedy's own social and economic philosophy has always been eclectic. He has never displayed any originality of mind, nor produced any notable ideas of his own. His qualities were those of an almost disembodied alertness and intelligence. True, he conveyed an impression of clarity and decision; but what he was being clear about or what, in fact, he had decided was difficult to discover.

Thus, summing up Kennedy's views on major issues in April 1960, the *Washington Star's* David Broder wrote: "The Senator's views on economic questions are, if not mysterious, at least not fully developed. Like most Democrats, he has criticized the Administration's 'tight money policy' and called for a 'stimulated rate of growth,' without telling how he would reverse the one or achieve the other."

And in the October 1960 issue of *Fortune,* after quoting Richard Nixon's economic views *in extenso,* John Osborne reported that "a search through the Kennedy record does not produce statements of general principle to place alongside these quotations from Nixon."

Kennedy, however, had a real facility for finding and recognizing bright people and adopting their ideas as his own. To a large extent, he found these people at his alma mater. But his attraction to brightness was not random. Though perhaps most famous—or infamous (among some alumni, at least) —for its Liberal thinkers, Harvard also has a distinguished company of intellectuals who would classify as Conservative. But it was decidedly not among this latter group that Kennedy did his brain-picking. The Harvard trio closest to Kennedy in the late Fifties, and the recruiters for him of other brain-trust talent, included Arthur Schlesinger Jr. of the history department, Archibald Cox of the Law School, and John Kenneth Galbraith of the economics department. Cox, now United States Solicitor General, was advising Kennedy all through the long effort to write a labor reform bill.

There were other so-called eggheads whom Kennedy recruited for his brain trust. Max F. Millikan, director of the MIT Center for International Studies (and co-author, with Walt Whitman Rostow, of books and articles on foreign aid), recalled that Fred Holborn—then with Kennedy's Senate staff —got in touch with him in January 1958.

"They were looking for ways to dramatize the foreign aid issue. They said, 'We want to find the right pegs on which to hang a real effort to do something legislatively.' The Senator wanted Fred to come up and find out just precisely what the India problem was."

According to Rostow, Kennedy made some strong and perceptive speeches on India. But he went further on a Rostow proposal. Persisting after an initial failure in 1958, Kennedy and Republican Senator John Sherman Cooper (who had succeeded Chester Bowles as United States Ambassador in New Delhi) reintroduced in 1959 their resolution calling for a multi-national Western aid study mission to South Asia.

Future historians seeking an insight into Kennedy's mind, therefore, would do well to read the books, essays, reviews, etc., of these Kennedy intellectuals, of whom—for a time—the most important appeared to be J. Kenneth Galbraith and Arthur Schlesinger Jr.

Now in his mid-fifties, a Canadian by birth, Galbraith's career has been in government, journalism, and academic life. Regarded by his professional colleagues more as a literary man with a gift for telling phrases than as an economic thinker, Galbraith has taught at the University of California, Princeton, and—until his appointment as the New Frontier's first Ambassador to India, as a reward for political services rendered—at Harvard.

Perhaps the most important year in Galbraith's intellectual development was the one he spent as a post-doctoral student at Cambridge University, England, the home base of that most influential economist John Maynard Keynes.

Those were the days of great ferment in economics, with Keynesian theories and New Deal practices challenging the traditional methods of combating depressions. To get some answers from the High Priest himself, Galbraith took a year off in 1937–38 to study under Keynes. But Keynes was recuperating from a heart attack and Galbraith, who spent the year in advanced economic study, did not see him. (The two finally met in Washington during the war.) Nevertheless, Galbraith did absorb Keynesian doctrine.

After Cambridge, Galbraith became an instructor at Harvard, where as a tutor at Winthrop House he first met the Kennedy brothers, Joseph Jr. and John F. Neither brother apparently had impressed the tall, sardonic, witty Galbraith—at least as potential economists.

With the coming of World War II, Galbraith jumped into the Washington scene in a big way. A paper he had written on price controls had attracted attention, and he was rapidly made Deputy Administrator in the Office of Price Administration, charged with the responsibility of keeping the lid on prices. Before long he discovered few of his theories would work. In one final and furious spat over the issue of whether the Government should order canned goods to be graded on quality—he insisted it should—Galbraith resigned. He was then thirty-five years old.

The next stop was *Fortune,* where as one of the editors he spent his time polishing his distinctive style and writing technically competent articles on economic subjects. In 1948 he returned to Harvard and a year later was named a professor of economics. His academic career since then has followed a constantly ascending curve, and his writing career also blossomed. His ideas, too, became better defined. He became famous for his theory of "countervailing power"—a phrase which he used to bless an economy of Big Business, Big Labor, and always Bigger Government. And he continued to cast himself in the role of a leading neo-Keynesian.

Galbraith's best-known book, of course, is *The Affluent Society.* Even before it was published in 1958, his views commanded respect in Liberal circles bordering on awe. Even market "pros" took him seriously. When he told a United States Senate Committee investigating the stock market in 1955 that a repetition of the 1929 crash could occur, the market obliged by falling twenty-five points. Headlined the *New York Journal-American:* AN "EGGHEAD" GIVES THE MARKET A THOROUGH SCRAMBLING.[12]

In 1952 Galbraith joined Thomas K. Finletter in the singular task of tutoring Adlai Stevenson in things that every would-be President should know. Once a month at five-hour sessions in Galbraith's book-lined Cambridge living room or in Finletter's Manhattan apartment, distinguished lawyers, professors, and writers gathered to prepare "position papers" on a wide variety of issues. These resulted in the famous "big black books" which Stevenson carried during the campaign as source material for speeches, policies, anecdotes, even ad-libs. And the group itself eventually evolved into the Democratic Advisory Council, which, in 1960, was doing the same things, but on a greatly expanded scale. The Advisory Council reversed Jefferson's old maxim to make it read: "That government is best which governs most." Galbraith was the chief instrument of the change.

Galbraith came out early for Kennedy on the mistaken assumption that Stevenson would not try again. He still numbers Stevenson as among his "closest friends in the world."

Curiously, Galbraith seems to have taken a rather cynical view of rich politicians like Kennedy. On pages 178 and 179 of *The Affluent Society,* for example: "The American rich . . . have long since found it wise, as well as more fashionable, to suppress the cruder manifestation of opulence. They now seek prestige not by determinedly adding to their hoard but in public toil and good works. The number of exceedingly well-to-do Americans who have made a success in politics as the accepted friends of the masses attests to the success of the formula. The rich may have their problems, but they are not insuperable."

As a stump speaker for Kennedy, Galbraith enjoyed himself much more than on the lecture platform because "it gives you a chance to be aggressive in a way that would be out of place in a classroom." And as a professor-politician he was far happier giving his own speeches than writing someone else's.

"Ghosting speeches," he complained in 1960, "is the world's most difficult literary form. You must at all costs avoid confessing authorship. You must be prepared to work all day and most of the night on a speech draft that the candidate may not only never use but never even see. Boise, Idaho, the campaign directors may conclude, is not the place for exegesis of the problems of natural resources. Rather, let the candidate talk on the place of women in the home.

"It can be pretty frustrating."

---

[12] Ironically, it was in the New Frontier's second year when the stock market tumbled in a fashion to frighten many memories back to 1929.

In another revealing clue to his character, Galbraith also observed, "No economist ever had the slightest influence who writes only for other economists."

And Galbraith has always sought to have influence. Though he has neither the character nor the personality to have played the role of Professor Higgins to Kennedy's Liza Doolittle, for a time it was he, and he alone, who appeared to be filling the vacuum in economics in Kennedy's mind. For Galbraith's ideas are tinged with telling phrases, vivid imagery, and sardonic insight. And this invariably appeals to quasi-intellectuals like Jack Kennedy. "The bland leading the bland" was a Galbraithian phrase borrowed by Kennedy to describe the Eisenhower Administration.

Well phrased rhetoric still impresses Kennedy. As President, he received a letter from Charles De Gaulle urging him not to negotiate with the Soviets over Berlin. The French leader, as usual, stated his case with supreme eloquence. "Upon what field shall we meet?" his concluding passage began. In De Gaulle's judgment there was no appropriate field. Kennedy, visibly excited, read the letter aloud to several friends.

"Isn't that beautiful?" he said at the end.

"You agree with it?" one of the listeners asked.

"Oh, no!" the President said quickly. "But what a marvelous style!"

Even Galbraith's severest critics concede that he can turn a phrase exquisitely. One of them, John Chamberlain, has observed, "There is no more entertaining writer in America."

The Affluent Society, a work which made a deep impact on Kennedy, was a trenchant criticism of American values. Behind the showy opulence of fin-tailed automobiles, free-form shaped swimming pools, safer deodorants, fresh-frozen Maine lobsters, over-booked luxury liners, and the weekend split-level ranch house, Galbraith saw a nation of social mendacity fast becoming a desert of the human spirit. While the private interests and material intake of the financially privileged gluts to obesity, the "public sector" (another phrase Kennedy used in his speeches) starves.

Meanwhile, education, welfare, housing, defense get only the stalest crumbs from the table creaking with the riches of our affluence. The prescription was simple: Take away from the private sector and give to the public sector. To right the imbalance between what he calls "private opulence and public squalor," government guidance is necessary.[13]

Needless to say, there was a germ of truth in each of Galbraith's com-

[13] In the foreword to *The Affluent Society* (Boston, Houghton Mifflin, 1958), Professor Galbraith acknowledged that a Guggenheim fellowship facilitated a visit to Switzerland where he worked on the book and "tried out the core of these ideas" on university students in Geneva. He was also able to elaborate them at the California Institute of Technology at the expense of the Haynes Foundation and "the chapter on poverty towards the end drew heavily on research financed by a grant from the Carnegie Foundation." Such is life in the Affluent Society. First class all the way.

plaints. And a germ was all he required to find his patient sick, sick, sick. The inability of our big cities to cope effectively with traffic congestion does suggest that here and there the area of public spending should be enlarged. And when Dr. Galbraith comments acidly upon the equanimity with which unemployment is viewed by those who have never been unemployed, he pleads a sympathetic cause, even though he has himself been criticized from the Left by Leon Keyserling for overestimating the extent of the world's—and even of United States—"affluence."

Keyserling symbolized the "old" as against the "new" Liberal approaches toward social goals. Whereas the Liberals from New Deal days sought to end poverty and to spread such material blessings as automobiles, deep freezers, garbage disposal units, etc., among the "underprivileged," the "new" Liberals now were out to curb the private amenities of life under the guise of "improving the public sector."

What they urged had another name, "compulsive public spending," applied by Eisenhower's Budget Director Maurice H. Stans.

But Dr. Galbraith's prescription for an ailing economic order is to make a free economy less free. His assumption is quite simple: People individually are incompetent to know how to spend their money, but people collectively—through government agencies—are thoroughly competent to spend everyone else's income. When the American people deserted the fin-tailed car without any coercion from Washington, D.C., Galbraith did not have the grace to admit that individuals were capable of upgrading their tastes without political interference.

Galbraith, though recently stationed in distant India, continues to sway President Kennedy through Arthur Schlesinger Jr., who takes his economics straight from his good friend "Ken." In a pre-election pamphlet written for private circulation, Schlesinger called for more Government spending so that the country can have what it needs. These needs, he added, can best be supplied by economic growth. "All that is involved is a marginal shift of resources—say some 10–12 billion a year more to be employed for public purposes. Such a shift in resources can easily be achieved within the framework of our present economic and political order. It would entail no interference with the existing freedom of investment or of entrepreneurial decision or of consumer choice."

Schlesinger, of course, did not achieve fame as an economist. His early ambition was to become a drama critic. Instead, he became an historian.

Arthur Schlesinger Jr. was born in Columbus, Ohio, in October 1917 —the eldest of two sons of Elizabeth (Bancroft) and Arthur Meier Schlesinger. The father, who was to win fame as an American historian, was installed at Harvard in 1924.

Arthur Jr., after attending public schools in Cambridge, prepared for college at Exeter. Even as a young man he had no compunction in calling people "idiots."

"At sixteen," a family friend recalled, "he knew everything and had no hesitancy telling you."

Gardner Jackson has a vivid memory of an evening at the Schlesinger home a year or so later. Arthur's mother, noticing a frown on her son's face, said, "Now, Arthur, I can say what I think, can't I?"

"Only if you know what you're talking about," the future Presidential adviser snapped.

Few people have neutral feelings about Arthur Schlesinger Jr. Though generally liked by those who know him, he usually creates an unfavorable impression with people who have heard him in debate. His scornful ripostes may win the argument but lose the audience.

After graduation from Harvard in 1938, he went off for a year's study in Cambridge, England, and returned to Cambridge, Massachusetts, as a Junior Fellow. In 1940, he married Marian Cannon, a daughter of Harvard physiologist Walter B. Cannon. During World War II he served, first, with the Office of War Information in Washington and, then, with the Office of Strategic Services in Europe. After a brief spell as a free-lance writer, he returned to Harvard as an associate professor.

"But he returned with a dismaying sense that Cambridge was remote from the stream of history," wrote Irwin Ross. It was a perpetual conflict between a life of scholarship and a life of action. "Each September he would take up his academic duties with groans of despair, hating the routine, yearning to escape his exile. But he stayed on, becoming an ornament to the Harvard faculty, an abundant intellectual resource for the liberal movement, and a leading social attraction for Cambridge."

His *The Age of Jackson,* published in 1945, turned out to be a backhanded panegyric to Franklin D. Roosevelt. In *The Age of Roosevelt,* of which three volumes have already been published, the panegyric was no longer backhanded; it was an overhead smash.

Though the Jackson book won the Pulitzer prize, some historians have expressed reservations, believing that Schlesinger forced facts too vigorously to fit a thesis. Most of the criticism centered around Schlesinger's handling of the struggle over the Bank of the United States. He made President Jackson out to be the champion of the common man, fighting the massed opposition of the rich. Actually, say other equally learned historians, bankers and businessmen were on both sides of the conflict.

Schlesinger is one of those historians who does not believe in making any facts public if they tend to embarrass the Democrats. In 1955 he denounced the State Department's publication of the Yalta documents, which recorded at least part of F.D.R.'s 1945 negotiations with Stalin. Though the documents were of undoubted historical importance, Schlesinger described their publication as "a classic example" of a determination to sacrifice the interests of peace and diplomacy for a "political point." Other Democrats complained it prompted disunity at home—meaning that it took some of the luster off the Roosevelt halo.

The Schlesinger method of political warfare was demonstrated in 1951, when the Truman Administration was being regularly embarrassed by scandals. As a loyal Democrat, Schlesinger tried to drag a red herring across the trail by pinning a corruption label on former President Hoover. In a letter to the *New York Times* he dragged out the ghosts of the Teapot Dome scandal which had rocked the Harding and Coolidge Administrations. "Far from objecting to corruption then," Schlesinger wrote, in response to the former President's criticism of the deep-freeze-and-mink disclosures, "Mr. Hoover sat in entire complacency as Secretary of Commerce while his colleague, the Secretary of the Interior, sought to loot the government. . . . Not only did Mr. Hoover fail to make any public objection to Secretary of the Interior Fall, or to Attorney General Harry Daugherty . . . but . . . eight days after Fall's hasty resignation [he later went to prison] . . . Hoover wrote him [a warm letter of commendation]." Schlesinger cited these as "indisputable facts."

These "facts," as Admiral Lewis L. Strauss replied in the *Times,* were strictly the product of Schlesinger's vivid imagination. Fall had not resigned hastily. His resignation had been announced two months before the finger of scandal touched him. So little suspicion had there been at the time that, as Admiral Strauss noted, the *Times* itself editorially deplored Fall's departure from the Cabinet. By the time proof of Fall's dishonesty was adduced, Mr. Hoover was President—and the prosecution was conducted by his own Attorney General.

As McGeorge Bundy, a former Harvard dean and now a White House colleague, has said of Schlesinger: "He's a terribly partisan man, to a degree rarely found in academic life."

Schlesinger's first major involvement in politics came in 1947 when he helped found Americans for Democratic Action. The ADA was founded to extirpate Communist influence among Liberals. According to Ross, Schlesinger's "larger concern was in helping create a political instrument which would provide the talent, ideas and *élan* to move the Democrats toward those larger social goals from which the war had deflected the New Deal."

Over the years he kept up parallel interests in both the larger orbit of the Democratic party and the more confined circles of the Liberal left. He took an active part in the American Committee for Cultural Freedom; and he waged an acrimonious battle to move the Committee to a more resolute anti-McCarthy stand. Within the American Civil Liberties Union he sought the removal of a Washington counsel whom he considered too much of a Red-baiter.

During the 1952 and 1956 campaigns Schlesinger was a speech writer for Adlai Stevenson. Though they were in substantial agreement, there were occasional disputes. In 1956 Arthur wanted Adlai to come out punching on civil rights; Adlai, however, was playing for the South. A typical example of a Schlesinger contribution was a 1952 speech, in which Stevenson denounced Old Guard Republicans as men "who have had to be dragged, screaming and kicking into the 20th Century." Schlesinger is still proud of the phrase.

"Arthur has always been extremely helpful—in writing, in ideas, in developing a program," Stevenson has said. "I've come closer to having a ghost writer in him than in anybody else."

Schlesinger has great zest for both work and play. As a bookish young man he was no great social success. But more recently he has been a demon on the dance floor. "You have to be sound of mind and limb to dance with Arthur," confided Mrs. Seymour Harris, wife of the celebrated Harvard economist.

"Arthur enjoys moving in society with a capital S," says another woman who knows him well. "He admires the ease, the graciousness that money and social status bring. He isn't interested in social prestige per se; he simply feels that these people are decorative and attractive, that they know how to live well. He admires elegance."

He also admires power.

Schlesinger's affinity for men of power is one of the most remarkable aspects of his altogether remarkable career. "Fascinated though he is by power," commented Irwin Ross, "it is the fascination of the counselor and confidant; he has never betrayed a desire to wield power personally."

Senator Hubert Humphrey observed that Arthur was never "pushy"; that, for example, at a banquet he was not the sort to push his way into the spotlight with the guest of honor. As an adviser, he seeks to influence. But he is willing to forego public credit.

"He is not a glory seeker," said Senator Humphrey.

Professor Galbraith said his younger colleague gravitated toward men of power effortlessly, less seeking than sought. And it was easy to understand why. "He is one of the best-informed men in the United States. He has an excellent sense of policy; he is highly literate, an able speech writer. And he has one other asset: most advisers are bores; Arthur is one of the rare individuals who is entertaining to the people he's helping."

In 1959, Schlesinger published a pamphlet, "The Shape of National Politics to Come," which claimed that the "Eisenhower lull" period was coming to an end and that the nation was probably ready for "a bold new advance." The document, which John F. Kennedy later seized upon as the "bible" for his Presidential campaign, held that in this nation's history there is "an inherent cyclical rhythm" in national affairs, "a predictable swing from periods of intense activity, which accomplish a lot of things but finally wear people out, to periods of apathy and passivity, which hold on until the national energy is replenished and forward motion can again be resumed."

Kennedy also borrowed heavily from another Schlesinger pamphlet published in early 1960, "The Big Decision: Private Indulgence or National Power," which eloquently argued the Galbraithian thesis that a reallocation of resources from the private to the public sector was necessary to meet social needs at home and responsibilities abroad.

At times, however, Schlesinger had his doubts concerning Kennedy. To him the coolly efficient types clustered around the Senator were not as congenial as the more intellectual advisers surrounding Stevenson. An old friend who saw him at the 1960 Convention said that Schlesinger was virtually immobilized by a conflict of loyalties.

"Arthur's attitude toward Stevenson," he said, "seemed to be similar to that of a man who has left his wife and run off with a new woman; later he encounters his wife and is suddenly afflicted with all sorts of memories and doubts. There was no mistaking Arthur's inner turmoil."

Author Norman Mailer recalls a Los Angeles lunch at which he asked Schlesinger why he was supporting Kennedy over Stevenson. The professor had just come from addressing the Pennsylvania caucus. In speaking for Kennedy, he had preceded Stevenson. Still caught up with the conflicting emotions of the event, Schlesinger downed his drink and then delivered an analysis of the character and abilities of the two men. At the end, two huge tears rolled down his cheeks, possibly in memoriam for the might-have-been of Adlai Stevenson.

Then came the final blow—the nomination of Lyndon Johnson for Vice President. Like many others in the "egghead" contingent, Schlesinger regarded it as a grievous betrayal; he and Galbraith "had been had."

Soon after the Convention, Kennedy invited Schlesinger to Hyannis Port. The two men had a long and earnest conversation, and Schlesinger returned to Kennedy's corner. Once again Kennedy's charm had worked its magic.

Within a short time Schlesinger was at work on a slender book entitled, *Kennedy or Nixon: Does It Make Any Difference?* It was primarily directed at those Liberals who answered the question in the negative.

Schlesinger, of course, enjoyed considerable prestige with a limited but articulate segment of American intelligentsia. Although many members of this group had misgivings about Vice President Nixon, they were unsettled by the repudiation of Adlai Stevenson at Los Angeles and by the harsh tactics and large sums of money spent by the Kennedy forces to achieve the nomination. Having serious reservations about Kennedy, they wondered whether the 1960 election did not really confront them with a Hobson's choice.

Schlesinger's literary contribution was clearly addressed to this group. Though extremely well written, it was an extraordinary volume to have come from a winner of the Pulitzer, Francis Parkman and Bancroft Prizes in history. Its serious defects as responsible literature—namely, its unwarrantable suppositions, inferences, and conclusions about the personalities of the candidates—were hidden in the author's unfailing style and urbanity. It was a strong—and undoubtedly persuasive—appeal to American intellectuals to cast their reservations aside and rally 'round the flag.

But it showed none of the intellectual objectivity that is supposedly characteristic of a careful historian. "A good many of his friends were dismayed by this performance," reported Irwin Ross, "feeling he had done a disservice to his own reputation as a serious writer." Schlesinger's treatment was emotional and subjective. It was, as Stewart Alsop noted, a prime example "of the total irrationality Nixon-hating produces among otherwise respected intellectuals."

Schlesinger's basic thesis was that "there is a considerable difference" between the personalities, policies, and parties of the two candidates. He found Nixon an utterly synthetic type, bereft of basic belief, opportunistic in method, eager for the Presidency merely as the capstone of a highly successful career.

By contrast, Kennedy was a man of conviction, experience, and wisdom, a good pragmatic Liberal animated by idealistic impulse; he sought the Presidency to effect noble ends. Though he did fault Kennedy on the McCarthy issue, Schlesinger—as Irwin Ross observed—"otherwise accepted his hero at his own valuation and wrote a portrait not totally recognizable by anyone who knew Kennedy. Quite apart from the ultimate merits, Schlesinger's criteria were clearly more relaxed in evaluating Kennedy than Nixon; in effect, he was guilty of applying a moral double standard."

For example, according to Schlesinger, Richard Nixon was "corny," "has no philosophy," "is not on record as a great reader," and delivers "jejune and boring" speeches. Kennedy, however, was "non-corny," has "read a good deal about poverty," "cares about the issues," "has a sense of history," and is "sharp, analytical, practical and unfettered."

In short, Kennedy was the "good guy" while Nixon was the "bad guy." When Kennedy changes his mind about something, it's because he's growing in wisdom. When Nixon changes his mind, it's further evidence of his lack of principle.

In a short paragraph on the economic policies of the two candidates, Schlesinger vividly argued for greater investment in the public sector of the economy and less in the private sector. Referring to Nixon's proposals that income tax rates in the higher brackets be reduced, that a general manufacturers' sales tax be substituted for our present system of excises, and that larger depreciation allowances and faster tax write-offs be allowed businessmen, Schlesinger said:

"One of the problems of growth rates is that 'gross national product' is a statistical measure which weighs a million dollars' worth of cosmetics equally with a million dollars' worth of hospitals or missiles. The Nixon proposals might well increase the gross national product by stimulating the production of more lipstick and eye shadow. But our present shortage in the United States is not a shortage of consumer goods. It is a shortage of things which the private economy does not and, in the main, cannot provide—everything from schools to atomic submarines. The problem obviously is to steer our fantastic wealth into areas where, instead of serving national self-indulgence, it builds national power."

This was an effective, though somewhat glib, statement of the Galbraithian point of view. Perforce it assumed that an intellectual elite, because of its infinite wisdom and understanding, could allocate economic resources better than the mechanism of more or less free markets. The intellectuals and the "sons of the rich," who, Schlesinger observed, "sometimes grow deeply concerned with the suffering of the poor and the inequities of society," were the hope of the Schlesingerian world. The Republicans, on the other hand, had become the "stupid party."

Inevitably, the translation of this viewpoint into public policy would mean curtailing the relative freedom of consumers and augmenting the relative power of the federal government. One must add, however, that it demonstrates a low estimation of the American people to characterize their choices in the market place as simply serving "national self-indulgence."

Nevertheless, this was an argument that was at least within the limits of proper controversy and fair debate.

Though Schlesinger purported to present "hard and verifiable facts" plus "reasoned analysis," roughly two-thirds of his book was devoted to the candidates' personalities. And insofar as he inquired into the inner life of Jack Kennedy one perhaps could not object too strongly. The two men, if we may take Schlesinger's word for it, were friends for many years. But he did not know Nixon.

The burden of much of the book was that Kennedy—unlike Nixon—was committed to a body of more or less coherent doctrine and that the reason can be found in the psyches of the two men. To say the least, the author's point would have been considerably strengthened had he given some evidence—however subjective—in support of his claim that some time after the bad old days of Kennedy's "McCarthyism" and "Bensonism" the Senator saw a white light on the road to Damascus.

"Let us try a test," Schlesinger challenged his readers. "Can anyone imagine Kennedy giving the Checkers speech?"

It was indeed a difficult thing to imagine, for a reason indicated by a story appearing in the Martin and Plaut book with respect to Kennedy's 1952 Senate campaign:

"After midnight once, on a freezing night, Kennedy drove for hours searching for a motel, finally found a tourist home in the town of Athol, got himself ready for bed when he spotted some dog hairs, got dressed again, piled back into his car, and drove on. He's allergic to dogs."

Road

17

The woods are lovely, dark and deep.
But I have promises to keep,
And miles to go before I sleep.
　　　　　　　　　—Robert Frost

There may have been a wistful note in the voice of John F. Kennedy as he quoted from the New England bard in taking his departure from a Wisconsin college in the Spring of 1959. The road that leads to the Presidency is long and arduous and a man who would dwell in the White House must travel many miles and make many promises.

For over two years the Junior Senator from Massachusetts had kept up almost a commuter's schedule between Washington and the rest of the nation. It was a body-bruising and brain-numbing experience. It was, he complained, "an endless treadmill of running around the country."

Besides, as one of his aides told Theodore H. White in early 1960, Kennedy wanted "to be President in the worst damned way." The implication, of course, was that he would do anything to achieve his ambition. "He has the F.D.R. instinct: when he gets into a fight, the instinct is to kill, not to wound," the aide added. "Being President is . . . not a panty-waist business."[1]

---

[1] The quotation appears in a White article on Kennedy's pre-Convention activities, published in the *Saturday Review* of March 26, 1960. Later, White wrote a more romanticized account of the 1960 campaign, entitled *The Making of the President— 1960* (New York, Atheneum, 1961).

In a December 1959 profile of Kennedy, London's *Economist* (one of J.F.K.'s favorite magazines) described him as "the Presidential candidate whose popular image contrasts most sharply with his real personality. The general impression is of a handsome, dashing, colorful Democrat who has many of the happy qualities associated with youth: high spirits, impulsiveness, a warm heart and an easy direct approach to life. Senator Kennedy is indeed handsome, but behind the boyish mask lies a convoluted and complex personality."

"A Liberal Senator who has worked closely with John Kennedy, and who is not unsympathetic to him, has described him 'as a pretty cold fish.' " commented Max Lerner in April 1960. ". . . No one as intensely competitive in his drive to power has come up in the Democratic political arena in our time, and no one has built a campaign machine to equal Kennedy's in its cold, impersonal efficiency. I don't mean that Kennedy is a natural politician; he isn't. He gives me the uneasy feeling of not really liking politics—in the way, for example, that Roosevelt liked it, or Truman, or in the way Lyndon Johnson likes it. But he has thrown himself into it with an almost frightening intensity, as if his life depended on his getting to the White House.

"If his life doesn't depend upon it, I suspect that his self-image does—which may amount to the same thing."

He was an enigma even to his biographer. True, James MacGregor Burns came to feel Kennedy was of "high presidential quality and promise." Nevertheless, he confessed misgivings. And he quoted a Capitol Hill observer as asking, "Where is the heart in the man—what makes it tick?"

Extraordinarily self-contained and seemingly self-possessed, Kennedy was capable of an emotional detachment about himself and those around him which was unusual in a relatively young man. Yet it is no secret in Washington that Kennedy hurts easily. In replying to Harry Truman's suggestions of immaturity on Convention eve, Kennedy displayed a wounded indignation which a more seasoned politician would have concealed—if he had felt it at all. As the *Economist* then noted, "Kennedy seems to lack that quality of relaxed unconcern which enables a man to bend under pressures just enough to save himself from cracking."

"The thing that bothers me most about Jack is this attitude that everybody is on earth for the sole purpose of helping him," a fellow Senator told the *Wall Street Journal*'s Robert Novak.

Another Senator, described as a famed member of the Foreign Relations Committee, in explaining why he was supporting Kennedy for the Presidential nomination, told the *London Observer*'s Philip Deane:

"For God's sake, don't attribute this to me, because he'd never forgive me. Jack is a bad enemy to have."

Why then was the Senator supporting Kennedy? Because, he said, like most Democrats, he wanted to win "desperately," and the Democrats felt they could win "biggest" with Kennedy.

"But," Deane reported, "they are uneasy about him. . . . He is not described as generous, charitable, hospitable, friendly, broadminded, compassionate, imaginative, faithful. Gossip is nearly always malicious but gossip about Kennedy is frequently vicious."

Gossip infuriated Kennedy. Few politicians, in fact, have ever been under such constant harassment—he didn't write any of his books; he was stricken with an incurable disease; he bought all his elections; he was just a tool of his father who, in turn, was putty in the hands of the Catholic hierarchy. But, he told a close friend in June 1960, he had become thick-skinned about such charges. He recalled how opponents had charged F.D.R. with having syphilis and General Eisenhower with being a "German Jew."[2]

Now, according to Kennedy, he was rolling with the punches, figuring—as he put it—"they never knock a loser." Anyway, he explained, jealousy was the mainspring of this criticism—from people who had never written books and from men who have had heart attacks.

This last, of course, was a slap at Lyndon Johnson who, in 1955, had been laid low by a heart attack. By late 1959, relations between Kennedy and his Majority Leader had become extremely bitter. Kennedy felt Johnson was trying to undermine him wherever possible. He saw the Texan's hand in the complicated maneuvering aimed at embarrassing him on the labor reform bill. Their feud became one of the hottest in the Senate. Johnson made no secret of his disgust with Kennedy's repeated absences at times he needed his troops.

Kennedy never moved close to the Senate's fabled "inner circle," the bipartisan after-hours group of distinguished Senators who make the deals and keep things moving. Jack, by now, was not highly thought of by his colleagues. In Senate popularity polls taken by the news media, he usually finished far down the list. Lyndon Johnson usually led the list.

"I sincerely fear for my country if Jack Kennedy should be elected President," Barry Goldwater told Westbrook Pegler. "The fellow has absolutely no principles. Money and gall are all the Kennedys have."

Kennedy had something else. "Egotism and a fierce will to succeed are his ruling characteristics," said the *Economist*. "In the service of his own ambition, he is wily and coldly calculating, but not hypocritical. Candor is probably his most engaging personal trait. Senator Kennedy is unashamedly a man on the make."

His candor was indeed remarkable—and revealing. For example, he told *Newsweek's* Benjamin Bradlee that he had a pet peeve about President Eisenhower. "He calls me 'Kennedy.' " he exclaimed. "How do you like that!"

"His intellectual qualities are his strongest point," according to the *Economist*. "He is the most widely-read of all the candidates. . . . Well versed in history, government, economics and foreign affairs, he has great intellectual

---

[2] Gerald L. K. Smith had alleged in 1952 that Eisenhower was a "Swedish Jew" and, therefore, according to that apostle of hate, obviously unfit to be President.

curiosity and is astute in 'picking the brains' of the many experts whom he cultivates."[3]

Judging from some news stories, there was scarcely a book published that Kennedy hadn't read or wasn't reading. "At home at night he dips into the Federalist Papers and studies history," reported Rowland Evans Jr. in August 1959. "He's reading 'Pilgrim's Progress' and a new book on Africa." Kennedy had taken a speedreading course in Baltimore (along with some soft drink salesmen) and was apparently devouring books by the libraries.

Lyndon Johnson, however, let it be known his Senate duties didn't permit him to do much outside reading.

Many a writer was pleasantly surprised to discover that Kennedy was familiar with his efforts. Upton Sinclair recalled receiving a letter from the Senator saying how much he enjoyed reading the works of the sage of Monrovia. Ian Fleming, here from London, was happy to hear from Kennedy's own lips how much he enjoyed following the adventures of British Super-Agent James Bond. (Bond, a love-'em-and-leave-'em type, included among his adventures the outwitting of the entire Soviet espionage network.) And Norman Mailer, interviewing Kennedy for *Esquire,* was struck most by "a passing remark whose importance was invisible on the scale of politics, but was altogether meaningful to my particular competence."

"As we sat down . . . Kennedy smiled nicely and said that he had read my books," wrote Mailer, somewhat aghast. "One muttered one's pleasure. 'Yes,' he said, 'I've read . . .' and then there was a short pause . . . in which it was obvious no title came instantly to his mind, an omission one was not ready to mind altogether since a man in such a position must be obliged to carry a hundred thousand facts and names in his head, but the hesitation lasted no longer than three seconds or four, and then he said, 'I've read "The Deer Park" and . . . the others,' which startled me for it was the first time in a hundred similar situations, talking to someone whose knowledge of my work was casual, that the sentence did not come out, 'I've read "The Naked and the Dead" . . . and the others.' If one is to take the worst and assume that Kennedy was briefed for this interview (which is most doubtful), it still speaks well for the striking instincts of his advisers."

Thus was the hipster vote won.

Kennedy was also engaged in buttering up the non-fiction intellectuals. He seems to have discovered that the way to an intellectual's heart is through his frustrations. Nothing pleases a thinking-man more than the idea that someone out there is actually taking him seriously.

[3] Kennedy's knowledge of history, however, is questionable. "For just as historians tell us," Kennedy declared in his acceptance speech, "that Richard I was not fit to fill the shoes of bold Henry II—and that Richard Cromwell was not fit to wear the mantle of his uncle—they might add in future years that Richard Nixon did not measure up to the footsteps of Dwight D. Eisenhower." Needless to say, Richard Cromwell was the son and not the nephew of Oliver.

In January 1960, shortly after he officially announced his candidacy for the nomination, Kennedy met with a group of Harvard and M.I.T. intellectuals. One of those present told John Obsorne that Kennedy had informed them with great earnestness: "I want to say things from now on that I can live with as President of the United States. All I am asking of you is your best thought on subjects in your fields of competence."

"And," said the professor who told the story, "that *is* all he asks."

Osborne's article in the October 1960 issue of *Fortune* was a major effort to establish the policy thinking of both Kennedy and Nixon. He wrote:

"On the question of how deeply and firmly these two men hold their beliefs an interesting difference appears. Nixon's advisers find in him a quality of deep conviction that conditions his public policies. Kennedy's advisers tend to give somewhat complicated answers when they are asked whether they consider him a man of 'conviction.' A typical reply goes: 'If you mean a set of preconceptions, a set of initial beliefs—no, Kennedy does not have that. It seems to me that he operates from acquired premises, from positions reached by conscious definition and choice. I admire that in him. It makes for positions that will be strongly held because they have been clearly formulated and are thoroughly understood.' An interesting variation of this analysis runs: 'He is a genuine liberal. But he is not a bleeding-heart liberal. He is a liberal of the 1960's—a rationalist, a man who deals in reality rather than in rhetoric. He's not what you would call an all-outer. He's not an all-outer in anything.'

"His staff's standard description of Kennedy as 'a fiscal conservative, completely dedicated to fiscal responsibility' strikes most of his economic intimates as about right. The adviser who shook his head in disbelief when this description of Kennedy was quoted and said, 'That's not the Jack Kennedy I know,' is an exception."

Usually Kennedy's closest advisers did not know—or at least were not certain—how he viewed a problem in their own field, even after discussing it with him time and again. "One never knows—one never should know—how Kennedy receives a viewpoint," was the characteristic comment heard by Osborne. "It is part of a politician's duty to protect himself from unnecessary commitments, even in discussions with friends."

Ideologically, Kennedy was a hard man to pin down. Depending which way the political winds were blowing, he could turn Left or Right. He always gave himself plenty of room to maneuver.

"On what issues does Kennedy feel deeply and respond to instinctively?" asked the *Economist*. "This awkward question must be asked of Presidential aspirants because in the American system of government so much depends upon the convictions and personal style of the man at the apex of power.

"The tentative answer in Senator Kennedy's case must be that he has no reservoir of deep feelings about public issues. His approach is almost cerebral. His tolerant, humane, liberal opinions are not nourished by any discernible hatred for injustice or any fellow feeling for the suffering and the deprived.

This emotional thinness is distressing to those liberals who regard the struggle for civil rights as the touchstone in politics and assistance to the underdeveloped countries as the touchstone in foreign affairs. Mr. Kennedy's stated views on both these great issues are adequate, but his critics fear that if he were burdened by the enormous weight of the Presidency he might have neither the self-consistent philosophy nor the emotional stamina to persevere in those views.

"These doubts may do Kennedy a serious injustice, but there is nothing he can do between now and the nominating convention to disprove them. It is in this sense that it is unfortunate that he has had no executive experience. Any public man can learn quickly enough the routines of administration, but only through the trial-and-error of executive action can he demonstrate the depth and character of his convictions. Unfortunately for Senator Kennedy, he seems destined never to acquire any proper preparation for the post of Chief Executive."

Kennedy never appeared to have doubts. His interest in history was one in which, according to *Newsweek*'s Samuel Shaffer, he had sought a "perspective on the art of politics and his role in it." After talking with Kennedy at length in June 1958, Shaffer reported that unlike Eisenhower, who first approached the Presidency as a soldier's high duty to be done, or Stevenson, who viewed it with unconcealed hesitancy, the young Senator "has weighed himself on the scale of the job and found himself not wanting."

"I've read a lot about the Presidency," Kennedy said. "All those jobs have to be done by humans."

Only he could provide the strong Presidential leadership the nation needed in the Sixties, or so he began to insist. And harping on this theme in addressing the National Press Club on January 14, 1960, Kennedy skated to the brink of political unseemliness when he specifically linked himself to Abraham Lincoln, Andrew Jackson, the two Roosevelts, and Harry S Truman, whom he characterized as "strong" Presidents. Sharply assailing what he described as President Eisenhower's policy of casual complacency, Kennedy declared:

"In the coming years we will need a real fighting mood in the White House. . . . In the decade that lies ahead, the President [must] place himself in the very thick of the fight, that he care passionately about the fate of the people he leads, that *he be willing to serve them at the risk of incurring their momentary displeasure*. . . . He must be prepared to exercise the fullest powers of his office—*all that are specified and some that are not*. . . . The President *alone* must make the major decisions of our foreign policy. . . . [The President] must act in the image of Abraham Lincoln, who summoned his wartime Cabinet to a meeting on the Emancipation Proclamation [and said]: 'I do not wish your advice about the main matter—that I have determined for myself . . .' " (author's italics).

The *Richmond Times-Dispatch* observed: "If Richard Nixon had delivered the speech, Left-wing Democrats might have thundered 'dictator!' and cited chapter and verse in an attempt to justify their fears of the Vice President's 'Fascist' ambitions."

What Kennedy said, in effect, was that the country needed a superman to end all supermen.

"Today a restricted concept of the Presidency is not enough," he said. "For beneath today's surface gloss of peace and prosperity are increasingly dangerous, unsolved, long-postponed problems—problems that will inevitably explode to the surface during the next four years of the next administration—the growing missile gap, the rise of Communist China, the despair of the underdeveloped nations, the explosive situations in Berlin and in the Formosa Strait, the deterioration of NATO, the lack of an arms control agreement, and all the domestic problems of our farms, cities and schools."

The Senator did not come right out and say how, if elected, he would deal with all these frightful problems. "Presumably," observed the *Washington Star*, "he felt it would take too long to go into those details. But he did say, or at least he intimated, that he had a concept of the Presidency which endowed him with some special qualifications for taking on the White House job. It was at this point that our sense of discouragement began to set in. Suppose that by some cruel stroke of fate, Senator Kennedy should be denied the nomination. Or, assuming the nomination, what if he should lose the election? Where would the country turn for the right man to deal with these problems before they explode to the surface?"

Kennedy's attitude was that, with the help of the best brains available, he would come up with the answers for all the enormous problems confronting mankind. First, however, he had to win the nomination. And when he candidly discussed his chances for getting the nomination, he would say, in effect, "Who else is there?"

There were, of course, Hubert Humphrey, whom no one was really taking too seriously; Stuart Symington, who couldn't seem to get off the ground; Lyndon Johnson, of whom critics said, "Can you imagine Lyndon campaigning in Harlem?"; and Adlai Stevenson, hopefully sitting in the wings polishing his prose—including, said detractors, his acceptance speech. ("Adlai wants to be appointed President," said a Kennedy partisan.)

As James Reston noted, Kennedy "has been lucky in that he has come to the center of the stage when the cast of Presidential characters is not the best in the history of the Republic. He has arrived, too, when political leaders . . . are impressed with the power of personality in an age of television campaigning."

Gore Vidal, the playwright, has suggested that the politician—to be successful—"must have that instinctive sense of occasion which is also the actor's art. . . . He is, in the purest sense, an opportunist. He must know in the marrow of his bones when it is right to make the large effort."

And Vidal cited as an example his good friend John F. Kennedy's near-miss in grabbing the Vice-Presidential nomination in 1956. "The moment was wrong, but the move was right."

"In a society like ours, politics is improvisation," Vidal contended. "To the artful dodger rather than the true believer goes the prize."

Kennedy had been campaigning and improvising without letup almost from the time he lost his dramatic bid for the Vice-Presidential nomination. There was literally no counting the total number of appearances he made in almost every state of the Union. Nor could any of his aides estimate the number of local Democratic leaders whom the Senator met and talked to in the course of his far-flung travels. No one who could possibly have an influence on the selection of a Presidential candidate was neglected. His 1956 bid had been hampered by lack of personal contacts in many state delegations; but this would most definitely not be the case in '60.

The pace was swift, well-timed and relentless. In almost perpetual motion, he obtained an avalanche of favorable publicity that made him seem almost omnipresent.

And it was the illusion of omnipresence and omnipotence that Kennedy sought to create.

News stories and favorable editorials almost everywhere helped in the mysterious but vital process of convincing voters throughout the nation that Jack Kennedy was indeed "their boy" for the Presidency.

"But the very fact that his publicity has generally been uncritical has done him anything but a service with other Democratic politicians," reported columnist William S. White in May 1958. "They suspect him, soundly or not, of running a vast public relations stable—or of letting his father run one for him."

White noted that at a recent Gridiron Club dinner this view had been put succinctly in a skit based upon the song "My Heart Belongs to Daddy":

> We send all the bills to Daddy,
> 'Cause Daddy pays them so well.

In June 1958 the Republicans began to pay attention to Kennedy. Meade Alcorn, the National Chairman, said: "Since the presidential bug first bit the Junior Senator, he has undergone some amazing changes. He has flip-flopped completely on some issues; on others he has compromised."

It was a booming discordant note in what otherwise had been a generally favorable reaction to Kennedy's White House ambitions. And it came as the Senator was preparing to run for re-election. Part of Alcorn's criticism was based on the fact that Kennedy, after voting in behalf of flexible farm price supports advocated by Secretary Benson, had the previous month voted to freeze those supports.

"If I were Kennedy's opponent in the upcoming election," said Alcorn, "I would ask him about his farm price 'freeze' vote over and over again. I would also put the spotlight on his curious flip-flop on the civil rights bill in 1957."

Which was precisely what Kennedy's GOP opponent, Vincent Celeste, tried to do that fall. He accused Kennedy of "opportunism" in his farm vote and of having given aid and comfort to the Faubuses and the Eastlands in catering to the South on civil rights.

Relatively unknown, and with little financial backing, Celeste also pictured himself as a man of the little people and Kennedy as a scion of great wealth.

"I'm running against that millionaire, Jack Kennedy," he repeatedly told folks on his handshaking tours.

Celeste kept pouring it on. He charged that Kennedy had severely hurt the Port of Boston by voting for the Seaway bill, and that the Senator was playing Walter Reuther's game by supporting a labor bill "dictated" by the UAW leader. But he always returned to the theme of the Kennedy family and their huge fortune.

"What right do Kennedy and his brother Bobby have to sit in judgment on labor without ever doing a day's work in their lives?" demanded Celeste, who still lived in a North Boston tenement house.

He also charged that Joseph P. Kennedy was calling the campaign signals. The senior Kennedy was, as usual, operating behind the scenes from a suite of rooms which he had rented for the purpose—staffed by political operators on his payroll. "Don't mention my name," he would caution his associates. "It might hurt my son."

During the campaign, a unique event occurred at Kennedy headquarters in Boston—a photographer was brusquely turned away at the door. He had come to photograph Joseph Kennedy on a rare visit.

The necessity of keeping the Ambassador out of the limelight had been a lesson well learned, indeed.

Meanwhile, according to the *New York Times'* Cabell Phillips, "the elder Kennedy is reputed to be not only underwriting the Massachusetts campaign to any extent necessary, but to be sending respectable contributions to the Democratic candidates in certain other states where goodwill for the Kennedy name may be important."

Cabell Phillips had this to say about Jack Kennedy: "Maturity—that vague hallmark of virtue which a prospective President is required to exhibit—is not today conspicuous among Kennedy's gifts. His youthful look and a certain glibness of speech and manner are against him on that count. And so is the fact that nothing in his background reveals any particular talent for leadership or executive management. The fact that he has never had to hold down a job, meet a payroll or run a city or state government—his entire professional life has been spent in Congress—marks him as deficient in the sort of rounded experience with which maturity is equated."

Not once during the 1958 campaign did Kennedy ever deign to publicly mention his opponent by name. Yet, according to the *Boston Globe's* C. R. Owens, he was seeking re-election "with a slick, expensive promotional apparatus which might indicate to the uninitiated that he is in a fight for his political life against someone of the stature of Vice President Nixon. . . ."

Kennedy had "the most plush political headquarters Boston has ever seen," according to Owens. In nominal charge was Teddy Kennedy, "who is customarily surrounded by a flock of young beauties."

Over the front door of Kennedy's headquarters a loud speaker spread music and words of praise for Senator Kennedy all through the day. The show windows were professionally decorated with mementos of the young Senator's active postgraduate life.

"One window," reported Owens, "as though putting the lie to rumors as to authorship, displays a photostat of a page of manuscript from *Profiles in Courage,* the Senator's tribute to some of his Washington predecessors. This page of manuscript is obviously in the Senator's hand."

The original manuscript, in Kennedy's handwriting, was kept in the Senator's Washington office. There it would be trotted out from time to time as proof positive to doubting Thomases that Jack Kennedy—and not some ghost—had written his Pulitzer prize-winning book.[4]

Aware that he had to rack up an impressive majority in 1958, the Senator left nothing to chance. He and his top strategists realized that winning was not enough. The Democratic king-makers would not be impressed by a narrow or a middling victory—particularly against a small-time opponent. Kennedy had to win—and win big.

Celeste accused Kennedy of using Massachusetts as a steppingstone to the Presidency—a charge which, by and large, backfired. For nothing would have pleased Bay Staters more than a Massachusetts boy in the White House.

Fighting almost singlehandedly, the voluble Celeste could light no fires. Not even with conservatives. For thanks to Kennedy's multi-millionaire father, as the *Washington Star*'s Gould Lincoln reported from Boston, "the Senator has the support of many conservatives among Republicans, Democrats and independents."

Again the Kennedys were getting at an opponent from both Left and Right.

Jack spent election night with his father listening to returns in the latter's hotel suite. This time he won with the extraordinary margin of 874,000, the largest margin ever obtained by any candidate for any office in the state.

One of the booby traps on the road to the White House had been defused. But there were others.

Eleanor Roosevelt, for example, refused to bow to the inevitable. Once again, she blasted Kennedy and derided his claims to courage. On TV's "College News Conference" on December 7, 1958, she did concede that Kennedy had "an enormous amount of charm." But to listen to her tell it, that was about all he had—besides his father's money.

"However," she insisted, "it has seemed to me that what you wanted in

---

[4] The rumor that Kennedy did not write the book persisted, however. In fact, according to Elie Abel, then with the *Detroit News,* when President-elect Kennedy asked Robert S. McNamara to become Defense Secretary, the Ford Motor Company president wanted something set straight first. Did Kennedy write *Profiles in Courage* himself? Assured that Kennedy had indeed written the book, McNamara then proceeded to discuss the business at hand.

your next President was someone whose courage in taking stands was unquestioned."

Then she charged that Kennedy's father "has been spending oodles of money all over the country and probably has a paid representative in every state by now."

In a frigidly polite letter dated December 11, Kennedy demanded substantiating facts. He asked Mrs. Roosevelt to name a single paid representative in a single state. On December 18, she replied she had heard his father quoted as saying that he would spend any amount to make his son "the first Catholic President" and that such preparations were common knowledge. On December 29, Kennedy replied that she was giving currency to unsupported rumors. Mrs. Roosevelt quoted from his letter in her newspaper column of January 6, 1959. This did not satisfy the Senator who, on January 10, noted that giving space to a denial did not constitute a commitment by her as to the truth or falseness of the accusation. On January 20, Mrs. Roosevelt conceded she had heard the allegations in casual conversation and that, anyway, her opposition to him was not based on them. On January 22, Kennedy wrote back saying, in effect, "Let's drop the subject."

Though she had expressed doubts about his ability to separate duties of Church and State, Mrs. Roosevelt later denied her opposition to Kennedy was based on religious grounds. She criticized his tendency to be heard on all the safe issues, but to be busy elsewhere when the tough ones come along—the kind of issues that separate the men from the boys. The consequence of this cautious selectivity was to leave his public posture—the question of what Kennedy really stood for or really believed in—in considerable doubt.

"He is still seeking to be amiable to all voters without being too specific about anything," reported the *New Leader*'s Julius Duscha in September 1959. And the *Providence Journal,* in an editorial February 15, 1960, observed, "Not many Americans today could say, if asked, what Mr. Kennedy stands for."

According to Joseph P. Kennedy, what his son stood for really didn't matter.

"Let's not con ourselves," the elder Kennedy told a Scripps-Howard man in March 1960. "The only issue is whether a Catholic can be elected President."

Joe Kennedy made the statement in response to a query as to whether he himself might not become an issue in the campaign. He denied he was playing any major role in his son's organization.

Some observers had different ideas. "Ambassador Joe Kennedy," reported Washington columnist Bill Henry in the *Los Angeles Times,* "has been spending and is willing to spend to see young Jack in the White House. He not only supplies the money but a lot of sound political knowledge and his part in the campaign so far has been mostly behind-the-scenes searching for delegates. He has thoroughly combed the prospective political delegations from every state in the Union and has probably a more accurate knowledge of the commitments and leanings of the various delegates than anybody in the Democratic

Party. He has a conviction that young Jack must make his own way, otherwise, and is inclined not to interfere too much in the Senator's personal campaigning."

Joe Kennedy's astuteness as a political operator can be seen from this quotation attributed to the Ambassador in the Martin-Plaut book: "The office of the President of the United States is the greatest and the most important in the world. And yet . . . do you realize that to get the nomination for that office candidates have the worst organizations? That's because good men— men who have important jobs—don't want to give up their jobs to work for a candidate before he gets the nomination, because it's too risky. He may not get it, and where are they? And the others—the ones you can hire, the ones who are available—they aren't any good and you can't build an organization with them."

What the elder Kennedy thus explained was the precise difference between son Jack's organization and those he kept defeating right up to his nomination. In the main the others had hacks, while Jack had experts. This, plus plenty of cash or, in some cases, the promise of rewards, spelled the difference. Though he minimized his own role, Joe Kennedy's part in getting the right help for his son was most invaluable.

"Well, I just call people," he explained. "You call people that you know and ask them to help in any way they can. I am seventy-one years old, and I've made a lot of contacts all over the country. You just ask them to help, that's all."

Casting his Croesus-like shadow over the proceedings, Joseph P. Kennedy was present at a meeting between Jack and his top lieutenants at which final plans for Operation Kennedy were devised. The date was October 28, 1959; the place, Robert F. Kennedy's summer home in the family compound at Hyannis Port. A little more than a year later this was to be the Kennedy command post on election night. But there was a lot of work to be done before that. Planning, far in advance, was always central to the well-ordered march of events in Jack Kennedy's political life.

Others present included brothers Bobby and Teddy (Bobby had just resigned his Senate Committee post); Ted Sorensen, anchor man on the Kennedy team; Senate probers Kenneth O'Donnell and Robert Wallace; Hy Raskin, silver-maned advance man for Adlai Stevenson's two unsuccessful campaigns; Larry O'Brien, a public relations man and compiler of a manual titled by insiders "How to Get Kennedy Elected to Anything."

Also present were Louis Harris, a public opinion pollster; John Bailey; Kennedy brother-in-law Stephen Smith, who helps manage the family's business interests in New York; Marjorie Lawson, in charge of Negro work; Dave Hackett, an old family friend; former Rhode Island Governor Dennis Roberts; John Salter, administrative assistant to Senator Henry M. Jackson; and Pierre Salinger, a refugee from the defunct *Collier's* magazine, in charge of press relations.

It was a raw, blustery New England day. Standing with his back to a roaring fire, John F. Kennedy proceeded to analyze the political situation from top to bottom, from Kennebunkport to Ketchikan. He spoke for three hours without a note or chart or map.

"We had not only the best candidate there," Sorensen said later, "but the best campaign manager, too. He knows the facts, who likes him and who doesn't, he knows where he should go and where he shouldn't, he has this incredible memory of places, names, dates, who should be written to and who shouldn't."

Since September 1956 Kennedy and Sorensen had traveled, separately and together, over a million air miles—studying Democrats, districts, election laws, local peculiarities. Gradually there was accumulated a card index of some 30,000 influential Democrats across the country—all punched into Addressograph plates for speedy action.

Another card file contained the names of every delegate—how he should be addressed (as Jack, or Doc, or Senator), his biography, and a résumé of any correspondence he might have had with the Senator. Meanwhile, Messrs. O'Brien, O'Donnell, Wallace, and Bob and Ted Kennedy had taken to the road to recruit people for local organizations. Hy Raskin was assigned to woo Stevenson supporters. By the time they met at Hyannis Port, there was a trusted Kennedy lieutenant in every state, and the beginnings of a full-fledged organization in the key primary states—Wisconsin, Oregon, West Virginia, Nebraska, Indiana, and New Hampshire.

In Washington a suite of nine rooms had been quietly rented in early 1959 at the Esso Building, a quarter of a mile from the Senate Office Building, and brother-in-law Steve Smith was placed in administrative charge. Also installed there was Pierre Salinger, who—in addition to handling press inquiries —began stockpiling a formidable array of Kennedy photographs, press releases, film clips, bumper strips, lapel buttons, and tons of reprints of the *Reader's Digest* article on Jack Kennedy's war heroism.

It was a young crowd, composed of *doers* as distinguished from *thinkers*. They arranged public appearances, transportation, distribution of copies of speeches, and the workaday chores such as organizing groups of young Kennedy volunteers to welcome the Man himself wherever he might be appearing. This GHQ also distributed a fourteen-page master plan for "Kennedy for President Organizational Procedure," which was as detailed as an Army training manual, and covered everything from the selection of local veterans' chairmen to techniques for giving away car stickers in supermarket parking lots. One of the office staff was an attractive young lady named Dierdre Henderson who acted in a highly important capacity as the Kennedy courier between Washington and scattered groups of New England braintrusters serving as speech writers, idea men, and apt-quotation-suppliers. Thanks largely to them, Kennedy was kept fully supplied with appropriate quotations from Great Men.

Operation Kennedy smacked of money—big money.

"One can only imagine how many open-dated blank checks have been given to strategically-placed individuals and interests to help Kennedy get where he is," wrote the *New Republic*'s Selig Harrison in June 1960. "How many of these checks, if any, would call for repayment by Kennedy as President, no one can foretell. One can only say that they are peripheral to the central issue, namely, the nature of the leadership Kennedy might give on the great issues."

But was the subject really peripheral to the central issue? Could not Kennedy's qualities as a leader have been deeply affected by the fact that, for the most part, he usually had things handed to him?

Money quite obviously played a key role in winning the nomination for Kennedy. "It is," commented the *Reporter*'s Douglass Cater, "a sad and sobering fact of life that Presidential politics in America is more than ever a sport for the rich or their protégés."

"Kennedy neither flaunts nor hides his wealth," reported Edward Kernan in the *Cleveland Plain Dealer* of November 15, 1959. "That it is nice to have was disclosed by an incident which happened in Chicago last month. His own plane was getting its regular checkup and a mixup developed over the rental of another plane to get him to Bloomington, Illinois. The Senator immediately took charge. In a telephone booth, he was overheard saying: 'Don't worry about the cost. Get the plane here. We're running late. . . .' "

"His money has given him advantages in this campaign," reported James Reston. "His father advanced him $270,000 to buy a plane. Six members of his family put up $15,000 each to complete the deal, and while they have a contract to return it to the seller for $260,000, there is no doubt that this—plus a great deal more for paid assistants and television—has given him opportunities his competitors have not enjoyed."

Cruising along in his private plane, well attended by heralds and outriders, Kennedy achieved a degree of gracious living almost unknown in campaign history. How better to deliver a profound discourse on the perils of an Affluent Society?

The plane, a twin-motored Convair, was furnished like an executive suite, with a bedroom in the rear. Not only was the Senator able to work in comfort at a large desk, but he could even watch his rivals perform on television. The sleek ship (costing about $15,000 a month to operate) rode at anchor, as it were, at the Washington National Airport, waiting for the candidate, ready, willing, and able to go anywhere, any time, staffed by two expert pilots and a secretary-stewardess, attractive auburn-haired Janet des Rosiers, who had previously worked for the senior Kennedy.[5]

Perhaps more than any other Presidential aspirant, Jack Kennedy was

[5] Following the election, a business deal between Miss des Rosiers and President-elect Kennedy came to light. Sometime in late 1959, according to the *Washington Post,* Miss des Rosiers paid Kennedy $2,400 for 75 per cent of the gas, oil, and mineral rights he owned on eight tracts of land in southern Louisiana. Kennedy had acquired 4 per cent of the royalty rights to 1,600 acres, located about 5 miles from the Lake Arthur oil and gas field, in 1952. According to Pierre Salinger, Kennedy had sold 75 per cent of his rights to Janet because the land was yielding only about $350 annually. Salinger, however, could not say why the President-elect had retained a 25 per cent interest in the royalty rights.

addicted to public opinion polls. For one thing, he could afford them. His polling organization was Louis Harris & Associates Inc., of New York. Its findings, neatly bound in celluloid covers and mimeographed on white paper, were impressive in their thoroughness. The cost of these services was reported by Marquis Childs to be in the neighborhood of $250,000 a year. Even if that figure was too high, as a Kennedy spokesman suggested, Harris certainly was providing valuable services.

For the motivations disclosed by the "in depth" polling techniques were more important to Kennedy than the resulting percentage points. "To me," Kennedy said, "polls are most useful as a gauge of people's feelings and ideas, as an indication of what they want, what they think and why. The figures only recapitulate these opinions and sum them up."

The first such polls were taken for Kennedy during the 1958 campaign. The results, as Kennedy put it, were "terribly accurate," and sold him on the use of depth interviews in polling technique. A voters' survey taken in May 1958 predicted that Kennedy would carry 72 per cent of the Massachusetts electorate. In September this was upped to 74 per cent. Kennedy actually got 75 per cent of the vote.

How the Senator reacted to the findings provided an interesting example of modern campaigning and was typical of the way in which Kennedy has been seeking to increase his popularity with the voters ever since.

Kennedy's 1958 election had been a foregone conclusion; and therefore his pollsters concentrated mainly on his public appeal and the state's major issues. The pollsters found that almost four out of ten people praised Kennedy because "he is honest, has fine personality, makes good impression, looks good [and] speaks well." Next on the list of his public appeal were words like "courageous," "hard worker," "good family," "knowledgeable," and "intelligent." No reference was made to what Kennedy stood for or believed in.

But what with recession worries diminishing, the pollsters found that most people were concerned about high taxes.

Putting two and two together, Kennedy and his advisers decided to make the most of the Senator's personality and his record on governmental economy. In his speeches Kennedy repeatedly called attention to his Government Budget and Accounting Reform Bill designed, he said, to save billions yearly for the hard-pressed taxpayer.

In August 1959 Kennedy permitted a correspondent to examine the results of polls taken in his behalf in the primary states of Pennsylvania, Ohio, Nebraska, and Oregon. Pennsylvania was chosen because of its size, political importance, large industrial population, and its location. In Ohio, Kennedy wanted to see how he would stack up against Governor DiSalle and Senator Lausche, the two potential favorite sons. Nebraska was included as a typical Midwestern farm state; and Oregon, a Farwestern state, as a supposed Humphrey stronghold. The findings were these:

In each of the states Kennedy ran ahead of all other potential Democratic aspirants (including Estes Kefauver, but not Adlai Stevenson; for a time Kennedy thought of the Tennessean as a possible rival).

Kennedy was the only Democrat with a nationwide appeal among Republicans. Of all the Democratic hopefuls, Kennedy was the only one who could beat Nixon or Rockefeller in at least two of the areas polled. In Oregon, Kennedy beat Nixon 45 to 41 per cent and Rockefeller 42 to 34 per cent. In Nebraska, the figures were almost the same.

Only a small fraction of people were apparently concerned with Kennedy's religion. Moreover, he was more popular among Protestants than among any other religious group. In Ohio, he was favored by 73 per cent of the Protestant voters questioned, 66 per cent of the Catholics and 63 per cent of the Jewish voters. The Kennedy people interpreted these and similar statistics from other states as indicating that the religious question lost most of its importance once it was associated with the Senator's name.

In spite of this overall popularity, the pollsters dug out areas where Kennedy was weak. Most important among them were the farmers, whose "image" of Kennedy was found slipping. Labor and low-income groups, generally, were found to have relatively slight acquaintance with Kennedy's name. While he was fairly well known to 85–90 per cent of white-collar and professional people, only 60–65 per cent of labor and low-income respondents recognized his name. Among men, especially in the older age brackets, there was less favorable sentiment for a Kennedy candidacy than among women. More than 80 per cent of the women questioned in Ohio indicated they would support Kennedy. Among men, however, the overall percentage was 72.

Kennedy took due notice of all these findings. Thus, to give his candidacy more appeal to men, he decided to feature Mrs. Kennedy more prominently in his travels. The apparent resistance of older voters, especially men, was given particular attention. The Senator attacked this problem on two fronts: on the one hand, he put out reprints of his "Bill of Rights for Our Elder Citizens," proposals for increased federal and local aid to the aged. On the other hand, in line with his effort to project a serious-minded, mature image, he weeded out jokes from his speeches.

Another weakness—the farm issue—was the subject of what was billed as a major Kennedy speech in April 1959. To "resuscitate the family farm" he proposed the encouragement of co-operatives to strengthen the position of farmers in the cost-price squeeze.

"It is doubtful that this nebulous Kennedy proposal made much of an impression on Wisconsin farmers," commented the *Washington Star*. "By all other indications, however, Senator Kennedy would defeat Senator Humphrey easily if the Wisconsin primary were held today."

The smoothly functioning, well-heeled Kennedy machine moved forward on various primary fronts. "If the whole picture of the Kennedy organization in all its details could be put together," Marquis Childs reported in January

1960, "and for a variety of reasons this will probably never be done, it would be a fascinating study in political power and influence."

Whenever challenged for his lack of administrative experience, reported his newsman friend Charles Bartlett, "Kennedy alludes to his campaign organization, which has been described as a powerful political machine in every primary state that it invaded."

And so it was.

In size, scope, and efficiency down to the precinct level in every state outside the South, the Kennedy machine was unprecedented in political history. It was a source of ceaseless speculation and even awe wherever practical politicians gathered. It was the cause of envious muttering from other Democratic hopefuls who had begun to feel its power.

Senator Kennedy took note of the muttering in an appearance on "Meet the Press." He said that his family's wealth did not help his candidacy since there were limits on how much a candidate could spend for his nomination.

He was immediately challenged by Senator Humphrey, who pointed out that there are no legal limits on how much can be spent for the nomination nor even, strictly speaking, on how much can be contributed to a candidate.

Unlike the other Presidential hopefuls, Kennedy never was forced to issue a single appeal to raise money for the primaries. "Kennedy's well-oiled political machine had everything but a fund-raising section," reported Arthur F. Hermann of Gannett News Service from the Democratic Convention. "Yet, the report is that Joseph P. Kennedy spent $7 million on this phase of the campaign alone."

How much was actually expended, however, will probably never be known. Officially, the Kennedy camp said it spent less than a million dollars between January 1959 and July 1960, when the Senator won the nomination. If this was so, it was like getting something at the bargain counter.

"His statements in regard to campaign expenses are further evidences as to his lack of qualifications for the Presidency," Senator Wayne Morse of Oregon said. "The American people should make clear to Senator Kennedy that the White House will never be put up for sale. It is obvious that the truth is not in him."

Senator Kennedy got off to a fast start in his race for the nomination when Governor Michael V. DiSalle personally—and surprisingly—handed him Ohio's 64 delegate votes six months before the Convention. DiSalle had never demonstrated any pro-Kennedy sympathies before; in fact, he had talked about running as his state's "favorite son" candidate. But the stern exigencies of politics sometimes make personal predilections irrelevant.

To put it bluntly, Mike DiSalle had been bludgeoned into making the announcement. Until then, Kennedy hadn't managed to crack any of the pivotal industrial states. And he felt he needed a big-state triumph before the early primaries.

The Kennedy forces had worked on DiSalle for nearly a year. Finally, they bared their brass knuckles. First, the pro-Kennedy Cuyahoga County (Cleveland) Organization threatened a party fight aginst DiSalle. Then, Bobby Kennedy laid down the law in terms one does not ordinarily use when talking to the Governor of a big state. Jack Kennedy himself moved in for the kill. In a secret meeting in a Pittsburgh hotel room, Kennedy showed DiSalle a Lou Harris poll which indicated that if the Senator opposed him in the Ohio primary the Governor would take a drubbing in his own state.

On January 5, 1960, DiSalle somewhat unenthusiastically announced for Kennedy.

And, as Senator Wayne Morse put it on a Cleveland visit, Ohio suddenly didn't have a "favorite son"—it had a "favorite stooge."

Some Ohio Democrats made no secret of their belief that DiSalle had permitted himself to be bullied by the Kennedys. Senator Frank Lausche came close to upsetting the applecart by allowing himself to be entered as a "favorite son." He gave this up only because there was no time to get petitions signed, not because of any enthusiasm for Kennedy.

"What could I have done?" DiSalle pleaded to his friends. "Those Kennedys play real rough."

It was Kennedy's first big psychological break in his relentless drive for the nomination. Another plus factor was involved. DiSalle had been listed as one of the Democratic Governors who, as Catholics, were concerned lest the religious issue be brought into the campaign. The others were California's Edmund G. "Pat" Brown and Pennsylvania's David Lawrence.

Even after DiSalle had broken the ice, Lawrence refused to buckle under Kennedy pressure. He publicly stated that Jack was far from ready for the nation's highest office and that his defeat could cause lasting party wounds. According to the *New York Herald Tribune,* Lawrence was "somewhat concerned that Kennedy may be placing his own future higher than the party's. He told the Kennedy camp that he believes a Catholic can be elected President—but that if the party is going to risk nominating one, he must be right in all other respects."

Moreover, Lawrence was quoted as saying that, in addition to Catholicism, Kennedy had certain "personal problems" with which to contend. What they were, however, he did not say.

Kennedy was playing the religious issue from all angles.

On the one hand, he was arguing passionately that the issue should have no place in politics so long as a candidate believes in the separation of Church and State.

Yet, as Doris Fleeson reported in April 1960, "at any given moment, Kennedy aides, and the candidate too, can tell anyone the figures of Catholic strength not only in a state but in a district or even a county."

As *Time* put it: "The political reality of 1960 in Jack Kennedy's starting point in his race for the Democratic nomination is his ability to deliver the heavy Catholic big-city vote much the way that John Bailey laid it down in

1956." This was a reference to the so-called Bailey Report (Appendix B) which said bluntly that there is, or could be, a "Catholic vote" which Jack could win for the hard-pressed Democrats.

Kennedy's strategy, simply, was to proclaim his strength and then let it be known that if he did not get the nomination it would serve notice on the nation's Catholics that he had been pushed aside solely on religious grounds. And he warned that the Democratic party would run the risk of losing the election.

The irony of all this, according to the *Economist,* was that Jack Kennedy "is close to being a spiritually rootless modern man. He performs the prescribed devotions of his faith, but his accession to the Presidency would no more mean 'the Pope in the White House' than the election of an Episcopalian would signify the coming to power of the Archbishop of Canterbury."

Almost to the last there was a widespread feeling that the Kennedy bandwagon was of a fairly fragile variety; that like some kind of jet-propelled plane it had to keep moving to keep from crashing. Carmine DeSapio, then New York political boss, alluded to this the night before the Democratic Convention opened.

"He outsmarted all the pros," DeSapio said admiringly. "But if he had ever stumbled just once, the wolves would have closed in on him."

Like Harry S Truman, the old pros thought all this Kennedy pre-Convention frenzy was just so much motion and that, as in the days of yore, it could be ignored. They could lick young Jack in the Convention in-fighting. They had done it to others.

This was Lyndon Johnson's feeling too. And like the other hopefuls, Johnson had a potent candidate for Vice President—Jack Kennedy.

"I can see it now," a Johnson aide told *Time.* "He'll be standing there in the hotel room after the nomination, and he'll say, 'We want that boy for Vice President. Go get him for me.' "

Was Johnson likely to wind up as a Vice-Presidential candidate himself?

"Not a chance," said the aide. "Can you imagine Lyndon sitting there watching someone else trying to run his Senate?"

All this overlooked the fact that Kennedy was not settling for second place. Even before he built up a commanding lead, one of his thorniest problems had been how to handle questions on the Vice Presidency.

"You bastards have got me either way," he told a journalist friend. "If I say I would accept the Vice Presidency, then I've got it. If I say I would not, then I'm a traitor to my party."

When a friend suggested there must be some good answer, Kennedy said, "Okay, let's hear it. You're Kennedy, and I'm Reston, and we're on 'Meet the Press.' " Obviously relishing the switch, Kennedy burst out with his first question, imitating Reston's wry voice: "Now look here, Lochinvar, what's all this nonsense about your not accepting the Vice Presidency?"

Also overlooked by his rivals was the fact that Kennedy and his colleagues were not amateurs. They represented a new professionalism in politics. Unlike the Kefauver insurgents of 1952 and 1956, the young Kennedy pros did not fight against the old-established pros unless it was absolutely necessary. While they bullied DiSalle in Ohio and Governor Tawes in Maryland, they proceeded cautiously in dealing with DeSapio in New York, Mayor Daley in Chicago, and even the bumbling Pat Brown in California.

With Governor Tawes, Kennedy had cracked the bullwhip in as tough-minded a manner as any Maryland Democratic leader had been subjected to in decades. The Marylanders were anything but pleased when Kennedy & Co. started to move in on them. Like all good politicians Tawes and other party nabobs wanted to go to Los Angeles free to bargain, free to make their own choice.

Kennedy was asked politely and pleasantly not to file in the Maryland Presidential primary. Just as politely and pleasantly, Kennedy told Tawes and the others that he understood their feelings.

But, he said, he wanted to be President.

And the only way he could get a good jump on other Democrats with identical ambitions was to enter the primary contests they were shunning.

Kennedy filed for the primary—and his shock troops set up a command post in Baltimore's Emerson Hotel. A soft-spoken Irishman from Boston, Joseph Curnane, was in charge. Liaison man between Baltimore and Washington was Congressman Torbert Macdonald of Massachusetts. Again, nothing was left to chance.

Local Democrats hopped on the bandwagon. Governor Tawes endorsed Kennedy's candidacy. It, of course, resulted in a romping victory over Senator Morse. Thus another 24 Convention votes were assured for Kennedy at Los Angeles.

"The biggest mistake that Kennedy's rivals could make," warned *Time,* "would be to judge the Kennedy campaign by the smiles, speeches and pretty pictures, and misjudge the strength and power of the organization that grimly aims to turn each smile and speech into hard votes."

Political analysts boggled at trying to understand how some of these "kids" playing politics knew what they were doing. Or how they got away with things they did. Thirty-four-year-old Bobby Kennedy, for example, consorted with governors and political bosses several decades his senior. Yet he handed out brutal ultimatums to some whom he deferentially addressed as "Sir."

Whatever Bobby's reputed genius for politics, it was tempered by a vindictiveness rarely seen before in public life. Following his brother's nomination at Los Angeles, Bobby Kennedy told Hubert Humphrey, who had given eleventh-hour convention support to Stevenson, that his number one objective would be the Minnesota Senator's political demise.

"I'm going to get you," Bobby angrily shouted at Humphrey.

Bobby also played rough with newsmen who failed to toe the Kennedy line in reporting the primary contests. One CBS correspondent felt the lash of his tongue for having suggested that Catholic voters were being taken for granted by the Kennedy forces in the Wisconsin campaign. Bobby went so far as to telephone CBS News head Sig Mickelson in New York and, as *Hollywood Daily Variety* put it, engaged in a "heated exchange" with him. Bobby reportedly denounced the CBS correspondent in ethnic terms reminiscent of his father—and as a no-good "Liberal" to boot.[6]

During the West Virginia primary, a *Baltimore Sun* correspondent—one of the best political analysts in the business—found himself cut off from official sources of information within the Kennedy camp after he reported he had personally witnessed the passing of money for votes. Rather than involve itself in a freedom-of-the-press battle with Kennedy, the *Baltimore Sun* pulled its man out of the Senator's entourage and assigned him elsewhere.

If anything, Robert F. Kennedy should have been everlastingly grateful to Hubert Humphrey. For his brother's decision to go the primary route required a half-way suitable client. Without Humphrey in the field as an active opponent, Kennedy would have been at a decided disadvantage—running by himself would prove little.

Nowadays, of course, primaries are less important for the delegates acquired than for the publicity they obtain. And with the active help of most of the press, Senator Kennedy utilized them to score an enormous personal publicity triumph. And he did it with "a toughness and a ruthless determination" that, according to London's *Economist,* "earned him the half critical name 'Jack the Knife' among reporters."

The Kennedy strategy for the primaries had been laid out with shrewdness and resourcefulness. At first it stressed Kennedy's position as an underdog. For a long time the Kennedy people encouraged feverish speculation about the Senator's Wisconsin intentions. Would he go in? Wouldn't he go in? Brothers Bobby and Teddy let it be known that they had advised their brother not to enter the race. After all, Wisconsin was Humphrey's backyard.

But if these statements were to be taken at their face value, they did not fit in with the picture the Kennedy camp had been painting—the picture of a fighting Presidential candidate ready to take on all comers in the Presidential primaries and attributing lack of courage to those unwilling to contest him.

The speculation continued. Friendly political analysts like the *Baltimore Sun's* Thomas O'Neill devoted entire columns to the perils Kennedy faced. "Wisconsin is a tough one for Senator Kennedy," O'Neill asserted.

This did not quite square with what Kennedy's full-time pollster Lou Harris was discovering as he roamed around the Badger State. Not only was he coming up with nothing but Kennedy victory findings, but he discovered

---

[6] Following the election, CBS President Frank Stanton visited President-elect Kennedy in a peace-making venture designed to heal campaign wounds, according to the trade paper. At the same time, there was a shakeup in CBS news operations.

that the Senator from Massachusetts was a far better known personality in Wisconsin than was the Senator from neighboring Minnesota.

According to columnist Ron May of the *Madison Capital Times,* Wisconsin Governor Gaylord Nelson had been shown a private Kennedy poll in January 1960 wherein the Massachusetts Senator was leading his Minnesota rival by 63 to 37. May also reported:

"A few days later columnist Joseph Alsop took up the 'underdog' theme in a big way and reported that . . . Lou Harris put Kennedy ahead by only 53 to 47. This somewhat bolstered the underdog claim, but—if true—still far from supported it.

"Told of the discrepancy between the two polls, Alsop conceded that he had got his figures from Kennedy and promised to check them—presumably with Harris, who is a close friend. Alsop reported back that he was sure his figures were authentic.

"But the leaks of poll 'results' did not stop. This column, which a year earlier had 'bit' on an inconsistent Harris poll on Pennsylvania, taken from Kennedy's file, got another one two weeks ago, allegedly from the same source.

"While this reporter was still checking the authenticity of the latest leak, pertaining to Wisconsin, it was presented as genuine in a syndicated column by Robert S. Allen and Paul Scott. Scott told this reporter that he was sure the new report was real.

"But the third 'poll' is different from either of the other two. It shows Kennedy with 57 per cent—not 63 or 53. However, its heading would seem to indicate that, like the first two, it had a specific political purpose—a message to 'sell.' The data is titled 'The Wisconsin Vote Steal.'

"The report says its contents are based on 'present polls.' Dated February 1, this would mean it was drawn up only a few days after both the 63-percentage and 53-percentage figures were circulated and was presumably based upon the results of the same early January questioning by Harris agents.

"The district-by-district estimates add up to Kennedy winning 4 of the 10 congressional districts (for 10 delegates) and the statewide count (for 5 delegates), while Humphrey takes 6 districts (for 15 delegates). The report argues that, under the figures given, Kennedy would get the same number of delegates as Humphrey—15—but would have more votes.

"The listed statewide totals are 323,000 for Kennedy and 242,000 for Humphrey.

"But the clear intent of amassing the figures to buttress an argument, rather than to report the truth, discredits the 'results.' "

The use of private polls as a "propaganda device" by political candidates was sharply criticized by Elmo Roper at the 1960 annual conference of the American Association for Public Opinion Research.

"I wonder," the dean of the pollsters observed, "if these polls are not being used to frighten people out of running for office or into getting aboard someone else's bandwagon."

Lou Harris, taking issue with "this thinly veiled charge," contended such polls were necessary to candidates as "operational tools" and indignantly denied that any taken by his organization had ever been for any other purpose.[7]

"The Kennedy boys are wonderfully engaging—and I keep telling myself, fundamentally decent," Murray Kempton wrote, "but I wish they'd stop saying, gee whiz, kids, we're outnumbered, but we're going to carry on. Jack Kennedy goes against Hubert Humphrey in the Wisconsin primary with most of the money, most of the charm, most of the killer instinct, and, we might assume, most of the potential votes. . . .

"And Bobby Kennedy goes around saying that Jimmy Hoffa will spend anything to beat Jack. This statement does not say outright that Hoffa is contributing money to poor Humphrey, but what other inference is possible?

"It would be foolish to deny that among forward-looking enlightened members of the party of progress there has been for at least seven years a longing for some Democratic candidate to come forward with an instinct for the jugular. Generally speaking, by actions of this sort, the Kennedys seem to have won professional approval. . . .

"Jack Kennedy's proclamations of desperation in the Wisconsin primary are a moral issue somewhat more delicate. . . . Kennedy has a pollster in whom he has every reason for confidence. He must therefore be as coolly confident in private as he is afraid in public. He is telling us something which he himself is better equipped than anyone else to think untrue, and, after that, he makes gentle little speeches to college kids talking about the need to revive the national morality.

"Couldn't the national morality begin at the bottom with candidates for the Presidency telling us what they believe to be the approximate truth? This is a bottom the national morality does not possess. Tiny deceptions of this sort are, in politics, not merely to be condoned; they are even to be described by every political commentator closer to earth than Walter Lippmann as sharp, tough and clever."

Still protesting about the risks he was running, Kennedy finally announced he would enter the Wisconsin primary. And he warned his supporters that a defeat might finish him off altogether.

From the first, it was obvious that Hubert Humphrey didn't stand a chance against the tightly knit, highly organized, plentifully financed Kennedy campaign, featuring—as the *Christian Science Monitor*'s Bill Stringer re-

---

[7] Apparently pollster Roper remained incensed. On February 19, 1962, the *New York Times* quoted him as saying that in the 1960 Presidential campaign some "so-called public opinion researchers" used their polls "rather openly for propaganda purposes," rather than to inform their candidate. In the early stage of the Wisconsin primary, he said, polls "were leaked to important Democrats showing that if they wanted to be on the bandwagon they had better go for Kennedy right now." And Dr. George Gallup, another leading public opinion analyst, was quoted as saying this type of misuse of private polls in election campaigns was the only one he could think of that went against the democratic process.

ported—"a young and personable candidate, intelligently tackling tomorrow's problems, and a hard-core religious following in every county."

In Milwaukee alone, Kennedy had 30,000 active supporters in that city of some one million souls. "Anyone who doubts this may go to the Kennedy headquarters at 330 W. Wisconsin Avenue and look through the card files," reported the *Baltimore Sun*'s Howard Norton. "The name, address, telephone number and other pertinent data on every one of the Kennedy enthusiasts is listed there. . . . The Kennedy people are vague on how much money has been poured into the campaign. They acknowledge only that the Massachusetts State Democratic Committee gave $50,000 toward the Wisconsin campaign and the Connecticut State Committee another $20,000."

"Lacking a cohesive organization," the *New York Times* reported in mid-March, "Senator Humphrey tries by sheer energy and boundless optimism to match the momentum of the powerful Kennedy machine. If politics is a war of words, victory could be Senator Humphrey's."

High resolves to avoid internal bloodletting faded at the onset when the Humphrey forces succeeded in increasing the number of delegates elected by districts and decreasing those elected on a statewide basis—a manipulation designed to aid the Minnesotan. Kennedy people immediately sounded the cry of "Vote Steal!"

Humphrey, meanwhile, played his poor-boy candidacy for all it was worth. He attributed his rival's political success to "a rich father. Let's face it." But, he added bravely, "I'm not complaining. These are the facts of life."

Soon Humphrey was being called a "windbag" backed by "ultra-Liberal money from New York." In turn, Humphreyites labeled Kennedy "soft on McCarthyism" and "tough and amoral."

At a Democratic dinner in New York, Jack cracked back, "I got a wire from my father that said, 'Dear Jack. Don't buy one vote more than necessary. I'll be damned if I'll pay for a landslide.' " Then he swiped at one of the candidates who had decided to sidestep the primaries: "Senator Symington said he hoped Wisconsin would be a good, clean fight—with no survivors."

The Manhattan Democrats were treated to another spectacle—that of Tammany Boss DeSapio solemnly reading a "Nixon nomination-acceptance speech," patterned after *'Twas the Night Before Christmas:*

> I'll wage a campaign that's hard and tough,
> As only Dick Nixon can really get rough.
> I'll smear and slander, vilify, attack,
> For of guts and spirit I sure have no lack. . . .

In Wisconsin, the smearing, vilification, and slander continued unabated. This time, the Kennedy men charged that the Humphrey campaign was being fueled by tainted Teamster and Texas money, the latter coming from oil-bloated billionaires who wanted to stop Kennedy so that Senator Lyndon Johnson would have a chance for the nomination.

Bobby Kennedy made it more specific. He informed horrified audiences that Teamster Boss Jimmy Hoffa was coming to Wisconsin to support Hubert Humphrey.

Humphrey denounced Bobby for raising the issue. And he questioned the right of the Kennedy brothers to pose as racket busters. He said it was one thing to serve on a Senate Committee, as Jack Kennedy did, and another to fight rackets as Mayor of Minneapolis, as Hubert Humphrey did.

"You're looking at a man who has fought the rackets all his life," roared Humphrey. "And I did so before some of the people who are doing all the talking about rackets were dry behind the ears." As far as efforts to link him with Hoffa were concerned, "whoever is responsible deserves to have a spanking. And I said spanking because it applies to juveniles."

At times, Humphrey wondered aloud whether he was not being ganged up on by Kennedy's friends in the press. He was particularly annoyed by a "Meet the Press" panel on which he was questioned by, among others, Charles Bartlett, of the *Chattanooga Times,* and Sandor Vanocur of NBC News. Their questions were revealing:

VANOCUR: Senator, for the last three weeks you have gone around the state attacking Senator Kennedy on his voting record. . . . Don't you think that if Kennedy does become the Democratic nominee this is going to hurt your party's chances in the November election?

HUMPHREY: I happen to believe that a discussion of the public record is about the only way that you can honorably carry on an election contest. Surely one wouldn't want to discuss extraneous issues.

VANOCUR: Senator, if you don't get the nomination, you are going to campaign for a third term as Senator. Don't you think the Republicans in your state are going to pick up the charges from your lips and throw them against you, running on the same ticket with this man you have attacked on agriculture?

HUMPHREY: I want to say that if I have no greater worry than the charges that will be hurled at me by partisans in the coming election I will be a very fortunate man. . . .

BARTLETT: I have heard you many times question the quality of Senator Kennedy's Liberalism. I think you once described him as "bland" and like "warmed-over tea." One of the letters circulating out here is a letter you wrote, a "Dear Jack" letter, on September 8, 1958.

HUMPHREY: Wait a minute. I have never said that Jack was "bland" or like "warmed-over tea." I said that I want to make sure that American politics doesn't become that way and that we don't indulge ourselves in sheer public relations. I can say many things about Jack, but he is not "bland" and he is not "warmed-over tea," I can tell you that.

BARTLETT: On September 8, 1958, you did write a "Dear Jack" letter: "Your fine work on behalf of liberal social legislation proves you believe in a government with a heart."

HUMPHREY: I surely did, and I think he deserved it. And may I say I have done a great deal since then to encourage Jack to be even more liberal.

What made the campaign particularly frustrating for Humphrey was that he was being forced to compete in what he dubbed a popularity contest. Others saw it that way too.

"And in that kind of competition the glamor of Senator Kennedy and the various members of the Kennedy clan, as they fan out across the state, is bound to win," Marquis Childs predicted from Madison. "It seems to get down to that Madison Avenue word, 'image.' The Kennedy image with all its attractiveness and appeal has been projected by the mass magazines and by television, and the hold that it has on large numbers of voters, particularly women and younger people, has little to do with issues or convictions."

Kennedy was greeted everywhere as a celebrity making a personal appearance rather than as a politician making a serious speech. "His supporters compared him to a movie star," a *New York Times* correspondent reported from Milwaukee. "He spent as much time signing autographs as he did shaking hands. Often he was almost mobbed by autograph seekers."

Humphrey, of course, was greeted as just another vote-seeking politician.

As D-day approached, Kennedy imported his "Massachusetts formula" of making every Kennedy meeting a social affair. Soon the entire clan, with the notable exception of Joseph P. Kennedy, was campaigning in Wisconsin. Three sisters, Mrs. Peter Lawford, Mrs. Stephen Smith, and Mrs. Sargent Shriver—with the Senator's mother—and his two brothers, along with assorted in-laws and friends, were crisscrossing the Badger State.

The voters in small towns received what looked like engraved invitations from Kennedy to come to his meetings (the lists prepared in advance from the telephone book). "There they find the cover-boy in person," reported James Reston, "not only glamorous but intelligent, well-informed, earnest, and literate. Maybe it's all a show, like Eddie Fisher and Liz Taylor coming to town, but the politicians don't think so, and the new polls coming up show Kennedy gaining on Nixon."

No bets were being missed. There were receptions for other Kennedys. Invitations sent well in advance gave the occasion a special touch. "The pleasure of your company is requested at such and such an hour on such and such a day to meet Mrs. Peter Lawford. . . ." This had the glamour of Bel Air and the chic fashion magazines. Its appeal can well be imagined. The resulting publicity was enormous. Perhaps Kennedy's greatest asset was his mother Mrs. Rose Kennedy, the target of the women reporters. Asked why she so enthusiastically endorsed Jack's interest in politics, she declared:

"It's a wonderful thing to serve your country. If you like it, there's nothing so rewarding. What rewards? Well, it's interesting, it's exciting, it enables you to meet a great many interesting people all over the world, and it brings prestige."

As an answer to the Kennedy socials, the Humphreyites arranged a $1-a-person "bean feed" rally in Milwaukee attended by some three thousand friends of the Minnesotan. It was his biggest campaign rally. Minnesota Governor Orville Freeman was there.

"Don't you think that beans and weiners are a much better motivation than tea and crumpets?" Freeman asked, jabbing at the Kennedy receptions. "I have a feeling they are."

Neither Senator reached heights of eloquence or rhetoric in his innumerable effusions. "If either Kennedy or Humphrey made one serious, considered speech on the great national issues it was, so far as my reading of the newspapers goes, not reported to the nation," complained Walter Lippmann.

Not that Kennedy didn't try to outegghead Adlai Stevenson. In a short talk at Wisconsin State College, he quoted Abraham Lincoln, Daniel Webster, Aristotle, George Bernard Shaw, Walter Lippmann, Sidney Hook, President Eisenhower, Thomas Jefferson, and John Quincy Adams.[8]

The effect, if not the intent, of his literary name-dropping was to blur the image of Adlai Stevenson as the sole Democratic egghead.

Kennedy told audiences that he had few ideological differences with Humphrey. "I just can't bleed all over the floor like Hubert does. If you check our records, you'll find that in 95 per cent of the cases, our voting has been the same. But we're temperamentally different. He likes to lambaste; I don't think it pays off. Does that make him more liberal than me? Hell, my voting record isn't perfect, but he's got soft spots too."

Humphrey did not agree. "I suggest we do not substitute popularity for leadership and mediocrity for principle," he said.

And he challenged Kennedy to debate the issues.

Kennedy refused, because, he told a Milwaukee TV panel, "we agree on almost everything."

"Well," said a panelist, "if that's the case, what can we vote on in the primary . . . your looks?"

"I think there is enough difference of emphasis and temperament on the issues so that the voters can make a judgment," Kennedy replied.

Kennedy's attitude was dramatized by a small incident that occurred on a press bus careening along an icy road near Fond du Lac in mid-February. Newsmen were probing the Senator on his strategy.

"Why don't you ever refer to Humphrey's voting record?" one reporter asked casually.

Kennedy recoiled as if from a treacherous attack.

"Voting record!" he snapped. "Why should I bring up his voting record?

---

[8] Small wonder, then, that the publishers of Bartlett's *Familiar Quotations* advertised: "Senator John F. Kennedy owns the modern Bartlett's. Do you?"

Then he'd bring up mine. What good would it do for me to chew him up or for him to chew me up?"

Toward the end, Humphrey began to discuss Kennedy's voting record in detail. And he distributed a pamphlet analyzing the records of both candidates.

"I hate to do this," he told a farm rally in La Crosse, waving a copy of the pamphlet. "But I'm tired of hearing that there's no difference between the two candidates."

The pamphlet claimed that while Humphrey voted *against* farm recommendations of Secretary Benson 27 times from 1953 to 1958, Kennedy had voted *with* Benson all 27 times. It also listed voting differences between the two Senators on taxation, civil rights and voting rights, housing and hospital construction, and public works. The material was designed to prove that Humphrey was a true Liberal while Kennedy's claim was decidedly suspect.

The *Chicago Tribune* commented as follows: "Humphrey may think that these allegations are sufficient to destroy Senator Jack, but, on the contrary, we feel that Howling Hubert has produced about the only favorable evidence that has yet come to notice about Kennedy's judgment."

Judging from the shouts of "foul" from the Kennedy camp, Humphrey appeared to be hitting pay dirt. However, if it was Humphrey's aim to lure his opponent into a personal slugging match, he was bound to fail. For Kennedy had been warned by Lou Harris not to accept the challenge.

"At all costs," Kennedy's pollster had warned, "Kennedy must avoid being looked upon as a politician. Anything approximating name-calling can only hurt Kennedy. He must make every effort to resist taunts and barbs thrown by Hubert Humphrey. Temptations inevitably will arise to slug it out with Humphrey. And slug it out Kennedy must, but on his own terms and in keeping with his own positive profile. The voters are confident Kennedy won't stoop to play the old political game with them. . . . The voters may not completely understand what he says, but they'll like and respect him for it."

Clearly nothing nicer could have happened to Humphrey than to be accused of something so reprehensible as campaigning on the issues.

"We're in politics," he said happily. "We're not making love."

And then he charged his "illustrious opponent" with the gravest of Democratic sins—being "soft on Nixon." And his headquarters issued another earth-shaking charge: namely, that Joseph P. Kennedy had contributed to Nixon's 1950 campaign. "For this reason," said the statement, "Jack is apparently reluctant to attack Nixon."

Kennedy replied he would not attack Nixon because "I never attack people personally." (Less than a month later, Kennedy was accusing Humphrey of "imitating Richard Nixon" by "playing fast and loose with smears and innuendos" in the West Virginia primary.)

Kennedy was obviously playing for a large Republican cross-over in the wide-open Wisconsin primary and, as the *Capital Times'* Miles McMillin reported, "he has been careful not to antagonize this potential vote."

"No one has been willing to estimate how much of the cross-over will be religiously motivated," he added, "but there seems little doubt at this point that Kennedy will be the chief beneficiary, largely because of the skillful and quiet way his organization has exploited the religious factor."

"The Catholics are 1,000 percent for Kennedy," a prominent Wisconsin Democrat told *Time–Life*'s Robert Ajemian. "We lost a lot of Catholics to the Republicans during the Joe McCarthy era, but Kennedy will get most of them back. It isn't just that he's a Catholic. It's because he's a damn attractive guy, and they're really proud of him."

Kennedy's other group of special supporters, his multitudinous family, was also giving his campaign a great lift. But, according to Ajemian, his campaign managers were closely watching public reaction.

"If it gets to be too much," said one aide, "we'll cut out the family right away."

The Kennedys had already discouraged a visit from one friend of the family—Frank Sinatra. But, though the Rat Pack Leader was not present in person, his voice boomed out from the Kennedy sound truck in a special campaign song:

> Everyone is voting for Jack,
> Cause he's got what all the rest lack. . . .

Then, almost inevitably, it happened.

In the closing days of the primary, vicious anti-Catholic literature began to appear in Wisconsin. Marquis Childs reported that it had been "sent largely to Catholics and often to individuals in care of the local chapter of the Knights of Columbus. While they seem to have originated with the lunatic fringe, the effect is naturally to create sympathy for Kennedy. . . . And this may well be true not only among Kennedy's fellow Catholics in Wisconsin but among others who have all along felt the injustice of discriminating against a candidate for the Presidency because of his religion."

The Humphrey organization angrily demanded that postal inspectors trace the source of the literature. Gerald Heaney, Humphrey's campaign director and a prominent Catholic layman, theorized the mailing may have been a guileful exercise in reverse psychology aimed at blackening Humphrey's name and enraging Catholic voters against him.

"This is the most despicable thing I've seen in my life," Heaney thundered.

When the final returns were in, Kennedy won, with a decisive 478,901 votes—56 per cent of the Democratic vote that took 6 of the state's 10 election districts, 20½ of the 31 delegate votes at the national convention. Humphrey obtained 372,034 votes, 4 election districts, 10½ delegate votes. Adding up the returns, the pundits and the politicians made them come out just about any way they wished.

But there were some unmistakable conclusions to be drawn.

One was that an attractive, hard-campaigning Catholic candidate could count on a powerful Catholic vote cutting across labor union loyalties, the farm problem and even—to a lesser extent—party lines.

Kennedy's support from Wisconsin's large Catholic population (32 per cent) almost amounted to a bloc vote. Voters in Democratic areas with a high concentration of Catholics gave Kennedy a top-heavy margin. More significant, he scored decisive victories in Catholic localities that usually voted Republican. "This means," reported the *New York Times* correspondent, "that Catholic Republicans in large numbers crossed over to vote for Kennedy, a Catholic. . . . Humphrey took many solidly Protestant localities handily, but not nearly as many Republicans crossed over to support him."

Kennedy also received huge margins in districts considered former strongholds of the late Senator McCarthy. Humphrey's efforts to link his rival with McCarthyism had paid off—for Kennedy.

James Reston opined that in Wisconsin Kennedy had "benefited . . . from the ancient feeling among Catholics that the Protestant majority in this country has wilfully denied the Presidency to anyone of the Catholic faith. It is not too much to say that, if he were not the beneficiary of this feeling, if the other leaders of his party were not fearful of losing the support of the large Catholic constituency in the large Northern cities, he would probably not be leading the race today."

And before he descended from his oracular heights to become a plain Kennedy Democrat, Walter Lippmann analyzed the results and proclaimed "there is no doubt that the religious issue was central and decisive." Looking ahead, he saw the disturbing possibility that this "ugly and dangerous" issue would become "much more acute and virulent in the national election itself."

As Lippmann saw it, if Kennedy headed the Democratic ticket, the religious issue would be critical, and if he were rejected by the party, that would antagonize millions of Catholics. Thus, the Democratic party found itself in the awkward position of being damned if it did and damned if it didn't.

According to Lippmann, the solution lay in nominating Kennedy for the Vice Presidency. In that position, the religious issue would not be paramount. "The office," he wrote, "is not one for which any man is too grand and certainly not any man who is 43 years old and has never occupied any executive office. Moreover, the nomination and election of a Catholic . . . would be absolute destruction of the taboo against electing a Catholic to the presidency."

The wide acceptance of the belief that Kennedy would be an asset to the Democratic ticket as a Vice-Presidential candidate was in itself a pronounced change in the political timidity about religious affiliation that followed the Al Smith campaign. As recently as the 1948 Democratic Convention, a proposal that Wyoming's Senator Joseph O'Mahoney become President Truman's running mate was peremptorily dropped at a leadership huddle on that single ground.

In retrospect, the division of the Wisconsin vote was another instance of Kennedy luck: had he won 7 or 8 of the state's 10 Congressional districts, instead of 6, Humphrey might well have dropped out of the race for delegates. As it happened, Humphrey's showing was enough to keep him in for the West Virginia primary. And a victory by Catholic Kennedy over Congregationalist Humphrey in the overwhelmingly Protestant Mountain State could go far toward removing the gnawing fear among some Democratic leaders that Kennedy could win only in states where the Catholic population was high.

Humphrey insisted on carrying the challenge to West Virginia. "We'll be out from under this Catholic thing," he said, "and we'll be dealing with real Democrats, not these one-day Democrats." (West Virginia forbids crossover voting.)

Kennedy had opened his West Virginia campaign headquarters in mid-March. He had spent five hours in Charleston that day. In the evening as he returned to Wisconsin in his Convair, the Senator asked accompanying newsmen how they thought things looked for him in West Virginia. Several correspondents said things looked tough.

"I'm not worried about West Virginia at all," Kennedy said, matter-of-factly.

The Senator tossed on the table a thick, mimeographed volume—a West Virginia poll completed for him in January by Louis Harris & Associates.

"This shows me winning 70 to 30 over Humphrey," Kennedy observed.

Reporters were allowed to read the Harris report. Earl Mazo, of the *New York Herald Tribune,* published huge chunks of it. The document Mazo reported, recognized that Kennedy's Catholicism would be a problem in some sections of the border state where hard-shell Presbyterianism makes for strong religious sentiments. But Harris' "final observation" was this:

"West Virginia sizes up as a safety valve for Jack Kennedy. He has a comfortable lead at the present which Humphrey will have difficulty cutting down, especially in the short time left between West Virginia and Wisconsin primaries.

"It is a state that will give Kennedy a chance to talk 'New Deal' and one where he can strike a great blow to the doubters on the matter of religion. He has assets and a powerful image working for him . . . a concentrated effort here can result in a handsome victory and a powerful weapon against those who raise the 'Catholic can't win' bit. . . .

"Here we learn again that while Senator Kennedy pulls strongly among Protestant voters, he makes a tremendous showing among Catholics. . . . With the exception of the religious issue there is almost a total absence of negatives in the Kennedy image. . . .

"The highest amount of anti-Catholic sentiment" was found in the Fifth [southern border] District where 33 percent of those polled had expressed some misgivings about voting for a Catholic—18 percent of them being "harsh" in their objections and 15 percent "milder." However, "anti-Catholic feeling does not appear to be enough to have any deleterious effect on the outcome."

Nevertheless, the Harris report recommended: "One, Kennedy must make a major effort in the Fifth District. He can counteract the religious issue with the ready-made bread-and-butter issue. Two, if Kennedy runs well in the Fifth District, it would seem likely that one or more syndicated columnists or commentators might do a post-primary piece on its significance. . . ."

"Though Kennedy does extremely well among wealthy and better educated people . . . ," the report continued, "there is, however, tremendous apathy among those in the lower-income groups—almost half of them undecided in a Kennedy-Humphrey race. . . . [To them] Kennedy can present himself as an all-out New Deal Democrat—a fighting liberal."

This was a switch. In Wisconsin, as Marquis Childs had reported, Kennedy had "set out to create the image of a warm, friendly, eager, able American who has at heart the interests of all the people and not just those of one party or one economic and social level. . . ."

Now Harris was calling for a new Kennedy, one tailored to meet the demands of West Virginia's depressed areas—"an all-out New Deal Democrat —a fighting liberal."

So Jack Kennedy changed images for the West Virginia run. Campaigning in the depressed mining regions, he stirred the dry leaves of the Great Depression in recalling F.D.R.'s first hundred days in office. He called for a rebirth of the New Deal—which was rather odd since Kennedy, at the same time, claimed only the Republicans looked backward. The New Deal pitch was further enhanced by the importation of Franklin Delano Roosevelt Jr., whom Jack had known as a Congressional colleague. "I have always found Roosevelt an amusing fellow," commented the irrepressible Murray Kempton, "but I would not employ him, except for reasons of personal friendship, as a geek in a common carnival." Formerly a registered public relations agent for the Trujillo dictatorship, F.D.R. Jr. had become a salesman of Italian automobiles. The talk was that he was seeking a political comeback.

Kennedy met the religious issue head-on. "Sometimes Kennedy raises the issue himself in his formal remarks; sometimes he waits to have it raised during the question period; or, if no one asks, he brings up the question himself," reported Douglass Cater in the *Reporter*.

"His answer is long and loose-jointed. He begins right off with the historic and Constitutional foundations for separation of religion and politics in America. He lists his 'coreligionists' both in this country and elsewhere who have served in high office without ecclesiastical hindrance. He emphasizes that Papal orders would be neither given nor listened to. He cites the patriotic and public-service record of himself and his brothers (curiously never mentioning Papa Kennedy's services) and declares, with the faintest touch of irony, that he cannot believe he was precluded at birth from holding the highest office in the land. Finally, having seized the issue by the scruff of the neck, he seeks to chuck it out of the primary altogether. 'I am going to live and die as a member of my church, but the problems of West Viriginia will be here long after I've left the state,' he announces flatly. He usually gets prolonged applause."

"While not exactly pulling 'I hold in my hand' techniques," commented Holmes Alexander, "Kennedy is using both the Stars and Stripes and the Constitution to smother the religious issue. It's no compliment to democracy when he asks his audience to agree with him that military service is a qualification for the Presidency or that the Constitution gave him the 'right' to their votes."

A native West Virginian, Alexander had another beef: "West Virginians are a proud, decent, conscientious people. They are not enjoying this campaign. For one thing, they do not like the 'Tobacco Road' image of their state as given in the faceless statistics of low income and persisting unemployment. Hard up they may be, but West Virginians object to being pointed at. They loathe being pitied."

And, above all, they objected to being called bigots. They objected to visiting correspondents who, by the dozens, were informing publications throughout the world of rampant religious prejudice in West Virginia.

"There seems to be some irrepressible desire on the part of American publications to explain, beforehand, that the vote next month will be shot through and through with ignorant prejudice," commented L. T. Anderson in the *Charleston Gazette.* "The constant din is calculated, it would seem, to shame West Virginia Democrats into voting for Kennedy. I regard this as very poor strategy and an almost personal insult."

But the strategy worked, serving to give the primary an importance it had not previously warranted. Throughout the country, the forces of righteousness mobilized their thunder against bigotry. Liberal pastors, not previously known for their fondness for Rome, preached sermons by the score against intolerance. And editorialists commented in dismay at the findings of their correspondents in the "cricks and hollers" of West Virginia.

As it turned out, according to W. E. Chilton III, also of the *Gazette,* "the issue of Kennedy's religion was a minor factor in determining the final results." Writing in the *New Leader,* Chilton said "The visiting press and pollsters had emphasized, sensationalized and distorted the religious question out of all reason."

A number of newspapers, including the *New York Herald Tribune,* displayed what they regarded as an outrageous example of bigotry—a headline from the West Virginia *Hillbilly,* reading: "Pa Ain't Going to Sell His Vote to No Catholic." But what the correspondents forgot to report was that the headline was satirical and had appeared over an anti-bigotry story. The

Washington Post subsequently apologized to its subscribers for using the story. Most papers, including the *Tribune,* did not.

"The out of town newsmen for the most part ate together, wrote together and relaxed together," the *Gazette's* Anderson later post-mortemed. "They talked to each other constantly about their discoveries in West Virginia. They traded bigotry stories. They marveled together about their awesome findings.

"They took polls. Many of them correctly showed Kennedy to be the leader. But as one correspondent confessed, 'We didn't have the guts to write it.' They couldn't believe their own polls. They couldn't believe persons who discussed religion so frankly could vote for a man with whose religion they disagreed."

Joseph Alsop, for example, was writing as much about the primary as he was about the "missile gap." After traveling with Lou Harris for several days, the widely syndicated pundit produced several columns on his findings. From Slab Fork (where he interviewed eighty families), Alsop reported that "the shoeless, the slatterns and the slobs" were for Humphrey, while most responsible citizens were backing Kennedy. He bluntly accused Humphrey of making use of ignorance and bigotry.

"In summary," Alsop wrote, "this critical West Virginia primary looks like a very ugly business, in which Humphrey can only win—if he does win— for very ugly reasons."[9]

Humphrey angrily demanded that Kennedy disassociate himself from Alsop whom he described as a close friend and active supporter of his rival: "When I see a columnist who refers to poor people as ignorant, and when I see my opponent associate with him, I say, 'Beware of people who judge others.' If there's anything I resent, it's a self-righteous, stuffy snob."

In the midst of the West Virginia campaign, Kennedy went before the American Society of Newspaper Editors in Washington and, in an eloquent, carefully drafted oration, appealed to the American people to take the religious issue out of the campaign.

"Is the religious issue a legitimate issue in this campaign?" he asked rhetorically. "There is only one legitimate question underlying all the rest: Would you, as President, be responsive in any way to ecclesiastical pressures or obligations of any kind that might in any fashion influence or interfere with your conduct of that office in the national interest? I have answered that question many times. My answer was—and is—no." He was opposed, he said, to federal aid for parochial schools ("clearly unconstitutional"), was opposed to sending an Ambassador to the Vatican ("It was last proposed by a Baptist

[9] As W. E. Chilton III later observed, "In the light of Slab Fork's 100 to 36 pro-Kennedy vote and in view of an Alsop remark to a Charleston editor that he disliked Humphrey intensely, it is obvious from whose typewriter the ugliest bit of campaign reporting emanated."

President"), and if confronted with a bill providing foreign aid funds for birth control, "I would neither veto nor sign such a bill on the basis except what I considered to be the public interest."

And he took up the charge that he was appealing to the "so-called Catholic vote."

"Even if such a vote exists—which I doubt—I want to make one thing clear again: I want no votes solely on account of my religion."

He denied he had ever suggested that the Democratic party was required to nominate him or face a Catholic revolt in November.

There was prolonged applause at the end of the speech; but no questions. The next day, James Reston raised some. In scoffing "at the indications of Catholic bloc voting in Wisconsin," Reston said, Kennedy was bucking some "convincing statistics." However, Kennedy's denial of a Catholic revolt if he was rejected by the Convention "helps remove the vague suggestion of blackmail that has hung over his campaign for the last few months."

In his speech Kennedy had specifically criticized the Wisconsin press for having failed to report his earth-shaking views in depth, but rather concentrating on "my theme song, family, haircut and, inevitably, my religion." He particularly accused the *Milwaukee Journal* of overemphasizing the Catholic vote in the primary.[10]

The *Journal* took issue with Kennedy's complaints. "The lack of hard issues in the campaign was best pointed up by Kennedy when, in refusing Humphrey's challenge to debate, he said that *there were no issues between them to debate.* . . . It was Kennedy who brought his family, his theme song, his coffee parties into Wisconsin. He certainly did it to attract attention, increase recognition of his name and candidacy and win votes. . . . As for the religious issue, Kennedy conceded that the press did not create it. In the first weeks, the issue was little mentioned. . . . In the last 10 days of the campaign the issue flared into the open. . . . Only then was public attention focused on an issue which politicians, newspapermen and pollsters knew was ever present (Wisconsin being a state in which the religious issue has frequently influenced politics). . . ."

Back in West Virginia, just to confuse things a bit more, a leading Roman Catholic clergyman announced he would not support Kennedy. Monsignor James F. Newcomb, of Huntington, said he favored Vice President Nixon. He was particularly critical of Kennedy's ASNE speech and said the Senator had needlessly stated he would not permit higher authorities of his church to exert pressure on him if elected President. "All he had to say was," Msgr. Newcomb said, " 'If I'm elected President, I'll abide by the Constitution absolutely and act according to my conscience.' "

Meanwhile the two rivals were campaigning doggedly—or underdoggedly—for votes. Across mine-scarred mountains, from Charleston to

---

[10] The *Milwaukee Journal* later endorsed Kennedy for the Presidency.

Charles Town, the plaints of John F. Kennedy and Hubert Humphrey echoed, mournful as a coon dog's cry.

Why Kennedy should be moaning didn't make sense to *Newsweek's* Harold Lavine: "His forces obviously are better organized than Humphrey's, and they obviously have money to burn. . . . Yet, Kennedy walks in gloom. Over and over again, he keeps saying, 'It's an uphill fight.' And he makes it clear that he thinks only a miracle can give him victory over Humphrey in the Democratic primary on May 10."

Lavine also noted: "Anti-Catholic sentiment did not prevent Alfred E. Smith from carrying the West Virginia primary in 1928; and besides, Kennedy, for understandable tactical reasons, grossly exaggerates the extent of the gang-up against him."

One reason for Kennedy's gloom, he let it be known, was his pollster's findings that bigotry had cut his lead over Humphrey. As a result, he climaxed a series of forthright speeches with a statewide television appearance in which he declared his independence of the Pope and also took a mock oath to uphold the Constitution, suggesting that he be impeached if it was found that as President he was taking orders from the Vatican.

Another reason for his gloom was his conviction that supporters of Adlai Stevenson, Stuart Symington, and Lyndon Johnson had formed an unholy behind-the-scenes alliance to "Stop Kennedy." Charging Humphrey with being the "hatchet man" for these non-candidates, Kennedy added: "Humphrey knows he can't get the nomination."

Skilled in underdoggery himself, Humphrey laughed out loud. "He's acting like a spoiled juvenile," he charged. "It has always seemed amusing to me to see Jack publicly challenge other candidates to enter the primaries. Then when someone else does enter, he complains there's a conspiracy to stop him and to deny him the nomination."

Humphrey spoke bitterly about the advantages that wealth gave his younger rival. "I don't have any daddy who can pay the bills for me," he said. "I can't afford to run around this state with a little black bag and a checkbook. I don't think elections should be bought. They're spending with wild abandon."

In Wisconsin, the *Baltimore Sun* reported, there had been "whispers of disapproval of the way Kennedy was exploiting his record as a war hero." In West Virginia, a state with a high percentage of war veterans, all stops were removed. Tens of thousands of copies of the *Reader's Digest* article about Kennedy's PT-boat heroism were distributed. And the growing number of Kennedy workers began sporting lapel buttons and tie clasps shaped like PT-boats, bearing the legend "Kennedy in '60."

"These depict not merely Jack's memorable World War II service—but they call attention to the fact that Humphrey was a wartime stay-at-home," noted Holmes Alexander. "Is this not an appeal to prejudice?"

The *pièce de résistance* came when the Kennedys pre-empted expensive

TV time for a reshowing of "PT-109," a sequence out of "Navy Log," detailing Kennedy's heroic true-life deeds in the South Pacific.

"Kennedy is the only veteran in the West Virginia primary," an announcer said emphatically just before the TV film rolled. Inadvertently or not the sponsors of this unusual political document left on the reel the message at the end saying the film had the endorsement and co-operation of the Department of Defense and the U.S. Navy. The camera cut instantly to Senator Kennedy in more recent scenes, telling hard-pressed West Virginians what he felt the Government should, and if he were elected, would do to alleviate their plight. After a few views of the nation's Capital and a stentorian announcement that this was a "time for greatness," there was a polite reminder that this was a paid political program.

For once, Senator Humphrey had no immediate comment. "There seemed to be little for him to say except perhaps, 'Banzai,' " commented that noted student of *One-upmanship,* Bob Considine.

Meanwhile, Franklin Roosevelt Jr. was inviting votes for Kennedy as "the only wounded veteran" among all Presidential aspirants. On April 27, however, he not only extolled his hero's war record, but added: "There's another candidate in your primary. He's a good Democrat, but I don't know where he was in World War II."

The implication was that while Kennedy was courageously defending the nation, Humphrey was a slacker hiding out in the hills.

The statement, the *Washington Star* said the following day, was "a new low in dirty politics." The *Star* said the publicly reported facts were that Humphrey, married and the father of three children, was first put in a deferred classification. When he tried to volunteer for the Navy he was turned down for physical disability. Then an Army physical in 1945 revealed a double hernia.

"If Mr. Roosevelt does not think these really are the facts, that is one thing," the *Star* said. "But to simply say that 'I don't know where he was in World War II' is a slur which all decent people will resent.

"It would not have been so bad, if Senator Kennedy had repudiated the Roosevelt remark. But he didn't. With an above-the-battle air, he merely said: 'I have not discussed the matter and I am not going to. Mr. Roosevelt is down here making his speeches. I'm making mine.' This, however, will not wash. For Mr. Roosevelt is making his speeches in Senator Kennedy's behalf. And Senator Kennedy cannot shrug his shoulders and escape all responsibility for what his campaigner says. . . ."

Moreover, Roosevelt could reasonably have construed Kennedy's comment as tacit approval of what was doing. On May 6, Roosevelt revived the issue—this time giving every indication that he knew very well where Humphrey was in World War II. At least, he came forward with a chapter-and-verse recital of what he described as Humphrey's efforts to obtain draft deferments—a recital that, incidentally, did not jibe with the Minnesotan's explanation of the matter.

"Whatever the facts may be as to this," commented the *Star,* "Mr. Roosevelt's second statement has been disapproved by Senator Kennedy—after it had been made and publicized."

What Kennedy finally declared was this: "Any discussion of the war record of Senator Humphrey was done without my knowledge and consent, as I strongly disapprove the injection of this issue into the campaign."

Later the same day, however, Kennedy said that no one had made a greater contribution to discussing the issues than Franklin Roosevelt Jr.[11]

As for Roosevelt's comment that he was "very upset that the *Washington Star* and *Time* magazine accused me of dirty politics," the *Star* observed: "For our part, we do not know why he should be upset. His original statement, we still think, was dirty politics. And so is the second one—flavored, this time, with a dash of disingenuousness."

"These boys play both the high road and the low road," Humphrey commented, "and they both get splashed. They cannot keep out of each other's ditch. But I am not running against Franklin D. Roosevelt Jr. I am running against Jack Kennedy, the son of Joe Kennedy who was a mortal enemy of F.D.R. Sr."

As the campaign neared the end, one local newspaper described it as "one of the worst name-calling campaigns in the history of Presidential politics."

On April 30, Senator Humphrey issued a veiled warning to Bobby Kennedy, who had compared the Minnesotan's campaign tactics with those of the late Senator McCarthy.

"I'd suggest," Humphrey told the Associated Press, "that Brother Bobby examine his own conscience about innuendoes and smears. If he has trouble knowing what I mean, I can refresh his memory very easily. It is a subject he should not want opened."

Asked to elaborate, Humphrey replied firmly, "No, sir."

The warning appeared to have fallen on deaf ears. For on May 2 Humphrey once again blasted Bobby Kennedy. This time, he accused his rival's brother and campaign manager of having learned "guilt by association" tactics "while working for the late Senator McCarthy's committee during its heyday."

What brought on the fireworks was Bobby's allegation that Jimmy Hoffa had instructed the West Virginia Teamsters to go all-out for Humphrey.

"This is just cheap, low-down, gutter politics," charged Humphrey, who

[11] Several months later, Kennedy gave Roosevelt a thank-you present in recognition of his primary services—a lucite cigarette box with a replica of a PT-boat, inscribed to "Franklin Delano Roosevelt Jr., commander of all forces south of the Kanawha," the river dividing the state's prosperous and depressed regions.

referred to his opponent as "the spoiled candidate" and to the brother as "that young, emotional, juvenile Bobby."

"I'm getting sick and tired of some of this stuff," said Hubert. "Some morning when I'm real tired I'm going to take his scalp off." The assumption was that anything endangering Kennedy's hair-do struck right at the heart of the Kennedy campaign.

"Anyone who gets in the way of teacher's pet—I should change that to Papa's pet—is to be destroyed. Bobby said if they had to spend half a million to win here, they would do it. He said that to a Senator in Washington."

Jack Kennedy immediately challenged the Minnesotan to name the Senator. He declared his entire spending in West Virginia would be in the "upper $40,000 or $50,000 bracket."

"I have never before been subjected to such personal abuse," Kennedy added. "I am puzzled that a candidate whom no observer thinks can be nominated by the Democratic party should indulge in such tactics."

Humphrey continued the attack.

"I don't think the people of West Virginia can be 'bought,'" he said, ". . . they are not going to be stampeded by reckless last-minute charges, wild and unfounded advertising, or the extravagant use of unlimited wealth. West Virginians don't want the Democrats to ape the Republicans by becoming the 'big money' party, relying solely on slick advertising gimmicks and avoiding the real issues that affect the people."

So dismayed was Arthur Schlesinger Jr. by the vituperation unloosed in West Virginia that he sat down at his typewriter to write a letter to both contenders deploring the "spectacle of the two liberal candidates swinging angrily on each other and trying to knock the other out of the ring while the conservatives . . . egg them on."

After months of trading insults with each other the rivals agreed to a debate. All of West Virginia awaited what was heralded as the greatest confrontation of feudists since the Hatfields and the McCoys perforated each other in the nearby hills. Instead, it turned out to be a tea party of mutual compliments and joint derision of Eisenhower and Nixon. Typical repartee:

INTERLOCUTOR: You now have five minutes, Senator Humphrey, for your rebuttal to Senator Kennedy.

HUMPHREY: I agree with everything he says.

KENNEDY: Me, too.

About which, Hearst correspondent Frank Conniff commented, "The tame exchange of love taps seemed to prove that Kennedy was correct in his Wisconsin attitude—that a 'debate' between the two liberals who generally agree on political issues would serve no useful purpose. But Humphrey proved such an amiable foil on the telecast that the Kennedy managers now regret their refusal to accept his challenge in Wisconsin."

In the final days of the campaign, Philip Potter reported in the *Baltimore Sun* that Kennedy was spending "most liberally for television and radio time, newspaper space and door-to-door advertising, and, according to knowledgeable Democrats, won the allegiance of many involved in local contests by giving their campaigns financial support."

The radio spots, broadcast at intervals throughout the day, featured a voice that poked fun at Humphrey's first name, Hubert, pronouncing it "Hyoobert," with a comical accent on the first syllable. The burden of the message was that no red-blooded Mountaineer would be caught dead voting for someone with a name like "Hyoobert."

There were unverified rumors that Kennedy's brother-in-law, Stephen Smith, had withdrawn all the $1 bills in Charleston's banks just before the May 10 primary, purportedly for vote-buying purposes. Hubert Humphrey announced he had hired an ex-FBI agent to look into all such charges.

Kennedy returned to Washington on primary morning. Later that night, he put in a call to brother Bobby in Charleston. "We're winning," he told his guests. He then placed a call to his father at Hyannis Port. The Ambassador, of course, never had any doubts about the outcome.

Kennedy flew back to Charleston where he shook hands with Hubert Humphrey who had already conceded. "It was very nice of you to come over, Hubert," he said. At a press conference, he said:

"I believe we have now buried the religious issue once and for all."

Brother Bobby picked up the theme: "We can now say that the religious issue was buried in the hills and mountains of West Virginia."

The final returns, showing Kennedy sweeping the Mountain State by 220,000 to Humphrey's 142,000, confounded the experts. Kennedy had carried all but seven of the state's 55 counties.

"It just proves you can't trust bigots," was the morning-after comment of *Baltimore Sun* correspondent Howard Norton.

A few days later, Norton published an authoritative report on how elections are really won in parts of West Virginia. And he discussed at length the role of the county politicians who, he said, had done more to get out the West Virginia vote for Kennedy "than did all the last-minute flood of newspaper and radio-television advertising, all the speeches and handshakes and all the alleged whispered instructions from labor and Negro leaders. It was also the activity of the pros that is credited with doing more to overcome this region's anti-Catholic prejudice than did the attractiveness of the candidate himself. . . . And here in brief is the story:

"The county politicians very frankly do not care much who wins in a Presidential primary. Their job is to keep their party in office in the county. . . . The pros are apt to regard out-of-state Presidential primary invaders chiefly as potential sources of revenue for the county campaign chests. This is true, particularly, when the party workers have no special fondness for the Presidential candidates who are entered in the primary. . . . This appears to have been the case in this year's primary; the politicians—and a lot of the people—were for Senator Johnson, Adlai Stevenson and Senator Symington. But they had to choose between Humphrey and Kennedy . . . it did not make much difference which one they voted and worked for, because the winner, under West Virginia law, cannot demand their convention votes. . . .

"Long tradition has built up a system of filling the county campaign chests by almost openly 'auctioning off' the support of the county machine to the highest bidder among the candidates for national office. This is a completely honest procedure. . . . It's put down as a county-level campaign contribution by the candidate for national office. And, in appreciation of the contribution, the county machine throws its support to the successful bidder.

"Once the bidding is completed, the party leaders . . . print up on little slips of paper the official 'slate' of candidates whom they urge the voters to accept. . . . For the purposes of last-minute political bargaining, however, these 'slates' generally are kept under wraps until the morning of election day. Then, when the organization's automobiles go out into the hills and start hauling the voters to the polls, copies of the official 'slate' are pressed into the hands of the party faithful. Only at this point does the average faithful member of the Democratic party in West Virginia suddenly come to know who he is going to vote for when he gets into the voting booth.

"This may explain why the five biggest hard-shell fundamentalist, conservative, Protestant counties of West Virginia went so overwhelmingly for a liberal Catholic candidate for the Presidency. It explains, too, why newspaper men traveling through these counties and talking to the people got such a wrong idea of what they would do on election day."

McDowell County, characterized by Norton as inhabited by "snake-handlers," offered its support to anyone, be he Kennedy or Humphrey, who offered the highest contribution. The bids appeared to have been sealed because Norton reported that Senator Humphrey "came right up to election day convinced that he had won the bidding in big McDowell County. His political scouts informed him that everything was 'absolutely safe' there.

"But only a matter of hours before the polls opened, word came that the McDowell County machine had switched to Kennedy. . . . By the same system, Raleigh County, another 'safe' Protestant area, gave Kennedy 10,141 votes to Humphrey's 5,242.

"Fayette County, where this correspondent saw loafers at the courthouse refuse to shake hands with Kennedy, gave him a 2 to 1 margin. . . ."

And so on down the line.

Since vote-buying is almost a tradition in West Virginia, as a rule nobody gets very excited about it. But the goings-on at the polls, particularly in Logan and Wayne counties, in the May 10 primary scandalized even West Virginians.

Editor Charles D. Hylton Jr. of the *Logan Banner* called the primary "one of the most corrupt elections in county history." He said the payoffs "ranged anywhere from $2 and a drink of whiskey to $6 and two pints of whiskey for a single vote."

FBI agents swarmed into the area; but their hands were tied. Just where state jurisdiction ends and federal jurisdiction begins was a tangled legal question.

"Since when," Senator Kennedy asked bitterly, "has the FBI been used as a political weapon?"

Kennedy, of course, was not without his journalistic defenders. His good friend Charles Bartlett reported that the Senator's rivals—including Stevenson, Johnson, and Symington—"are looking with extreme hopefulness to the reports out of West Virginia, where a combination of Republicans, newspapermen and Senator Robert Byrd, a Johnson supporter, is pressing for evidence of illegal spending by the Kennedy camp in the primary. The big hope is that a local grand jury may be induced to indict the Senator's brother, Robert Kennedy."[12]

Other factors, besides "the heavy outpouring of funds by the Kennedy forces," contributed to the Senator's showing, according to *Wall Street Journal*'s Paul Duke. "The outcome was a remarkable personal triumph for Kennedy whose buoyant youth, clean-cut appearance and polished, Boston-accented speechmaking were vote-getting ingredients of a more private nature. . . . Pre-primary interviews with West Virginians favoring Kennedy brought responses of amazing similarity. Time and again voters would smile and say they 'liked' Kennedy, but couldn't say exactly why. . . ."

This was no new phenomenon, according to Duke. He cited, as an example, the 1920 selection of the likable Warren Harding as the GOP Presidential candidate.

"And it is this image of a bright young man who is also likable which Mr. Kennedy obviously intends to try to sell the American public if he runs in November."

West Virginia cast a pall over the hopes of the other Democratic aspirants. Nevertheless, the bitterly fought primary did raise some new doubts about Jack Kennedy personally. "The most alarming weakness which showed up in West Virginia," wrote Robert Hartmann in the *Los Angeles Times,* "was an inability on Kennedy's part to 'take it' as well as dish it out, a tendency to rattle and come unglued when the heat was on.

[12] On the opening day of the Democratic Convention, Drew Pearson published what he claimed was a Justice Department report into alleged West Virginia improprieties. The following day, the Department denied Pearson's statement that an indictment against Robert F. Kennedy was under consideration. On November 23, 1960, several weeks after Kennedy's election as President, it was announced in Logan, West Virginia, that eleven persons had been indicted by a special grand jury on charges growing out of the May 10 voting irregularities. But the jury, in a report of its work, said West Virginia election laws were unrealistic and because of this it was difficult to obtain sufficient evidence against other suspected violators.

"Kennedy's low Irish boiling-point and condoning of some rather low blows did not seem to disenchant West Virginia voters, but the professional politicians were appalled."

Nevertheless, Hartmann continued, "one must conscientiously report that the Kennedy bandwagon is rolling and will be hard to stop before November, if then." Still there were as many doubters as there were statistics to support a contrary opinion. Is one, after all, invincible because he beat Hubert Humphrey? Or because he beat Wayne Morse in Oregon and Maryland?

Presidential nominations, after all, are simply a matter of statistics. Of the 1,521 delegate votes at the Los Angeles Convention, 761 would be needed to win. By mid-May John F. Kennedy still needed several hundred more delegate votes to go over the top.

Consequently, he began to eye the tidy bloc of 50 to 80 delegates still held by his most recent deadly enemy Hubert Humphrey. And in true Honey Fitz tradition, he swallowed his pride and asked to meet with Humphrey. They met secretly in the latter's offices. The key episode came when Kennedy musingly inquired how Humphrey would react if the Convention gave him the Vice-Presidential nomination on a Kennedy ticket. Humphrey indicated he might accept. Kennedy said it was helpful to know what was on Humphrey's mind.

Humphrey, however, made no commitment on his delegates. He made it clear that the wounds of the primaries were not all healed.

One tangible outcome of the meeting was an apology to Humphrey by Franklin Roosevelt Jr., who had questioned the Senator's wartime activities. Both in person and in a letter, Roosevelt assured Humphrey his statements were "unnecessary and unwarranted."

Another Roosevelt—Eleanor—still refused to endorse Kennedy. In fact, she let it be known that if the choice in November were between Kennedy and Nixon she might not even vote. Her heart, she indicated, still belonged to Adlai.

And Congressman James Roosevelt of California was for a time under the impression he might be Kennedy's running mate.

Breathlessly he telephoned Adam Clayton Powell, informing his New York colleague that Kennedy had "practically" offered him the Vice Presidency. What should he do?

"Get it in writing," was Powell's laconic reply.

Powell, of course, was aware that Kennedy and his top commandos were planting Vice-Presidential hopes in the minds of others who controlled votes at the Convention. Usual procedure was for Kennedy or an aide—often brother Bobby—to confer with a hopeful and analyze the situation. The conclusion was inescapable: the hopeful had just the right qualities and, moreover, Jack liked him. Since almost any respectable, non-Irish, non-Eastern, non-Catholic had these basic qualities, the field was wide open.

For example, in Nevada, Kennedy told reporters it would sure be fine to have a Western Governor as a running mate. Nevada's Governor Grant Sawyer got the word. Since the other Western Governors were either Catholics or Republicans, the logical conclusion was that Kennedy meant Sawyer. As the Sawyer pride swelled, so did his enthusiasm for Kennedy.

Barnstorming through Kansas, Kennedy let it be known that Governor George Docking stood "near the top" of any list of Vice-Presidential choices; and Kennedy pointedly refrained from naming any others as "outstanding" as the fifty-six-year-old Governor.

In Michigan, Kennedy told a news conference he would like to balance the ticket with a Midwestern Governor whose Liberalism could be counted on to woo the votes of labor, Negroes and other minority groups. But, he added, he would let the Convention decide. And if the Convention happened to decide on his then host Governor G. Mennen "Soapy" Williams, he would be overjoyed.

The same "liberal Midwestern Governor" message also reached Iowa's Herschel Loveless and Minnesota's Orville Freeman, and it fit them just as aptly. Farther West, Kennedy's commandos spread the word that they were also considering Washington's Senator Henry "Scoop" Jackson, New Mexico's Senator Clinton Anderson, California's Senator Clair Engle, and even Arizona's Congressman Stewart Udall. Below the Mason-Dixon line, the only live entry appeared to be Florida's Governor Leroy Collins.

With the smell of victory in the air, the Kennedy bandwagon became crowded. One Governor who refused to hop aboard was New Jersey's Robert B. Meyner, even though the Kennedy camp had offered him a Cabinet-level post as a reward.[13]

Meyner made no bones about his distaste for the behind-the-scenes activities of Joseph P. Kennedy who, through the long Spring of 1960, had won the votes of north New Jersey politicians for his son. Meyner felt that by bypassing him, Joe Kennedy threatened his control of New Jersey Democracy.

Though the newspapers and magazines were filled with pictures of energetic young Kennedys romping around the country, some observers felt that Ambassador Kennedy's efforts in heading off a Stop Kennedy movement were more important. Joseph Kennedy's largess toward his party and individual Democrats over the years thus became no small weapon in his son's race for the nomination. As was well known, Joe Kennedy never gave a nickel to anyone without expecting something in return.

Joe Kennedy paid a visit to Albany's Democratic boss Daniel O'Connell in March 1960. The O'Connells, of course, have dictated upstate New York Democratic politics for half a century. They were expected to control 20 to 35 of New York State's 114 delegate votes at the Convention. After a short talk, Dan O'Connell assured the elder Kennedy of his machine's support.

[13] For failing to jump through the hoops on signal, the out-of-office Meyner paid the penalty following the election. After a visit to the White House, Meyner disclosed that he was not getting a job on the New Frontier.

Sometimes Joe Kennedy had really important things to worry about. There was an episode involving Frank Sinatra, The Leader of the Rat Pack, who had hired a screen writer said to have Communist affiliations from here to Moscow. The resulting uproar in patriotic circles reverberated in Hyannis Port. The Leader, after hearing from Peter Lawford's father-in-law, arranged to dispense with the screen writer's services forthwith, lest—he declared— Senator Kennedy be further embarrassed. As Broadway columnist Dorothy Kilgallen reported, "the situation was becoming especially delicate in Massachusetts where rather important church figures don't quite understand the Sinatra-Kennedy connection."

It was an extraordinary connection, indeed.

Frank Sinatra was one of the first prominent Americans to endorse John F. Kennedy for President.

On October 24, 1958, he explained why: "Senator Kennedy is a friend of mine."

The occasion was a London press conference at which newsmen questioned him about a statement made by French actress Brigitte Bardot who had announced she was flying to England to discuss making a movie with him.

"We should make interesting chemistry together," Miss Bardot proclaimed.

"Sorry," Sinatra told the reporters, "I gotta be in Boston to see Senator Kennedy. I promised."

Sinatra and Kennedy were drawn together by Kennedy's brother-in-law Peter Lawford, who had been an intimate friend of The Leader for years. Lawford had met Patricia Kennedy at the 1952 Republican Convention in Chicago. Lawford, though not yet a citizen, then considered himself a Republican. When they became engaged, Joseph P. Kennedy made a characteristic comment: "The only thing I hate worse than an actor as a son-in-law is an English actor." But he finally gave his blessing to the nuptials.

And before John F. Kennedy discovered the promotional values of *Culture* (Pablo Casals and all that jazz), he was the Rat Pack's most eminent fan. There was one memorable—and well-photographed—evening Las Vegas will never forget, when Sinatra, Dean Martin, Peter Lawford, and Sammy Davis Jr. put on a special performance for John F. Kennedy. The time was March 1960. The Senator had taken a day off from his campaigning to be with his show-business friends. The show went on and on until the group, all of whom had been drinking on stage, nearly dropped from exhaustion. Dean Martin kept sipping from an ice bucket in which Frank Sinatra had poured a gargantuan highball. The jokers really went wild.

Typical Rat Pack dialogue: When Peter Lawford asked Sammy Davis Jr. to dance with him, the latter said:

"*You* want to dance with *me?* Do you realize I happen to be the greatest Jewish Mau-Mau dancer of all time?"

"I'm not prejudiced," said Lawford.

"I know your kind," Davis replied. "You'll dance with me but you won't go to school with me."

From all accounts—and judging from the photographs—the future President of the United States enjoyed the evening immensely.

Con

18

When the deed was done—when a shrewd, slick, well-financed operation finally put John F. Kennedy over as the Democratic candidate for President—editor Carey McWilliams reported to the *Nation* from Los Angeles:

"So the paradox of this Convention has been that a young man without an impressive political record, without a program, without broad rank-and-file support, backed by not a single interest group with the possible exception of labor, not merely won the nomination of a great party without substantial opposition, but took possession of it, lock, stock and barrel. The delegates were victims of a default of political leadership which was premised, of course, on their own default as citizens."

According to McWilliams (who later endorsed the Democratic ticket with "two cheers"), Kennedy had met with only "a kind of token opposition" on the road to the nomination. "Late in the game," he added, "when the opposition realized what was happening, it refrained from organizing a 'Stop Kennedy' movement not out of chivalry, but because it knew that any such movement would be said to rest solely on Senator Kennedy's religion, which the Senator had converted into a formidable defense weapon."

As the race went into the stretch, John F. Kennedy appeared to have a hammerlock on the nomination. So overwhelming was his bandwagon propaganda after he piled up majorities in seven primaries (of which only two, Wisconsin and West Virginia, could possibly be described as contests) that it was difficult for Kennedy's rivals to see how he could be stopped. If anything could deprive the New Englander of his goal, however, it would be a desperate, last-minute onslaught by Lyndon B. Johnson's forces. But the effectiveness of the Kennedy machine was again demonstrated in the six weeks between the primaries and the Los Angeles Convention, when the Kennedyites whipped the Texan's forces at caucuses and conventions in Arizona, Colorado, Montana, and other Western states.

In many of these states the battles took on the aspect of a "war between the generations," with the Kennedy campaign generally enlisting the enthusiasm of the younger politicians, while Lyndon Johnson's cause was defended by men past their peak of political power.

"We're a young group and we're going to take over America," is the way Robert F. Kennedy put it, with an exuberance born of success.

Perhaps Lyndon Johnson never had a chance. Perhaps it could also have been said of him that because of an accident of birth he was precluded from holding the highest office in the land. At any rate, he was a lot less single-minded about pursuing the nomination than was his younger rival. He had repeatedly rejected suggestions that he declare himself a candidate, travel around the country, and enlist Democratic Governors and county chairmen to his side. He claimed that if he began campaigning he would, of necessity, have to neglect his duties as Majority Leader of the Senate.

Nevertheless, his unannounced candidacy attracted plenty of money (mostly Texan); many potential delegate votes (mostly Southern); and an extraordinary array of supporters ranging from Sam Rayburn and Dean Acheson to the old Roosevelt team of Tommy Corcoran and Ben Cohen. The main reason for this support appeared to be the almost mystical but rather widespread conviction that whatever Lyndon wants, Lyndon gets. And Lyndon Baines Johnson wanted the Presidency desperately.

Moreover, the contrast between Johnson and Kennedy—both as leaders and as legislators—was that between day and night. During his six years as Majority Leader, facing a Republican President, Johnson—as *Time* put it— "proved himself to be one of U.S. history's ablest masters of the subtle, complex art of legislative leadership. And he exercised that leadership with statesmanlike responsibility. . . ." Kennedy, however, was conspicuous in the Senate "not for achievements of legislation or leadership but for youth, good looks, wealth, and the aura he exuded of being bound for higher places still."

In June 1960, the non-partisan *Congressional Quarterly* polled Senators and Representatives on who they thought would be the Democratic party's "strongest possible" Presidential candidate; of the 220 members who replied, 54 per cent named Johnson; only 20 per cent named Kennedy; and Adlai Stevenson came in third with 14 per cent.

This may help explain in part the embarrassing inability of President Kennedy to get an overwhelmingly Democratic Congress to co-operate during the first half of the New Frontier Administration. Rarely has any Chief Executive demonstrated such paralysis and ineptitude in dealing with the Hill. Surely this extraordinary state of affairs did not come as any major surprise to Lyndon Johnson who, while pursuing the Presidential nomination, frequently warned of Kennedy's incompetence and juvenile qualities.

For his part, Johnson demonstrated a limitless capacity to manage everything but his own candidacy. For one thing, he waited too long. But there were other compelling reasons why Johnson could not have bridged the gap between the 400 or so first ballot votes he expected at Los Angeles and the 761 needed to win. First, he was a Southerner—even though he had tried to rearrange his geography by calling himself a Westerner. Second, Organized Labor considered him a foe. Third, he was considered the tool of his state's oil and gas interests.[1] Fourth, there was his civil rights record that left him on the floor between two stools, the more extreme Dixiecrats dubbing him a "traitor" for having nursed two civil rights bills through Congress, and the NAACP leaders who considered him, at best, a compromiser. Fifth, there was his medical record—a massive heart attack in 1955, which lurked in the background despite the reassurance of the plastic-encased cardiogram which he could whip from his pocket to prove his recovery.

In May 1960 came the collapse of the Summit Conference. The downing of the high-flying, U-2 reconnaissance plane on Soviet soil culminated in Chairman Khrushchev's furious, obscene, and Hitlerian attack on President Eisenhower in Paris. Alone among the Democratic hopefuls, Lyndon Johnson responded from his viscera that Nikita had better stop "being sanctimonious" in "making pious protestations of outraged innocence." And every American who had ever heard of Davy Crockett and the Alamo knew that Lyndon was back in business again. Though he may have regarded the Eisenhower Administration as nothing but a bunch of Republicans, Johnson felt that when an American President reaps insults from "a dirty s.o.b." like Khrushchev, the only self-respecting response is, "I don't care if he is a hound, you gotta quit kickin' my dog around."

The U-2 episode sharply divided the Democrats. Even before the vilified and abused President had returned from Paris, Adlai Stevenson reacted. He directly blamed the Eisenhower Administration for the summit breakup. And he questioned the morality and truthfulness of the Administration.[2]

Kennedy's response to the summit blowup came when he was asked in Eugene, Oregon, whether he would "apologize" to Khrushchev for sending

---

[1] Difficult to fathom is why Johnson should have been pilloried for acting in behalf of his state's economic interest. There were no major outcries when Hubert Humphrey fought for his state's agricultural interests; or when Kennedy, in Congress, battled for his state's textile industries.

[2] A year later, Stevenson himself, as United States Ambassador to the United Nations, was caught relaying untruths in connection with the Cuban fiasco. His excuse was that he did not know he was telling untruths; the White House had not informed him of what was going on.

the high-flying U-2 plane over the Soviet Union. Dispatches published May 18 quoted the Senator as having said: "I certainly would express regret at the timing and give assurances that it would not happen again. I would express regret that the flight did take place."

Kennedy regretted the statement almost immediately. Stung by charges of appeasement, he defended himself May 23 on the Senate floor. He denied he had suggested that President Eisenhower apologize to Khrushchev, then added: "But I did state that, if necessary, to keep the summit going, I would have been willing to express regret at the timing of the U-2 incident."

The next morning, May 24, he appeared on the Dave Garroway television show and tried again to explain just what he did say in Oregon. From the transcript:

KENNEDY: What I said was, if he, Mr. Khrushchev, had merely asked that the United States should express regret, that would have been a reasonable term. In other words, Mr. Khrushchev asked for two conditions on continuing the summit. One, that we express regret, whatever phrase he may have used—

GARROWAY: It was "to apologize," sir.

KENNEDY: What did you say?

GARROWAY: He said, "apologize."

KENNEDY: No, he didn't even use the word apologize or regret. The words were different than that. . . . Now what I said, was that the President should express—could have expressed regret. We could have met that first condition, and therefore, quoting me, if he had merely asked that the United States should express regret, then that would have been a reasonable term. I do regret it. I do regret it.[3]

Then, in a letter to the *New York Herald Tribune* on June 15, Kennedy declared: ". . . I never advocated either expressing regrets or offering apology as a method of saving the summit. . . ."

But a few weeks later the *Washington Post* quoted him as saying, "I did say . . . that it might have been useful to express regret."

This persistent inability to articulate precisely what was on his mind also raised questions as to Kennedy's political stamina. His verbal contortions, as Selig Harrison noted in the *New Republic,* made him appear "perhaps overly sensitive and concerned about the damage he may have suffered by his candor."

[3] On May 17, 1960, the *New York Herald Tribune*'s page one dispatch from correspondent B. J. Cutler in Paris read (emphasis supplied): "Soviet Premier Khrushchev demanded in an ultimatum that the United States humiliatingly *apologize* for sending spy planes over his country, and thereby seemed to have wrecked the summit conference at its start today. . . . President Eisenhower rebuffed the ultimatum and refused to crawl before Mr. Khrushchev by *expressing regrets* for having sought intelligence against surprise attack."

At any rate, Kennedy was clearly on the defensive. And this was what Lyndon Johnson had been waiting for. On a delegate-hunting safari out West, the Man from Texas won the loudest applause by booming out: "I am not prepared to apologize to Mr. Khrushchev—are you? I am not prepared to send regrets to Mr. Khrushchev—are you?" Invariably, the audiences boomed back, "NO!"

Johnson was obviously hoping to benefit from a widespread public suspicion that Khrushchev, if he met Kennedy, would simply pat him on the head.

Senator Symington, meanwhile, joined with the Democratic Advisory Council in briskly demanding a whole new foreign policy without making it entirely clear whether they wanted to renew negotiations with Khrushchev— as did Stevenson—or return to the barricades of the cold war.

Wheeling up a battery of charges against the White House, the Advisory Council termed the Eisenhower foreign policy "chaotic" and "in shambles"; and specifically criticized the President for going to the summit meeting, despite his earlier stand that some clear signs of progress toward agreement must be visible, "in the full knowledge that no progress had been made towards the settlement of the issues which most threaten the peace of the world: Berlin and the arms race."

This was an extraordinary statement coming from a body whose leading lights had been loudly pressuring for a summit conference.

"If there ever was a time for national debate, that time is now," the Advisory Council added. "We urge that this debate be carried on without rancor and without motivation of mere partisan advantage."

After "communing with his muse and his poll-takers," as London's *Economist* put it, Senator Kennedy announced that although he concurred in the Advisory Council's over-all position, he dissociated himself from the Council's apparent belief that Eisenhower should not have gone to the summit. Announced Kennedy:

"I would like to make clear my view that while summit meetings should be preceded by meaningful negotiations, given the state of world opinion and that of our allies, the President, under then-existing circumstances, could not have avoided attending the conference without harm to the prestige of the United States."

The statement was a good example of *Kennedyese,* an effort to have the best of two opposite worlds in a single paragraph.

The standard pattern of Kennedy's prose went something like this: statement of one side of the case (a), followed by a statement of the other side of the case (b). Although the bridge from (a) to (b) is usually the word "but," other familiar locutions such as "at the same time," "on the other hand," and "however" also enabled him to take a position and warn against it at the same time.

"I am not a believer in the omnipotence of Federal bureaucracy; I see no magic attaching to tax money which has flowed to Washington and then back again," he wrote in the *New York Times Magazine* of May 18, 1958. "But as long as our State Legislatures are not fully responsive to the urban areas and their needs, there is no practical way in which Congress can avoid its responsibility for meeting problems that are national in concern."

Less than a year before—on October 15, 1957—he had argued that Government programs alone would not produce or maintain prosperity for the New England states. "No bill," the Senator told the Fitchburg, Massachusetts, Chamber of Commerce, "can ever replace community leadership and spirit as essential ingredients for maintaining and rebuilding our economic prosperity. No federal program could ever solve all the problems of the New England economy without action on the state and local levels—and particularly without assistance from private organizations, industry, and individuals."

His remarkable ability to work both sides of the street was also seen in his statements regarding the wisdom of inviting Nikita Khrushchev to this country. Prior to the Soviet dictator's visit to the United States in September 1959, Kennedy was all for it, saying it was a "good idea" that Khrushchev "would have a chance to talk to the President of the United States." And Kennedy was all for a "summit conference" that would bring Eisenhower and Khrushchev together with heads of government of the other allies.

Following Khrushchev's visit, Kennedy spoke at the University of Rochester. He said that he didn't mean to minimize the value of the talks at Camp David for, after all, it was "far better that we meet at the summit than at the brink."

"But," he asked, "what are the results of Mr. Khrushchev's visit? What has been its contribution, if any?" And he replied to himself: the United States "gained nothing tangible, nothing enforceable, nothing essential to the achievements of our foreign policy objectives."

Of this piece of *Kennedyese,* with the inevitable "but," the *Washington Star* suspected "it means nothing more than that Senator Kennedy, at this stage of the game, does not know which way to jump. If we were in his shoes, we wouldn't know either."

It was at the University of Rochester that Kennedy fired his opening shot at the Soviet dictator: "Let Mr. Khrushchev try to surpass the United States in the production of corn and butter, homes and TV sets. Let him turn his nation's energies to this pursuit."[4]

It was a shot *not* heard 'round the world. Yet, it is interesting because it

---

[4] On August 24, 1960, in an Alexandria, Virginia, speech, Kennedy scoffed at Richard Nixon's "kitchen debate" with Khrushchev. "In the Soviet Union he argued with Mr. Khruschev in the kitchen, it is true, pointing out that while we may be behind in space, we were ahead in color television." (The laugh-producing line later became the high point of Arthur Schlesinger Jr.'s campaign speeches.) Actually, Nixon had made the same point as Kennedy—that it would be better to compete in consumer goods than rockets.

constituted a defense of the capitalist system which, Kennedy said, "with its unique combination of public effort and private competitive enterprise, is dynamic, progressive and still evolving." True, "it may from time to time, pause or show weakness. But it is still capable of building all the defenses we need *and* all the schools and homes and industries, too—and at the same time helping to build situations of strength and stability throughout the non-Communist world."

"This is no atrophied capitalist system, declining, splitting, failing," added Kennedy. "We do not live under a dying system, fading from the scene as feudalism faded some centuries ago."

In February 1960, five months after he had challenged Khrushchev to surpass the United States in the production of corn and butter, Kennedy told a Spokane Democratic dinner: "In agriculture, while we are weakening our farm economy and penalizing our farms for their increased efficiency and productivity, the Russians—as Mr. Khrushchev made clear—are determined to pass us. Already their agricultural production is expanding faster than their population. Their grain production is up an estimated 30 per cent; their production of fertilizer has expanded, on the average, some 11 per cent every year since 1951. And now they are out to match us in meat, butter and milk. If our agricultural economy collapses, if our surpluses remain a liability to the taxpayers instead of a blessing to the hungry world, then they, not we, may become the world's greatest arsenal of food. But this need not happen—and I am hopeful that a new Administration, and a new Secretary of Agriculture, would see that it does not happen."

In Kennedy's prose—as is obvious from the foregoing—the straw man emerges as more than a debating device: it is an innate feature of his thinking. But what makes Kennedy's 1960 analysis of Soviet agriculture even more interesting is that the Kennedy Administration now argues that because Khrushchev—and, for that matter, Mao Tse-tung—cannot solve their agricultural problems, the United States is winning the cold war.

Inconsistency, of course, is not new in the Kennedy spectrum. His chameleon-like qualities are by now taken for granted. Rarely has anyone bothered to compare past Kennedy attitudes with his current stances; somehow he has managed to transmute the differences into matters of personal growth or new-found maturity about which it would be churlish to complain.

In foreign policy, for example, he has seesawed between calls for cold-war belligerence and proposals for peaceful accommodation. He would frequently denounce the Eisenhower Administration for failure to arm to the teeth and, at the same time, for failure to disarm. Likewise, he would warn of the Communists' "nibbling away" at the free world positions and, at the same time, condemn United States over-extension of military commitments abroad. At Rochester he had stated: "We need to think through more carefully our own positions on such questions as disarmament and troop withdrawals, instead of offering only proposals which we know in advance must be rejected."

He always implied that things would be better once he was in the White House. At a California Democratic Council meeting in Fresno on February 12, 1960, Kennedy said, "We cannot afford in the turbulent sixties the persistent indecision of a James Buchanan, which caused Ohio's Senator Sherman to say: 'The Constitution provides for every accidental contingency in the Executive—except a vacancy in the mind of the President.' "

On July 31, 1959, Kennedy declared that the United States should keep its troops in West Berlin even if it touches off a nuclear war. Interviewed on the *Milwaukee Journal* TV station's "Open Question" program, the Democratic front-runner said the United States must convince Moscow of its "willingness to go to the ultimate weapon" in the Berlin crisis.

"Our position in Europe is worth a nuclear war," he said, "only because if you're driven from Europe, you're driven from all of Asia and Africa and you're back to the United States and our time will come next."

These off-the-cuff remarks on Berlin inevitably produced denunciations of "war-mongering" by Liberal elements whom the Senator was going out of his way to impress. He said his remarks had been misinterpreted. But if they had been, the videotape of his performance must have been doctored.

Foremost among the Superman roles that Kennedy assumed was that of Military Expert. He had read various columns about a so-called "missile gap," and it sounded like a good issue.

Shortly after the Russians had launched their first Sputnik, Kennedy had told a New York audience that while he did not "underestimate Soviet achievements in a wide range of fields . . . neither do I believe that each Soviet success should cause us to shape our own effort solely in terms of matching each new Russian move. We will not prove our inherent strength and value as a nation simply by outdoing the Russians at every turn."

"On the contrary," he had said, "we will compete successfully with the Russians only if we possess, independent of any cold war, inherent strength and value as a people. We are not going to conscript scientists or engineers or turn our nation into an armed camp. We are not going to bid against the Russians for the privilege of seeing who can send the most aid to a wavering nation."

A few months later, this was exactly what Kennedy was advocating. The Senator joined the politically motivated chorus that was turning the Washington air blue with criticism of the Eisenhower Administration's defense policies.

And to have heard Jack Kennedy talk, one would have gotten the idea that the President was a man of conscienceless indifference to national safety; and what the nation needed was a less callous and more humane leader— like, for instance, Senator Kennedy—to save us all from destruction. Whereas Eisenhower was "gambling" with survival, Kennedy—if President—would reduce the element of risk by spending more and turning our nation into an armed camp.

Senator Kennedy's major debut as a Military Expert came on August 14, 1958. In a full-dress Senate speech he compared the American situation with that of the British who, four hundred years before, were forced to withdraw from Calais, the last foothold of English power on the Continent.

"Once they had recovered from their initial panic, the British set about adjusting their thinking and their policies to the loss they had suffered," he told his colleagues. "The old power, the foundation for old policies, was gone —but new policies had brought a new power and new security."

"The time has come for the United States to consider a similar change," he added, "if we, too, are to depend on something more than deep convictions and pious motives to guide the state aright. For we, too, are about to lose the power foundation that has long stood behind our basic military and diplomatic strategy.

"That foundation . . . has been, since Hiroshima, our nuclear power. We have possessed a capacity for retaliation so great as to deter any potential aggressor from launching a direct attack upon us."

And now, said Kennedy, we were quickly losing our one-time lead. And, he added, the greatest danger would come in what some Pentagon experts called "the gap"—the period between 1960 and 1964 in which this country's missile development was expected to lag so far behind the Russians as to cause a great threat to our national existence.

"There is every indication that by 1960 the United States will have lost its Calais—its superiority in nuclear striking power," he declared.

Coming from a voracious reader of history books, Kennedy's Calais analogy was far-fetched. By no stretch of the imagination could the position of the British in 1558 be likened to that of the United States in 1958. After Calais, the British turned to exploiting backward areas of the world and England became the world's leading imperialist power. Kennedy, of course, was not advocating similar policies. What he called for was devoting more of United States resources to building up backward areas without imperialistic considerations.

But all wasn't lost—if the United States only followed the Kennedy formula for peace and salvation. Basically, he urged the United States to adopt "the classic strategy of the underdog," in the face of mounting Soviet missiles, rockets, and other armaments. In addition, he called for new major spending to build bigger and better missiles; more air tankers to refuel our SAC bombers; a redesigning of our continental defense system, et cetera, et cetera.

"Once the Soviets are in the driver's seat . . . the question again arises as to what basic strategy we employ during the years of the gap," Kennedy continued. "The best and most recent example is that provided by the Soviets themselves during the years of their gap—when American might was superior. While we would not imitate the Communists per se, they demonstrated the classic strategy of the underdog—and soon we will be the 'underdog.'

"It is basically a strategy of making the most of all remaining advantages and making the most of the enemy's weakness—thus to buy the time and opportunity necessary to regain the upper hand."

The strategy called for new aid programs to bolster such nations as India and Tunisia; reducing our military commitments abroad; disowning unpopular rulers of paper governments (that is, Chiang Kai-shek of Nationalist China); and using foreign aid to wean her satellites from the Soviet Union.

And wrapping himself in the mantle of Sir Winston Churchill, John F. Kennedy quoted Britain's wartime leader as having said in a dark time of history: "Come then—let us to the task, to the battle and the toil—each to our part, each to our station. . . . Let us go forward together in all parts of the [land]. There is not a week, nor a day, nor an hour to be lost."

Kennedy's sense of history was somewhat out of kilter when he implied his role resembled that of Churchill warning England against Hitlerite aggression in the thirties. The British were then practically defenseless—apart from the Channel. The United States by the late fifties, was expending some $40 billions a year for military purposes. Nevertheless, from the *Congressional Record:*

SYMINGTON: I should like to congratulate the distinguished Senator from Massachusetts for one of the finest statements on this all-important subject to which it has been my privilege to listen . . . I notice in the remarks of the Senator he has quoted from the great Sir Winston Churchill . . . with respect to the situation in Britain in 1938. Would my able friend from Massachusetts agree that the situation which the United States faces in the late 1950's may have considerable comparability with the situation faced by the British in the late 1930's?

KENNEDY: The Senator is completely correct.

It was an extraordinary speech coming from a young man whose military experience included having the PT boat of which he was the skipper, rammed and sunk by a much slower Japanese destroyer.

Kennedy admittedly had neither the experience nor the information on which to base broad strategic military judgments. Admittedly he was merely arguing that there was some risk, and therefore we should have more insurance. And admittedly he would have left the implementing of decisions to the President whose competence in such matters was somewhat higher than that of the Junior Senator from Massachusetts.

Apparently he was only concerned with creating a political issue, or so Republican Senator Homer Capehart implied:

CAPEHART: Does the Senator believe that we ought to increase our defense appropriations from $40 billion to perhaps $45 billion or $50 billion?

KENNEDY: I do not believe it is necessary for me today to attempt to give such details, although I shall be glad to get some figures together for the Senator. . . . I am not a member of the Committee on Armed Services and therefore I am not privy to confidential information which is available to that committee. . . .

However, I will say I have seen some information, published in a responsible column appearing in the *Washington Post;* and to answer the Senator's question, I should like to have the Department of Defense give us some idea about the accuracy of these facts which have been published recently: to quote from this article, whether it is true that the Soviet Union will have 500 intercontinental ballistic missiles by the end of 1960, as against 30 intercontinental missiles of the United States by the end of 1960. . . . These figures have been published. Whether or not they are true, I do not know. . . . I believe the Soviet Union knows the answers. I think it would be well for the United States to know. In any event, as I say, we have not done enough. I hope the Senator will agree with me. If he does not, that is his responsibility.

CAPEHART: I do not agree and I do not disagree. I again wish to say that I find a tendency on the part of Members of Congress to sell the United States short. It is always being said that Russia is making great progress, and we are not doing enough; that Russia is all-right, and what Russia is doing is all right. . . . I do not know on whose authority those statements are based. I notice that every so often Members on the other side of the aisle stand up and read speeches. I do not know by whom those speeches have been prepared, and I do not care. They quote General Gavin—

*   *   *

KENNEDY: I do not believe there is any doubt who prepared the questions of the Senator from Indiana. They could come only from him, and I give him full credit for them. I will not yield to him any further at this time. . . .

SYMINGTON: There has been some talk about selling America short. My question to the able Senator from Massachusetts is this: Does he think that giving the American people all truth which will not help a possible enemy, or at least in trying to do so, is in any manner selling America short?

KENNEDY: I would not think so. I believe the record of the past six years, the frustration of every attempt to develop what the real facts and situation are, and our failure to act, all indicate that as time moves against us, it is important that we do so, regardless of what the reaction may be.

But the "missile gap" was a good issue while it lasted.

In fact, it was Senator Symington's one big issue. In one respect, the Missourian went even further than Kennedy by charging the Eisenhower Administration with "deliberate deception" on defense matters.

"I do not charge anyone with intentionally misleading the public for the purpose of deception," said Kennedy. But "our crumbling defenses" became one of his main speech staples. "We began the fifties with overwhelming military superiority—strength enough to ensure that no one would attack," he said on January 30, 1960. (The fact was that we began the fifties bogged in Korea in a war for which we were lamentably unprepared.) "But during the past eight years our military strength has deteriorated—the Russians have taken the lead in missiles, in space, in armies, and in conventional weapons."

On February 11, Kennedy changed his tune. "Militarily," he declared,

"I would not say that the Russians possess an overall superiority." And on February 29: "This year, our mix of forces undoubtedly is far superior."

In fact, Kennedy even complained that while we were pouring vast resources into weapons of destruction, the Eisenhower Administration had less than one hundred persons working on disarmament problems. "The harsh facts of the matter are that we are not prepared to undertake that kind of [disarmament] effort today . . . ," he declared March 7. "No plea for disarmament can be complete without planning for the reconversion of our economy—for diverting our resources to the constructive channels of peace." The urgency for disarmament preparations (Kennedy had proposed an Arms Control Institute for the purpose) rested on this evaluation of the East-West situation: "I do not say that our dangers have receded or that our enemy has become less benevolent. . . . But I do believe that today's international climate, more than ever before, holds out the possibility for an effective start on arms control."

Images and imagery were constantly on Kennedy's mind. On June 21, touring New Jersey, Kennedy told audiences that a "solid, creative program for peace" was essential to project the nation's "image." He said that "goodwill tours and personal charm merely project the President's own image." And, he insisted, the President could not shift his responsibility to Congress "under the guise of bipartisanship—asking our support for an unknown policy on Quemoy and Matsu, asking for our support for a Middle East doctrine that was more public relations than policy.

"For, bipartisanship does not mean—and was never designed to mean—rubber-stamping every executive blunder without debate. Next year will be different—with an overwhelming Democratic Congress and a Democratic President."

To Kennedy, the U-2 fiasco was precisely such an executive blunder. But he never made clear whether he meant Eisenhower's original authorization of the flights or the Administration's bungling of the "cover story" that followed the downing of the CIA aircraft. With a firmness that did it credit, especially in light of Soviet successes in stealing A-bomb secrets, the Eisenhower Administration sanctioned the use of the high-flying Lockheed plane for flights over Russia that went on for an uninterrupted span of four years. The U-2s brought back what a recent book described as "breath-taking information." Could we have had any valid diplomacy without this information?

The success of the U-2 flights in convincing Eisenhower that the Russians weren't nine feet tall obviously had a stiffening effect on our policies. Without this effect, Berlin probably would have been lost to the West long ago. When the Powers-piloted U-2 crashed on Soviet soil and the news leaked out that the flight had been merely one among many, it advertised to the world that the United States could be both strong and purposeful in the business of blunting the cutting edge of Soviet imperialism. With all the talk about the importance of "images," was that really a bad thing for the United States? Kennedy thought so.

The viability of the Kennedy image was never better demonstrated than on the war-and-peace issue. Before some groups he was the big, bold cold warrior (Remember PT-109!) who could do a much better job of standing up to Khrushchev than Nixon. ("Mr. Nixon may be very experienced in kitchen debates. So are a great many other married men I know.")

For groups on the other side of the ideological fence, Kennedy was the man of peace, skilled in foreign affairs, troubled about Strontium-90 in baby's milk. Hadn't he opposed Nelson Rockefeller's call for a renewal of United States nuclear testing? But he never explained how the nation was supposed to outstrip the Soviets militarily without such testing.

Trying to be many things to many people is, of course, not uncommon in the great game of American politics, where getting more votes than the other guy is essential for survival. "The art lies in being able to project double images without getting accused of being two-faced," commented *Time* on Convention eve. "In this political art, Presidential Hopeful John F. Kennedy, for all his youth and boyish charm, is already a master."

But it was more than trickery. "Kennedy's double imagery seems to be one more instance of his keen political sixth sense," *Time* continued. "Knowing well the strength of his family anchor in conservatism, he senses how far he can loop toward liberalism to bring the liberals into camp, without getting so far out that he can't get back."

Thus, as his principal foreign policy adviser he selected Chester Bowles, a former United States Ambassador to India and a conspicuous Liberal who advocated, among other things, a "two-Chinas" policy (that is, the United States should cease to recognize Nationalist China as the legitimate Government of anything but Formosa) which would, in effect, imply recognition of the Peiping regime as the true Government of mainland China, and undermine Washington's long campaign to keep Red China out of the United Nations.

Probably no other Presidential hopeful could have gotten away with it. But, as a Roman Catholic, Kennedy obviously felt he was immune to charges of being "soft" on Communism.

The Bowles selection was obviously aimed at disarming those Stevenson supporters who—despite the Galbraith-style build-up—continued to question John F. Kennedy's commitment to Liberalism. The wave of the Liberal future was with Adlai, they insisted, and not with Joe Kennedy's son, Jack, who at heart was a Conservative like his father.

This sort of talk irked the Senator who had gone out of his way to mollify Stevenson by offering the Man from Libertyville the opportunity to be Secretary of State. But Adlai temporized. Perhaps he thought a miracle might occur at Los Angeles. At least his supporters were beginning to make a lot of noise as the Convention neared. The *New York Post* and Eleanor Roosevelt thought that a Stevenson-Kennedy ticket would be just dandy.

Among those who talked with Kennedy about the increasingly annoying Stevenson situation was Arthur Goldberg, the special counsel to the AFL–CIO and the Steel Workers. Goldberg, who had thrown his considerable prestige as *Mr. Labor Lawyer* behind Kennedy, arranged for the Senator to meet with leaders of New York's Liberal party, a peculiar amalgam of Morningside Heights intellectuals and Seventh Avenue labor czars.

The meeting provided another example of Kennedy's remarkable ability to keep a foot in every camp. However, he was embarrassed by the publicity resulting from what he thought was an off-the-record session with New York's Liberal party leaders.

On June 24, the *New York Times* reported that the Senator had assured the Liberal party policy committee that he hoped to win the nomination without a single Southern vote at the Convention. Asked about a possible trip to the South, Kennedy shook his head and remarked: "I understand they favor another candidate." He also indicated that, if elected, he would take a stronger position on civil rights than did President Eisenhower. The Liberals cheered in jubilation, and Kennedy was cheered by what amounted to a promise to support him if he received the Democratic nomination.

But Kennedy's cheer was short-lived. The statement hit the South like a bombshell. "Kennedy May Be Writing Off South in His Nomination Bid" the Richmond *Times-Dispatch* headlined a Frank van der Linden dispatch from Washington.

And, once again, Lyndon Johnson pounced. His campaign headquarters termed the Kennedy statement "incredible."

It was particularly "incredible" since many Southern delegates had received what appeared to be a personal letter from Kennedy asking their support on the same day he was quoted in New York that he was not seeking Southern support.

"I am told that certain of [name of state] delegates, out of personal friendship, have pledged to vote for one of my distinguished opponents for the nomination for President," the Kennedy letter read.

"You may be so obligated. If not (or as soon as you feel that he has insufficient chance for victory), I would deeply appreciate your support. Your vote for me at the earliest moment will mean much to my candidacy."

Dated June 22, the Kennedy letter was signed by pen by "John F. Kennedy." It asked the Southern delegates to write to Kennedy "giving me any thoughts or advice you may have" at the Kennedy campaign headquarters in the Biltmore Hotel in Los Angeles.

"Apparently," wrote publisher John S. Knight, "Kennedy wants the New York eggheads to believe that he has no truck with the 'benighted South.' And yet Kennedy, with private blandishments, pressure and cash is slickering up to every impressionable political leader below the Mason-Dixon line. . . . So 'John Boy' is neither as noble nor as agile as we had thought."

Oscar Chapman, chairman of Citizens for Johnson, asked why, if Kennedy did not want Southern support, he and his brothers, Bobby and Teddy, had invaded Texas, Alabama, Florida, and North Carolina in recent weeks. In fact, press dispatches disclosed that Bobby had met secretly in early June in Raleigh with Terry Sanford, the front-running candidate for Governor in the Democratic run-off primary in North Carolina. At first Sanford had denied having seen Bob Kennedy, but later he admitted it. Both sides, however, claimed no pledges of delegates were asked or given.

The newly nominated Sanford arrived in Los Angeles at 9:00 P.M. At a press conference at 9:00 A.M. the next morning, he announced for Kennedy. "His statement was part of Kennedy's winning psychological warfare," observed Drew Pearson.

Oscar Chapman also reminded Kennedy how he had sought Southern votes for Vice President at the 1956 Convention; and how nine Southern states had given him their support for the nomination. After this needling implication that Kennedy was ungrateful, Chapman said his own man, Lyndon Johnson, would welcome Dixie votes. "The man who is going to be President of this nation and lead the free world should be one who desires and seeks the support of all sections of America," he said.

Then, mentioning the breakfast date Kennedy once had with Alabama Governor John Patterson, Chapman wondered aloud whether the Senator had explained his position then "in the same spirit as he did to the Liberal party in New York."

Perhaps the least livid of Dixie's newspapers was the *Atlanta Constitution,* of which Ralph McGill was publisher. The Kennedy statement "was rather unexpected," it said editorially. Kennedy had been "fairly well regarded in the South. Many recalled his friendliness from the time he sought the 1956 vice-presidential spot."

The *Constitution* added: "The young Senator's need for support in New York, Pennsylvania and California makes his barb understandable politically, if he is playing by the rule of win-at-all-costs. We are nevertheless disappointed in his tactic. We had not expected him to play the game by this rule. There has been enough prejudice in the last decade—racial, religious and regional—to last the Democratic Party forever. The attitude of Southern politicians on the racial issue has been unbecoming and hurtful to the South, laying it liable to national scorn. There have been signs that the South is moderating a little; certainly efforts are being made, and the harshness of 1948, 1952 and 1956 is diminished. We had hoped this election year would mark a time of some healing. But a concurrent moderating of regional prejudice is desirable and necessary. We are disappointed in Senator Kennedy for using it as a tool, however indirectly."

Arriving at the Governors' Conference at Glacier National Park, Governor Ribicoff—Kennedy's spokesman—found the fatback was really in the fire. Johnson's supporters had circulated copies of the *New York Times* story concerning Kennedy's Liberal party statement. Ribicoff conferred with Kennedy by telephone. The result was that Liberal party members in New York who had read in the *Times* of June 24 that "Kennedy Assures Liberals He Seeks No Help in South," four days later read that "Kennedy Appeals to South for Support at Convention."

It was all a "misunderstanding," Ribicoff told the Southern Governors. What Kennedy had meant to say, he said, was that since the South seemed to favor Lyndon Johnson, Kennedy expected to win without Southern votes. Not that he didn't want those votes. "Nothing could be further from the truth," said Ribicoff.

The episode helps illustrate the cynicism of politics. Commented the *Wall Street Journal:* "[Ribicoff's] statement, since ambition is ambition, a delegate is a delegate and a vote is a vote, is probably as accurate as any we've run across in a long time. But our guess is that this won't by any means end the misunderstandings about what sort of image the Senator has managed to create for himself either below the Potomac or east of the Hudson."

Johnson headquarters also distributed copies of a satirical "Dear Jack" letter to Kennedy from Pennsylvania's witty Republican Senator Hugh Scott, deriding the New Englander's absenteeism from the Senate. Scott was moved to write the letter, when, after fourteen weary hours on the Senate floor, he came home after midnight and flicked on his TV set. On the screen appeared the face of John F. Kennedy, looking happy, rested, and relaxed. The Senator was exchanging witticisms with entertainers on the Jack Paar show.

"I thought you would like a fill-in on some important developments you might have missed while you were absent from the Senate," Scott wrote. "We in the Senate took very seriously the lecture you had delivered to us only two days before on the importance of leadership and the need to do something about the missile programs and about modernizing the armed forces. Your leadership was felt all the way from Cambridge, Mass., and we passed a $40.5 billion defense bill.

"We are going to wait until you return before we tackle the foreign aid bill because your colleagues over on the House side have knocked off $750 million from that bill, and we know how you feel about it. So, when you get back, please exert the leadership you called for and see that our foreign aid program won't be seriously impaired.

"That wasn't the only thing we did, Jack. We passed a constitutional amendment to give citizens of the District of Columbia the right to vote for President. We know you wanted this because we had heard you advocate it.

"We also took care of the housing bill for you, Jack, since you as a Presidential candidate have strongly advocated more and better housing. So we passed a one and a quarter billion dollar housing bill and hope you will like it. There were a couple of close votes but we knew you were busy and we did the best we could.

"We know you must have enjoyed your college reunion back at Harvard because we read all about your being there and how you were dressed in the traditional top hat and tails of an overseer.

"That was nice. What fun it must have been!

"Well, it was a long day, Jack. A number of Senators had made sacrifices to stay here in the Senate. Some canceled speeches, some postponed mending of political fences back home and one Senator declined an honorary degree to be able to vote on three big tax-heavy bills.

"We know that you have called for sacrifices by everybody in your speeches around the country, and we want you to know, Jack, that we were very glad to make these sacrifices. You would have been proud of us, Jack.

"It was real refreshing to come home dog tired after 14 hours of Senate debate and turn on our favorite TV show, presided over by one of your most enthusiastic admirers. You and the other Jack were also selling something called 'Lestoil.'

"With what joy we observed your sparkling answers to the happy, responsive audience. We were glad you looked so relaxed and so 'unwearied of toil.'

"Since I did not see you around on Friday, either, perhaps I'll get a chance later to report to you about the debate on the Federal and postal employees pay raise bill.

"Well, we don't want to bore you, Jack. If you have the time, drop in, and, if not, just send one of the other Kennedys down."

On June 29, the Senate exchanged words over Kennedy's long absences. The row was touched off by a Republican Senator who noted that Kennedy had missed 120 out of the previous 159 roll calls. Kennedy's attitude was expressed by Senator Paul Douglas, who argued that "there is nothing more important than campaigning for the Presidency of the United States."

Lyndon Johnson, however, thought differently. In formally declaring his candidacy a week before the Convention, he said he had waited that long to announce because he had "a post of duty and of responsibility here in Washington as the Majority Leader. . . . Because of that duty, a duty to all the people, I cannot be absent when there is public business at stake. Those who have engaged in active campaigns have missed hundreds of votes. This I could not do. . . . Someone has to tend the store."

Off stage, Lyndon put it more bitterly: "Jack was out kissing babies when I was passing bills." He could scarcely contain his not-so-secret dislike for "young Jack," and his awareness that the dislike was mutual. No secret either was Kennedy's threat that if elected President he would try to kick Johnson out of his majority leadership.

"When Senator Johnson said to him, 'I'll get even with you at the Convention,'" reported Joan Younger in the *Ladies' Home Journal,* "Jack laughed and said, 'You'll have to get in line, Lyndon.'"

In his announcement, Johnson also pointed up Kennedy's comparative youth and inexperience by warning that the "forces of evil," meaning global Communism, "will have no mercy for innocence, no gallantry toward inexperience." And with another sly jab, Johnson hit at Kennedy's drive to corral Convention delegates: "I would not presume to tell my fellow Democrats that I am the only man they should consider for this job or to demand that any delegate or delegation vote for me. I am not going to go elbowing through 179 million Americans—pushing aside other Senators and Governors and Congressmen—to shout, 'Look at me, and nobody else!' I only want my fellow Democrats and my fellow Americans to look long, to look hard, and to look wisely to find the right man."

But Kennedy kept swooshing across the political skies on his jet-propelled bandwagon, seemingly oblivious to criticism and last-minute efforts to knock him down. His was a campaign so finely machined, so thoroughly organized, so carefully fashioned for a single purpose that the professionals still could not believe what they saw. "Kennedy's got this country laid out like one big switchboard," marveled Illinois' old pro Jake Arvey. "I marvel at his organizational ability."

Open-mouthed wonderment was exactly what the pilot of the bandwagon wanted. For John F. Kennedy well knew that most of his delegate support sprang not from any real deep-down belief in him as the best possible candidate, but from the politicians' normal desire to be with the winner in time to earn rewards or at least to escape punishments. And this Kennedy crowd was the roughest most politicians had ever seen. And the best-heeled.

A NANA correspondent, talking to a Kennedy staffer, reported he had "encountered Southern politicians who were hired by the Kennedy organizations. They all had good expense accounts. They would take friends to Las Vegas for weekends."

"Yes," said the staff man. "We hired these men. They could talk to delegates. They had pools of influence."

As usual, nothing was being left to chance.

Harry S Truman was so disturbed about the probability of Kennedy's nomination that from Independence, Missouri, he launched a last-ditch effort to prevent it. It was the same old Truman—salty, unpredictable, bumptious.

"I want to read this statement," he told a July 2 news conference that had been summoned for the purpose, "and then I'll let you fellows who are curious ask questions, and I'll answer them if I want to."

Mr. Truman said he had resigned as a delegate-at-large because he refused to be a party to proceedings that bore a look of "prearrangement," with one clique riding herd over the Convention. He said that this would reduce the deliberations to a mockery.

In addition to this implied charge that the show was rigged, the former President accused Kennedy and his supporters of having improperly brought pressures of various kinds on various party workers. And while he did not say it in so many words, Truman also seemed to be charging that the Kennedy money and its dollar-power had been improperly exerted to win the nomination for the son of an ambitious, multi-millionaire father.

"Senator, are you certain that you are quite ready for the country, or that the country is ready for you in the role of President in January 1961?"

That, said Mr. Truman, was what he had written to "Senator Joseph Kennedy." The error passed unnoticed until a reporter asked him "if that was a Freudian slip." All Mr. Truman would say was that the name "of the young man is John."

Mr. Truman's "Last Hurrah" was a "tragic story" for James Reston to write. For, in trying to warn the American people against placing their destiny in the hands of an inexperienced son of a rich man, Mr. Truman—said Reston—had "followed his natural combative instincts back into the political pit, and took the Presidency back to the precinct." By dramatizing "the fierce personal and ideological divisions within the Democratic party," the former President "thus exposed its weakness and helped the cause of Richard M. Nixon."

"This," Reston conceded, "does not mean that Mr. Truman did not have a case to make. Senator Kennedy, and particularly his brother Robert, have run a very tough campaign. They have been as ruthless in their own way behind the scenes in gathering delegates as Mr. Truman was in the open this afternoon. It is true, as Mr. Truman implied today, that money and religion have been exploited to aid Senator Kennedy's cause."

Mr. Truman, needless to say, was opposed to religious bigotry. But he noted that the "religious issue" had been repeatedly injected by the Kennedy forces. After lying dormant since the West Virginia primary, it had been re-injected by Democratic National Chairman Paul Butler, a pro-Kennedy man, in an appearance at the National Press Club. Supporters of other candidates felt he had issued a thinly veiled threat that Democrats would lose the Catholic vote unless they supported Kennedy. In his own defense Butler said he was merely responding to a question.

Complaints about other pro-Kennedy maneuvers by Butler were piling up:

Item: His refusal until very late to grant Convention space to supporters of Adlai Stevenson. In refusing the request for space, the party chairman said that Stevenson was not a candidate. But he also refused a request that Stevenson be invited to address the Convention on the ground he *was* a candidate.

Item: Butler's supposedly not-for-attribution dinner with newsmen at which he predicted Kennedy's probable nomination. Reporters who had not attended the small private dinner—which had been initiated by Butler— named the party chairman as the source of the stories, and Butler subsequently acknowledged this.

Item: A 1959 tightening of Convention rules, which placed almost all power of decision in Butler's hands. His critics charged him with using this power to appoint a rubber-stamp appointments committee which approved allegedly pro-Kennedy choices for some key Convention posts. Cited as evidence was the appointment of Chester Bowles, Kennedy's foreign policy adviser, as platform committee chairman. The freezing out of Congressman Hale Boggs as permanent chairman was cited as another instance. The theory was that Butler, a Catholic, did not want Boggs, also a Catholic, presiding over a Convention that picked a Catholic as its Presidential candidate.

Item: Supporters of other candidates complained that they had been discriminated against in the allotment of Convention hotel space. "If you're not for Kennedy you are parked miles away from everything, in a hotel nobody ever heard of," said one. The effect could well have been the hindering of any anti-Kennedy conspiracies. In a town where a taxi ride could cost up to $15, it was not easy for conspirators to meet conveniently for last-minute Stop-Kennedy plotting.

Item: Disclosure that Butler had informed veteran House Doorkeeper William L. (Fishbait) Miller, who had volunteered his services to every Democratic Convention since 1948, that his presence at Los Angeles was not needed. Miller, of course, had worked closely with House Speaker Sam Rayburn, unofficial manager of the Lyndon Johnson campaign.

Item: Tight control by Butler of staff people from the Democratic National Committee who could go to the Convention, with anyone who leaned toward a candidate other than Kennedy being left at home. Butler explained that the move was prompted by limited party finances. But a Butler memorandum to the staff forbade Committee personnel from going to the Convention on their vacations at their own expense. In fact, all vacations were canceled.

"Nasty, mean, vicious rumors," snapped Paul Butler at the allegations.

"An absolute falsehood," he said of another well circulated report—that he had been offered a business connection with an establishment controlled by the Kennedy family. "I deeply resent and repudiate any such report. I have had no contact from the Kennedy family."

On July 4—two days after Truman's blast—Kennedy held a televised press conference of his own. As he stood before the forest of cameras and the rows of correspondents in New York's Roosevelt Hotel, Senator Kennedy seemed icily calm. His voice never rose as he replied to Mr. Truman's challenge. His face never flushed. His eyes never blazed.

But hidden behind the microphones, his hands gave away his inner tension. His fists clenched and then unclenched. To emphasize a point, he tapped the podium. His hands never stopped moving. They appeared to be trembling slightly.

With his wife Jacqueline sitting by his side ("she arrived looking very much like a movie starlet on a personal appearance," one correspondent wrote), Jack Kennedy allowed himself one witticism—his remark about how Mr. Truman considered a Convention open only when all the delegates meet, carefully weigh all the candidates, and then select the man Mr. Truman designates.

"I do not intend to step aside for anyone," he said, thumping the podium.

Then he went into the matter of his youthfulness. He said he was at least as seasoned as many a great statesman at many a great moment in history. He mentioned George Washington at the time he assumed command of the Continental Army; Thomas Jefferson when he wrote the Declaration of Independence; the younger Pitt when he carried England through the Napoleonic wars; and Alexander the Great when he conquered the world. Then he fashioned an eloquent rhetorical bit about the need for a young national "image" (the emerging African nations, after all, had them); and he reminded everyone he was only four years younger than Nixon and had been in Government every day as long as the Vice President.

When the news conference ended, everyone was thinking and talking about how the Senator had handled the question of his youth—and the question seemed even more on people's minds than it had been before.

The *New York Herald Tribune* found Kennedy's rebuttal to be weak: "For all his claim to stature he again bogged down in the old irrelevancy of his naval service and in new ones about the youth of Jefferson, Washington, Napoleon, and Christopher Columbus. What all this has to do with the serious business of appraising Kennedy's Presidential ability we are at a loss to understand. . . . And in plugging youth for youth's sake, Kennedy has missed another magnificent opportunity to answer a growing number of doubts about his qualifications for the nomination and the tactics he is using in seeking it."

Moreover, the point about men like Washington, Jefferson, Hamilton, and others was not their chronological age in given circumstances, but the breadth of their intellects, the range of their knowledge, and the maturity of their perceptions and judgments. These are qualities that could be possessed by a man of thirty-five and absent in a man of seventy—or vice versa.

And the *Wall Street Journal* commented: "Youth is not by itself a drawback, but it is not by itself a virtue, either. Senator Kennedy exhibits a deficient grasp of human nature when he notes that most of the world's leaders are over 65 and then goes on to say that they have been less than successful in improving the fate of the world. That is a sophomoric argument; we can all remember the days when we superciliously complained of the messy world our elders were bequeathing us. Young people who talk in such fashion usually have not had time to comprehend the enormous complexities, the intractable problems, facing national leaders—particularly in today's circumstances of having to deal with the menacing phenomenon of international Communism. These new problems, Mr. Kennedy argues, demand a young President. Not so. The problems confronting a President demand maturity and experience, regardless of age—which is what Mr. Truman was trying to get across."

Otherwise Kennedy's rebuttal was generally well received. But by declaring that the Presidency demanded "the strength and health and vigor of young men," Kennedy inadvertently dragged in the "health issue." Lyndon Johnson's supporters leaped to the conclusion that J.F.K. was making a not-so-subtle allusion to L.B.J.'s 1955 heart attack.

John B. Connally, a Fort Worth lawyer who was Citizens-for-Johnson director, called in the press and charged that Senator Kennedy secretly suffered from Addison's Disease, an incurable but now controllable deficiency of adrenal secretions.[5]

India Edwards, another top Johnsonite (and former Democratic National Committee Vice Chairman), observed that Kennedy was the only man "offering himself for President who has been absent eight months in one year because of illness." This was a reference to Senator Kennedy's 1954 illness when he underwent surgery for a spinal disc condition.

Mrs. Edwards informed newsmen that she had been told by physicians in "close touch" with the Lahey Clinic in Boston that Senator Kennedy was completely dependent on cortisone.

"Doctors have told me that he would not be alive today were it not for cortisone. It is no disgrace to have Addison's Disease. He has it now."

She said that she did not consider the disease to be a "serious defect" in a Presidential candidate "if it can be controlled."

"But I object to his verbal muscle-flexing with regard to his youth," she added, "as if he had better health than anyone else."

Connally said he would be "delighted" to enter Johnson in a comparison of medical records with any of those seeking the Presidential nomination, adding he would like to see Kennedy undergo an examination by Johnson's own physician.

The discussion of his brother's health by the Johnson camp was bitterly assailed by Robert F. Kennedy. "These are desperation tactics employed by those who are trying unsuccessfully to stop my brother's nomination. These charges show how really desperate they are."

Actually, rumors about Senator Kennedy's health had been circulating for years. On June 14, 1959, Fletcher Knebel reported in the *Des Moines Register* that a "whispering campaign aimed at discrediting Senator Kennedy as a Presidential candidate has gained increasing momentum in recent weeks. The whisperers have been stating as a fact that Kennedy has Addison's Disease. So virulent is the power of gossip that even Governor Edmund G. [Pat] Brown of California was impelled to ask Kennedy personally about it. In an interview Kennedy said there is no basis to the rumor. He said he has tried in vain to learn the source."

The public record on Kennedy's health is incomplete and contradictory; and the statements which have been made appear to have evaded rather than clarified the legitimate questions which are of public concern.

[5] Connally became the New Frontier's first Secretary of the Navy. He resigned to enter the 1962 race for Governor of Texas.

For example, *Time* magazine has stated bluntly that Kennedy had Addison's Disease in 1954. Yet, on July 4, 1960, replying to the Edwards-Connally allegations, Robert F. Kennedy declared, "The Senator does not now nor has he ever had an ailment described classically as Addison's Disease, which is a tubercular destruction of the adrenal gland. Any statement to the contrary is malicious and false. It has been explained on numerous occasions and there is a full exposition on the matter in James MacGregor Burns' book, *John Kennedy: A Political Profile.*"

The Burns biography says this, however: "While Senator Kennedy's adrenal insufficiency might well be diagnosed by some doctors as a mild case of Addison's Disease, it was not diagnosed as the classic type of Addison's Disease, which is due to tuberculosis. Other conditions, often not known, can cause inadequate functioning of the adrenal glands. As in Kennedy's case this can be fully controlled by medication taken by the mouth and requires a routine endocrinologic checkup as part of regular physical examinations once or twice a year."

The *New York Times* of July 5, 1960, quoted Kennedy's chief assistant, Theodore Sorensen, as saying, "He is not on cortisone." Asked what other drugs, if any, the Senator might be using, Sorensen replied: "I don't know that he is on anything—anymore than you and I are on."

Time, in its July 18, 1960, issue, quoted Kennedy, himself, as saying he had taken regular doses of cortisone from 1947 to 1951 and again from 1955 to 1958 to combat what he called a "partial adrenal insufficiency." He said he still took oral doses of corticosteroids (cortisone-type medication) "frequently, when I have worked hard."[6]

If raising the health issue by Johnson's supporters was "outrageous and irresponsible," as Bobby Kennedy had stated on July 4, the medical bulletin released by Kennedy headquarters later that evening was, at best, vague and unresponsive. Signed by Dr. Travell and another New York physician, the bulletin said in part:

"Your fine record of accomplishment during the primary campaigns for the Presidential nomination speaks for itself. . . . Your superb physical condition under severe stress indicates that you are able to hold any office to which you aspire."

A supporter of Senator Symington asked the *New York Herald Tribune's* David Wise, "Is that a medical report or a nomination speech?"

---

[6] On June 22, 1961, following an attack of virus after the Vienna summit meeting, President Kennedy authorized his physician, Dr. Janet Travell, to meet the press.

CORRESPONDENT: Dr. Travell, are any corticosteroids being used [in treatment of the President] at this time?

DR. TRAVELL: Yes. . . . I would like to say that the doses that are given from time to time are minimum.

CORRESPONDENT: Corticosteroids are used for what, in the President's case?

The Kennedy doctors' statement continued: "With respect to your old problem of adrenal insufficiency as late as December 1958 when you had a general checkup with a specific test of adrenal function, the result shows that your adrenal glands do function."

Here, the Senator's problem was referred to as an "old problem." Yet, it was reported that he had been under treatment just one month earlier. Also to have said that the Senator's adrenal glands "do function" may have been misleading. If a man has had a coronary attack, his heart continues "to function." The question really involves the seriousness of the impairment and its present or future effect. Moreover, a "general checkup" in December 1958 (a year and a half earlier) does not stand up against the statement by James Mac-Gregor Burns that Kennedy "requires a routine endocrinologic checkup as a part of regular physical examinations once or twice a year."

The health issue was to be brought out again in the closing days of the Presidential campaign. On November 5, 1960, Republican Congressman Walter H. Judd demanded that Candidate Kennedy follow Candidate Nixon's lead in making full disclosure of his "true physical condition."

"Unless this is done," said Judd, himself a former medical missionary, "I can only conclude that a cover-up job is being done to hide the drugging and consequent side effects frequently associated with long-standing Addison's Disease."

According to Judd, "It is well known that adrenal insufficiency requires an artificial supply, affecting a patient's physical and mental health, and that medication for Addison's Disease can have all sorts of side effects which I, for one, would consider dangerous beyond calculation in a President of the United States.

"For one thing, I would like a flat answer to rumors in medical circles that Case Number Three in the American Medical Association's Archives of Surgery, Volume 71, relates to Senator Kennedy. If so, this represents information which Senator Kennedy is duty-bound to make freely available to the consideration of every voter. This can be done if the Senator will simply release his doctors from their patient-doctor secrecy bond."

Case Number Three related to a young man who had suffered for many years from Addison's Disease, and who also suffered from a back injury which caused much pain and required surgical correction and relief.

Judd termed the July 4 Kennedy doctors' report "nothing less than shocking," adding: "Any layman, let alone a doctor, can read it and see the political nature of the omissions. Doctors know that Addison's Disease tends to create the adrenal insufficiencies that are disturbing to physical and mental

---

DR. TRAVELL: Mild adrenal insufficiency. There has never been any other statement on that matter.

To some correspondents the statement sounded like there might have been more to say on the matter than had been said. Still unanswered was a question concerning possible side-effects from the President's use of corticosteroids.

health. If drugs of the large dosage indicated were required some years ago, it is not unreasonable to suppose that even more massive and more critical dosages are required today. This is the sort of fact voters are entitled to have, and to have now."

Judd noted that in the 1956 campaign, Candidate Eisenhower had instructed his doctors to release an "extremely comprehensive" medical report a week before the election.

However, full disclosure of John F. Kennedy's physical condition and the course of medical treatment he has taken, and is taking, has never been made. The matter is considered not fit for public discussion, and the White House resents any questions on the subject.

The pre-Convention flurry of medical exchanges demonstrated that most of the anti-Kennedy activity progressively centered around Lyndon Johnson. In large measure, this was due to the belief that Senator Symington had been abandoned by his most illustrious advocate, Harry S Truman, and that Lyndon was now the former President's favorite.

Then there was the joint announcement by Lyndon and his mentor, Speaker Rayburn, that the Congress would recess and return for a majestic session of statesmanship as soon as the smoke was cleared from both party Conventions. Thus, Johnson served notice that his would be the dominant Democratic voice in the formative months of the campaign. And many Democrats, who knew that Lyndon rewards his friends and punishes his enemies, wondered what would happen to their pet money bills if they were identified with Kennedy. Moreover, the recess had given Lyndon a few extra days for his last-lap drive to catch up with the solid-gold Kennedy bandwagon.

It was a desperate gamble for Johnson. The recess infuriated many Congressmen who had their own campaigns to worry about. Also, Johnson's strategy of delaying issue-building legislation could backfire if he were unable to deliver when Congress reconvened in August.

As Lyndon moved westward toward Los Angeles, he desperately sought to counteract the phenomenal Kennedy bandwagon fever. In Chicago, he pounced on Bobby Kennedy's prediction that the outcome would be decided by noon, Monday, July 11, five hours before the Convention officially opened. "This will come as a great surprise to the delegates," rumbled Johnson in Chicago. "Most of them thought they were going to Los Angeles to confer with their fellow Democrats to help select the next President."

"There are countries in the world where such pure arrogance is customary in politics," he added. "This is not that kind of country."

As the delegates began moving into the City of the Angels for their quadrennial hootenanny, the practical Johnsonians on the scene confessed they couldn't see how their tiger could possibly do it. No combination of delegates adding up to the winning total of 761 votes was in sight. Nevertheless, they were moved by a remarkable faith in the legend that the impossible was no obstacle for Lyndon Johnson, and that he might have something big up his very wide sleeve. This was a very valid point to those who had watched Lyndon's magic at work in the Senate.

Even before he arrived in Los Angeles, Lyndon displayed his magical powers by confusing those observers who felt that no Negro of stature would endorse him for President. But—lo and behold!—that was precisely what occurred when Adam Clayton Powell said, in effect, any candidate was better than Jack Kennedy.

Ironically, Johnson had played into Kennedy's hands by making it appear that the contest was between them. This, according to Doris Fleeson, was "a thesis eagerly promoted for months by Kennedy. It had already pushed much northern liberal and labor support into the Kennedy camp before the delegates gathered." The ADA, for example, had warned that Johnson's nomination for President "would make a mockery of the Democratic party's profession of liberalism." Its national chairman, Dr. Samuel H. Beer, had written the delegates that for the Democrats to "write a liberal platform" and then nominate Johnson would be "political hypocrisy of the worst sort." The ADA, of course, was vigorously opposed to hypocrisy.

Johnson replied by observing that the ADA was not known for "the good judgment of its expressions." And, recalling Jack Kennedy's one-time dislike of the ADA, the Majority Leader added: "As a matter of fact, I would not feel very *comfortable* if I had their support."

On Friday, July 8, Lyndon Johnson swept into Los Angeles with his Texas sombrero filled with jibes at the candidate with the "Madison Avenue toothpaste smile." The first of the Presidential contenders to arrive on the scene, Johnson immediately denounced "the constant, crude efforts to smear candidates by guilt by association." He referred to well circulated rumors that he was being supported by Jimmy Hoffa and the Teamsters Union.

"I really think," he told a mammoth press conference at the Hotel Biltmore, "that Mr. Kennedy, his father, and his brother have been running against Mr. Hoffa for several years now . . . the closer we get to the nomination, the hotter their breath becomes."

At the same time, he indicated that he would not reject Senator Kennedy as his Vice-Presidential running mate. "The Vice Presidency is a good place for a young man who needs experience," he observed.

But Lyndon Johnson—old "pro" that he was—knew that the only hope of stopping Kennedy lay in a deadlock that, in all probability, would result in Adlai Stevenson (whom he disliked intensely) as the compromise candidate.

The hurriedly organized Stevenson movement had unsuspected "grassroots" strength, in New York and California particularly, and enclaves of Liberal support around the country; but it lacked organized power. The inner contradiction of Stevenson's position—he remained aloof, unwilling to campaign, and yet was obviously anxious to be "drafted"—made it difficult for his supporters.[7]

Finding themselves largely outside the political machines (and often in blatant opposition to them), the Stevenson supporters had to rely upon public demonstrations. In New York, more than half a million were said to have signed Draft Stevenson petitions, and when the Man from Libertyville put in an unexpected appearance at the Convention, the demonstrations in his behalf interrupted the proceedings for twenty minutes.

Not that John F. Kennedy had the nomination nailed down when the Convention opened. The *New York Times* estimated he was 160 votes short of the 761 needed to win. But his team oozed with supreme confidence perhaps born of the knowledge of the inevitability of victory.

"We took for granted that good politicians are smart politicians," said Organization Insider Larry O'Brien. "They have their ear to the ground. They know what is going on."

What was going on was that Kennedy had strength in every section of the country. He came to Los Angeles with a thick wad of promissory notes. The cashing of these notes took place at a series of Hotel Biltmore press conferences at which local potentates declared their support for Jack Kennedy. Everything was done with efficiency and dispatch. The Kennedy machine rolled through the Convention almost without a hitch. Its progress marked the rise and triumph of the college-cut, button-down-collar business technicians in politics: the new men of power, Jack Kennedy's "boys," made the old "pols" look like country bumpkins.

They played every angle to win votes for Jack. They used any argument. They used different approaches to different people. According to the *Washington Post*'s Edward T. Folliard, the Kennedy professionals used "a strategy worthy of a Machiavelli."

"It is a strategy that seems to be contradictory since it involves both bullishness and alarm," Folliard added. "But like everything the Kennedy people do, it has been carefully thought out—and what's more, it seems to be effective."

The way it worked was this:

In talking to uncommitted delegations arriving for the Convention, the Kennedy pros made this argument: "Jack's got it. It looks now as if he will go over on the first ballot. All this Stop-Kennedy talk is— Well, it's just talk. We've got the votes, and Lyndon knows it. If you want to be with a winner, hop aboard the Kennedy bandwagon now."

With delegates who favored either Stevenson or Symington, the Ken-

---

[7] Mort Sahl described the arrivals of the Presidential Hopefuls for his Los Angeles audiences: "Jack Kennedy got off the plane and said, 'I came here to accept the nomination.' Lyndon Johnson got off the plane and said, 'I'm sorry I'm late, but I've been busy running the country,' and Adlai Stevenson said, 'I don't want the nomination and I'm not here.' "

nedy salesmen turned the argument completely around. Here they used the scare technique. They told these Stevenson or Symington supporters that Lyndon Johnson was not only strong but was gaining all the time.

"Don't kid yourself that Lyndon's strength is limited to the South," they said. "He's picking up delegates in the Midwest and elsewhere above the Mason-Dixon line. Now if you want Lyndon, if you think he can carry your state in November and help elect your local candidates, well, that's your business. But if you don't want him, and if you want to head him off, you'd better line up for Jack now."

Political historians will also have a time for themselves in analyzing the contrasting ideological pitches made in Kennedy's behalf by widely differing organizational associates.

Among Liberals, and notably Stevenson devotees, men like Professor John Kenneth Galbraith pointed to Kennedy's qualifications as shown on the voting index of Americans for Democratic Action. What disturbed some Liberals, however, was that Kennedy's apologists were constantly reminding them of how much growth potential there was in Jack. Was the White House ever intended to be a national laboratory, a test center, where promising young men could try out?

Among Conservatives, especially Southerners, the pitch was in the opposite direction. They used the voting index of ACA—Americans for Constitutional Action, the right-wing group—which, according to Kennedy's backers, showed that the Senator was "one per cent less liberal" than Stu Symington.

A special drive was made among the Dixie delegations. It was handled by Robert B. Troutman Jr., an Atlanta attorney who had been at Harvard with Jack, who worked under the direction of the candidate's hard-driving brother Bobby. The basic aim was to cut into Johnson's Southern support.

"Just before the Convention opened, Room 3115 at the Biltmore hung out a shingle 'Southern Hospitality' and proceeded to pass out anti-Johnson literature," reported Drew Pearson. "Some of it was poisonous. It branded Johnson a 'traitor to the South' and called him responsible for the Civil Rights Bill."

Circulating among the Dixie delegations was Senator James O. Eastland, of Mississippi, who indicated that while he was still in Johnson's corner he would not be unhappy if Kennedy obtained the nomination. "Jack was with us in 1957," he told his cohorts. "He knows the score."

Rarely before had professional politicians seen a Convention operation like the one staged in behalf of John F. Kennedy. "It's the greatest snow job ever pulled off in a Presidential year," a Johnson supporter told the *Philadelphia Inquirer*'s John C. O'Brien. "It's positively oppressive the way Kennedy has hemmed us in. You can't move ten steps in the headquarters hotel without encountering a Kennedy banner, a Kennedy poster, a Kennedy brother or a Kennedy staff man."

Typical of the omnipresence of the Kennedy people was a story told with glee by Michigan Governor "Soapy" Williams, a Kennedy backer. He was about to slip a coin into a vending machine in one of the Biltmore's public rooms, when a hand reached out, slipped a coin into the machine, and a cheery voice called out, "Governor, have one on Senator Kennedy."

The startled Governor turned around and there stood a smiling young man wearing a Kennedy staff badge.

Once the coffee machine in Kennedy headquarters went dry for three-and-a-half minutes. "Consternation reigned," reported Arthur Hoppe in the *San Francisco Chronicle.* "It was the first time in the memory of most observers that any machine remotely connected with Senator Kennedy's campaign for the Presidency had failed to function at peak efficiency."

"The Kennedy operation has a lavish money's-no-object aura," reported Gladwin Hill in the *New York Times.* "But economy is not being forgotten behind the scenes. Forty cases of the Senator's book, *The Strategy of Peace,* being distributed as campaign literature, were shipped from a Scranton, Pa., warehouse, under the Senator's Congressional postage frank."

To Ralph McGill, there was something disturbing about the Kennedy operation. "It had a great deal of the electronic age in it," he reported in his column. "He used polls, computers and many IBM machines. His efforts were exacting, painstaking and careful. Data were fed into computers and results obtained. . . . Kissing babies wins few votes nowadays.

"It was the presence of the IBM machine in his campaign which disconcerted and disturbed some of the delegates and perhaps some of the voters. The Kennedy preparation was smooth, rehearsed and efficient. Not one tactical mistake was made."

Nerve center of the Kennedy operation, which reached into each of the fifty state delegations, was a suite of rooms on the eighth floor of the Biltmore. Here shirt-sleeved Bobby Kennedy was directing Convention strategy with the brisk passion of a man confidently engaged in a proxy fight. He and his assistants, Kenny O'Donnell, Larry O'Brien, and others of the tight inside group had only one objective—to keep the show rolling, stay out of trouble, and reap the rewards of four patient years of cultivating the political soil.

These were non-ideologues. Their only concern was to win—and win big. Issues were only of importance if they would help Jack win. A revealing episode occurred the Friday night before the Convention opened. Bobby Kennedy, interviewed on TV, was asked what he thought about the Connally Amendment. Bobby, who was already being touted as Attorney General if his brother won the Presidency, confessed he had never heard of the amendment.

The amendment, under which the United States could not be hailed into the World Court without its permission, was explained to the future chief law officer of the United States. Bobby was also advised his brother favored its repeal.

"In that case," said Bobby, "I presume it should be repealed but, frankly, that's not my province. I'm just on the team and Jack's the captain."

The heart of the Kennedy operation was a file, known reverently as "the box," which contained the names of some 3,200 delegates and alternates. Every one would be seen, pressured, cajoled. Each was listed on an individual card, blue, four by six inches. Each card noted the delegate's contact and Presidential preference when last seen. On the back of each card were attached excerpts from correspondence to and from Kennedy. As fast as any delegate changed his views, the fact would be promptly noted. And the news was usually flashed by one of the liaison men attached to each delegation.

"These are my delegate cards," a liaison man told the *New York Herald Tribune*'s Rowland Evans Jr. "I'm responsible in precise detail for knowing the political views of every name on my cards. There's a secret telephone in the Kennedy headquarters, manned around the clock, twenty-four hours a day. I call that phone every day to make my daily liaison report.

"An organization man at the other end of the phone has a duplicate card that exactly matches mine. I not only call once a day, but I call the instant that I know of any change in attitude of any one of the delegates listed on my cards. Immediately, not in five minutes.

"After reporting the change, I note it on my own copy."

The Kennedys were allowing for mischance, miscalculation—the sudden outbreak of an emotional riot, perhaps, that could conceivably start delegates stampeding in the wrong direction. In the back of their minds was the remembrance of those cheering gallery crowds who, in another year and in another party, won the Presidential nomination for Wendell Willkie. The sharpest spur to the Kennedy camp's intense drive to put Jack over on the first ballot was the lurking fear that Lyndon Johnson might be right in predicting that if Jack failed to win early his strength would start to wane.

Bobby ran the Los Angeles operation in a manner that soon earned him the nickname "Raul," after Fidel Castro's younger brother. He barked orders at the staff like a drill sergeant. His undiplomatic approach toward politicians many years his senior created resentment. "He talked to us like he was talking to Jimmy Hoffa," one politician complained.

A British correspondent who happened to observe Bobby in action reported somewhat apprehensively that the candidate's brother "looks like a Sioux brave about to take a scalp." (Asked whether she minded this description, Bobby's wife—Ethel—replied, "Why should I, since he generally is about to?")

The key to Bobby's character, wrote Stewart Alsop, was probably disclosed when the *Saturday Evening Post* writer suggested that Nixon would be a pretty hard man to beat. "Nixon," Alsop told Bobby, "is a man who likes to win." Bobby's rather thin lips parted in a chilly smile. "We like to win too!" he said grimly.

According to columnist Jim Bishop, Bobby Kennedy is "an irritable and irritating little man [who] condemns and praises men as though all of us were serfs on some big Kennedy estate." He is also "tactless, impatient, ruthless. . . . When he concludes a short, confidential chat with a political leader, the man is left with the feeling that his suit is hanging in tatters and, if he doesn't do exactly as Robert tells him, God will strike him dead. I would not like to see the young man appointed to high office."

Once he gave his staff a dressing-down in Los Angeles that has become legendary. Bobby discovered that his "serfs" had visited Disneyland. They had taken time, he reminded them icily, which could have been put to better use for "my brother, the Senator." They weren't brought to Los Angeles to frolic in the sun. Henceforth, Disneyland was off-limits. Moreover, he was distressed about the tardiness of some staff members. When he called a meeting, he expected his troops to appear at the appointed time—not five minutes before or five minutes afterward. "And that's the way it's going to be if you want to remain on the Kennedy team," he barked.

Everything was pretty well under control by the time John F. Kennedy arrived in Los Angeles. It was Saturday, July 9, and on hand to greet "Lochinvar"—as James Reston persisted in calling him—were some 2,000 very girlish fans who squealed with delight as their hero consented to say a few historic words.

"A few days ago another candidate [Johnson] said that we needed a man with a little gray in his hair," said Kennedy. "We put that gray in *his* hair and we will continue to do so."

And then to business. His first act on arriving at the Biltmore was to call on Governor David Lawrence whose big Pennsylvania delegation (81 votes) was still a question mark. Jack left Lawrence with a wide grin. "The ball game is over," a Kennedy aide whispered happily to a friendly newsman.

Monday morning Jack got into a white Cadillac to drive to Pasadena where, at the Huntington-Sheraton Hotel, Lawrence was playing host to the various contenders. "Stu" Symington, who had another breakfast to get to, spoke first and got a good hand by promising, if nominated, to really raise hell with Nixon. Lyndon Johnson promised "experienced leadership"—the accent on *experienced*—and then, almost with a note of resignation, offered to back the winner whoever he might be. Then came Senator A. S. "Mike" Monroney, in behalf of Adlai Stevenson. The Oklahoman pleaded for Pennsylvania to support a "Stevenson-Kennedy ticket to match the greatness of the challenge."

It was a speech aimed directly at Governor Lawrence, whose heart had long belonged to Adlai. But it was too late. Wiping away a tear, Lawrence introduced Kennedy.

Kennedy launched into a brief dissertation of the nation's dwindling prestige abroad. And he wondered "why it was that Africans who some years ago quoted Thomas Jefferson and Lincoln and Franklin Roosevelt now quote Karl Marx in the Congo." The Congo, of course, had just erupted onto the front pages, but the cigar-puffing delegates obviously couldn't have cared less about who was being quoted in the jungle. They only showed interest when Jack said he was "gonna make this election the most significant in 25 years." And Pennsylvania was going to rise to new heights when Jack was going to take over the country. Translated, that meant that Pennsylvania's politicians could count on considerable patronage if they hopped on the Kennedy bandwagon.

When Kennedy finished, Lawrence called his delegation into caucus and —without explanation—announced he was supporting Kennedy. Sixty-four delegates dutifully fell into line. One of them was Senator Joseph Clark, who warned that Kennedy would have to make it on an early ballot. Clark said that he agreed with Lawrence that Stevenson was the best qualified man for the Presidency. "But," he added, "I felt he had no chance to be nominated. Accordingly, I voted for my good friend Jack, who would make a splendid President. But if he doesn't make it on the first ballot, we will all reconsider our position."

Taking nothing for granted, Jack Kennedy prowled the far reaches of Los Angeles, invading caucus after caucus with his plea for support, a plea always tempered with a recognition of the regional needs of the delegates to whom he was talking. Thus, he told Iowans he intended to return to Washington to introduce a bill during the special session to put the farmer on his feet. "You see," the *Dallas News* commented, "a quick survey at the Convention showed him a little weak in the Farm Belt. About all that this young millionaire socialite knows about farming is that there's votes in them thar fields. He is about as qualified to legislate on agriculture as a Japanese jujitsu artist. . . ."

On and on rolled Kennedy's white Cadillac through miles and miles of sun-drenched streets. From hotel to hotel, from caucus to caucus, Jack Kennedy brought his basic message: He could win. And everywhere he went, he shook every outstretched hand, autographed every paper in sight, and all the while he was being pursued by perspiring, panting newsmen and photographers who, on one occasion, even surrounded him in the men's room.

There was an unscheduled stop for Massachusetts; and the Honorable John W. McCormack, who was in the chair, proclaimed that a Man of Vision had come to visit. What he actually thought of the young man he was introducing was another matter. The dislike was mutual. "Kennedy habitually refers to that old Roman as the Chairman of the Legion of Decency in the House," reported Murray Kempton. "The Democrats are nominating, after all, the most anti-clerical candidate since Millard Fillmore."

Kennedy, however, accepted the McCormack eulogy with the same sincerity with which it had been offered. "John McCormack," he told the "pols" from home, "will from now on be in charge of all our activities in Los Angeles. We could not be in better hands."

The fact was that John McCormack, Majority Leader of the House, a proud and deeply religious man, had not intended to go to the Convention. He fully agreed with old crony Harry Truman's estimate of Jack Kennedy. But Kennedy went to McCormack and pleaded for his support. McCormack agreed to attend the Convention and, in a belated gesture of respect, was designated as Kennedy's floor manager.

As the Bay Staters pondered their long-determined Presidential choice, a scantily clad girl wandered among them, passing out Chinese fortune cookies. In each cookie was a slip of paper asking the delegates to vote for "Stu—he's good for you—Symington."

Speaking before the Michigan delegation, Kennedy said that he wanted his candidacy to be judged by the fact that a man of "Soapy" Williams' great stature was supporting him. And "Soapy" returned the compliment by saying that in Jack Kennedy the progressive people of Michigan had, at long last, obtained a champion for all those things Walter Reuther held precious —like civil rights, for example.

Next came South Carolina, presided over by Governor Ernest Hollings, an old friend of Bobby Kennedy. They had met when both were among those honored by the Junior Chamber of Commerce as outstanding young men of the year. That was the occasion when Bobby stomped out rather than listen to a McCarthy-baiting oration by Edward R. Murrow. For a long time "Fritz" Hollings thought there were some Northerners with sense. If Jack was anything like Bobby, then the South had nothing to fear. Consequently, Hollings was a staunch pro-Kennedy man.[8]

After Kennedy made his pitch, Hollings asked if he would mind a few questions. "Of course not," replied the candidate. A delegate wanted to know whether Kennedy thought President Eisenhower had any right to send federal troops into free states—meaning, of course, Little Rock.

Kennedy didn't say yes and he didn't say no. He just mumbled something to the effect that if he had been in the White House it would never have come to that. However, he didn't want to mislead the delegates. He was for the Supreme Court decision and, as President, he would enforce it. At any rate, it was time for him to go.

Next stop was Florida, where another good friend—Senator George Smathers—played host. Introducing Kennedy, Smathers noted he had been an usher at Jack's wedding in 1954, said the appropriate things about Jacqueline waiting for her baby at Hyannis Port, and concluded by recalling that

[8] Hollings had a change of heart in mid-1962. He felt betrayed by the Kennedys when they refused to support his candidacy against incumbent Senator Olin D. Johnston in a bitterly fought primary contest. Hollings, who ran on an ultra-conservative program, was trounced.

only three years ago Jack had voted with the South on the jury trial amendment of the civil rights bill.

After thanking Smathers for his "gracious introduction," Kennedy said he knew that the Floridians were for Lyndon Johnson but that he was looking forward to working with them as their nominee. One Southerner suggested that Kennedy was already giving Lee back his sword.

Last stop that busy Monday was Alaska, to which Kennedy promised a new dam. And Murray Kempton—who had been tagging along waiting to record words of historical import—asked the Senator just what it was he said about Little Rock to the South Carolinians. According to Kempton, Kennedy explained he had said that "he would have used the muscle on the Governor of Arkansas and then he would have depended on the Little Rock cops and then he would have used U.S. marshals. . . ." But he felt sure it would never have come to troops.

"What Eisenhower did at Little Rock," Kennedy exclaimed suddenly and coldly, "was what all weak men do. When they have waited too long, weak men do desperate things." He tapped Kempton on the chest. "That is what weak men do. Desperate things too late."[9]

He then returned to his Biltmore suite (Apartment Q) where he held court for a parade of politicos. And Murray Kempton concluded his dispatch, "Jack the Knife was back from the prowl."

For four days it was the same wearying routine, seeing delegation after delegation, answering questions and more questions. The Hawaiians, some of them wearing Stevenson buttons, dropped in for a talk. One said: "We don't have anything against you, Jack, but Stevenson is better known around the world than you, and we need someone who is well known. Very well known."

"I think I'm pretty well known," the Senator said. "If you have followed my travels, you know that I've been around. In any case, a man who is elected President of the United States becomes well known immediately."

The Hawaiians, not all of whom were entirely satisfied, then asked Kennedy about McCarthyism and he said he didn't think that it was an issue any longer. "Maybe not," a man said, "but we'd like to know your position on it."

Kennedy hesitated, then said: "At the last Convention, Governor Stevenson asked me to nominate him and I doubt that he would have done that if he did not think I was in accord with his views."

Still evading a direct answer, Kennedy added, "I think the issue today

[9] Little Rock was a minor skirmish compared to what occurred under President Kennedy two years later in Oxford, Mississippi. Two persons, including a foreign journalist, were killed; scores were injured; and hundreds were arrested in riots that swept the campus area when a Negro, James H. Meredith, sought admission to the University of Mississippi. An estimated 15,000 federal troops and U.S. Marshals finally ended the bloody riots. At Little Rock no one was killed or injured, and there were few arrests.

is, who is strong enough to win and, having won, will be strong enough to present the cause of the United States forcefully—forthrightly."

In the evenings while the Convention droned on downtown at the Sports Arena, the Senator would manage to dodge his press entourage to drive secretly to the plush Beverly Hills villa of former movie star Marion Davies. There, secluded from the world, was Joseph P. Kennedy, unavailable for interviews but always working a battery of poolside phones, talking confidentially to various powers-that-be, making sure that the script was being followed.

A newspaperman who got into the closely guarded villa by a fluke heard the Ambassador's Boston twang, "How many votes do you figure in that total. Good. There should be some Southern votes in there, too . . . Well. . . ."

Joe Kennedy nodded at his visitor, but he made no effort to lower his voice or terminate his conversation. Finally, he finished and walked over, tall, erect, and curious. He seemed to mirror momentary disappointment when the visitor did not turn out to be an emissary from Kennedy headquarters.

"Sorry," he said agreeably, "but I've agreed not to say anything."

And he kept his word. Too much was at stake for a wrong word to be uttered at that time.

The visitor wondered whether Joe's hopes were high for his son and how he was bearing up under the strain.

"If I answer that, you'll print it and then what would happen? I'm not saying anything about politics."

But his weight was being felt in places that count. At a breakfast for Presidential contenders, the late Sam Rayburn said he had been asked, "Where's Joe?" And Mr. Sam, fighting desperately for his boy, Lyndon, had replied, "I haven't seen him but he is in the bushes around here. Those of us with other candidates felt his power."

Meanwhile, to avoid the mobs, Kennedy shifted from the Biltmore to an eight-room penthouse in a rose-colored apartment building which, shaped like a ship in a series of three decks, was called the Mauritania. Kennedy called it his "hideout." Before long its location was the worst-kept secret at the Convention. And, to avoid newsmen and snooping TV cameras, he was forced to scramble down a fire escape and leap over the back fence.

"I'm so tired," he told brother-in-law Steve Smith, "I wonder if I'm exuding the basic confidence."

It wasn't all work and no play for Jack, however. There were parties galore, and the candidate managed to hit a few. And he managed to ignore a few. He failed to show up at a shindig given by Mrs. Perle Mesta, a conspicuous Johnson rooter. Out of another party came a then little-known fact about Jack Kennedy. He is a "wonderful dancer." That was the considered judgment of actress Janet Leigh, who announced to the press that Jack had asked her to dance at a party at the home of Jack's brother-in-law, Peter Lawford.

"Imagine a possible President dancing with just a girl like me," she said.

Frank Sinatra was there too. He disclosed that Kennedy was "real relaxed and let his hair down. He didn't talk too much about affairs of state, though."

Frankie-boy was somewhat piqued that Jack couldn't make it to the pre-Convention bash he hosted at his Beverly Hills pad. Other Kennedys were there, however. Even Joe Kennedy came out of hiding for the wing-ding.

Sinatra and the other Rat Packers were featured at the Convention's opening ceremonies at the Sports Arena. When Sammy Davis Jr. bounded on stage in his skin-tight pants, a group of delegates booed him. Sammy looked as if he had been whipped. "What can you say when people boo you?" he asked tearfully.

The opening session also was marked by a keynote speech by Senator Frank Church of Idaho. It was an encyclopedia of clichés. What is the United States? "The showcase of democracy." Where do we live? "On a shrunken planet." What have Eisenhower's economic policies done? "Sapped our vitality and shackled our economic growth." What should our military strength be? "Second to none." And what must we do? "Speak softly and carry a big stick."

The text was a parody of the Galbraithian thesis of The Affluent Society, and it contained a particularly disagreeable passage in which Church spoke of "festering sores," "rotting cores," and "the stench from our polluted public rivers." The text also called for the Idahoan to denounce the Republicans for spending too much money on "liquor and tobacco," but somehow it came out "liquor and alcohol."

As the proceedings droned on, the assembled critics of The Affluent Society dispersed to parties all over town, at which liquor and alcohol flowed like water. Some parties even boasted movie stars. But the party which had everything—movie stars, intellectual tigers, literary lions (that is, Norman Mailer), and New York delegates—was the one hosted at Romanoff's by Gore Vidal. The evening was inspired, the playwright confessed, by a whimsical desire to find himself saying: "Mr. DeSapio, this is Christopher Isherwood."

It was quite a party. Adam Clayton Powell, in a beautifully cut white jacket, could be seen in animated conversation with Gina Lollobrigida; and Arthur Schlesinger Jr. could be heard giving a history lesson to Diana Lynn and Lauren Bacall.

Despite such pleasant company, the Convention was one of the "most agonizing" weeks in the life of Arthur Schlesinger Jr. Kennedy's managers had asked him to lobby among Stevenson's supporters. But he couldn't do it. For one thing, his wife Marian had remained loudly faithful to Adlai. Another was the hostility he sensed among Stevensonians at the Convention. Many of them regarded him as a traitor; and Arthur was apt to open a conversation, "Are you at least still speaking to me?"

Schlesinger was a bundle of mixed emotions. He was convinced that Lyndon Johnson would be a disaster if nominated: and the Texan could well win out if the Liberals were divided. But while he wanted Kennedy as the nominee, he couldn't bring himself to work against Adlai.

"Ken" Galbraith, however, evidenced no such inner turmoil in working for Kennedy among the delegates. The professor demonstrated great talents in the practical workings of politics. He managed to swing several delegates with Liberal doubts over to Kennedy.

Despite the reluctance of their dragon, the Stevenson forces mounted a huge demonstration outside the Sports Arena. All through the Convention, thousands of Adlai's supporters paraded in front of the hall shouting, "We want Stevenson! We want Stevenson! WE WANT STEVENSON!"

To Bobby Kennedy, then running things from the Convention hall, the demonstrators didn't mean much. His scouts had reported that they consisted of "beatniks, comrades and a few movie stars thrown in."

On Tuesday, July 12, Bobby Kennedy—that "brash young man," the *New York Times* called him—was singing a different tune. His scouts now reported that California was splitting wide open and that Governor "Pat" Brown was unable to control the delegation. Later that day came the bad news. At a caucus, the Californians had given 31½ votes for Stevenson, 30½ for Kennedy, and the rest were scattered.

Meanwhile, back at the ranchlike décor of the Statler-Hilton, the Minnesota delegation was enjoying its traditional tear-marked 'emotional binge. Senator Humphrey, who had come to Los Angeles inclined to vote for Kennedy, now encountered stiff, rural delegate opposition to the Bay Stater. Senator Eugene McCarthy remained adamant for Adlai. But Governor Orville Freeman, assured by Kennedy he had the inside track for the Vice Presidency, was even more adamant for Kennedy. Freeman had words with Humphrey, who said: "If you get a commitment from Kennedy in writing that you will be his Vice President, then I'll declare for Kennedy."

Nor was calm and equanimity achieved when Herbert Lehman of New York suggested that if the Minnesotans couldn't support his man, Stevenson, they should insist on running Hubert as a serious candidate. Dabbing a moist eye, Humphrey declined with thanks.

Humphrey also faced repeated ultimatums from Walter Reuther: either come out for Kennedy or face the possibility of no labor support in his own Minnesota re-election campaign. Another factor was the anti-Kennedy feeling of Humphrey's wife, Muriel, who could not forget nor forgive what the Kennedy forces had done to her husband in his short-lived campaign for the nomination in Wisconsin and West Virginia.

Finally, Hubert made up his mind. He announced for Stevenson, saying the future of the world would be better entrusted to the Man from Liberty-ville.

John F. Kennedy, informed of the Minnesota development, conceded it was a "reverse," adding: "You know you can never bank on Hubert." Then he announced that Orville Freeman would make the principal nominating speech in his behalf. This, of course, was a tip-off that the Governor had probably been eliminated from consideration as Kennedy's running mate.

For days the Kennedy forces had tried to persuade Adlai Stevenson to make the nominating speech, Robert F. Kennedy surmising that he would have so few votes himself he would not want his own name placed in nomi-nation. Asked about Stevenson's reluctance to nominate his brother, Bobby said, "Just like always. He can't make up his mind."

Lyndon Johnson, however, had made up his mind to keep fighting. The Man from Texas refused to lie down. As he faced the various delegations, he stacked his own experience against the neophyte's—and wondered why in an age when the right leadership is so essential, there was even a contest.

The break that Johnson had been waiting for came on Tuesday. In routine fashion, Kennedy headquarters had sent wires to various delegations request-ing an audience for Jack. This was the sort of miscalculation which Kennedy had feared. Johnson replied with a telegram suggesting a joint caucus of the Texas and Massachusetts delegations and a debate on the major issues. Ken-nedy declined the honor and assumed the debate was off. Lyndon assumed no such thing and announced that Texas would hold an important business meet-ing at 2:15 P.M., and that the delegation would expect Kennedy and the Massachusetts delegation in the grand ballroom of the Biltmore. The spider was spinning his web.

A regiment of newsmen and television people took over the ballroom for what was being billed as something like the Lincoln-Douglas debates. This could well turn out to be the high spot of an otherwise tedious Con-vention. About 2:30 P.M. Bobby Kennedy arrived, wondering what was going on. (Someone said that Bobby had a habit of showing up whenever it looked as though there might be a rumble.) Bobby said that he had heard about a "so-called debate," but neither he nor any other Kennedy had re-ceived an invitation. After all, he added, there are proper ways of doing these things. Translated, that meant that Bobby didn't like Johnson's *One-upman-ship*.

Who said the feud between the dude from Harvard and the fastest gun in Texas had been settled?

At 2:45 P.M., Lyndon rode in with his boys from the cattle country. Dressed in TV blues, he was all set for the showdown. Unlimbering his ora-torical artillery, Lyndon asked whether anyone who could speak for Kennedy knew where the Senator was. The Senator was upstairs in Apartment Q, not knowing what to do. The phone rang. It was Governor Hollings. "You're going down to that debate, aren't you?" Hollings asked. Jack said he didn't think so. "You'd better get down there," drawled the South Carolinian. "I'm watching that commentator on TV and he'll ruin you if you don't."

It was 3:12 P.M. before the author of that book on political courage arrived in the jam-packed ballroom. And Lyndon was right glad to welcome him. Lyndon, in presenting his colleague, said he was "a man of unusually high character," a "great intellect" as well as "a dedicated and devoted public servant." Lyndon sounded very sincere.

As he rose to speak, Kennedy's trembling legs made his trousers flutter, and beads of sweat tumbled from his upper lip. He made a set speech about the need for developing natural resources, facing up to new problems, and so forth. We stand, he said, on the Razor Edge of Decision.

Against Kennedy's conciliatory remarks, Lyndon unloosed a barrage of sarcasm, the likes of which have rarely been heard in a face-to-face encounter. Johnson pistol-whipped his guest unmercifully. He repeatedly drew attention to Kennedy's voting record and Senate absenteeism. He questioned Kennedy's devotion to the farmer and reminded his audience that he was for rural telephones long before some people had ever seen an outhouse. And he brought up the religious issue, an action that did not appear to appeal to Kennedy. "I think, Jack, we Protestants proved in West Virginia that we'll vote for a Catholic," he bawled. "What we want is some of the Catholic states to prove that they'll vote for a Protestant."

With each sharp shaft—and they were coming quickly—the Johnson-loaded room hooted and cheered. The back of Kennedy's neck began to redden; though his face remained expressionless. His hands trembled as he appeared to be making notes on the back of an envelope.

And, bellowed Johnson, where were certain people during all those quorum calls on the civil rights bill? "There were 45 roll calls on civil rights in recent months," he observed. "Lyndon Johnson answered every one of them." But, he added, there were some people who would like to be President who failed to set much of a record. "I know Senators who missed as many as 34 of those roll calls," he thundered.

Bobby whispered into brother Jack's ear. Kennedy's face remained expressionless. And when Johnson finally concluded, Kennedy arose and made jokes.

"The Senator wasn't specific in his remarks about voting on civil rights legislation," said Kennedy, "so I presume he was talking about some other candidate."

Then, accompanied by brother Bobby, Jack Kennedy hurriedly rushed out of the Texans' den of iniquity. Superman had more than met his match in Big Daddy.

"Flogged and whimpering, Kennedy bit it off and departed," reported Murray Kempton from the battle scene. "This is the posture to be expected of all Booth Tarkington adolescents. The Kennedy boys are essentially punks. As he himself said to this repository of the affectations of politicians yesterday, this is the way weak people act.

"There are men and there are boys. Lyndon Johnson, say of him what you will, is a man; Jack Kennedy is a boy. No matter what anyone else might say, Lyndon placed Jack across his knee and spanked that shrunken bottom. This report on the experiment could help no one but Richard Nixon, but I earn my keep singing about what I saw, rather than about what I expected. I do not respond to John Fitzgerald Kennedy. He does not rise to occasions. If I must die for people who do not rise to occasions I would far, far rather go out with Adlai Stevenson who has failed, with unforgettable grace, to rise to more occasions than any politician that I have ever known."

Though Johnson had scored the points, the fact still remained that Kennedy had the votes.

Nevertheless, future historians may record as the political paradox of the century the extraordinary fact that while Kennedy had the votes to win the nomination, few of the delegates were happy about him. "It is a strange thing but no matter to whom one talks here," reported Alexander F. Jones, Executive Editor of the *Syracuse Herald-Journal,* "there is often a private wish, expressed almost, at times, in a whisper that another candidate, Senator Johnson or Adlai Stevenson, may in some miraculous manner upset the relentless steamroller steered by the ambitious young man from Massachusetts."

"Again and again," reported columnist David Lawrence, "as one talks to delegates of the independent type, they bemoan the fact that deals and trades inside the states have brought Kennedy his delegate strength. They tell of the early efforts of pro-Kennedy men extending back for four years.

"It takes time and money to line up a first-ballot victory as Kennedy has in sight. Some estimates are that $5 million has been spent in the Kennedy movement. This means that commitments were made months ago. It shouldn't be inferred that votes were actually bought, but in politics the ambitious are ready to give their support for what they can get out of it later. . . ."

"If, as seems today overwhelmingly probable," wrote Editor-in-Chief Price Day of the *Baltimore Sun* on July 10, "Senator Kennedy gets the nomination, and if he loses to [Nixon], the weeping will not be general. The Kennedy family might cry—a thing of no small consequence in a community of that size. Most other Democrats would feel regret rather than sorrow. Senator Johnson's grief at such an outcome would undoubtedly be mitigated by the memory of how his Massachusetts colleague got the nomination. . . . The [Kennedy] machine's very efficiency works against the rise of any heartfelt surge of feeling here for Kennedy. Many Democrats believe he would make an attractive candidate, but sense a cold calculation in his methods of operating, and are able to refrain from fainting in his personal presence."

In short, the Convention lacked passion. It was a Convention without real heroes. Excitement was lacking. There was no sense of drama. Rarely had any Convention been so foregone in its result. Everything appeared cut and dried—"prearranged," in Harry Truman's word. Sulking in his Missouri tent, Harry reckoned it was too late to stop Kennedy. Again he declined to attend the Convention. "I cannot lend myself to what is happening," he wired his friends in Los Angeles.

"This Convention has been one of a cold and absolutely fixed order," wrote William S. White. "Democrats have for years complained of the Organization Man, of The Man in the Gray Flannel Suit, of Madison Avenue and of all the various techniques of shaping and controlling opinion. In Los Angeles, it is not perhaps Madison Avenue—for Madison Avenue is commonly supposed to mean Republican Avenue. But if it is not Madison Avenue, it is much more. For this is a place in which at a single moment has been gathered, all in one piece, every possible modern tactic of pressure and persuasion, gentle and otherwise."

As Kennedy's push-button politics clicked toward a decision, his opponents mounted a remarkable last-minute effort to stop him by will power. Tuesday evening, without announcement, Adlai Stevenson turned up at the Convention hall, presumably to join the Illinois delegation, of which he was a member. A twenty-minute, ear-splitting demonstration ensued. The propriety of his appearance was questioned by Governor Mike DiSalle. "It has been traditional," said the Ohioan, "that candidates do not appear on the floor." Another Kennedy supporter, then Congressman Stewart Udall, confessed that "after about eight minutes some of us got a funny feeling in the stomach that it might be Wendell Willkie all over again." Mrs. Roosevelt, still madly for Adlai, was in the audience during the demonstration. A TV camera pointed her way. "Later I received many letters from people who said they sympathized with my tears after Adlai's defeat," she reported. "As a matter of fact, it was not tears I was having wiped off my cheek but someone's lipstick."[10]

The next morning the Stevenson forces joyously proclaimed that the tremendous Convention floor demonstration proved the tide had turned for their hero. Senator Mike Monroney, the Stevenson campaign boss, gravelvoiced from endless caucuses and exuding cheer despite only a few hours of sleep, told newsmen there had been "a vast swing," that many Kennedy delegates had "begun to rebel," and that he expected the Kennedy bandwagon to be deserted by delegates "looking for a new bandwagon."

He was joined by Mrs. Roosevelt, who was conspicuously wearing a Stevenson-Kennedy button. "I had not planned to come to this Convention," she said. "Then I saw that Mr. Galbraith, Mr. Schlesinger and other intellec-

---

[10] Stevenson supporters complained bitterly that Paul Butler had neglected to provide Mrs. Roosevelt with a Convention ticket. "We thought it odd," a Stevenson Committee spokesman said, "that it was necessary for us to have to intercede to obtain a ticket for the widow of Franklin D. Roosevelt."

tuals had said that while they knew Stevenson was the best man, they would be for Kennedy because they believed he would win." Then the punch line: "It seems absurd to accept anyone as second best until you have done all you can to get the best."

In her newspaper column that day, Mrs. Roosevelt declared: "Whatever happens, I am a Democrat and I will abide by the decision of even a controlled Convention."

Lyndon Johnson started the day of decision—Wednesday—by announcing with great joy that the delegates were revolting against Kennedy. The Majority Leader was in top form, sharp-tongued, and superbly confident. "The Convention today is wide open," he dramatically told newsmen. He charged that great pressures were being applied by the Kennedy forces in a "feverish effort" to save the nomination.

"What sort of pressures?" a Chicago newsman asked.

"Son, where you been all this week?" Johnson replied.

Johnson drew a rosy picture of delegates changing their minds. "Minnesota refused to flop," he said. "California turned into a real setback. Indiana is restive. New Mexico has shown that Kennedy support is as mythical as Minnesota. Iowa refused to go over. Look at Delaware. The Canal Zone went for me. Kansas refused to flop. Ohio and Maryland don't want to be hog-tied. They want to rise up and express themselves.

"Obviously the bandwagon is not rolling this morning. Delegates have started to ask themselves, 'Who would be the best nominee' and not 'What's in it for me if candidate X should win.' "

It sounded convincing. But even as Lyndon spoke, 31½ New Jersey votes broke for Kennedy.

Johnson fought desperately right down to the wire. The whiplash of his rawhide sarcasm had not lost its cutting power. He threw everything he had against the foe, hitting at the wealth of the Kennedys, his rival's record on McCarthyism, and even the prewar attitude of Joseph P. Kennedy toward Hitlerism.

"I never thought Hitler was right," he shouted at one state caucus. "I was never any Chamberlain umbrella man."

Regarding the Kennedy wealth, he said, "I haven't had anything given to me. Whatever I have and whatever I hope to get will be because of whatever energy and talents I have."

On civil rights, an issue which was a factor in his rejection by leaders in delegations from big-city states, the Texan mounted a strong counterattack: "I've tried to be a doer and not a talker." He added that he was "liberal enough for Franklin Delano Roosevelt; he gave me some of the highest appointments available."

"When Joe McCarthy was on the march and someone had to stand up and be counted, I was a voting liberal," he continued. "Every Democratic

Senator stood up and voted with the leader. That is, all those who were present."

He even brought up a new charge: that Kennedy was the creature of "Brown, Bailey, Butler, Daley, DiSalle and DeSapio"—party bosses who without exception were Catholics. He challenged the idea that "these five or six men can get together and divide this thing up." Of course, this overlooked the fact that at least four of the gentlemen had to be practically bludgeoned into hopping on the Kennedy bandwagon.

But it was all too late. Even before Johnson completed his visits to delegations the nominating speeches in the Convention hall had begun. And Johnson knew, after returning to the Biltmore and making a few phone calls, that his drive had stalled.

Still the Kennedy high command was taking no chances. Even toward the end, an elaborate "spy-proof" communications setup—never before seen at any other political Convention—linked the Kennedy high command with all parts of the Convention floor. The Kennedy camp did not intend to be taken by surprise. The high command was located in a heavily guarded, model display cottage several hundred feet from the Sports Arena. Telephones linked the cottage with special conference telephones fixed on the backs of seats of friendly delegations. Hy Raskin was in charge of the telephones. Meanwhile, eight commandos roamed the Convention floor with walkie-talkie units. Robert Troutman, of Atlanta, was prepared to use a calculating machine once the balloting began. In charge of the whole operation was Robert F. Kennedy.

The Kennedy communications network, observers agreed, was the best system ever used to maintain contact despite the noise, impassable aisles, and the confusion of a Presidential nominating session. It was capable of coping with emergencies that in this case never occurred. An example of how it worked out was reported by the *Chicago Tribune*'s George Tagge:

Long before the balloting began, the telephone light in the Illinois delegation began flashing. James L. O'Keefe, a Chicago lawyer, picked it up.

"Butler says this is Kennedy's night," O'Keefe told Chicago's Mayor Richard Daley. "If Kennedy wants to come here and make a speech, it's all right with Butler. But Butler wants us to let him know."

O'Keefe went to work on the matter. This was an early indication that Kennedy might appear at the Convention before the long night was over. "Paul Butler, outgoing Democratic National Chairman," observed Tagge, "was being extremely solicitous of Senator Kennedy. . . ."

The conversation also meant that the Kennedy steamroller had completely and effectively flattened all opposition.

Yet the Stevenson challenge was not altogether dead. In what was probably the most stirring speech of the Convention, Minnesota's Eugene McCarthy placed in nomination the name of Adlai E. Stevenson. "Do not turn away from this man," he pleaded. "He spoke to the people. He moved their minds and stirred their hearts. . . . Do not leave this prophet without honor in his own party. Do not reject this man." With that, the hall exploded into the noisiest, most determined demonstration of the week. The aisles were jammed with Stevenson people far above the number of organized demonstrators for Kennedy, Johnson, or Symington. It was the closest thing of the night to an emotional surge.

Over at the New York delegation, aging Herbert Lehman had to put up a fight to get the Empire State standard for the demonstration. The former Senator, who was then eighty-two years old, got his licks within the delegation even before he went up to the platform to second Stevenson's nomination. He told reporters that things might have been different had there been a secret ballot in the 114-vote New York delegation. He said that instead of only three-and-a-half votes Stevenson would have received from 40 to 50.

Then as the Stevenson demonstration erupted, Lehman and Stanley H. Lowell, another pro-Stevenson delegate, reached for the New York standard. There was a tussle with three heavy-set Tammany types who, holding the standard, would not budge. Mayor Wagner appeared on the scene. "Let them have it," he barked.

Bobby Kennedy dashed from his command post into the Arena to put out any Stevenson fires that might have been lit by McCarthy's appeal. He quickly discovered that the Stevenson revival was largely confined to the aisles and gallery, and had not moved any delegates. Bobby phoned Jack. "Don't worry," he advised his brother. "We're in." Gene McCarthy had the decibels; but Jack had the delegates.

Jack had spent the afternoon with his father at the Marion Davies place some eleven or so miles from the Convention hall. There he had his hair trimmed by that tonsorial artist from the Beverly Hills Hotel, Mr. Euripedes K. Papanicolau, who is called Pete for short.

Earl Wilson, who obtained an exclusive interview with Pete, asked him what sort of coiffure he would call Kennedy's. "It's like Perry Como's," he said. "In New York, we call it 'The Madison Avenue.' "

"He's got a lot of gray hairs," Pete went on. "They don't show because his hair is light, but they're there. He looks young but he's not young."

According to Pete, Kennedy had a hamburger in front of him as he sat watching the nominating speeches on television.

"Eat it before it gets cold," his father urged.

Kennedy returned to his "hideout" for the roll call. A small army of newsmen and TV people were camped outside the apartment building. The ordinarily quiet and sedate avenue was lined with electronics equipment trucks, press cars, and floodlights. This clearly astonished most of the neighbors.

One of Kennedy's neighbors was actor William Gargan, hero of a hundred Grade B thrillers. The Gargans were in pajamas watching the Convention on television. Just as the roll call got to California, there was a knock on the door. It was Senator Kennedy.

"May I look at your television set?" he asked. "Mine won't work."

According to Gargan, Kennedy was "nervous and tense." It was almost as if he did not know the outcome. When Washington cast its vote, making the count 710 of the 761 needed to win, Kennedy jumped up and excused himself.

"I've got to get upstairs," he said. "Bobby will be calling me. And I want to call my wife."

Moments later, in the Sports Arena, the clerk bellowed "WYOMING!" and Delegation Chairman Tracy McCracken, his white hair glistening in the spotlight, started to speak as a hush descended on the huge arena.

"Mr. Chairman," the voice rocked over the hall, "Wyoming's 15 votes makes the majority for Senator Kennedy."

And so it did. (The final roll call tally: Kennedy, 806; Johnson, 409; Symington, 86; Stevenson, 79½.) Through the tumult came Missouri's move to declare the nomination by acclamation. Despite a chorus of noes, the chair ruled that Kennedy had been unanimously nominated.

Senator Olin Johnston of South Carolina immediately sprang to his feet and made a dramatic effort to correct the record. The vote for Kennedy was not unanimous. South Carolina stood steadfastly against Kennedy even after he had won. When the party leadership refused to recognize Johnston, the Senator rushed to the platform, which was blocked so that nobody could enter without the consent of the platform bosses.

Chairman Paul Butler refused to let the South Carolinian in, so Olin Johnston stood on the floor and yelled his denunciation at Butler. "Some will think we ought to jump on the bandwagon," he shouted, "but I for one will not jump." He carried the pledge against Kennedy to the bitter end, even declining the nominee's invitation to sit with him for the acceptance speech.

The significance of the episode was not lost on the victorious nominee who already was on his way to the Sports Arena.

As the Kennedy cavalcade raced at over sixty miles per hour to the hall, the defeated candidates were composing their congratulatory statements.

Over in Room 620 ("The Presidential Suite") of the Sheraton-West Hotel, Adlai Stevenson had been watching the proceedings on television along with a dozen or so friends. While Speaker Rayburn, in his nominating speech, was extolling Lyndon Johnson's greatness, the Chief of Police called. Agitatedly, the Chief reported that several thousand angry Stevensonians outside the Sports Arena were threatening to break into the hall. Violence was feared. Would Mr. Stevenson stop them? The suggestion was made that the Chief talk either to Senator Monroney or to one of his assistants at the hall.

Adlai Stevenson after all was not directing these people from his hotel command post by push button.

People kept dropping in all through the evening. Marquis Childs arrived from Convention hall and reported his observations. Only a miracle could stop Kennedy.

When the balloting began, Stevenson sat holding a pencil and a tally sheet but he made no serious effort to keep abreast of the voting, relying mainly on the TV computation.

Stevenson was on the telephone talking to Mike Monroney on the Convention floor when Wyoming put Kennedy over. What was he thinking about at that moment? Someone observed he was silent for about thirty seconds after hearing the news. "I was just reflecting on what you might think I was thinking," Adlai quipped.

Defeat, after all, had not come unexpectedly.

"And now for the purple prose department," smiled Adlai as he began writing a statement of congratulations to Kennedy in longhand. In it, Stevenson said he was "enthusiastically" for the nominee and called on his supporters to bring about a Democratic victory.

In his suite at the Biltmore, Lyndon Johnson turned off the TV set. He dictated a congratulatory statement, and sent a telegram to Kennedy.

"We have a winner—he has proved it here," said Johnson, who had worked until the very last to try to stop the Kennedy blitz. "Senator Kennedy has my sincere congratulations and my solemn assurance that in the coming months of this campaign, no one will be more dedicated than I. No one will work harder than I to [see] that John F. Kennedy will be elected. . . ."

The statement was released to the press and Lyndon Johnson went to bed.

In Independence, Missouri, Harry S Truman had watched the Convention on television and when the worst struck he turned off the set. Newsmen who called were informed by Mrs. Truman that the former President would have nothing to say.

In Washington, Richard M. Nixon, who had previously forecast Kennedy's first ballot nomination, said through an aide he had no comment.

It was John F. Kennedy's night. It was also the night of the Kennedy clan. Bobby Kennedy excitedly kept pounding his right fist into the palm of his left hand. He called his father, who told him, "It's the best organization job I've ever seen in politics."

Disappointment was obvious in the ranks of the supporters of Adlai Stevenson, who had staged the most raucous demonstration of the day's session, and among the Southern delegations, whose leaders had expressed doubts about the possibility of Kennedy's carrying their states in the November election.

"To this writer, who has seen every political Convention since 1944, the nomination of Kennedy seemed the least enthusiastic of the past 16 years," wrote AP's news analyst James Marlow. "The answer may be that it is difficult to get emotional about a technician."

"This Convention has made a political decision to nominate the Senator from Massachusetts," reported Doris Fleeson, "but while it has given him its hand, it has still to give him its heart." And the not unfriendly *Washington Post* said that "the nomination was more a triumph of organization and evaluation than of deep dedication."

"Kennedy was clearly the most electable candidate," reported the *Economist*'s man in Los Angeles. "The question was whether he would also make the best President for the conduct of foreign policy. The doubts that already existed in some people's minds on this score were brought to the surface at the beginning of the week by the news that the Russians . . . were threatening to help Castro against any American intervention in Cuba. It cannot be said that Kennedy helped his case at this point. Some delegates were plainly irritated by his confident prediction on Monday that he had already tied down more than enough votes to win. He has also displayed in interviews and television appearances, a boyish tenseness which hardly recommends him as a negotiator-in-chief."

Despite the promised in-person appearance of John F. Kennedy, the Southerners began leaving the vast arena; and the visitors' galleries, which had been full during the tense balloting, soon had many empty seats. And before he left, the Honorable Herbert H. Lehman turned to Congressman Charles A. Buckley, the Bronx leader, friend of Joseph P. Kennedy and an original backer of son Jack, and said, "This is the greatest calamity that the Democratic party has had in my lifetime." Then the aging, but still defiant, Lehman drove to the Sheraton-West where, after being embraced by Adlai Stevenson, he joined the other mourners.

Their mourning was not assuaged by what the triumphant John F. Kennedy had to say before the remaining delegates and guests. Flanked by his beaming mother and sister Pat Lawford, the weary conqueror arrived just to say hello.[11] But he also expressed his sympathy for his opponents, Senators Johnson and Symington, for that awful moment when they knew he had been nominated.

The fact that the just-nominated candidate neglected to mention Adlai Stevenson was not lost in Room 620 at the Sheraton-West. It was taken as a pointed reminder that John F. Kennedy even in victory was not a magnanimous man.

But, Kennedy is, above all, a practical man—"pragmatic," as he likes to describe himself. He demonstrated this quality dramatically the next day when he announced his running mate.

---

[11] This was one of Rose Kennedy's most thrilling moments. She never had any doubt of the Convention's outcome. "I think every American mother looks at her baby and thinks of the time when he might become President," the daughter of Honey Fitz said. "My son was rocked to political lullabies."

When ageless James A. Farley strode into a broadcasting studio at the Sports Arena that Thursday afternoon, he was asked, "What do you think of the new ticket?"

"I think Symington will do just fine," replied Farley.

"But it's not Symington," he was told. "It's Johnson."

Farley's jaw dropped. "Why," he exclaimed, "that's impossible."

Jim Farley's reaction was typical of the stunned disbelief that swept over the delegates to the news that John F. Kennedy had announced, in the tones of a corporation executive announcing a shift in staff personnel, that Lyndon B. Johnson would be his running mate.

Actually the news was first disclosed by Senator Henry M. Jackson of Washington. Jackson, who along with Senator Symington was most often mentioned as Kennedy's running mate, spoke at a news conference attended by more of his supporters than newsmen. He opened the conference by saying, "At about 3:20 this afternoon Senator Kennedy called me and advised me that after careful and thoughtful consideration he had decided Senator Johnson should be the Democratic Vice-Presidential nominee." His announcement brought tears to the eyes of most of his supporters at the Statler-Hilton. Jackson said he was naturally disappointed, that he had had high hopes of being the nominee.

The most astonished people in Los Angeles were in the Texas delegation, before whom Johnson had appeared that Thursday morning to express his gratitude. He had given no inkling of coming events.

As Jack Kennedy was announcing his running mate at the Biltmore, "Soapy" Williams was assuring a secret Michigan caucus at the Statler a few blocks away that the Senator would never be so foolhardy as to pick the Texan for Vice President; and rumors to the contrary should be taken with a grain of salt—or pepper.

When the news hit the Symington people, they were thunderstruck. "Partner," said Missouri's James Blair, "we've just been run over by a steamroller."

A California lady buttonholed John McCormack. "Please," she argued plaintively, "you're ruining the party. This is too cynical. The people will revolt and elect Nixon."

"I'm sick," announced Arthur Schlesinger Jr.

"I'm shocked," gasped Robert Nathan, former ADA National Chairman. "The Liberals that I have talked to here feel that this is a complete violation of an understanding."

What he meant was that Kennedy and his associates had given assurances, or what appeared to be assurances, that Johnson would definitely not be Kennedy's running mate.

"We were warned we had to support Kennedy to stop Johnson, and now we have both of them," exploded one delegate. "It's somewhat dishonest."

"It blurs the picture," Kennedy biographer James MacGregor Burns was telling anyone who cared to listen. "It takes the liberal edge off the image."

"Soapy" Williams' wife, Nancy, showed her contempt by publicly turning in her Kennedy buttons.

Many Dixie delegates demonstrated *their* contempt for the "sellout" by wearing their "all the way with L.B.J." buttons. There were men of principle on both sides of the struggle. As Senator Olin Johnston put it, "I voted for Lyndon, but I'm against Kennedy and against the platform. This ticket is like the tail wagging the dog." In damn-Yankee terms, it was as if Abe Lincoln had been nominated for Vice President in 1860 on a ticket headed by Hannibal Hamlin of Maine.

The party platform, which had infuriated most Southerners, contained a civil rights provision believed the strongest ever issued by any political party. In its sweeping promises of Government-enforced equality for Negroes, the plank flatly declared: "The time has come to assure equal access for all Americans to all areas of community life, including voting booths, schoolrooms, jobs, housing and public facilities." If the platform were translated into action, every school district in the country would undertake "at least first-step compliance" with the Supreme Court's school desegregation decision by 1963. The plank's most controversial proposal: a federal Fair Employment Practices Commission "to secure for everyone the right to equal opportunity for employment."

The document, prepared under the direction of Platform Committee Chairman Chester Bowles, was joyously described by Hubert Humphrey as "the most liberal in the party's history."

But "liberal" was an understatement for its economic provisions. They out-reached Roosevelt and Truman in laying down a blueprint for a complete welfare state and for government control of the economy. The blueprint was to be carried out regardless of cost.

"Its promises," commented Norman Thomas, "are in considerable degree Utopian, if they are not insincere." Only under a system of planned production, the Socialist leader argued, could the Democratic pledges be kept. Otherwise, said Thomas, the platform must be considered "a tale for simpletons."

Apparently the delegates didn't take the platform too seriously. Anyway, few of them were in the mood to pick a fight over economic policies, civil rights, or anything else. Everything was prepared for them in advance. Like it or lump it.

"It was a perfect setup for Kennedy, a candidate determined to win," wrote Vermont Royster in the *Wall Street Journal.* "And equally so for those with strong ideas on civil rights and economic issues who . . . would have taken almost any candidate to get the platform. Mr. Kennedy would have taken almost any platform to be the candidate. The result was almost foreordained."

On the day he was nominated, July 13, Kennedy gave unstinted praise to "the vigorous platform"—a platform "which I can stand on without reservation and which I pledge the Democratic party to carry out if I am nominated."

The following day Kennedy was reliably represented as having misgivings about portions of the platform. William Battle, a Virginian and a personal friend of the nominee, said that Kennedy had told him "there is a lot about this platform he is sick about as we are—and he authorized me to say that."

Battle (a PT-boat buddy of Kennedy who in 1962 was named Ambassador to Australia) had relayed Kennedy's sentiments to pro-Johnson Virginia delegates in an effort to get them behind the party nominee.

When the story was published in the *Washington Star,* there was a minor flap at Kennedy headquarters and Battle refreshed his recollection. Battle said he never meant to say that Kennedy was "sick" about the platform. What he meant to say, he said, was that Senator Kennedy "had been unaware of the planks calling for establishment of a fair employment practices commission and for 'first-step' plans for integration of every school district by 1963."

Battle said he might have said that Kennedy was "surprised" by those two planks, but never that he was as sick as the Southerners—"because some of them were very, very sick."

A Kennedy-Johnson ticket had long been the dream of Joseph P. Kennedy. In 1959, he had talked to Sam Rayburn on the subject. At that time Johnson, informed of the conversation, uttered a short ugly expletive.

After his son was nominated, Joseph P. Kennedy was reported by Robert S. Allen to have called Johnson to urge him to run with his son. Johnson declared he preferred to stay in the Senate.

"A vote is a lot more important than a gavel," he said.

The elder Kennedy contended that this was a "narrow view," according to Allen, and that as Vice President, Johnson would exercise much more influence than "one vote." In the end, Johnson remarked:

"The thing for Jack to do is to make up his mind who he thinks would be best for the country and for the party, and ask him to be his running-mate. I don't think any patriotic American would refuse such a call."

The next morning, Jack Kennedy went to Johnson's apartment and offered him the Vice Presidency.

It was Jack Kennedy's first act of leadership as Presidential nominee. It was an act that shed a good deal of light on the candidate's political quality.

"It must be set down as an act of major political cynicism by a man who is confident that he will get away with it," wrote Max Lerner from the scene. "Put most baldly, Kennedy was faced by two choices. . . . One was to pick a running-mate who would symbolize his concern about the liberal and civil rights vote, on both of which his support is pretty shaky. The other was to pick one who would symbolize his concern about the disaffected Southern States and the economic conservatives within the party.

"He made his choice clearly and dramatically. What it amounts to is a political gamble that he can count on the liberal voters because, given the Nixon alternative, they have nowhere else to go, but that he must woo the South and the conservatives.

"I don't know whether it was the result of pressure from Johnson and the Southerners or whether Johnson had to be persuaded. You can buy both versions here at Los Angeles.

"But this first act of Kennedy's was a crucial symbolic act. If he capitulated to pressure, his courage must be questioned. If he took the initiative, then his basic drive toward liberalism must be questioned."

The choice of Johnson, reviving the Roosevelt-Garner combination of a rich intellectual young Easterner and an older, more conservative Texan, sought also to revive the old coalition between northern city machines and southern traditionalists which had kept the Democratic party in power for so long. "It was as if a computer-machine had told him that the South needed his earliest attention," said the *New York Post* in sorrow, "regardless of any inconsistency between this move and the language of the platform."

However, the combination of a Northern Catholic and a Southern Protestant was by no means unprecedented in Presidential politics. In 1928, Al Smith's running mate was Senator Joe Robinson of Arkansas. Nor was the merger of two bitterly contending factions, immediately after what seemed a struggle to the death, unusual. That it happened in Los Angeles only "emphasizes the dominant role of political expediency in Senator Kennedy's campaign to date," the *St. Louis Post-Dispatch* said sadly.

"Obviously it was not Johnson's qualifications that put him on the ticket. He was put there to carry Texas and persuade the South to hold still for a liberal program, especially on civil rights, which it doesn't like at all."

The implication that Kennedy anticipated running under one standard in the South and another in the North was not lost among those Liberals who saw trouble selling a Kennedy-Johnson ticket in Negro communities. They said the addition of the Texan to the ticket might sabotage all of Kennedy's careful efforts to convince Negroes he really was a champion of civil rights— and not a mere opportunist seeking their votes. At a pre-Convention rally of the NAACP, mention of Johnson's name triggered spontaneous booing.

The Johnson decision also gave *New York Post* editor James Wechsler the shakes. "To the liberals and laborites who had prematurely committed themselves to Kennedy and had helped him destroy the Stevenson draft movement, the news was a special blow; just one day after his nomination, Kennedy had seemingly turned his back on them in reaching his first fateful conclusion," the *Post* wailed.

Top labor leaders, including George Meany, let it be known that they were not consulted on Johnson's selection—a choice they obviously disapproved. Many AFL–CIO officials said it made them wonder if Kennedy could be "trusted" to consider their interests in the future if he bypassed them within twenty-four hours after getting the nomination.

Passing George Meany at the Ambassador Hotel swimming pool, former New York Governor Averell Harriman greeted him hopefully, "It's a great ticket."

"I'm glad you think so," replied the AFL–CIO president without so much as turning his head.

A Negro delegate from Washington, D.C., the Reverend John Wesley, pastor of the A.M.E. Zion Church, declared: "Mr. Johnson is not the man to fill the cracks in the Kennedy armor. Mr. Kennedy already was a man we had to sell. This will make the selling job even more difficult."

But Jack Kennedy was aware of the brutal realities of political life. He had no compunction about ignoring the anguished cries from the Liberal-Labor bloc. Those people were always shouting about something or other. Though they still made him feel uncomfortable, he had come to understand them and their mentality. He was aware of their almost pathological obsession with Richard M. Nixon. And he knew there would be no significant defections.

One Liberal who defected was Harold Tipton, Helen Gahagan Douglas' manager in the California Senatorial campaign of 1950. Tipton, who got out a pamphlet explaining why he intended to vote for Nixon, said that many prominent Liberals found themselves in "political boxes from which they cannot escape—some in boxes of their own building, others in boxes carefully constructed around them by the Kennedy kids and Lyndon Johnson. For example, Bowles is in a box he built for himself in the conviction that as Secretary of State he could lead Kennedy, the country and the world to better things. Harriman built his own box in the conviction, probably, that as Secretary of State he could lead Kennedy, the country and the world to better things. Stevenson, on the other hand, is in a Kennedy-built box—a prisoner of his political past—hoping that, as Secretary of State, he will be given the opportunity of leading Kennedy, the country and the world to better things. How many others may have been promised, directly or by implication, the office of Secretary of State in a Kennedy administration may be exceeded only by the number promised the Vice-Presidential nomination prior to July 14."

Except for a few non-conformists like Tipton, the Liberals and the Laborites—(the Lib-Labs, as Dwight MacDonald once described them)—began to talk of Kennedy's decision as an act of tremendous political statesmanship—something akin to F.D.R.'s 1932 selection of Texan John Nance Garner as a running mate. In fact, the episode became part of the Lib-Labs' mythology which saw in Kennedy the Roosevelt of 1960.

Lieutenant Governor Phileo Nash of Wisconsin, who on Monday had been plugging for Hubert Humphrey for second place on the grounds that he could not sit on the same platform with Lyndon Johnson in his state, said on Friday that he thought he could do it after all, "perhaps a little uneasily, but . . ."

Ironically, John F. Kennedy had a little trouble, at first, with brother Bobby who was opposed to Johnson. For one thing, Bobby had given complete assurance to numerous Liberals that—cross his heart and hope to die! —Jack would never, never, never consider naming Lyndon as his running-mate. (Such unspeakable deviationists as Richard Nixon, Harry Byrd, and Thruston Morton had publicly predicted a Kennedy-Johnson ticket.)

One of those to whom Bobby had made the pledge was none other than Joseph L. Rauh, ADA bigwig, Walter Reuther's lawyer and vice chairman of the tiny but noisy District of Columbia delegation. On hearing the news, Rauh went on television with an appeal to his wandering boy. "If anyone out there knows the whereabouts of Jack Kennedy," he pleaded, "or if Jack Kennedy is within reach of my voice, I implore him to consider the seriousness of this step." Various emissaries were sent to Rauh to plead for no public display of pique. He said he would fight the nomination.

The Liberal uproar gave concern to Bobby. At one of the all-day conferences Thursday, Bobby turned to Jack and hurled another anti-Johnson argument at Jack: "I don't see how you can include Lyndon after what he has said."

This, of course, was a reference to the vigorous Johnson attacks on Kennedy and his family in the closing stages of the Convention.

"What interests me . . . is how Kennedy squared putting Johnson on the ticket one day after he struck one of the foulest blows of the 1960 campaign," wrote Robert Spivack in the *Nation*. "Johnson's assertion that 'I never was for Hitler,' was an attempt to destroy Kennedy in New York by bringing Father Joe's skeleton out of the closet. Kennedy pretended it never happened; at least he sought no public retraction.

"Another revealing aspect of the Kennedy campaign has been his belated wooing of the 'clean government' Democrats in New York. When he sought delegates, he did nothing to encourage the hard-put Democratic reform movement. Ironically, this is one aspect of F.D.R.'s early career his researchers must have overlooked; F.D.R. fought Tammany from the beginning. But now Kennedy is trying to win his way back into the good graces of the Lehmans, Roosevelts and Finletters. Yet the moment Democratic State Chairman Michael Prendergast reminded Kennedy how 104½ machine votes were cast in his behalf—it 'was no accident,' Prendergast said—Kennedy promptly referred to Prendergast as 'the leader' in New York."[12]

It was inevitable that the question would arise: How was it possible to reconcile Johnson's hearty embrace of Kennedy as the top candidate, and as

---

[12] As President, Kennedy gave Mike Prendergast the knife by supporting successful efforts to remove him as Democratic State Chairman. "That's gratitude!" commented Prendergast, who had battled the Stevensonians in order to get the New York delegation to back Jack at the Convention.

the ideal in Leadership, when, only twenty-four hours before, Lyndon had denounced Jack as immature and unqualified for the Presidency.

"Oh, that!" exclaimed Chester Bowles. "That was in the heat of politics."

The former Madison Avenue advertising executive was submitting to interrogation following the Convention and his remark drew a gasp from the *Nashville Banner:*

"The difficulty of such explanation is that it doesn't explain. From the nominee's standpoint and that of his backers, it leaves them under the shadow of a public doubt. For if as an expedient of politics they misrepresent their true feelings, how is one to appraise the good faith of any conviction or opinion asserted? Or is one supposed to just assume that because Senator Johnson suddenly wanted to be a Vice-Presidential nominee, just as suddenly all that he had been saying in disparagement of Senator Kennedy was untrue?"

Also inevitable were questions concerning Lyndon Johnson's motives in accepting second place to a junior colleague not hitherto high in his regard. Generally his motives were said to be these:

He was persuaded that only he and he alone could keep the South in the party and that, therefore, it was his "duty" to accept.

He was also assured that as Vice President he would play the same major role as did Nixon under Eisenhower, attending National Security Council meetings, presiding over Cabinet meetings in the President's absence, and making official trips abroad. He further saw the possibility of a "dynamic" Vice Presidency in which he would wield an authority over the Senate in terms similar to those he exercised as Majority Leader.

Finally, Lyndon Johnson has had a lifetime dream to be President. As Majority Leader he never could have made it. But as Vice President fate could always intervene.

Then there was the theory that Johnson took second place, even though he had previously insisted he would not exchange a vote for a gavel, in order to exercise a restraining influence on Kennedy if he should become President.

At least that was the explanation offered to David Lawrence by one of Johnson's top advisers. "Bear in mind that Kennedy will make a campaign on virtually a socialistic platform," the adviser told Lawrence. "He may be less radical if elected, but he will be plenty radical in the campaign. . . . If elected, Johnson will have considerable power inside the Senate. . . . I tell you his influence will be exerted toward safe and sane policies, and he will be in there pitching. We told him he just had to accept the nomination. He had nothing to lose if defeated, because he would remain as Majority Leader."

By way of reply, a Kennedy man told the *Wall Street Journal:* "Jack doesn't owe Lyndon a thing. We won the nomination without his help, and we gave him the Vice Presidency. Jack's going to be the President."

As the delegates headed for their last session in the Sports Arena, a bitter floor fight over Johnson appeared in the making.

Politics even crept into the invocation that evening as the Reverend

E. A. Anderson, pastor of the McCoy Memorial Baptist Church, hailed Kennedy as the nation's saviour and pronounced him fully equal to the task of coping with the problems of the world. The early hours of the session were devoted to such formalities as the introduction of past National Committee Chairmen by retiring Chairman Paul Butler. A long string of resolutions were approved, including one of appreciation for limousines furnished delegates by General Motors, a corporation occasionally assailed by Democratic orators as tainted with Republicanism.

Then came a long motion picture, which had for its theme the nation's frightening descent into poverty and unemployment under Republican rule. The movie presented scenes of slums, unemployed workers, picket lines, and deserted farms to challenge optimistic statements by Eisenhower and Nixon on the health of the economy. The narrator, Wisconsin's Governor Gaylord Nelson, also spoke of the shocking state of the nation's defenses under the GOP, referring, of course, to the "missile gap."

What was really on the delegates' minds, though, was Lyndon Johnson. Despite all the caterwauling, however, no floor fight developed when Lyndon was officially—and finally—nominated. A swift and almost decapitating maneuver by John McCormack crushed a mounting wave of anti-Johnson feeling before it could be fully mounted. At the end of the nominating and seconding speeches, McCormack abruptly moved that the Convention rules be suspended and Senator Johnson be named by a voice vote.

When Chairman LeRoy Collins called for the nays vote, the 152-member Michigan delegation, with "Soapy" Williams leading the chorus, broke into a tumultuous "NO!" Others, including Joe Rauh, joined in the shouting. The nays were nearly as loud as the ayes.

Chairman Collins hesitated, unable to tell whether the ayes had it (the rules called for a two-thirds majority in this form of action). The Convention's venerable parliamentarian, Congressman Clarence Cannon of Missouri, whispered into Collins' ear and he turned back to the microphones:

"Two-thirds have concurred, the motion is adopted," Collins announced solemnly. Boos shot through the Arena from all directions, drowning out the Chairman's concluding words ". . . and Senator Lyndon B. Johnson of Texas has been nominated for the Vice Presidency of the United States, by acclamation." The booing continued. And thus, on a note of rancor, the Democratic party brought its official deliberations to an end.

The next night, the Democrats concluded the Los Angeles bloodletting with a love feast of "unity" in the Coliseum. And in his acceptance speech Kennedy sought to launch his campaign with a rousing battle cry. In so doing, he did a surprising—even baffling—thing when he called for a "New Frontier," which, he said, "is not a set of promises—it is a set of challenges. . . . It holds out the promise of more sacrifice instead of more security." He also decried "promises to this group or that" and "assurances of a golden future, where taxes are always low and subsidies ever high," and then amazingly added: "My promises are in the platform you have adopted."

The platform, however, had promised something to every group in society. It called for no sacrifices. It promised to "unshackle" American enterprise—apparently by imposing new controls in every direction. It presented an "economic bill of rights" which included the "right" not only to a job but to a "remunerative" job. Everyone had the "right" not only to a home but to a "decent" home, even to "recreation"; and, of course, "the right to adequate medical care." For the cities, a new Democratic Administration would help "clear their slums, dispose of their sewage, educate their children, transport suburban commuters . . . and combat juvenile delinquency." After pledging new and bigger expenditures in every direction, the Democratic platform blandly declared that "these needs can be met with a balanced budget, with no increase in present tax rates, and with some surplus for the gradual reduction of our national debt." However, *"if* . . . the unfolding demands of the new decade . . . cannot be fulfilled without higher taxes," the Democrats promised to impose them.

As the *Christian Science Monitor* observed: "Anyone who has read that platform must ask: Has the candidate seen it?"

To the London *Economist,* it was a "somewhat disappointing" speech, "made more so by his harsh, jerky delivery and by the contrast with the polished inspiration of Mr. Stevenson's introductory remarks, which generously hailed a new beginning for the Democratic party and the country."

The speech had eloquent and noble passages which contrasted strangely with its glib personal attacks on Richard Nixon. "We know that our opponents will invoke the name of Abraham Lincoln on behalf of their candidate—despite the fact that his political career has often seemed to show charity toward none and malice for all," he said. "We know that it will not be easy to campaign against a man who has spoken and voted on every side of every issue. Mr. Nixon may feel it is his turn now, after the New Deal and the Fair Deal—but before he deals, someone is going to cut the cards."

The candidate concluded: "It has been a long road . . . to this crowded Convention city. Now begins another long journey, taking me into your cities and homes all over America. Give me your help [cheers], give me your hand [more cheers], your voice and your vote [still more cheers]."

Across the continent, in Washington, D.C., Richard M. Nixon was attending a small dinner party at the home of a friend. The TV set had been turned on for Kennedy's speech. Nixon smiled when Kennedy unloosed his personal attacks. He said nothing. He knew that, despite the speech, John F. Kennedy would make a formidable opponent. He knew he had an uphill fight on his hands.

In New York, Joseph P. Kennedy watched his son's acceptance speech at the home of *Time-Life's* Henry Luce. His absence from the vast Coliseum was noticeable that night as, one by one, the Kennedys were introduced by Chairman LeRoy Collins.

"If there are any Kennedys I have omitted, please let me know," Collins concluded.

There was a titter in the huge crowd. "Where's Joe?" people asked.

"As someone observed," wrote Randolph Churchill, " 'It was a lovely party, but where was the host?' "

The host had conveniently flown to New York, so as not to embarrass his son's Presidential chances. "It was," wrote Murray Kempton, "a sad and bitter experience for a man who had struggled forty years to make some son of his President of the United States."

Mort Sahl that night announced he had sent a wire to Joseph P. Kennedy: "You haven't lost a son; you've gained a country."

Camp

19

As the captains, king-makers, and rank-and-filers departed from Los Angeles, only the litter of their quadrennial brawl—tattered posters, battered noisemakers, shattered traditions—remained. The attention of Americans was turning to Chicago where the Republicans were beginning to gather.

That it would be a hard campaign—and demanding to the last—few observers doubted. The alliance of John F. Kennedy and Lyndon Johnson had been accomplished at a high price. The candidacies of Senator Symington and Adlai Stevenson lay in ruins. The allegiance of party extremists, both North and South, was still precarious. And facing the ticket, inevitably, was the prospect of a head-on battle with Vice President Richard Nixon.

Kennedy's nomination had produced no feelings of exultation among the Democrats. "To the very end," reported James Reston, "doubt persisted in every honest mind." They had him now, but what did they really have? The long look at John F. Kennedy began.

Edward R. Murrow[1] gave his CBS television audience this analysis of the Democratic nominee: "Senator Kennedy's record in the Senate will not be labeled 'brilliant' by historians. He headed no powerful committees, he drove through no major legislation. . . . However, this is a very considerable young man, and he will be a most formidable campaigner. He doesn't panic, he's tough. . . . He appears to approach the prospect [of being

---

[1] Appointed head of the United States Information Agency by President Kennedy.

President] with absolutely no sense of awe or inadequacy. If he has any inner doubts, they are buried—and buried very deep. His ambition appears to be unlimited. . . . He did not tell the Convention he would *try* to be worthy of their confidence. He said he *would* be worthy. Now, all of this ought to add up to an arrogance of personal manner that would destroy any politician running for justice of the peace. But with Kennedy it adds up to what I can only describe as a degree of detachment. He seems somehow able to stand off and look at himself and his party. . . . I do not know whether this quality is good or bad, only that it undoubtedly helped him get the nomination."

Kennedy began to put his political house in order as soon as he reached Hyannis Port for his post-Convention "vacation." His first major problem was to make sure that the Democratic organization—powerful as compared with the Republicans, who in many states were largely letterhead affairs—would be operating at top efficiency. His chief asset was the numerical and qualitative superiority of the Democratic organization. Added to this was the nation's labor movement which had grown more powerful and affluent in the Eisenhower years.

The party's left flank was Kennedy's major headache. Liberal disaffection with Kennedy–Johnson was expressing itself freely. New York's ADA denounced Kennedy's choice of Johnson as "an affront to liberals." Joseph Barry, columnist for the *New York Post,* wondered hopefully if 1960 might not go down in history as "the year nobody voted." New York's Liberal party prepared to endorse Kennedy–Johnson, but a vocal minority sought to postpone endorsement until the candidates had "proved" themselves on labor and civil rights at the forthcoming special bobtail session of Congress. Though Negro leaders appeared to acquiesce in the Democratic ticket (Jackie Robinson, however, described it as "loathsome"), their primary concern was how to hold Kennedy and Johnson to their platform commitments. Forlorn Stevensonians were circulating petitions asking Kennedy to pledge that, if elected, he'd make Adlai his Secretary of State.

As Stewart Alsop observed, the Liberals were rather like the Victorian lady and the handsome stranger—"Does he really love me, or is it only my fair body that he wants?"

Kennedy was not overly worried about his right flank. True, Johnson's nomination was not greeted with joy throughout the South. James Jackson Kilpatrick, editor of the Richmond *News-Leader,* for example, branded Lyndon a "counterfeit Confederate." The *Nashville Banner* called him a "political charlatan." And Georgia's Governor S. Ernest Vandiver reflected widespread Dixie opinion when he observed that Johnson made the ticket "a little more palatable," more palatable, that is, than a Liberal like Hubert Humphrey or a "Soapy" Williams would have been.

"But despite such lukewarm reaction," *Newsweek* reported on August 15, "Johnson evidently does offset some anti-Kennedy, anti-civil-rights feeling, and he will help keep the bulk of the South in the Democratic column in November. This was the over-all picture pieced together by *Newsweek's Listening Post* in 11 states that comprise the so-called Solid South."

From his own reports, Kennedy was reasonably sure he had things definitely under control in Dixie-land. The South's reconciliation to the Democrats seemed attributable less to Johnson's presence on the ticket than to the concession it implied—an apparent assurance that a Kennedy Administration would not act "beastly" toward "the land o' cotton."

It was a new Johnson who arrived in Hyannis Port in late July.

"I have come to see my Leader," he announced as he stepped off a chartered Viscount plane loaded with newsmen from the Lone Star State.

It was a Johnson who no longer called Jack Kennedy "Jack" but now referred to him as "John." It was a Johnson who had been telling folks back home, "It's a privilege to run with John Kennedy. I can tell a man by looking in his eyes. I looked in John Kennedy's eyes and I liked what I saw."

It was a "new" Johnson in more ways than one.

The labor leaders who trekked to Hyannis Port swallowed all their past unpleasant remarks about Lyndon and pointedly exclaimed, in the presence of The Leader, that L.B.J. would make an "excellent" Vice President.

The first week in August was the time appointed for homage; and one by one the labor leaders walked out on the Kennedy front lawn to tell the world what a great fellow the Senator from Texas really was. In fact, they now proclaimed that Johnson's record as Majority Leader was an outstanding one.

Of course, Johnson had a long and consistent record of voting for bills that Organized Labor had invariably certified as "anti-Labor"—as, for example, the Taft-Hartley "slave labor" bill.

Circumstances, of course, now required that people like Walter Reuther —usually so adept at sniffing out "anti-labor" heresies—discover and praise the hitherto hidden virtues in Johnson's formerly "reactionary" background. As a former Socialist, Reuther did not feel he was selling out to the class enemy. One has to be practical in manipulating bourgeois politics and politicians. Or one will find himself sitting out in the cold. And after eight years of Eisenhower, Reuther wanted to get warm.

Reuther made his submission before the microphones on Kennedy's lawn. It was a ritual grown familiar to newsmen.

The candidate began to speak. "I've invited Mr. Walter Reuther, who is Chairman of the Economic Policy Committee of the AFL–CIO, to talk to me about high unemployment in July."

"He has presented me," Kennedy went on, "with a memorandum."

The "memorandum" turned out to be a seven-page press release slugged "News from the UAW." It was handed to newsmen when Reuther emerged from his conference with the candidate and then, as an afterthought, presented to John F. Kennedy himself. Before the press conference ended, the historic "memorandum," describing the plight of the toilers under Republican rule, lay on the grass—crumpled and unread.

The script called for a session of grunts and smiles from Kennedy and "Do you mind if I comment on that, Jack?" from Reuther. The UAW leader happily reported that economic conditions might worsen, which would win votes for the Party of the People.

Kennedy was asked if he had any comment on Richard Nixon's observation that he had sold out to the labor goons. He noted Nixon had not given details, but suggested that since the Vice President said he was running a "high level" campaign, he might provide some specifications.

"May I comment on that, Jack?" Reuther interrupted, going on to explain that Kennedy had won labor backing, not by buying it, but by backing "the things that all America needs, not what organized labor wants."

Reuther and the steelworkers' David McDonald could always be expected to play the game, but their public testimony to Johnson's "excellence" took a bit of crow-eating.

When Michigan's "Soapy" Williams took his turn, the humiliation could not have been greater; the man who had made a spectacle of himself at Los Angeles, trying to bellow down Johnson's nomination, now meekly walked out on the lawn to extol the ticket as the best the Democrats had to offer.

The Stevenson fraternity was also dealt with—by the public patronization of its fallen hero, Adlai himself, on the stretch of green where the Kennedys and Senator Joe McCarthy used to play baseball with the neighbors.

Other callers included a group headed by Professor Archibald Cox of Harvard Law, who was co-ordinating the "egghead" contributions to the Kennedy campaign. With him were four economics professors: John Kenneth Galbraith and Seymour Harris of Harvard, Richard A. Lester of Princeton, and Paul A. Samuelson of MIT. The candidate took them out for a two-hour spin aboard the family yacht *Marlin* (an excellent symbol of the very Affluent Society that Galbraith and friends had been railing against).

"Frankly, I think the braintrust has produced more publicity than help," commented a Kennedy staffer at Hyannis Port. Another complained, "The professors give us old clichés instead of new ideas."

Though at times the "eggheads" would get insufferable, Jack liked to have them around anyway, according to *Time,* "to add prestige, a tone of earnestness, and appeal to Liberal voters." And Professor Galbraith himself, when asked why Harvard brains were so much sought after by political candidates, gave a one-word response.

"Prestige," he snapped.

At any rate, Galbraith went on to say (and somewhat wistfully for Galbraith), "Sometimes I read with awe and surprise about how influential I am supposed to be."

Kennedy's brain-picking activities were never intended solely to help him form policy positions. A basic purpose was to overcome the considerable

distrust of him by many intellectuals who regarded him as a brash opportunist. In that respect, he succeeded. As the wife of a Kennedy braintruster
put it, "The best way to get an intellectual on your side is to ask his opinion."

As the campaign progressed, it became increasingly obvious that the
candidate was ignoring the tons of memoranda flowing in from the nation's
campuses. "In the end," Kennedy told Nixon in their post-election meeting,
"I found myself relying more and more on Sorensen, who was with me on
the campaign tour and who therefore could react to and reflect up-to-the-
minute tactical shifts in our basic strategy."

One Kennedy enthusiast had gone so far as to propose an "Operation
Academic" which would have had Harvard Professor Samuel Beer, head of
Americans for Democratic Action, issue an appeal to thousands of professors
to send their views to Kennedy. "The Senator rejected the plan as too blatant
a device to win 'liberal' support," according to the *Wall Street Journal.* "Anyway, Beer is one Harvardian who has not formally climbed aboard the
Kennedy bandwagon."

Dr. Beer, however, had distinguished himself for having described the
Eisenhower era as a period of "glacial immobility—the Ike Age." At an ADA
meeting in Cleveland, he not surprisingly declared that the American people
live in "private opulence and public squalor." Then he added: "You'd be
surprised how many families get along with outdoor toilets in Cambridge,
where I live."

The *Cleveland Plain Dealer,* which indeed was surprised, sought en-
lightenment from the Mayor of Cambridge, Massachusetts, the Honorable
Edward A. Crane. He replied that Professor Beer's statement "staggered me."
"I assure you none of this type exists in this city," the Mayor added.

"Dr. Beer is professor of government and general education at Harvard
College," the *Plain Dealer* commented. "We trust, for the sake of the undergraduates he teaches, that his lectures contain more accurate facts than his
political diatribes."

Finally, Dr. Beer announced that the ADA had endorsed Kennedy. The
name of Lyndon Johnson, Kennedy's running mate, was conspicuously missing from the statement approved by the ADA's national board. But the statement did call for support of the Democratic platform and ticket.

Then, political hat in hand, Candidate Kennedy made the long and
painful trek to Hyde Park to visit the Queen Mother of the Democratic Liberals, Eleanor Roosevelt. Jack had pleaded for her support four years before,
but had been reminded that he had failed the test on Senator McCarthy. This
time he had won the nomination in spite of Mrs. Roosevelt, but he still needed
her help at the polls.

Mrs. Roosevelt looked down at the youthful Senator and delivered a
new judgment, one as cruel as it was patronizing. Yes, she proclaimed, she
would help him and the ticket. After all, she was a Democrat.

Commenting on the meeting in her column, she wrote: "Kennedy has a quick mind, but I would say that he might tend to arrive at judgments almost too quickly." She suggested that Kennedy lean on Adlai Stevenson's "more judicial and reflective type of mind." "I was pleased to learn that the Senator already had made plans much along these lines. It gave me a feeling of reassurance."

She added: "I think Kennedy is anxious to learn. I think he is hospitable to new ideas. He is hard-headed. He calculates the political effect of every move. . . ."

That he hadn't learned yet was hardly the strongest recommendation for the leadership of the free world.

Kennedy swallowed more pride and made plans to visit still another of his critics—Harry S Truman. It was not the most pleasant of tasks. In fact, he described his anticipated meeting with the former President as follows: "I guess he will apologize for calling me an SOB and I will apologize for being one."

Some politicians have short memories when it comes to their own actions. Mr. Truman did everything he could to keep the nomination from Kennedy, even to depriving the Convention of his presence, on the basis that the Senator was immature and inexperienced. Now, Mr. Truman had had a change of heart. And he told Kennedy so at the Truman Library, Independence, Missouri, on August 20, 1960.

QUESTION: What caused you to decide that Senator Kennedy was ready for the country?

MR. TRUMAN: When the Democratic National Convention decided to nominate him for President. That is all the answer you need. The National Democratic Convention is the law for the Democratic party. I am a Democrat and I follow the law.

QUESTION: On July 2, I believe you said that you thought the Convention was fixed. Have you changed your opinion?

MR. TRUMAN: I did not say that. I said it looked to me as if the Convention was already made up the way it was supposed to go, and that is what the trouble was. And it was, and it has been done all right, and they nominated this man, and I am going to support him.

What are you going to do about that?

*   *   *

QUESTION: You say that as a good Democrat, you of course will support Senator Kennedy. You told us out here before Los Angeles that you felt that Senator Kennedy was too young and inexperienced.

MR. TRUMAN: I said the National Democratic Convention solved that, and that is all there is to that.

QUESTION: You now feel that he is?

MR. TRUMAN: That is all there is to that.

At their make-up meeting, Kennedy promised a beaming Harry Truman that he would conduct a "give 'em hell" campaign.

"I'm taking a page from your 1948 campaign," he told the former President. "I've studied it closely and I am going to do exactly what you did and give the Republicans, and especially Nixon, hell."[2]

Kennedy also held a series of conferences with his Southern colleagues, who were still disgruntled. He offered them reassuring words. The Democratic platform, he told them, was merely window dressing. They need have no fears. If elected, he said, he would ignore most of the platform. The important thing, he insisted, was to win in November.

One of the Southerners to whom he paid a visit, accompanied by Lyndon Johnson, was that old apple farmer from Viriginia, Harry F. Byrd. The story was first told by Frank van der Linden, Washington correspondent for Southern newspapers, including the *Nashville Banner,* and then was given national circulation by *Newsweek's* Raymond Moley.

When Kennedy and Johnson marched into his Senate office to solicit his blessing, Senator Byrd told them he could not go along with the Democratic plank calling for abolition of state right-to-work laws. Kennedy and Johnson then offered not to press the issue if they were elected.[3]

"To us," commented the *Charleston* (S.C.) *News and Courier,* "the cold offer to ignore a key issue of the campaign in exchange for the support of another politician, no matter how powerful, is a measure of the faith that the public can place in Messrs. Kennedy and Johnson. Their offer not to press for repeal of the right-to-work law would be worth no more, in our judgment, than their promises to uphold the platform. In fact, we find difficulty believing in their sincerity about anything except the quest for votes. Political expediency is a poor basis for choosing the top leadership of a great Republic."

And while Kennedy was assuring Southern Democrats that the Los Angeles platform was just a bunch of rhetoric, the *New Republic's* "T.R.B." was assuring worried subscribers that "this writer's personal judgment is that Kennedy is way to the left of Stevenson."[4]

The *New York Post,* smarting over the rejection of its proposed Stevenson-Kennedy ticket, adopted a wait-and-see attitude toward the Kennedy-

---

[2] In that famous campaign against Thomas E. Dewey, Mr. Truman said, among other things, "If the Republicans win they will tear you apart. . . . The Republicans dare not tell you their aims since they [the people] would take them out and hang them if they did—and that would be disastrous—or would it? . . . The Republican gluttons of privilege are cold men, cunning men. . . . [Thomas E.] Dewey is a ruthless man who considers shooting at sunrise as a cure for inefficiency. . . . When a few men get control of the economy of a nation, they find a front man to run the country for them [referring to Dewey and citing Mussolini, Hitler and Tojo]."

[3] One campaign "pledge" they have kept.

[4] "T.R.B.," who writes with such Liberal militancy, is actually Richard L. Strout, who writes more mild-mannered prose for the *Christian Science Monitor.*

Johnson ticket. "Johnson's selection symbolized," the *Post* contended, "the recreation of the alliance between the Northern party bosses and the conservative Southern bloc."

"So, despite its uniquely liberal program," the *Post* added, "the Democratic party emerged from Los Angeles still vulnerable to the ancient cry that it was a two-headed donkey after all. In the aftermath one heard all the ancient bromides about 'realism,' 'long-range strategy' and 'the art of the possible' being used to justify an arrangement that cast doubt on the integrity of the week's work.

"Are things exactly what they seem? Some answers may come swiftly. The August session of Congress will provide a stern trial and a great chance.

"This will be Johnson's opportunity to prove he places his Vice Presidential candidacy above his race for re-election in Texas (which will occur simultaneously) and that he feels liberated from provincial politics. It will give Kennedy abundant occasion to affirm both his leadership and his earnestness—in civil rights and other matters. By the time the session is over, the country may know much more about the future of Mr. Kennedy."

The special session, of course, had been arranged by Lyndon Johnson and Sam Rayburn to give a weary Congress a month's recess for the Conventions—and also to help the Majority Leader politically.

Returning as his party's nominee, Kennedy sought to ram through a much heralded list of "gut" measures intended to be billed as Democratic accomplishments in the fall campaign.

"Hopes ran high in every corner of Kennedy-land," commented the *Cincinnati Enquirer*. "From the West Coast, where the self-styled 'Clan' is fighting for the New Frontier under the inspiring moral leadership of Frank Sinatra and Sammy Davis Jr., all the way to the French Riviera, where the eminent retired philanthropist Joseph P. Kennedy is sitting out the campaign in exile, it looked very much as though Senator Kennedy might get his first bill through Congress—his first bill in 14 years of legislative life."

The Kennedy bill pertained to the minimum wage. It provided that it be increased from $1 an hour to $1.25. It also provided that it be extended to cover several million additional Americans.

Few bills were ever introduced in Congress under more favorable circumstances. In unmistakably clear language, the Democratic platform declared that "we pledge to raise the minimum wage to $1.25 an hour and to extend coverage to several million workers not now protected." There was no challenge to this pledge. From every indication, it was a pledge to which every Democrat was committed.

The Kennedy bill went into the hopper, moreover, at a time when the Democrats were more firmly in control of Congress than they had ever been since the early days of the New Deal. In the Senate, Democrats out-numbered Republicans by a 2–1 margin. In the House, the Democratic majority was only slightly less top-heavy.

"But most important of all," the *Enquirer* noted, "the minimum wage bill enjoyed the magic of that celebrated Kennedy leadership—the inspiring, dynamic, irresistible leadership of which the Democratic orators have been speaking as the salvation of America and Western civilization."

For a time, it looked very much as if the Kennedy bill might make it. It actually passed the Senate—after a long battle against weakening amendments, proposed mainly by Kennedy's fellow New Frontiersmen. The bill ran into trouble in the House, which was willing to increase the minimum wage only to $1.15. But Kennedy, in a pique, flatly refused to accept the $1.15 bill, declaring it did not represent progress. The Kennedy bill was dead.

"Quite aside from the wisdom of the minimum wage increase," commented the *Enquirer,* "the manner in which the Democratic Congress dealt with it should give the American people a new insight into Senator Kennedy's stature in his own party, among the lawmakers who know him best. It looks more and more as though the New Frontier died at birth."

Kennedy and Johnson had repeatedly stated they were running on a platform that contained a generous, far-reaching civil rights plank. So the Republicans in the Senate offered the Democratic majority a chance to make good on some of their platform's promises. A bill introduced by Senator Everett M. Dirksen would have prevented racial discrimination in plants working on government contracts and would have earmarked federal funds to help school districts abolish segregation—measures proposed in President Eisenhower's message.

And when, on August 8, a civil rights group inquired about an "August down-payment" on his platform's promises, Candidate Kennedy declared, "I stand ready now, as I have in the past, to vote for all these measures."

But the next day Kennedy voted against the Dirksen proposals.

What happened was this: Lyndon Johnson, as Majority Leader, had pulled one of his famed parliamentary fast ones to get the bill tabled. "With a grin of delight on his face, Johnson forced the Republicans to a quick vote in which the Dirksen proposal was killed 54–28," reported the AP. "After a brief conference with Johnson, Senator Kennedy, the Democratic Presidential nominee, added a soft-voiced 'aye' to support the motion." Only four Democrats had gone along with the Republicans.

Lyndon Johnson had persuaded the others that the Republicans were only playing politics. So most of the Liberal Democrats decided to play politics. Or rather, they played Johnson's politics. And Kennedy defended all this on the ground that raising the civil rights issue would block the whole legislative program because the Southerners would filibuster against it.

"The Senate," commented the *Chicago Tribune,* "doesn't have to permit a filibuster and if the Democrats were sincere in their platform promise they would not tolerate one. Together with the Republicans, they could block it."

The *New York Post,* on the other side of the ideological fence, was similarly horrified. "Was it, after all, a Johnson-Kennedy ticket? Is Johnson the master in Kennedy's house?" the *Post* asked in anguish on August 10. " 'Wait till next year,' cry the Kennedy adherents. But will there be a next year? Can Kennedy win the election if the image he offers is that of a calculating, passionless man, dedicated only to the pursuit of power? Is that not fundamentally the case against Mr. Nixon? It is the kind of performance that dims all luster in the Kennedy campaign and strengthens the neutralism so widespread now among independent liberal voters. . . . Civil rights gave Kennedy a unique chance to overcome much of the cynicism created by his choice of Johnson. . . . It gave Johnson the occasion to prove that he is liberated from provincial Texas politics. Neither man rose to the challenge. . . . No decision is irretrievable; there are still many August days left. What matters now is that Mr. Kennedy recognize that his deed has affronted thousands who care deeply about the quest for human equality, and that it has stirred grave doubts about the quality of his convictions."

Kennedy felt trapped. No matter what he did, he was bound to lose votes. So he left the matter open—indicating he might make a counter-move on civil rights before the rump session ended.

Thus Kennedy managed to make the worst of both worlds. He irritated the Southerners and failed to pacify the civil rights advocates.

"This is the first time I've ever seen Jack so inept," a Kennedy admirer told the *Wall Street Journal*'s Robert Novak. The "most frightening aspect" of the civil rights "nightmare" to many Democrats was not the certainty that votes would be lost no matter what Kennedy decided to do. "It is the apparent unwillingness of Mr. Kennedy to make any firm decision," Novak reported.

To gain time, Kennedy denounced the Eisenhower Administration for the cardinal sin of "playing politics." And he played politics in turn by demanding that Eisenhower immediately issue an Executive Order forbidding discrimination in federal housing projects. "He could do it today. . . . If he does *not* do it, a new Democratic Administration *will*. . . ."

Kennedy's militant rhetoric, however, did not satisfy the Leadership Conference on Civil Rights, composed of labor leaders, ADA officials, and other Liberals. The Conference demanded deeds—not more words—from Kennedy. "This anti-Nixon coalition turned down flat a secret Kennedy proposal that might have extricated him from the trap with a minimum of damage," reported Novak. The proposal was for Kennedy and Nixon to join in calling for the creation of a bipartisan commission headed by Michigan's Governor Williams and New York's Governor Rockefeller to draft a civil rights program for enactment by Congress in early 1961.

By August 12, the *New York Post* concluded: "The truth is that Senator Kennedy has apparently been deluded into believing that he can ride out the storm in the crucial areas where civil rights is deemed the great human issue of our time. We believe this is a dangerous delusion. . . ."

As it turned out, it was no delusion.

The real delusion was the belief, as expressed by such newspapers as the *New York Daily News,* that the Republicans "by doing their best to expand and enlarge civil rights for minority groups without waiting for election" would find a payoff at the polls in November. "We wonder how friendly the Negro voter now thinks Kennedy and Johnson are to Negroes," said the *News.*

"We're also intrigued by a parliamentary stunt which Kennedy performed recently on his own, without visible help from Johnson," the *News* continued. "As chairman of a Senate Labor subcommittee, Kennedy in one minute flat engineered approval of a bill which would seriously weaken the Taft-Hartley and Landrum-Griffin labor laws' provisions against secondary boycotts. He did it while Senator Barry Goldwater stood outside of the committee room yelling that there wasn't a quorum inside. That was true, but Kennedy declared the bill approved nevertheless, and apparently nothing can be done about it."

Despite Kennedy's parliamentary maneuver, the bill did not get through the Congress.

As the session wore on, accomplishing nothing, Kennedy became increasingly irritable. His Senate behavior under misfortune and strain was described in a revealing dispatch by the *Washington Star*'s Mary McGrory, who was not unfriendly to Kennedy. "He darts in and out of his Capitol hideaway. . . . When he is on the floor, he paces around nervously. When he stops by a Senator's desk, he compulsively tidies everything. He lines up the pencils in the tray, straightens the edges of piles of papers. When he sits down, he nervously drums with his fingers, smooths his hair, fingers his tie. He gives a powerful impression of wishing to be elsewhere."

Lyndon Johnson did not appear too unhappy about the misfortunes befalling his Leader. His job was to carry the South in November and the more concessions the South got, the easier his job would be. *Newsweek* reported that Lyndon "lolled through most of the proceedings in his front-row seat, long legs outstretched, a look of inward amusement flickering across his face. Only rarely did he seem pained—notably when Pennsylvania's sharp-tongued Republican Hugh Scott repeatedly referred to Kennedy as 'the Majority Leader's leader.' "

Rarely has Washington witnessed anything like the spectacle in the Senate Chamber when a Kennedy-backed proposal for Social Security-financed Medical Care for the Aged came up for a vote. Every Democrat had been rallied to vote against an alternative plan sponsored by Liberal Republicans; it received 28 GOP votes and no others. Then Jack Kennedy, who had refused to yield an inch on the GOP measure, realized he could not rally all Southern Democrats to his Medicare bill. He needed "at least five or six" Republican votes.

"So, just before the vote," as New York Senator Jack Javits recalled the scene, "Kennedy turned to the liberals on the Republican side of the aisle and asked for our support; he told us that a true liberal *has* to vote for a liberal measure regardless of defect, if it comes down to a choice of that bill or nothing at all for the time being. But liberal Republican views had been neither considered nor reflected in the Kennedy supported bill. So understandably, we were not a sympathetic audience."

After having failed to obtain passage of any of the other pieces of legislation he had dubbed "must," Kennedy was counting on passage of Medicare to provide him with the glorious victory that he could take before the electorate as an example of his superb Leadership.

When Kennedy finished his appeal to the Republicans, Senator Javits arose to reply: "You ask us to endorse this. I am sorry, sir, but this is not the season for that. . . ."

Kennedy wearily sat down in his rear seat on the Democratic side. The moment of truth had arrived.

As the roll call progressed, tension mounted. Kennedy sat somber-faced, his chin propped on one hand, his other hand nervously fiddling with a pencil. His rival, Vice President Nixon, took a seat beside Javits, who was keeping a tally. Nixon was waiting to see whether his vote would be needed to break a tie. It was not. The vote was 51 to 44. Kennedy had been deserted by 19 of his fellow Democrats, nearly one-third of the Democrats present.

When the voting was over, Kennedy threw his pencil down on his desk in disgust, stood up, and stalked out of the chamber with Lyndon Johnson, presumably to discuss how soon he could be released from bondage on Capitol Hill.

The medical care plan enacted—the Kerr-Mills bill—provided for a federal-state matching arrangement instead of Kennedy's proposed Social Security financing.

There were other "must" items which Candidate Kennedy had hoped to get through the special session. But the "greatness," with which his partisans said he was so abundantly endowed, could not prevent each of them from being pulverized: his aid-to-education and housing programs didn't even get out of the appropriate committees. Although Kennedy had promised at the Convention to pass a farm bill to give farmers "full parity income," saying January would be too late for such vital legislation, no farm program was ever presented in the special session. The Democratic leadership had complained loudly about inadequate defense and promised to vote more billions for arms; but no additional money came out of the August session.

Finally—and mercifully—the disastrous session reached its graceless end. Nothing bearing the Kennedy endorsement got through the Democratic-controlled Congress. By any measurement, the bobtail session proved to be a devastating defeat for John F. Kennedy. Rarely had any Presidential candidate so quickly exposed his built-in weaknesses—the same weaknesses that Kennedy was to demonstrate in his first years as President.

"In the dead-end session," *Time* noted, "Kennedy embarrassingly showed what a lot of his fellow Senators already knew: that he was never a real leader in the Senate, had never mastered its nuances. Accordingly, he greatly over-estimated his capacity, as his party's Presidential nominee, to control the course of legislation."

His travail over, Kennedy flew off to Hyannis Port to nurse his bruised ego.

When asked whether he thought the Democrats had made a mistake in scheduling the special session, Kennedy showed the strain.

"I didn't recess it," he snapped to newsmen, "and I didn't bring it back."

It was difficult, indeed, to forget the taunts of the opposition. Senator Scott, the Republican poet laureate, had got under his skin with this "unfinished parody":

> This is the tale of the session,
>   The Texas two decreed,
> To ease the folks of their taxes,
>   To gain them votes in their need.
> The lords of their party assembled;
>   East and West they came—
> Lyndon and Scoop and Hubert,
>   Jack and Mister Sam.
> Some were faithful to farmers,
>   Some were devoted to toil,
> Yes, some were loyal to labor,
>   And some were loyal to oil.

The poetical outburst had been triggered by the rare event of a United States Senator reading Kipling to his colleagues. Senator Keating, Republican of New York, quoted from the English bard's "Road Song of the Bander-Log" as a tribute to what he termed "the spirit of the present session":

> Here we sit in a branchy row,
>   Thinking of beautiful things we know.
> Dreaming of things we mean to do,
>   All complete, in a minute or two—
> Something noble and wise and good,
>   Done by merely wishing we could.

Keating cited "one positive and affirmative accomplishment" of the session. "It has given Members," he noted, "the chance to get better acquainted —not with the great issues of the day—but with each other."

Then Scott recited the forgettable prose that he had composed in three minutes.

KEATING: I must say that your verse is very descriptive. If Kipling were alive today he would have real competition in my friend from Pennsylvania.

SCOTT: I do not wish to compete with Kipling. Those of us who have spent most of the month of August here have been doing nothing more than kippling and piddling anyway.

The session has been long because of the tragic failure of leadership. We came here hoping that the Majority Leader's Leader would guide us into paths of enlightenment, that we would see great gains accomplished for the people of the country, that we would see at least a part of the promises made so gaily at Los Angeles realized at least to a minor degree of fulfillment. . . .

We had hoped that the Majority Leader's Leader, the Junior Senator from Massachusetts, who was absent on official business in Hyannis Port last Saturday, while we were debating the medical care for the aged bill, would give us some leadership and some enlightenment and some guidance. We had hoped that as we gathered here, he would lead and unite his party. Having failed in August to lead and unite his party, one wonders whether . . . he will be able to do any better in January. . . .

KEATING: I do not wish to yield the floor without saying that I bear for both the distinguished Senator from Massachusetts and the Majority Leader a very real affection. I hope to serve in this body with them for many years to come.

SCOTT: . . . However, does not the Senator agree with me that it is indeed deplorable that 1,400,000 citizens will be deprived of coverage under the minimum wage bill because of . . . partisan or petulant reactions on the minimum wage bill, [which] caused us to substitute a demogogic issue in a political campaign rather than sincere and effective legislative action? Would it not have been better to have a bill to benefit many plain, average people, than to have an issue for two political candidates?

KEATING: I quite agree with the views expressed by the distinguished Senator from Pennsylvania. . . .

SCOTT: Does the distinguished Senator from New York know why the distinguished Junior Senator from Massachusetts has been unable, so far, to exert his leadership over the Members of his own party in the other body? To me, this is a puzzlement, a matter which I cannot understand. I followed with great interest the proceedings at Los Angeles and was under the impression that the Junior Senator from Massachusetts, whom we all respect, was greeted as the leader of a united party; that the Members of his party in both Chambers of Congress would hasten to follow his merest nod, indeed, his slightest beckoning, his mildest wish. But all of a sudden we find that the entire picture in the other body is a repudiation of the leadership of the Junior Senator from Massachusetts, to say nothing of this body—of which, perhaps, the less said the better—with regard to the leadership of the Senator from Massachusetts.

KEATING: It is inexplicable to me why the distinguished Junior Senator from Massachusetts, as the leader of his party, has not been able, at least, to convince his own party in the House of Representatives that they should produce action on at least one of the five major matters which we were called back into session to consider. I have no answer for it. The distinguished Junior Senator from Massachusetts will have to answer that question himself. I am not able to answer for him.

SCOTT: . . . As the Senator knows . . . I am a strong supporter of the Phillies baseball team, which is now at the bottom of the National League. However, although the batting average of the Phillies is unfortunately low . . . it is considerably in excess of the batting average of the Junior Senator from Massachusetts. (Laughter.)

KEATING: It is not only in excess of his batting average, but also in excess of the batting average of Congress in this special session.

SCOTT: Indeed, it is; and it makes me feel better about the future of the Phillies.

KEATING: I am sure it should.

SCOTT: Meanwhile, I rejoice in the prowess of the Pittsburgh Pirates, "than whom there is no whicher." (Laughter.)

KEATING: I agree with the Senator from Pennsylvania.

"Since young Mr. Kennedy fell on his face with everything in his favor, what leadership could he possibly be expected to exert if he were President?" asked the *St. Louis Globe-Democrat.* "His Administration would be doomed to disaster from the very day it took office."

"The Democratic Presidential candidate who emerged from this unhappy session is a far cry from the all-powerful executive that Senator Kennedy envisions as necessary in the White House," observed the *San Diego Union.*

"We do not agree with those who interpret the session as a defeat for Senator Kennedy. . . ." said the *St. Louis Post-Dispatch.* "True, the Kennedy legislative program was rejected. But this program could not have survived a sure Presidential veto anyway. Furthermore, Kennedy showed that he was not passionately interested in immediate legislation when he junked the minimum wage bill rather than accept the narrower House version—thus delaying for millions of workers a 15 per cent rise of the minimum wage in order to sharpen a campaign issue. . . ."

"The liberal promises of the Democratic platform have now met their first test," commented *New America,* the Socialist publication. "On the floor of the Senate they have been shown to be empty and meaningless. Kennedy's strategy of trying to ride two horses—the platform and unity with the Dixiecrats—has proved itself to mean unity with the Dixiecrats, period."

"Having gotten exactly nowhere in the grandiose plans he had made for turning the rump session of Congress into his own image," said the *Chicago Sun-Times,* "Senator Kennedy says he will now carry his fight to the country.

"What fight? With whom?

"The fact is he was thwarted by the conservative members of his own Democratic Party, mostly Southerners. They are, or should be, his targets. But Kennedy hopes to keep the South loyally Democratic. He can't tilt at his own Southern flank."

In retrospect, the surprising thing about the rump session was that it did

Kennedy much less damage than most Washington observers, with their parochial preoccupation with Congressional minutiae, had thought.

One reason was that many vacationing Americans were simply unaware of what was happening in Washington. In fact, during the closing days of the post-Convention session, the remark, "Why the people back home don't even know Congress is in session," was frequently heard in the corridors and cloak-rooms on Capitol Hill.

"Of those who do," commented the *Economist*, "most have the vague impression that Mr. Kennedy fought for what he thought right and was over-come by the legions of darkness. . . . If Senator Kennedy wants to be entirely cynical, he can also reflect that it is better to have a bunch of practi-cally unbitten carrots to dangle in front of the electorate in November than to have fed the donkey already."

Soon the painful memories of the August session were being drowned in a flood of campaign oratory. Hardly had the session ended before Candi-date Kennedy took to the hustings to bemoan "the lack of leadership" of the Eisenhower Administration and to insist that only he could save the nation—and the free world—from certain doom.

Kennedy also managed to salvage a useful campaign issue from the wreckage of the session. He claimed that all that was proved by his legislative defeats was the necessity for electing a Democratic President who would not suppress legislation by the threat of a veto. The argument would have been stronger had Kennedy been able to muster even a simple majority on a single issue and force an actual White House veto.

But logic loses its potency when it comes to political campaigns. For example, addressing a Labor Day throng in Detroit's Cadillac Square shortly after the rump session, Candidate Kennedy had this to say:

"Next January, we will have four more votes in the United States Senate to give us medical care under Social Security. And next January, there will be no threat of a Republican Presidential veto."

The official record noted "applause" after both these predictions. Candi-date Kennedy added:

"The man and the party who oppose medical care for the aged have no more compassion for the small farmer or the small businessman, or hungry families here in the United States or around the world. That kind of man and that kind of party likes things the way they are."[5]

[5] Two years later, President Kennedy was still unable to get a Democratic-controlled Senate to pass his Medicare program. In July 1962, the Senate killed the Administra-tion's bill with 21 Democrats voting against it, each one presumably the "kind of man" Kennedy was talking about in 1960 as totally lacking in "compassion" for unfortunate folk and definitely preferring "things the way they are." This time, however, Kennedy had a new excuse for his failure. Reeling under the impact of the 52–48 Senate defeat, the President permitted himself a large absurdity. In his moment of pique, he said, "Nearly all the Republicans and a handful of Democrats joined with them to give us

Kennedy argued that his election would mean the end of "divided government"—with Congress Democratic and the Presidency Republican. "Every objective observer agrees that the Congress will continue to be strongly Democratic—that a continuation of divided government will mean continued inaction on vital problems—and that a Democratic President, with long experience in both the House and the Senate, and with a mandate from the people, would be better able to work in harmony with the Congress to get this country moving again."

At least one objective observer didn't think so. William H. Stringer, Chief of the Washington News Bureau of the *Christian Science Monitor,* wrote: "It could be argued that Mr. Nixon, representing a less radically liberal stance than Senator Kennedy, would be more in tune with Congressional sentiment and more likely to get along with it."

The thesis that Kennedy's influence in Congress would increase because, as President, he would be in a position to dispense favors to the Democrats was scoffed at by David Lawrence. "The conservatives aren't the kind who are influenced that way," wrote Lawrence in *U.S. News & World Report.*

And the *Cleveland Plain Dealer* noted: "While it is true that Kennedy as President would have vast powers over appointments which could be used to line up support in Congress, there is nothing in the record to indicate that he possesses the magnetic qualities of leadership that would unite the two Democratic parties (North and South) behind his projected legislative programs."

The "divided government" theme was explored in a pamphlet published by the Democratic National Committee. "As Abraham Lincoln so eloquently stated in the Gettysburg Address, 'A house divided against itself cannot stand.' "

As the boys at the other National Committee quickly noted, Lincoln uttered the phrase at the Republican State Convention in Springfield, Illinois, in 1858. The Gettysburg Address was delivered five years later.

"The rest of the Democratic pamphlet continues along the same inaccurate line," the Republicans added. "For instance, it describes Senators Kennedy and Johnson and a Democratic Congress as 'the strongest possible team.' Only sorcery could reconcile Kennedy and Johnson as a team and only magic could depict a Democratic Congress as part of that 'team.' In the Senate since 1953, Kennedy and Johnson divided on 238 roll call votes—including such basic issues as the defense of Quemoy and Matsu. And in the

---

today's setback." The Loyal Opposition quickly pointed out that the "handful" added up to 21 Democrats, about one-third of all Senate Democrats. Among the "handful" were the Democratic President pro tempore of the Senate (Carl Hayden of Arizona), a former Vice Presidential candidate (John Sparkman of Alabama), the Secretary of the Senate Democratic Conference (George Smathers of Florida), and 10 of the 16 Democratic Committee Chairmen.

special session, Kennedy and Johnson failed to deliver on even one of the seven major items they had promised.

"Blithely ignoring this record of discord—both between their nominees and between their nominees and their own Congress—the Democratic National Committee pamphlet carried, with a straight face, the title 'United We Stand.' "

They were united on one thing—winning the election. One of their big weapons was the so-called People Machine—a big, bulky electronic monster that busily forecast voter responses and outlined the most productive campaign strategy for Kennedy.

The People Machine—also known as the People Predictor—was perfected by several distinguished social scientists with $65,000 provided by the Democratic Advisory Council. It was manufactured by the Simulmatics Corporation under the guidance of Dr. William McPhee of Columbia, Dr. Ithiel de Sola Pool of MIT, Dr. Robert Abelson of Yale, and Edward L. Greenfield of Madison Avenue.

The story of how this computing device was secretly designed for the Democratic Presidential campaign was related in full detail in the January 1961 issue of *Harper's* in an authoritative article by Thomas B. Morgan. At first Kennedy's press representative, Pierre Salinger, denied any knowledge of the People Machine. "We did not use the machine," he said flatly. "Nor were the machine studies made for us."

Pierre's recollection was somewhat refreshed, however, after it was disclosed that Bobby Kennedy had helped finance the People Machine by a sum of $20,000 and that reports based on its findings went directly to Bobby.

According to Morgan, the Democratic Advisory Council used the People Machine for a report on how to woo the Negro vote. He said the computer concluded there would be mass defections from the Democratic party unless a strong civil rights plank was adopted.

The basic premise of the People Machine is that "people are predictable," wrote Morgan. This is the premise of regular public opinion polling too, but polls are essentially static—they speak only for the polled subject's current opinion. The People Machine eliminated this imponderable by having built into it the capacity to simulate new, even unexpected, circumstances, and then test the result of a change before it occurred.

Morgan said that information, designed to outline voters' attitudes, was assembled by Dr. Abelson in the summer of 1959. It consisted of 100,000 interviews with voters, the results of 66 nationwide polls made since 1952. The interviews were divided into 480 "voter-types" such as "Midwestern, small-town, poor, Catholic, female" and "Western, metropolitan, Jewish, male."

Armed with this kind of information, the People Machine provided the Kennedy strategists with important information about the "images" of Kennedy and Nixon and about voters' attitudes toward issues. Here are some recommendations contained in a report to Bobby Kennedy on August 25, 1960:

On the upcoming TV debates: Nixon has been less effective on TV than Kennedy. The crucial TV debates are therefore a risk for him. Should he be able to trap Kennedy into approaching the debates at his own level of super-coolness, he can "win" the debates. The danger to Nixon is that Kennedy can make use of his more personable traits—including a range of emotions such as fervor, humor, friendship, and spirituality beyond the expected seriousness and anger—and thus cause Nixon to "lose" the debates.

On the foreign affairs issue: . . . This issue is Kennedy's area of greatest weakness, but it is also an area in which he has positive opportunities. . . . Should he or should he not attack the Republican (foreign affairs) record? We conclude that the answer is: he should attack. As part of an aggressive, partisan campaign, Kennedy can materially affect party feeling among the electorate and enhance his own image by: (1) talking and acting about foreign affairs in a way which conveys a sense of knowledge and power; (2) unmistakably exposing the degeneration of prestige and power which the United States has suffered under the Republican Administration.

On Nixon's probable style of campaigning: Nixon can be hurt if his campaign style does not capitalize on his personal assets (self-confidence, competence, sober-mindedness). Should Nixon campaign intensely, but above party strife and personal attack . . . he can gain among the undecided Democrats and Independents.

The People Machine was considered a significant advance over other public opinion methods because it gave answers to "what if" questions—those concerned with changes from the present situation. One question put to it, according to Morgan, was "what if the religious issue becomes embittered close to Election Day." The machine's answer (supplied to Bobby Kennedy) was this:

. . . Kennedy today has lost the bulk of the votes he would lose if the election campaign were to be embittered by the issue of anti-Catholicism. The net worst has been done. If the campaign becomes embittered he will lose a few more reluctant Protestant votes to Nixon, but will gain Catholic and minority group votes. Bitter anti-Catholicism in the campaign would bring about a reaction against prejudice and for Kennedy from Catholics and others who would resent overt prejudice. It is in Kennedy's hands to handle the religious issue during the campaign in a way that maximizes Kennedy votes based on resentment against religious prejudice and minimizes further defections. On balance, he would not lose further from forthright and persistent attention to the religious issue, and could gain. The simulation shows that there has already been a serious defection from Kennedy by Protestant voters. Under these circumstances, it makes no sense to brush the religious issue under the rug. Kennedy has already suffered the disadvantages of the issue even though it is not embittered now—and without receiving compensating advantages inherent in it.

In short, Kennedy was advised to play up the religious issue for all it was worth on the premise he could only gain from it. Which was exactly what he did that fall when he repeatedly urged American voters to forget his religion by constantly reminding them of it.

"If by now people don't know his stand on that they never will," commented David H. Beetle in the Albany (New York) *Knickerbocker News* early in the campaign. "Repeating it can only serve to stir up once again a question that doesn't seem pertinent."

Bobby Kennedy was placed in charge of making sure that the voters would be constantly reminded of the necessity of forgetting the religious issue.

Richard Nixon had hoped to keep the issue out of the campaign. His attitude was that there would be a religious issue only if the candidates and their spokesmen persisted in talking about it. Nixon said that as far as he and the Republicans were concerned, it would not be raised. And he kept his pledge.

The Kennedy attitude, as brother Bobby explained it at the start of the campaign, was that "my brother, the Senator" would continue to discuss religion "as long as there are questions about it."

The Kennedy brothers did not need the findings of the People Machine to know the political potency of The Issue. After all, it had played a major role in winning them the nomination. The findings merely confirmed what they already knew.

Bobby raised the issue at the opening of Kennedy Headquarters in Cincinnati on September 13.

"Did they ask my brother Joe whether he was a Catholic before he was shot down?" he asked.

He couldn't go on. What appeared to be real tears gushed from his eyes, and he sat down. The audience broke into applause.

It was a well publicized episode. Later, Bobby said, "I hope Jimmy Hoffa doesn't hear about it."

Again, Hoffa was being used against a Kennedy opponent. As Lyndon Johnson had stated—shortly before the identity of his Leader was made known to him—the Kennedys had been running against Hoffa for years.

Four days later, Bobby toured the resort areas in New York's Catskills, this time reminding audiences that "it is not important as to what church a candidate attends on Sunday, but whether or not the prestige of the United States, as leader of the free world, can be restored."

Franklin Roosevelt Jr., who accompanied Bobby, reminded their largely Jewish audiences that "If religious prejudice is raised against one minority today, it can be raised against another minority tomorrow."

Special efforts were being mounted to turn out the Jewish vote. Reports reaching Kennedy headquarters suggested that the vote—so crucial in the big cities—was not responding properly. Reprints of Drew Pearson's Convention columns, recalling Joseph P. Kennedy's pre-war attitudes, were still being circulated; and rumors about Old Joe's more intemperate remarks—stirred up by Lyndon Johnson and others at the Convention—were becoming troublesome.

Old Joe, of course, was being kept out of sight. He refused to grant interviews to newsmen. At Cap d'Antibes, where he and Rose had repaired following the Convention, he did, however, promise to "speak up. . . . I'm not going to do it before the election. However, I assure you that I will do it after that, and that it will be something worth while. People may even see a flash of my old-time form."

The elder Kennedy's seeming absence from the political wars was noted in "Where's Joe?" editorials around the country.

"Is Senator Kennedy somehow ashamed of his father, or does he think that the elder Kennedy would lose him votes?" asked the *Chicago Tribune.* "If so, why? Because the presence of a rich and somewhat conservative parent would not accord too well with the 'image' of a candidate speaking for the union bosses and the left? We cannot be sure, but Kennedy Sr. has proved almost invisible since his son was nominated. He is in the file of the political bureau of missing persons. The major mystery of the 1960 campaign may prove to be: Where is Joe?"

Actually, Joe was not all that invisible. In September he turned up in Manhattan where, according to the *New York World-Telegram,* he huddled privately with various Democratic bosses at the plush Hampshire House. The senior Kennedy's presence was being felt elsewhere, too. "He never comes into a campaign," Rose Kennedy explained. "He just works in his own way—and very successfully."

All of which gave rise to the couplet:

> Jack and Bob will run the show,
> While Ted's in charge of hiding Joe.

Actually, Ted Kennedy was ordered to San Francisco to supervise campaign operations from the Rockies to the Pacific Coast. And Bobby was placed in charge of running the whole show. Senator Henry Jackson, named Democratic National Chairman for the campaign's duration, soon discovered that he was nothing more than a titled figurehead, taking orders from Bobby. And that was the way Jack Kennedy wanted it. The Kennedys don't trust outsiders.

As his brother's campaign manager, Bobby Kennedy offended almost everyone with whom he came into contact. His attitude was perhaps best summed up in the remark he made to New York Reform Democrats who were warring with the regular Tammany organization: "Gentlemen, I don't give a damn if the state and city organizations survive after November, and I don't give a damn if *you* survive. I want to elect John F. Kennedy."

Many of his listeners were offended. The Reform group had its mass following in the old Stevenson clubs, which had worked so enthusiastically in 1952 and 1956.

Bobby's interference in the internal affairs of New York Democrats only resulted in widening the split between Tammany, headed by Carmine DeSapio, and the so-called Reformers, whose leading lights were Mrs. Eleanor Roosevelt and Herbert H. Lehman. Finally, an agreement was reached whereby Bobby was to stay out of New York. Acting in his behalf, however, would be a Kennedy buddy, artist William Walton, a former newsman who had worked on the now-defunct *PM* and later for *Time*.

"Significantly enough," wrote columnist Ralph de Toledano, "some Democrats agree with the Republicans that Bobby Kennedy is Nixon's secret weapon. They suspect that the American voter will be frightened off by visions of a family dynasty taking over the White House. They know the extremely tight bonds which link the Kennedy brothers to each other and to their father. To suggest that Bobby take a long vacation until election day— something these Democrats would like to see—would court swift and massive retaliation. They also realize that to separate Jack from Bobby would be just as difficult as driving a wedge between Fidel and Raul Castro."[6]

Bobby hadn't helped matters in New York when, in a radio interview, he threw caution to the winds and took on his brother's enemies in a free-wheeling verbal brawl. In an hour-long appearance on the Barry Gray show, Bobby assailed Dixie Democrats for having blocked so-called progressive legislation at the special session, identifying Senator Harry F. Byrd, Finance Committee Chairman, and Congressman Smith, Rules Committee Chairman, both Virginians, as the chief culprits.

Bobby also sailed into Jackie Robinson for having dared to question his

---

[6] Bobby Kennedy may have been Nixon's secret weapon, but the Republican candidate did not use it. Nor did Nixon ever refer to Joseph P. Kennedy. As he explained, "The decision not to drag Kennedy's father and other members of his family into the campaign was one for which I take sole responsibility and for which I have no regrets. Throughout my political career, I have always held that a candidate's public record should be exposed and attacked in as hard-hitting a fashion as possible. But his personal life and that of his family are not fair subjects for discussion unless they somehow bear directly on his qualifications for office.

"I put this policy into practice at the time of the Republican National Convention, and I stuck to it throughout the campaign. At the time of the Convention, some of my Chicago supporters reported to me that the Merchandise Mart—which is owned by Kennedy's father and his brother-in-law Sargent Shriver, now head of the Peace Corps— hired no Negroes at anything above the very lowest, most menial level. They reported that there was great resentment over this policy in the Negro community of Chicago. And they suggested that this issue be dramatized during the Convention by means of a mass-picketing demonstration at the Mart. I rejected the proposal on the ground that I was running against Jack Kennedy, not against his father and brother-in-law."

brother's commitment to civil rights. He had brought a dossier containing what the FBI would call "raw"—unevaluated—materials on the former baseball star. And Bobby used these materials to make a sharp personal attack on Robinson.

As the *pièce de résistance,* Bobby pulled still another document from the dossier and charged that the owner of Chock Full o' Nuts, a chain of refreshment shops of which Robinson was personnel director, had always supported Republicans and "is a great booster of Mr. Nixon."

Robinson's reply was scorching. "If the younger Kennedy is going to resort to lies, then I can see what kind of campaign this is going to be. I don't see where my company has anything at all to do with his brother's having had breakfast with the head of the White Citizens Councils and the racist Governor of Alabama."

On the labor relations matter, Robinson said: "This is something that happened in 1957 and the charges were brought up by the head of a union local who has since been indicted for alleged illegal activities."

Robinson said that his employer was a registered member of the Liberal party who, during the primaries, had made a $5,000 contribution to Hubert Humphrey.

"To me," Robinson added, "the most revealing part of the whole attack was Robert Kennedy's reference to 18 million Negro Americans as 'his Negroes'—meaning Jackie Robinson's. Apparently young Bobby hasn't heard that the Emancipation Proclamation was signed 97 years ago. I don't run any plantation and I suggest to Kennedy that he stop acting as if he did."

Bobby Kennedy's criticism of Southern Congressmen aroused anger among Dixie Democrats. So much so, in fact, that Jack Kennedy did an uncharacteristic thing—he apologized for his brother's behavior. The story was told by Roulhac Hamilton, Washington correspondent, in the September 4, 1960, issue of the *Charleston* (S.C.) *News and Courier:*

"Last Tuesday South Carolina and Florida Democratic leaders met separately with Senator Kennedy. Both groups brought up the New York radiocast.

"Senator Kennedy told the two Southern groups that his brother's remarks were 'unfortunate.' The senator was quoted as saying Robert was 'young and very hot-headed.' He implied he already had had words with Robert about the outburst. And he promised the Southerners he would try to see that it didn't happen again.

"But the Southerners wanted more. They extracted from the Democratic presidential nominee a promise to give them what they wanted: A flat agreement that Bobby Kennedy would (1) keep his hands absolutely off the Florida and South Carolina campaigns for the national Democratic ticket, (2) stay out of the two states, and (3) quit attacking publicly state political leaders who might happen to disagree with him or with the senator.

"As far as can be learned here, it was the first time Senator Kennedy had said to anybody that his brother's attitude toward opponents of the Kennedy presidential aspirations might be wrong. It certainly was the first time the Senator had apologized to anybody, except possibly privately, for the conduct of the former chief counsel of the Senate Labor Rackets Investigating Committee."

As far as Kennedy was concerned, nothing was too good for the South when votes were at stake.

In fact, he agreed to a campaign entirely different from that conducted in other parts of the country. No effort would be made, for example, to defend the Democratic platform. The objective was to ignore the platform. Should discussion be unavoidable, the line was this: The Southern leaders never accepted that platform. While any Convention could write a platform, no Convention could make it law. Only Congress could do that—and, no matter what happened in November, the South would still have power in Congress.

This strategic approach was worked out by Florida's Senator Smathers, whom Kennedy and Johnson had named as campaign manager of the Southern and border states. True, Smathers, one of Jack's closest friends, had voted against all of Kennedy's pet projects in the special session. But George spoke very highly of Kennedy's "leadership," even when disregarding it.

According to William S. White, the heart of the Smathers' plan contemplated these things:

A policy of non-interference in the South by Northern Democrats.

A minimum of talk about the Democratic presidential candidate and a maximum of talk about the South's old allegiance to the Democratic party as a collective institution.

No harsh attacks on bolters or potential bolters on the theory that the more such people are pushed the more they will broaden the bolt by soliciting other resentful Democrats.

Unlike the North, in Dixie the campaign would be completely geared into the traditional organizations of established Southern leaders—Governors, Senators, legislators, sheriffs, and so on.

Smathers traveled throughout the South, accusing Vice President Nixon of having once held an honorary membership in the National Association for the Advancement of Colored People. Up North, meanwhile, Harlem's Adam Clayton Powell was accusing Nixon of having failed to repudiate an endorsement of the Florida Ku Klux Klan.

As usual, the Kennedy camp was having it both ways.

The Kennedys were also having it both ways on Lyndon Johnson. They were all for him in the South. Up North, they acted as if they had never heard of him.

"While Kennedy campaigns in the Pacific Northwest the almost unmentioned man is his running mate, Lyndon B. Johnson," reported the AP's Jack Bell from Eugene, Oregon, September 7. "The voters of Washington, Oregon and Idaho—as well as those in Maine, Alaska and Michigan—who have heard the Massachusetts Senator speak in the last five days could be excused if they thought Kennedy was running alone on the Democratic ticket."

This was in sharp contrast to the tactics of his GOP rival. At almost every opportunity, Nixon brought up the name of his running mate, Henry Cabot Lodge, praising Lodge's accomplishments as United Nations Ambassador.

"It seems rather obvious," reported Bell, "that the Democratic high command has decided that the less emphasis placed on Johnson in civil rights-conscious states the better their ticket is likely to fare. . . . Nearly everywhere on his current campaign trips the signs and literature have featured Kennedy and haven't mentioned Johnson. "There was a stir in the press when a reporter discovered an 'L.B.J.' sign in the crowd and remarked it was the first he had seen in days."

The effort to downgrade Lyndon Johnson went into high gear.

Arthur Schlesinger Jr., his faith restored in Kennedy, told a New York news conference on September 26 that "Johnson has dropped out of the campaign, but it does not really matter." Moreover, the Harvard historian said, the Vice Presidential candidate had very little voice in the national campaign. "No one hears from him any more, but it doesn't make much difference," he said, adding he did not believe Presidential candidates win or lose on the strength of their running mates.

But history failed Schlesinger. As it turned out, Johnson made all the difference for Kennedy.

If Johnson was annoyed by such discourtesies, he never said so. He was having enough troubles without adding to them. On September 18, the *New York Post* reported that "Johnson has been ducking on civil rights. Last weekend in New York City, three reporters sought unsuccessfully for four hours for comment on Rodman Rockefeller's suggestion that he ought not leave town without explaining why he voted to table GOP civil rights bills last summer. From a private reception, the candidate sent out word that he had already discussed the subject at a press conference earlier that day.

"When this was disputed—since the press conference had been cut short at the first mention of civil rights—a speech writer promised to get some kind of statement. The statement never materialized. Johnson thereby achieved his apparent purpose: no statement, no story."

L.B.J. had another bad day in Phoenix, Arizona, which was not the best place to trot out the Democrats' 1960 platform. When Lyndon got up to speak in Goldwater-land, he sounded, according to the *Washington Post,* "like a Republican going after the Roosevelt and Truman Administrations." He accused the Eisenhower Administration of being the costliest in nondefense spending of any administration in history (which begged the fact that Johnson's party was planning to spend at least twice as much). Arizona has a right-to-work law it's rather proud of, and a reporter asked Lyndon whether he supported his party platform's plank for repeal of such laws.

Well, yes, said L.B.J.—but (did he wink at his audience?), "there are a lot of things said in party platforms that are not realized." As a matter of fact, he continued, as regards labor, the 1960 platform was more conservative than previous platforms, as witness its failure to call for repeal of the Taft-Hartley law.

Then, in evident desperation, he demanded, "Tell me one thing that Dick Nixon or Henry Cabot Lodge have *ever* done for the State of Arizona!"

The next day, in Las Vegas, Johnson assailed the Republicans as a party of "two faces." One face, in the North, was that of Governor Rockefeller "who rewrites the Republican platform" to appeal to Liberals. The other, in the South, was that of Senator Goldwater assuring the people of conservative government.

This was sheer hypocrisy and Lyndon Johnson, of course, was firmly opposed to hypocrisy.

Goldwater, campaigning for the Nixon-Lodge ticket, was scoring heavily among Southern audiences with barbs directed at Johnson's forthright ambivalence toward the 1960 Los Angeles platform.

"Lyndon has always been acrobatically inclined," smiled Goldwater.

Johnson countered with, "They can dress him in a frock coat, a string tie, and put a mint julep in each hand, and hang a Confederate flag on him and we'll still know him."

Goldwater raised a question dealing with Johnson's dual candidacy—his bid for both the Vice Presidency and a third term as Senator from Texas. In April 1959 the Texas legislature had passed a special bill permitting Lyndon to run for both jobs.

Goldwater's question was: Which platform was Johnson running on—the ultra-Liberal national platform adopted at Los Angeles or the conservative platform adopted by his party's state convention in Texas?

The documents were quite dissimilar. In fact, on basic issues—civil rights, labor policy, school aid, internationalism and taxation—the Texas platform was virtually a point-by-point repudiation of the Los Angeles platform. The Texans deplored "the growing concentration of power in the central government and socialistic proposals which could rob our people of their initiative and freedom." They called for law enforcement "to protect private property from unlawful boycotts, forcible entries or physical occupation" (meaning Negro sit-ins); backed the state's right-to-work law; called for retention of the Connally Reservation; supported the oil depletion tax allowance; and demanded "strict adherence to all state laws guaranteeing local determination in the operation of the public schools."

Johnson also ran on a third platform. He went to New York to "accept" the nomination of the Liberal party, an organization which prior to Los Angeles had placed the Texan in a separate category among Democratic hopefuls—"unacceptable."

Now the Liberal party said Johnson was eminently acceptable. The group, which accounts for half a million votes in the Empire State, hadn't much choice. Johnson hadn't much choice either. Struggling for some point in common, the Texan remarked that "you are against the sweatshop and I am against the sweatshop."

Perhaps, as the *New York World-Telegram & Sun* suggested, if he had thought a little harder, he could also have "risked opposition to depressions, pulmonary tuberculosis and hurricanes." Johnson, the newspaper noted, "admitted he wasn't familiar with the details of the Liberal party platform, and that probably was just as well. Sometimes a man has to stick out his neck, but there's no point to stretching it."

The Democratic and Liberal platforms called for all-out war on "loopholes in the tax laws" which, most observers assumed, referred to "depletion allowances" granted oil and mine operators, many of whom were Texans; while the Texas platform declared all-out war against any miserable damn-Yankees who wanted to monkey with those laws.

Johnson was asked where he stood on the matter in a TV panel interview on October 2. In effect, he said he was opposed to reducing the depletion allowances on oil. He insisted that the Los Angeles platform "doesn't mention oil in any respect" but referred to 105 other depletion allowances. Moreover, he claimed it was the Republicans—led by Delaware's Senator John J. Williams—who were seeking to reduce the depletion allowance.

Johnson's defense of the oil interests shocked the *New York Post*. The *Post* was also dismayed by Johnson's equivocation on repeal of right-to-work laws. Johnson "adroitly stated that such a plank had appeared in every Democratic platform since 1948, as if to wink at those who feared that any platform plank should be taken seriously while he is around.

"Perhaps the cruellest cut Johnson administered to Kennedy came when he described him as a 'careful, prudent, cautious man.' These are hardly inspiring words; they are the ancient GOP clichés. If this is all Johnson has to offer, Kennedy will have to go it alone, and speak out even more firmly and resolutely on the fighting issues of the campaign. His heralded ally is more than ever an albatross."

The Kennedy strategy, from the start, had been to let Liberal spokesmen blow off steam and gradually get used to the idea of Lyndon Johnson. Then, when the campaign was really under way, they would be reminded of the awful choice: Nixon or us.

If this weren't enough, they were told that getting Johnson on the ticket was all part of a clever plot to remove him as Senate Majority Leader, a post where he could continue to obstruct their pet programs.[7]

---

[7] On August 4, 1962, White House correspondent Marianne Means reported that President Kennedy's "unexpected troubles with a balky Senate, despite its heavy Democratic majority," could be traced to the fact that Lyndon Johnson had been "promoted into oblivion." She added: "The basic reason the Senate cannot be counted on to rush through Kennedy bills is that the power has drifted from the Majority Leader to the 16 committee chairmen, who prefer to exercise their own independence, rather than bow to party unity."

The Johnson matter was apparently discussed when Kennedy paid a visit to the offices of the *New York Post*. The visit paid off. On October 17, the *Post* declared for Kennedy–Johnson, conceding that Kennedy "will be guilty on some days of the week of evasion, compromise and double-talk."

The front-page editorial, signed by publisher Dorothy Schiff and editor James Wechsler, predicted that "a decisive Kennedy victory would almost certainly expand the Democratic liberal bloc in both the Senate and the House. A decisive Nixon victory would almost certainly expand the right-wing Goldwater faction."

The "deadly bottleneck" to the passage of all sorts of legislative goodies, the Schiff-Wechsler manifesto contended, was that awful coalition of Southern Democrats and conservative Republicans. "Under Nixon, as under Eisenhower, that coalition is likely to flourish, with Lyndon Johnson retaining his power as Senate leader; under Kennedy, it may be finally challenged. Fearful as we were of Johnson's possible effect on the tone and substance of the Kennedy campaign, his replacement as Senate chieftain may finally enable liberal Democrats and Republicans to end the stalemate on civil rights."

Thus, *Post* readers were urged to vote for Lyndon Johnson for Vice President—a heartbeat away from the Presidency—in order to get rid of him in the Senate.

The *Post* editorial also noted "that over the years we have frequently criticized Mr. Kennedy for his evasion of the McCarthy issue." But it was an evasion "over which Kennedy has at least voiced a deeply troubled conscience."

Presumably he voiced his "deeply troubled conscience" in private conversation with Mrs. Schiff and Mr. Wechsler. *Newsweek,* on September 26, 1960, reported that Kennedy had told associates he had made a bad mistake in not taking a firm public stand against the late Senator McCarthy. "Had I known then that I was going to run for President," Kennedy asserted, "I would have gone on crutches to vote for censure."

"We have had the chance to get to know the man better," Mrs. Schiff and Wechsler added. ". . . We believe he exhibits vast capacity for growth and the potential for great leadership. . . . In opposing a pointless and dangerous over-commitment on Quemoy and Matsu, he has shown a great degree of political valor." Nixon, however, demonstrated "his essential political recklessness" in his attempt to depict "Kennedy's plea for sanity in the Quemoy-Matsu conflict as a symptom of craven 'appeasement.' "

The question of United States policy toward the Chinese offshore islands emerged as one of the big issues of the 1960 campaign. How John F. Kennedy handled the issue, in retrospect, was more important than the issue itself. For it demonstrated Kennedy's inability to stand firm under political fire.

Only one reporter appeared to have understood that the sound and fury engendered by the Nixon-Kennedy dispute on Quemoy and Matsu would be dissipated by the actual test of events no matter who became President.

On October 15, 1960, Frank Conniff, National Editor of the Hearst Newspapers, wrote: "I will make the following bet with any of [Kennedy's] partisans or any member of his entourage: American policy toward the off-shore islands will be largely the same a year from today as it is at the moment." And, as it turned out, Conniff was proved absolutely right.

Kennedy had argued for several years that the United States should "make decisions now about vacating Quemoy and Matsu, which are indefensible and which provide a needless irritant that could drag us into a struggle with Red China. . . ."

The matter had come before the Senate in January 1955, when Kennedy was recuperating from his back operations. The Formosa Resolution, which was adopted with Lyndon Johnson's backing, permitted the President to defend Quemoy and Matsu if an attack on these islands was believed to be part of an attack on Formosa. Senator Herbert Lehman tried to get the bill amended to limit the authority of the President to the defense of Formosa and the Pescadores, thus excluding Quemoy and Matsu. The Lehman amendment was defeated 74–13. Interestingly, Johnson voted against the amendment, but Senator Kennedy was announced as paired in favor.[8]

Thus, Kennedy was consistent when he told a National Press Club audience on January 14, 1960, that the United States should "make it clear that we should not engage in the defense" of Quemoy and Matsu. "I think the line ought to be drawn clearly at the island of Formosa," he said, adding: "If a military action occurred we would not then be involved in it."

The issue was thrust into the Presidential campaign on October 1, 1960, when NBC's Chet Huntley asked the Democratic candidate whether he agreed with the "present policy with which it seems to me we are committed now to the defense of the tiny islands off the coast of China, Quemoy and Matsu?"

"I have always thought that was an unwise place to draw the line," Kennedy replied. ". . . We should draw the line very exactly and precisely, so that any aggressor knows that if he moves into this area that it would mean war. . . . Under the Eisenhower doctrine, we have stated we would defend Quemoy and Matsu if it was part of an attack on the island of Formosa. How are we going to make that judgment? On what basis? Quemoy and Matsu are not essential to the defense of Formosa. . . ."

What Kennedy appeared to be saying, with unusual precision, was that if elected President his policy would be to eliminate the islands from the defense pattern in the Taiwan Straits.

In his second so-called Great Debate with Richard Nixon on October 7, Kennedy was asked whether "a pullback from those islands" could not be

---

[8] This was the period in which Kennedy said he was too ill to make known his position in regard to the censure of Senator Joe McCarthy.

interpreted as appeasement. Kennedy denied any such interpretation. He said he believed "strongly" in the defense of Formosa. And he added:

"We have never said flatly that we will defend Quemoy and Matsu if it's attacked. We say we will defend it, if it's a part of a general attack on Formosa but it's extremely difficult to make that judgment. . . . I believe that if you're going to get into war for the defense of Formosa it ought to be on a clearly defined line. . . . To leave this rather in the air—that we will defend it under some conditions but not under others—I think is a mistake. . . . It's been my judgment ever since 1954 that our line should be drawn around Formosa."

Nixon, in replying, noted the analogy to Korea, where another "line" had been drawn and Communist aggression had followed almost immediately. And he added: "These two islands are in the area of freedom. . . . We should not force our Nationalist allies to get off of them and give them to the Communists. If we do that, we start a chain reaction because the Communists . . . are after Formosa. . . . This is the same kind of woolly thinking that led to disaster for America in Korea. I am against it. I would never tolerate it as President of the United States and I will hope that Senator Kennedy will change his mind if he should be elected."

Three days later, Kennedy spoke scornfully of Nixon's position: "He wants us to be committed to the defense of every rock and island around the world but is unwilling to admit that this may involve American boys in an unnecessary or futile war, as he sought to have us involved in Indochina in 1954."

The truth was that Nixon had never denied the risks inherent in a no-retreat policy vis-à-vis Red China. Nor did he ever advocate defending every rock and island around the world even at the risk of a "futile war." Moreover, Quemoy and Matsu were not "rocks." Quemoy alone is 70 square miles in territorial extent, with some 125,000 Free Chinese inhabitants. As for the islands being "strategically indefensible," Quemoy and Matsu were still free, although the Chinese Reds began threatening them—and Formosa—in 1949.

Nixon appeared to be scoring on the issue. If the Chinese offshore islands were to be abandoned because they were "strategically indefensible," the Republican candidate asked, then what about *onshore* areas of freedom such as Hong Kong and Berlin? In the Formosa Straits, the biggest danger to peace was not the fate of a couple of islands, Nixon argued, but the cocky bellicosity demonstrated by a regime which is daily proclaiming the United States is a paper tiger and daily shouting—with relish—about the inevitability of war. A retreat anywhere to such a nation would be bad enough. But to do so on the grounds that an area is militarily exposed would open the door to retreat anywhere the same situation obtains. Today Quemoy. Tomorrow Berlin.

Kennedy, incapable of defending himself against the Nixon onslaught, called his rival "trigger-happy," willing to chance a nuclear war over these "indefensible islands." Needless to say, the Republicans did not like this remark. It gave them the opportunity to recall that several Democratic Presidents had been elected after promising to keep the United States out of war —notably Wilson in 1916 and Roosevelt in 1940.

Kennedy, however, kept asserting we should not defend Quemoy and Matsu. He quoted Admiral Yarnell, former commander of the U.S. Asiatic Fleet as having asserted that "these islands are not worth the bones of a single American."

The quote apparently had been taken from a 1955 symposium conducted by the *Manchester* (N.H.) *Union Leader,* in which the Admiral, then eighty years old and retired from the Navy before World War II, was asked along with other military leaders, about Quemoy-Matsu. Twelve other military men, including General James Van Fleet, Admiral Arthur Radford, General Claire Chennault, Lieutenant General George E. Stratemeyer, Admiral Louis Denfeld, and Admiral William H. Stanley, backed the Eisenhower-Nixon position on the islands—that they could be important to the defense of Formosa and should not be surrendered.

Kennedy did not refer to the other quotations. Nor did he explain that Admiral Yarnell, who died in 1959, had made the observation in 1955.

Kennedy also quoted Admiral Raymond A. Spruance as having once said the islands shouldn't be defended. The retired Admiral had made such a statement in 1955, but he didn't feel that way in 1960.

"I'm sorry it has been injected into the campaign," the Admiral told newsmen. "The less said about it the better." A former United States Ambassador to the Philippines, Spruance thought it "would be a mistake to try to convince Chiang Kai-shek to back off. Chiang has never had any illusions about getting along with the Communists. You have to admire him for that."

Kennedy's extraordinary reliance on carefully selected quotations to prove a point was nowhere better demonstrated than in his third television encounter with Nixon on October 13. Kennedy quoted a single sentence from an October 1958 letter that President Eisenhower had sent to Senator Theodore Green: "Neither you nor any other American need feel the U.S. will be involved in military hostilities merely in the defense of Quemoy and Matsu." Then Kennedy said:

"Now that is the issue. I believe we must meet our commitment to Formosa. I support it in the Pescadores Islands. That is the present American position. The treaty does not include [Quemoy and Matsu]."

President Eisenhower then got into the act. Press Secretary James Hagerty, distributing copies of the original letter, said the President "believes that to correctly state his position requires reading the entire letter, not just one sentence."

Any objective reading of the entire letter would indicate that Kennedy had misunderstood its meaning. Mr. Eisenhower had reassured Senator

Green that he would "scrupulously observe" the limitation not to order the military defense of Quemoy and Matsu unless it was clear that attacks upon the offshore islands were part of an attack on Formosa.

However, the President cited the Chinese Reds as authority for the belief that seizure of the islands would "open the way for them to take Formosa and the Pescadores."

"I cannot dismiss these boastings as mere bluff," he added.

Nor was Kennedy's case helped by a telegram to Secretary of State Herter from William vanden Heuvel, Democratic candidate for Congress in Manhattan, asking about reported negotiations for withdrawal of Chinese Nationalist forces from the beleaguered islands. Kennedy joined in that query.

"There is a report—and I demand to know whether it is true—that the Administration has begun secret negotiations for withdrawal of troops from the two islands," Kennedy said on October 12. "I repeat my stand—those islands are strategically indefensible. . . . They jeopardize Formosa. . . . The position taken by Mr. Nixon is the road to irresponsibility."

The State Department flatly denied that any such negotiations were in progress.

Even as Kennedy was making a long speech on the subject in New York, Governor Rockefeller leaped into the melee by asserting that Kennedy's advocacy of surrender of the islands had placed him "in an extremely difficult position to negotiate with Red China should he be elected President."

And from the Democratic side, Senator Lausche of Ohio, who had only that week come out for Kennedy, publicly approved Richard Nixon's position on the Quemoy-Matsu argument. And Harry Truman, campaigning for his new-found friend, refused to comment publicly on Kennedy's call for abandoning Quemoy and Matsu. In the past, of course, Mr. Truman had unequivocally supported the defense of the offshore islands. As the former President had stated in October 1958: "The islands are symbols, if not steps, to test our policy of firmness and our determination to resist—with force if necessary—the Communist technique of piecemeal conquest."

The *New York Times* reported from Hong Kong that Kennedy's position had caused dismay among top officials there. "Senator Kennedy, these analysts say, has shown his hand in a game where the stakes are too high for incaution, and bluff is sometimes the best weapon. In their opinion, President Eisenhower showed more astuteness by declining to indicate what action the U.S. would take if the Chinese Communists tried to grab Quemoy and Matsu." They described his advocacy of a new defense line in the Formosa Straits as "a tactical blunder."

Nixon, by this time, was slashing away at his opponent. He contended that the foreign policy issue was now clear. Senator Kennedy talked much of military strength, he said, but of what use is strength if the enemy knows you will shrink from using it? What Senator Kennedy advocated was a policy of weakness and of hope that appeasement would placate the enemy. Any realistic student of history, Nixon observed, knows that dictatorships are never satisfied.

Meanwhile, Samuel Lubell, whose personal research into voter opinion had proved highly accurate, reported that more people agreed with Nixon than with Kennedy on the basic question of giving ground to the Communists without a struggle. In fact, Lubell reported, "Nixon's chances of squeezing through to victory have been boosted significantly by his dispute with Kennedy over the offshore islands. . . ." Nixon, finally able to get his rival in his sights, was clearly determined to press the advantage.

Feeling the tide of political opinion was running against him, Kennedy took a run-out powder and called upon his rival to quit talking about Quemoy and Matsu and "return to the real issues of the campaign." Kennedy now claimed he had supported President Eisenhower's position on the two islands since 1955.

Having raised the issue, and having had it boomerang in his face, Kennedy suddenly discovered that continued discussion of Quemoy and Matsu would only aid the Communist enemy and would not be in the best interests of the foreign policy bipartisanship he had rarely before advocated. All of a sudden, too, he became an advocate of national unity. To Kennedy, national unity becomes imperative whenever necessary to get him out of a jam. His previous views on national unity in regard to Quemoy and Matsu had been expressed in Tulsa, Oklahoma, on September 16, 1959: ". . . The repeated calls for national unity, the repeated assertions that such unity exists, the attempt by Mr. Nixon to silence those who would admit that public opinion is negative, all this cannot and should not conceal the present actual disunity over our policy in the Formosa Strait—a disunity which is not limited to any one party, but which finds critics within the defense establishment itself, within both parties, and among all Americans. I might mention in this regard, in making my present position clear, that I was one of fourteen Senators in 1955 who supported an amendment to the Congressional resolution sought by the President—an amendment which would have specifically excluded Quemoy and Matsu from its jurisdiction."

Desperately seeking to close debate on Quemoy–Matsu, he now insisted that Nixon did not understand the Eisenhower policy.

As Ernest K. Lindley observed in *Newsweek,* Nixon "sat in the National Security Council when what to do about Quemoy and Matsu was under consideration at various times. Many in Washington know from personal conversations with him over the years his familiarity with this problem."

But Kennedy contended it was Nixon, not he, who was in disagreement with President Eisenhower. "I have always been in agreement with the President's policy toward Quemoy and Matsu," he told a "Meet the Press" panel on October 16 with a straight face. "I agree with the President and the Administration, so that, I think—it is my hope, as I would not want any issue to endanger the security of the United States, I would certainly feel that in the tradition of bipartisanship no area in the field of foreign policy should be used for political advantage. If we both agree with the President, in my opinion, the matter is then closed."

QUESTION: Senator, you said yesterday, "Let the debate return now to the real issues of the campaign." Yet today you have continued to discuss Mr. Nixon's attitude on the—

KENNEDY: Because last night I said I was prepared to close, in my official statement. Then last night after he said he supported the President, in his speech given last night, in his release, he attacked me for my position on these islands and said that I was working against the interest of the country and all kinds of statements. I don't know what the issue now is, providing he supports the President's position; so do I, but I think that is an entirely different position than he took a week ago. In my opinion if we are both in support of the President and there are great issues which disturb our country, it would seem to me that I would be prepared to move on to the discussion of those issues. . . . As long as he will support the President and I do, I think that in the interests of bipartisanship I would not endanger the situation in that area by attempting to drag it into a political campaign. That is my view, and I am prepared to rest on it and make this the last word.

"If Senator Kennedy, as he now claims, really supports the Administration position," commented the *Los Angeles Times,* "then certainly some more explanation of his past statements should be forthcoming. He has left the impression with some sensitive Americans that he would appease the Communists by calling off the Nationalists and letting the islands go by default."

And the *Chicago Daily News* observed that "one is entitled to doubt that Kennedy would have tried to drop the issue so fast had he believed it was working in his favor. The indications are that, having raised the issue in the first place, he discovered he had touched the wrong side of a sensitive nerve."

Nixon's polls indicated that the voters generally, Democrats as well as Republicans, overwhelmingly supported his position on the issue. As he later wrote in his book, *Six Crises,* "Kennedy apparently was receiving similar reports from his own surveys. Shortly after the third debate, at any rate, Fred Seaton received a curious message from Washington. Chester Bowles . . . now one of Kennedy's top foreign policy advisers, had called on Secretary of State Chris Herter at the latter's Georgetown home. The purpose of the call was to indicate Kennedy's concern over the way the Quemoy-Matsu debate was developing. Kennedy, according to Bowles, did not want to give the impression during the campaign that the American people were divided in their support of the Eisenhower Administration's firm stand against Communist aggression. Kennedy had long disagreed with the Eisenhower-Dulles policy on Quemoy-Matsu—a disagreement that went back at least to the Senate debate of January 1955 over the so-called Formosa Resolution and his support of the Lehman-Morse amendment. . . . But now, Bowles went on, the issue had been raised in the campaign by questions during the debates and not on Kennedy's own initiative. He was prepared under the circumstances to modify his position so that there would be no appearance of opposing Eisenhower on this issue and so that we could present a united front to the Communists.

"I asked Seaton what he thought the real purpose of this message might be. His reaction was that Bowles and Kennedy—if Kennedy was aware of what Bowles had done—were using this device for the purpose of getting me to lay off on an issue that was becoming increasingly unpopular for Kennedy. My own reaction was that if Kennedy did modify his position, I would have no choice but to drop the issue—except for continuing to point to the whole 'shoot first, think later' approach as indicative of his lack of experience in the foreign policy area. This was the course of action I eventually followed. While I recognized that I had Kennedy over the barrel on an issue which was turning sour for him, I believed that he had a right to change his mind. It was important that the Chinese Communists be given no encouragement to start trouble in the Formosa Straits because of a hassle in the American presidential campaign."

But Kennedy had another foreign policy issue which was just "t'rrific"—Cuba. Originally Kennedy and other Democratic leaders had brushed Cuba aside as a campaign issue, saying it was one of the few places where Eisenhower had been following the correct course. For the most part, the Democrats stuck to generalized and mainly intellectual criticisms of the handling of foreign policy. Then, William S. White wrote on September 14, Lyndon Johnson "began to go beyond the generalities and to hammer at what has happened in Cuba. . . . The Democrats believe they have got hold of something—the charge that a Republican administration permitted a pro-Communist bridgehead to rise within 90 miles of the American coastline—which well might hit the Republicans with violent impact in November."

The pollsters' findings confirmed the feeling that Americans, by and large, were deeply troubled by the spectacle of a Communist dictatorship sitting, as the Democratic orators put it, "just 90 miles off our coast."

Kennedy picked up the theme, adding his own embellishments.

"I wasn't the Vice President who presided over the Communization of Cuba," he snapped in Jacksonville, Florida.

"I'm not impressed with those who say they stood up to Khrushchev when Castro has defied them 90 miles away," he said at Evansville, Indiana.

Kennedy made a major address on Cuba in Cincinnati on October 6. He charged that Nixon had been in Cuba in 1955, but "could not see then what should have been obvious . . . and as a result the Communists took over Cuba with virtually no opposition from the United States."

Nixon had been in Havana for a few days in 1955—a year before Fidel Castro landed in Cuba. But Kennedy himself had been there a number of times in 1957—and even as late as January 1958—to visit his good friend and Palm Beach neighbor, Ambassador Earl E. T. Smith, our man in Havana from June 1957 to the time of Fidel Castro's takeover in January 1959.

Yet, there is nothing on the record to indicate that Kennedy ever foresaw or ever warned about the dangers of Communism in Cuba. In fact, there is nothing in the record to indicate he ever showed the slightest interest in Cuban affairs, despite the fact he was a member of the Senate Foreign Relations Committee. His visits to Havana during the period of the Castro revolution were purely social—night clubs, golfing, and sailing. In April 1960, on "Face the Nation," he said he had supported the Eisenhower policy toward Cuba, "with which I agree." And in May, he said in another TV interview that "for the present, I support the Administration" even though "the situation in Cuba . . . continues to deteriorate." The only previous comments he had made on Castro appeared in his book *The Strategy of Peace,* published not in 1955 but in 1960. After comparing the Castro revolution to the American revolution, Kennedy observed:

"Fidel Castro is part of the legacy of [Simón] Bolívar [the great Latin American liberator] who led his men over the Andes Mountains, vowing 'war to the death' against Spanish rule, saying, 'Where a goat can pass, so can an army.' Castro is also part of the frustration of that earlier revolution which won its war against Spain but left largely untouched the indigenous feudal order. 'To serve a revolution is to plow the sea,' Bolivar said in despair as he lived to see the failure of his efforts at social reform.

"Whether Castro would have taken a more rational course after his victory had the United States Government not backed the dictator Batista so long and so uncritically, and had it given the fiery young rebel a warmer welcome in his hour of triumph, especially on his trip to this country, we cannot be sure."

But we can be sure of one thing: anyone who in 1960 was still describing Castro as a "fiery young rebel" was hardly qualified to condemn Nixon for supposedly failing in 1955 to see what should have been obvious.

"And what was it, really, that was obvious before Castro came to power?" asked the *Washington Star.* "To us at least, it is far from obvious that a warmer welcome to Castro would have diverted him from his Communist course, or that greater American economic aid to the Cubans would have prevented the Castro dictatorship. On these points, we think, Senator Kennedy has, or had, his head in the clouds."

What was obvious, too, at the time Kennedy was visiting Havana was that a choice had to be made between trying to uphold Batista or accepting the risk that Castro would come to power. As Kennedy friend Ambassador Smith later observed, "We helped to overthrow the Batista dictatorship which was pro-American only to install the Castro dictatorship which is pro-Russian."

During 1960 Kennedy made these contradictory statements: While he agreed with the Eisenhower policy on Cuba, he believed "Cuba is gone." And while "I realize that it will always be a cardinal tenet of American foreign policy not to intervene in the internal affairs of other nations—and that is particularly true in Latin America," he also believed that the United States should have pressured Batista into "free elections." (The fact was that an election was held in Cuba in 1958, mainly at United States insistence, but Fidel Castro insisted that the people boycott it.)

In his Cincinnati speech, Kennedy blamed the Eisenhower Administration for supporting Batista and, at the same time, for failing to heed warnings of former Ambassadors Gardner and Smith "that Communism was a moving force in the Castro leadership." This, of course, was a prime example of *Kennedyese*—trying to have it both ways.

Kennedy's arguments seemed to be a curious blend of Chester Bowlesian uplift and Senator Tom Dodd's more practical hard-headed anti-Communism. Alluding to comments by Senator Dodd and other members of the Senate Internal Security Subcommittee that had probed the Cuban situation, Kennedy said:

"It is not enough to blame it on unknown State Department personnel. Major policy on issues such as Cuban security is made at the highest levels— in the National Security Council and elsewhere—and it is the party in power which must accept full responsibility for the Cuban disaster."

According to Kennedy, it was the United States failure to give Cuba sufficient economic aid that turned the people against us, paving the way for conversion of Cuba to "Communism's first Caribbean base." Kennedy said that (1) "We refused to help Cuba meet its desperate need for economic progress" and (2) "We used the influence of our government to advance the interests and increase the profits of the private American companies which dominate the island's economy." And he spoke of a gold telephone which had been presented to Batista by "the American-owned Cuban Telephone Company . . . as an expression of gratitude for the excessive telephone rate increase which the Cuban dictator had granted at the urging of our government."

At this point, at least one correspondent fully expected him to cry out, "Cuba sí, Yanqui no!"

Actually, Cuba had one of the highest standards of living in the Caribbean. And as Ambassador Smith testified, "The year 1957 was the best economic year that Cuba ever had." Yet Fidel Castro won.

"The Batista Government was overthrown because of the corruption, disintegration from within," Mr. Smith testified on August 30, 1960. "The Castro forces themselves never won a military victory. The best military victory they ever won was through capturing Cuban guardhouses and military skirmishes. . . ."

In effect, Kennedy had adopted the Castro line, which was that the United States had been robbing the Cuban people blind. The fact was that

Cuba long enjoyed a tremendous annual subsidy by means of the special high price paid for its sugar crops. Moreover, United States investors helped the Caribbean republic raise its standard of living.

Yet, Kennedy seemed to be promoting a new doctrine: That "to advance the interests and increase the profits" of private American companies in Cuba was somehow wrong. It was odd, indeed, to hear an American Presidential candidate advance the notion that a nation should not protect the interests of its nationals abroad.

There was always the possibility, of course, that in the heat of the campaign Kennedy did not have enough time to study the implications of the speech, which had been handed him by Ted Sorensen.

Another disturbing element in Kennedy's views was that he appeared to be blaming the United States Government for not curtailing United States private investments in Cuba and concentrating on economic aid. Whether Kennedy was aware of it or not, he was using the same arguments Castro was making for expropriating American-owned companies in Cuba.

"From now until election," commented the *Chicago Daily News,* "a good deal of disgusting nonsense will be uttered by many candidates of both parties, but there is not much reason to expect anything worse than Senator Kennedy's speech in Cincinnati. Everything that's now wrong in Cuba is the Republican Administration's fault, Senator Kennedy says. We supported Batista and protected American investments too long, he says. The implication is that we should have done something (Kennedy doesn't say what) to throw Batista out long ago, and put somebody in power (maybe Castro himself) who would have divided American property among the people before Castro actually got around to it.

"How we were to accomplish Batista's downfall without sending in the Marines he does not explain. Perhaps he thinks we should. have marched in and done the job by force. We don't believe for a minute that Kennedy, had he been President, would have done any of those things. Kennedy has been in public life a good long while, as he is fond of pointing out. We can find no record that he advocated doing any of these things—or anything at all—at any time when (by his schedule) it was 'time' to do them."

At no point in his Cincinnati speech did Kennedy say what *he* would have done about the situation in Cuba, its poverty, or its "exploding population," as he termed it. But he did promise, if elected, to go back to Franklin Roosevelt's "Good Neighbor" policy. What Kennedy apparently did not realize was that support of pro-American dictators like Trujillo and Batista was a cardinal tenet of the so-called "Good Neighbor" policy. "He may be an S.O.B.," F.D.R. once said of a Latin American dictator, "but he's *our* S.O.B."[9]

---

[9] Generalissimo Rafael Trujillo's radio station in the Dominican Republic endorsed Kennedy for President. In a broadcast over La Voz Dominicana, the late dictator's personal network in Ciudad Trujillo, Kennedy was described as "a dynamic, angry young

The curious thing about all this was that Richard Nixon had long been urging a stronger policy, within the Eisenhower Administration, against Castro. Back in April 1959, when Castro visited Washington, Nixon had a three-hour conference with him. The Vice President then prepared a confidential memorandum stating flatly that he was convinced Castro was "either incredibly naive about Communism or under Communist discipline" and that the United States would have to treat him and deal with him accordingly— with no further illusions about "fiery rebels" in the "tradition of Bolívar." Copies of the memorandum went to the CIA, the State Department, and the White House.

At first the memorandum received a lukewarm reception. Trying to "get along with" and "understand" Castro continued to be the State Department line. "Early in 1960," Nixon later wrote, "the position I had been advocating for nine months finally prevailed, and the CIA was given instructions to provide arms, ammunition and training for Cubans who had fled the Castro regime and were now in exile in the United States and various Latin American countries. The program had been in operation for six months before the 1960 campaign got under way. It was a program, however, that I could say not one word about. The operation was covert. Under no circumstances could it be disclosed or even alluded to. Consequently, under Kennedy's attacks and his new demands for 'militant' policies, I was in the position of a fighter with one hand tied behind his back. I knew we had a program under way to deal with Castro, but I could not even hint at its existence, much less spell it out."

Was John F. Kennedy aware of the CIA's covert operation aimed at getting rid of the Castro regime?

"Suffice it to say at this point that neither Vice President Nixon nor Senator Kennedy were wholly unaware of the CIA's efforts," reported Tad Szulc of the *New York Times* and Karl E. Meyer of the *Washington Post*. "Knowledge of this lends a revealing retrospective dimension to what both men said during the campaign."[10]

On October 19, in a speech before the American Legion in Miami, Nixon called for a policy of all-out "quarantine"—economic, political and diplomatic—of the Castro regime. The time for patience was over, he added, and the United States must move vigorously—if possible, in full association with our sister American republics—to eradicate this "cancer" in our hemi-

---

man who likes to call a spade a spade, a fighting man whose words and actions could be very helpful to remedy the errors, ineptitude and weakness which have caused the United States to lose the world leadership which the last world war placed in its wealthy hands." Kennedy was particularly praised for being "aware of the dangerous Russian interference in the Caribbean area. . . ."

[10] *The Cuban Invasion,* by Tad Szulc and Karl E. Meyer. New York, Ballantine, 1962.

sphere. He announced the United States was planning "a number of steps" and "will very promptly take the strongest possible economic measures to counter the economic banditry being practiced by this regime against our country and our citizens."

The next day, Kennedy hit back with a statement that produced big black headlines:

KENNEDY ADVOCATES U.S. INTERVENTION IN CUBA

CALLS FOR AID TO REBEL FORCES IN CUBA

Kennedy's statement began: "Mr. Nixon's new Cuba policy is too little and too late. After ignoring the repeated warning of our Ambassadors that the Communists were about to take over Cuba—after standing helplessly by while the Russians established a new satellite only 90 miles from American shores—Mr. Nixon and the Republicans, after two years of inaction since Castro took power, made no attempt to make up for this incredible history of blunder, inaction, retreat and failure. . . ."

Then Kennedy called for what amounted to direct intervention in Cuba: "We must attempt to strengthen the non-Batista democratic anti-Castro forces in exile, and in Cuba itself, who offer eventual hope of overthrowing Castro. Thus far these fighters for freedom have had virtually no support from our Government."

The statement shocked Nixon. For, as columnist Ted Lewis later reported in the *New York Daily News,* "Nixon had been told earlier in 1960 by a source he considered unimpeachable that Kennedy was to be briefed throughout the campaign on everything going on in the foreign field—not just some things. It was his definite understanding that Kennedy would have exactly the same complete secret information he himself had."

As soon as Nixon read the story, he called in Fred Seaton, then Secretary of the Interior traveling with the Vice President. Nixon asked Seaton to call the White House on the security line to find out whether or not Kennedy had been briefed by CIA Director Allen Dulles on the surreptitious training of anti-Castro Cubans for the eventual purpose of supporting an invasion of Cuba itself. The briefings on this and other intelligence matters had been ordered by President Eisenhower so that Kennedy would be as informed as the Vice President.

In fact, Eisenhower considered these briefings so serious that he got into a three-day tug-of-war with Kennedy regarding them. This was over Kennedy's announcement that Adlai Stevenson and Chester Bowles would sit in for him during the CIA sessions. President Eisenhower objected, saying only the candidates themselves would be briefed. And he won the argument. "However," reported Larry G. Newman in the *New Bedford Standard-Times,* "there are many who believe that Senator Kennedy and his staff are just as happy that this is one battle they lost. The President's firm position that

Stevenson and Bowles could not and would not receive CIA briefings gives the Kennedy forces a chance to ease Stevenson out of the picture for the present, if not altogether. . . . So the President has taken Kennedy's staff off a rather hot spot early in the campaign."

Kennedy's first briefing by CIA representatives had been at Hyannis Port on July 23, 1960. Press reports characterized the briefing as a "nothing-with-held rundown" on the "two hot spots, Cuba and the Congo." The *New York Times* reported on July 24 that ". . . such secret information as was added to the Senator's fund of knowledge about world affairs will remain secret. But it provides guidance for his campaign utterances dealing with foreign policy and defense, and it puts him on the same footing as the Administration's candidate, presumably Vice President Nixon."

Within an hour after Nixon had instructed Seaton to call the White House, he reported back to the Vice President that, yes, the White House said that Kennedy had been fully briefed on the covert Cuban operation.

"For the first time and only time in the campaign," Nixon later said, "I got mad at Kennedy—personally. I understand and expect hard-hitting attacks in a campaign. But in this instance I thought that Kennedy, with full knowledge of the facts, was jeopardizing the security of a United States foreign policy operation. And my rage was greater because I could do nothing about it."

Nixon said he could not attack his opponent for making public and advocating a policy already under way, for this would disclose the "secret operation and completely destroy its effectiveness." To protect the planned operation, therefore, Nixon took a softer course than intervention—the "quarantine" of Cuba.

Nixon gave his version of the story in his book, *Six Crises*. Shortly before its publication, the White House denied Kennedy had violated security restrictions in the campaign, thus jeopardizing the planned invasion of Cuba. Press Secretary Pierre Salinger told newsmen on March 20, 1962 that ". . . the then Senator Kennedy was not told before the election of 1960 of the training of troops outside of Cuba or of any plans for 'supporting an invasion of Cuba.' Mr. Nixon's account is apparently based on a misunderstanding. Senator Kennedy received two briefings from Mr. Allen Dulles of the CIA. The first, on July 23, 1960, and the second on September 19, 1960. The two briefings covered an overall review of the world situation during which Cuba was mentioned. But Senator Kennedy was first informed of the operation to which Mr. Nixon refers in a briefing by Allen Dulles and Richard Bissell, of the CIA, given in Palm Beach, Florida, on November 18, 1960."

The White House denial was supported by a CIA press release stating that Allen Dulles, the former CIA chief, had read both the Nixon version of the Kennedy briefings and the White House statement. The release quoted him as adding:

"There has been here, I believe, an honest misunderstanding. This was probably due to the nature of the message Mr. Nixon writes he received as to these briefings. The Cuban situation was, of course, dealt with in the briefings I gave to Senator Kennedy. The last briefing I gave him was over a month before the debate in which the issue arose. My briefings were intelligence briefings on the world situation. They did not cover our own Government's plan or programs 'overt or covert.' "

What was the "nature of the message" Nixon received? According to Fred Seaton, he had telephoned the White House on October 20, 1960, to ask "whether Kennedy had been briefed on the covert operations in Cuba, and the answer came back to me that he had." Seaton told the *New York Times* on March 24, 1962: "A check was made, and the reply came back—a categorical reply." He had talked to "the appropriate official" at the White House, "one who we could expect to either know the answer or be in a position to get it."

"I cannot say categorically that he knew," he explained. "I can say that he thought he knew, or he would not have told me flatly that [Kennedy] had been told."

Nixon's 1960 press secretary, Herbert G. Klein, had a similar recollection. Klein's version of the incident was published in the March 24, 1962 issue of the *San Diego Union,* of which he is editor. According to him, four members of Nixon's staff knew that refugees were being trained for an assault on Cuba. "Frequently we debated among ourselves the handling of the Cuban issue within security bounds. We heard that the Kennedy staff feared the beach assault would take place before the election. We suspected this was the reason why, on October 20, Mr. Kennedy proposed direct intervention.

"For the Vice President and his staff, the angriest moments of the campaign took place on October 20 on the eve of the fourth television debate. We were in New York when Mr. Kennedy made a proposal which directly outlined the exact program which was being carried out—and which we had, for security reasons, kept secret. Here is what we thought had happened:

"First: On July 23 Allen Dulles, then head of the Central Intelligence Agency, and Mr. Kennedy had concurred in announcing that he had been briefed in depth, with particular emphasis on Cuba and Africa. Nothing was withheld, the two told reporters. And we knew that this was in accord with orders given Mr. Dulles by President Eisenhower.

"Second: Nixon had captured the initiative on the Cuban issue with his Miami statement urging a quarantine against Castro. And, in the best coordinated part of the campaign, the Administration had followed with quick orders putting this into effect.

"It seemed obvious to us that Mr. Kennedy was striking back after realizing he was losing points at a crucial point of the campaign, was striking back with secret material he had been given at the Dulles briefing. The White House was queried and we were told Mr. Kennedy had been informed about the troop training. Others told us President Eisenhower was angry over the disclosure.

"In the light of what I know of happenings at that time, I was, of course, surprised last week at Mr. Dulles's statement which corroborates President Kennedy's position that he wasn't told about the troop training."

Even more surprised by Dulles' statement was Dwight Eisenhower. The former President authorized Nixon "to state that, following the practice he had established in 1956, he had given instructions that in regard to U.S. intelligence activities abroad Senator Kennedy was to be as fully briefed on our foreign problems as I was."

All of which, according to Raymond Moley, raised these most serious questions: "Did or did not Allen Dulles obey the orders of President Eisenhower and tell Mr. Kennedy about the most important Cuban preparations? If so, why does Mr. Kennedy now deny that he knew what he was supposed to know? (A matter of veracity is involved here, or at least a matter for clarification.) Just what does Mr. Dulles' mealy-mouthed word 'misunderstanding' mean? Who is misunderstanding whom? Does he mean that the 1962 White House statement is due to a lapse of memory? Does Mr. Nixon 'misunderstand' what the two-and-a-half hour briefing covered? If so, how does Dulles explain that he omitted from that briefing the most crucial operation in which the CIA was involved?"[11]

President Kennedy, however, refused to be drawn into further discussion of the matter. At a news conference, he declined to say whether he thought the CIA should have briefed him on the invasion plan.

"The amazing disclosure that former CIA chief Dulles held back from briefing John F. Kennedy fully about the Cuban crisis deserves more examination than the usual teapot-tempest variety of post-election revelations," reported columnist Ted Lewis.

"Because Kennedy was kept ignorant before his election of the Ike-Nixon plans for mounting an anti-Castro invasion, it now turns out paradoxically that the Democratic nominee benefited from a phenomenally lucky political break. But for it, he could well have been defeated, and Richard Nixon would now be in the White House. . . .

"The villain in the whole tragi-comic affair is Dulles, the 'master-spy,' and a Republican from way back. If Dulles had informed Kennedy of what was going on, Kennedy, as the Presidential campaign reached a climax, would have been forced to soft-pedal the Cuban issue. He would have known better.

"Instead, it was an issue that Kennedy, out of ignorance, made one of his most effective. He was able flatly to charge that Ike and Nixon had had a do-nothing policy toward Red Cuba. He sounded an alarm over Communism having a foothold 90 miles from our shores. He said, if elected, he would do something about it, not just stand still.

---

[11] Following the ill-fated Cuban invasion attempt in April 1961, similar "misunderstandings" developed as a result of contradictory White House stories about the Eisenhower Administration's responsibility for the fiasco. As the *New York Herald Tribune* reported, it "seemed a case of eating one's cake and having it, too."

"The vote-producing response pleased the Kennedy camp. It disturbed Nixon, who knew he had the answer that would cut his opponent down to size—even win the election. But silence had been imposed upon him, and he was a patriot."

In the fourth so-called Great Debate, Nixon pinned down Kennedy's interventionism as "dangerously irresponsible." It would violate United States agreements with Latin America, he said, and "probably" get us condemned at the United Nations.

Kennedy's rebuttal on this point did not come through very clearly, except that he thought the United States needed to strengthen its prestige in Latin America.

Nevertheless, Nixon—as he later wrote—was "in the ironic position of appearing to be 'softer' on Castro than Kennedy—which was exactly the opposite of the truth, if only the whole record could be disclosed." In effect, at a crucial period of the campaign, he was being clubbed with his own weapon.

Also ironical was that the pro-Kennedy columnists and editorial writers, for the one and only time in the campaign, gave Nixon the better of the argument. "The Vice President's criticism of Senator Kennedy's program for assisting the anti-Castro forces to regain power in Cuba was approved by well-informed people here tonight," reported James Reston. And one week after he had praised him to the skies, Walter Lippmann declared he had "not liked Mr. Kennedy's making so much of a campaign issue of Cuba. . . . The policy of the Administration since the fall of Batista has been, so I believe, about the best that was possible given all the circumstances." The *Washington Post* said: "Mr. Nixon accused Mr. Kennedy of recklessness and there is a good deal of point to this obsevation. Mr. Kennedy has been rather extravagant in his criticisms and rather unsatisfying as to just what to do."

"I really don't know what further demagoguery is possible from Kennedy on this subject," wrote Murray Kempton, "short of announcing that, if elected, he will send Bobby and Teddy and Eunice to Oriente Province to clean Castro out."

The vehemence of the editorial reaction to Kennedy's interventionist position, particularly from sources friendly to him, was so great that two days after the Great Debate, Kennedy completely changed his line. And again he berated Nixon for having supposedly distorted his views and for "attacking me for things I never said or advocated." In a telegram to Nixon, he added:

"I have never advocated and I do not advocate intervention in Cuba in violation of our treaty obligations and in fact stated in Johnstown, Pa., that whatever we did with regard to Cuba should be within the confines of international law. What I have advocated is that we use all available communications—radio, television and the press—and the moral power of the American

Government, to let the forces of freedom in Cuba know that we are on their side."

This, of course, was a far cry from Kennedy's statement of September 23 that "the forces fighting for freedom in exile and in the mountains of Cuba should be sustained and assisted."

The new statement was greeted with approval by the *New York Times:* "The use of propaganda and diplomacy is immensely different from force of arms. Mr. Kennedy was . . . well-advised to clarify his position." The *Nashville Banner,* in a front-page editorial, noted that this was "not the first time Kennedy has sought by evasion and tedious circumlocution to cancel out a positive utterance, reverse his field, and charge misrepresentation of views glibly stated. That is his campaign technique, not confined to debates but more noticeable there because of being subject to instant challenge."

And Norman Thomas later recalled that "a highly-placed Democrat assured me" that the original interventionist statement "had been sent out from Kennedy's office by mistake."

All of which proved of little political comfort to Richard Nixon. Some 60 million people had observed his rival on television demanding a tougher stand against Castro. Only a small percentage of that number noted Kennedy's reversal. The general feeling toward the end of the campaign was that Kennedy was stronger and tougher than Nixon on Castro and Communism.

Even after Kennedy had reversed himself on Cuba, George Sokolsky —whose influence was strong among Conservatives—commented that, concerning Cuba, Kennedy "has been on the right side throughout. He has been speaking in the voice of American history much closer to the spirit of Theodore Roosevelt than Franklin D. Roosevelt. He is closer to the nationalist attitude of the Republican party than to the internationalism of the Eisenhower Administration. Certainly this country must carry a big stick or we shall become the laughing-stock of the Western world which watches little Cuba mock and twit the great United States that does not know what to do."

Senator Dennis Chavez, Democrat of New Mexico, meanwhile, said that "when John Kennedy is elected President the Cuban problem will be settled in six months."

And on the other side of the ideological fence, Corliss Lamont, whose friendship for the Soviet Union goes back to the early thirties, remained firmly in Kennedy's corner. True, Corliss was "stunned and miserable" after Kennedy "made his deplorable statement of October 20." But then, said Corliss, "the Senator later stated he meant that the U.S. government should render merely moral support to the anti-Castro gang; and he gave indications of recognizing that his declaration on Cuba was a blunder. At the same time it became clear that Kennedy's suggestions about the Castro regime had been primarily political eye-wash, with little possibility of practical actualization."

"So," as Corliss concluded a letter to the Trotskyite *Militant,* "I stand by my original position in the *National Guardian* that Kennedy will make a far more progressive, intelligent and effective President than the unspeakable Nixon."

Nikita Khrushchev thought so too. Returning from Moscow, labor leader Joseph Curran reported that the Soviet ruler had told him that Kennedy "made sense" while Nixon was "not a politician but a grocery clerk." To which Nixon replied he'd rather be a grocery clerk in the U.S. than a politician in the U.S.S.R.

It was a strange campaign. It was a campaign in which Kennedy put together a winning coalition of diverse elements in his own party—a majority of Southern segregationists, Protestants, states' righters, and conservatives combined with Northern desegregationists, Roman Catholics, unionists, Negroes, and Liberals. He won votes in Alabama, where his name appeared on the ballots in the column headed "white supremacy," wiring them with the votes of Negro militants in Harlem impatient with civil rights progress.

It was a campaign in which Kennedy's supporters included such hitherto incompatible souls as Senator James Eastland of Mississippi and Congressman Adam Clayton Powell of New York; Corliss Lamont, a founder of the Russia-is-rarely-wrong school, and Congressman Francis E. Walter, Chairman of the House Un-American Activities Committee; and oilman H. L. Hunt and columnist Walter Lippmann. (Kennedy, wrote Lippmann, "has outgrown many of his mistakes and vacillations of his youth and today his position in domestic and foreign affairs is substantially the same as Stevenson's . . . judging by the one long talk I have had with him, I would say that he knows the score." Nixon, however, was "an indecisive man who lacks that inner conviction and self-confidence which are the mark of the natural leader and governor of men."[12]

It was a campaign in which Mrs. Eugene Meyer and Harry Truman discovered virtues in Kennedy they had not previously suspected. "Nixon has always been a slick opportunist," said the widow of the publisher of the *Washington Post.* "Kennedy has been a consistent liberal. Nixon will use any

[12] Just how valid are Lippmann's judgments? How do his previous punditries stack up in the light of events? In July 1960, Lippmann declared he considered Franklin Roosevelt one of the great Presidents and Winston Churchill "the greatest man of this century." Lippmann hadn't always felt that way. In 1920, he wrote that Churchill and other public figures opposed to Soviet Communism should stand up "like men to confess their follies and ask forgiveness." Lippmann further described Churchill *et al.* as "duds." On January 8, 1932, the columnist found Governor Roosevelt lacking in the qualities required of a Presidential candidate: ". . . Franklin D. Roosevelt is no crusader. He is no tribune of the people. He is no enemy of entrenched privilege. He is a pleasant man who, without any important qualifications for the office, would very much like to be President." On April 28, 1932, Lippmann wrote: ". . . the people of the East know about Mr. Roosevelt, and gradually have taken his measure. They just do not believe in him. They have detected something hollow in him, something synthetic, something pretended and calculated. . . . They would like the next President to ring true. Mr. Roosevelt does not ring true. . . ." In 1960, Lippmann said he had been wrong about Roosevelt, that F.D.R. "grew up" in office.

means to get power. Kennedy seeks power as an opportunity for service."
And Mr. Truman now said he liked Kennedy because "he is not a chameleon
and he doesn't change his colors every time a pollster tells him to."

It was a campaign in which Lyndon Johnson assured troubled audiences
in the South that "my leader" was really a Conservative at heart; while
Arthur Schlesinger Jr. was assuring troubled audiences in the North that
Jack was basically a dedicated Liberal.

It was a campaign in which Lyndon Johnson accused the Eisenhower
Administration of "sitting in a rocking chair" instead of facing up to pressing
problems.

It was a campaign in which an actress introduced John F. Kennedy to a
radio audience as follows: "This is Tallulah Bankhead, ladies and gentlemen.
I am an actress, I am a Southerner, I am a Protestant, and I am a Democrat
with a Capital D. I am here to introduce John F. Kennedy, who as of January
20 will be a resident of 1600 Pennsylvania Avenue, Washington, D.C. That's
the White House, darlings. . . ."

It was a campaign in which Kennedy's mother lectured women's groups
on the subject "My Son, the Senator." Stumping the Bronx, Rose Kennedy
disclosed that her son Jack had begun his political education when he was
"knee high" and he was already intimate with world affairs at an age "when
most young men were spending their time in just the irresponsible outdoor
sports."

It was a campaign in which Jack's sister, Mrs. Eunice Shriver, denied
rumors that her husband, Sargent, had his eye on a cabinet job as Secretary
of Health, Education and Welfare. "We don't even talk about cabinet jobs
at home," she told the *Chicago Tribune*'s Louise Hutchinson. "All we talk
about is winning." Then she picked up her year-old son, Timothy, held him
aloft and cooed to him in a chanting fashion, "Win, win, win."

It was a campaign in which Joseph Alsop was able to see in his hero,
Kennedy, all the admirable traits he had once found in Adlai Stevenson—and
one more. Kennedy's "image," Alsop wrote, seemed so masculine.

It was a campaign that got a big uplift when it was announced that the
Princess of Monaco, the former Grace Kelly of Philadelphia and Hollywood,
would campaign for Jack among U.S. servicemen in Europe. Some undecided
GI voters, it was believed, were bound to be impressed by *her* image.

It was a campaign in which Kennedy repeatedly claimed he did not want
votes "under the expectation that life would be easier if I were elected." And
yet, when it was all over, *Congressional Quarterly* toted up Kennedy's campaign promises and found the grand total to be no less than 220 "musts,"
priorities, and pledges of action. These ranged through every conceivable
field of endeavor. Nothing was too great or too small to escape the Kennedy
eye or to elicit a promise. There were 54 promises on foreign policy, 21 on
agriculture, 15 on national security, 41 on labor and welfare, 24 on natural

resources, 14 on commerce, 16 on economic policy, and 35 on general government and judiciary.[13]

Kennedy promised greater military strength, "full employment," more billions for foreign aid, bigger handouts for farmers, slum rebuilding and subsidized housing, huge expenditures for hydroelectric development, federal subsidies for teachers, old age medical care for all, and other lavish benefits for practically everybody.

"Kennedy has got away with murder on his domestic program," commented James Reston, who continued to support him. "His promises to the farmer, to labor, to old people, are all very exciting, but he has not given anybody the slightest idea of how they are to be financed."

Actually, Kennedy did not know how.

But, as a famed Washington hostess, quoting H. L. Mencken, observed: "There are some politicians who, if their constituents were cannibals, would promise them missionaries for dinner."

In the second Great Debate, a reporter pointed out that in his acceptance speech Kennedy said he intended to stress not what the country could do for the people, but what the people must do for the country. "Since that time you have spelled out many of the things that you intend to do; but you have made only vague reference to sacrifice and self-denial."

Kennedy's answer was: "I merely say that they—if they elect me President, I will do my best to carry the United States through a difficult period but I would not want people to elect me because I promise them the easy soft life. I think it's going to be difficult but I am confident that this country can meet its responsibilities."

The next day Kennedy was telling the tobacco farmers in Kentucky what he intended to do for them. "We will sweep away tight money and restore the Democratic policy of abundant farm credit," he said in Bowling Green. "We will protect REA against the Republican threat of increased rates. And we will move forward again on one of the Democratic party's proudest achievements—the TVA."

Kennedy's disregard of his own anti-TVA voting record did not go unnoticed following an appearance in Nashville, where he referred to TVA as a monument to the "nation's courage and capacity and as a reminder that the past eight years have seen stagnation and retreat in nearly all aspects of our national life."

The *Nashville Banner* observed that Tennessee was not "unacquainted with the TVA, whose major miracles are not those of the quantitative blessings it has wrought and the economy it has enriched, but in perennial resort to it by candidates plugging in for political juice. As one of these, seeking an 'issue' for variety's sake to localize, Mr. Kennedy tapped the circuit to let

[13] The Republican National Committee came up with a listing of 500 Kennedy campaign pledges, promises, and programs. The indexed study was prepared by the Research Division headed by Dr. William B. Prendergast.

his own light shine; and if that didn't blow a fuse or two, it was only because nobody bothered to ask him just when he became a TVA fan."

The *Banner* concluded: "The people of Tennessee needed no campaign testimonial by Senator Kennedy to identify Andrew Jackson as a great Democrat and Tennessean, and to confirm his place in history. They could have enlightened the present aspirant, however, employing that tribute as an oratorical crutch in support of his own candidacy, that any similarity of cases and stature is as remote as the resemblance between Jackson's Democracy and his."

Meanwhile, Henry A. Wallace, Secretary of Agriculture and Vice President under Roosevelt, said he had analyzed Kennedy's farm program and found ". . . it boils down to a rehash of the proposals put forward by the left wing of the Farmers' Union in 1933. Those proposals were so fantastic and impossible of attainment without tight licensing and controls that Franklin D. Roosevelt was furious at the men backing them. He shouted so loudly and vehemently at the committee that his secretary came running in fear he was in trouble."

Speaking solely as "an agriculturalist" and not a partisan in what he called the "Presidential controversy," Wallace suggested the Kennedy program "may be just a vote getter." Of course, he added, the farmer was in a difficult position, "but if the Kennedy proposals went through I think it would be a very disheartening experience for everyone." They would provide for "stricter controls than they have in most Communist countries."

In his post-election meeting with Nixon, Kennedy said the farm problem had been the most difficult of his domestic issues. "It is terribly difficult to develop a farm program that is both politically appealing and economically sound," Kennedy told him.

Basically, the Democratic campaign was one of ambiguities. They were all things to all men. They wished the electorate to believe they favored big spending and economy; a balanced budget and an unbalanced budget; inflation and no inflation; higher taxes and lower taxes; enforcing the civil rights of Negroes and continuing to deny them in the South; a hard line toward Communism and a conciliatory one.

Kennedy's speeches were custom-tailored for his audiences. One day he would be running against Herbert Hoover. The very next day he would be quoting from a letter Mr. Hoover had sent him praising his work in behalf of Government economy.

Before labor audiences, Kennedy also campaigned against McKinley, Landon, and Dewey. He claimed that only the Democrats favored progress and implied that the Republicans were somehow in a sly conspiracy to cause people to die in the gutter of disease and malnutrition, or words to that effect. Invariably, he tended to rely on pretested exhortations of the Rooseveltian faith. As he looked over the land, he overlooked prosperity and he saw a country even more shrunken than Nikita Khrushchev's vision of the United States as "a limping horse."

"Seven million Americans have an income of less than $2,000," he said. "There are 15 million on a substandard diet; 17 million are not covered even by the $1 minimum wage. We have more than 3,000,000 unemployed workers with jobless benefits averaging less than $31 a week."

But Kennedy's most dramatic claim—one he had to drop—was this: "The facts are that 17 million Americans go to bed hungry every night." And, naturally, it was all the Republicans' fault. "We'll admit the young Senator's figures are startling—but where did he get them?" the irreverent *New York Daily News* asked. "Did that amazing total include citizens on diets or ginmill patrons who plain forgot to order a sandwich?" Apparently Kennedy—or one of his ghost writers—seemed to have misunderstood a 1955 Agriculture Department study of the nation's eating habits. It found that many American families do indeed suffer from nutritional deficiencies. But again, while such deficiencies are most common in low-income groups, it was also found that between 13 and 17 per cent of households with incomes of $10,000 and over suffer from various nutritional shortages.[14]

Kennedy also made an appeal to business. He appointed Governor Luther H. Hodges of North Carolina as head of his Businessmen-for-Kennedy Committee.[15] The appointment was supposed to emphasize the Democratic nominee's middle-of-the-road approach to economic matters despite the ultra-Liberal Los Angeles platform on which he said he was campaigning "without any reservation."

The fact that Organized Labor was bitterly opposed to Hodges did not seem to trouble Kennedy. After all, where would the labor leaders go? W. Millard Barbee, president of the North Carolina AFL–CIO, considered Hodges terribly anti-Labor. "The way he feels about unions shows me his stature, which is very small," Barbee told the *Washington Star*. There was a personal feud involved, however. Hodges had declared Barbee *persona non grata* in the Governor's office at Raleigh.

Although Hodges had criticized President Eisenhower for sending troops to Little Rock and to the Caribbean (after Vice President Nixon was attacked in Venezuela), he nevertheless had sent the National Guard to Henderson, North Carolina, during a textile strike. Hodges said he had done so to prevent violence, but the Textile Workers said it was to break the strike. Both appeared to be correct.

Hodges, a self-made man who "stands for the free enterprise system,"

---

[14] Another Agriculture Department report averaged out United States food consumption in the election year of 1960 at 1,488 pounds per person, which, allowing for the 17 million Americans Jack Kennedy said go to bed hungry every night, meant that certain gluttons must have downed 8 pounds or more a day.

[15] Hodges was later appointed Secretary of Commerce by President Kennedy.

had asked Kennedy about certain of his "economic advisors whose views are unpopular with businessmen." Kennedy had replied:

"Anybody who aspires to the Presidency must have the objectivity and detachment to listen to and evaluate every responsible point of view. I have always endeavored to do this. I consult advisors of both liberal and conservative thought, just as any corporate executive seeks the advice of all of his associates. Then I make up my own mind."

Kennedy's major appeal to businessmen was made before the Associated Business Publications Conference in New York. "I do not know whether to regard with alarm or indignation the common assumption of an inevitable conflict between the business community and the Democratic party," he said. "That is one of the great political myths of our time, carefully fostered."

And Kennedy proceeded to tell the conferees that his was a "conservative policy." The contradictions in his speech were so numerous, however, that the question could well have been raised—but wasn't—as to whether Kennedy really agreed with his own program.

"I believe that the budget should normally be balanced," he said. "In boom times we should run a surplus and retire the debt." The government, he added, should refrain from "unjustified and unnecessary intervention in the economy," and the Federal Reserve Board should remain "removed from political pressure." Yet both he and his party were pledged to a program which would make balanced budgets impossible; which held that government control of the economy was both justified and necessary; and which would force the Federal Reserve Board arbitrarily to reduce interest rates and expand credit.

How could the Board be influenced to do what it didn't wish to do? By "co-operation," according to Kennedy, and by "strong and well considered leadership which expresses the responsible will of Congress and the people." Which sounded a little like the sort of co-operation that exists between Moscow and, say, Budapest.

Moreover, Kennedy said, "a Democratic administration" would use these monetary controls (the Federal Reserve Board apparently would co-operate itself out of business) to foster the industrial investment which, he claimed, the Eisenhower Administration had prevented since the Fall of 1957.

"We must make certain," he added, "that there is proper encouragement to plant modernization. Postwar Europe has a new and modern industrial plant. So has the Soviet Union. We cannot compete if our plants are out of date and second rate. . . . It is sound policy to see that our productive plant is the best and most modern in the world."

Only three years before, in addressing Chicago's Economic Club, Kennedy hadn't thought that United States plants were becoming second rate. In fact, he then was alarmed at "the unprecedented use of available capital" and the "huge investment in new plants and machinery." He urged a greater willingness to invest United States capital abroad, particularly in the less developed nations. "The almost insatiable demands of our own consumers," he said in the Fall of 1957, "aided by record levels of long-term consumer credit and extremely liberal mortgage credit, have soaked up some 100 billion dollars in this country alone in the past ten years."

Kennedy's views on foreign trade had also changed. In 1957 he was urging a boost in imports; in 1960 he said "it is vital that we keep our exports well ahead of our imports," and he urged more protection for United States industry under existing laws.

Which Mr. Kennedy was right? The Kennedy of 1957 or the Kennedy of 1960? Obviously, in 1957 Kennedy was blind to the evils which he later claimed had been present since before then. If his 1957 diagnosis was as wrong as he later suggested, then his more recent diagnosis should also have been suspect.

In his Economic Club Speech in 1957, Kennedy had also discussed the Arctic lemmings who plunge blindly ahead into the Atlantic Ocean to their death. But this is not the "age of the lemming," he added. "For this is an age of prosperity, an age of abundance. It is an age characterized by full employment, rising wages, rising prices and profits, increased productivity, growing international trade, increased national income, rising standards of living, record levels of production, tremendous gains in research, high demand and consumption, accelerated investment and continued plant expansion. . . . Our own record boom here at home makes any warning about the fate of the Arctic lemming seem very remote and very absurd to most of the American people."

Three years later—election year—it wasn't so absurd. For Kennedy saw crises everywhere—in a flabby economy, growing unemployment, reduced productivity, educational inadequacies, lagging scientific research, etc. etc. etc. What had caused Kennedy to completely reverse himself on the state of the economy? Since he never explained, one was forced to assume it had something to do with his seeking the Presidency.

"We don't find fault with Mr. Kennedy for changing his mind when there is good reason for doing so," commented the *Chicago Tribune*. "But, having apparently changed his mind, is he now justified in condemning the decisions which he condoned at the time? Having seen no need for action when it was his responsibility, can he in good conscience accuse the Administration of inaction? And, having changed his mind on so many matters with no more explanation than a weather vane offers for swinging around, can he now honestly pose as a leader who will point out firmly and infallibly the road ahead? We don't think so."

Kennedy's shifting views were always expressed with a righteous indignation that would normally indicate an enormous personal concern about the subjects involved. In his first so-called debate with Nixon, Kennedy began by saying:

"I'm not satisfied to have 50 per cent of our steel mill capacity unused.

"I'm not satisfied when the United States had last year the lowest rate of economic growth of any major industrialized society in the world—because economic growth means strength and vitality. It means we're able to sustain our defenses. It means we're able to meet our commitments abroad.

"I'm not satisfied when we have over $9 billion worth of food, some of it rotting even though there is a hungry world and even though 4 million Americans wait every month for a food package from the Government which averages 5 cents a day per individual. I saw cases in West Virginia, here in the United States, where children took home part of their school lunch in order to feed their families, because I don't think we are meeting our obligations toward these Americans.

"I'm not satisfied when the Soviet Union is turning out twice as many scientists and engineers as we are.

"I'm not satisfied when many of our teachers are inadequately paid or when our children go to school in part-time shifts. I think we should have an educational system second to none.

"I'm not satisfied when I see men like Jimmy Hoffa, in charge of the largest union in the United States, still free.

"I'm not satisfied when we are failing to develop the natural resources of the United States to the fullest. . . .

"I'm not satisfied until every American enjoys his full constitutional rights. If a Negro baby is born, and this is true also of Puerto Ricans and Mexicans in some of our cities, he has about one-half as much chance to get through high school as a white baby. He has one-third as much chance to get through college as a white baby. He has about a third as much chance to be a professional man, and about half as much chance to own a house. He has about four times as much chance that he'll be out of work in his life as the white baby. I think we can do better. I don't want the talents of any American to go to waste."

Wherever Kennedy looked—both at home and abroad—he saw nothing but wreckage caused by eight years of Eisenhower "blunders."

Everything was going to pot in Latin America, the Middle East, Quemoy and Matsu, and the Congo, to mention a few hot spots. Yet, at the time these mistakes were presumably being made, John F. Kennedy appeared to be remarkably unaware of them.

Thus Candidate Kennedy spoke a great deal of African problems, making much of the Administration's asserted indifference to them. "As Chairman of the Senate Subcommittee on African Affairs," he said on September 22, 1960, "I have been disturbed by recent evidence of Russian infiltration and subversion in the Congo." But apparently he was not "disturbed" enough to have called a single meeting of his Subcommittee for fifteen months, despite the chaotic conditions which he claimed he saw developing in the Congo in that period.

"Jack Kennedy has spoken extensively on disarmament," Nelson Rockefeller observed during the campaign, "but he has been a member of the Senate Disarmament Subcommittee for over two years and has never been at a single meeting of that Subcommittee."

As a candidate, John F. Kennedy talked much about other grave problems. But as a Senator he failed to use his opportunities to do something about them:

Item: In Sioux Falls, South Dakota, on September 22, 1960, he told a campaign crowd: "We must use our excess productive capacity to feed the hungry and undernourished here and abroad. We cannot allow food to rot in our warehouses as long as there are men and women and children anywhere in the world without a decent diet." BUT Kennedy failed to support this proposal three times on September 4, 1959, and voted AGAINST this plan as a part of the Mutual Security Act of 1953.

Item: In Billings, Montana, Kennedy said: "No state, no region, no nation in the world today can be economically strong without an adequate supply of water. . . . But already the water shortage is nationwide in scope. . . . And the American people have a right to hear not only our goals but how we intend to reach them—not only our principles, but how we intend to apply them—not only our rhetoric, but the deeds we plan to match our words." BUT on April 20, 1955, Kennedy "paired" himself AGAINST the Upper Colorado River Storage Project—the largest reclamation project ever enacted in a single piece of legislation.

Item: In Alaska, September 3, 1960, Kennedy spoke of public power projects: "Our policy has been one of timidity. We have neglected our greatest sites. We have wasted our most valuable resources. We have substituted for a positive program an empty policy labeled 'no new starts.' . . . The tragic fact is that if Alaska belonged to the Russians today, Rampart Canyon Dam would be under way. I don't think it is going to take the Russians to do it. I think we can do it. . . ." BUT in 1952 and 1955 Kennedy voted to reduce funds for the Tennessee Valley Authority. In 1951 he voted to reduce Bonneville Power funds and to eliminate funds for Southeastern power development.

Item: In Pocatello, Idaho, September 6, 1960, Kennedy said: "Our research in the peaceful uses of atomic energy has fallen far short of expectations. There has been too much bureaucratic red tape and too little budget." BUT on May 10, 1960, when the Senate debated and passed the Atomic Energy Appropriations Act, Kennedy was reported to have spent the morning in West Virginia and the afternoon at a luncheon for Mrs. Eleanor Roosevelt. The previous year, too, when these funds were provided by the Senate, Kennedy was listed as ABSENT.

Item: "We will begin a sound system of soil conservation," Kennedy pledged on September 22, 1960. BUT on June 2 and 3, 1959, when the Senate voted on measures to reduce the Soil Conservation Program, Kennedy was ABSENT. And when the vote was taken to reduce the Conservation Program in June 1957, Kennedy voted "yea."

Item: On Rural Electrification, Kennedy told a Bismarck, North Dakota, audience: "I say it is a tragic fact that the kind of dynamic leadership and initiative REA needs in the Executive Branch is lacking today at the very time we need it most. Instead of new help, we get new handicaps. Instead of more funds, we get more restrictions." BUT in June 1954 Kennedy voted twice against REA funds, and while in the House on July 13, 1949, he voted AGAINST establishment of the REA Rural Telephone System.

Item: "We must put to work the wonders of automation in a way which will be a blessing for all America—not merely a curse for the workers," he said in Detroit, September 5, 1960. BUT as a member of the Joint Subcommittee on Automation and Energy Resources, Kennedy had not attended a single one of the five meetings devoted to discussing ways and means of solving these problems.

Item: "If we're going to grow the way we should grow we must adopt fiscal policies that will stimulate growth and not discourage it," he said. BUT as a member of the Joint Economic Committee of Congress, Kennedy attended only the first meeting on March 20, 1959, and thereafter had not attended a single one of forty-four meetings dealing with United States and Soviet economic growth and price levels. Nor did he attend any of the six meetings that studied the Economic Report of the President.

Throughout the campaign, Kennedy frequently consulted his "Nixonpedia," a 1,000-page, single-spaced book containing his rival's stated views on every conceivable subject. Every Nixon vote was recorded. A special section dealt with the Vice President's frequent travels—what he said in each country and what happened there afterward to confirm or contradict his on-the-spot judgments.

Kennedy knew much less about his own record. For example, this is what was said at a Pocatello, Idaho, press conference early in the campaign:

QUESTION: Senator Kennedy, we here in this part of the state are interested in Burns Creek. We know that although most people are for it, it was defeated and did not even get out of the House. How do you feel about the Burns Creek and other reclamation projects?

KENNEDY: I don't know enough about it to give you a comment on it.

QUESTION: Senator Kennedy—

KENNEDY: It did not come to the Senate, did it?

QUESTION: It passed the Senate.

KENNEDY: You will have to inform me again. It is early in the morning.

QUESTION: The Burns Creek bill passed the Senate. It was defeated in the House by the committee. The committee did not take it up before the House adjourned.

KENNEDY: Frank Church and I are flying out together. I am sure he will tell me about it for the rest of the morning.

The curious thing was that Kennedy had actually voted for the Burns Creek Project twice. Apparently someone had forgotten to brief him on how he had voted. Or why.

Throughout the campaign, Kennedy proudly boasted that the Democrats had always had better slogans than the Republicans.

"You can tell, by contrasting the slogans of the two parties what the two parties stand for," he said. " 'Stand Pat with McKinley'; 'Retain Normalcy with Warren G. Harding'; 'Keep Cool with Coolidge.' " (Laughter.) " 'Had Enough?'; 'Time for a Change.' The weakest slogans in the history of American politics." (Applause.)

"Contrast the slogans of which we are proud: Woodrow Wilson's 'New Freedom'; Franklin Roosevelt's 'New Deal'; Harry Truman's (applause)— Harry Truman's 'Fair Deal.' (Applause.) And Adlai Stevenson's 'New America.' " (Applause.)

"And I will respectfully contrast the so-called slogans of the 1960 campaign: The Vice President's 'Send a Man to Do a Man's Job' versus a slogan of a 'New Frontier' for the United States." (Applause.)

The slogan bit became a standard part of his repertoire—always good for a laugh. He used it numerous times during the campaign. Sometimes he added to the slogans: " 'Two Chickens in Every Pot with Herbert Hoover.' (Laughter.) These are the great rallying cries of the Republican party in the twentieth century. (Applause.) 'Repeal Social Security with Alf Landon'; 'Had Enough?' with Tom Dewey; and 'You've Never Had It So Good' with Dick Nixon."

Then there was Kennedy's well publicized rivalry with James Hoffa. In rattling off things he found deplorable, Kennedy named the Teamsters boss as a national menace comparable to farm surpluses, underpaid teachers, hungry children, unused resources, and the rate at which Russia produces scientists.

But Kennedy hit a peak of righteous authoritarianism during the first debate when he shuddered for his country because Hoffa was still at large. One reason Hoffa was not behind bars was because he hadn't been convicted of anything. Kennedy's instinctive disregard for legal processes should have caused a storm among those citizens who always protest the slightest invasion of Civil Liberties.

The fact is that Kennedy was using Hoffa for political advantage. Among other things, he said he doubted whether "the Department of Justice had carried out the laws in the case of Mr. Hoffa with vigor." And everyone knew the Department was headed by a Nixon friend, Attorney General William Rogers. "In my judgment," he added, "an effective Attorney General with the present laws on the books could remove Mr. Hoffa from office."[16]

---

[16] How "effective" then is brother Bobby? After three years as Attorney General, Bobby—and the Justice Department which he heads—had yet to show the necessary "vigah" to deal with the wily and resourceful Hoffa. In fact, the labor leader grew even more powerful and cocky in the Kennedy years.

As Kennedy expected, Hoffa let loose with a blast that the Senator was not fit to be President of the United States. Kennedy got across his point: if Hoffa was opposed to him, obviously he was for Nixon.

At the same time, Kennedy reverted to Red-baiting. He made a big thing out of the fact that Harry Bridges, pro-Communist leader of the International Longshoremen's Union, had bitterly condemned him as a foe of Labor.

"It is an interesting fact that neither the Teamsters Union nor the Longshoremen's Union dominated by Mr. Bridges is supporting me in this campaign and that both unions are opposing me," he said. "Now, in regard to Mr. Reuther, I consider Mr. Reuther an honest union leader. . . . I want to get the crooks and the Communists out of the union movement, like Mr. Bridges. . . ." And he promised that, if elected, he and brother Bobby would do so.

Thus Kennedy got across his point: Richard Nixon was being supported by "crooks and Communists."[17]

There were other gimmicks in Kennedy's Hoffa-baiting. By concentrating on Hoffa, he avoided touching on equally shocking facts involving certain other labor leaders. At the same time, he posed as the champion of those who were tired of labor abuses. And all it cost was Hoffa's enmity. Politically speaking, it was just perfect for *One-upmanship.*

Kennedy's approach to serious problems was also demonstrated by a little-publicized episode involving a short television film he made on Medicare. The idea was—as they say in show business—a real "gasser." Jack was to pay a visit to Mr. and Mrs. John McNamara—just plain folks residing in Newport, Kentucky. McNamara was recovering from a fractured hip—the result of a fall. And the idea was for Jack to show how interested he was in problems of medical care for the old folk—compassion, sympathy, and all that jazz.

Everything in the little drama went fine. The McNamaras looked the part. The lighting was great. As the TV cameras recorded the event for showing all over the country, Jack interviewed the McNamaras on the husband's ordeal. Then Jack looked into the eye of the camera and summed up earnestly: "What I think is a serious problem for Mr. McNamara and Mrs. McNamara is he's retired, and then because he had an accident . . . he incurred a debt of over $600 to pay for his medical bills."

Later, the truth leaked out. McNamara's medical bills—except for $146—had been covered by Blue Cross–Blue Shield. (All but $63 would have been covered had McNamara not chosen a semi-private hospital room.) When McNamara was asked whether he had informed Kennedy of the insurance benefits, he said he certainly had. In fact, he had explained the situation to the Democratic Presidential candidate shortly before the inter-

[17] The Communist party, however, had endorsed Kennedy as "the lesser evil," taking the attitude that Richard Nixon was incapable of being pressured from the Left.

view was filmed. And how had Kennedy responded? According to McNamara, Kennedy said, "We won't talk about that now!"

Well, as they say, that's show biz.

And it demonstrated Kennedy's approach to the campaign. It was one based largely on half-truths. Thus, he sought to make it appear that the Republicans were opposed to all such programs as aid to education, aid to depressed areas, and medical care for the aged. He always cited what he called "the record." His arguments, however, were a distortion of the record. What he cited were votes in Congress on specific provisions of specific bills— whether, for example, aid to education should include teachers' salaries. To say that a "no" vote on that one facet meant opposition to all aid to education was not the whole truth—and Kennedy knew it.

Needless to say, it is axiomatic for the party out of office to denounce the party in office for its mistakes—alleged and real. But the quantity and quality of Kennedy's oratory and mimeography against the Eisenhower-Nixon Administration reached farcical proportions.

The bizarre theme to which Kennedy pitched his campaign—"the degeneration of prestige and power under the Republican Administration"—had been proposed by the People Machine. Every United States reverse abroad was greeted exuberantly by the Kennedy camp. Kennedy himself could hardly contain his joy when someone leaked out a U.S. Information Agency "prestige" poll confirming—so Kennedy said—what he had been alleging. The joy was catching. At a New York rally, according to the *Reporter,* "when Carmine DeSapio announced that American prestige abroad had fallen to an all-time low, the audience, apparently recognizing only a hallowed party issue, responded to the news with a resounding cheer."

Kennedy's passionate concern about America's "image" abroad was all the more remarkable because he had never before indicated any such concern. In fact, in reviewing a book by Arthur Larson, former head of U.S.I.A., for the *New York Times* in February 1959, Kennedy stated:

"Finally, Mr. Larson is perhaps too worried about America's image abroad. Here two issues should be distinguished. On the one hand, it is inevitable that foreigners, to a degree, fail fully to understand American society and its dynamics. After all, we are guilty of similar over-simplifications and misunderstandings of how other people organize their lives. And while we should all strive to understand each other better, too much should not be made of this point. What really matters is whether our policies and actions in the world appear to overlap significantly with the aspirations of other peoples."

Yet, Kennedy managed to make "prestige" one of his major 1960 issues. He charged that "State Department polls on our prestige and influence around the world have shown such a sharp drop that up till now the State Department has been unwilling to release them." The fact that all such studies had always been considered confidential did not deter Kennedy from implying that the

Eisenhower Administration was trying to hide something. Kennedy argued over and over that we were in a bad way and slipping still more.

Nixon denied any merit to this scare story. He said we were in good shape all around and were respected, and that the tide of history was on our side because we serve the cause that is right. Moreover, he argued, national policy cannot be based on polls or on centering all efforts on the creation of "images." Strength is what it is; it is not what people may choose to think it is.

And so the argument—one of the most incredible ever raised in any political campaign—raged.

In late October the disputed prestige polls were filched from the files of the U.S. Information Agency and published by the *New York Times.* Though most helpful to Kennedy, they said little of importance. Taken at face value, they did confirm Kennedy's contention that United States prestige had declined.

The polls, designed for the purpose of guiding U.S.I.A. policies, measured public opinion about the relative power of the U.S.S.R. and the United States. About a thousand or so Europeans were polled. A majority felt that by 1970 the Soviets would surpass the United States in military power. These opinions were in part the result of press reports on speeches about the "missile gap" by leading Democrats and unhappy Generals.

The documents did not entirely refute Nixon's case, if by "prestige" was meant esteem and popularity. For the polls showed the United States still highly popular, even among people who thought the Soviets more powerful.

The most sensible word on the issue came from London's *Daily Telegraph:* "The truth is that prestige abroad is an absurd issue on which to fight the election at home. It is tantamount to giving foreigners the right to choose the next President."

But in repeating again and again that the United States had lost ground militarily, economically, and in prestige, Kennedy deliberately overlooked a basic fact of which he had been well aware as a young Congressman—namely, that the ground was lost to the Communists during the Roosevelt and Truman administrations.

Moreover, there was a fatal flaw in Kennedy's arguments which would haunt him as President; this was the assumption that the United States, alone and by itself, could influence every global development.

Throughout the campaign Kennedy emphasized every weak spot in the economy. The words "idle plant capacity," "unemployment," "recession," "rising inventories," and "1932" filled the autumn air. He repeatedly invoked the name of Franklin Delano Roosevelt—demonstrating a fervent, though belated, admiration for the departed President.

Nevertheless, according to Raymond Moley, Kennedy's knowledge of F.D.R. was deficient. "Kennedy was only 15 when F.D.R. was elected," Moley wrote. "I was then F.D.R.'s major economic adviser. In F.D.R.'s instructions to me about drafting his inaugural speech he said he wanted to banish fear and instill confidence in the economy. There it is: 'There is nothing to fear but fear itself.' Action followed."

A week before the election, Kennedy spoke to Douglas Aircraft workers in Long Beach, California, where several hundred had just been laid off because of defense cutbacks. And Kennedy warned them that there was worse to come. "I came here," he said, mocking Nixon, "to make sure that you never had it so good." The workers hooted. "I wish," a Kennedy man muttered to the Manchester *Guardian*'s Alistair Cooke, "there were more places like this —God forgive me."

But the height of campaign extravagance was reached when Kennedy concentrated on "economic growth," a subject as mysterious to the average voter as differential calculus. Intoned ponderously, however, it was cleverly designed to create the same alarm as the excited whisper that the boys and girls are practicing coeducation up there in Greenwich Village.

During the primaries Kennedy had affirmed that the Soviet Union's rate of growth was four times that of the United States under Eisenhower. By the time he officially opened his campaign, he had reduced this differential to three times the American rate. On October 12, he said: "The first and most comprehensive failure in our performance has been in our rate of economic growth. . . . Our average annual increase in output . . . has been only 2.4 per cent a year. The rate of increase in the Soviet Union . . . has been better than 7 per cent." Kennedy was constantly changing the figures but the import was the same.

Nixon's reply was most succinctly stated in the television debate of September 26: "The Soviet Union has been moving faster than we have. But the reason for that is obvious. They start from a much lower base. Although they have been moving faster in growth than we have . . . their total gross national product is only 44 per cent of our gross national product."

Kennedy countered by saying that the 44 per cent was causing the United States a good deal of trouble and added that he wanted to make sure that the Soviet figure would not increase proportionately.

One of the difficulties with the whole "growth" argument was the tendency to accept Soviet statistical assertions at face value. That Soviet statistics are compiled primarily for propaganda purposes—and consequently are padded—need not be belabored here. What was curious, in retrospect, was the relish with which Kennedy kept reciting them for campaign purposes.

As President, however, he sees things differently. Within six months of taking office, President Kennedy repudiated Senator Kennedy on "growthmanship." There is little to fear, President Kennedy assured the country on June 28, 1961, from Mr. Khrushchev's threat that the U.S.S.R. will outproduce the United States by 1970. "We agree with Mr. Kennedy," commented the *Chicago Tribune*. "We agreed with Mr. Nixon last fall when he said exactly the same thing."

Kennedy's favorite slogan throughout the campaign was, "It's time for

America to start moving again." The bland assumption was that the country had been standing still for eight Eisenhower years. These were years that covered one of the biggest periods of relatively non-inflationary growth in United States history. Nobody needed statistics or esoteric percentages to prove that. It was just a visible fact.

"By any honest index of measurement," commented the *Chicago Daily News,* "the last eight years have brought phenomenal gains in almost any field one might name. In 1952, the nation's gross national product was $348 billion. This year, it has passed $500 billion and the gain is magnified by the fact that inflation has been slowed from a gallop to a crawl in the same space of time. More people, riding in more cars on more highways, can see more homes and more factories rising on every hand. More jobs are providing more personal income than ever before. If this is stagnation, it is certainly the liveliest stagnation the world has ever seen. If the factual rebuttal presented by Vice President Nixon can't stem this flood of nonsense about moving out of stagnation, what can? It's difficult to combat something that doesn't exist."

Such opinions didn't disturb Kennedy in the slightest. He went on promising—or was it "threatening"—to "move" America. *"I* want to get America moving," he said. He went even further in the closing days of the campaign with what amounted to a promise to "move the world down the road to peace."

One Kennedy statement delivered on Labor Day aroused considerable interest: "With an average rate of growth in this country every workingman in the last eight years would have received $7,000 more than he has received— for an education, or a new house, or a rainy day, or his old age. With a really healthy rate of growth this country can have full employment for all who want a job." How to get this $7,000 and this rate of growth? Very simple: "Elect an administration that will do something about it."

Columnist Holmes Alexander was fascinated by this speech, which reminded him of Huey Long who was going to "make every man a king." He tried to find out how Kennedy had concluded that the average American family had been shortchanged by $7,000 during the Eisenhower era.

"Oh, Jack!" he wrote. "You had a couple of us beginning to believe in you. I went around to your research office on L Street and asked them where you got that figure. Oh, they said, it was just a matter of 'arithmetic.' If you hike the growth rate from umm-umm-umm per cent to blah-blah per cent, you automatically lift the Gross National Product by ug-ug-ug per cent and it comes out to about $7,000 per four-member family. Just like that! It must have been a long time since a Socialist collectivist, using 'social engineering' and 'planned economy,' ever made the formula come out so pat."

Nixon estimated the cost of the various Kennedy programs at between $13 and $18 billion over what was already being spent yearly. Kennedy termed the Nixon figure "wholly fictitious," but declined to offer his own estimate.

Lyndon Johnson, who termed the Nixon figures a "phoney," was unable to explain why on "Meet the Press." Instead Johnson concentrated on the point that Democratic Congresses had reduced the appropriations requests of the Eisenhower Administration by $12.5 billion. He indicated that if Congress had gone along with all the proposals the national debt would have been increased by $31 billion.

"Well, no doubt it takes all kinds of approaches to make a campaign," commented the *Washington Post,* "and perhaps this was intended to impress those persons who have had misgivings about Senator Kennedy's devotion to a balanced budget. . . . It is something of a surprise, though, to have the No. 2 Democrat singing what sounded like a pronounced economy tune when Mr. Kennedy and the party platform have so plainly called for more spending. . . . And it seems just a bit inconsistent to have from the same party one leader advocating more spending . . . and to have another criticizing the present Administration for proposing too much."

Meanwhile, Kennedy kept promising. He promised that "within 90 days" after assuming the Presidency he would reassert American leadership at home and abroad. Within that space of time, he would propose a program to deal with "wiping out poverty here in the United States," a plan for getting the country a "nuclear capacity second to none" which will make us "invulnerable to surprise attack." And he promised to rally all our prosperous European allies in a regional program to get long-term capital into underdeveloped countries all around the world so that they will be prepared for self-government.

"If you question Kennedy about the lack of specific proposals in his speeches, his answer is both surprising and significant," reported Henry Brandon, the *London Sunday Times'* man in Washington, on election eve. "He says he re-read Churchill's ringing warning of the thirties and found that he limited himself to issuing a challenge and asking the nation for a mandate, but that otherwise he was quite unspecific. And that, says Kennedy, is the example he has tried to emulate."

"The Republican party," Kennedy declared, "is the same party which gave us the missile gap, and the economic gap, and a performance gap, and that is the gap which will bring about the rejection of the Republican party this November." (This was "gapsmanship.")

The broader and vaguer the allegations, Nixon discovered, the more difficult they were to disprove. And when Nixon rebutted charges of lack of action, or of insufficient action, during the Eisenhower years, Kennedy reacted by crediting Democratic-controlled Congresses with every advance and blaming the White House for everything that didn't get done. As the *New York World-Telegram & Sun* noted, "Kennedy is using one of those trick coins— heads I win, tails you lose—on Mr. Nixon."

But as he continued to bound about the country mixing slogans and wild-eyed promises, he terrified the world's financial interests. For if his campaign speeches were to be believed, a Kennedy victory would be followed by inflationary policies. As the *London Times* then put it, the Kennedy campaign led to doubts about the future of the dollar. The price of gold, which had consistently been very close to $35 per ounce, rose one day in October to $36, and soon reached $40. The news sped around the world. The panic was on. Only quick intervention by the Eisenhower Administration restored confidence in the dollar.

Naturally, Kennedy strongly denied that he had anything to do with "the recent flurry of speculation on the London gold market." He issued a special statement on the subject, pledging "stability of the dollar." He attributed the "flight of gold" partly to *low* interest rates, but further on charged that the United States had "an *artificially high level* of interest rates—stifling investment, expansion and growth." Kennedy also pledged to balance the budget, shun deficit spending, and curb inflation.

Lucius Beebe, that most elegant columnist, took sharp issue with Kennedy. In the *San Francisco Chronicle,* he wrote: "Can anybody contemplate the hysterical flight from the dollar . . . and attribute it to anything else but the universal and well justified fear that, if the Democrats prevail, the U.S. is headed for the cataclysmic crackup of all time? What else but a Democratic edge reported by pollsters could send gold rocketing on the bourses of the world and the shin plaster dollar still further down the drain?

"If ever there was a spectacle of a political party begging and entreating a supposedly enlightened electorate to vote itself out of jobs, this is it. . . . The full dinner pail may be an archaic symbol of sufficiency in the age of the proletarian Cadillac, but there would seem no rational reason for rejecting it solely on the basis of the television personality of a boy Democrat whose only assets are juvenile charm and $300 million."

The swing to Kennedy is widely believed to have started in Chicago on the evening of September 26, 1960, when he and Nixon appeared in the first of the so-called Great Debates. Most analysts claim that before this event Kennedy wasn't getting anywhere but that after the encounter he gained strength rapidly. The keen edge which Kennedy had when he took the primaries and then the nomination was gone after he showed his helplessness during the short post-Convention session. "Even friendly observers see that he is more nervous, that his hands are more in movement, and that he is weary," reported the friendly Ralph McGill on September 13, 1960. "A spot check across the country reveals that while the religious issue is everywhere a factor, Kennedy's seeming youth and relative inexperience are as frequently mentioned."

Before September 26, the Nixon camp was cautiously optimistic. Huge, enthusiastic crowds were turning out for the GOP candidate; Republicans were wearing broad victory smiles even in the Deep South; and the Nixon campaign organization was full of zest. The Kennedy campaign, on the other hand, had not gotten off the ground. He was not getting the crowds that Stevenson had gotten before him. Party people everywhere seemed lackadaisical toward their standard-bearer.

There was an immediate change in both camps after the first debate. The Kennedyites walked on clouds; while the Nixonites turned grim and nervous, talking only of "recouping." The Kennedy TV image that first night sparkled; while Nixon's was a disaster.

After the election, President Kennedy opined that he couldn't have been elected without television. But in view of the fact that he was elected with the smallest margin of votes in the twentieth century, it can be argued with equal force he couldn't have been elected without the Negro vote, the Southern vote, the Catholic vote, or the Labor vote. While Nixon and his associates agree the debates cost the GOP cause dearly, they contend that other negative factors were more decisive in the Vice President's defeat. "Conceding the worst of everything else," said Robert Finch, Nixon's campaign director, "we still would have won if 400,000 people had not become unemployed during the last thirty days of the campaign."

"My own view," wrote Earl Mazo, National Political Editor of the *New York Herald Tribune,* "based on an analysis of surveys and polls I consider reliable and on a first-hand acquaintanceship with much of the campaign and its participants, is that if there had been no debates on television, Nixon would have been elected President."[18]

"Wherever this reporter traveled in the 1960 campaign, he heard the same story from Democratic professionals," Edward Folliard wrote in *Nation's Business.* "It was to the effect that the first TV debate was the turning point. These pros said that it exploded the idea that Kennedy was simply an immature hero of the bobby-soxers. They said that it persuaded many of the skeptical that he had a good mind and a fine grasp of the issues of the day, and that he would be just as good a man as the Vice President to 'stand up to Khrushchev.' "

The Great Debates, of course, were not debates. They were what Daniel J. Boorstin has called "pseudo-events."[19]

"A perfect example of how pseudo-events can dominate is the recent popularity of the quiz show format," wrote Professor Boorstin. "Its original appeal came less from the fact that such shows were tests of intelligence (or of dissimulation) than from the fact that the situations were elaborately contrived —with isolation booths, armed bank guards, and all the rest—and they purported to inform the public.

"The application of the quiz show format to the so-called 'Great Debates' between Presidential candidates in 1960 is only another example. These four programs, pompously and self-righteously advertised by the broadcasting networks, were remarkably successful in reducing great national issues to trivial

---

[18] Mazo's highly informative report is contained in a symposium on "The Great Debates" published by the Center for the Study of Democratic Institutions of The Fund for the Republic, of Santa Barbara, California. Other participants included Malcolm Moos, Hallock Hoffman, Harvey Wheeler, and Harry S. Ashmore.

[19] *The Image,* by Daniel J. Boorstin. New York, Atheneum, 1962.

dimensions. With appropriate vulgarity, they might have been called the $400,000 Question (Prize: a $100,000-a-year job for four years). . . . Public interest centered around the pseudo-event itself: the lighting, make-up, ground rules, whether notes would be allowed, etc. . . . The pseudo-events spawned in turn were numberless. People who had seen the shows read about them the more avidly, and listened eagerly for interpretations by news commentators. . . . Numerous interviews and discussion programs were broadcast exploring their meaning. Opinion polls kept us informed on the nuances of our own and other people's reactions. Topics of speculation multiplied. Even the question whether there should be a fifth debate became for a while a lively 'issue.' "

Far less interest was being shown in what was being said. In fact, the big issue that came out of the first debate was whether or not a makeup man sabotaged Nixon's appearance. As Theodore H. White noted in copious detail in his *The Making of the President: 1960,* Nixon suffered a handicap that was serious only on television: he has a light, naturally transparent skin. On an ordinary camera that takes pictures by optical projection, this photographs well. But a television camera projects electronically, by an "image-orthicon tube," which has an x-ray effect. This camera penetrates Nixon's transparent skin and brings out (even just after a shave) the tiniest hair growing in the follicles beneath the surface. For the decisive first "debate," Nixon wore a makeup called "Lazy Shave" which was ineffective under these conditions. He therefore looked haggard and heavy-bearded by contrast to Kennedy, who looked pert and clean-cut.

"What one's face looks like—how one's face corresponds to television's laboriously created stereotypes for good guys and bad guys—becomes critical," observed Harvey Wheeler of the Center for the Study of Democratic Institutions. "This first became apparent in the 1960 West Virginia primary. For the first great television debate was . . . between Kennedy and Humphrey. There it was Humphrey who adopted the offensive and Kennedy who said 'me too.' But somehow Kennedy came through with a stronger impression. Humphrey has the disadvantage of looking like Cassius. He has a lean and hungry ambitious look. But Kennedy happens to look like a composite figure of all the good stereotypes television has created. . . .

"There is little doubt that in his debates with Nixon, Kennedy profited from his fortuitous facial correspondence with television's pre-established model of the 'good guy.' It seems likely that in the future one of the tests of a candidate's 'availability' for political nomination will be his correspondence with the then current image of the good guy."

There was an added factor. The electronics media have conditioned audiences to what Madison Avenue calls the *positive sell.* "Here," reported the *Washington Post*'s Lawrence Laurent, "Kennedy had a clear advantage: the most popular word in advertising is 'new' and Kennedy was ready with a 'New Frontier.' In the harshest commercial terms, Kennedy was able to pitch for a trial of a new product. Nixon, defensively, was forced to argue that the old product is still good."

The chief issues of the campaign were America's defense posture, her prestige and rate of economic growth, and the accidental intrusion of what to do about Quemoy and Matsu. These were Democratic issues. In other words, the campaign was waged on Democratic terms.

"In politics," as Professor Wheeler has written, "the advantage accrues to the side able to maintain the offensive. In politics this is compounded by the fact that the average voter votes against rather than for a person or issue." Thanks largely to the TV debates, the Democrats were able to exploit these two advantages. For without the debates it would have been almost impossible to publicize the issues fully and to force the Republicans on the defensive.

"On another score," Wheeler added, "the effect of the debates on sub-stantive issues is of doubtful benefit. The two most instructive examples con-cern Cuba on the one hand and Quemoy and Matsu on the other. . . . Con-cerning Cuba, we now know that Kennedy had been given prior briefing about some general preparations for the overthrow of the Castro regime. We also now know exactly what these preparations were and that the precise form of American participation had not yet been decided. In the television debates, Kennedy committed himself to an attempt to do in Cuba what had been achieved by the CIA before in Guatemala. He outlined in advance the precise mode of operations that was later followed in the Cuban invasion. He is the man who really 'planned' the venture. It is not surprising, therefore, that when President Kennedy asked for advice on Cuba he got back mirror-versions of his own position. A gratuitous television reference to a serious policy matter seems to have played a crucial role in shaping one of the most grievous diplo-matic blunders in American history."

Kennedy had prepared for the debates as if he were preparing for a quiz show. Most of the preparation consisted of devising answers for questions which his handlers anticipated. How many broadcasts were we beaming to Cuba? How many African students are studying in the United States? What was the party breakdown in the House vote on the housing bill? How much surplus food has the Government accumulated in warehouses the last eight years? How many countries voted to admit Red China into the United Nations? All that was missing was the isolation booth.

An added fillip made the Kennedy warm-up unique. A Kennedy Organi-zation man followed Nixon almost everywhere to record his speeches and off-the-cuff comments, and, prior to each debate, selections from the Nixon tapes were played to Kennedy to help put him in a properly aggressive mood.

Another curious thing: "In all four debates" reported the *Washington Star,* "the Senator was not asked a single substantive question that had not been covered in the briefing." Kennedy's advisers had unusual facilities for determining what kind of questions would be asked. As a result, Kennedy was rarely at a loss for words.

Nixon had one uncomfortable moment during the first debate. A question asked by one of the panelists—of little substantive value—was to plague the Vice President all through the campaign. It was put by NBC's Sandor Vanocur, who appeared to be making a career out of needling Kennedy's opponents. Vanocur, whose friendship for Kennedy was no secret, noted that at his news conference President Eisenhower had been "asked to give one example of a major idea of yours that he adopted. His reply was, and I am quoting, 'If you give me a week, I might think of one.' Now, that was a month ago, sir, and the President hasn't brought it up since,[20] and I am wondering, sir, if you can clarify. . . ."

The day Eisenhower made the remark he phoned Nixon to express chagrin at the way it was being handled by the press. "He pointed out he was simply being facetious and yet they played it straight and wrote it seriously," Nixon later wrote. "I could only reply to Vanocur's question in the same vein, but I am sure that to millions of unsophisticated televiewers, this question had been most effective in raising a doubt in their minds with regard to one of my strongest campaign themes and assets—my experience as Vice President."

Kennedy's great strength in the critical first debate, according to Teddy White, lay in the fact that he was not "debating" at all, but "was addressing himself to the audience that was the nation"; while Nixon stuck close to the issues, rebutting one by one "the inconsistencies or errors of his opponent." Few voters know enough about contemporary affairs to listen intelligently to a debate about them. Ordinary people, worried mainly about how they are faring in their own lives, are rarely given to wondering about such matters as "the flight of gold," G.N.P., or oil depletion allowances. Such complex issues have no direct meaning for most voters. In any case, they do not allow for three-minute answers. Kennedy was not much interested in "debating" complex questions. Instead, he sought to impress his views by the way he *seemed* to answer the questions—the formula proposed by the People Machine.

Thus, in the first debate, Kennedy sometimes talked pure gibberish. Rebutting Nixon's argument about how under Eisenhower the "price line has been held very well," Kennedy declared: "Well, I would say in the latter, that the—and that's what I found somewhat unsatisfactory about the figures, Mr. Nixon, that you used in your previous speech. When you talk about the Truman administration, you—Mr. Truman came to office in 1944, and at the end of the war, and the difficulties that were facing the United States during that period of transition, 1946, when price controls were lifted, so it's rather difficult to use an overall figure of those 7½ years and comparing them to the last 8 years. I prefer to take the overall percentage record of the last 20 years of the Democrats and the 8 years of the Republicans, to show an overall period of growth. . . . So that I don't think that we have moved . . . with sufficient vigor."

[20] The reason Eisenhower hadn't brought it up was that no one, at later press conferences, had asked him about it.

But, incomprehensible as it was, the verbal outpouring was rendered with such "fervor"—the People Machine term—that no one seemed to notice.

Another issue that was rendered totally incomprehensible by Kennedy was that of oil depletion allowances. One would have correctly assumed that the Democratic Platform, on which Kennedy ran "without reservation," had called for their curtailment. From the transcript of the third Great Debate:

QUESTION: Senator Kennedy . . . your running mate is from Texas, an oil-producing State and one that many political leaders feel is in doubt in this election year, and reports from there say that oil men in Texas are seeking assurance from Senator Johnson that the oil depletion allowance will not be cut. The Democratic platform pledges to plug loopholes in the tax laws and refers to inequitable depletion allowance as being conspicuous loopholes.

My question is, do you consider the 27½ per cent depletion allowance inequitable and would you ask that it be cut?

KENNEDY: There are about 104 commodities that have some kind of depletion allowance, different kind of minerals including oil. I believe all of those should be gone over in detail to make sure . . . that no one is getting away from paying the taxes he ought to pay. That includes oil, it includes all kinds of minerals. It includes everything within the range of taxation. . . . Now the oil industry recently has had hard times, particularly some of the smaller producers . . . but I can assure you that if I am elected President, the whole spectrum of taxes will be gone through carefully, and if there's any inequities in oil or any other commodity, then I would vote to close that loophole.

I have voted in the past to reduce the depletion allowance for the largest producers for those from $5 million down to maintain it at 27½ per cent. . . .

NIXON: Senator Kennedy's position and mine are completely different on this. I favor the present depletion allowance. . . . Why do we have a depletion allowance? Because this is the stimulation, the incentive for companies to go out and explore for oil, to develop it. . . . He suggests that there are a number of other items in this whole depletion field that could be taken into account . . . that we would get more money to finance his programs by revising the tax laws, including depletion. I should point out that as far as depletion allowances are concerned, the oil depletion allowance is one that provides 80 per cent of all of those involved, so you're not going to get much revenue insofar as depletion allowances are concerned, unless you move in the area that he indicated. . . .

*   *   *

KENNEDY: Just to correct the record, Mr. Nixon said on depletion that his record was the opposite of mine. What I said was that this matter should be thoroughly gone into to make sure that there aren't loopholes. If his record is the opposite of that, that means that he doesn't want to go into it. . . .

Which, of course, was another superb example of Kennedy *One-upmanship*.

Of course, a man's ability to answer in several minutes a question kept secret until that moment had only the most dubious reference—if any at all—to his real qualifications to make deliberate Presidential decisions on matters of earth-shaking importance. One wonders how television debates might have altered United States history. Henry Steele Commager believes that George Washington would have lost a televised debate, and even Jefferson, "for all his erudition and his literary gracefulness," would have done poorly under the klieg lights of a television spectacular.

"And what of Stevenson and Eisenhower?" wrote Earl Mazo. "My conjecture is that the eloquent, articulate, and witty Stevenson would probably have torn his opponent to ribbons on radio—but on television most eyes and hearts would have been won by the Eisenhower smile and 'image.' "

Significantly, the radio reaction to the Kennedy-Nixon encounter was just opposite from that on television. All polls gave Nixon the advantage. Ralph McGill of the *Atlanta Constitution,* a Kennedy supporter, ran an actual test. "Kennedy looked better. . . ." he concluded. "But I had a number of persons listen on the radio. . . . They unanimously thought Mr. Nixon had the better of it." Also, Nixon did best on Election Day in areas that had the biggest radio audiences for the debates, especially the first one. For instance, in the West, which Nixon carried, 9 per cent of the adults heard the debates on radio; in the East, which Nixon lost, the radio audience was about 2 per cent.

The night of the first encounter Earl Mazo was in Hot Springs, Arkansas, covering the Southern Governors' Conference. "At the time, the Hot Springs television station was not linked directly to a network and its telecast of the debate was a re-play an hour or so after the actual performance. But Hot Springs did have network radio. The reactions of the governors and reporters with whom I first heard, then saw, the debate pointed up the difference between hearing and seeing. Before the encounter on radio was half finished every Kennedy partisan in the room was disparaging the whole idea of a fine, up-standing young man like Kennedy having to clash verbally with a crusty old professional debater like Nixon. But the attitude changed immediately when the magic lantern of television came on."

Nixon did considerably better in the last three debates. He disguised his "five o'clock-shadow," and was more forceful in getting across his points. But he found Kennedy difficult to pin down. Kennedy fired away with all sorts of facts, names, and dates, talking so fast that it was difficult for Nixon—let alone the average listener—to keep up with him. As the *Richmond News Leader* observed: "Quick to seize opportunities for ridicule, for misstatement, and for shrewdly planned confusion, Kennedy has managed nimbly to skip from side to side of questions dealing with Cuba, Quemoy and Matsu, and a wide variety of domestic policies. He has demonstrated the classiest footwork since Conn got in the ring with Louis.

"Mr. Nixon has failed to counterpunch effectively. He has two great areas of superiority over Mr. Kennedy in his deeper maturity and in his sounder political philosophy, but he has projected neither of these to best advantage. The Vice President clearly has reserves of dignity, calmness and temperateness that his voluble opponent does not have; in his essential reliance upon the private enterprise system, and his dedication to limited government, he is far closer to the heart of America than Mr. Kennedy stands in advocacy of a welfare state."

Following the fourth debate, Nixon's pollster, the late Claude Robinson, told the Vice President: "Kennedy, however, started the campaign as the less well-known candidate and with many of his adherents wondering about his maturity. He has done a good job of dissipating the immaturity label and has increased his standing on every test issue. Kennedy has succeeded in creating a victory psychology."

President Eisenhower had privately objected to Nixon's debating with his Democratic rival. But Nixon felt he had no choice, even though he knew he had practically nothing to gain and that his opponent would come off best merely if he held his own and avoided visibly serious blunders. Still, Nixon could find no graceful way out. To have refused to debate would have made him appear to be a kind of coward. It would have given Kennedy the opportunity to use the "empty chair" technique.

That television is better suited to the attacker than to the defender was recognized by Bobby Kennedy. Shortly after the election Bobby expressed doubt that the President would agree to debate his GOP opponent in 1964. But at one of his earliest press conferences as President, Kennedy said he would so debate.

"That was said three years and seven or eight months before the next campaign," commented Earl Mazo. "I suspect that President Kennedy's decision when the time comes will depend on the identity of his opponent, and that, more likely than not, he will manage to find the excuses not to debate that Richard Nixon failed to come up with in 1960. And I wouldn't blame him at all."[21]

Nixon's main problem, of course, was simply the fact that across the country there were three registered Democrats for every two Republicans. From the organizational and statistical standpoint, therefore, any Democrat should have overwhelmed any Republican. Moreover, the Democrats controlled the major power centers—the governorships, both Senate seats, all the Congressmen, and both houses of the legislature—in 11 states, while the Republicans enjoyed that amount of power in only New Hampshire. The Democrats had 34 Governors; the Republicans, 16. In Congress, the Democratic majorities were 66–34 in the Senate and 280–152 in the House. Democrats

---

[21] Two opposing views have been expressed on this question by important Republicans. In a CBS interview in October 1961, Dwight Eisenhower stated that a President running for re-election should never engage in televised debates with his opponent. In February 1962, Richard Nixon in an NBC interview, said: ". . . debates between the Presidential candidates on television are a fixture, and in all the elections in the future we are going to have debates between the candidates."

dominated the legislatures in 29 states, the Republicans in 7. In 128 of the nation's 177 cities, the mayors were Democrats.

And organizationally, the Republican party was in its worst shape since the 1936 Roosevelt landslide which almost swept it out of existence. This, of course, was largely due to the fact that President Eisenhower had rarely involved himself in the grubby work of building party organizations around the country. He felt a Chief Executive should not be that partisan.

The fact that Nixon came within an infinitesimal margin of victory demonstrated that he personally was much more acceptable to the nation's voters than was his party. According to Earl Mazo, a private poll taken in his behalf immediately after the Democratic Convention showed that the Kennedy-Johnson ticket would beat any that Nixon led by a decisive 5 to 6 per cent. Subsequently, Nixon's leadership at the GOP Convention and his unusually well-received acceptance speech brought a shift. In early August, the private surveys showed the two candidates to be running almost even among voters who expressed a preference. However, there was an extraordinarily large "wait and see" element.

In the final analysis, such issues as foreign policy and United States prestige abroad proved relatively unimportant in the 1960 outcome. At least, that is what Richard M. Scammon, Director of Elections Research for the Governmental Affairs Institute, thought.[22]

"I think these two men [Kennedy and Nixon] could have talked about the World Series," said Scammon. "It was the way they talked that counted."

According to Scammon, "The real weights on the scale were the return of the Democratic Catholics to the Democratic party and the departure from the Democratic party of rural Protestants who were Democrats for historical reasons."

Thus, according to a pro-Kennedy authority the "religious issue" could be considered a major factor—if not *the* major factor—in Kennedy's election.

"Like it or not," reported Stewart Alsop in the *Saturday Evening Post* at the height of the campaign, "Kennedy's Catholicism is a vitally important factor in this campaign, partly because there is no great domestic issue between the parties to smother and override the 'religious issue.' "

And Kennedy played upon the issue, with enormous skill, to establish the advantage that he had publicly boasted about four years before when he said he could win with the Catholic vote.

Kennedy's religious strategy was outlined in the so-called Bailey Report of 1956 (Appendix B). The states with big electoral votes were the keys to victory. In those states the "Catholic vote" in the large cities could tip the scales. Kennedy had argued that he could win back the large number of Catholic voters who had deserted the Democrats for Eisenhower. Moreover,

[22] Scammon was appointed Chief of the Census Bureau by President Kennedy in 1961.

he argued that the states where his religion could hurt have relatively few electoral votes.

Strangely enough, this memorandum of reverse bigotry excited little attention in the press and so far as can be determined neither Kennedy nor his various brothers and sisters were ever asked about it.

In contending that a candidate's Catholicism would be an asset, the Bailey analysis counted on the fact that efforts of good citizens of all faiths to "get religion out of politics" had changed the situation which had made it a handicap for Al Smith. The reasoning was that anyone who raised the issue would be labeled a bigot while, at the same time, Kennedy's "religious affiliation" could be used to decisive advantage by the Democrats. (The 1956 Kennedy view was reiterated in a poll released on the eve of the 1960 Democratic Convention by New York State Chairman Michael Prendergast. The Prendergast poll stated that the "key" to New York State was "the Catholic vote.")

Unique in its frankness, the Bailey Report, however, made no mention of Kennedy's qualifications for higher office. It simply treated him as an agent for capturing the "Catholic vote." In effect, therefore, what Kennedy told his party in 1956 was: Nominate me because I am a Catholic.

Four years later, Kennedy repeatedly asserted he wanted no one to vote either for him or against him because of his religious faith.

This, of course, is another example of Kennedy having it both ways. It was the sort of doubletalk described by the Liberal Catholic weekly, *Commonweal:* "Candidates who by devious means accent their religious affiliations where it helps and play them down where it may be a handicap are cheating."

As a result, Nixon got it from both ends: Republican Catholics were being urged to vote for Kennedy because he was of their religion; and Republican Protestants were being urged to vote for him to prove they were not biased against Catholics. For Kennedy, it was a "heads-I-win, tails-you-lose" proposition.

Leading Catholic churchmen were well aware of Nixon's predicament. They were deeply appreciative of his super-human efforts to keep the lid on the boiling cauldron of anti-Catholicism. Needless to say, they maintained a scrupulous neutrality between the candidates. In no way did they indicate that the future of the Church depended on whether or not Joe Kennedy's life ambition was fulfilled. Their attitude was perhaps best expressed by Boston's Cardinal Cushing, a friend of the Kennedy family, who on January 13, 1961, nominated Nixon as "Good Will Man of the Year." The Cardinal said: "During the recent campaign which tested and taxed all his powers, physical and mental, he never exploited the religious or any-other issue that would tend to divide the American people."

Kennedy and Nixon were co-speakers at Cardinal Spellman's annual Alfred E. Smith Memorial Dinner at the Waldorf during the campaign. "Kennedy," according to Ted White, "originally, had been reluctant to accept the invitation to this strictly Catholic affair; he felt it would accentuate the religious issue. Evidently he decided finally to speak with a light touch, and for two days before the engagement his aides had been circulating through the press, asking, 'Do you know any jokes?' "

Kennedy, who spoke first, read a speech that sparkled with the best humor money could buy. (A professional gag writer had been impressed into service.) Kennedy began:

"I am glad to be here at this notable dinner once again, and I am glad that Mr. Nixon is here, also. [Applause.] Now that Cardinal Spellman has demonstrated the proper spirit, I assume that shortly I will be invited to a Quaker dinner honoring Herbert Hoover. [Laughter.]

"Cardinal Spellman is the only man so widely respected in American politics that he could bring together, amicably, at the same banquet table, for the first time in this campaign, two political leaders who are increasingly apprehensive about the November election [laughter], who have long eyed each other suspiciously, and who have disagreed so strongly, both publicly and privately, Vice President Nixon and Governor Rockefeller [laughter].

"Mr. Nixon, like the rest of us, has had his troubles in this campaign. At one point even the Wall Street Journal was criticizing his tactics. That is like the Observatore Romano criticizing the Pope. [Laughter.]

"But I think the worst news for the Republicans this week was that Casey Stengel has been fired. [Laughter.] It must show that perhaps experience does not count. [Laughter and applause.]

"On this matter of experience, I had announced earlier this year that if successful I would not consider campaign contributions as a substitute for experience in appointing ambassadors. Ever since I made that statement I have not received one single cent from my father. [Laughter and applause.]

"One of the inspiring notes that was struck in the last debate was struck by the Vice President in his very moving warning to the children of the Nation and the candidates against the use of profanity by Presidents and ex-Presidents when they are on the stump. And I know after fourteen years in the Congress with the Vice President that he was very sincere in his views about the use of profanity. But I am told that a prominent Republican said to him yesterday in Jacksonville, Florida, 'Mr. President, that was a damn fine speech.' [Laughter.] And the Vice President said, 'I appreciate the compliment but not the language.' And the Republican went on, 'Yes, sir, I liked it so much that I contributed a thousand dollars to your campaign.' And Mr. Nixon replied, 'The hell you say.' [Laughter and applause.]

"However, I would not want to give the impression that I am taking former President Truman's use of language lightly. I have sent him the following wire:

DEAR MR. PRESIDENT: I have noted with interest your suggestion as to where those who vote for my opponent should go. While I understand and sympathize with your deep motivation, I think it is important that our side try to refrain from raising the religious issue.

[Laughter and applause.] . . ."

Kennedy wound up his speech with partisan political overtones which did not go well at what was supposed to be a strictly non-political, non-partisan affair. Then Nixon spoke extemporaneously and avoided any statement that smacked of partisanship. The effect was easily predictable. Kennedy had received polite applause. Nixon received a prolonged ovation.

"Kennedy himself referred ruefully to this incident when we met in Miami immediately after the election," Nixon later recalled. "He was discussing voting patterns among Catholics and he pointed out that economics rather than religion primarily determined how people voted. And then he added with a smile, 'You saw how those wealthy Catholics reacted at the Al Smith Dinner in New York.' "

From the day of his nomination, Nixon had laid down the firm line that no one directly or indirectly connected with his campaign should initiate or even engage in any discussion of the religious issue. He made it clear that he did not believe that Kennedy's Catholicism should be an obstacle to his serving as President. He also proclaimed his faith in Kennedy's unqualified and undivided loyalty to America's interests and to the Constitution. He called for an end to the discussion.

"What more can he do?" asked the Chicago Tribune. "What more can the most devoted of Mr. Kennedy's followers ask or expect Mr. Nixon to do to put this matter to rest?"

But Kennedy's supporters would not give up. "There is no doubt in my mind," said Governor Almond of Virginia, "that the Republican leadership, by innuendo, is seeking to capitalize on the religious issue. Furthermore, I think Mr. Nixon has done that by repeatedly referring to it, ostensibly to deprecate it."

Governor Almond's comment demonstrated Nixon's unenviable position. Certainly if he had failed to condemn the injection of the religious issue, he would have been damned as one who condoned bigotry and intolerance. But by contending whenever he was asked that religion was not an issue, he was also damned, by Governor Almond's standards, for the same offense.

One Kennedy supporter, Governor Orval E. Faubus of Arkansas, was not as pessimistic about the religious issue. At Hot Springs, where he was host of the annual Southern Governors' Conference, Faubus said he was "one of those who disagree" that religion would be a big factor in the South. He said most of Dixie, including Arkansas, would stick with the Democratic ticket.

Kennedy had stated that he would discuss the religious issue only when he was asked to do so. But the Associated Press correspondent, traveling with him in Texas in early September, reported that "he has sometimes seemed almost eager to be asked. Twice during this western swing he has invited questions from his audience. These have been written out and screened by his staff. Each time a question on religion was included."

"No one is doing more than the Hon. John Kennedy himself to keep the religious issue alive. It might be said that Mr. Kennedy brings up the subject at the drop of a hat," the *Richmond News Leader* noted, "but this would not be accurate; Mr. Kennedy does not wait for the hat to be dropped. From Oregon to West Virginia, without visible provocation of any sort, he has gone way out of his way to assert his political independence from the Catholic hierarchy, and to invite sympathetic applause by urging that he be accorded fair play. He himself has let no one forget the issue."

Shortly after his nomination Kennedy created a special bureau in his campaign organization to publicize his position on religion. Heading the bureau was James W. Wine, who had resigned as associate general secretary of the National Council of Churches to become Kennedy's special assistant on community affairs. But the *Louisville Courier-Journal* described him as "the man responsible for corralling Protestant support for Kennedy."

In October 1962 President Kennedy appointed James Wine Ambassador to the Republic of the Ivory Coast.

The new bureau, according to an August 17, 1960, dispatch in the *Baltimore Sun,* had as its purpose the answering of questions raised about Kennedy's Catholicism, the writing of letters to the press to make clear his position on the separation of church and state, and the dissemination of films in which he dealt with the religious issue. Interviewed in Louisville on September 10, Wine said his job was to organize statewide groups of clergymen to answer questions on the religious issue. He said that talks with "people from about every state" had convinced him that religion was the "No. 1 presidential campaign issue in the nation today."

"If Kennedy should lose in November," he said, "we feel right now that the principal cause would be because he is a Catholic."

The religious issue worked various ways. Governor Luther Hodges of North Carolina warned: "We had to choose between a Catholic and a Quaker in 1928. We elected a Quaker and lived to regret it. And if you vote for a Quaker this time, you will live to regret it horribly."

And Adlai Stevenson, at his home in Libertyville, was quoted as "wondering out loud" why nobody had raised a question about Nixon's Quaker faith, since "many Quakers are pacifists." Stevenson, of course, knew how pointless his observation was because Nixon was no pacifist. On the other hand, letters were being circulated among Quakers, citing Nixon's war record and regular attendance at a Washington Methodist Church as evidence that the Vice President was a poor Quaker, not to be trusted by Friends.

At the same Libertyville meeting, Robert F. Kennedy informed the audience that his brother's Catholicism had become a campaign issue in the South. He then went on to say that the candidate was not questioned about his religion when he entered the Navy or in his subsequent career in Congress. "Of course he wasn't; but why orate about these matters in Illinois if the issue is more important only in the South?" asked the *Chicago Tribune*. "And why keep the subject going anywhere in the country if it is irrelevant everywhere in the country?" The answer was obvious. "Mr. Kennedy's managers must have come to the conclusion that he has more to gain by keeping the issue alive than by agreeing with Mr. Nixon to drop it. . . . These calculations . . . may be correct but it is no credit to Mr. Kennedy. . . . He is promoting exactly the kind of voting that he professes to deplore and which men of good will, regardless of religious affiliations, genuinely do deplore."

Kennedy did nothing to discourage his supporters from making these false charges of bigotry against Nixon and the Republicans. On September 6, at a press conference in Pocatello, Idaho, the subject arose:

QUESTION: Senator, in Indianapolis yesterday, former President Truman, speaking in behalf of the ticket, said of Vice President Nixon, "While he stands at the front door proclaiming charity and tolerance, his supporters are herding the forces of racial, religious, and antiunion bigotry in by way of the back door. And no one will ever make me believe he is not smart enough to know what is going on." Do you have any comment on that?

KENNEDY: No. I did not see the statement of the President. I think you are familiar with the fact that I did not plan to comment on Vice President Nixon or any of his actions until he is out of the hospital. Therefore, I am not participating in any way in any attack on the Vice President at this time.

But Kennedy had not been asked to comment on "Nixon or any of his actions." He was asked to comment on Truman's false imputation of bias to the Vice President. And Kennedy ducked the question.

In his third face-to-face encounter with Nixon, Kennedy took another tack:

QUESTION: Mr. Kennedy, Representative Adam Clayton Powell in the course of his speaking tour in your behalf is saying, and I quote: "The Ku Klux Klan is riding again in this campaign. If it doesn't stop, all bigots will vote for Nixon and all right-thinking Christians and Jews will vote for Kennedy rather than be found in the ranks of the Klan-minded."

Gov. Michael DiSalle is saying much the same thing.

What I would like to ask Senator Kennedy is: What is the purpose of this sort of thing? And how do you feel about it?

KENNEDY: Well, the que—Mr. Griffin, I believe, who is the head of the Klan who lives in Tampa, Fla., indicated, in a statement I think 2 or 3 weeks ago that he was not going to vote for me and that he was going to vote for Mr. Nixon. I do not suggest in any way, nor have I ever, that that indicates that Mr. Nixon has the slightest sympathy, involvement or in any way imply any inferences in regard to the Ku Klux Klan. That's absurd. I don't suggest that. I don't support it. I would disagree with it. Mr. Nixon knows very well that this whole matter has been involved—this so-called religious discussion in this campaign. I have never suggested even by the vaguest implication that he did anything but disapprove of it and that's my view now. I disapprove of the issue. I do not suggest that Mr. Nixon does in any way.

Kennedy, however, got it across that the self-styled head of the Klan whom he identified as a man named Griffin had said he would vote for Nixon.

The Vice President, in his turn to speak, repudiated the Klan and all who would use the religious issue in furtherance of his candidacy. "I will not tolerate it," he said.

But Kennedy did not repudiate Adam Clayton Powell. This, of course, was the same Powell who shortly before the Democratic Convention endorsed Lyndon Johnson on the basis that anyone would make a better President than Jack Kennedy. This was the Powell who, opposed by Tammany Hall in the 1958 Congressional primary, charged that his Negro opponents were allied with the Church. (At least four of the six Harlem leaders were Catholic.) In 1959, Powell fought these men and defeated three of them, again under conditions making their religion a specific campaign issue.

On October 12, Powell was host at a hastily-gathered affair called "Senator John F. Kennedy's National Conference of Constitutional Rights and American Freedom" in front of Harlem's Theresa Hotel. While a cadre of Elijah Muhammad's Black Muslims hawked their Leader's wares among the spectators, Robert Wagner, Soapy Williams, Carmine DeSapio, Herbert Lehman, Billy Eckstine, Averell Harriman, Hulan Jack, and Mrs. Roosevelt entertained the waiting crowd.

After Kennedy arrived, Adam Powell, who never disappoints a crowd, gave one of his better performances. Alternately thundering at and sweet-talking his audience, Powell gave the "low-down" on Richard Nixon, telling how he had failed to repudiate a KKK endorsement, how he represented "the worst forces of bigotry in America."[23] It was one of the most intemperate speeches of the campaign, but it served to introduce Kennedy to Harlem.

"After that speech," Kennedy began, "I am ready to put the question right now. Are we going to vote Democratic? [Response from the audience.] Adam, I am going to sit down and turn it all over to you. [Laughter.] Congressman Powell says he is my senior. I respect age. I admire his speech. It was very good."

At an International Ladies' Garment Workers Union rally, former Senator Lehman expressed alarm over the "current out-croppings of religious bigotry in a way that has not been equaled in my experience since 1928," adding: "I trust and hope that the American people . . . will respond to this

---

23 Powell knew better. Back in the late forties, at Powell's request, then Congressman Nixon was made a member of a five-man subcommittee which had one mission: it was to answer immediately anything said by Congressman John Rankin, the vehement racist from Mississippi. Powell's relations with Congressman Kennedy at that time were minimal.

bigotry in the best and finest American tradition—by repudiating it" at the polls.

This theme was developed by AFL–CIO's COPE—the Committee on Political Education—in a booklet saying the issue in the campaign was not Kennedy vs. Nixon but "liberty vs. bigotry."

"Senator," Kennedy was asked on "Meet the Press" by Elie Abel, "some of your supporters in the labor movement are distributing a four-page broadsheet which seems to suggest that a vote against you is a vote for bigotry. . . . The key theme seems to be, 'Which do you choose, Liberty or Bigotry?' —a vote for Kennedy being a vote for liberty, presumably. Do you believe this is a proper appeal for your supporters to the people?"

"I haven't seen it," replied Kennedy, "so I would be reluctant to characterize it. I have attempted in all my statements—I don't think there is any doubt of that—to try to keep the religious issue from becoming a matter of dispute between the parties or between the candidates."

But this was no repudiation of an appeal to prejudice in his behalf.

The leaflet in question, which carried on its cover a picture of the Statue of Liberty and a caricature of a Ku Klux Klansman, was promptly denounced as "bigotry in reverse" by the Michigan Fair Election Practices Commission, made up of a Catholic priest, a Protestant bishop, and a rabbi.

Shortly afterward Tallulah Bankhead, introducing Kennedy on a broadcast presented by the ILGWU, said: "In desperation, the Republicans have harped on Senator Kennedy's age, and his religious faith. They will be well advised to take another look at history. Senator Kennedy is 43—remember Christopher Columbus, the 41-year-old Catholic who discovered America in 1492? If it wasn't for Christopher, next Tuesday's election might be academic. Kennedy's qualifications for the Presidency are best expressed by Walter Lippmann, '. . . It has been truly impressive to see the precision of Mr. Kennedy's mind, his immense command of the facts, his instinct for the crucial point, his singular lack of demagoguery and sloganeering. . . .' Hear! Hear! Mr. Lippmann."

Again, the low blow was condoned through silence by the man who, of course, was opposed to demagoguery and sloganeering.

Many Northern Liberals, who had never before defended the Church of Rome, hysterically bewailed attacks on Kennedy's religion. These Liberals did not scruple to use the anti-Catholic weapon against the late Senator Joseph McCarthy. As Murray Kempton noted in the *New York Post*, "those liberal bigots who are our worst Catholic baiters" made political hay against McCarthy by harping on his religious faith.

"It is an irony of the situation," Ralph de Toledano wrote on September 3, 1960, "that the most concerted attack on the Catholic Church in the past two decades came from Liberals and Leftists—many of whom now support Kennedy for their own good reasons—who made a national best seller of Paul Blanshard's book, *American Freedom and Catholic Power.*" The book put together every accusation ever made against the Catholic Church—and the intellectuals applauded. "That Blanshard should have fanned the flames of bigotry is not nearly so important as the reaction of the Liberal gentry—now bleating that the GOP is 'anti-Catholic'—to this vulgar and rabble-rousing book."

The Blanshard book was reviewed approvingly by most Liberal publications. The *New Republic,* for example, said it was "written with careful objectivity—a patient, honest attempt to break through a hush-hush smoke screen . . . the Catholic Church permits no questions."

But the *New Republic* changed its tune in 1960 and actually excoriated a Protestant group which had raised the kind of questions that the magazine had praised when Paul Blanshard had first suggested them. The group, of mysterious antecedents, had as its spokesman the Rev. Dr. Norman Vincent Peale, author, columnist, lecturer, and minister of the Marble Collegiate Church of New York.

Dr. Peale, the apostle of positive thinking, had presided over a conclave of clergymen and laymen calling themselves the Citizens for Religious Freedom, out of which came a 2,000-word manifesto which, though aimed at keeping Kennedy out of the White House, did a great deal to put him in there. The statement expressed concern over whether a Catholic President could resist pressures from the Pope. Apparently the Peale group had never heard of Charles De Gaulle, Konrad Adenauer, and other world leaders who happened to be Catholic.

"Mr. Kennedy is a disappointment and a serious threat," commented *National Review,* of which William F. Buckley Jr. is editor, "but not, as Dr. Peale so recklessly suggests, because he is a Catholic. . . . In the age of Communism we do not want as leader of the West a man who speaks in such faltering accents about the Soviet menace; a man whose instinct was to apologize to Nikita Khrushchev when the national honor was at stake. In an age when the machine, the bureaucracy and mass-culture threaten to dehumanize life, we do not want a man who seeks to accelerate the tendencies toward centralization; whose understanding of the intricate predicament of the individual is as mechanical and inhuman as his close adviser's, John Kenneth Galbraith. We do not want, in an age when heroic leadership is required, a man who will submit so passively to the presumptuous demands of a Walter Reuther; whose Brave New Frontier is symbolized by his call for a protective tariff for New England."

The Peale episode could not have been better for the Democrats had the Kennedys arranged it themselves. This was what they had been waiting for. This was not the statement of an unknown crackpot preacher. Dr. Peale was a long-standing Republican, with a large Protestant following. True, Dr. Peale quickly disassociated himself from the statement; but it was too late. The Democrats were going to town. Kennedy's personal New York campaign representative, William Walton, said: "It was not Nixon, but it smacked of Nixonism."

As the uproar intensified—with ministers, rabbis, and editorialists vying with one another in condemning Dr. Peale—the Kennedy camp made a major decision, probably the most important of the campaign. An invitation for Kennedy to address a group of Protestant ministers in Houston, Texas, was quickly accepted.

"We can win or lose the election right there in Houston on Monday night," said Ted Sorensen, who of course knew a great deal about how religion could be used to political advantage. He was, after all, the author of the "Bailey Report" which laid down the strategy employed on Kennedy's road to power.

The importance of the Houston meeting on September 12 could be seen from the fact that the Kennedy people paid for the large ballroom in which it was held.

Kennedy's speech before the Houston ministers was eloquent. He said he would not take orders from the Vatican; and that he would resign as President rather than do so. He said that there were far more critical issues in the campaign and that they should be discussed.

But when Nixon proposed a "cut-off date" on any further discussion of religion, Kennedy came back and said it was a candidate's responsibility to "submit himself to the questions of any reasonable man." And so it went.

Democratic leaders were jubilant over the upswing for their candidate in the big cities. From New York, Doris Fleeson reported that "Democrats offer several reasons why their original pessimism about the biggest state has vanished. They credit Dr. Norman Vincent Peale with shattering the apathy which had gripped many liberal Democrats and independents after Los Angeles. Dr. Peale has walked away from his original fundamentalist ukase, but it was too late. Too many New Yorkers did not want to be caught in such company, even by abstaining from activity."

The *New York Times* reported that the Peale statement was "said to have steadied wavering support for the Kennedy-Johnson ticket among Jewish and minority groups."

According to *Time* (in a cover story based on extensive interviews with Bobby Kennedy): "Hard-boiled Kennedyites run a continual poll on the Catholic vote, know that Jack's confrontation by the Houston Protestant ministers helped them with Nixon-minded Northern Catholics—and know that a fall-off of interest in religion will weaken them in the same area. Bobby plans to show a film of Jack Kennedy's session with the Houston clergy in every state."

Bobby's plans were indeed carried out. In New York, Baltimore, Chicago, and other Northern cities where there were large Catholic populations, expensive television time was purchased by the Democrats to broadcast and rebroadcast the selected portions of the speech made by Kennedy before the Houston ministers.

"While we see that it may be desirable to distribute to Protestants who misunderstand and fear Catholicism the film clips of Mr. Kennedy's reply to the Texas ministers, we see little need to show the film before Catholics who, presumably, have no such fears," observed the *Commonweal*.

"This has brought up the question as to whether there now is a campaign effort to keep the issue alive and to take advantage of the natural resentment many Catholics feel when the so-called religious issue is raised," commented David Lawrence.

"Our precinct workers are gaining access to the homes of Republican Catholics that they have never been able to get into before," a Democratic spokesman told *U.S. News & World Report*. "Our workers go in and talk about the candidates for Governor and Senator. Finally they raise the question: 'Do you think they are going to keep Kennedy from being President just because he is a Catholic?' It gets a good response. We are winning lots of new votes." Shades of James Michael Curley.

The absolute cynicism of those masterminding the use of the religious issue was demonstrated when Bobby Kennedy accused the Republicans of distributing vile anti-Catholic literature. He told newsmen the GOP was spending over $1 million on anti-Catholic literature. This charge was checked out after the campaign by the Fair Campaign Practices Committee and was found to be without foundation. "Repeated observation, examination and study has convinced this Committee that the Republicans—with only rare and short-lived exceptions—were scrupulously careful to avoid abuse of the religious issue," the non-partisan group said.

Needless to say, this didn't prevent Lyndon Johnson from telling audiences that the Republicans were spreading bigotry. And one of Lyndon's acquaintances, a fellow Democrat named Billie Sol Estes—who later became renowned for his fertilizer deals—paid for a full-page advertisement in his home-town paper in Pecos pleading with West Texans to "Show the World Texans Are Not Religious Bigots." A few months later Billie Sol paid for an ad for an upcoming revival at his church which said, "Come and hear about the two biggest threats to Western civilization today—Communism and Catholicism."

The volume of printed matter addressed to the religious issue was unquestionably greater than what was circulated in the 1928 campaign.

"We have received large amounts of this so-called anti-Roman literature," commented the *Greenville* (S.C.) *News*. "Not all of it is scurrilous by any means, although its accuracy and the motives of its originators are open to question in many instances. Some of it is demonstrably false." Much of it originated in the North. "The origin of this material makes us all the more curious as to just who is mainly responsible for its distribution. Some of the more extreme arguments are falling on fertile soil both here and elsewhere.

But it is causing an opposite reaction in pivotal Northern states and many Southerners are coming to be of a like mind.

"The question is: who is making the most use of the religious issue, and for or against whom?"

Another question, never fully answered, arose out of the fact that large numbers of Catholic families in the North received particularly vile pieces of literature concerning their faith. Who was responsible? Who benefited?

As the noted pollster Samuel Lubell observed after the election: "Too much publicity and attention was given the circulation of so-called 'hate' literature. Of course, these 'hate' sheets were disgusting and sickening. But how important were these anti-Catholic tracts? And didn't the enormous publicity given these 'hate' sheets leave a distorted, one-sided view of the campaign which ignored that on both sides deeply-rooted religious prejudices were constantly at work?"[24]

In the end, the massive swing of Catholic votes to Kennedy—as the Bailey Report had predicted—was the biggest factor in Kennedy's election. As Louis Bean put it, the statistics showed that "Catholic pride" was a stronger factor than "anti-Catholic prejudice" in bringing about Kennedy's victory.

With some 78 per cent of the Catholics and 70 per cent of the Negroes and 80 per cent or more of the Jews voting for him, Kennedy took lopsided majorities in the big cities, and thus in the big electoral-vote states they controlled. Looking at the Catholic vote as a whole, according to figures provided by Dr. George Gallup, the Democrats got 56 per cent of the total in 1952, and 51 per cent in 1956, but the figure went up by 27 percentage points to 78 per cent in 1960. No other religious group showed a switch of that proportion.

It was significant that the Republican ticket got more Catholic support from better-educated Catholics with higher incomes, where the percentage went up to 31 for Nixon, whereas among the lower-income groups and farmers the Nixon percentage of Catholic voters went down to around 16 per cent.

In the final analysis, Kennedy got his squeaked-through victory from a coalition of Northern big-city bosses, labor and urban minorities, plus a big section of the South (thanks to Lyndon Johnson).

"One thing is certain," pollster Elmo Roper commented in the *Saturday Review*. "If there was a net victim of religious prejudice it was Nixon more than Kennedy. All but one of the states most heavily populated by Catholics went for Kennedy. Only one of the states most heavily populated by Protestants went for Nixon. This brings into sharp focus the fact that the term 'religious bigot' has come to mean to liberals a White Protestant who doesn't like Catholics or Jews. Perhaps the concept, politically, can now be broadened to include anybody of *any* religious faith who votes for a coreligionist largely because he is a coreligionist.

[24] Lubell's statement was made before the 47th annual meeting of the Anti-Defamation League of B'nai B'rith, January 14, 1961, during a panel discussion on "Bigotry and Politics."

"Certain it is, from our polls and from actual voting on November 8, that Catholics thought Kennedy better than Nixon by some place between a three-to-one and a four-to-one majority. Protestants, on the other hand, leaned to Nixon by a two-to-one majority in September and by a somewhat smaller margin in late October."

In the industrial cities of the North, Negro voters, largely Protestant but traditionally Democratic, gave Kennedy a powerful assist in achieving his narrow victory over Nixon. The return to Democratic ranks by many of the Negroes who bolted in 1956, largely in protest over the treatment of their brethren in the Democratic South, was attributed by the *New York Times* to these factors:

Item: Intensive registration drives and campaign activity by labor groups and Democratic organizations in Negro areas. In contrast, Republican campaigning was lackadaisical and poorly financed. For example, the Democrats blanketed the Negro press with political advertising while Republican advertising was held to a minimum.

Item: Kennedy's move, in the closing days of the campaign, to intercede in behalf of Dr. Martin Luther King Jr., Negro integration leader who had been jailed in Georgia on a charge of violation of probation in a traffic case. "Vice President Nixon's refusal to comment on the episode," reported the *Times,* "tarnished what many Negroes felt was a good civil rights image and bolstered Mr. Kennedy's previously weak civil rights image."

Later President Eisenhower, in discussing the episode, said that "a couple of telephone calls" had swung the Negro vote to Kennedy and gave him the election. And Nixon later was quoted as crediting Kennedy with an astute political move in telephoning the Rev. Mr. King's wife with his sympathies. "I just didn't realize such a call could swing an election," Nixon told Simeon Booker of *Ebony.* "In a political campaign, I guess talking pays off most."

Shortly after the election Bobby Kennedy told newsmen, "The Houston Ministers' Conference helped us, and so did Norman Vincent Peale. They helped us a lot." He felt the Republicans had lost because (1) they had neglected the Negroes; (2) they failed to make a real issue of Adlai Stevenson; (3) they did not use President Eisenhower soon enough; and (4) "while the vast majority of newspaper publishers were for Mr. Nixon, the working press was for Senator Kennedy." And this he implied, showed in their copy—one Kennedy pronouncement with which the Republicans agreed completely.[25]

The subject of biased campaign coverage damaging to Nixon was raised by prominent Republicans and some newspapers and newsmen. The *New*

[25] Bobby discovered late in the campaign that a Nixon supporter had infiltrated his household. His then five-year-old son, David, told visiting newsmen that he was for Nixon. "Now, David," Ethel Kennedy remonstrated in front of one reporter. "You know you don't mean that!" "Yes, I do," he said. David persisted until his mother made clear by the stern tone of her voice she would stand for no more such nonsense. "All right, then—Kennedy," David said in surrender.

York Daily News, for example, said editorially that 75 per cent of the newsmen who traveled with Nixon were opposed to his election and many of them "slanted their dispatches against Nixon." And Raymond Moley reported that "in general what Mr. Nixon had to say in his whirlwind campaign was badly reported in the press by most of those assigned to his campaign."

William H. Stringer, of the *Christian Science Monitor,* in a dispatch from Washington to his newspaper on January 5, 1961, reported: "Some members of the Republican high command feel there was press bias. There comes to mind a moment in the campaign when a member of the Republican high command expressed anguish over the prospect that reporter X from one of the big-city newspapers was being reassigned to the Nixon campaign. The reporter was regarded by Nixon officials as being overly critical and hostile.

"The incident also comes to mind of a small group of reporters on a Nixon press bus reading aloud the dispatch of one purportedly pro-Kennedy reporter who had let his critical faculty show through his writing. In these dispatches some of Mr. Nixon's campaign statements were qualified by such a phrase as 'without offering proof.' Crowd estimates, too, were examined critically. The main news got through all right, but with a querulous tone."

Nixon himself was reported by Fletcher Knebel in the Cowles newspapers as having "made it clear in private talks with friends that he thinks a pro-Kennedy attitude by reporters covering the campaign provided Senator Kennedy with his narrow victory margin."

The official tabulation showed that Kennedy defeated Nixon by 119,450 votes. Counting write-in votes and other votes for minority tickets, Kennedy did not receive a majority of the 68,836,385 votes cast. The official tally gave Kennedy 34,227,096 votes and Nixon 34,107,646. In electoral votes Kennedy had 303 and Nixon 219. Senator Byrd of Virginia received 15.

From the early morning hours of November 9, when Vice President Nixon decided to go to bed after provisionally conceding his own defeat in case further returns showed his rival's victory, there was a tentative quality about the results of the election.

One of Kennedy's strongest supporters couldn't take the uncertainty. "It was unbearable," said Frank Sinatra. All through that long night he telephoned the Ambassador Hotel in Los Angeles, where Nixon was staying, trying to get through to the Vice President. "I wanted him to concede," the Leader of the Rat Pack explained. "The suspense was killing me."

Though Nixon soon recovered from his grueling experience, Dr. William Prendergast, Research Director of the Republican National Committee, was still using slide rules to see whether he could squeeze out a GOP victory, at least on paper, nearly a year after the election. And this is what he came up with:

"A record-breaking 69 million voters went to the polls last year. Yet fewer than 12,000 persons actually determined which man won the Presidency. Only 24,000 more votes for Vice President Nixon—properly distributed, of course, among the five states of Hawaii, Illinois, Missouri, New Mexico and Nevada—would have given him the needed electoral margin. Thus a switch of only 11,871 votes cost Richard Nixon the White House."

The *New York Times,* on reflection, found itself pleased with the results. "While we supported Mr. Kennedy," it said, "we think it is a good thing that the election was so close. It should serve as a restraining force, as a reminder to the Kennedy Administration that it should proceed with caution and that it has no mandate to embark on drastic changes of policy, either foreign or domestic."

The *Times,* rather late in the campaign, had endorsed Kennedy in what columnist Morrie Ryskind described as "a rather amazing editorial that sums up his palpable weaknesses and would lead you to think it was heading for a totally different conclusion. But, the paper argued, Kennedy would be able to get along better with a Democratic Congress than would Nixon; ergo, one reluctant vote for Kennedy. If the *Times* editorial is a love-letter, it is one that even the homeliest old maid would not keep among her souvenirs."

Meanwhile, complaints mounted throughout the country—but particularly in Illinois and Texas—that the election had been "stolen."

"A tempest in a teapot," scoffed Bobby Kennedy.

The charges had substance, however. Illinois had cast 2,377,638 votes for Kennedy and 2,367,837 for Nixon, a difference of only 9,801 votes. Despite the furor caused by known frauds and vote piracies, the state's electoral votes —27 of them—went to Kennedy. There was little, under the law, the Republicans could do.

The major "ambiguities" occurred in Democratic-controlled Cook County (Chicago). In one place 100 votes were tabulated before the polls opened. The first legal vote cast was recorded as vote No. 101. In another Chicago voting place where an election board was convicted of fraud it was proved that 71 ballots were cast by persons who gave false names; 34 persons voted twice and one voted three times. In that voting place, residents of Chicago flophouses were hauled in to vote the names of absent or dead voters.

"Those people know enough to take care of these matters themselves," said Bobby, in denying the Democratic National Committee was advising Cook County Democrats in any way.

Without exception, Chicago's newspapers took the position that, as the *Tribune* put it, "the election of November 8 was characterized by such gross and palpable fraud as to justify the conclusion that [Richard Nixon] was deprived of victory."

Perhaps the strangest case occurred in a Texas precinct where 86 persons received ballots. But when they were counted the score was: Kennedy 147, Nixon 24. All over Texas similar situations were reported. Tens of thousands of ballots disappeared overnight. In two adjoining precincts in Fort Bend County, Texas, this occurred: in one county which voted Nixon over Kennedy, 458 to 350, 182 ballots were declared void at the "discretion of the judges." But in the other, 68 to 1 for Kennedy, not a single ballot was declared void.

On December 14, 1960, the *Washington Post* reported that Republican efforts to upset the election in Illinois and Texas had met rebuffs in the courts. The *Post* said there could be no "complacency over court decisions to the effect that there is no judicial remedy for alleged vote frauds. Certainly some means ought to be at hand for checking controversial returns before the electoral votes are cast and the new President is inaugurated. . . ."

In the end, Richard Nixon disposed of the whole question. In the face of mounting Republican demands that he demand recounts in Illinois and Texas, he decided against doing so because, as he said, "the organization of the new Administration and the orderly transfer of responsibility from the old to the new might be delayed for months. The situation within the entire Federal Government would be chaotic. . . . Then, too, the bitterness that would be engendered by such a maneuver on my part would have done incalculable and lasting damage throughout the country."

One week after their bitter Presidential campaign, Kennedy paid a visit to the man he had so narrowly beaten. Nixon was vacationing at Key Biscayne, just below Miami, and—as a mark of courtesy—Kennedy flew down from his father's home at Palm Beach.

According to Nixon, the two had scarcely met when Kennedy said, "Well, it's hard to tell who won the election at this point." Nixon agreed the verdict was close, but he said the final result had been pretty well determined. This, of course, was the first time that Nixon indicated he would not contest the election results.

Kennedy expressed concern about the probable fate of his domestic programs, in view of the makeup of the new Congress. He told Nixon: "A Republican President can probably get more out of a Congress where his domestic policies are concerned because of his ability to get support from the natural coalition of conservative southern Democrats and most of the Republicans, who also have conservative views. On the other hand, a Democratic President, unless northern and western Democrats make up a clear majority of the House and Senate—which, of course, will not be the case in the new Congress—will find that his more liberal programs will fall short because of the strength of the conservative coalition arrayed against him." [1]

In other words, Kennedy predicted—and correctly so—that "divided government" would continue under the New Frontier.

They then discussed public opinion polling. Nixon said he had found his private pollster, the late Claude Robinson, "miraculously accurate." Kennedy said that Lou Harris had done a good job too. (Harris, for example, had discovered that Medicare was "a major issue working in Kennedy's behalf," but that control of nuclear testing stressed by Stevenson in 1956 was no issue at all. Only one in 50 voters was interested.)

Finally, the President-elect sounded out Nixon on what part he and other leading Republicans might be willing to take in the incoming Kennedy Administration—in the interests of national unity, of course.

"In view of the closeness of the election," he said, "there have been suggestions that it might be well for me to appoint some Republicans to positions in the Administration. . . . What I had in mind were appointments to posts abroad which would create an impression of unity and bipartisanship as far as our allies and potential enemies are concerned."

Then he added: "I wondered, in fact, if after a few months you yourself might want to undertake an assignment abroad on a temporary basis."

As Nixon said later, he sensed that Kennedy was making the suggestion mainly because he thought it was expected of him—"the thing to do"—and not because he was fully convinced in his own mind the idea was a useful one.

Nixon told Kennedy he appreciated his "thinking of me in this connection." However, he pointed out that taking such an assignment might be misinterpreted and could be damaging to the concept of a two-party system and party responsibility. Kennedy appeared considerably relieved that Nixon had answered the question that way; and the subject was quickly dropped. It was obvious to Nixon that the suggestion had originated elsewhere.

The private meeting on the Florida coast had been arranged by Joseph P. Kennedy, working through Herbert Hoover in New York. The former President had telephoned Nixon in Key Biscayne to ask whether the meeting would be acceptable. Soon afterward, Nixon got a call from the President-elect.

Only when the victory had been finally achieved had Joseph P. Kennedy emerged from the shadows. He posed for the family victory picture.[26]

It was a picture of defiance—albeit somewhat delayed—of a family described by *Time* "as handsome and spirited as a meadow full of Irish thoroughbreds, as tough as a blackthorn shillelagh, as ruthless as Cuchulain, the mythical hero who cast up the hills of Ireland with his sword."

For a time, there was an orgy of father-son photos. They were photographed laughing it up at the airport, on the golf course, and going to church. Then there was the photo of a top-hatted Joseph P. Kennedy standing next to his son on Inauguration Day, as the nation paid homage to the new President. The son of East Boston, whose family had emigrated at the time of Ireland's potato famine, had come a long way. Having suffered all the slights and indignities Brahmin Boston could contrive for its despised minorities, Joseph P. Kennedy had set out to beat his persecutors at their own game. Combining intense ambition and shrewdness, he had amassed enormous economic and political power. Now his son was President of the United States.

Here was revenge on traditionalist Boston, the home of the bean and the

---

[26] A California lady (obviously an unreconstructed Republican) saw the photograph in *Life* and wrote to the editors, thanking them for "the family portrait of the victorious Kennedy team. It is the picture of a happy family with a new toy—*us*."

cod, where the Lowells talk only to the Cabots and the Cabots talk only to God.

Here, too, was an end to make-believe. No longer would Joseph P. Kennedy need to absent himself from the public scene.

"Now," he told the *New York Times,* "I can appear with Jack any time I want to."

And as a new sun rose in a shabby ward of old Boston, an ancient, beery Irish pol thought he heard someone shuffle a ghostly old-country jig and rasp out the strains of "Sweet Adeline."

Begin

20

And more important than winning the election is governing the nation. That is the test of a political party—the acid, final test. When the tumult and the shouting die, when the bands are gone and the lights are dimmed, there is the stark reality of responsibility in an hour of history haunted with those gaunt, grim specters of strife, dissension, and materialism at home, and ruthless, inscrutable, and hostile power abroad.

> —Adlai E. Stevenson, in accepting the Presidential nomination of the Democratic Party in Chicago in 1952.

On December 6, 1960, six weeks before his Inauguration as President of the United States, John F. Kennedy met with President Eisenhower at the White House. The subjects discussed were (1) NATO nuclear sharing, (2) Laos, (3) the Congo, (4) Algeria, (5) disarmament and nuclear test-ban negotiations, (6) Cuba and Latin America, (7) United States balance of payments and the gold outflow, and (8) "the need for a balanced budget."

President Eisenhower, who had said some rough things about Kennedy during the campaign ("the young genius," he called him at one point), was impressed by the scope and flair of his successor. But over a Scotch and soda, he later remarked to a few friends:

"I don't believe that young man knows what he is up against."

In fact, one of Kennedy's biggest surprises as President was that the job was really as tough as he said it was during the campaign.

After having survived a blizzard, an unbelievable traffic jam, an Inaugural parade, five Inaugural balls and the Rat Pack, Washington was officially into the New Frontier. "Well," commented Fletcher Knebel, "it's nice to settle down into the Kennedy Administration. That Sinatra Administration, however brief, was a bit trying at times." The humor was good-natured. John Kennedy had entered the White House with the all but universal good will which Americans customarily extend to a new President. There were no crabbed reminders that his margin over Nixon was a mere 119,450 votes, and that, when the minor party votes were counted in, Kennedy was a minority President.

Yet, as the London *Economist* noted, "the biggest among the many burdens now taken up by the new President may be the burden of great expectations. No new President has been so heralded." No new President, it might have been added, had come to office after promising so much.

The main motif of the new Administration was to obtain what the *New Republic's* T.R.B. so trenchantly and admiringly described as "Kennedy's real goal"—"to achieve a transition to . . . Presidential rule . . . to activist government." And James Reston predicted, though in his Inaugural Address Kennedy did not hint it, that "in the long run Kennedy's solutions are likely to be more radical than anything in American politics since the first Administration of Franklin D. Roosevelt." However, "for the moment nobody knows what these solutions will be—not even Mr. Kennedy—but it is not too difficult to identify the problems. . . ."

A conservative pundit, Frank S. Meyer, made these observations in *National Review:* "Early as it is, and despite the difficulties created by modern political rhetoric, I think one can predict fairly clearly the major lines of policy of the new Administration. There will be much talk of the great challenge of Communism, much drum-beating about frontiers and missions; but there will be no firm anti-Communist policy. Instead there will be a grandiose shadowboxing endeavor in which Communism will be the excuse for massive unproductive expenditures of energy and money in every far-flung corner of the globe. There will be no Rooseveltian Hundred Days of dramatic extension of domestic welfarism. Instead the Galbraithian prescription of increasing the sphere of government power and contracting the sphere of the individual's control over his own life and fortunes, will be implemented by welfarism on a world scale, while in the real war we continue to lose position after position to Communism."

"But let no one be misled," wrote the *New York Post's* William Shannon, "the new President and his able, aggressive associates in the new Administration intend to conduct the affairs of government at a break-neck pace. Every problem is to be tackled as soon as humanly possible. Progress on twenty different fronts simultaneously will be the expected order of the day. . . . President Kennedy intends to get around all obstacles, focus public attention upon himself and his program, and reach the largest possible audience. He is keenly aware that a shift of only a few thousand votes would have made him the loser and Mr. Nixon the winner. He believes there is no margin for safety and no time in which he can safely coast. For the next four years, he intends to woo public attention and public support just as assiduously and untiringly as he did in the previous four years seeking the nomination.

"The President intends to bombard Congress and the public with special messages, frequent press conferences, televised speeches, and dramatic gestures. He likes to make quick trips as he did this week to New York for one day. This practice will continue in the White House. He also likes to use the homes of private friends for conferences as he did when he spent several hours at the Georgetown home of William Walton. . . . He made use earlier in the month of the Cambridge home of Professor Arthur Schlesinger. This is an unconventional practice which he also will continue during the next four years. He intends to be a President on the move."

From the first, Kennedy told his top officials that he wanted "all the communication we can get" with the public through the press and other media. And he got it. Rarely had any incoming President been ushered into office with such fanfare and indiscriminate eulogy. The early months of the New Frontier found the press and television reveling in details of the transformation of the White House into a political powerhouse.

The first three months, particularly, were halcyon months for Kennedy. The nation appeared to exult in the glamour and vigor radiated by the new tenants in the White House; and the President appeared to glory in the range his new office permitted an energetic young man.

As a calculated matter, Kennedy was out to demonstrate to the public that he was the active, articulate and visible leader of the United States Government. And no one can dispute the fact that he appeared to be in perpetual motion. But motion does not necessarily mean progress. It was, in fact, motion largely without movement. Never before had so much public relations effort been expended to convey an impression of great activity.

During the campaign, Kennedy had pledged "100 days of action" to establish the leadership he claimed the nation had lacked during the Eisenhower years. He promised to take executive action and push through legislation that would "get America moving again," that would "move America forward," that would get this country in proper shape to meet "the complex challenges of the sixties." There was his constant chiding of President Eisenhower for withholding a mere stroke of the pen by which racial segregation could have been barred forever from federally aided housing. There was the commitment to other bold and far-reaching civil rights action by Congressional legislation. He pledged repeatedly that all this would begin with a massive thrust in the first one hundred days following his Inauguration. In short, between January 20 and May 1, 1961, America was to begin crossing the New Frontier.

During the first one hundred Kennedy days, there was a flood of speeches, statements, special messages and legislative requests—close to fifty, spaced properly for maximum press coverage—which conveyed a *sense* of momentum and constant progress. People felt things were happening under Kennedy, when they really weren't.

There was this revealing episode: on September 22, 1962, while Kennedy was in Newport, Rhode Island, his associate press secretary, Andrew T. Hatcher, told newsmen that the President had conferred by telephone with two Cabinet officers. However, Hatcher declined to say who they were.

When a reporter remarked, "Why tell us about it at all?" Hatcher replied, amid laughter, "I have to convey the impression—that the President is working—convey the true impression that the President is working."

Adding to this sense of motion was Kennedy's own restlessness. Unlike Eisenhower and Truman, who had regarded themselves as something of a "prisoner" in the White House, Kennedy from the beginning of his reign wanted to get around and do some of the same things he used to do as a Senator. He made the rounds of the various "events" in Washington, such as the Alfalfa Club dinner and the inauguration of new officers of the National Press Club. One night he slipped out to see the movie *Spartacus* at a downtown theater; and on another occasion he attended a public *première*. Sometimes he strolled along public streets in the vicinity of the White House, usually after dusk in the evenings.

His activities, of course, gave the Secret Service considerable concern. Aware that the number of threats against the President had risen greatly since Kennedy had taken over, the agents assigned to protect his life preferred to take no chances. But he made it plain that he felt entitled to a private social life in the evenings, immune from the eyes of prying reporters. He partied, sometimes into the early morning hours, at the homes of friends.

In those early months, the new President demonstrated a partiality for the social companionship of certain newspapermen. Those he was chummy with, however, were usually wealthy or influential members of the Georgetown "smart set," rather than the more mundane working reporters who regularly cover the White House.

Some newsmen were particularly annoyed by Kennedy's attendance at a small dinner party given by Rowland Evans Jr. of the *New York Herald Tribune*. They felt that in the easy discourse of a cozy little group the President could, intentionally or otherwise, give his favored friend the makings of an exclusive dispatch known in the parlance of the trade as a "beat."

"What seems to be developing here is an after-hours elite corps," reported Paul Martin, of Gannett Newspapers, "a sort of unofficial oligarchy of wealth and wit and intellect. Kennedy avoids the matronly social hostesses of Washington."

According to Martin, the New Frontier "seems to get started later than the Eisenhower Administration. Whereas Ike, an old soldier, was up at the crack of dawn, and in his office by 7:40 A.M., the Kennedy machine rumbles into action around 9:00 o'clock. But the staff also is pinned down later at the White House, with no one leaving before 'the boss' gets away.

"White House visitors are being hustled in and out the back doors nowadays, with no opportunities for press interviews which used to take place regularly in the lobby. The Kennedy public relations people, for both Mr. and Mrs., have a gay and carefree disregard for punctuality, and a seeming indifference to accuracy about names, identifications, facts, dates, and places. Almost nothing happens 'on time' around the White House."

Except for Old Frontiersmen like Paul Martin, dissenting voices were few and far between in those halcyon days. On March 12, 1961, Robert J. Donovan, Washington bureau chief of the *New York Herald Tribune,* reported in wonderment: "In these last seven weeks Pierre Salinger has been getting his chief publicized on a scale that makes a piker out of James C. Hagerty, who only recently was regarded by many as perhaps the master publicist in White House history." The truth is that J.F.K. handled his own press relations. (Early in his reign, President Kennedy let it be known he preferred that editors use J.F.K. in their headlines, rather than Jack. Under Roosevelt, editors relied on the initials F.D.R.)

Later in the year, Donovan came out with a best-selling book on Kennedy's wartime experiences in the South Pacific, *PT-109.* The best-selling tome, extolling Kennedy's courage, did no harm to the Presidential "image." Other benefits were yet to come. Hollywood purchased the book for a film, the deal having been worked out by Joseph P. Kennedy, a former movie producer himself.

Still another adoring book about the President was published in September 1962. William Manchester's *Portrait of a President: John F. Kennedy in Profile* (Boston, Little, Brown, 1962) did not pretend to be an objective biography. But author William Manchester was compared to "the dazzled artist [who] has gazed upon the subject with loving eyes and found redeeming beauty in his every flaw."

The comparison was made in a *New York Times* book review by Tom Wicker of the *Times'* Washington staff. Wicker raised this profound point:

"The question is whether any President is well-served by the sort of adulation that Mr. Manchester allows himself and Mr. Kennedy has too often been accorded in the press. May it not tend to give both him and the public a sense of euphoria? And when trouble comes, as it always will, the fall from glory will be just that much harder. President Kennedy deserves better of his chroniclers. . . ."

In September 1962, *Chicago Sun* cartoonist Bill Mauldin reported on a visit to Washington. He had lunch with Pierre Salinger. ("The Kennedy Administration wants cartoonists to know that J.F.K. has got a sense of humor," wrote Mauldin.) At lunch, Salinger asked if Mauldin would like to visit the President.

"So," Mauldin reported, "at 4:00 P.M., I reported to Pierre's office. He told me to wait in the Cabinet Room. I tried out some of the chairs around the big, boat-shaped table (in the South they'd say I was walking in tall cotton), inspected some ship models and was staring out the French doors at the garden when the President popped in.

"Physically, he's a lot skinnier than I used to draw him. Those jowls fool you. (I made a mental note: 'Narrow from Adam's apple down.') He has a warm smile and a cool eye. (Add mental note: 'If Pierre offers to fix you up with a presidential poker game, decline.')

"He had had a rough summer and when I said I was pleased to meet him he actually looked as if the words meant a lot to him.

"We exchange some small talk about newspapers, a subject he seems to enjoy. I remembered hearing somewhere that he was a frustrated journalist. He needn't be. Most papers will take on men with political savvy at the age of 52. His chances would be even better at 48. I didn't want to take up more of his time telling him all this, so I left the message with Pierre on the way out."

Another Kennedy innovation that has annoyed reporters has been his refusal to release the guest list of small dinner parties he occasionally hosts while he is out of town. Newsmen who inquire as to the names of the President's guests are informed it's none of their business.

And in the early months of the New Frontier, the correspondents didn't know that the President was sneaking over to the Burning Tree Club to play golf on the sly. Only after Kennedy's afternoon disappearances became the subject of wild rumors was the story officially confirmed. Yes, said Pierre, Kennedy was a pretty good golfer. But the less said about it the better, lest he be compared with *The Great Golfer,* as Kennedy's chum Gore Vidal had tabbed Eisenhower.[1]

Even after his "addiction to golf" was disclosed, Kennedy refused to be photographed swinging a Number Five Iron. The rule, handed down by Pierre Salinger, was that photographs could be taken of the President standing on the first tee, but not swinging a club.

Kennedy's fear of being caught swinging a club was described by Under Secretary of the Navy, Paul B. "Red" Fay, a pal from PT-boat days. Before he was nominated, he was relaxing with Fay on the golf course at Pebble Beach, California. On the 15th hole, as Fay recalls it, the candidate-to-be teed off with a Seven Iron and almost got a hole-in-one. As the ball rolled across the green, Kennedy leaped up and down, shouting frantically at the ball, "Get out of there!"

"What's the matter?" asked Fay, bewildered. "Are you nuts, or something?"

Kennedy wasn't nuts. "If the ball drops in," he said quickly, "everybody in the country will know about it in five minutes, and they'll think another golfer is trying to get into the White House. Get *out* of there!" And with typical Kennedy luck, the ball stopped only inches from the cup.

---

[1] By November 1961, Gore Vidal was parodying President Kennedy (and in ringing Kennedyesque tones): "Ask not what you can do for your country, but what your country can do for you!"

In May 1961, the White House took an anguished view of reports that Mrs. Kennedy had given the President, as a birthday gift, a small golf layout at their Virginia country estate. "The story is ridiculous and untrue," said Acting Press Secretary Andrew Hatcher, in a lengthy statement which seemed to protest too much.

What really got Kennedy's goat was when the Associated Press dispatched an army of reporters to dig up an answer to this question: "Is Jack Kennedy really a better golfer than Dwight Eisenhower?" And the AP reported: "Not all the returns are in, but from what old-hand White House reporters have learned from authoritative stories, we are led inescapably to the conclusion: Yes, he probably is."

One boon result was that political pitchmen who used to worry lest the nation be lost on the back nine weren't worrying out loud any more.

Somehow or other the Kennedy Administration generally managed to avoid the deadly label of "Madison Avenue," in itself no mean public relations achievement. Reporters who thought that Eisenhower's techniques smacked of Advertising Row didn't believe Kennedy's did. It was, as the still unchastened Senator Hugh Scott put it, "an era of good fooling."

There were, of course, various reasons for this. As already suggested, many Washington correspondents are of the Democratic persuasion and, unavoidably, some of their political prejudices seep into their copy. Then, Kennedy's more youthful personality and style set much better than did General Eisenhower's. Mostly, reporters liked the innovations that brought about greater accessibility of the President. This, of course, meant more publishable stories and photographs. That much of the early copy smacked of the movie fan magazines did not deter the press corps. Scarcely a week went by, in those early months, without some news organization offering an exclusive account with photographs of, usually, a day in the life of the President. Even *U.S. News & World Report* published ten pages of such photographs, space which amounted to one-tenth of the March 6, 1961, issue of that usually serious publication.

On another occasion a *Washington Star* photographer was admitted to the President's office to take a picture of Kennedy working at his desk on a Sunday night. In walked Caroline Kennedy. The result was a series of charming photographs of his three-year-old daughter conferring with the President and using the Presidential phone to call grandfather.

The *Star* photos, made available to the nation's newspapers, obtained a big play Monday.

All of this encouraged imitators to stage their own little dramas along the New Frontier. "The other day," wrote Douglass Cater in the *Reporter,* "a White House assistant having some important business to transact with a Cabinet member took along a cameraman who was covering him that day. When he arrived, he found that the Secretary already had a reporter spending the day with him. And so, the four of them sat down to confer."

The fact is that President Kennedy likes to have his picture taken. He is probably the most picture-conscious Chief Executive in United States history. And he made very effective use of the photographic medium in his race for the Presidency.

Authority for all this was Jacques Lowe, Kennedy's official photographer during the campaign. "This is probably the first time there has been a concerted effort to use and coordinate photography into a political campaign," Lowe told *Editor & Publisher* after the election.

Lowe's job was to help build the visual image of Kennedy as a man truly concerned about people's problems. The idea was to identify Kennedy with people and their various needs. "When the Senator went to visit some of the aged," Lowe recalled, "I went along and we would get pictures that would talk, that would make sense. We did the same thing with the miners, farmers, big business, labor and the urban problems."

Kennedy rarely missed an opportunity to gaze at Lowe's handiwork. Not even the exigencies of campaigning would prevent him from deciding what pictures to send to which magazine and which to use on campaign posters.

"Let's face it," Lowe said. "We're in an age when the visual means more than the word to the great mass of people who decide an election one way or another. They looked at the debates but many didn't listen to what was said but they studied how the candidates looked."

"The image a candidate projects is the most important thing," he added.

As Kennedy's quasi-official Court Photographer in the first half of 1961, Lowe roamed about the inner offices of the White House, taking candid photographs freely. His presence infuriated the regular White House photographers. "But," reported Douglass Cater, "Mr. Kennedy seems to enjoy having Lowe hovering in the background. Once when a high-ranking politician wanted to communicate something private and suggested that Lowe leave the room, the President abruptly turned him down."

If anything, the new boy was getting finer press notices abroad than at home. "Suddenly, splendidly, America has been captured by a man inspired," rhapsodized Rene MacColl, United States correspondent of the *London Daily Express.* "What a transformation has taken place in Washington. Where before there was doubt, dreariness and defeatism, now a great wave of excitement and eagerness has transformed the United States. When Kennedy and Khrushchev finally meet—wow!"

Across the Channel, the French press was no longer doubtful about Kennedy, particularly when it became known he had enough sense to take unto himself a French-descended bride. "His virile language," wrote Roger Massip in *Le Figaro,* "is designed to stir up the energies of a great nation which is threatened by the excesses of her prosperity." And the normally skeptical *Le Monde* added: "There is every reason to believe that Kennedy diplomacy will result in spectacular developments in the near future." (The following month came the Bay of Pigs.)

In West Germany, a widespread pre-election anxiety about Kennedy's youthfulness had been coupled with Chancellor Adenauer's concern that some of the new President's advisers would be soft on Berlin. All this was forgotten.

"The free world has a leader again," exulted Cologne's *Neue Rhein-Zeitung*—and it didn't mean Adenauer. The *Frankfurter Allgemeine* hailed Kennedy's cabinet selections as "a masterpiece of natural political talent."

Even the Soviet press was giving Kennedy the benefit of every doubt. Terminating the anti-Eisenhower tirades which had begun with the U-2 episode, Soviet newspapers were so gentle with Kennedy that *Pravda* even referred to his "beautiful wife."

Still more favorable publicity accrued when these foreign reactions were cabled back to the United States. It was nice to know that the folks beyond the pond were so impressed with young Jack.

But some of Jack's admirers were beginning to worry.

"The Kennedy build-up goes on," wrote James MacGregor Burns, Kennedy's biographer, in the *New Republic*. "The adjectives tumble over one another. He is not only the handsomest, the best-dressed, the most articulate, and graceful as a gazelle. He is omniscient; he swallows and digests whole books in minutes; he confounds experts with his superior knowledge of their field. He is omnipotent."

Burns was worried, as were other Kennedy admirers, that Kennedy and his family might soon suffer ill effects from public overexposure. "The build-up is too indiscriminate," Burns added. "The build-up will not last. The public can be cruel, and so can the press. Americans build their triumphal arches out of brick, Mr. Dooley said, so as to have missiles handy when their heroes have fallen."

"I don't really believe that you can 'overexpose' the President of the United States," Pierre Salinger replied. "I think when people talk about 'overexposure' they are talking about show business—about jugglers and comics getting too much TV time."

President Kennedy himself was plainly unworried about competing with jugglers and comics. The week the Burns article was published another hour-long glimpse into the life of Jack and Jacqueline was televised by NBC. The fact that it was sponsored by Crest toothpaste led wags to wonder if Pepsodent, Ipana, and Gleem might not demand equal time. This was the *Just Plain Jack* show in which Jacqueline complained that the fish-bowl life of the White House was "very hard" on the kids, that she was striving to provide "normal" and "private" lives for them. "Someday Caroline is going to have to go to school, and if she is in the papers all the time, that will affect her little classmates, and they will treat her differently."

Less than a month after the Inauguration, CBS beat out the competition by presenting an "Eyewitness to History" which the network hailed as "the first time television has ever been permitted" in the White House "during the actual conduct of official business." The half-hour taped telecast was billed by Walter Cronkite as a "candid glimpse" of the "fulcrum, the balancing point in which national crises come to rest, to be swung one way or the other by decisions made in the office of the President of the United States." (Music up.)

The big scene showed President Kennedy receiving a telephone call on February 15, 1961, the day that Lumumba supporters rioted in the U.N. Security Council:

CRONKITE (his voice hushed): "The waited call from U.N. Ambassador Adlai Stevenson. . . ."

KENNEDY: "Governor . . ."

CRONKITE: ". . . whom he—the President—customarily addresses by his former title of Governor."

KENNEDY: "Oh, yes, yes. How is that up there? Yes, that'd be fine. Oh, who is— Who has withdrawn?"

(While Kennedy, thoughtful-looking, listens to Stevenson, Cronkite gives a fast run-down on "fast-moving developments" at the U.N.)

KENNEDY: "Have they announced that they're going to give the assistance or they're prepared to give it? I see. That's ah . . . Right, fine. Look, now let me ask you, what is the legitimacy of Gizenga?"

(Cronkite explains that Antoine Gizenga was the political heir of Patrice Lumumba in the Congo.)

KENNEDY: "Right. Well, I'll get ahold of that. If there's any further questions on this matter of the delegation—I'll get on this business of getting it to the Senate, and, ah, I'll have Kenny O'Donnell talk to some member of your staff if there are some questions further about it. Okay. Good. Thanks, Governor."

While CBS had promised "an unprecedented look at the making of a President's decisions . . . ," it was left for ABC to show how a Presidential judgment was actually reached at the White House:

ANNOUNCER: "The hour is late, the official day is ending, and now you will see the President in the more intimate moments of evening—moments that reveal his personal charm, the workings of an extraordinary mind and the warmth with which he treats his close associates . . . Now Ted Sorensen is posing a question. For an insight into the workings of the Kennedy mind, watch how and when Sorensen finally gets his answer."

Viewers could see Sorensen place what appeared to be a list of names in front of the President. Kennedy glanced at the list. Then, without saying a word, he got up, and walked to his secretary's office. There, he jiggled the TV set, and waited for a picture to appear. Unhappily for ABC, Chet Huntley of NBC emerged. Huntley was barely able to say a dozen newsworthy words before Kennedy snapped him off. Still without saying a word, Kennedy headed back to his office where Sorensen was still waiting.

KENNEDY: "That's okay."

Thus was a Presidential decision made.

The sequence involving Walter Heller was not as candid. The Chairman of the Council of Economic Advisers was shown handing the President a letter. The President, after reading it, broke into loud laughter. The scene dissolved, but the Presidential belly-laugh continued to be heard. Later, the producers admitted to Douglass Cater that the laugh had been stretched out by technical means to cover the video transition.

During "Adventures on the New Frontier"—an ABC production starring John F. Kennedy—McGeorge Bundy appeared ill-at-ease as he tried to brief the President on National Security Council business. He kept making oblique references to "the thing we discussed last week."

At a meeting of the Joint Chiefs of Staff, the then Chairman Lyman Lemnitzer was horrified when—with the television equipment grinding away —the President brought up certain classified matters. A Presidential aide finally asked the TV crew to leave the room. (Ironically, one of the matters under discussion was the then upcoming invasion of Cuba. When the invasion failed, Kennedy was to level much of the blame on the American press for failing to observe security.)

"Adventures" also showed the President conferring with Disarmament Chief John McCloy. Under discussion was the question of when the United States would be ready to begin to negotiate with the Soviets. The transcript included the following dialogue:

MCCLOY: "I think it probably would be pretty early fall, but from the way I can sense attitudes around town here, there's an awful lot of pessimism and an awful lot of studies that have to be resolved. We've got studies all over the place."

KENNEDY: As far as saying anything to them, that would look pretty late. I thought at least we ought to indicate our. . . . Otherwise, everybody's going to begin to assume that we're not as serious as . . ." (deletions by the network).

That television posed a number of problems in discretion, if not security, was the point of a Douglass Cater article in the *Reporter* (April 27, 1961): "The films are cleared by Salinger, but no one has cleared the cameramen to make sure they don't repeat anything they may pick up. So far Salinger has been lenient. The 'Adventures' editors themselves decided to eliminate the sound track of the meeting with the Joint Chiefs. They left in the dialogue with McCloy, fully expecting it to be disapproved at the White House, but it wasn't. Even after the clearance, Kennedy's remark was cut, reportedly by ABC news chief James Hagerty, who has had a certain amount of experience in the censorial duties of a President's press secretary."

Kennedy's inordinate use of the television medium had other dubious aspects. "For one thing," said Cater, "television tends to hoke it up, to try to make a big show out of the Presidency. The real drama of decision making is a great deal more subtle and secluded. What the viewer is apt to see is a reality without substance. No matter how unrehearsed, it is shadow acting. When carried too far, it bastardizes the business of government and tempts the public to regard a President's job as less awesome than it is."

According to Cater, Kennedy showed "a shrewd awareness that the only way to develop trust among most reporters is to trust them, or at least some of them. He has also been shrewdly aware that government in the words of the old adage is a vessel that *ought* to leak from the top."

One such leak, eighteen days after Kennedy took office, caused him considerable dismay. After a background briefing by Defense Secretary Robert McNamara, favored correspondents wrote that the "missile gap," which had played such a large role in the 1960 Democratic campaign, was non-existent.

The revelation, needless to say, touched off a small storm. Republicans, still indignant over their claims that the Presidential election had been "stolen," now charged that the missile gap was the "grand deception" of the 1960 campaign. Minority Leader Everett McKinley Dirksen went so far as to term it a "yap-gap."

Yap-gap or not, it was terribly embarrassing to the Administration. As Senator Hugh Scott so unkindly observed, all it took to close the alleged gap was eighteen days of Mr. Kennedy in the White House.

Perhaps even more important than the controversy itself was the way President Kennedy handled its embarrassing aspects. Less than a month after taking office, the new President provided a case history in how the New Frontier deals with facts; and how those facts invariably become subordinated to the interests of Jack Kennedy.

First, Secretary McNamara held a "background briefing" for the nation's top military analysts. They reported in stories published on February 7, 1961, that studies by Kennedy's defense command had tentatively concluded that there was no missile gap at the present time. The stories differed in some minor particulars, but they all agreed upon that central fact.

Second, Pierre Salinger, on the same day, denied the stories. At one point, the White House press secretary said the stories were "inaccurate." Then he went further, contending that "no government official" had given out the information on which the stories were based and that the reports were "absolutely wrong."

Third, at his own press conference, Kennedy at first seemed to deny there had been a McNamara meeting with the press ("if such a meeting took place"). He said that McNamara had told him that no study on the missile gap possibility had been completed. Therefore, he added, he would make no comment on whether or not a missile gap existed until his audit of United States defense forces was completed.

The *fourth* step came when Secretary McNamara replied to a letter of inquiry from Minority Leader Dirksen, who had asked (1) whether Mc-

Namara had held a background briefing with newsmen and (2) whether the February 7 stories were correct.

In his reply, McNamara admitted the briefings, saying that "during the past month I have met on a background basis with reporters, individually and in groups." This admission varied considerably from the statements attributed to Salinger.

As to the accuracy of the February 7 stories, McNamara ducked. He was not responsive to Senator Dirksen's query, limiting his answer to saying that "I have not said with respect to missile power that the United States is either in a superior or inferior position vis-à-vis the Soviet Union." McNamara thus did not address himself to the main point of the newsmen's stories.

McNamara enclosed a number of newspaper stories which he said reflected his point of view. These stories, it turned out, were published several days after the snafu developed and after the White House had denied the original stories.

One of the men who had written one of the challenged February 7 stories, John G. Norris, military expert for the *Washington Post,* made these observations on McNamara's reply to Dirksen: "McNamara did not answer Dirksen's questions directly. . . . He did not deny that he had said there was no 'missile gap.' . . . He did not answer Dirksen's questions asking whether quoted statements from the stories in the *Washington Post* and *New York Times* were correct or incorrect. . . ."

Norris also reported that "the newsmen who wrote these stories (the original February 7 reports) said yesterday they have found no reason to change their original reports."

All of which came down to this: President Kennedy contradicted Candidate Kennedy; Kennedy contradicted Salinger; McNamara contradicted Salinger; and Kennedy and Salinger contradicted what McNamara apparently said originally.

"The inescapable fact remains," Fulton Lewis noted, "that Candidate Kennedy spoke with every outward assurance and gave the clear impression of certain knowledge of a missile gap—in order to be elected President. GOP spokesmen have failed to charge Kennedy with this unforgivable irresponsibility which placed personal ambition high above the requirements of truth and the national interest."

"Apparently," Lewis continued, "President Kennedy understands that the GOP attacks are not all-out and sustained. He thus even permitted himself his little joke, by publicly stating there will be sufficient budget 'to start closing what the Democrats and this Administration used to call the missile gap.' "

Some Republicans didn't think it was a joking matter. Congressmen John Rhodes of Arizona and Melvin Laird of Wisconsin demanded that Kennedy apologize or, at least, "express regrets" to President Eisenhower who had called the missile gap a "fiction."

The *Nashville Banner,* which had supported Nixon, could not forgive Kennedy for having "fabricated" the missile issue "out of the whole cloth as a scare device." Kennedy "owes his election to the fact that many accepted his screaming accusations at face value. He either believed what he was saying, based on amateur judgment of facts beyond his grasp, or he did not—and all things considered the latter is the logical explanation. . . . The nation is treated to political caprice at its worst when people can be lied to with straight face—with the earnestness of avowed candor, a 'profile of courage,' no less—and then three weeks after the inauguration witness the wakening and hear the admission that, in substance, it was all campaign oratory.

"America was taken for a political ride, with John F. Kennedy at the wheel. The truth eventually catches up; meanwhile, what assertion—earnestly proclaimed—does one believe?"

And the *London Observer,* ultra-Liberal weekly, said "it is already clear that this gap, which was always exaggerated by the more warlike Democrats, has been closed by the brilliant work done by American scientists. . . . It is no doubt politically embarrassing for Mr. Kennedy to have to admit that some of his severest criticisms of the Eisenhower Administration were unfounded."

By November 1961, President Kennedy was able to say, "In terms of total military strength, the United States would not trade places with any nation on earth. . . ." The reason for Kennedy's total reversal on the "lagging defense" issue was explained by the *Detroit News'* Washington bureau chief, J. F. Ter Horst: "Russia's superbomb blackmail made it necessary, in Mr. Kennedy's opinion, to publicly affirm this country's superiority" in missile strength and total retaliatory might. "The result has been to discard the gap theory as a military figment and also to cancel it out as a Democratic issue. The decision to do so publicly was reported to have been difficult for the Administration. . . ."

Yet, President Kennedy never conceded that his campaign oratory was what it was—campaign oratory. "That is what we call it in polite and parliamentary language," commented the *Richmond News Leader.* "Out on the sidewalk, when a man repeatedly asserts that a thing is so, when he knows it is not so, we call it something else."

Understandably, Kennedy was embarrassed about informing the American people that it was the United States—and not the Soviet Union—which held the big punch; that our nuclear delivery power was far greater than that of the Soviets.

"The great truth—far from being emphasized—is only allowed to trickle to us, as if enough time should pass to make it appear our security was achieved by President Kennedy," wrote Henry J. Taylor on November 3, 1961. "If this is unintentional, it is nevertheless the effect. When an early trickle came from Secretary McNamara last February, his good news was slapped down immediately at the White House. Now we have heard from

Deputy Secretary of Defense Roswell L. Gilpatric. He has blandly informed a business group at Hot Springs, Virginia, that the famous 'missile gap,' of which Mr. Kennedy made such an issue in the campaign, is on the Soviet side, not ours.

"Mr. Kennedy had this information in detail when he set out to win the Presidency, and knew how greatly the situation favors America, in briefings President Eisenhower ordered before the campaign started. Allen W. Dulles, chief of the Central Intelligence Agency, told Mr. Kennedy every fact Mr. Gilpatric now renders.

"The damage done is serious business. In all good conscience President Kennedy has a duty to correct it. He owes it to us to reverse himself at the top of his voice—not in small asides which do not penetrate—and relieve our hearts and the hearts of the whole free world by a great, ringing recital of the truth."

Taylor's comments deserve further exploration. Did Allen Dulles brief John Kennedy on the facts of United States defense superiority? If not, why not? He had been under direct orders from President Eisenhower to do so. Dulles had also been instructed to brief Kennedy on the covert Cuban operation; yet, Dulles said later he had not done so.

Still more questions could be explored: If Kennedy had been properly briefed on the superiority of United States defense vis-à-vis the U.S.S.R., then why did he persist in making a campaign issue out of alleged inferiority?

President Kennedy's failure to repudiate his various campaign misstatements on the nation's defenses prompted David Lawrence to denounce "the politician—in and out of public office—who betrays the citizens generally, misleads the voters, and by misstatements of fact damages the prestige of his own country throughout the world."

The *New York Times,* whose dicta enjoy an air of infallibility along the New Frontier, had the final word December 27, 1961: "The 'missile gap'—the prediction of an overwhelming Soviet superiority in intercontinental ballistic missiles in the early 1960s—was the product of partisan politics and service (primarily Air Force) pressures. The same forces and the same congressional and journalistic mouthpieces who manufactured an alleged bomber gap in the 1950s sponsored, and indeed invented, the alleged missile gap in the 1960s. . . . The Democrats, on the political out, used the alleged 'missile gap' as a club with which to belabor the Administration. The result was that a ghost, a shadow, became a synthetic issue, which obscured real national defense problems and confused the voter."

But the people of the United States were not the only ones confused. Abroad, the so-called prestige of the United States supposedly had declined enormously; but no one took the trouble to analyze how much of the decline could be attributed to the fault-finding and the moaning of ambitious United States politicians making speeches about not being satisfied about this country falling behind the Soviets in everything from missiles to parchesi sets.

Once in power, the Kennedy Administration solved the "prestige gap" in short order. It quickly abolished the prestige polls. These were the polls that Kennedy, as a candidate, had made one of his biggest issues, insisting that they showed United States prestige in Europe to be further down the scale than it had ever been. He demanded the confidential polls be publicized. President Eisenhower declined on the ground that they were of no real value. Following Kennedy's lead, the Democrats tried to blow up the refusal to an issue of major importance. Eventually, copies of the documents—stolen from the files of the U.S. Information Agency—were published in the *New York Times.*

In announcing the discontinuance of the polls, Edward R. Murrow, the new USIA chief, said the Kennedy Administration had "no desire to spend the taxpayers' money running what might be called a rating system of relative popularity as between the United States and the Soviet Union."

This did not satisfy Congressman Frank Bow, Ohio Republican, who in a closed-door meeting of the House Appropriations Committee asked Murrow, "Is the Kennedy Administration worried about its prestige abroad?"

"The polls are being discontinued," said Murrow. "We found they had little depth. Some were inaccurate and of little use to the Government."

Two years later, the "discontinued" polls were again in the news.

As it turned out, they were continued.

At his February 14, 1963, press conference, Kennedy was asked whether official prestige polls "are now being taken." Kennedy said they were, but he dismissed the polls by saying, as did Nixon in 1960, that the United States "is known to be a defender of freedom and is known to carry major burdens around the world." He conceded the United States was having "difficulties" with its allies. "We will have to wait and see," he added somewhat obtusely, "both what our prestige is abroad and at home when we get clearer ideas in the next two years."

An inquiry to the United States Information Agency the following day by the *Washington Star* drew the statement that the polls were "classified." And a day later, Pierre Salinger backed up the USIA and suggested the President "misspoke himself" in saying such polls even existed.

At his February 21 press conference, JFK was asked whether he thought the USIA was justified in keeping the polls secret.

"No, I don't," the President replied.

Some polls—those involving personalities or policies of other countries "which might provide some diplomatic embarrassment"—would not be in the public interest to release, he noted. Otherwise, the polls were not "embarrassing" to his Administration, and the results would be released "at periodic intervals."

Finally, the USIA agreed to release the polls to the public, but only two years after they were taken, unless "national security interests" required them to remain classified.

This did not prevent the Administration from breaking its own self-imposed restrictions. In March 1963, the Associated Press published excerpts from a confidential USIA document purporting to demonstrate the popularity abroad of Kennedy policies.

Aside from some muttering from the Republicans, nobody seemed to care. It was different during the 1960 campaign when "prestige" was played big in the nation's newspapers—particularly in the *New York Times*.

No polls were needed, however, to determine that United States prestige —after three months of the New Frontier—had really hit bottom all over the world.

What had happened, of course, was Cuba. And, as Theodore Draper wrote, "The ill-fated invasion of Cuba was one of those rare politico-military events—a perfect failure." Cuba shattered the magic of the first few months of the New Frontier. It even shattered Kennedy's faith in himself.

Everything had appeared to be so simple while he was seeking the office. Get the best brains working on the nation's problems, provide strong Executive Leadership, and the nation would begin to move again.

But as Kennedy soon learned to his sorrow, the prescription had flaws. Sometimes the best brains get fuzzy or the leadership itself falters. Or people involved in problems don't play their roles the way the Administration would like.

Actually, Kennedy had begun to feel the frustrations of a lag between decision and action after only two weeks in the White House. The man who had pledged to get the country moving again was finding it difficult to get the giant federal bureaucracy to move. Asked at his second press conference what particular problems he had encountered which he had not expected, Kennedy gave this revealing reply:

"I think the problem is the difficulty in securing a clear response between decisions . . . which affect the security of the United States, and having them . . . instrumented in the field. It is easier to sit with a map and talk about what ought to be done than to see it done, but that is perhaps inevitable."

Inevitable or not, his experiences were not unique. As an amateur historian, he could have found plenty of precedents in the experiences of his predecessors.[2]

Kennedy soon learned, too, that even when a President clearly sees a course of action he would like to take, literally dozens of political, diplomatic, military, or other considerations may prevent him from taking it. For example, all through the campaign he had questioned why it wasn't possible to get rid of

[2] F.D.R. once told a visitor: "If you ever sit here, you will learn that you cannot, just by shouting, get what you want all the time." Harry Truman remarked of his successor: "He'll sit here, and he'll say, 'Do this! Do that!' And nothing will happen. Poor Ike—it won't be a bit like the Army. He'll find it very frustrating." And Poor Ike did. Once, Eisenhower became so exasperated with his own Republican party's failure to support him that he began to talk about forming a third party.

more United States food surpluses by giving them to more hungry people abroad. As President, he discovered that dumping United States surpluses would create havoc among our food-exporting allies. In other words, things were not as simple as they had appeared to be to the eager young candidate.

Cuba, however, provided a perfect example of how conflicting advice led a young President, thoroughly inexperienced in diplomacy, military affairs, and psychological warfare, into a doomed adventure that would have world-wide repercussions long after its tragic denouement.

Basically, Kennedy failed in Cuba because he tried to ride two horses, and fell between them.

One group of advisers urged him to throw the full resources of the United States military forces behind the invasion attempt. These *activists* warned Kennedy that the landings by Cuban exiles must not be allowed to fail—even if United States military power had to be committed.

The other group, the *inactivists,* opposed the invasion. They opposed a Presidential policy of insuring it against failure. What bothered them was the "immorality" implicit in what they termed "masked aggression." They argued that the plan would probably not succeed; that if it did succeed, it would be difficult to disguise United States involvement. And this would have an embarrassing effect among the neutralists of Asia and Africa, whose good opinion Kennedy's advisers were most eager to cultivate. In Latin America, support of the exiles—particularly with massive United States air and naval support—would be widely regarded as old-fashioned Yankee Imperialism. It would provoke enormous resentment in an area where, as Adlai Stevenson had put it in reporting to Kennedy on his ten-nation South American tour, the "principle of nonintervention is a religion."

Whether Kennedy should or should not have approved the invasion attempt is not at issue here. That was for him to decide. He was President of the United States. Only he could have made the decision—one way or the other. But having made an affirmative decision, John F. Kennedy had no alternative but to assure victory. This he failed to do. Instead, he tried to compromise between the views of the *activists* and *inactivists* in his entourage, and the result was catastrophe.

The argument has since been made that Kennedy had no alternative but to approve the invasion plan blueprinted by his predecessor. For one thing, the training by CIA of thousands of Cubans at secret camps had long been completed. The invaders were, in fact, overready. To call off the invasion could well have demoralized the anti-Castro exiles and opened the new Administration to charges of appeasement.

The argument was hardly flattering to Kennedy's qualities as a leader. He was the President. He was privy to top-secret information regarding the security of the nation. If he had any doubts about the program devised by the previous Administration, his duty was either to disband or, at least, to postpone it. Moreover, the argument doesn't hold water since it was Kennedy who, in the latter stages of the 1960 campaign, had taunted the Eisenhower Administration for having permitted a Communist regime to seize a base "less than ninety miles from the coast of the United States."

The plan that Kennedy had "inherited" from Eisenhower was based on the assumption, as Charles J. V. Murphy reported in *Fortune,*[3] "that a landing force could not possibly be brought off unless the expedition was shepherded to the beach by the United States Navy (either openly or in disguise), and covered by air power in whatever amount might be necessary. Eisenhower, the commander of Normandy, understood this well enough."

As envisaged by Eisenhower, every effort was to be made to avoid overt United States intervention, except on a "contingency basis." That is, for example, United States carrier-based jets would be employed only if necessary to maintain control over the beachhead and prevent the destruction of the invaders.

The situation inside Cuba had grown so bad from the viewpoint of United States security that at one of their pre-Inaugural talks, President Eisenhower told Kennedy, "It's already a bad situation. You may have to send troops in."

Thus, the new President was faced with making a major command decision as soon as he took office. As a result a spirited debate took place within the new Administration as to what course the President should adopt.

According to Stewart Alsop, in a *Saturday Evening Post* article on June 24, 1961, entitled "The Cuban Disaster: How It Happened," President Kennedy had, from the beginning, strong doubts about the operation. But just why was not made clear—whether Kennedy judged the invading force to be too small to take on Castro or because he was reluctant to take on, so soon, a nasty job that was bound to have unfortunate repercussions internationally— and perhaps on his own "image."

On April 4, 1961, the day before Kennedy was to give his final go-ahead decision, a dozen insiders met with the President to thresh out the matter. Only one of them passionately opposed the venture. He was not exactly an insider; but he was a man greatly admired by the President—Senator J. William Fulbright, Chairman of the Senate Foreign Relations Committee on which Kennedy had served. (Fulbright, in fact, had been the President's first choice as Secretary of State. But when the story leaked out that he was being considered for that all-important post, all hell broke loose. Negro leaders pointed to Fulbright's staunch segregationist record; Zionist leaders claimed he was pro-Arab and anti-Israel; and anti-Communists contended Fulbright was appeasement-minded.)

Fulbright pleaded with Kennedy that the wise course was not to over-

---

[3] A superb piece of journalism, Murphy's article, "Cuba: The Record Set Straight," in the September 1961 issue of *Fortune,* will provide historians with source material for a long time to come. Its historiography can be determined from the vehemence with which President Kennedy characterized it as inaccurate.

throw Castro but to work constructively elsewhere in Latin America. He repeated, in effect, what Kennedy had sometimes said during the campaign: "The road to freedom runs through Rio and Buenos Aires and Mexico City." By then, however, it was too late.

One of the curious aspects about the lengthy secret debate within the Administration which had preceded Kennedy's decision was that at no time had the President ever discussed the matter with either Adlai Stevenson or Chester Bowles, who had been billed as Kennedy's chief foreign policy advisers during the campaign. What made this even more strange is that Kennedy had sent Stevenson on a good-will tour of Latin America, another purpose of which presumably was to obtain first-hand information on what the leaders were thinking down there.

Under Secretary of State Bowles learned about the proposed invasion purely by accident. He happened to be Acting Secretary the day documents about the project crossed Dean Rusk's desk. "Horrified," as he later told friends, Bowles immediately dashed off a memorandum of protest for Dean Rusk. Rusk, who took a dim view of subordinates involving themselves in top-level policy-making, placed the memorandum in his desk and forgot it.

Rusk, who considers himself an implementer rather than an innovator in the making of foreign policy, voiced no objections to the invasion plan at that final April 4 meeting. Neither did Secretary of Defense McNamara; Secretary of the Treasury Dillon; General Lyman Lemnitzer, Chairman of the Joint Chiefs; McGeorge Bundy, Special Assistant to the President for National Security Affairs; CIA Director Allen Dulles (who along with assistant Richard Bissell had briefed the conferees); Paul Nitze, Kennedy's strategic planning specialist at the Pentagon; Thomas Mann, then Assistant Secretary of State for Latin-American Affairs; and three of Kennedy's specialists in Latin-American affairs—Adolf A. Berle Jr., Arthur M. Schlesinger Jr., and Richard Goodwin.[4]

Rusk, Schlesinger, and Bundy had previously voiced their doubts about the operation, but at this fateful meeting they all went along. Except, of course, Fulbright, who argued passionately about the immorality of it all and, besides, it was the sort of thing the United States always did poorly.

However, Adolf Berle, the veteran New Dealer and Roosevelt's Assistant Secretary of State for Inter-American Affairs, argued with equal passion that "a power confrontation" with Communism in the Western Hemisphere was inevitable anyhow. The sooner it was faced up to, the better, was Berle's counsel.

[4] Significantly, Vice President Lyndon Johnson appeared to have played no major role in the tragic events. His advice was not sought. As an older man wiser in the ways of Washington bureaucracy, Johnson undoubtedly could have backstopped his youthful leader and pointed out some of the pitfalls in proposed courses of action. Kennedy's failure to utilize his Vice President's extraordinary knowhow to greater advantage is one of the puzzling features of the New Frontier.

Thus, Kennedy was torn between two opposite points of view—to invade or not to invade. Finally, and typically, he compromised between the extremes. He ordered changes in the original Eisenhower plan which, to say the least, considerably weakened the effort.

First, he ruled that *under no circumstances whatever* were United States forces to become involved. This, of course, meant a ban on United States air support for the invaders. The air strikes were to be conducted against the Castro Air Force by Cuban pilots flying B-26 bombers from bases in Guatemala. The sorties were to be publicized as the work of defectors from Castro's Air Force. The military specialists were aghast. The round trip would take more than six hours and that would leave the ancient bombers with fuel for less than an hour of action, for bombing and air cover, over Cuba. In contrast, Castro's planes could be over the beachhead and the invading craft in a matter of minutes, thus greatly increasing his relative air advantage.

The Joint Chiefs reportedly advised Kennedy that without United States air support the rebels might not be able to hold the beachhead. But in that case, they said, the invaders could make their way to the Escambray Mountains, fifty miles away, where they could form guerrilla bands to harass the Castro regime. As it turned out, fifty miles was quite a piece for defeated, disillusioned soldiers to travel.

Kennedy appeared determined to further weaken the invasion plan. On April 12, two days after the invasion craft had begun to steam north, the President told a press conference that "there will not under any conditions be an intervention in Cuba by United States armed forces." He added that the United States Government would do "everything it possibly can . . . to make sure that there are no Americans involved in any actions inside Cuba." Dean Rusk made sure the idea got home by repeating the same things on April 17, the morning of the invasion. It was all good propaganda for world consumption, of course, but the effect was to serve notice on Cubans in Cuba, who were waiting for an encouraging signal from the United States, that if they rose up against the Castro tyranny, it would be at their own risk.

Shortly after 6:00 o'clock on the morning of Saturday, April 15, a pair of B-26's on which CIA had painted Cuban Air Force markings flew low over Havana, making diving passes at the Camp Libertad airfield on the outskirts of the city. Minutes before, the attacking aircraft had strafed the big air force base at San Antonio de los Baños, not far from Havana. About an hour later a third B-26 made passes over the airfield at Santiago, on the eastern part of the island. The effectiveness of air strike number one is still a matter of debate. What was puzzling about it, in a strategic sense, is why a softening-up operation should have been planned forty-eight hours before the all-out amphibious attack, thus giving Castro plenty of warning as to what was coming.

The air strike came just as the United Nations Political Committee was discussing a Cuban charge that the United States was waging "undeclared war" against the "Cuban people." Castro's Foreign Minister Raul Roa had the floor. "I have been instructed by my government," Roa declared, "to denounce before this committee the vandalistic aggression carried out at dawn today against the territorial integrity of Cuba, with the most grave implication. The responsibility for this act of imperialistic piracy falls squarely on the Government of the United States."

The crowded room buzzed as Roa charged that the aerial bombings were "undoubtedly the prelude to a large-scale invasion attempt, organized, supplied, and financed by the United States with the complicity of satellite dictatorships of the Western Hemisphere."[5]

Ambassador Stevenson indignantly protested Roa's "false" accusations. He categorically denied that United States planes had bombed the Cuban airfields. He held up a photograph of one of the planes which had landed in Florida after it had attacked Camp Libertad. "It has the markings of Castro's air force on the tail," Stevenson asserted, pointing to the picture, "which everybody can see for himself. The Cuban star and the initials FAR—Fuerza Aérea Revolucionaria—are clearly visible. The two aircraft which landed in Florida today were piloted by Cuban air force pilots. These pilots and certain other crew members have apparently defected from Castro's tyranny. No United States personnel participated. No United States planes of any kind participated. These two planes to the best of our knowledge were Castro's own air force planes, and, according to the pilots, they took off from Castro's own air force fields."

With firmness springing from an apparent conviction he was telling the truth, Stevenson summed up the United States case: "As President Kennedy said just a few days ago, the basic issue in Cuba is not between the United States and Cuba, it is between the Cubans themselves. . . . The history of Cuba has been a history of fighting for freedom. The activities of the last twenty-four hours are eloquent confirmation of this historical fact."

It has been said that an Ambassador is a Government servant who is sent to lie for his country. To make matters worse, Stevenson thought he was telling the truth. Little did he know that he was mouthing a "cover story," which had been prepared for him by President Kennedy. And like the "cover story" in the U-2 affair—that the high-flying aircraft had lost its way over Russia while on a weather mission—the Stevenson story was soon exploded as a tissue of lies. What is strange, however, is that Stevenson was apparently not informed the story was a phoney.

From that hapless moment on, Stevenson's actions become unclear. According to Andrew Tully: "When Stevenson learned that the story about the

---

[5] On April 5, Raul Roa had denounced the State Department's White Paper on Cuba, a 36-page pamphlet written by Arthur Schlesinger Jr., in his new role as apologist —so the Castroites insisted—for "Wall Street Imperialism." The document outlined in detail how Castro had promised a democratic revolution but delivered a totalitarian regime. Roa dubbed Schlesinger's handiwork a "McCarthyite" document.

strike being the work of Cuban defectors was a lie and that the American Ambassador to the U.N. had had his credibility impaired before the world, he hit the roof. He demanded of Kennedy that there be no more air strikes, and Rusk supported him. Thereupon, Kennedy canceled the second strike."[6]

But according to Murphy in *Fortune*, "Stevenson has flatly denied, and continues to deny, that he even knew about the second strike, let alone that he demanded that it be called off. But there was little doubt about his unhappiness over the course of events in the Caribbean and he conveyed these feelings to Washington. Before Sunday was over McGeorge Bundy was to fly to New York, to see Stevenson and still wearing, in his haste to be off, sneakers and sport clothes. This sudden errand followed a shattering order that went out to [Richard] Bissell."

Bissell, director of CIA's operations section, had received a telephone call from Bundy on the White House line. The President, he told Bissell, had decided that there would be no air strike the next morning—the morning of the invasion. The B-26's were to stand down; this was a Presidential order. If Bissell wished to appeal, he could do it through Rusk. According to the Murphy article:

"Bissell was stunned. In Allen Dulles' absence (he was in Puerto Rico), he put his problem up to CIA Deputy Director Charles Cabell, an experienced airman. Together they went to the State Department to urge Rusk to reconsider a decision that, in their judgment, would put the enterprise in irretrievable peril. Cabell was greatly worried about the vulnerability to air attack first of the ships and then of the troops on the beach. Rusk was not impressed. The ships, he suggested, could unload and retire to the open sea before daylight; as for the troops ashore being unduly inconvenienced by Castro's air, it had been his experience as a colonel in the Burma theatre, he told the visitors, that air attack could be more of a nuisance than a danger. One fact he made absolutely clear: military considerations had overruled the political when the D-minus-two strike had been laid on; now political considerations were taking over. While they were talking, Rusk telephoned the President at Glen Ora to say that Cabell and Bissell were at his side, and that they were worried about the cancellation of the strike. Rusk, at one point, put his hand over the mouthpiece, and asked Cabell whether he wished to speak to the President. Cabell shook his head. Perhaps that was his mistake; it was certainly his last chance to appeal a lamentable decision. But Bundy had made it clear that Rusk was acting for the President, and Cabell is a professional military man, trained to take orders after the facts had been argued with the man in command."

By this time, it was too late for any re-examination of the operation. The first assault barges, still unobserved, were even then approaching the beaches; and the planes carrying paratroopers had already taken off. At

[6] *C.I.A.: The Inside Story*, by Andrew Tully. New York, Morrow, 1962.

4:00 A.M., Cabell went back to Rusk with another proposal. "It was mani-
festly impossible for the Brigade's small force of B-26's (only 16 were
operational) to provide effective air cover for the ships from their distant
base against jets that could reach the ships in minutes," Murphy wrote.
"Cabell now asked whether, if the ships were to pull back of the three- or
twelve-mile limit—whichever distance U.S. legal doctrine held to be the
beginnings of international water—the U.S.S. *Boxer,* a carrier on station
about 50 miles from the Bay of Pigs, could be instructed to provide cover for
them. Rusk said no. . . . The President was awakened. Cabell registered
his concern. The answer was still no."

At 5:15 A.M., Monday, Brigadier General Chester Clifton, the President's
military aide, heard by phone that the invasion had begun. But the invaders
had little chance. "They were without the ranging fire power that the B-26's
with their bombs and machine guns had been expected to apply against
Castro's tanks and artillery as they wheeled up," wrote Murphy. "Castro's
forces came up fast. He still had four jets left, and they were indeed armed
with powerful rockets. He used them well against the ships in the bay. Before
the morning was done, he had sunk two transports aboard which was the
larger part of the reserve stocks of ammunition, and driven off two others,
with the rest of the stock."

By midafternoon it was obvious that the Cuban uprisings expected by
the CIA had not materialized. (It later developed that the Cuban underground leaders had not been informed of the date of the landings.)

Kennedy and his strategists became alarmed. According to Murphy,
Bissell was told that the B-26's could attack Castro's airfields at will. "Orders
went to the staging base for a major attack next morning. But the orders came
too late. Most of the pilots had been in the air for upwards of 18 hours in an
unavailing effort to keep Castro's planes off the troops and the remaining
ships. That night a small force was scratched together. It was over Cuba at
dawn, only to find the fields hidden by low, impenetrable fog. Nothing came
of the try."

Tuesday, the second day, was the turning point. The 1,500 or so men
who had landed had fought bravely and had gained their planned objectives.
They had even seized an airfield. But they were running short of ammunition
and food, and under pressure of Castro's superior fire power they were being
forced back to the beaches. Three B-26's trying to help them were shot down.
The only hope lay in two small landing craft that had taken on food and
ammunition. The odds were, however, they could not reach the beaches until
after daybreak, at which time they would be wide open to attack. However,
the U.S.S. *Boxer* was anchored offshore in international waters. The release
of a few of its jets would see the two craft safely to shore; and the courageous
men clinging tenaciously to the beaches would have another chance.

As the fates would have it, Tuesday night Kennedy was caught up in his
first big White House reception—the traditional white-tie affair for members

of Congress, cabinet members, and their wives. At 10:15 P.M., the President and Mrs. Kennedy made their entrance down the grand-stairway to ruffles and flourishes and "Hail to the Chief." Mrs. Kennedy, a diamond clip in her bouffant hairdo, was attired in a sleeveless white-and-pink lace sheath with a low scalloped neckline. They then dispensed with a receiving line and mingled with the 1,200 guests. At a signal, the Marine Band struck up *Mr. Wonderful* and the President and his lady whirled around the East Room, smiling graciously at the applauding guests. A huge buffet had been set in the State Dining Room. One aide who had been on the White House staff since 1921 said it was the most elaborate he had ever seen. The fare included chicken à la king with rice, cold pheasant, turkey, ham, tongue, roast beef, tiny sandwiches and breads, French pastry and huge punch bowls with a champagne-spiked brew. Senator Hubert Humphrey found the relaxed atmosphere "wonderful," and Senator Albert Gore, with a broad smile, declared, "It's very democratic."

It was a night that John F. Kennedy will not soon forget. An aide informed him that Richard Bissell wished to see him. Bissell was asked to come to the White House. Calls went out to others. Dean Rusk was called from a formal dinner for the Greek Premier, and he arrived at the President's office with Secretary of Defense McNamara, General Lemnitzer, and Admiral Arleigh Burke, then Chief of Naval Operations. An intense discussion lasted until the early morning hours. One of the participants told Murphy: "Two men dominated that singular occasion—the President and Bissell. Bissell was in the unhappy posture of having to present the views of an establishment that had been overtaken by disaster. He did so with control, with dignity, and with clarity."

With Admiral Burke concurring, Bissell made a strong plea to President Kennedy to permit the use of United States air power to save the otherwise doomed invaders. In substance, he asked that the *Boxer*'s planes be put into the air in order to save the entire operation. Dean Rusk vigorously dissented, pointing out that the President himself had pledged no direct United States intervention.

The outcome of the session was a strange compromise. According to Murphy, "Jets from the *Boxer* would provide cover next morning for exactly one hour—from 6:30 to 7:30 A.M., just long enough for the ships to run into the shore and start unloading, and for the remaining B-26's to get in a hard blow." But the next morning, by an incredible mischance, the B-26's came too early and the *Boxer*'s jets remained on the carrier.

Castro's jets were ready, however. And that afternoon, Richard Bissell received word of the melancholy end in the Bay of Pigs. The men on the beaches had fought bravely. They had been solemnly assured of air cover. Once on the beaches, they were shocked to learn that the promised air cover would not be forthcoming. More implausible was the fact that no provision had been made for alternative courses of action in case of disaster. Despite such incredibly demoralizing conditions, the Cuban exiles fought bravely, firing as best they could against Castro's encircling troops. All Fidel had to do was wait until the invaders' ammunition ran out before mopping up with scarcely a fight. And this was exactly what occurred in an invasion that was doomed to failure by White House blunders.

In the waning hours, as Castro's forces were taking hundreds of prisoners, a radio ham in New Jersey heard a faint signal. "This is Cuba calling. Where will help come from? This is Cuba calling the free world. We need help in Cuba."

Bissell went to the White House to report the end. Kennedy gave orders for a destroyer to move in to pick up survivors. Only a few men were saved; the rest of the 1,500 were either killed or captured. Tens of thousands of Cubans within Cuba were rounded up by the panicky Castro regime and dumped in makeshift jails. Instead of eliminating Castro, the abortive invasion strengthened his position at home and inflated his prestige throughout the world.

And, as the *New York Times* observed, "the outcome of that battle was a blow to American pride and prestige which was certainly unmatched in the history of our relations with Latin America."

Meanwhile, the neutrals, whose sensibilities Kennedy had sought to placate by curtailing direct United States involvement, had a field day condemning the United States. In New Delhi, the peace-loving Nehru government—even then preparing its own peace-loving invasion of Goa—quickly expressed disapproval. In Caracas, the Venezuelan legislature unanimously condemned "any armed intervention in Cuba or in any other American country." And as was not entirely unexpected, mobs gathered before the U.S. Embassy in Moscow, shouting "Cuba da, Yankee nyet!"

At the United Nations, Ambassador Stevenson found himself in a defensive position, arguing the technical distinction: "No offensive had been launched from Florida or from any other part of the United States." But no one really believed him.

As Kennedy himself observed several days later, "Victory has a hundred fathers, and defeat is an orphan." Yet, for all his outward calmness at his moment of defeat he was never quite the same. Instinctively, he turned to his brother Bobby.

The rapport between the brothers was poignantly illustrated that terrible Tuesday night when the dimensions of the disaster in the Bay of Pigs became clearer. Bobby had been attending the state dinner at the Greek Embassy. Late in the evening, as Marquis Childs told the story in *Good Housekeeping,* Bobby turned to his wife Ethel, and said, "I've got to be with him. I know he needs me."

At the White House, Bobby found his brother surrounded by tense, dismayed advisers, trying to figure out what to do next. Though the President appeared outwardly reserved, Bobby could see the signs of anguish. At last, late in the night, the brothers were alone. Bobby, close to tears, put his hands on the President's shoulders.

"They can't do this to you," he said, his voice choked with emotion, "those black-bearded Communists can't do this to you."

From the tone of the outburst, one would have thought that Bobby was angry with those "black-bearded Communists" for not having co-operated with the United States-launched invasion aimed at ridding the island of Castroism.

The outburst was remarkable for what it demonstrated about the Kennedys. The Cuban tragedy—one of the greatest defeats ever suffered by the United States—was viewed primarily as a personal affront. The fact that 1,500 young Cubans were being slaughtered or captured on the beaches apparently was a secondary consideration.

In the days following the fiasco, Bobby Kennedy played a major role in trying to pick up the pieces. One of his chores was to take care of Chester Bowles, who had gotten under the President's skin for having advised newsmen he had opposed the invasion effort. There ensued the incredible scene of the Attorney General of the United States poking his finger in the chest of the Under Secretary of State, twenty-four years his senior, and snarling:

"So you advised against this operation. Well, as of now, you were all for it."

And President Kennedy passed the word to his top officials the less said about Cuba, the better. Cuba, of course, had been his first major either-or decision, and it came out neither. A catastrophe of such magnitude, it made the U-2 affair of the previous year pale in comparison. If anything, the downing of a high-flying United States photographic plane deep inside the Soviet Union demonstrated United States strength.

Cuba, however, demonstrated United States weakness.

After some initial hesitation, President Kennedy did assume full responsibility for the worst reverse suffered by the nation since Pearl Harbor. In fact, he almost had to insist he was the man who made the basic decisions leading to the disaster. Kennedy had no choice. Like Eisenhower in the case of the U-2, Kennedy had to assure the nation that—however maladroitly—he was in complete charge of the Government. Otherwise, the assumption could have been that the making of such life-and-death policies was in the hands of faceless bureaucrats.

Walter Lippmann was horrified by what had occurred. To him, the only man who came out with honor in the catastrophe was Senator Fulbright. "President Kennedy is in grave trouble," he wrote on May 2, 1961. And his inquiries on how the "misjudgment" had been made led him to believe that the President "was not protected by the New Hands—Bundy, Rostow, Schlesinger, and Rusk—against the Old Hands, Bissell and Dulles, of the CIA, Lemnitzer and Burke of the Joint Chiefs of Staff, and Berle of the State Department."

Added Lippmann: "When there is a disaster of this kind—as for example the British disaster at Suez—the mistake can be purged and confidence can be restored only by the resignation of the key figures who had the primary responsibility and by candid talk which offers the promise that the mistake will not be repeated. In the immediate wake of the disaster the President took the position that he would accept all the blame and that nobody else was to be held responsible. This was generous. It was brave, and in the sense that the Chief Executive must stand by those under him, it was right. But it is not the whole story. Under our system of government, unlike the British system, the Chief Executive who makes a great mistake does not and cannot resign. Therefore, if there is to be accountability in our government, the President must hold responsible those whose constitutional or statutory duty it is to advise him."

In retrospect, the most extraordinary aspect of the Cuban tragedy seems to be the fact that President Kennedy managed to escape the political consequences and emerged an even more popular figure—if the public opinion polls are to be credited. And how he did so tells much about the President. As a noted columnist observed privately at the time, had Richard Nixon pulled that kind of catastrophic blunder, he would have been "crucified," and deservedly so, by the press. But, by and large, Kennedy was treated kindly. Much more kindly, in fact, than President Eisenhower was treated following the U-2 episode.

Undoubtedly the U-2 affair crossed Kennedy's mind in the dark hours when word was coming through of the disaster in the Bay of Pigs. His immediate reactions were instructive. First, he moved in quickly to curb criticism from the Loyal Opposition. In rapid succession, he conferred with Richard Nixon, Barry Goldwater, Nelson Rockefeller, Herbert Hoover, and Dwight D. Eisenhower—just about every Republican leader in the country, with the exception of Harold Stassen. Bipartisanship, which Kennedy had denigrated as a candidate, was found to have its uses. His Liberal supporters were chagrined at Kennedy's instinctive turning to the Republican leadership for comfort. But Kennedy knew what he was doing. He averted a bruising debate on his abilities as the leader of the free world. And his all-important image —somewhat tarnished, to be sure—remained fairly intact.

At the same time, Kennedy assigned brother Bobby and General Maxwell Taylor to investigate the role of the CIA in the disaster. Presumably, the President was investigating himself. At any rate, Kennedy appeared to be shifting the blame from himself to the CIA. And then efforts were made to shift the blame to former President Eisenhower. And the latter efforts were undertaken on the very same day Kennedy was "romancing" Eisenhower at Camp David. Such was the atmosphere on the New Frontier those hectic days.

"While the Kennedy-Eisenhower conference was under way at Camp David," a front-page dispatch in the *New York Herald Tribune* reported on

April 23, "reporters in Washington were told by an excellent source that Eisenhower once urged Kennedy to follow through on the Cuban assault. The story was hardly out before the White House denied it.

"According to this source, Eisenhower and Kennedy discussed the plan when they met after the November election but before the Jan. 20 inauguration. Without reference to the source, assistant White House press secretary Andrew Hatcher issued a statement which said: 'Any report of an Eisenhower-Kennedy discussion of the Cuban refugee invasion plan prior to the inauguration is totally and completely inaccurate.'

"What did all this mean? It seemed obvious that the Administration has not yet quite recovered from being rocked back on its heels by the blowup of the invasion attempt. Here it was working at cross purposes. On the one hand, President Kennedy was at pains to win from top Republicans a promise not to make a painfully partisan issue of the failure. That is why he conferred at length with Eisenhower, former Vice President Nixon, Senator Barry M. Goldwater and others. . . . But on the other hand, here were informed sources telling reporters it was an idea conceived a year ago by the Eisenhower administration, and later strongly recommended to Kennedy by Eisenhower, the Joint Chiefs of Staff and the Central Intelligence Agency as well as other 'holdovers.'

"So it seemed a case of eating one's cake and having it, too. While President Kennedy publicly accepted full responsibility, the word was being quietly passed that the idea was really an inheritance and perhaps Kennedy, in office only three months, was talked into it by the old regime.

"Hatcher's denial, issued after a check with the President, sought red-facedly to set the record straight. Its obvious aim was to keep Eisenhower and the others from crying foul and otherwise giving vent to criticism.

"The word now is that the subject of the Cuban invasion scheme never came up in the Kennedy-Eisenhower meetings prior to the inauguration."

But the word was wrong; the matter had indeed come up for discussion. And the plan which Kennedy "inherited" was based on a simple premise: the key to a military outcome, in terms of holding a Cuban beachhead and then breaking out from it, was largely control of the air. And the fact remained that President Kennedy, in his first major command decision, refused proper air cover to the invading forces. Only obsolete prop-driven planes were supplied the invaders. Finally, at the last minute, a second air strike aimed at crippling Castro's air power was canceled. The net effect of these self-imposed restraints, ostensibly ordered to conceal United States participation, was to hand Fidel Castro a stunning victory. No wonder, then, that General Eisenhower said privately some time later, "Any second lieutenant with combat experience could have done better."

Soon after the Camp David meeting, Interior Secretary Stewart L. Udall said that the abortive Cuban invasion scheme had originally been planned by the recent Republican Administration, specifically by Eisenhower and Nixon. "They started it and handed it over to Mr. Kennedy," Udall said in a television interview. "Eisenhower directed it; another Administration carried it out."

Thus the political trial balloon went up, bobbed along on the winds of controversy for a day or so, and then was punctured by none other than Udall's boss President Kennedy who, the White House announced, had assumed full responsibility for the "events of the past days."

"Udall's remarks, clearly, were being disowned," the *Los Angeles Times* observed. "But how, in an Administration which insists on clearing all policy statements beforehand, could the remarks have come to be made in the first place?"

Added the *Los Angeles Times:* "It is possible that the Udall statement might have been allowed to stand, had it not aroused such violent Republican reaction. The President, after all, went to great lengths to win GOP backing for his Cuban policy. . . . But the unity which existed on the Cuba question was now threatened by politics. Udall, therefore, had to be disowned. But if, in the process, the President took on an aura of magnanimity by assuming all blame himself, well, consider that a fringe benefit. Udall, who is a pretty good politician, understands these things and probably feels no hurt. He who plays with balloons, after all, must expect to come down hard now and then."

But even after Udall's trial balloon, if such it was, Dwight Eisenhower refused to indulge in a partisan blast in the "Give 'em hell" tradition. "For a lesser man," the *New York Herald Tribune* editorialized, "the temptation might have been too great. Only last year Mr. Eisenhower himself was being assailed by opposition critics (including Kennedy) for everything from the U-2 episode to the tailfins on Detroit cars. And he was given little quarter."

At a Washington press conference, Eisenhower called upon the American people, at this low moment of the United States world position, to stand by President Kennedy. He said vehemently that the last thing they should want is any immediate public airing of the Cuban fiasco, likening such demands to witch hunting. Typical was his reply to the suggestion that he compare United States prestige under Kennedy with prestige under his Administration. Eisenhower said that popularity at any one moment was not the test, and that no strong Administration was ever really popular in a crisis. The achievement of respect for our words and the actions which must implement them, he said, would always be filled with risks.

As Doris Fleeson noted: "The immediate effect of Eisenhower's comments must be to encourage and cheer the young President, who has taken such a beating and reacted with something less than the grace expected of him. Democrats who never really managed to work up a partisan fervor against Eisenhower will count themselves justified."

Despite Eisenhower's gracious comments, some Kennedy partisans continued to snipe at the former President. Senator Joseph Clark, the Pennsylvania Democrat, said he thought that Eisenhower had conceived "a very foolish plan" to attempt to topple Fidel Castro with United States military forces. He said the outcome of the landings might have been more successful "from the military point of view," but would have been "disastrous insofar as our relationships with other Latin American states are concerned."

All of which made Holmes Alexander so angry he could hardly type his column denouncing "the despicable alibis for Mr. Kennedy by some of his followers." He particularly referred to the line that it all was conceived by Eisenhower and that Kennedy wasn't around and deserves no responsibility.

"This is wholly false," wrote Alexander. "For the record, candidate Kennedy was fully briefed by Allen Dulles before the fourth Nixon-Kennedy debate last autumn. Actually, if JFK had done as Ike did at Lebanon and in the defense of Quemoy-Matsu, the Cuban invasion would have succeeded.

"President Eisenhower (a) put on a strong display of U.S. military power and (b) kept the enemy in doubt as to our willingness to shoot it out. President Kennedy (a) made no military display and (b) announced in advance that the U.S. would not intervene in Cuba. The contrast is between a mature man who had already lived amid world events, taken great tasks, made enormous decisions, and an underdeveloped younger man whose greatest decisions to date had been to enter the West Virginia and Wisconsin primary elections.

"As a personal opinion, backed by testimony of those who have sat with JFK in the torture chamber on the Avenue, I venture that Kennedy will come away from this experience a better man. My faith will be fortified on the day he expels Allen Dulles, downgrades or dismisses all the eggheads with Adlai Stevenson as the first to go, and fires a few shots heard round the world in defense of the American position."

Considering the scale of the disaster, it is surprising that there were no firings or major resignations. True, he tried to get rid of Chester Bowles, but "Chet" wasn't buying the proposed ambassadorship. And Kennedy was frightened off by the fury of the Liberal protests. He waited for a more propitious moment in which to slip in the stiletto. Allen Dulles, of course, had no Liberal claque concerned about his particular fortunes. In fact, the head cloak-and-dagger man had no outside backing. Before the year was out, Allen Dulles was out. And Kennedy picked as his successor a Nixon Republican, John A. McCone, California industrialist and Chairman of the Atomic Energy Commission under Eisenhower. The appointment did not satisfy the Liberals. McCone, to them, was a "cold warrior" who viewed Khrushchev with too much distrust. The Liberals had hoped that CIA would be given to one of their own. For a time, in fact, there had been pressure on Kennedy to appoint someone like New York attorney Telford Taylor; and when the story leaked out that Taylor was actually being considered for the number one intelligence job, one noted anti-Communist exclaimed the time had come to consider going into exile.

The week of the Cuban fiasco John F. Kennedy was a frustrated, frantic man. And while he said there would be no scapegoats, he chided the press for not having hidden the Administration's daggers under their cloaks during the Cuban operation. (A few weeks later, Kennedy marked the first United States astronaut flight by boasting to the world that the strength of this country, in contradistinction to the Soviet Union, lay in being an open society, with a vigorous free press.)

His first public appearance following the disaster took place before the American Society of Newspaper Editors on Thursday, April 20, two days after he had learned the worst. The strain on him was evident. His speech was far from immortal. His tone was not one of disappointment as much as nervous belligerency. Rejecting contrition, he took an aggressive tack which unavoidably inspired the expectation of something dramatic to come which would erase the humiliating defeat. His words were those of a thwarted leader finding release from a sense of defeat.

But not once in the speech did he suggest any of the policies he has since followed toward Cuba. "We do not intend to abandon" Cuba to the Communists, he said. Rather, he proposed outright unilateral intervention should "the nations of this hemisphere fail to meet their commitments against outside Communist penetration. . . ."

"Should that time ever come," he warned, "we do not intend to be lectured on 'intervention' by those whose character was stamped for all time on the bloody streets of Budapest."

Strong words, indeed—but they were not soon backed by deeds. And in the international arena, a great power should not resort to threats unless its leaders are fully prepared, without any inner reservations, to back them up with acts of strength. This is what it known in diplomatic parlance as "credibility."

Nevertheless, Kennedy's strong words did serve a purpose. Designed largely to let off public steam, they were based on the Churchillian maxim: "In defeat, defiance." There were ominous overtones in the speech. In fact, at times he sounded like the spokesman for other ideologies: "The complacent, the self-indulgent, the soft societies are about to be swept away with the debris of history. Only the strong, and the industrious, can possibly survive." These were not the instinctive words of a man who believes in freedom. Similar words had been uttered before by men who themselves had been swept away with the debris of history. The fact that they were uttered by the President of the United States—with little, if any, criticism—was, in retrospect, an extraordinary episode.

"We intend to profit from this lesson," the President promised.

"The lesson," Mr. Arthur Krock observed coldly the next morning, "was plain long before the latest crises arose."

"One incidental item of profit that Mr. Kennedy might draw from his lesson is the need for a measure of humility," wrote James Burnham in

National Review. "How scornful he and his colleagues were last year at the confusion in Washington, and the fall in U.S. prestige, following the U-2 exposure! That confusion was clarity itself, that fall a positive ascent, compared to the aftermath of the Cuban affair. And the U-2 operation itself had been an astounding success, not a catastrophic failure."

Chaos reigned in Washington the fateful week of the Cuban invasion. Rarely had so many top officials told so many contradictory stories on what was occurring. The American press was deliberately fed untruths.

"When the landings started," reported the *New York Times'* James Reston, "American reporters in Miami were told that this was an 'invasion' of around 5,000 men—this for the purpose of creating the impression among the Cuban people that they should rise up to support a sizable invasion force.

"When the landing, not of 5,000 but of around 1,000 men, began to get in trouble, however, officials here in Washington put out the story—this time to minimize the defeat in the minds of the American people—that there was no 'invasion' at all, but merely a landing of some 200–400 men to deliver supplies to anti-Castro guerrillas already in Cuba.

"Both times the press was debased for the Government's purpose. Both times the Castro Government and its Soviet advisers knew from their own agents in the anti-Castro refugee camps and from their own observation on the beaches that these pronouncements were false and silly. And both times the American people were the only ones to be fooled."

Even more incredible was President Kennedy's April 27 speech before the American Newspaper Publishers Association in New York. At one point, he admonished: "Every newspaper now asks itself, with respect to every story: 'Is it news?' All I suggest is that you add the question: 'Is it in the national interest?'. . . And should the press of America consider and recommend the voluntary assumption of specific steps or machinery, I can assure you that we will cooperate wholeheartedly with those recommendations."

It was a speech that baffled his auditors. What was he trying to say?

According to the *St. Louis Post-Dispatch,* Kennedy's meaning was clear: "He suggested . . . that the press submit itself to a system of voluntary censorship under government direction, as has been customary during shooting wars. Such a system would make the press an official arm of the government, somewhat as it is an official arm in totalitarian countries."

"It was obvious," said the *Indianapolis Star,* "that the President was trying to intimidate the press into going easy on criticism of his policies and actions. At the same time he was trying to make the American people believe that if it had not been for the press the Cuban affair might have succeeded. This is nonsense. Until the President finds a clear case of injury to national security as a result of newspaper publication, he should stop trying to accuse the press of errors that are his alone."

"The saddest consequence of a month of adversity is that some Americans have been led to question the very validity of our free institutions," said the *Washington Post*.

Commented the *Los Angeles Times:* "When Mr. Kennedy wondered about censorship before the publishers he was smarting with chagrin. The Cuban fiasco raised world-wide echoes of derision. The President would not have been human if he had not, at least for an angry moment, sought a scapegoat. The press had overstated the U.S.-backed invasion—but it had not understated the defeat. Mr. Kennedy may have felt that he, personally, was being pilloried and that this was not in the interest of national security. It was easy for him to forget, perhaps for the moment, that much of the stuff about the invasion was printed in good faith, it having been put out by the Central Intelligence Agency, a potent arm of Mr. Kennedy's administration. Mr. Kennedy chided the press when it should have been twitted for having its leg pulled."

In London, Malcolm Muggeridge, the acidulous critic of royalty, said of Kennedy's speech, "These are ominous words. Some variant of them has been the prelude to every assault on the freedom of the press."

On May 9 a committee of newspaper editors and publishers met with the President at the White House to discuss his plea for self-censorship. Leaning forward in his rocking chair, Kennedy said that he felt the nation was now in the most critical period of its history.

"Do you accept that view?" the President asked his guests.

"No," replied Felix McKnight, executive editor of the *Dallas Times Herald* and president of the American Society of Newspaper Editors, and most of the other newsmen seconded him with firm shakes of the head.

Kennedy's visitors told him flatly they saw no present or future need for censorship, short of "a declaration of a national emergency, or something like that." And Kennedy said he had no intention of declaring a national emergency.

The seventy-minute session left everyone as baffled as before. The President still insisted that he did not intend to restrict the flow of news. And the editors and publishers were clearly at a loss to know what the President had in mind.

"The puzzled committee, having met with the President, has agreed to go home and think about this question for several months," reported the *Baltimore Sun*. "But the feeling grows that the President hadn't thought his suggestion through before he made it—and that whatever he had in mind, if it went beyond a vague feeling of dislike for the publication of uncomfortable facts, is not consistent with the way a free society operates."

The day after the White House meeting, James Reston wrote in the *New York Times,* "It is unfortunate that President Kennedy chose to raise this problem of a free press in a cold war immediately after the Cuban episode. . . . The trouble with the press during the Cuban crisis was not that it said too much, but that it said too little. It knew what was going on ahead of the landing."

The same day, Reston's indictment was heartily seconded by a *Times* editorial, "The Right Not to be Lied to." It said: "A democracy—our democracy—cannot be lied to. This is one of the factors that make it more precious, more delicate, more difficult and yet essentially stronger than any other form of the government in the world."

President Kennedy's preoccupation with the press and what it says about him and his Administration is, by now, one of the major characteristics of the New Frontier. He himself will spend hours trying to trace down a "leak" in the White House. On occasion he has gone out to spend an entire evening at a columnist's home to try to "straighten out" the writer on an article he did not like. And the President has been known to call newspaper editors and publishers in an effort to have a reporter rebuked. Thus, he telephoned Henry Luce to personally protest the publication of Charles J. V. Murphy's *Fortune* article on Cuba. And he sent General Maxwell Taylor to New York to argue sheepishly with Luce executives about alleged misstatements in the article.

The sensitivity of Kennedy and his aides to criticism is by now almost legendary in Washington. "They are almost psychopathically concerned about that dreadful modern conception of their image," wrote James Reston.

And John F. Kennedy goes to unusual lengths to influence public opinion.

Take the case of E. M. "Ted" Dealey, publisher of the *Dallas Morning News,* who toward the end of Kennedy's first year in office told the young President to his face that he and his Administration appeared to be "weak sisters." The extraordinary episode occurred at a White House luncheon, one of a series at which Kennedy entertains statewide groups of newspaper people.

Presumably these get-togethers enable the President to provide his guests with an off-the-record low-down on the shape of affairs. In return, the President hopes to be filled in on grass-roots sentiment. As Kennedy had put it, he feels isolated in the White House and wants to know what the people are thinking. And what with wine, French cuisine, and Presidential witticisms, the luncheons are generally pleasant little affairs. All that is missing is a group of strolling violinists.

Enter Mr. Dealey—by invitation, of course. Asked how things were down Lyndon Johnson-way, the veteran publisher saddled up and began reading a five-hundred-word statement he just happened to find in his pocket. As President Kennedy smiled inscrutably, the publisher intoned:

"The general opinion of the grass-roots thinking in this country is that you and your Administration are weak sisters."

The President's face flushed. His inscrutable smile disappeared. The other guests cringed in embarrassment. But Dealey continued to read.

The American people, he told J.F.K., were "aroused and rightly so" about Khrushchev and were opposed to symptoms of aid and comfort flowing his way from Washington.

"They do not want to see this nation make any concessions to Russia," Dealey added.

Then, in a remark since misinterpreted by Liberal viewers-with-alarm, Dealey said that "we need a man on horseback to lead this nation," a phrase not used in the usual depiction of dictatorship, but implying the need for leadership "from strength, not from weakness," as befits a great nation far more powerful than the Soviet Union.

Continuing to address the President, Dealey added that "many people in Texas and the southwest think that you are riding Caroline's tricycle."

The statement, in Dealey's words, "caused sort of a ruckus."

"But," he told newsmen right after the luncheon, "the President assured me that he was not mad."

All Kennedy did, in fact, was to turn to Pierre Salinger and say half-jestingly, "Don't subscribe to his paper. I'm tired of reading its editorials."

"But I have to read them," Salinger replied.

Only after publication of Dealey's comments in the morning newspapers did Kennedy get mad. For the Dealey statement, which had bluntly summed up what a lot of people were beginning to think, had definitely tarnished the Kennedy "image."

Something had to be done.

At this point, entered Charles Bartlett, Washington correspondent of the *Chattanooga Times*. A long-time confidant of the President, Bartlett had, in fact, introduced Mr. Kennedy to Mrs. Kennedy. He is always turning up as the guest of the President at such places as Hyannis Port.

At any rate, Bartlett obtained an exclusive fill-in on what President Kennedy supposedly said when he told off "Ted" Dealey. Bartlett, who was not present at the luncheon, used exact quotations even though no one is supposed to quote the President at these luncheons.

Thus, ten days after the unique luncheon an exclusive story by Bartlett was published on the front page of the Chattanooga paper, a sister publication of the *New York Times*. "The President's reply," he wrote, "a spontaneous expression of his basic philosophy, has been partially reconstructed from the recollections of some of those who were present."

According to Bartlett, the President, after being challenged for the first time at his own table, replied in a low voice that everyone in entitled to his own opinions in this country and that this was a healthy thing.

"But the difference between you and me, Mr. Dealey," Bartlett quoted the President as saying, "is that I was elected President of this country and you were not and I have the responsibility for the lives of 180 million Americans, which you have not."

Then Kennedy was quoted as observing that men tend to like the idea of war until they have tasted it, but that they quickly get enough of it.

"Wars are easier to talk about than they are to fight," the President was further quoted as having said. "I'm just as tough as you are, Mr. Dealey. And I didn't get elected by arriving at soft judgments."

These were indeed Presidential remarks designed for the history books. And, needless to say, they obtained wider currency than the statement that prompted them. For example, the *New York Times* which had ignored the Dealey statement published a full account of the Bartlett story and an editorial, too.

But the big question was: When did President Kennedy make his forthright reply to "Ted" Dealey?

"Bartlett's quotations are unfamiliar to me," said Dealey. He had absolutely no recollection of the President uttering any of the remarks attributed to him by Bartlett. And neither did any of the other eighteen Texas newsmen present at the luncheon—though a few did take issue with Dealey for being so frank with the President.

"I think the whole story was cooked up by the Administration and by Bartlett stating what Kennedy wanted to say to me in rebuttal to my statement," said Dealey. "Only the President didn't say it at the time."

Though aware of the close relationship between the President and Charles Bartlett, Dealey believes that the episode demonstrated "pretty sorry newspapering."

Perhaps it demonstrated something more important: the lengths to which the Kennedy Administration is prepared to go to keep the Presidential "image" untarnished.

President Kennedy's sensitivity to the press was explained by brother Bobby in an interview with Paul Martin of Gannett Newspapers. The Attorney General said bluntly that his brother was "annoyed" by criticism of his Administration in some newspaper editorials and columns.

"What bothers him most," Bobby told Martin, "is when he sees misstatements of fact, unfair criticism, or where a pundit poses an easy solution to a difficult problem, without knowing all the facts."

President Eisenhower, however, had never showed public annoyance by any newspaper criticism. In fact, he was not an avid newspaper reader. President Truman never seemed to care what columnists and editorial writers said about him. The only time he got really sore was when a music critic wrote something disparaging about daughter Margaret's singing abilities. And Truman sent the critic a stinging personal letter. "When you're in the kitchen," Harry Truman used to say, "you've got to learn how to take the heat."

President Kennedy has yet to learn how to take the heat. A voracious reader of newspapers, he doesn't miss a thing written about him. "How they can spot an obscure paragraph in a paper of 3,000 circulation 2,000 miles away is beyond me," gasped the senior White House correspondent, UPI's

Merriam Smith. "They must have a thousand little gnomes reading the papers for them."

Bobby Kennedy also told Paul Martin that some advisers have told the President he ought to "quit reading the newspapers and just do what he thinks is best."

"That would be the ideal solution," Bobby added. "But newspapers are important in influencing public opinion. We have to pay attention to them."

Thus, "influencing public opinion" becomes more important than doing what is best.

Talking with another correspondent, the Attorney General said it was only "blatant inaccuracies and dishonest reporting that cause irritation," and not columns of opinion. The reason his big brother called several editorial writers, he said, was because "the editorials were based on inaccurate data."

"Perhaps we could just let inaccurate statements go by," he said. Then, he grinned. "My father told us once that we shouldn't complain because so many of the inaccurate stories were the ones that praised us."

Bobby Kennedy himself has been known to chew out offending newspapermen. Thus he called Roscoe Drummond to protest a column on the Billie Sol Estes case. And he telephoned columnist Robert S. Allen several times to challenge the accuracy of a series of columns he had done about the Ted Kennedy-Ed McCormack battle for the Senatorial nomination in Massachusetts. (The columns reported on White House pressures, threats and strong-arm methods employed to win a Senate seat for Teddy.) And Bobby "blew his stack" in arguing with Earl Mazo about the *New York Herald Tribune* man's stories on Billie Sol Estes.

"Bobby's so-called 'lecture,' as it has been described, was in reality a childish outburst," said Mazo, a veteran correspondent. "He was so enraged over our coverage of the Billie Sol Estes scandal that I expected at any moment he would throw himself to the floor, screaming and bawling for his way. Insead, he paced back and forth, storming and complaining. It was something to see!" (Apparently that was the week when the President exercised his leadership in banning the *New York Herald Tribune* from the White House.)

Actually, Bobby has been serving the President in many capacities. His freewheeling in government was demonstrated following the assassination of Dominican dictator Trujillo when anarchy threatened in the Caribbean island. With President Kennedy in Europe for the Vienna meeting with Khrushchev, Bobby moved to a command post in the State Department. There, he authorized the dispatch of U.S. Navy ships off Santo Domingo in a show of force.

The fact is that when President Kennedy runs into trouble, he instinctively turns to brother Bobby for help. In the large Kennedy family, such extensive mutual reliance—and dependence—has always been taken for granted. This, of course, has made it difficult over the years to determine to what extent a specific action has been Jack's or the product of a family undertaking.

Thus, when the Communists began raising The Wall in Berlin one Sunday morning in the summer of 1961, President Kennedy cut short a cruise and raced back to shore.

"Get Rusk on the phone," he ordered. "Go get my brother."

Arthur Schlesinger Jr., undoubtedly a future chronicler of The Age of Kennedy, explains Robert F. Kennedy's extraordinary role as follows:

"Bobby has been a kind of troubleshooter for the President in many fields. No Attorney General in history, for instance, has sat in on as many State Department meetings. He's certainly closer to the President than anyone else, and the President has great reliance on his judgment—he feels more secure about any situation if Bobby is involved in it. This doesn't mean that the President agrees with him all the time. . . . Not only the President depends on him, but often, when some of us here in the White House see things that ought to be done, we call on Bobby."

Not all of Professor Schlesinger's fellow Liberals have been so entranced. Fears have been expressed about Bobby's "insensitivity" to issues involving civil liberties. Conservatives, too, have questioned Bobby's crack-down on Big Business.

"Bobby gets things done," the President says.

Sometimes he gets things done without finesse or regard for the rules. Thus, his improper use of the FBI during the flap about steel prices in the spring of 1962 was properly condemned by the *New York Times* as smacking of a "personal vendetta."

"Looking back at the whole episode," wrote the *New York Post*'s pundit, Max Lerner, "there was one thing I found distasteful about the administration's behavior. It was the use of FBI agents to track down aspects of the steel story by dawn interviews of reporters. This may make sense if you want to catch a spy before he vanishes, but these were reporters, not spies, and this invasion of their privacy suggested a police operation."

All this was done without any warrants, only orders from the Attorney General of the United States.

At the same time, Bobby Kennedy ordered a grand jury inquiry into possible violations of the anti-trust laws. And what with the Government throwing all its vast legal resources against the steel men and their companies, Big Steel caved in.[7]

Whatever the merits of the dispute, it was at most a mild crisis, hardly calling for hysterical night-riding tactics more reminiscent of totalitarian powers. "This indefensible abuse of personal power by a hired public servant . . . ," the *Richmond Times-Dispatch* commented, "highlights the

[7] Comedian Dick Gregory, referring to the Kennedy brothers as Matt Dillon and Chester, commented on the steel dispute, "I love to see millionaires fight."

intemperate reaction of the Brothers Kennedy toward any and all who presume to cross their ambition."

The dual role played by the White House and the Justice Department during the frenzied seventy-two hours of the steel "crisis" served to demonstrate that there really were two Kennedys to deal with in Washington.

What is significant about Bobby's emergence as the number two man in the United States Government is that Joseph P. Kennedy planned it that way. Like his father, Bobby Kennedy is touchy, partisan, passionate, and unforgiving. "There was never a tougher one than Joe Kennedy, nor a more unscrupulous opponent," wrote Robert Ruark. "Young Bobby, even more than Jack, shows more outer smudges of the parental stamp, but there is a lot of he-coon ingrained in the hide of the new President. He strikes me as practically cold all the way, with a hard blue eye on Valhalla."

At any rate, the Swahili-speaking columnist was not opposed to Bobby's being named to the Cabinet. "A lot of people don't like Bobby, but nobody has to love an Attorney General," said Ruark.

"Bobby hates the same way I do," his father once said. And as he observed on another occasion, Bobby is the cop in the family. "Bobby's a tough one," he told Bob Considine. "He'll keep the Kennedys together, you can bet."

Bobby's extraordinary talents in this direction were demonstrated at one of those informal dinners which the President and Mrs. Kennedy like to attend. According to Marquis Childs, Bobby nearly caused an incident when, seeing a childhood friend with his arm around Mrs. Kennedy, he summarily removed it. The Attorney General angrily told the guest that this was no way to behave toward the wife of the President.

"Oh Bobby," Jacqueline said loudly, "you're so sweet to want to protect me, even when protection isn't necessary."

Despite reports to the contrary, there never was any real doubt following Kennedy's election that he would appoint Bobby to some high post in government. True, some aides had expressed misgivings about possible public relations repercussions. After all, during the campaign Kennedy had loudly and vigorously decried "nepotism."

"Nepotism," candidate Kennedy had said on October 18, 1960, "is dangerous to the public interest and to our national morality."

Also, during the campaign, Robert F. Kennedy himself was asked this question during a TV interview: "If your brother is elected, how much truth is there, if any, to the persistent rumor that you will be appointed U.S. Attorney General?"

"There is absolutely no truth to that, at all," replied Bobby. "That would be nepotism of the worst sort!"

But when an election is over people tend to forget what was said or promised. Nevertheless, Bobby hesitated about accepting. He said he was much more interested in running for governor of Massachusetts in 1962. But

Father Joe resolved all doubts when he reminded all parties concerned that Jack would need someone in high position whom he could trust implicitly when the chips were down. "For the father," wrote Marquis Childs, "the request to serve is an order."

Thus after an exhaustive search for the man best equipped to be the nation's chief law officer, John F. Kennedy selected Robert F. Kennedy. And with a spirit instilled in him by his father, Jack Kennedy explained, "There have been, of course, members of the same family who have served the government in positions of responsibility. The two Dulles', of course, were both valuable public servants, one in State and the other the head of the Central Intelligence Agency. President Eisenhower and his brother, of course, Milton Eisenhower, served the people of this country in a number of important positions."

But the facts remained that neither Dulles appointed the other, and Milton Eisenhower served only in temporary positions. Moreover, the historic precedents were in the other direction. George Washington brushed off a nephew who wanted a government job by observing that such an appointment might be twisted into "a supposed partiality for friends or relations." Woodrow Wilson, in fact, rejected his own brother for a postmaster's job after "a struggle against affection and temptation."

When reminded there was no historic precedent for appointing a brother to the Cabinet, President Kennedy declared, "We're going to start one."

Though their father's advice may not always have been heeded, his children have treated him with the deference due the patriarch. *Parade* magazine reported in 1957, "When the clan gathers at Hyannis Port, Old Joe's word is law. Meals are served the exact moment he orders them. No one drinks. If Father wants to see a movie, everyone dutifully troops up to his private projection room. One day Jack and Bob were playing touch football when Old Joe wanted to take a nap. From an upstairs bedroom came his majestic bellow: *'Shut up!'* Jack and Bob abruptly stopped their horseplay and spoke softly until the nap was over." Jack Kennedy was then thirty-nine years of age.

The night after the election, the senior Kennedy invited his sons and their guests to go over to his private screening room at Hyannis Port to see a double feature, *North to Alaska* and *Butterfield 8*. Though the President-elect was in no mood, he nonetheless obliged his father. Since the Ambassador had seen the films, he did not hang around. Twenty minutes after the lights went off, the President-elect led his guests out into the night.

Some months later, there appeared to be a shift in the clan's power relationships. "A member of the family," reported Hearst correspondent Marianne Means, "recalls the day the patriarch acknowledged that he, as head of the Kennedy clan, the man who bowed to no one, would bow to the head of the United States, his own son."

It happened at lunch. The elder Kennedy suggested that the family go sailing. Usually that would have been the signal for everyone to make for the boats. But the new President said he didn't feel like it. Anyway, he had a few things to do. There was a sudden silence. Everyone waited for Father Joe's customary outburst. It never came.

"I don't think the President should have to go if he doesn't want to," said Joseph P. Kennedy.

According to Murray Kempton, an occasional visitor to Hyannis Port, episodes such as this meant that "Jack Kennedy is no longer a little boy."

"It was not always like this," added Kempton. "Jack Kennedy was a grown man and a member of the United States Senate when he still used to have to go back to his father's house and like a schoolboy sit and endure his father's violent opinions."

Naturally, there has been great public curiosity about the influence Joe Kennedy has supposedly exerted on the New Frontier. The official story is that it has been very little. Nevertheless, until he was stricken Joe would talk to his son almost every day. And any person who regularly has a President's ear is in a position to exert influence.

The President's father had also handled certain ticklish assignments in his usual behind-the-scenes manner. Thus, he helped arrange the post-election meeting between his President-elect son and the man he defeated, Richard Nixon. And later Joe Kennedy's influence was felt in the abortive attempt to rid the New Frontier of the increasingly irritating presence of Adlai Stevenson. The idea was to interest Adlai in running for the Senate seat occupied by Illinois' Everett Dirksen. This would have meant his resignation as the U.S. Ambassador to the United Nations. The suggestion was made by Mayor Richard Daley of Chicago, an old friend of Joe Kennedy.

Stevenson, unhappy about the secondary role he was playing in foreign affairs, actually gave the matter some thought, until he came to realize what lay behind the proposal. After conferring with the President, Stevenson announced he would remain at the U.N. And Kennedy publicly reassured the Ambassador how valuable he considered his services in the great cause of peace and global understanding.

With his eye on '64, Jack Kennedy was taking no chances on creating disaffection among the loyal Stevensonians who, though small in number, play a key role in Democratic party affairs. Without their support, he could hardly have won the big cities in 1960. And the big cities provided the small margin which carried him to victory.

The victory was made possible nationally by a coalition of diverse elements with no common denominator except a disposition to come together every four years to preserve patronage and perquisites.

This explains why Kennedy, early in his administration, insisted on the nomination of Alabama's Charles Meriwether as a director of the Export-Import Bank, despite charges that he was linked to the Ku Klux Klan. To the Liberals this was a shocking appointment. Senator Wayne Morse, for one, denounced it as "a horrendous, inexcusable mistake." The *Washington Post* urged the President to withdraw the nomination.

Instead, Kennedy exerted tremendous pressure to get it through. Meriwether finally was confirmed by the Senate by a 67 to 18 roll call vote. And, as Kennedy had expected, the matter was soon largely forgotten.[8]

The episode demonstrates that there is a good deal of Joe Kennedy in Jack Kennedy; that Presidential decisions now reflect the moral and intellectual fiber which through the years Father Joe passed on to each of his offspring. Shrewdness, vitality and ambition—combined with a don't-give-a-damn attitude, plenty of brass, and a sense of cool detachment—had early shaped the character of the sandy-haired Irishman whose appealing toothy grin can be observed in his children.

With the passing of the years, Joseph Kennedy came to recognize the importance of keeping a foot in all political camps. He is probably the only man in America who enjoyed friendships with Senator Joe McCarthy and such New Deal types as Associate Justice William O. Douglas, with whom he served on the Securities and Exchange Commission.

"The point about my father is that he is interested in the man, rather than in his ideas," Jack Kennedy once explained.

Similarly, the President sees nothing incongruous in friendships ranging the entire spectrum of politics—from an Arthur Schlesinger Jr. to a Senator George Smathers. Neither does he consider it odd for a President to remain on good terms with a Frank Sinatra or a Porfirio Rubirosa.

Sinatra, according to correspondent Marianne Means, "showed up last year three times for private affairs at the White House, and once at Hyannis Port for good measure."

Rubirosa, diplomacy's most celebrated exponent of *la dolce vita,* was a conspicuous guest of the President at Hyannis Port in September 1961. Their friendship dates back to Jack's most-eligible-bachelor days. On January 10, 1962, Murray Kempton managed to slip a column into the *New York Post,* by now a Kennedy house organ, which began: "Porfirio Rubirosa yesterday added to his other distinctions that of being the first house guest of the President of the U.S. ever to refuse to sign a waiver of immunity before a New York grand jury."

At the time he was President Kennedy's guest, Kempton continued, "one assumes he was relaxing between his efforts to convince our State Department of the determinedly democratic impulses of the junior Trujillos. In those days he was the Dominican Inspector of Embassies, a position from which he was removed . . . after 24 years of carrying his diplomatic passport into some of the most distinguished boudoirs in the architecture of international relations."

[8] One wonders how President Eisenhower would have fared had he had the temerity to appoint someone like Meriwether. One thing is certain—had he done so, the matter would not have been so quickly cast into oblivion.

The day after he lost his diplomatic immunity, Rubirosa was slapped with a subpoena from New York's District Attorney Frank Hogan.

"Rubirosa had been Generalissimo Trujillo's son-in-law, and, throughout the distractions of his personal life, a career member of the Dominican foreign service. The Generalissimo always maintained the Renaissance concept that murder is an instrument of foreign policy and Hogan wondered whether Rubirosa had any special knowledge of the workings of the Dominican Governments West Side shooting gallery for exiles."

At any rate, Rubirosa told his story to a grand jury after being careful enough not to sign a waiver of immunity.

The significant thing about Rubirosa's visit at Hyannis Port is that, except for the nonconforming likes of a Murray Kempton, no other journalist appears to have commented on it.

Also, no one appeared to have raised a journalistic howl when President Kennedy showed up at a gay party given by Charles Patrick Clark, Generalissimo Franco's $100,000-a-year man in the capital and an old friend of the President. Normally, such associations would be the kiss-of-death in the pages of Liberal publications. But not a peep out of them. For some reason, Jack Kennedy manages to escape the usual Liberal censure in such matters.

Then there was the summary firing of Jack Romagna as chief White House stenographer, after twenty-one years of faithful service to Presidents Roosevelt, Truman, and Eisenhower. Romagna had slugged a transcript of President Kennedy's telephoned remarks to a Florida convention as having originated from the White House swimming pool. For some reason, Kennedy found the reference offensive; Romagna was out of a job; and the White House correspondents—perhaps because of the grim look on Kennedy's face —failed to raise the question at the Presidential press conference.

Another question they failed to ask the President was about his decision to cancel not only his own subscription to the *New York Herald Tribune,* but twenty-one others. This could only have left the impression that the President decides the reading habits of his associates. As Robert G. Spivack has put it: "President Kennedy grimly believes in the right to dissent. In fact, he will tell you what you can dissent about."

Of course, there was always that former dissenter, Arthur Schlesinger Jr., who snapped over the phone to columnist Henry J. Taylor, who happened to be a former United States Ambassador to Switzerland, "You are an idiot!" And Arthur followed that up with the observation, "It is obvious to me that I write for people who have higher intellectual qualities than you possess."

What Jack Kennedy discovered during his first One Hundred Days was that being President and facing up to the Communists—whether in Cuba or in the Far East—was far more difficult than subjugating the Democratic party or impressing the American people with his rhetoric. There was no doubting Kennedy's energy or ambition to Get Things Moving in the Sixties; but he quickly learned that with all the authority of the Presidency he still lacked the effective power to do many of the things he said he wanted to do.

The education of John F. Kennedy must have been a far harsher experience than could have been anticipated by him or the Schlesingers, Rostows, Bundys, and Galbraiths who had accompanied him into the seats of the mighty. On November 25, 1961, Ambassador Galbraith, speaking at the University of Mysore in India, made a rare confession: "Whereas a year ago, I was never in doubt as to what to do, the problems of late have been more puzzling. I notice also that I become rather more tolerant of imperfections and even of compromises when I am associated with them myself. Such is the effect of responsibility."[9]

Basically, Galbraith *et al.* had overestimated the capacity of words and style to influence the stubborn political and economic realities of the times. Problems do not go away when stated in fine rhetoric. A press release, no matter how excellently worded, is no substitute for a foreign policy. A slogan —*Alianza para el Progreso*—does not solve the age-old problems of Latin America.

Exhortations to restraint, President Kennedy also discovered, rarely restrain the self-interest of economic groups. But appeals for sacrifice on the part of the American people should at least be matched by practicing what one preaches. It ill behooved the President to ask for an understanding of the balance of payments problem on the part of wives, separated from servicemen husbands, at the very moment that his own wife, daughter, two sisters, and mother were vacationing abroad and contributing to the problem.

The President sets the example. Either he is serious about what he is saying or he isn't. A President who is serious, for example, about getting a Medicare bill through the Senate, and who knows that its passage that week may depend on a single vote, does not take off for a long weekend of sun and fun at Cape Cod.

Of course, the line of the New Frontiersmen was to blame Congress for the President's inability to cope with his legislative responsibilities. In fact, Mike Mansfield, the Democratic Senate Leader, was reported to have "blown his stack" in September 1962 after repeated quorum calls were required to get enough Senators in the chamber to transact business.

"It was not a very heartening spectacle," he said, "to see the world's most deliberative body making a spectacle of itself."

This raised an interesting question. With the world in desperate crisis, what with the Soviets setting up a formidable military base in Cuba, among

[9] On August 19, 1962, columnist Charles Bartlett reported that Ambassador Galbraith had reached the end of his usefulness in India. The word was, according to Bartlett, that Galbraith "has grown unpopular with the government and key private citizens in New Delhi and is no longer an effective intermediary. His problem is described as largely one of personality in that he is inclined to lecture the Indians, including Nehru, and to seem somewhat arrogant." That's what President Kennedy's newspaper chum reported. The following April word leaked out that Chester Bowles would replace Galbraith in Delhi.

other things, where was the President, the man charged with the greatest responsibility in any free government anywhere in the world?

He was attending a yacht race.

The fact was that in his first two years in office, President Kennedy was out of the White House almost as much—if not more—than he was in it. In this, of course, he was a creature of habit. After all, his absenteeism record as a member of the Senate was one of the worst in that body.

During the campaign and in the first few months of his Administration, Jack Kennedy had encouraged the belief that he had new ways to handle the old problems of aggression, infiltration, and disunity abroad; and unemployment, inflation, and education at home. Kennedy said he knew "what happens to a nation that sleeps too long." He said he wanted to be "a President who works full time." He would be a President, moreover, "who does not speak from the rear of the battle, but who places himself in the thick of the fight."

"I have heard all the excuses," Candidate Kennedy had stated, "but I believe not in the America that is first *but,* or first *if,* or first *when*—but an America that is first—*period."*

Before the year was over, President Kennedy was offering excuses. As Arthur Krock reported in December 1961: "When the Kennedy Administration is under heavy attack for a foreign policy, it seeks to demonstrate, by official statement or helpful unofficial hint, the identity of this policy with Eisenhower's."

As examples, Krock cited Cuba and the Congo.

"After the President's refusal of air cover to the anti-Castro invasion," Krock noted, thus dooming "any chance of the invasion's success, the word went out unofficially that the project with the same design had been initiated in the Eisenhower Administration.

"And when widespread and diverse public sentiment in this country arose against the U.N. war against Tshombe in Katanga that the United States had supported in both their policy and military aspects, the same point was made."

According to Krock, while Eisenhower had supported "properly constituted mechanisms" of the United Nations "as the chief hope of restoring stability to the Congo," he had steadfastly refused to provide United States planes for use *within* the Congo. Nor did he support U.N. measures, by armed force or otherwise, against secessionist Katanga.

By the end of the year, United States air power—inexplicably withheld at the last minute from the anti-Castro invasion of Cuba—was being used to transport U.N. troops in a bloody war aimed at crushing anti-Communist Moise Tshombe in far-off Katanga. An incredible end to an incredible year. But the Tshombe story was not over. All through 1962 it plagued the Kennedy Administration. And it took on the earmarks of a personal vendetta against Tshombe. For one thing, at President Kennedy's instruction, the State

Department refused to allow Tshombe to enter the United States in order to plead his case.

Another of the U.N.'s "peace-keeping efforts" that President Kennedy supported was the Dutch-Indonesian agreement on West New Guinea. If anything, this was a surrender to Indonesian aggression. Indonesia has no more claim to West New Guinea than Hitler did to Czechoslovakia, but President Sukarno had been preparing an invasion with heavy Soviet military aid. The Dutch, for their part, were not trying to hold on to the colony; they wanted a plebiscite in which the natives could decide their own future. But the United States and the U.N. decided that the wave of the future was with the Indonesians. And the Dutch Premier bitterly observed, "The Netherlands could not count on the support of its allies, and for that reason we had to sign."

Meanwhile, Kennedy appeared to have forgotten Cuba. In his 1962 State of the Union message, in which he assured the country the nation's prestige was never higher, Kennedy failed to mention the Communist base "only ninety miles away from our shores." Kennedy had promised Cuba's exile leaders he would do everything in his power to save the freedom fighters who had been captured by Castro, thanks largely to White House blundering. The pledge was the genesis of the President's subsequent decision to take up Castro's impulsive offer to swap the prisoners for tractors. The negotiations came to nothing. And President Kennedy lost interest, becoming testy whenever the subject arose. He also issued an order to his top aides that Cuba was not to be discussed publicly.

Castro refused to let Kennedy—and the American people—forget. In April 1962, he staged a Communist-type show trial in Havana of the 1,179 invaders who had been captured in the Bay of Pigs. In effect, these courageous men had been abandoned by the Kennedy Administration. Though taunted by their captors, they refused to condemn the United States for having "betrayed" them by failing to back them up. All of which prompted the *Chicago Tribune* (one of the newspapers President Kennedy reads daily) to say:

"While we continually hear paeans to the quality of leadership we are getting these days from Washington, let no American forget that the conscience of the United States is also, in some measure, on trial. For the men in the dock were equipped, trained and transported by the United States to the invasion beach, and it was a failure of will in the Kennedy inner circle which deprived them of the air cover which alone could have made the landing successful."

The *Tribune* also noted that Castro had released photographs "of these forlorn victims of a cause that was lost even before it was well begun. . . . They might be matched against the pictorial record of the peacock opulence of Mrs. Kennedy on her recent progress through India and Pakistan. What is our 'image' before the world to be—that of a lady with a dozen daily changes of wardrobe, spread in color through the picture magazines, or of a nation which cravenly washes its hands of a thousand men it tenders to the hangman? Even the Government of Canada calls for open trial and for justice. Our Government does not even do that little."

There could be no doubt, however, that Jacqueline Kennedy's traveling habits did interest many Americans—otherwise the newspapers would not have devoted so much space to them. There was some criticism that the First Lady, in India, had hobnobbed only with the aristocracy. But, as Mrs. Kennedy observed later, "the Indians decided our trip. . . . They could have shown me their deepest poverty, hoping I'd go home and say they needed more aid, but they were too thoughtful for that. They just wanted us to have magical memories of an enchanted visit."

Interviewed by Joan Braden for the *Saturday Evening Post,* Mrs. Kennedy said that Prime Minister Nehru had made a deep impression on her: "We never talked of serious things, I guess because Jack has always told me the one thing a busy man doesn't want to talk about at the end of the day is whether the Geneva Conference will be successful or what settlement could be made in Kashmir or anything like that. Only once did Goa come up. And that was one evening before dinner when we were all sitting around eating nuts. . . . Ken Galbraith asked where they came from. There was dead silence, and finally Ambassador B. K. Nehru said, 'From Goa.' Then Galbraith said, 'Oops, I didn't realize I'd dropped such a brick,' and everyone laughed.

"Ken Galbraith really was a saint on the whole trip," Mrs. Kennedy continued. "Do you know what Pamela Mountbatten said about him? 'I've read the Ambassador's books and, if you skip the part about economics, they really are terribly witty.' So is he. Whenever we were tired and thought we couldn't take another step, he always made us laugh and gave us courage to go on."

Mrs. Kennedy told Mrs. Braden how anxious she was to visit a bazaar, but "the Secret Service would look aghast and say 'No! No!' and before I knew it a bazaar was set up outside my front door. Once I spent almost $600 when I thought I was only spending $50. Ken Galbraith kept saying, 'Oh, I'm sure that sari is only about $5,' or an evening bag 'only $10,' or a piece of raw silk for Jack 'only $15'—and when I found out that night what I'd really spent, I nearly died.

"Only an economist could make such a mistake," she added.

Mrs. Kennedy also greatly admired Pakistan's President Ayub Khan, who had been a White House visitor in July 1961. "Ayub is like Jack—tough and brave and wants things done in a hurry," she said. "Wasn't he magnificent in his uniform? I asked him why he hadn't worn it to meet me. He said it wasn't a military occasion, but he promised to wear it on Pakistan's Independence Day. I told him he ought to wear it all the time.

"On the way to the airport we talked about his Astrakhan hat, and he promised to send me one. Then I asked to try his, and it was just right so he gave it to me. . . .

"Maybe," she went on, "I can talk Jack into wearing one . . . when he meets me! He always carries such a pathetic gray one in his hand."

Apparently Mrs. Kennedy failed to convince her husband to wear an Astrakhan hat. Perhaps it was because he had other problems on his mind. For the President had begun to tell visitors how different world problems now looked from his White House rocking chair than they had from the candidate's rostrum. There were fewer certainties, far more complexities. Old illusions and swift judgments had to be modified. He had also discovered that there are irrational forces loose in the world. Copious doses of foreign aid, for example, were not leading our little brothers in Asia and Africa into instant prosperity and political stability. Algeria—at last free from the chains of French colonialism—appeared to be forging new chains for herself. The first months of Algerian independence, for which Senator Kennedy had militantly crusaded, had brought only political and economic chaos and the threat of a Nasser-type dictatorship with an anti-Western orientation.

There was also the problem of disarmament. During the 1960 campaign, Kennedy had suggested the United States might get along better with the Russians if only it would put more people to work on disarmament and more "real effort" on the atom-test-ban negotiations at Geneva. Six months after Kennedy came to power, the Russians announced they would resume nuclear testing. Kennedy promptly charged "atomic blackmail" and he seemed to have learned about Communists the hard way. But had he really?

President Kennedy at first appeared to be almost helpless during the 1962 buildup of Cuba as a Soviet military base. The following developments reflect the positions he took during his second year in office:

February 3: Kennedy ordered an embargo on United States trade with Cuba.

March 21: At a news conference, he said he saw no evidence of a buildup in Cuban military strength around the United States Guantanamo Navy base. "We are always concerned about the defense of American territory wherever it may be, and we take whatever proper steps are necessary," he said.

August 22: Kennedy confirmed that during July and August, the Soviets had begun shipping to Cuba substantial quantities of modern war equipment and military technicians. "What we are talking about are supplies and technicians of rather intensive quantity in recent weeks," he observed.

August 24: Government intelligence sources reported that Soviet arrivals included 3,000 to 5,000 specialists, at least half to two-thirds of them military technicians; guided missiles similar to the United States Nike antiaircraft missile; transportation, communications, and electronic equipment.

August 28: At a news conference, Kennedy said: "I don't know who told you at the State Department that they are going to operate Nike missiles, because that information we do not have at this time. . . . But on the question of troops, as it is generally understood, we do not have evidence that there are Russian troops there."

September 5: After Republican Senator Keating of New York announced that Soviet ships had landed at least 1,200 troops wearing "Soviet fatigue uniforms" in Cuba, Kennedy acknowledged that the Soviets had brought in antiaircraft guided missiles "with a slant range of 25 miles similar to early models of our Nike," along with motor-torpedo boats carrying "ship-to-ship guided missiles having a range of 15 miles." However, the President said: "There is no evidence of any organized combat force in Cuba from any Soviet bloc country; of military bases provided to Russia; of a violation of the 1934 treaty relating to Guantanamo; of the presence of offensive ground-to-ground missiles; or of other significant offensive capability either in Cuban hands or under Soviet direction or guidance. Were it to be otherwise the gravest issues would arise."

September 13: "If the United States ever should find it necessary to take military action against Communism in Cuba, all of Castro's Communist-supplied weapons and technicians will not change the result or significantly extend the time required to achieve that result," said President Kennedy.

But what did he mean? No one could say for sure. One thing was certain, however. Kennedy was playing for time, hoping against hope that somehow the Cuban dictatorship would crumble without outside intervention. He appeared to view the Soviet threat in the Caribbean with extraordinary equanimity. He seemed to be promoting a "hands-off" policy while the Soviet military base in Cuba was permitted to expand. And with few exceptions, most editorial opinion viewed Kennedy's revised position on Cuba with dismay.

Significantly, even Max Lerner of the *New York Post* found something profoundly amiss in the new White House line on Cuba. Commenting on Khrushchev's threat to unleash a nuclear war in the event of a United States attack on Cuba, the Liberal pundit observed: "The importance of the recent Soviet statement is that the Russians have now made a daring move to appropriate Cuba as one of their own don't-touch-me areas. That is why it is, to put it mildly, astonishing for President Kennedy to say that nothing has happened in the recent Soviet moves to threaten American vital interests. Nothing has happened except Khrushchev's attempt to steal the Monroe Doctrine so far as Cuba is concerned, and turn it upside down and inside out, so that Russia assumes the role of protector of the outraged integrity of a Latin American country and the U.S. is put into the role of the big bad foreign power."

Actually, President Kennedy did leave the door open for United States intervention in the Caribbean. He had drawn a very thin line between "defensive" and "offensive" threats, saying the United States would meet the latter. He had stated he could not see a serious offensive threat to any part of the hemisphere, but added that the United States was ready to take "whatever action the situation will require."

Two days after Kennedy had stated his position, Washington correspondent Charles Keely reported to the *San Diego Union* (September 15th) that should Castro provide the pretext the United States would take military action. "This," wrote Keely, "Mr. Kennedy would like very much to do before the congressional elections on November 6."

The election campaign did not appear to be going too well for the Democrats. Poll soundings taken in his behalf convinced the President that Cuba had emerged as a foremost issue. On September 18th his former rival, Richard Nixon, seeking the Governorship of California, called for a "quarantine" of Cuba, possibly taken unilaterally. Nixon suggested this would involve use of a naval blockade.

On October 13th President Kennedy, speaking in Indianapolis for Birch Bayh, Democratic opponent of Senator Capehart, condemned "self-appointed generals and admirals who want to send someone else's sons to war." The remark was widely interpreted as a slap at Capehart who had earlier called for a blockade or invasion of Cuba. Previously, the rarely heard-from Vice President, Lyndon Johnson, had told a $40-a-plate Democratic dinner in Albuquerque that those who wanted to blockade Cuba were courting World War III.

"Stopping a Russian ship is an act of war," Johnson said. "Some people have more guts than brains and some don't have either."

Not all blockade advocates were Republicans seeking political advantage. Democratic leaders were becoming increasingly apprehensive over the seeming helplessness of the Kennedy Administration toward Castro's Cuba. They feared such "do-nothingism" would cost the Democrats votes at the polls. The "do-something" demands snowballed. Wherever Kennedy went on his campaign tours, political signs taunted his Administration about Cuba. "More profile than courage" was again raised against him. "Castro loves Democrats" was another slogan. These signs irritated President Kennedy greatly.

Kennedy had his journalistic defenders. Columnist Ralph McGill, for example, on September 30th denounced those political partisans who were seeking "deliberately to arouse public opinion by insisting that the United States Navy blockade Cuba. . . . To imply that this is an easy and simple solution is either ignorant or contemptible."

Easy or not, ignorant or not, contemptible or not, this was the solution that President Kennedy announced on October 22, 1962, when he took a new view of the seriousness of the Cuban threat. The latest intelligence had showed construction of offensive missile sites in Cuba—just as Senator Keating had been saying for months—sites which could hurl nuclear warheads on targets from Canada to Peru.

As it turned out, the *San Diego Union*'s Charles Keely proved right. Just two weeks before the 1962 elections, President Kennedy—at long last—ordered a naval blockade of Cuba. (This was the kind of affirmative action Candidate Kennedy had feared from the Eisenhower Administration in the fall of 1960. Had President Eisenhower engineered a successful overthrow of Castro in the closing days of the 1960 campaign, Richard Nixon might well have been elected President of the United States. Eisenhower, however, had held up invasion plans so that they would not become enmeshed in domestic politics. He held to the old-fashioned thesis that political considerations should not influence foreign-policy decisions.)

Kennedy's forthright stand in the closing days of the 1962 campaign resulted in Khrushchev's agreeing to remove his deadly missiles from Cuban soil. And for a time Kennedy looked ten feet tall. He looked like a Khrushchev-killer. Which, of course, did not hurt the Democrats at the polls. Among other things, Kennedy was able to accomplish the political destruction of his former rival, Richard M. Nixon, in California, and he prevented a large loss of Democratic seats in the House of Representatives. The final score—nationally —was clearly in the President's favor.

"As to why it is in the President's favor, the answer is equally clear," post-mortemed Joseph Alsop three days after the 1962 election. "Until only a fortnight ago, the atmosphere of the Democratic campaign was downright dank, to put it mildly. The President's barnstorming on domestic issues had lighted no bonfires among the voters. There was no enthusiasm, no spark to ignite the faithful with excitement.

"Then came the Cuban crisis. The President . . . took the kind of action most Americans wanted to see taken. . . . Cuba was the spark that had been lacking before. In some states the way the resulting fire singed the Republicans was easy to see."

Actually, the Cuban problem remained unsolved; and following the election it remained a Number One issue in national life as well as President Kennedy's Number One headache. Getting rid of Castro and Cuban Communism was not as simple as Candidate Kennedy had suggested during the 1960 campaign.

And no matter how hard he tried, the President appeared to be incapable of stemming the flow of criticism of his Cuban policies. The golden glow of his great October "victory" over Khrushchev wore off quickly. The more JFK protested, the more he created doubts. There was, in short, a crisis in credibility.

The reasons went back to the previous fall when the Administration was tardy in acknowledging the presence of Soviet missiles in Cuba, as well as in the Administration's stated policy to "manage" news.

President Kennedy's inability to convince the American people that his Administration knew what it was doing on Cuba had alarmed even his supporters. In fact, Walter Lippmann began speaking of a "crisis of confidence." In February 1963, Lippmann pointed out that JFK had stated categorically on September 13, 1962, that Soviet shipments to Cuba "do not constitute a serious threat to any other part of the hemisphere."

Two weeks later, Undersecretary of State George Ball told a Congressional committee there were no offensive weapons in Cuba.

"But in fact there were," commented Lippmann. "A week later, on

October 10, Senator Keating insisted that there were intermediate-range missiles in Cuba, and five days later the President received the photographs that confirmed the charge. This is how Senator Keating won the right to be listened to. . . ."

Whether or not Keating won "the right to be listened to" was not so important as whether the Administration had won that right. The New Frontier made no secret of its desire to manage the news.

Thus, following the Cuban crisis, the Pentagon's Arthur Sylvester bluntly acknowledged that the news was being deliberately manipulated by the Kennedy Administration. This, he said, was "part of the arsenal of weaponry."

On December 6, 1962, Sylvester, who used to be a newsman himself, made himself even clearer: "The inherent right of the Government to lie—to lie to save itself when faced with nuclear disaster—is basic."

No one in the communications media was arguing that the Government did not have the right to lie when it came to the enemy. The question was whether the Government had a right to lie to the American people.

Sylvester, Assistant Secretary of Defense for Public Affairs, put it this way in discussing the manner in which the Kennedy Administration had denied the Cuban buildup prior to the great confrontation: "When it [the Administration] is on the defensive under our political system, I would always be suspicious of what it said, or any other administration—and I do not expect virtue to come out of men, complete virtue, or even 75 percent virtue. If any of us are virtuous 51 percent of the time in life, that, I say, is a good record, and in politics, an amazing record."

It was an amazing statement. In effect, Sylvester was arguing that politicians had a right to lie in order to save their political hides.

Arthur Sylvester, however, termed "hogwash" charges that the Kennedy Administration "managed" the news. Appearing before a House subcommittee investigating government news policies, he denounced previous testimony that the Administration had issued distorted information or suppressed facts to give the Kennedy regime a favorable "image."

"I have not seen much documentation of these charges," Sylvester said.

The Pentagon spokesman should have been referred to an article by Hanson W. Baldwin, military analyst of the *New York Times,* in the April 1963 issue of *Atlantic.* In the article, Baldwin contended that "the blatant methods used by the administration and its tampering with the news deserve considerably more criticism and discussion than they have received." And he described the methods and cited the examples.

One form of news control, Baldwin wrote, was "the tremendously strengthened influence in government of the federal police power (the FBI and especially the Central Intelligence Agency) and of the 'intelligence mentality,' which tends to enshrine secrecy as an abstract good." The freewheeling use of federal cops to investigate leaks has grown to menacing proportions. Some of the most respected reporters in Washington have experienced "the treatment," which included visits by the FBI to their homes, tapping of telephone lines, shadowing of reporters, investigations of their friendships, and other forms of intimidation.

"In all these cases the newsmen concerned have told the FBI in effect that their sources were their business," reported Baldwin. ". . . These investigations have ranged throughout the Pentagon, the State Department, and other executive branches of government. And Mr. Kennedy has been the first President to send the FBI into the Pentagon, superseding the services' own investigative and internal security agencies."

(Baldwin did not say so, but he himself had been visited by federal snoopers, after he had written an article displeasing to the powers-that-be.)

Another method of news manipulation, according to Baldwin, is the personal reprimand, request, admonition, complaint, or compliment. When the respected and experienced Charles J. V. Murphy published his brilliant article on the Bay of Pigs fiasco in *Fortune,* he was not only personally denounced by JFK but also found most doors closed to him in official Washington. Later, Murphy, a colonel in the Air Force reserve who for years had a mobilization assignment in the office of the Air Chief of Staff, found that under White House pressure the Air Force had been compelled to shift him to a minor post elsewhere.

A third method is blocking the press from access to the news. Arthur Sylvester issued an order requiring the presence of a third person during any interview, or, alternatively, the filing of a report by the person interviewed. This rule, said Baldwin, "has gone a long way toward restricting news to the 'Poppa knows best' kind, to stories and data which the government *wants* to release."

Still another tactic used by the Kennedy Administration is the calculated leak, described by Baldwin as "the carefully disseminated canard or half-truth from someone close to the throne." The most famous example was the account in the *Saturday Evening Post* by Stewart Alsop and Charles Bartlett which purported to depict the "softness" of Adlai Stevenson during the 1962 Cuban crisis and which also added "hawks" and "doves" to political parlance.

"There was a time when the word of the government was its bond; the people could have faith . . . in what Washington told them," Baldwin continued. "Public confidence has been severely shaken many times since World War II; the U-2 case exposed the dangers of governmental falsehood for all to see.

"But the Kennedy Administration does not appear to have learned from these past horrible examples. . . ."

Another technique employed by the Kennedy Administration is the deliberate withholding of news. Baldwin tells how this technique was used during the Cuban crisis, with the result that the American people were deceived concerning matters which the Russians knew all about. Administration propaganda was so adroit, he said, that few Americans realized "the possibility, even the probability, that some long-range missiles are still concealed in Cuba" and, for that matter, "the greatly increased military strength of the Communist-Castro regime. . . ."

What are the dangers of news management?

"One of them is internal," wrote Baldwin. "The mania for secrecy often prevents the right hand of government from knowing what the left hand is doing."

But the greatest danger is the impairment of the constitutional right of press freedom. No people can be really free if its press is spoon-fed with government propaganda, said Hanson Baldwin.

President Kennedy, however, feigned ignorance when he was asked about managed news. And his press secretary, Pierre Salinger, said: "I don't know what managed news is. Nobody has ever defined this to me."

Pierre may not have known what managed news is, but he certainly knows how to manage the news.

Take the episode that occurred the morning of September 4, 1962, when Senator Keating was interviewed by Martin Agronsky on NBC-TV's "Today" show. Among other things, Keating stated he had been "reliably informed" that some 1,200 men in Soviet Army uniforms had landed in Cuba in August; and he suggested the American people had not been sufficiently alerted to the dangerous situation existing just 90 miles from our shores.

Even before Keating left the studio, Salinger was on the phone with the network, berating Agronsky. The White House hadn't liked the way the questioning went. Pierre claimed it showed Agronsky knew little about Cuba. The White House also resented Keating's "erroneous" estimates of the Cuban threat.

As it turned out, Keating's estimates were "erroneous" only insofar as they were decidedly on the conservative side.

"White House pressures are nothing new," the New York *Daily News'* Washington man, Ted Lewis, reported the following day. "But by dusk it was clear to NBC that the White House would not be happy unless an Administration Democrat had a chance to rebut Keating on the same show. Senator Clair Engle was picked quickly by the White House, for he had just received a complete fill-in on the Administration's Cuban line."

And the line simply was, as expressed by Senator Engle, that "my good friend from New York, Ken Keating, was just as wrong as he could be. . . . He didn't get his facts right."

At the very same time, in an off-the-record briefing, Pierre Salinger was telling newsmen "the general information that he [Keating] made public has been made public by the government before."

Then came Defense Secretary McNamara's now famous television show of February 6, 1963—an extraordinary effort on the part of the Administration to stem the flow of criticism of its Cuba policies.

Suddenly, everything was out in the open—the high-flying photographic planes and other United States intelligence techniques were laid bare on the idiot box. These were areas which Government officials had previously refused to discuss even on an off-the-record basis.

What had happened? What had changed?

"Nothing but the political pressures," reported Warren Rogers, Jr., in the *New Republic*. "Senator Keating . . . had made the heat in the political kitchen intolerable. The window was opened just long enough to cool things off.

"The question arises as to how Mr. Kennedy and other critics of 'the missile gap,' which never existed when they said it did in 1960, might have reacted if the Eisenhower Administration had exposed missile and intelligence secrets to drown them out. Perhaps that is when this new technique was born, since the Eisenhower Administration, electing to take the rap in silence, was clobbered."

Despite this unprecedented TV show and consequent reassuring statements by the President, much of the public, by and large, appeared bewildered, if not distrustful. The moral, as the Chicago *Tribune* editorialized, was supplied by these lines of Sir Walter Scott:

> O, what a tangled web we weave,
> When first we practice to deceive!

The Republicans, however, were not overly joyful about JFK's Cuban predicament. In fact, a specter began haunting the GOP's high command. And that was the fear that JFK would stage a repetition of the 1962 Cuban crisis on the eve of the 1964 Presidential election—and thus guarantee his own reelection.

That is why, Senator Margaret Chase Smith told a Republican Lincoln Day rally in February 1963, "the seeming ardor of Republican Presidential possibilities to do battle with Jack in 1964 has seemingly cooled down."

The Maine Republican, who has never cottoned to JFK's undisputed charms (particularly after he sought her defeat in 1954), added:

"Really you can't blame them when they are faced with such brilliant political timing as the sudden brace stand on Cuba just before the November 1962 election when it had become so apparent that the American people were fed up with the way the Cuban threat was being handled. After all, who knows but that there may be a repetition of such brilliant timing just before the November 1964 election."

Other things were not as simple as they had appeared to a candidate who on numerous occasions had bitterly protested he was "not satisfied" with things as they were. After two years of the New Frontier, foodstuffs were still piling up in United States warehouses while people abroad went hungry; James Hoffa still ran around "free"; the Soviets were still turning out more scientists; the growth rate still suffered in comparison with other industrialized powers; Communism, more than ever, was entrenched in our former good neighbor Cuba; and Kennedy didn't know what to do next.

"The truth is that U.S. relations with Western Europe are at present very bad, and that they are likely to become worse and not better in the near future," wrote Michael Padev, foreign editor of the *Indianapolis Star* on August 4, 1962, following a tour of European capitals. "All this is due to the fact that President Kennedy's foreign policy advisers, obsessed as they are with the supposed importance of the newly independent Asian and African nations, tend to ignore Western Europe almost completely."

Mr. Padev's perception was extraordinary. In less than six months, the unity of the Western Alliance was threatened as it never was before. From Ottawa to Karachi, thanks to incredible diplomatic ineptness, United States prestige—which concerned JFK terribly in 1960—appeared to have toppled to a new low.

The weather had abruptly changed in Washington from the high buoyancy of the post-Cuba-crisis days of the fall of 1962. Wherever one looked, the Western Alliance appeared in shocking disarray. To begin with, there was the debacle in Brussels. In vetoing Britain's entry into the Common Market, General de Gaulle blocked—if not wrecked—JFK's "grand design" for an Atlantic community with the United States in the driver's seat.

Then all of a sudden—to the amazement of most Americans—the United States found itself in an unseemly row with its indispensable close neighbor Canada. The United States, through a misguided State Department press release, brought down the government of Prime Minister Diefenbaker, who thereupon publicly warned Washington not to consider Canada as "part of the New Frontier"—a direct slap at JFK. A West German official, visiting the United States, privately told a group of newsmen, "Most Europeans do not take your President too seriously."

Why this "crisis in confidence" in President Kennedy?

Only a few short months before, JFK seemed to be on top of the world. He had scored what appeared to be an impressive victory over Khrushchev in Cuba. He became cocky and—in European eyes—arrogant. European leaders were outraged when Mr. Kennedy, at a Palm Beach background briefing for newsmen, let it be known that the United States intended to pursue its own role in world affairs even at the expense of treading on allied toes.

The President repeatedly went out of his way to irritate our allies. There was his disregard of European interests in such areas as the Congo. Over the protests of knowledgeable Europeans, JFK authorized a U.N. military adventure aimed at smashing a pro-Western regime in Katanga. "Kennedy will undoubtedly be applauded by the world's neutrals," commented *Le Monde* of Paris, "but he is showing how little regard he has for his allies."

Then there was the President's decision to hamper, or restrict, the growth of a truly independent nuclear deterrent in Europe. In London, where Whitehall announced it would develop its own air-launched missile to fill the gap left by United States cancellation of Skybolt, a British official commented: "The day has long gone when the American President sneezed and Europe caught pneumonia. If the United States now intends to place relations with the Afro-Asians, and even the Soviet Union, ahead of relations with Europe, the reaction on this side of the water is apt to be 'thank God for de Gaulle.' "

The truth is that de Gaulle became the most important spokesman for the new Europe. On the world stage he emerged as at least the equal of President Kennedy. And no one knew that unpleasant fact better than JFK who seeks to go down in history as the greatest of American Presidents. But *le Général* refused to play ball. He had failed to see any "greatness" in the young man from Hyannis Port. He was unwilling to entrust the future of France—and the Europe he now dominates—to the trigger finger of a youth responsible for the Bay of Pigs.

It has been difficult for de Gaulle to take the Kennedy Administration very seriously. While JFK kept saying that the Cuban threat had diminished, the Soviet buildup continued. And when the President was asserting the indivisibility of the NATO Alliance, United States diplomats were engaged in bilateral, secret negotiations with the Soviets. Suspicious Europeans began to ask if the United States was about to make a nuclear deal with Moscow over Europe's head.

As the pro-Alliance Paris newspaper, *La Croix,* put it: "Instead of a direct telephone between the White House and the Kremlin, what seems more essential is a permanent line between Europe and the United States."

In short, just two years after President Kennedy entered the White House, the world was in a real mess. All the glib pronouncements, the stirring slogans, and numerous promises had failed to turn the tide. The rhetoric was truly superlative; the performance virtually nil.

About JFK's performance on the domestic front, Richard Nixon put it this way in March 1963: The President has demonstrated "great salesmanship," but the product thus far has failed to live up to the promises.

Later that month, William V. Shannon discussed "the discontent of many liberals with the Kennedy Administration.

"These liberals," Shannon wrote in the *New York Post,* ". . . support the Administration but they do not identify with it. These liberals are presently an inchoate and almost leaderless group, partly because so many of their natural leaders and spokesmen have taken office in this Administration."

Their discontent could be summed up as follows:

"First, they expected that foreign policy would be shaped up by men such as Adlai Stevenson, Hubert Humphrey and Schlesinger himself. They did not expect Kennedy to turn for advice instead to . . . such as Dean Rusk, Dean Acheson and McGeorge Bundy. . . .

"Second, they expected the Peace Corps and the Alliance for Progress, both of which all liberals heartily approve, would be the models rather than almost the isolated exceptions in Administration approaches to foreign policy. . . .

"Third, liberals expected the President to reform the Central Intelligence Agency and give it enlightened political direction. They did not expect him to turn the agency over to reactionary John McCone. . . .

"Fourth, liberals expected the President to live up to his 1960 campaign speeches in which he stated that the Chief Executive should first of all be a great educator and that the Presidency is 'a place of moral leadership. . . .' "

Also giving the Liberals concern was the specter of Bobby Kennedy as the Democratic Presidential candidate in 1968. And, of all people, it was playwright Gore Vidal, a Presidential chum, who warned the public of this dread possibility.

Vidal, whose stepfather, Hugh D. Auchincloss, is also Jackie Kennedy's stepfather, reported in *Esquire* that the big buildup is already well under way for Bobby to succeed Jack in the White House.

Vidal cited Bobby Kennedy's books, his global tours, his civil-rights activities, and other elements as factors in a campaign to give him wide appeal.

"There is no doubt," he wrote (after blithely assuming JFK's reelection in 1964) "that when Bobby goes before the convention in 1968 he will seem beautifully qualified and from the point of view of sheer experience, he *will* be qualified." But, he adds, it would "take a public-relations genius to make him appear lovable. He is not. His obvious characteristics are energy, vindictiveness, and a simple-mindedness about human motives which may yet bring him down. To Bobby the world is black or white. Them and Us. He has none of his brother's human ease; or charity."

Bobby, added Vidal, "would be a dangerously authoritarian-minded President." And he quotes an "associate in the government" as saying: "It's not as if Bobby were against civil liberties. It's just that he doesn't know what they are."

Then why should anybody vote for him? "The general public," says Vidal, "can't have too much of their favorite family."

It was a portrait that will not be quickly forgiven in the White House, for it hits a little too close to the mark. The "Them and Us" quality has tended to be a Bobby Kennedy trademark in his career to date, and whatever uses it may have in lesser offices, vindictiveness is not a quality voters like to associate with the Presidency.

At any rate, after writing the piece, Vidal took off for Rome where he planned to stay for at least a year. One thing is certain: had he remained in the United States the White House invitations would no longer be coming.

That the New Frontier has no sense of humor became the considered judgment of satirist Mort Sahl.

And he's bewildered by the cool reception of his jibes at the Kennedy Administration.

"I had eight years with Ike and Nixon," the comedian told Hollywood correspondent Vernon Scott. "I got rich on the Republican Administration. The Democrats laughed at my jokes about the President and Vice President, and the Republicans enjoyed a laugh on themselves.

"But things are different now. The Republicans are still laughing but the Democrats aren't.

"Some people ask me, 'What's happened? You used to be on JFK's team,' " reported Democrat Sahl. "It is said the President is willing to laugh at himself. That is fine. But when is he going to extend that privilege to us?"

Victim of Sahl's most merciless cannonading was Richard Nixon.

"We recently met in a restaurant and had a long talk," recalled Sahl. "Mr. Nixon said he held no grudges at all and encouraged me to continue to light fires under both parties.

"I guess I'm an irritant to the Democrats because I remind them of their predicament, that the New Frontier isn't making it. Presidential jokes still get laughs built on my license to kid Presidents—but the license hasn't been renewed lately."

In other words, the New Frontier can dish it out but can't take it.

A more kindly appraisal of the New Frontier was provided by the Reverend Charles E. Coughlin, one of the most controversial American figures in recent history. The once-famed radio priest, in an exclusive interview with the *Detroit News,* still insisted he was right in his caustic denunciations of FDR in the thirties.

On the Kennedy Administration, however, Father Coughlin felt "it is doing better than anyone expected it would. Perhaps the President and his advisers have made some mistakes, but everybody does that. They are doing their best in a difficult situation."

Listen to novelist Herb Gold expound on the glories of the New Frontier:

"It's really quite a Roman administration—great dinners, great tours, great redecoration. Kennedy is undoubtedly talented, but ever since he was a tiny boy he's had one idea—succeeding. His speaking style is pseudo-Roman: 'Ask not what your country can do for you . . .' Why not say, 'Don't ask . . .'? 'Ask not . . .' is the style of a man playing the role of being President, not of a man being President."

Doesn't Kennedy invite dissent?

"Exactly," said Gold. "He's been sending messages to people like Paul Goodman, saying, 'Go out and dissent!' It makes dissent 'nice,' another consumer product. Dissent should be a threat to an administration. Kennedy sees it as a way of broadening his pitch. What value is dissent unless it is destructive? Dissent which is merely a way of demonstrating the broadmindedness of the man in power is not dissent any more. Maybe the moral is that if you eat the President's chicken you tend to become chicken."

Those who talked with Kennedy at the end of his first year—as did the *London Daily Mirror*'s Cassandra (William Connor)—could not help coming away with a feeling of sympathy for the President in his extraordinary difficulties. Cassandra concluded his account of his White House visit with these words: "But the harsh fact remains that the realities of brutal power politics cannot be erased by sympathy and that an older and more experienced man might be a better occupant of the lonely place in the White House."[10]

The frustrations implicit in Kennedy's private remarks continued to crop up in his public utterances. He became more "philosophical," more aware that the President of the United States can't solve all the world's problems.

The new Kennedy—or was it the *new* new Kennedy?—emerged publicly in November 1961. In a speech in Seattle, he observed:

"We must face the fact that the United States is neither omnipotent nor omniscient, that we are only six per cent of the world's population and that we cannot right every wrong or reverse each adversity, and that therefore there cannot be an American solution for every world problem."

Within a year, the image had shifted from that of a can-do-anything Chief Executive full of vim and "vig-ah," to that of a sadder-but-wiser man laboring under grave demands, cautiously, seriously, in an almost fatalistic mood.

The exultation Kennedy had felt on Inauguration Day had gone out of the man. The man with all the answers had finally discovered his answers didn't answer very much.

"What do they want me to do?" he asked of his critics. "Why don't they put it down on paper?"

Or as Ben B. Seligman, in an article in *Dissent* (Winter, 1962) criticizing the New Frontier from the left, reported: "Whenever a high Administration functionary is asked, 'When will something be done?' the reply is, 'Give us some ideas.' Now, who elected whom?"

Seligman's chief complaint was that Kennedy was corrupting his Liberal advisers into apologists for the status quo. He claimed that Seymour Harris, the Harvard economist who acts as consultant to the Treasury, had emerged as chief expositor of the political difficulties faced by the Kennedy economic program. "Harris' heart has always been with the angels, that is on the liberal or slightly left side," wrote Seligman. "Yet one can detect in his most recent popular writings a tone of resignation to the harsh requirements of Washington *realpolitik*. He evidently has tried hard to impress his perhaps old-fashioned

---

[10] On August 28, 1962, Cassandra came to the defense of Jacqueline Kennedy, whose frequent public appearances in a bathing suit had come under criticism. "Since when has youth and grace and gaiety at the White House been improper?" he demanded.

New Dealish views on government officials, but they keep coming out as pure New Frontier."

"And New Frontier," said Seligman, "these days is comprised of one part thought, two parts hope, three parts rhetoric, and four parts political buck-passing."

Seligman also complained that "all of the Presidential economic advisers appear to be of one cut—sophisticated, non-utopian, even bland, and very quick to learn the ways of practical politics. None lacks a ready justification for his retreat from 'text-book idealism.' Such accommodation, we are repeatedly told, is what Washington needs these days. But part of Kennedy's appeal to intellectuals, at least between the summer of 1960 and Inauguration Day, was his apparent sense of history. He seemed able to trace the roots of our difficulties and called for fresh ways of dealing with them. Only a few observers noticed that rhetoric is a poor substitute for genuine proposals. . . .

"There was a promise that vigorous action—a favorite Washington expression—would be taken. But somehow assessments of situations as preludes to judgements got in the way—so much so that Paul Samuelson had to admit that the adventures in New Frontier economics constituted a 'placebo program for recovery.' The cocktail party circuit and car-pool riders began to talk about the Third Eisenhower Administration. . . .

"Why this harsh reaction? Quite plainly, the Kennedy Administration has been unable to break the bonds of its milieu. We have now a society in which the ostensible end of ideology is welcomed and in which serious political debate is frowned upon. Existence under Kennedy is unchanged: it is what it was under Eisenhower. . . ."

There was one difference, however: Under Eisenhower considerable legislation was enacted. Under Kennedy, nothing of major consequence bearing his stamp made much headway in the early years of the New Frontier. Seldom before in United States history has any President been so consistently rebuffed by the legislators—not of the Opposition party, but of both parties. The hostility to Kennedy's "must" proposals was not partisan. It was bipartisan.

And what made it particularly embarrassing for Kennedy was that, in large measure, it was a repeat of the post-Convention short Congressional session of 1960. At that time, he had excoriated "divided government" as the reason for his legislative failures. Now he was in the White House and, despite overwhelming Democratic strength in Congress, he still couldn't get legislation through.

William Shannon, of the *New York Post,* accused the President of having made no great decision, of involving himself in no "irrevocable commitments," and of evoking no serious controversies. And he compared Kennedy with "the stylish young man at the end of the high diving board whose sole actions consisted of impressing upon the audience that the water down below is hellishly cold," reminding onlookers "that he has read all the books on diving, that he knows how important it is to dive, that diving is the key to the whole show, etc., etc.

"All that remains for him to do is dive."

Shannon wanted immediate action on the numerous campaign pledges Kennedy had made. Civil rights, for example. During the campaign, Kennedy had said that President Eisenhower could have ended discrimination in federally supported housing "with a stroke of his pen" on an Executive Order.

Finally, after enormous pressure, JFK managed to stroke his pen. This was two years after his election.

"Decisions cannot, of course, be long postponed," Shannon had written. "The exercise of power means drawing blood and raising blood pressure; it means making enemies; it means arousing anger."

Which was precisely what Kennedy was seeking not to do.

In the spring of 1962 he had drawn blood by going after United States Steel. He said his daddy had told him that "all businessmen" were of doubtful parentage. And he triggered off a "crisis in confidence" which was reflected in the near-panicky mood of May 1962, when stock prices on Wall Street collapsed. On Black Monday (May 28) many older businessmen thought they were hearing echoes of the Great Crash of 1929. It was somewhat disturbing to recall that during the long bull market of 1950–62 there had been a lot of "New Era" talk very much like that of the Twenties.

At any rate, the economic situation frightened President Kennedy. He quickly decided that a quick tax cut was needed to pep up the sluggish United States economy. Most of his economic advisers agreed. Yet, in mid-August, when he went on television to explain his policy, the President came out not with a tax-cut proposal, but rather with a statement that emergency tax legislation "could not now be either justified or enacted." The operating word, of course, was "enacted." The President knew he could not get his proposal through his Democratic-controlled Congress.

Clearly, under Kennedy there has been a failure in leadership at the White House level. There was, as the *London Times* phrased it in Kennedy's first year, "complete political disarray" in the nation's capital. The Government was being badly run. However, when one considers the way in which a well run Kennedy Administration might occupy its time, perhaps one should be grateful for a badly run one.

The truth is that despite Kennedy's personal popularity (and every time he got into trouble his rating went up), the President has yet to win popular support for his programs. Some of his Liberal critics contend that he runs away from fights rather than dissipate some of his popularity which, they claim, he is hoarding for 1964.

The central theme of Kennedy's first two years in office was not so much venturing toward new frontiers as the systematic exploitation of the rich political and publicity assets of the Presidency. Scarcely a day went by without Huntley and Brinkley televising a little feature of the President in the Rose

Garden handing out medals to worthy citizens or shaking the hand of some exchange student from Nigeria.

The President deliberately sought to focus attention on himself and his personality, obviously believing it was easier to change the minds of hostile voters about a man—a friendly, reasonable man with a lovely wife and vivacious children—than to convert them through the abstractions of a program.

Kennedy's preoccupation with his image is, of course, shared by his aides. As William Shannon observed in the *American Scholar:* "The politics of those closest to the President, the group sometimes called 'the Irish Mafia,' is personal, not programmatic. . . . Their first criterion, sometimes their sole criterion, on every important problem is: How will this help 'The Boss' get re-elected in 1964?"

Kennedy has also spent an inordinate amount of time worrying about how to undercut potential 1964 GOP opponents like Rockefeller, Nixon, Goldwater, and Michigan's George Romney. He has conducted a talent search for someone to oppose Rockefeller in New York; and he tried to pin the John Birch label on Richard Nixon.

According to Joseph Alsop, Kennedy pollster Lou Harris had come up with the findings that the great majority of California voters disapproved of the Birchites. "On the basis of the Harris soundings, President Kennedy himself pressed Nixon's Democratic opponent, California Governor Pat Brown, to challenge Nixon briskly to disavow the Birch Society. Governor Brown, though not normally given to briskness, thereupon proceeded to say Nixon would wear the Birch label unless he disavowed Birch."

There had been a time, before the Age of Kennedy, when Alsop was a determined foe of those who, for political advantage, sought to pin false labels on opponents. Now things were different.

To what extent does President Kennedy continue to rely on polls for guidance? The question was raised by publication of an item in the *New York Herald Tribune:* "Private polls made for the Administration indicate that the American public is willing to fight to preserve West Berlin. The polls were conducted by Lou Harris. . . ." Early in October 1962, Joe Alsop reported that President Kennedy, "apprehensive about the power of the Cuban issue to poll votes for the Republicans" was "taking one of his private soundings of public opinion to get a better measure of the potential danger." (Apparently, to Kennedy, the potential danger lay not so much in the Soviet military buildup in Cuba as in losing votes.) Does this mean that Kennedy's foreign policy decisions are based on popularity polls? And a related question: Who is paying for the polls? Efforts to determine the answer at the White House have been unavailing.

The fact that Kennedy's popularity remained high—despite repeated setbacks both at home and abroad—has fascinated observers. "Professional polling people have been seeking the answer for both Republican and Democratic groups," Roscoe Drummond reported on March 2, 1962. "Their findings are remarkably uniform; they may well be arguable, but they agree substantially on one point: That the widespread doing-a-good-job rating Kennedy is receiving is not an in-depth approval, could turn out to be quite fragile."

As the glitter of the New Frontier wore off, it became increasingly obvious that Kennedy had little else than his personality to sell to the American voter. Except perhaps for his October 1962 "brinkmanship" in the Caribbean, he had not scored any outstanding domestic or foreign successes. Rather, it could be said, the reverse had occurred.

So far, Kennedy has shown himself to be much more adept at activity than at achievement, to think in terms of politics than principles. And though he was supposed to excel at the political arts, his admirers have been shocked at his almost complete paralysis in dealing with Congress. Frustrated by continuing defeats, he placed the major blame on the Republicans. Which prompted the *Christian Science Monitor* to comment on July 25, 1962: "Mr. Kennedy respects both logic and objectivity but in this case he seems to be taking leave of both. Why should he blame members of the opposition party for predictably voting against bills with which they traditionally disagree? He could more logically blame the voters. The voters gave him an insufficient number of Democrats who agree."

Also, for whatever reason, perhaps a rising political self-confidence resulting from the high popularity ratings, Kennedy's approach to Congress had radically changed. Whatever the merits of the proposed new Department of Urban Affairs, the fact is that President Kennedy's highly political efforts to obtain its creation assured its doom.

Kennedy's first endorsement of the plan was in October 1960 when, as a Presidential candidate, he addressed an "urban affairs conference" in Pittsburgh, which he had called to give himself a forum. He made a speech about the "shameful record of neglect" of the cities, and charged that the Republicans in Congress had kept them from getting larger grants of federal tax funds for urban renewal, public housing, private housing, public schools, hospitals, mass transportation, stream pollution, air pollution, and to combat juvenile delinquency.

In 1961, as President, Kennedy repeated the proposal for an Urban Affairs Department, but he did not press the matter when it was sidetracked in the House Rules Committee.

The House Rules Committee, still a stronghold of cranky conservatism in spite of Kennedy's widely celebrated "victory" over it in 1961, again killed the proposal after the President had insisted on an immediate showdown. In effect, this was a rebuke administered to a Democratic Chief Executive by members of his own party.

The Democrats controlled Congress by a heavy majority of almost two to one in the Senate, and four to three in the House. The division was even more lopsided in the House Rules Committee—of its 15 members, 10 were

Democrats. Yet, in assessing the blame for the defeat of his bill, Kennedy told a press conference:

"I am somewhat astonished . . . that all of the Republican members of the Rules Committee opposed the bill. . . . I had gotten the impression . . . they shared our concern for . . . the problems of two-thirds of our population who live in cities."

Next Kennedy announced he would create the Department of Urban Affairs by executive order, and that unless the Congress vetoed the plan within sixty days, he would name Robert C. Weaver as the Department's first Secretary. Weaver, head of the Federal Housing Administration, would thus become the first Negro in the Cabinet.

The idea was to twist things around so that a vote against Urban Affairs could be construed as a vote against having a Negro in the Cabinet. The Republicans cried "foul." They argued that the proposed Department would be an unnecessary enlargement of the Federal bureaucracy and would allow Washington to bypass the states in dealing with the cities, and they insisted they had no objection to Weaver; that he'd be all right in some other Cabinet post. They pointed out that when Weaver's nomination as Housing Administrator came before the Senate, five Republicans—Dirksen, Javits, Bush, Miller, and Cooper—spoke in his behalf. Not one GOP voice had been raised against him. But six Democrats denounced him.

Even more satisfying were the paeans of the Personality Cultists. And such was the similarity of the eulogies that it almost suggested a prima facie case for conspiracy among the laureates.

"President Kennedy's masterly political skills," wrote the *Baltimore Sun's* Thomas O'Neill, "the same that confounded all competition on his way to nomination and election, were again on parade in the swift moves which maneuvered congressional Republicans into an uncomfortable and probably untenable corner for the forthcoming elections."

"If there was any political trap in all this," wrote Walter Lippmann, "the Republican leaders have laid the trap into which they have fallen."

". . . He strode into his press conference and started swinging on the first question . . .," wrote James Reston. "There was something about the way the President handled this brisk maneuver that indicated he was going to have a good day—and he did."

Both the Washington and New York *Post*s ran ecstatic editorials on the President's shrewdness. "The Chief Executive in a few brief moments at his Wednesday press conference, deftly demonstrated that he is still the master politician . . .," said the *Washington Post*.

"The President's announcement," said the *New Republic*, "that he will establish the Department by executive fiat and appoint a Negro to head it has been called a mean political trick. It surely is; for [it] has blown the GOP-Dixiecrat coalition sky-high."

And Bill Mauldin, then cartoonist for the *St. Louis Post-Dispatch*, depicted Kennedy as a happy elephant hunter, laughing as the GOP lumbered toward a pitfall.

Well, he who laughs last, and all that. The strategy was so raw that Kennedy found himself speedily accused of racism. It was quickly recalled that during the 1960 campaign, after Henry Cabot Lodge, the Republican Vice Presidential candidate, had predicted a Negro in the Cabinet in the event of a GOP victory, Candidate Kennedy had stated:

"I am not going to promise a Cabinet post or any other post to any race or ethnic group. That is racism at its worst."

And now Kennedy himself was practicing what he had preached against. "For in indicating in advance that a Negro would occupy the new cabinet seat, Kennedy is seeking to make use of the same bigotry-in-reverse technique that helped win him the Presidency," commented the *Cincinnati Enquirer*.

Of course, as Thomas O'Neill had observed, "these maneuvers pushed into the background whether there is merit in the creation of a new Cabinet Department."

Majority Whip Hubert Humphrey didn't seem to care. He was on the phone talking to Negro leaders, whipping up telegrams like the one sent by Roy Wilkins, executive secretary of the NAACP, to Republican National Chairman William E. Miller: "[The Republicans'] action will be interpreted as racially motivated."

The President's reorganization message had hardly hit Capitol Hill before it became clear that the new Department he proposed would give Weaver a position of minimum authority and little stature. The plan was limited to housing. No longer did it include the long list of programs such as air pollution control, snow removal, water supplies, recreation, social services, sewage disposal, airports, etc., which would have come under Weaver's bailiwick in the original proposal.

Kennedy's strategy was to get the question to a vote in the Senate first. It had a chance of winning there, and Senate approval would conceivably sway some votes in the House, where hopes were slim. Also, if the House voted first and killed the plan, no Senate vote would be necessary, and the Administration would lose a chance to put Republican Senators on the spot.

But somehow Kennedy's vaunted Leadership slipped up. Senator John McClellan, the Arkansas Democrat who heads the Government Operations Committee, refused to rush consideration of the plan and get it onto the Senate floor. The White House, unwilling to await the accustomed procedure, instructed Majority Leader Mike Mansfield to move for an immediate vote. Party leaders then introduced a motion to force the measure out of the McClellan Committee.

For the first time since 1936, every Senator showed up to vote. Senator Edmund Muskie, Maine Democrat, victim of an auto accident, arrived in a wheel chair. The vote was 58 to 42 against the motion, thereby killing the plan. In effect, the Senate told the President to keep his cotton-pickin' hands off its affairs. The Presidential intrusion had affronted the inner "club" of the Senate, estranged all but one of the Committee Chairmen, and incurred resentment except from the most submissive New Frontier Democrats and four Republicans from states with large Negro constituencies.

The vote was taken during the very minutes that Astronaut John Glenn on his third orbit of the earth was gladdening the hearts of every American, and giving the Administration its happiest day. The contrast between the simple heroism of Colonel Glenn and the bold executive attempt to frighten Senators with the bogey of a resentful Negro vote was heightened by their coincidence.

The next day the House delivered the *coup de grâce*. The 264 to 150 vote included a score or more of Western and Northern Democrats who voted against the President. In other words, his own party divided almost 50–50 on the issue—which was astonishing in view of Kennedy's reported popularity.

It was a walloping rebuff for President Kennedy. It brought into sharp focus the whole question of his leadership.

Even *Newsday,* whose editor had supported Kennedy in 1960, said the President "has suffered the defeat he deserved." The influential Long Island daily added: "There is no denying the need for such a department, with the problems of the cities being what they are. Had Kennedy tried to sell his new department on the basis of need alone, he surely would have at least come closer to achieving it.

"But Kennedy chose to obfuscate the issue. . . . To forewarn a racially divided Congress that a Negro would join the Cabinet for the first time in American history via this new department was legislative suicide, and a gross attempt by Kennedy to inject the racial issue into a subject which needed no additional barrier to its passage by Congress. Kennedy's attempts to label those Congressmen voting against the measure as anti-Negro fortunately didn't cow Congress into voting out of fear.

"A Department of Urban Affairs and Housing would be a natural, modern-day extension of the Cabinet and one which should be established, just on its own merit. Kennedy, when he came into office, had 10 opportunities to name a Negro to his Cabinet but chose not to do so. It is at the expense of a vitally needed new Cabinet department that he selected this time to inject the totally unrelated racial issue. In this case, he may have won the battle, but he unquestionably lost the war."

At a press conference, Kennedy served notice he would still try to get political mileage out of his defeat. He pointedly noted that the Department would have served the "70 to 75 to 80 per cent" (actually two-thirds, the Census Bureau said later) of the nation's population living in cities. And he added, sarcastically, that Weaver would be "grateful for those good wishes for a Cabinet position where there is no vacancy."

Of course, as everyone knew, Abe Ribicoff was about to resign as Secretary of Health, Education and Welfare. The Republicans suggested Kennedy appoint Weaver to this post, and said that no Republican would raise any objection to Weaver's appointment.

Kennedy had other ideas. He had made his point with Weaver. But he was in trouble with the Italian-American community, some of whose leaders had publicly accused him of having ignored their compatriots in selecting New Frontiersmen for high office. The word went out that Dr. Weaver, distinguished as he was, did not have the background necessary for HEW. But neither did the man Kennedy selected to succeed Ribicoff—the Mayor of Cleveland, the Honorable A. J. Celebrezze who, among his other qualifications, happened to be Italian-born.

Having proposed to play rough on Urban Affairs, Kennedy asked for precisely the rough treatment he received. "The President," commented Holmes Alexander, "deserves to be punished whenever he appeals to the lower instincts of Congressmen. He does this when he tempts them to vote against their better judgments on peril of political defeat. He does this when he appeals to their venality by buying their support with judgeships and other political sweetmeats. He does so when he appeals to their vanity by personal telephone calls and the like."

Kennedy had gained absolutely nothing in political advantage from the hurly-burly he had created. But the Congress felt it had gained a good deal. By winning this contest against a popular President, the Congress was encouraged to take him on again and again. As a result, despite all its brave words, John F. Kennedy's Administration has proved to be one of the weakest in American history.

And one reason has been the superficiality of its programs and actions. This is odd. For the New Frontier had been widely touted as one of the most intellectual Administrations in many years—and if the often-abused term should not be entirely debased it should signify not so much academic brilliance as a capacity for serious, logical, mature thought. Yet, what has been coming out of the New Frontier, no matter what the problem at hand may be, has been a thinness of thinking, rather than intellectuality. Consider the proposal for a Department of Urban Affairs. It was simply assumed that the Federal Government could provide remedies that have baffled municipal specialists for years. The fault is not too much intellectuality, but, in the real sense, too little. As the *Wall Street Journal* put it: "The most obvious explanation would be that many of the new men in Washington were overrated to begin with. It would seem that, rather than some kind of intellectual super-elite, we just have some shallow thinkers dominated not by any particular high-mindedness but by an intense concern for the main political chance in each case.

"A further explanation is that the 20th-century liberal, in sharp contrast to the 19th-century liberal, is apparently incapable of profound philosophical thought about the nature of man and man's institutions. Today's liberal invariably takes the path of least mental resistance, which in political terms means dumping every problem, no matter how small or local, on the Federal Government.

"It would be surprising if the appeal of such thinking, if that is the word, had not faded. There was much shallow thinking and intense politicking in Franklin Roosevelt's days too. But Mr. Roosevelt at least seemed to be doing something new. He seemed to be moving the country, even though its economy remained on dead center. There was a dash, a style, a quality about the New Deal that is absent in the New Frontier."

In foreign affairs, too, the New Frontiersmen have demonstrated incredible naïveté. They had come into office, hoping that the Soviet Union would be more tractable in dealing with a Liberal Administration. After all, hadn't Chairman Khrushchev released the RB-47 pilots just in time for Kennedy to make the announcement at his first press conference? And hadn't the Chairman said he could have released them during the campaign, except he didn't want to help that blankety-blank no-goodnik, Richard Nixon?

In fact, the new President had even sent a personal communication to Khrushchev pleading with him to give the New Frontier team a six-months' reprieve from crises in which to formulate new policies designed to reach a *modus vivendi* with the Soviet Union. This, of course, turned out to be a horrible diplomatic blunder; it was like waving a red flag before a bull; it convinced Khrushchev that the new Administration was unsure of itself and the time was ripe for some heavy-handed pressure tactics.

And Kennedy—or rather, the United States—suffered blow after blow. For a time it was almost too much for Kennedy to bear. "After seven months in office," Karl E. Meyer, editorial writer for the *Washington Post*, reported in the *Progressive*, "President Kennedy is not a notably relaxed man—and the anxiousness and occasional uncertainty on his face have also marked the appearance of his Administration."

Until he assumed the Presidency, the road to success had been comparatively easy and, like other young men who've had few setbacks, Jack Kennedy thought he knew all the answers. As Hubert Humphrey had stated during their primary contests: "Jack lacks humility." And humility might in turn have suggested the propriety, in times of crisis, of more silence. The President, in short, has talked too much. He thereby cheapens what he says, and casts doubt as to his credibility. In the rhetoric of an ultimatum, he demanded a cease-fire in Laos. But he failed to back up his strong words uttered at a televised press conference on March 23, 1961.

Addressing himself somberly to a map of that small Southeast Asian nation, Kennedy warned that a Communist takeover would "quite obviously affect the security of the United States." In effect, he warned Khrushchev to be prepared for a fight.

Four days later, Andrei Gromyko visited the White House. Taking the Soviet Foreign Minister into the Rose Garden, Kennedy warned Gromyko against pushing the United States too far in a situation where its prestige is at stake.

"The United States does not intend to stand idly by while you take over Laos," the President said sternly.

Gromyko listened politely—and the Communist Pathet Lao kept gobbling more of Laos. And Kennedy, his bluff called, began to downgrade the importance of Laos vis-à-vis United States security. The new line was that Laos was a strange faraway land of elephants, parasols, and pagodas, definitely not worth fighting a war over. And, what's more, Kennedy now was saying, "We can only defend the freedom of those who are ready to defend themselves."

The failure of the Kennedy Administration to go to the aid of Laos—and its insistence on a coalition government including Communists and pro-Communist neutralists—did not mean United States non-involvement in Southeast Asia. By 1962, United States forces were participating in one of the bloodiest non-wars in recent times—in South Vietnam, where Communist guerrillas were infiltrating through Laos. As a result of reverses from Laos to Cuba, the United States lost enormous "face"—or prestige—from the Philippines to Pakistan. Asked what he thought of Kennedy, Pakistan's President Ayub Khan, one of Asia's greatest leaders, replied: "An excellent young man. With a little experience, he'll do better."

Following the Cuban debacle, President Kennedy—in European eyes—emerged as a baffling and disappointing figure. Most disheartened were those who had been led to expect a fresh and vital new force in international relations. His words and activities first perplexed, then confused and finally (after Cuba) reduced to incredulity a substantial number of European well-wishers. These included many critics of Eisenhower who had felt that any new American President would be an improvement. For example, as Jean Daniel reported in the *New Republic,* General Charles DeGaulle, no matter what differences he had with Eisenhower, had "never forgotten that the latter was the Commander in Chief of the Allied Forces" in World War II. But, Daniel reported from Paris, "DeGaulle refers spontaneously to the 'young man' who is presiding over the destiny of the North American nation. On the lips of an illustrious elder statesman, the expression 'young man' is not necessarily a flattering one."

On April 20, 1961, Kennedy called Richard Nixon to the White House to discuss the Cuban debacle. He assured his former rival—as he did other Republican leaders—that he intended to "take care" of Castro. Among the steps he was considering was a Naval blockade that, among other things, would prevent Soviet shipments of armaments, jet planes, and other articles of war to Cuba. He appeared to be fully determined to face up to the problem.

At the same time, he told Nixon that the Cuban episode might have given Nikita Khrushchev a wrong idea—that he might keep pushing us around all over the world. The President said he had to try to convince him of United States determination in the cold war.

True, during the 1960 campaign, Kennedy had been scornful of gad-about diplomacy and had promised to be a stay-at-home President. "If I am elected next Tuesday," he declared at the New York Coliseum on November 5, 1960, "I want to be a President known . . . not by tours and conferences abroad, but by vitality and direction at home. My opponent promises, if he is successful, to go to Eastern Europe, to go perhaps to another summit, to go to a series of meetings around the world. If I am successful, I am going to Washington, D.C., and get this country to work."

Kennedy had met Khrushchev on a previous occasion. That was in September 1959 when the Red ruler, visiting the United States, had dropped in to say hello to members of the Senate Foreign Relations Committee. Though Khrushchev did not recall the historic encounter, Kennedy referred to the episode in a speech at the University of Rochester in October 1959. He declared, ". . . the Khrushchev with whom I met . . . was a tough-minded, articulate, hard-reasoning spokesman for a system in which he was thoroughly versed and in which he thoroughly believed. He was not the prisoner of any ancient dogma or limited vision. And he was not putting on any act—he was not engaging in any idle boast—when he talked of the inevitable triumph of the Communist system. . . . The fact is that we can find certain basic interests or objectives which the United States and the U.S.S.R. have in common—and we should concentrate our efforts on those potential areas of agreement. We need a new approach to the Russians—one that is just as hard-headed and just as realistic as Mr. Khrushchev's, but one that might well end the current phase —the frozen, belligerent, brink-of-war phase—of the long Cold War."

In short, Khrushchev was a reasonable man who, if approached properly, could be persuaded he couldn't have everything his way.

This was not the Khrushchev with whom President Kennedy met in Vienna for two days in June 1961. Kennedy's faith in his own rhetorical powers of persuasion was soon badly shaken. He knew Khrushchev would be tough—but not that tough. When, for example, Kennedy made clear his determination to defend Berlin at all costs, the Soviet boss did not appear to be listening.

But if diplomacy failed Kennedy, publicity didn't. The personable young President and his glamorous wife scored a huge personal success in Europe. There were encouraging stories that he had made a favorable impression on Charles DeGaulle, who had been referring to him as *Jacques l'enfant*. And sophisticated commentators—short of hard news of any real accomplishments —discoursed on the psychological benefits of the trip on Kennedy's maturing Presidential personality. Some said he was beginning to learn from his grave mistakes. And the national pride back home was touched by Europe's homage to the First Lady as the American Queen of Hearts.

Forgotten was the humiliation in the Bay of Pigs as the newspapers of the world began to read like movie magazines with reams of gushing, girlish copy about Jacqueline Kennedy's clothes, her various hairdos, and excellent linguistic talents. And who could forget the dazzling sight of Jack and Jacqueline—young, rich and handsome, straight out of the American dream—standing so graciously beside the dumpy, dowdy Nikita and Nina on the receiving line at the glittering Palace in Vienna!

"If anyone thinks *that* won't stop the Communists cold, then he had better read 'Beauty and the Beast' again," commented the *Richmond News Leader*. "Why did Khrushchev ogle Jackie so obligingly; why did he talk so courteously with the Harvard freshman, all the while drinking in his profile of courage? There were a thousand reasons.

"It is good strategy to encourage any illusion in one's enemy, especially an illusion so crippling and total as the American idea that the Cold War is a popularity contest. A Harvard freshman, dancing with the belle of the Vassar ball, does not invade Cuba (except with an autograph pencil). A king and queen of movieland are ideal enemies, in Khrushchev's realistic world of brute strength. The spirit of Camp David had its uses as a smoke-screen; but the Klieg-lit dazzle of 'Operation Jack and Jackie' can be put to a much wider variety of uses."

The editorial was entitled "Silver Screen vs. Iron Curtain."

A joint communiqué issued at the end of the Vienna meetings described them as frank, courteous, and useful. But useful to whom? From Kennedy's viewpoint, the confrontations had failed. *U.S. News & World Report* said that Khrushchev had sized up Kennedy as a "pushover"; and Henry J. Taylor wrote, "Khrushchev concluded we are a people who first shake our fists, then shake our fingers, and then shake our heads."

The truth, as it later filtered out, was that Khrushchev had refused to withdraw any of his unreasonable demands—on Germany, nuclear testing, the U.N., Cuba, and Laos. In effect, Khrushchev demanded that Kennedy give in on every point. Unable to budge Khrushchev on a single item (except Laos, where both men agreed on a "neutralist" coalition government), Kennedy said finally, "It's going to be a cold winter."

A small grin appeared on the Chairman's face. Later, it was widely reported on the diplomatic circuit that Khrushchev had boasted to the East Germans, "I think that I have taught that young man what fear is."

"Flying back to the United States the next night," reported *Time,* "John Kennedy sat in his shorts, surrounded by his key aides. He was dead tired; his eyes were red and watery; he throbbed with the ache of a back injury that the nation did not yet know about but that had forced him to endure agonies on his European trip. Several times he stared down at his feet, shook his head and muttered how unbending Khrushchev had been. He hugged his bare legs and wondered what would come next."

A month after the event, Kennedy's chum, Joseph Alsop, reported: "High in the air above France . . . Kennedy first addressed himself to the . . . hardest question of our time . . . the question whether it is better to risk a war with modern weapons in order to avoid surrender. . . . So he mused about the problem for a while, unburdening his mind almost at random for his closest staff members.

"If one could think only of oneself, he remarked, it would be an easy problem. He was 44. He had had a full, rich, lucky life. He had never, in any case, been troubled by the deep, anxious fear of dying that afflicts some men. In that way, too, he supposed he had been lucky. For the individual, in any case, the duty to make any sacrifice to avert a great national defeat was crystal clear. 'If you could think only of yourself,' he remarked, 'it would be easy to say you'd press the button, and easy to press it, too.'

"Yet as President, he went on, he could not think only of himself. He had also to think of the next generation and of those who would come after. 'That makes it damned hard,' he said. He concluded bluntly that it was a choice, none the less, which might have to be made."

Almost as soon as he returned to the White House on June 5, Kennedy called for an estimate of the number of Americans likely to be killed in a nuclear war; the number was seventy million.

The next day Kennedy used one word to describe the outlook for the United States. That word was "somber." That same day Nikita Khrushchev cavorted and clowned at a diplomatic party in Moscow. UPI correspondent Henry Shapiro reported that the dictator looked more exuberant and relaxed than he had seen him in years. The Soviet boss acted like a winner.

Khrushchev's behavior baffled Kennedy. Every rule of logic dictated that it was in the Soviet's self-interest to calm the Berlin crisis before it reached the point of no return. Still, Khrushchev kept heating it up.

As a politician, Kennedy owed a measure of success to his ability to put himself in "the other fellow's position" and figuring out how the "other fellow" would react to certain situations. Kennedy tried to do this with Khrushchev. Instead of enlightenment, the result was more confusion.

Somehow he had to get through to Khrushchev, to make him understand.

On the night of July 25, 1961, President Kennedy went before the television cameras to answer Khrushchev's challenge on Berlin. Kennedy told the American people he was firmly rejecting the dictator's ultimatum. This meant that thermonuclear war was possible by the December deadline Khrushchev had given. Among the emergency measures he advocated for meeting the crisis was a program of fallout shelters. "In the event of attack," he said, "the lives of those families which are not hit in a nuclear blast and fire can still be saved—if they can be warned to take shelter and if that shelter is available. We owe that kind of insurance to our families—and to our country. . . . The time to start is now."

"The deliberate, somber way he addressed himself to the teleprompter," reported Robert T. Hartmann, of the *Los Angeles Times,* "the word-fumbling which caused paroxysms of mirth among the literati when similar pressures bore on his predecessor, the seeming dryness of mouth and constriction of vocal muscles visible to the television audiences were not the John F. Kennedy they thought they knew. . . ."

This was not the same supremely self-possessed and coolly confident young man who only six months before, in his Inaugural speech, had urged: "Let us begin!"

Nineteen days after Kennedy's Berlin speech, the Communists gave their reply. They began to erect The Wall which slashed Berlin—"the great testing place of our courage and will," according to Kennedy—in half. And once again, Kennedy was caught off balance. As usual, on a weekend, he was elsewhere than Washington. This time he was sailing off Hyannis Port when word flashed through from Berlin. Soon Kennedy was complaining bitterly that no one had even warned him that such a dreadful thing could happen.

But happen it did. And the United States did nothing. In fact, it took two days before the Allies could agree on a statement of protest. By that time, it was too late. The sealing-off of East Berlin had left the United States without a policy. The President and his advisers had assumed that the Reds would return to the 1948 strategy of blockade. That miscalculation, Walter Lippmann pointed out on September 7, "led the Administration to concentrate its energy on convincing Khrushchev that the West would fight if he interfered with physical access to West Berlin." This was true, and "it was a prudent precaution to make this plain to Khrushchev. But it should not have been sold to the American people and to the world as a policy. . . . On August 13 we had no policy, and there is reason to ask whether we are on the way to having one now."

In calling for a do-it-yourself shelter program, however, Kennedy had again shot from the hip. The truth was that prior to his July 25 speech, the White House had given the subject little thought. It took five months for the Government to produce a simple booklet on "Fallout Protection"—and that proved to be of little value.

Rarely had Kennedy rhetoric created more confusion than on this subject. Conflicting voices only added to the confusion—climaxed by Kennedy's statement of September 25 before the United Nations that "nuclear war would make a flaming funeral pyre" of the world. Theological debates resulted: Should you shoot your neighbor if he tried to get into your shelter? And it was not clear what kind of shelters Kennedy wanted; or who would pay for them.

At the height of the 1961 Berlin crisis, "Red" Fay received a telephone call from Kennedy. "Have you built your bomb shelter?" the President asked. "No," replied Fay, "I built a swimming pool instead." "You made a mistake," the President said.

"And," Fay added, "he was dead serious."

Finally, on November 29, Kennedy said he favored community shelters, adding he "never" thought the Government should build a shelter in each home. For four tense months people thought he was saying otherwise.

When the policy was changed, James Reston observed: "The home shelter system favored the rich over the poor, the single-house dweller over the apartment dweller, the home owner over the renter. It was unequal, unfair, divisive, and therefore politically dangerous. Moreover, once the President and his aides in the White House belatedly put their minds to the problem of civil defense they began to see other objections to urgent appeals for an immediate home shelter program.

"It helped create a war psychology in the country. It encouraged all kinds of commercial exploitation by shelter builders who were going around door to door showing movies of atomic explosions and scaring people into buying shelters and stocking food they often couldn't afford.

"Also," Reston concluded, "the shelter scare in America weakened the confidence abroad in Kennedy's judgment."

Following the Los Angeles convention, Edward R. Murrow had remarked gloomily that Candidate Kennedy appeared to have no sense of awe or inadequacy. Toward the end of his first year in office serious concern was expressed as to whether President Kennedy had not been rendered "immobile" —to use Marquis Childs' characterization—in the face of repeated setbacks.

Of course, the Presidency is an impossible job. No one man could possibly keep on top of everything the job entails. Wilfred E. Binkley, an outstanding authority on the American Presidency, has suggested that "the fantastic expansion of Federal functions (under Roosevelt) initiated a trend toward disintegration of the executive function. . . . Thus an observer of Franklin Roosevelt was to remark, 'It is a mystery to me how each morning he selects the few things he *can* do from the thousands he *should* do.' "[11]

There were times when Kennedy, alone in the quiet of the night, might have wondered whether Richard Nixon was not the more fortunate in having lost the Presidency. Occasionally, Kennedy has wondered aloud as to why he had fought so hard to win the literally back-breaking job.

"Sure," he once said, commenting on the unexpected resignation of Brazil's President Janio Quadros, "there are times when I'd like to go off to the South of France and take in the sun, but no man can just quit his responsibilities and walk away."

And while talking with Mike DiSalle in mid-1961, Kennedy asked the Ohio Governor if he intended to run again. DiSalle said he wasn't sure. "There are days," he said, "when I think it's great, and other days when I'd like to chuck it."

And DiSalle quoted the President as replying: "I have days like that, too."

And in concluding his Berlin report to the nation, Kennedy said he had found the burdens of the Presidency even greater than he thought when he ran

[11] From Professor Binkley's *The Man in the White House* (Baltimore: Johns Hopkins Press, 1959). In December 1961, President Kennedy announced that Professor Binkley had been replaced as a member of the American Historical Association by Arthur Schlesinger Sr. This wasn't nepotism. It was *pa-ola*.

for office. He asked for suggestions and for the public to help him. The President's plea was enormously appealing and his sincerity unquestionable.

But what was surprising about his new-found humility was that Kennedy appeared to be truly surprised, on entering the White House, to find things as bad as he had claimed them to be during the campaign. In fact, in his first State of the Union Message, January 29, 1961, the new President had stated:

"No man entering upon this office . . . could fail to be staggered upon learning—even in this brief ten-day period—the harsh enormities of the trial through which we must pass in the next four years. . . . I speak today in an hour of national peril. . . . The outcome is by no means certain. The answers are by no means clear. . . . Each day the crises multiply. Each day their solution grows more difficult. Each day we draw nearer the hour of maximum danger. . . . The tide *is* unfavorable. The news will be worse before it is better. . . ."

The new President drew as dark a picture of the United States economy as he could find statistics for. "The American economy is in trouble. . . . Our national household is cluttered with unfinished and neglected tasks. . . . Life in 1961 will not be easy."

It was a foreboding speech. He pictured an America slipping out of its days of greatness and its people wondering whether "a nation governed and organized such as ours can endure. The outcome is by no means certain. . . ."

By his own admission, the enormity of these problems had only loomed so great to Kennedy in his first ten days in office. Why they should have "staggered" the new President is difficult to fathom. There was nothing in his message which he hadn't said during the campaign.

"There were moments," observed the *Wall Street Journal,* "when we thought President Kennedy was trying to scare the nation out of its wits."

But Joseph Alsop was thrilled. "The language of the long message," he enthused, "was concise, masculine, and elevated."

Before the year was out, Kennedy was complaining even more bitterly about the "can of worms" which, he claimed, the Eisenhower Administration had left him. Resenting his inheritance, he referred to left-over problems as "not of our making." One morning, shortly after Cuba, McGeorge Bundy opened a staff meeting with the announcement that four urgent matters were to be discussed.

"Are these problems which I inherited?" Kennedy asked. "Or are they problems of our own making?"

"A little of both," Bundy replied tactfully.

The President's personal tragedy is that although he inherited the critical situations in the Caribbean, the Congo, and Southeast Asia, he worsened them. Surrounded by a brain trust of Ivy League intellectuals, not one of whom has demonstrated any real capacity thus far to deal with the relentless nature of world Communism, President Kennedy has exposed a dangerous gullibility to the enemy. Far too solicitous of "world opinion," he has put all his African eggs in the U.N. basket; a U.N. negatively controlled by Soviet demands; and he has snubbed European members of NATO in pursuit of a reverse racism in Africa. "Africa for the Africans," Kennedy's "second-to-none" Assistant Secretary of State for African Affairs, "Soapy" Williams, had demanded. And Williams later confessed he did not know what the slogan meant.

"In the meantime," Irving Kristol wrote in *Encounter* of January, 1962, "American sentiment, unmoblized and undirected, shows signs of turning actively sour. Left without guidance from its natural preceptor, the President, confused and frustrated by the inimical trend of world affairs, bewildered by the high-falutin' legalisms that befog all statements of American foreign policy, exasperated by the immense publicity given to such an obviously minuscule project as the Peace Corps, bored with the United Nations and its petty politicking—this public opinion is veering dangerously towards an odd kind of belligerent isolationism. The emergence of such organizations as the John Birch Society and the Minutemen is a symptom of this political disorder.

"If the country's natural leader is not going to define the national purpose and direct the national energies, then there are plenty of unnatural and monstrous candidates for this mission. So far, they are still circulating around the crackpot fringe, more a nuisance than a danger. But unless something is done to transform the popular mood, they may yet have an influence utterly disproportionate to their present numerical strength."

The truth is that all Presidents inherit problems. Dwight Eisenhower inherited a bogged-down war in Korea. Harry Truman inherited the Cold War. And Franklin D. Roosevelt inherited the Great Depression. No President has ever taken office with a blank pad waiting to be filled with the fresh-ink policies. The reach of current events is such that the actions of any President become a continuing part of national policy. That policy may be altered. It can rarely be reversed.

The fatal flaw in Kennedy's assumptions as a Presidential candidate was the belief that the United States, alone and by itself, can influence every global development, can change all river courses, can start and stop revolutions.

"The notion that John Kennedy has become dictator of the world's destiny is fallacious," David Lawrence observed on January 16, 1961. "His hands are tied—just as were those of President Eisenhower. All the hysterical rantings of the critics about lowered 'prestige' and lack of 'leadership' by President Eisenhower ignore a simple fact—that the head of the American government is not the boss and that he has only one choice, between war or peace."

Before the Presidential year was over, Kennedy was saying: "There's no reason why we should do everything."

The fact is that no matter what its political complexion, any United States Administration in recent times has been sharply limited, particularly in the conduct of foreign affairs. It is limited by Soviet intransigence; by the complexities of dealing with numerous allies; by the unprecedented confusions of a world in which new nations are being created all over the map. And it is limited by the very limitations of United States political, economic and military power, which cannot be deployed everywhere at once.

Despite continuing setbacks all over the world, the Administration kept seeking to convince the American people that thanks to President Kennedy's policies the United States was winning the cold war.

This gambit, known in New Frontier parlance as Operation Counterattack, was devised in the wake of the Bay of Pigs fiasco to accent our Cold War successes and gloss over our defeats.

When, for example, there was a lull in the Berlin crisis, the word was bruited about that the situation had improved.

And when the Wall went up in Berlin, Undersecretary of State Chester Bowles actually crowed that it represented "an extraordinary fantastic defeat" for the Communists. Some Berliners thought that a few more such Communist "defeats" and we had all better study Russian.

Arthur Schlesinger, Jr., White House apologist-historian-in-residence, once went so far as to suggest we owe a debt of gratitude to Castro because the bearded dictator had alerted us to the dangers of Communism in our hemisphere. Thus the Cuban disaster was converted into a big break for our side.

Another foreign-policy success, according to Administration spokesmen, was Katanga. Here the crushing of a pro-West regime by U.S.–backed U.N. forces was somehow translated into a defeat for Communism.

Then there was the supposed significance of the ideological split in the Communist world and the nasty exchanges between Peking and Moscow. Kremlinologists do not agree on the importance of the split; but it was cited as an example of how our Cold War position had been improved since You-Know-Who entered the White House.

The truth is that what Peking and Moscow were arguing about was how best to bury capitalism.

In March 1963, Walt Whitman Rostow, the State Department's chief policy planner, opined there was "quite a lot of reason for satisfaction" in international accomplishments during the Kennedy Administration. He told correspondents that United States policy had checked the momentum of a powerful Communist offensive. "In addition to sealing off the crises," he added, "the positive aspects of U.S. policy in Latin America, in Africa, in the Middle East, in Asia have all gained strength."

Such is Operation Counterattack. Everything comes up roses.

Back in February 1960 a noted political figure told the California Democratic Council Convention in Fresno:

"The President's responsibility is to all the people. If he rejects Operation Candor as politically dangerous—if he constantly reassures an imperiled nation that all is well—if he answers all critics with an air of infallibility—or, worst of all, if he himself is not informed and therefore cannot inform the people—then the Presidency has failed the American people."

That noted political figure was none other than John F. Kennedy.

Many have been President Kennedy's feelings of irritation and frustration since January 1961. Very little has seemed to work out as he had hoped. The "best brains," which he had assembled, weren't coming up with the right answers. The Democratic-controlled Congress, for a time in 1962, appeared to have gone haywire, what with Conservative Democrats voting against him and Liberal Democrats filibustering against him. No wonder the Republicans were laughing out loud.

The extraordinary phenomenon was that the President's personal popularity seemed to remain high. "Yet," as Carroll Kilpatrick observed in the *Washington Post* on March 18, 1963, "in this Capital the complaints about his effectiveness as a leader are louder than at any other time."

At JFK's March 6, 1963, press conference, the *New York Times'* Tom Wicker put it this way to the President:

"Your policies in Europe seem to be encountering great difficulties. Cuba continues to be a problem. At home unemployment is high. There seems to be more concern in the country over a budget deficit than for a tax cut. In view of all these things, there is some impression and talk in the town and country that your Administration seems to have lost its momentum and to be slowing down and to be moving on the defensive."

Kennedy gave a sort of philosophical reply that wound up with a quip that made use of the line from Shakespeare's *Richard III* (Act I, Scene I)— "Now is the winter of our discontent."

"There is a rhythm to a personal and national and international life and it flows and ebbs," said JFK. He conceded "a good many difficulties at home and abroad," but he insisted they were in the process of being solved.

"So that if you ask me whether this was 'the winter of our discontent,' I would say no. If you would ask me whether we were doing quite as well this winter as we were doing in the fall, I would say no."

Kennedy's statement satisfied few commentators. Bill Shannon, who had cited the Shakespearean passage two days before the President, wrote: "The Presidential press conference, once a tiger burning bright in the forests of the Washington night, has become a toothless old animal."

James Reston chimed in as follows: "In other words, [JFK] is insisting that he has done all right, and if some things have not gone well, why, that's the way life is, and nothing much can be done about it.

"As a public relations stance, this attitude has its advantages. It gives the impression of being cool under attack, and confident that somehow today's problems will yield to patience and persistence, but will they? This is the question that disturbs his own closest advisers."

And the irrepressible Doris Fleeson put it this way: "President Kennedy has come out for the rhythm method of controlling reactions to the New Frontier."

Some Administration stalwarts conceded things had not gone well for their leader. "Okay," *Time* reported their argument, "maybe Kennedy has had to compromise on a few issues that he considered basic. But that is because he is a first-term President who must, to see his ideals come to bloom, be reelected. Kennedy's second term . . . will be his last. And so, unhampered by political considerations, he will be able to go all out for the policies and programs in which he believes.

"In other words, wait until the year after next."

The interesting thing about this argument is that some Liberal historians claim that Eisenhower's more productive Presidential years were during his first term; that because he was a lame-duck President he couldn't accomplish much in his second term.

In one area of endeavor, John F. Kennedy has outshone any of his predecessors. Persons barely literate say the Kennedys have created a cultural rebirth in Washington. There have been state dinners for such notables as Pablo Casals and Igor Stravinsky. These supposedly have led us to a great cultural renaissance. The eggheads have come of age, and all that jazz.

There have been a few dissenters.

Thomas Hart Benton, for example, suggested it was the artists rather than their art that the White House has placed on exhibition.

The artist said he "approved" in principle the interest the Kennedys had demonstrated in the cultural field. "But," he added, "they're making a dilettante show out of it."

Asked whether Robert Frost's role in the President's inauguration had not been good for American culture, Benton—reported the *New York Times*—agreed that it had, but precisely because the bard's poetry reading had been an integral part of the ceremony.

Very touching, indeed, were the well-publicized bonds of affection and admiration that bound the youthful President and the nation's uncrowned poet laureate, Robert Frost. On January 20, 1960, JFK had shared his greatest triumph with the then eighty-six-year-old Frost, who hailed the New Frontier as "an Augustan age of poetry and power, with the emphasis on power."

"Yet within two years, the poet and the President were estranged," wrote Walter Trohan. "The President, who had used the poet to launch his Administration against a background of culture, ignored the poet during his fatal illness, which lasted almost two months."

Not once had JFK written to Frost, who had entered a Boston hospital for an operation on December 3, 1962. No letter of condolence was received by the poet's family, at least as of February 3, 1963, when memorial services were held for Frost. No member of the vast Kennedy family attended the rites.

True, the White House had issued the usual Presidential statement on Frost's death, but such statements are the work of an alert and responsive staff rather than of the Chief Executive.

"The poet who had starred at the Inaugural was snubbed in death and the story can now be told," wrote Trohan.

The story, according to Trohan, was that JFK was displeased with a quotation attributed to Frost after the poet had visited the Soviet Union. Frost said that during an hour-long visit with Nikita Khrushchev, the Communist ruler "said he feared for us because of our lot of liberals. He thought that we're too liberal to fight. He thinks we will sit on one hand and then on the other."

Subsequently, the American Embassy in Moscow denied that Khrushchev had made the remark. And Kennedy felt that what had happened was that Frost had made the remark and Khrushchev had agreed with it.

"Frost made it known he carried a message from Khrushchev to the President but he was never invited to the White House to deliver it," Trohan reported. Frost did go to the White House on the eve of his 88th birthday in March 1962 to receive from the President a medal voted him by the Congress.

"Mr. Kennedy described Frost as 'our very good friend,' but there was a chill in the air, not as cold as the wind that riffled Frost's white air on Inaugural Day, but it was there. The weather on Inaugural Day was more of a test than an 86-year-old man might have been expected to meet but he took it in stride and recited a poem dedicated to the new President in a voice which was resonant.

"Frost's family was described by one who attended the Amherst memorial services as 'livid' over Presidential neglect during his illness and in death. Yet, Mr. Kennedy was not setting a precedent in neglect.

"Those who hang on the favors of a prince cling to a precarious perch. The prince is ever ready to brush them off for his own advantage or even to satisfy whim or caprice."

Malcolm Muggeridge, the anti-royalist observer for London's *New Statesman* has reported from Washington:

"The personality cult is going strong, and likely to go stronger yet. It is very like popular monarchy. There is the same mixture as with our royal family of contemptuous ridicule and imbecile adulation.

"All America, one reads, longs to hear that Jackie is pregnant again. The children's birthdays and outings are frontpage news. People surge round the President wanting to touch him in the manner described by the Duke of Windsor in his memoirs. At the same time, a long-playing record taking off the whole Kennedy clan is an immediate best-seller, and a decidedly malicious Caroline's Colour Book is in brisk demand.

"This, I suppose, is the kind of leadership required in our time. People want to admire what they despise and despise what they admire. When the

Kennedy administration becomes hereditary, the title of the heir, equivalent to our Prince of Wales, will presumably be the Senator for Massachusetts.

"The young Teddy Kennedy, who went through the formality of getting elected as such at the recent Congressional elections, had no evident qualifications apart from being a Kennedy and rich and having a pretty wife. From this a hereditary title would be an easy transition."

"The world public figure who seems to me most like John F. Kennedy is the Duke of Edinburgh," observed Murray Kempton. "Each is energetic in ceremony, informal in conduct, and each is a symbol of royalty beloved for being outside the struggle."

One informal day was the day in August 1962 when President Kennedy went for a democratic swim on a public beach at Santa Monica. To the dismay of the Secret Service, Kennedy was mobbed by several hundred fans as he made a personal appearance on the sands adjacent to the home of brother-in-law Peter Lawford. On this historic occasion, several ladies dived into the ocean, fully clothed, to be near his presence. The next morning the nation's newspapers published a photograph of the Presidential navel.

"I think we should all snip out the picture and paste it on the wall," commented *San Francisco Chronicle* columnist Art Hoppe. "Then when people imply reverently that we should all have blind faith in The President, we could all look at it. For there is nothing that renews one's belief in political equality and the fallibility of any leadership than contemplating The Presidential navel. After all, I've got one myself."

Peter Lawford, as the President's brother-in-law, has become privy to many non-state secrets. A future Carl Sandburg (who chronicled the life and times of a previous President) may well be indebted to Lawford for the actor's firsthand glimpses into John F. Kennedy as provided in a *McCall's* article entitled "The White House Is Wondering What to Do with Me."

According to Lawford, the President sees *Variety* every week, "which helps keep him up on show business and my business. Not long ago he wanted to know if I planned to concentrate on drama or comedy. Then he came up with one of those bits of obscure knowledge that never fails to astound me. He said: 'I hear "Oceans Eleven" is going well in Manchester, England.' "

Well, that's show biz.

Gore Vidal has described President Eisenhower as *The Great Golfer*. His successor, however, may go down in history as *The Great Party Giver*.

A quaint description of one Kennedy-hosted affair has been left for posterity by Mrs. Jacob K. Javits, wife of the senior Senator from New York:

"The Kennedys held a party at the White House last night for 1,200 people. It was the kind of party the President seems to like best, with Senators, Congressmen and Cabinet officers on the guest list. The President's party chatter was about his favorite subject—politics. . . . The First Lady was stunning in a white satin sleeveless dress embossed with brightly-colored flowers into which tiny pearls were sewn. She wore long diamond and emerald earrings and a diamond hairclip. . . .

"Adam Clayton Powell's attire was unique. He wore a green Austrian evening jacket with a black velvet collar and four buttons, Franz Josef coins. . . . This was by all odds the most chic of the many receptions I have attended at the White House. . . . On elegant White House china, the guests could pile truffle-glazed ham, cold roast beef, smoked salmon, *pâté*, raw vegetables and lots of *petits fours*.

"Before departing, the President graciously asked my husband to bring me to Washington more often. With all respects to New York, he jocularly observed that Washington was a much jazzier town these days."

And down by the Potomac, rustling through the trees, you could hear the Shakespearean laughter of James Michael Curley, who could see the humor in almost anything.

Appendix A

China—Statement of Hon. John F. Kennedy, of Massachusetts

EXTENSION OF REMARKS

OF

HON. GEORGE J. BATES

OF MASSACHUSETTS

IN THE HOUSE OF REPRESENTATIVES

Monday, February 21, 1949*

Mr. BATES of Massachusetts. Mr. Speaker, under leave to extend my remarks in the RECORD, I wish to include the timely and interesting address delivered in Salem, Mass., on January 30, by my colleague, Hon. JOHN F. KENNEDY, of Boston, on the tragic story of China:

Over these past few days we have learned the extent of the disasters befalling China and the United States. Our relationship with China since the end of the Second World War has been a tragic one, and it is of the utmost importance that we search out and spotlight those who must bear the responsibility for our present predicament.

When we look at the ease with which the Communists have overthrown the National Government of Chiang Kai-shek, it comes as somewhat of a shock to remember that on November 22, 1941, our Secretary of State, Cordell Hull, handed Ambassador Namuru an ultimatum to the effect that: (1) Government of Japan will withdraw all military, naval, air, and police forces from China and Indochina; (2) the United States and Japan will not support militarily, politically, economically, any government or regime in China other than the National Government of the Republic of China.

It was clearly enunciated that the independence of China and the stability of the National Government was the fundamental object of our far eastern policy.

* Congressional Record.

That this and other statements of our policies in the Far East led directly to the attack on Pearl Harbor is well known. And it might be said that we almost knowingly entered into combat with Japan to preserve the independence of China and the countries to the south of it. Contrast this policy which reached its height in 1943 when the United States and Britain agreed at Cairo to liberate China and return to that country at the end of the war Manchuria and all Japanese-held areas, to the confused and vacillating policy which we have followed since that day.

In 1944 Gen. "Vinegar Joe" Stilwell presented a plan to arm 1,000,000 Chinese Communists, who had been carefully building their resources in preparation for a post-war seizure of power, and with them to capture Shanghai and clear the Yangtze. This plan was supported by some State Department officials, including Ambassador Clarence Gauss. Chiang Kai-shek refused to cooperate with this plan, which would have presented the Chinese Communists with an easy coup. Chiang requested that Stilwell be recalled, which caused such bitter comment in this country; and Gauss resigned. From this date on our relations with the National Government declined.

At the Yalta Conference in 1945 a sick Roosevelt, with the advice of General Marshall and other Chiefs of Staff, gave the Kurile Islands as well as the control of various strategic Chinese ports, such as Port Arthur and Darien, to the Soviet Union.

According to former Ambassador Bullitt, in Life magazine in 1948, "Whatever share of the responsibility was Roosevelt's and whatever share was Marshall's the vital interest of the United States in the independent integrity of China was sacrificed, and the foundation was laid for the present tragic situation in the Far East."

When the armies of Soviet Russia withdrew from Manchuria they left Chinese Communists in control of this area and in possession of great masses of Japanese war material.

During this period began the great split in the minds of our diplomats over whether to support the government of Chiang Kai-shek, or force Chiang Kai-shek as the price of our assistance to bring Chinese Communists into his government to form a coalition.

When Ambassador Patrick Hurley resigned in 1945 he stated, "Professional diplomats continuously advised the Chinese Communists that my efforts in preventing the collapse of the national government did not represent the policy of the United States. The chief opposition to the accomplishment of our mission came from American career diplomats, the embassy at Chungking, and the Chinese Far Eastern divisions of the State Department."

With the troubled situation in China beginning to loom large in the United States, General Marshall was sent at the request of President Truman as special emissary to China to effect a compromise and to bring about a coalition government.

In Ambassador Bullitt's article in Life, he states, and I quote: "In early summer of 1946 in order to force Chiang Kai-shek to take Communists into the Chinese Government, General Marshall had the Department of State refuse to give licenses for export of ammunition to China. Thus from the summer of 1946 to February 1948 not a single shell or a single cartridge was delivered to China for use in its American armament. And in the aviation field Marshall likewise blundered, and as a result of his breaking the American Government's contract to deliver to China planes to maintain eight and one-third air groups, for 3 years no combat or bombing planes were delivered to China—from September 1946 to March 1948. As Marshall himself confessed in February 1948 to the House Committee on Foreign Affairs, this "was in effect an embargo on military supplies."

In 1948 we appropriated $468,000,000 for China, only a fraction of what we were sending to Europe, and out of this $468,000,000 only $125,-000,000 was for military purposes. The end was drawing near; the assistance was too little and too late; and the nationalist government was engaged in a death struggle with the on-rushing Communist armies.

On November 20, 1948, former Senator D. Worth Clark, who had been sent on a special mission to China by the Senate Committee on Appropriations, in his report to that committee said, "Piecemeal aid will no longer save failing China from communism. It is now an all-out program or none, a fish or cut bait proposition."

Clark said this conclusion was confirmed by Ambassador J. Leighton Stuart and top American Army officers in China.

On November 25, 1948, 3 years too late, the New York Times said: "Secretary of State George Marshall said today the United States Government was considering what assistance it could properly give to the Chinese Government in the present critical situation."

On December 21 a Times headline was: "ECA Administrator Hoffman, after seeing Truman, discloses freezing of $70,000,000 program in China in view of uncertain war situation."

The indifference, if not the contempt, with which the State Department and the President treated the wife of the head of the nationalist government, who was then fighting for a free China—Madame Chiang Kai-shek—was the final chapter in this tragic story.

Our policy in China has reaped the whirlwind. The continued insistence that aid would not be forthcoming unless a coalition government with the Communists was formed, was a crippling blow to the national government. So concerned were our diplomats and their advisers, the Lattimores and the Fairbanks, with the imperfections of the diplomatic system in China after 20 years of war, and the tales of corruption in high places, that they lost sight of our tremendous stake in a non-Communist China.

There were those who claimed, and still claim, that Chinese communism was not really communism at all but merely an advanced agrarian movement which did not take directions from Moscow.

Listen to the words of the Bolton report: "Its doctrines follow those of Lenin and Stalin. Its leaders are Moscow-trained (of 35 leading Chinese Communist political leaders listed in the report, over a half either spent some time or studied in Moscow). Its policies and actions, its strategy and tactics are Communist. The Chinese Communists have followed faithfully every zigzag of the Kremlin's line for a generation."

This is the tragic story of China whose freedom we once fought to preserve. What our young men had saved, our diplomats and our President have frittered away.

Appendix B

The "Bailey Report"

1. THE SIGNIFICANCE AND LOCATION OF THE CATHOLIC VOTE

The voter surveys of Lasarsfeld ("The People's Choice"), Lubell ("The Future of American Politics"), Bean ("How to Predict Elections") and others —as well as the statistics contained within on the 1928 election and the 1952 vote for Catholic candidates—all indicate that there is, or can be, such a thing as a "Catholic vote," whereby a high proportion of Catholics of all ages, residences, occupations and economic status vote for a well-known Catholic candidate or a ticket with special Catholic appeal.

As Lubell has pointed out: "Catholic voting strength is currently at its peak, in view of the maturing of the offspring of the Italians, Poles, Czechs, and other former immigrant elements."

But the Catholic vote is far more important than its numbers—about 1 out of every 4 voters who turn out—because of its concentration in the key States and cities of the North. These are the pivotal States with large electoral votes, which vary as to their party support and several of which are inevitably necessary for a victory in the Electoral College. And the strength of the Catholic vote within these States is considerably increased by the findings of Gallup, Campbell of the University of Michigan ("The Voter Decides") and others that Catholics consistently turn out to vote in greater proportion than non-Catholics.

The proportion of Catholics in the adult population and 1952 two-party vote in these key States, with a total electoral vote of 261 (266 is a majority) is shown in Table 1, compared with the margin by which Eisenhower carried these States.

These are the key Democratic States where elections are won or lost. Of these 14 pivotal Catholic States with their 261 electoral votes:

—In 1940, 13 of these States with 240 electoral votes went Democratic, *without which the Democrats would have lost the election.*

—In 1944, 12 of these States with 221 electoral votes went Democratic, *without which the Democrats would have lost the election.*

—In 1948, 8 of these States with 125 electoral votes went Democratic, *without which the Democrats would have lost the election.*

—In 1952, none of these States went Democratic, all 261 of their electoral votes went to Eisenhower, thus making possible the first Republican victory in 24 years.

Equally important are the major urban areas in these States and the concentration of Catholic voters in those areas. As shown by Table 2, *the Catholic voters in each of these cities can usually determine the size of the Democratic margin in those cities; the size of the Democratic margin in those cities usually determines whether these States go Democratic; and whether these States go Democratic usually determines whether the Democrats win the election.* For example, taking the past four elections:

—In 1940, without net margins in New York, Chicago, Hudson County (Jersey City), Philadelphia-Pittsburgh, Providence and Milwaukee, the Democrats would have lost New York (47), Illinois (29), New Jersey (16), Pennsylvania (36), Rhode Island (4), and Wisconsin (12), or a total loss of 144 electoral votes.

—In 1944, without their net margins in New York, Hartford and New Haven, Chicago, Baltimore, Detroit, Hudson County (Jersey City), Minneapolis–St. Paul and Philadelphia, Democrats would have lost New York (47), Connecticut (18), Illinois (28), Maryland (8), Michigan (19), New Jersey (16), Minnesota (11), and Pennsylvania (35), or a total loss of 172 electoral votes—*and the Republicans would have won the election.*

—In 1948, without their net margins in Chicago, Los Angeles, Cleveland and Providence, the Democrats would have lost Illinois (28 electoral votes), California (25), Ohio (25), and Rhode Island (4), or a total loss of 82 electoral votes—*and the Republicans would have won the election.*

—In 1952, as shown on Table 2, the Democratic vote in all of the major cities except Philadelphia fell sharply, and these cities for the first time in 24 years did not contribute a single electoral vote to the Democrats, thus making possible the first Republican victory in 24 years.

2. ARE THE DEMOCRATS LOSING THE CATHOLICS?

Every analyst agrees they are, in terms of the national ticket. The Catholic Democratic vote was noticeably off in 1948—and showed a critical decline in 1952. Gallup, Roper, the University of Michigan Survey and others all reported this trend. Gallup said only 34 per cent of all Catholics considered themselves Republicans in 1950, but at least 44 per cent voted for Eisenhower in 1952. Harris of the Roper organization ("Is There a Republican Majority") said that Roper polls showed the following shifts to have been decisive in Eisenhower's election:

—Catholics in general, normally over 65 per cent Democratic, went 47 per cent for Ike.

—German Catholics, previously 82 per cent Democratic, went 55 per cent for Ike.

—Poles, normally over 70 per cent Democratic, went 50 per cent for Ike.

—Irish, normally 65 per cent Democratic, went 53 per cent for Ike.

The Democratic era and political base begun by Al Smith, said Harris, ended in 1952. The "immigrant base," which had begun cracking in 1940, split wide open, probably permanently, he said. He predicted that the important Irish and German votes in particular would become largely an independent group, sharply affecting Democratic majorities in the Northern cities.

The University of Michigan nation-wide survey showed that, of those voting for one of the two major candidates, over 66 per cent of the Catholics voted Democratic in 1948 but fewer than 51 per cent did in 1952. (There is a striking similarity between these figures and those of Gallup and Roper.)

Thus Catholics in 1952, roughly 25 per cent of the voting population, went approximately 1 out of 2 for the Republican candidate, whereas in 1948 they had gone 2 out of 3 for the Democratic nominee; and, though they had constituted approximately one-third of the Democratic vote in 1948, they were only 28 per cent of Stevenson's vote and constituted 21 per cent of Eisenhower's tremendous vote. Approximately 30 per cent of these Catholics for Eisenhower were "shifters"—that is, even on the basis of 1948 when the Catholic vote was already slipping away from the Democrats (the Republicans carried New York, New Jersey, Pennsylvania, Connecticut, Michigan and Maryland), they would have been expected to vote Democratic in 1952.

These shifters—whom we shall call "normally Democratic Catholics"— constituted approximately 7 per cent of Eisenhower's total nation-wide vote. If Stevenson could have held in 1952 *only* those Catholics who had voted for Truman in 1948 but for Ike in 1952—or if he could recapture them in 1956 —this would, as shown in Table 3, *add 132 electoral votes to the Democratic column, enough when combined with the Solid South to provide a majority of electoral votes!*

3. CATHOLIC CANDIDATES.

What may be the clue as to the means of recapturing those votes—as well as further evidence of the national ticket's loss of Catholic votes in 1952— is provided by Table 4, showing how Democratic Catholic candidates for Congressman, Senator and Governor ran consistently ahead of their national ticket, in a striking example of ticket splitting on the part of Catholic voters.

Outside the South, according to Gallup and Roper, the Democratic presidential vote and the Democratic congressional vote ran approximately even, the same over-all percentage behind the Republican presidential and congressional candidates. Specifically, voters on the average cast Democratic ballots for President at a rate only *1/10th of 1 per cent* (Gallup) or 1.6 per cent (Roper) behind their votes for Democratic congressional candidates. But Table 4 shows how selected Catholic Democratic candidates ran much further ahead of the national ticket in their areas.

Table 1

	Proportion of Catholics in Adult Population	Estimated Proportion of 1952 Two-Party Vote Made Up of Catholic Voters	Eisenhower's Margin Over 50% of the 1952 Two-Party Vote	Electoral Vote
NEW YORK	32%	40%	6.0%	45
PENNSYLVANIA	29	39	3.0	32
ILLINOIS	30	34	5.0	27
NEW JERSEY	39	47	7.5	16
MASSACHUSETTS	50	57	4.4	16
CONNECTICUT	49	55	5.9	8
RHODE ISLAND	60	65	0.9	4
CALIFORNIA	22	27	6.9	32
MICHIGAN	24	30	5.8	20
MINNESOTA	24	27	5.6	11
OHIO	20	25	6.8	25
WISCONSIN	32	38	11.2	12
MARYLAND	21	31	5.8	9
MONTANA	22	26	9.7	4

261
(NEEDED TO WIN: 266)

NOTES:

Column 1—Selected States: Not included are seven other States where the Catholics are an important part of the adult population: New Hampshire (37%), Louisiana (34%), New Mexico (46%), Arizona (30%), North Dakota (22%), Maine (26%), and Vermont (29%). If these seven States were included, the total number of electoral votes would be 295. They are excluded from this analysis, however, either because they are not considered to be among the key swing States or because it would be speculative to translate the proportion of Catholics in their adult population into important voting strength for a Democratic Catholic candidate.

Column 2—Proportion of Catholics in Population: These figures are taken from "The Official Catholic Directory" (1955, P. J. Kenedy & Sons). They pertain to actual members of the church—and surveys have indicated that the actual number of those classified as Catholics would be approximately 10% higher in each State. Survey analysts have found that the proportion of Catholics in the total population approximates the proportion of Catholics in the adult eligible-voter population.

Column 3—Proportion of Catholics in 1952 Two-Party Vote: This column is calculated by applying Campbell's national-average figures for the turnout of Catholics and non-Catholics to the official turnout figures for 1952 for each of the 14 States.

Column 4—Eisenhower's Margin over 50% in 1952: This figure represents the number of votes which must be shifted to the Democratic column for a Democratic victory in 1956.

Some of the examples shown are particularly instructive. Had Stevenson run as well as Pastore (and Roberts), Lausche, Kennedy and Mansfield, he would, of course, have won an additional 49 electoral votes. His lags behind O'Brien in Albany and Delaney in New York City were greater than his lag behind Eisenhower for the State of New York as a whole; and the same is true of his lags behind Rodino in Newark, Zablocki in Milwaukee, Eugene Mc-Carthy in St. Paul, and Price in East St. Louis.

Especially revealing of the picture of Catholic voters leaving the Democratic Party, except where a Catholic is on the ticket, are the following normally Democratic districts where Catholic voters are a major element:

— Zablocki won in Milwaukee by 29 per cent while Stevenson was losing by 4 per cent.

— O'Brien won in Albany by 7 per cent while Stevenson was losing by 9 per cent.

— Delaney won in New York City by 2 per cent while Stevenson was losing by 13 per cent.

— Addonizio and Rodino won in Newark by 4 per cent and 14 per cent respectively while Stevenson was losing by 4 per cent and 7 per cent.

— Rabaut won in Detroit by 6 per cent while Stevenson was losing by 2 per cent.

— Dodd won in Hartford by 8 per cent while Stevenson was losing by 1 per cent.

4. HOW MUCH WOULD A CATHOLIC VICE-PRESIDENTIAL NOMINEE HURT THE TICKET?

On June 24, 1956, the Gallup Poll feature was headlined "Qualified Catholic Could Be President." Nearly 3 out of 4 respondents said they would vote for a well-qualified Catholic nominated by their party *for the Presidency itself*. Of those who thought they would be opposed, a large share lived in the South—and if one of three Democrats stayed home (or even voted Republican) in the South due to a nominee's religious affiliation, few if any Southern electoral votes would be lost, even though Democratic margins in several States might be diminished.

A large share of the remainder appeared to be Republicans who would not support the Democratic ticket under any circumstances, and Northern "liberal intellectuals" who will certainly vote Democratic without regard to the Vice President's religion. In short, even a Catholic nominee for President would be judged by most people on his qualifications for the office—and it is apparent that a Democratic Catholic vice-presidential nominee, though admittedly prejudice would be stirred, would lose no electoral votes for the ticket simply because a handful of Southerners or Republicans would not support him. Particularly in the key States and cities where he might be expected to concentrate his campaigning, his religion would be irrelevant to most.

5. HOW ABOUT AL SMITH?

This is the cry raised by professional pessimists opposed to a Catholic on the ticket. But, as Bean and others have shown, *the "Al Smith myth" is one of the falsest myths in politics.*

(a) 1928 was a Republican year, regardless of who was on either ticket. It was a year for "drys" like Hoover, not "wets" like Smith. Prof. William F. Ogburn, after a statistical study of 173 Northern counties, concluded that "prohibition sentiment was three times more decisive an influence in the election than the religious issue." Moreover, studies showed Midwestern and Southern voters opposing Al Smith as a Tammany product from the streets of New York, a portly, cigar-smoking stereotype of the immigrant-base political boss. If Al Smith had been the Republican nominee and a dry, he would have won the election regardless of his religion.

Table 2

	Estimated Proportion of 1952 Two-Party Vote Made Up of Catholic Voters	Decline in Democratic Proportion of Two-Party Vote 1948 to 1952
NEW YORK CITY	38%	3.6%
BUFFALO	62	8.6
ROCHESTER	38	9.8
ALBANY	38	Not Available
PHILADELPHIA	42	(gain) 8.0
PITTSBURGH	46	5.0
SCRANTON	49	Not Available
CHICAGO	49	4.2
NEWARK–JERSEY CITY	53	5.4
TRENTON	46	Not Available
BOSTON	55	11.8
HARTFORD	59	Not Available
BALTIMORE	31	3.1
SAN FRANCISCO	33	4.2
LOS ANGELES	22	5.2
DETROIT	39	1.4
MINNEAPOLIS–ST. PAUL	30	9.0
MILWAUKEE	41	9.4
CLEVELAND	36	4.6
CINCINNATI	25	5.5
TOLEDO	25	4.0

NOTE:

Column 2—Catholic Voters in Cities: These figures are derived by applying the appropriate State-turnout figures for these dioceses in "The Official Catholic Directory" (1955, P. J. Kenedy & Sons).

(b) Of the States his two predecessors as Democratic nominees had both carried, Smith lost *only 4* (Florida, North Carolina, Texas and Virginia, all of which the Democrats also lost in 1952 except for North Carolina), despite the usual assumption that Smith's Catholicism caused the Solid South and numerous other States to go Republican.

(c) The nation has changed since 1928. There are more Catholics— their political role, as seen above, is more crucial—their leadership in the Democratic Party and in Statewide offices from California to Maine is both frequent and accepted—and the nation is considerably more tolerant on religious matters. Gallup's 1956 poll found an increasing acceptance of a Catholic President in just the last 15 years. The support for Frank Lausche for President among prominent Southern Democrats is most indicative. An Ambassador to the Vatican is not likely to be a major campaign issue, regardless of the candidates; and the question of federal aid to parochial as well as public schools has been largely avoided by concentration on the problem of public-school construction instead of operation.

(d) Most important of all, and least known, is the fact that Al Smith helped the Democratic Party far more than he hurt it:

—Of the States his two predecessors as Democratic nominees had both carried, Smith lost *only 4* (Florida, North Carolina, Texas and Virginia, all of which the Democrats also lost in 1952 except for North Carolina), despite the usual assumption that Smith's Catholicism caused the Solid South and numerous other States to go Republican.

—Smith carried Massachusetts and Rhode Island which had never previously returned a Democratic majority in the twentieth century.

—Smith carried a majority of the counties in every section of the country but one (East North Central); and increased the number of counties in the Democratic column in the Northeastern, Middle Atlantic, West North Central, Mountain and Pacific States. 122 Northern counties (77 of them predominantly Catholic) were captured from the Republicans.

—Smith increased the Democratic vote by fantastic proportions in most States and particularly urban counties. For example:

DEMOCRATIC VOTE, IN THOUSANDS

	1924	*1928*
Massachusetts	281	792
Suffolk County	79	205
Connecticut	110	252
Rhode Island	76	118
New York	951	2,090
Bronx County	73	233

DEMOCRATIC VOTE, IN THOUSANDS

	1924	*1928*
Pennsylvania	409	1,060
Philadelphia	54	276
Ohio	478	864
Cuyahoga County	24	166
Hamilton County	35	110
New Jersey	298	616
Hudson County	91	153
Minnesota	56	396
Hennepin County	11	81
Michigan	152	397
Wayne County	23	157
Maryland	198	224
Illinois	577	1,300
Cook County	226	716

Thus Lubell has written: "The Republican hold on the cities was broken not by Roosevelt but by Al Smith." And Louis Harris concluded: "Al Smith marked the beginning of the Democratic era *which ended in 1952*. . . . [He] created a new political base in the large Northern metropolitan areas."

CONCLUSION

Has the Democratic era ended? Has the party permanently lost its political base among the Catholics and immigrants of the large Northern cities that made a Democratic victory possible in 1940, 1944 and 1948? The above indicates that a Catholic vice-presidential nominee could refashion this base as Al Smith did, and begin a new era of Democratic victories, without costing even the few electoral votes Smith did.

His campaign would be largely concentrated in the key States and cities listed above, including also on his itinerary such cities with high Catholic populations as St. Louis, Gary, Omaha, Denver, Dubuque and Reno. No further State-by-State analysis should be needed—but it should be re-emphasized as a major example that, by reducing Republican up-State majorities in New York by virtue of his vote in Rochester, Albany and Buffalo, and by increasing the declining Democratic vote in New York City, such a candidate could assure return of New York's 45 electoral votes to the Democratic column in 1956 for the first time in 12 years.

If he brought into the Democratic fold only those normally Democratic Catholics who voted for Ike, he would probably swing New York, Massachusetts, Rhode Island, Connecticut, Pennsylvania and Illinois—for 132 electoral votes. If he also wins the votes of Catholics who shifted to the Republicans in 1948 or earlier, he could also swing New Jersey, Minnesota, Michigan,

California, Wisconsin, Ohio, Maryland, Montana, and maybe even New Hampshire—for a total of 265 electoral votes (needed to win: 266). Thus Ike could and would be defeated.

Table 3

	Estimated Per Cent of Eisenhower Vote in 1952, Made Up of Catholic Voters	*Proportion of Eisenhower Vote Constituting Margin by Which He Carried State*	*Estimated Per Cent of Eisenhower Vote in 1952, Made Up of "Normally Democratic" Catholic Voters Who Shifted*	*Electoral Votes*
NEW YORK	35%	11%	11.0%	45
PENNSYLVANIA	36	6	11.0	32
ILLINOIS	31	9	9.3	27
MASSACHUSETTS	51	8	15.3	16
CONNECTICUT	48	11	14.4	8
RHODE ISLAND	63	15	18.9	4
NEW JERSEY	40	13		16
CALIFORNIA	23	12		32
MICHIGAN	27	10		20
MINNESOTA	23	10		11
OHIO	21	12		25
WISCONSIN	30	18		12
MARYLAND	27	10		9
MONTANA	21	16		4

261
(NEEDED TO WIN: 266)

NOTES:

Column 2—Proportion of Eisenhower Vote Consisting of Catholics: This column is calculated by applying to Table 1 the findings of the University of Michigan nationwide survey (Campbell, "The Voter Decides") that roughly 49% of voting Catholics voted for Eisenhower and roughly 51% for Stevenson.

Column 3—Eisenhower's Margin: The percentage listed is not to be confused with the percentage by which Eisenhower carried the State (which can be determined from Table 1, Column 4), but is the percentage of his own total vote represented by that margin, in order to make it comparable with figures portraying the percentage of his total vote made up of Catholics and previously Democratic Catholics.

Column 4—Catholics Shifting to Eisenhower: This column is calculated by applying to Table 3, Column 2, and Table 1, Columns 3 and 4, the findings of the Michigan survey that over 66% of the Catholic two-party voters in 1948 supported the Democratic ticket, as compared with fewer than 51% in 1952. Figures are provided only for those States where a shift of the State to the Democratic column by means of a return of these Catholic voters is indicated.

Table 4

	Candidate	Number of Percentage Points of Two-Party Vote by Which National Ticket Ran Behind Candidates Listed (*Norm: 0.1% to 1.6%*)
NEW YORK		
30th (Albany)	O'Brien	16.0%
7th (New York City)	Delaney	15.0
10th (Brooklyn)	Kelly	5.0
9th (Brooklyn)	Keogh	3.0
14th (Brooklyn)	Rooney	11.0
NEW JERSEY		
11th (Newark)	Addonizio	8.0
10th (Newark)	Rodino	21.0
14th (Jersey City)	Hart	4.0
MASSACHUSETTS		
	Kennedy	12.0
	Dever	8.4
RHODE ISLAND		
	Pastore	12.0
	Roberts	7.0
OHIO		
	Lausche	26.0
	DiSalle	5.0
19th (Youngstown)	Kirwan	21.0
20th (Cleveland)	Feighan	25.0
WYOMING		
	O'Mahoney	19.0
WISCONSIN		
4th (Milwaukee)	Zablocki	33.0
PENNSYLVANIA		
2nd (Philadelphia)	Granahan	2.0
3rd (Philadelphia)	Byrne	2.0
5th (Philadelphia)	Green	1.0
28th (Pittsburgh)	Eberharter	1.0
MINNESOTA		
4th (St. Paul)	E. McCarthy	12.0

Table 4 (*Cont.*)

MICHIGAN	Candidate	Number of Percentage Points of Two-Party Vote by Which National Ticket Ran Behind Candidates Listed (Norm: 0.1% to 1.6%)
1st (Detroit)	Machrowicz	6.0
13th (Detroit)	O'Brien	4.0
14th (Detroit)	Rabaut	8.0
15th (Detroit)	Dingell	7.0
16th (Detroit)	Lesinski	8.0
CONNECTICUT		
1st (Hartford)	Dodd	9.0
ILLINOIS		
2nd (Chicago)	O'Hara	1.0
5th (Chicago)	Kluczynski	6.0
6th (Chicago)	O'Brien	4.0
8th (Chicago)	Gordon	7.0
24th (East St. Louis)	Price	11.0
MONTANA		
	Mansfield	21.0

NOTE: Columns 1 and 2—Catholic Candidates, States and Districts: These columns list only those members of Congress or Governors elected in 1952 who are known to be Catholics and elected by areas with large Catholic populations. There are, of course, many others where these facts could not be as easily determined.

SPECIAL APPENDIX

Which would add the most strength to the Democratic ticket—an appeal to the Catholic vote, the Southern vote or the farm vote?

1. COMPARATIVE ELECTORAL STRENGTH

States with important Catholic votes which were lost by Stevenson in 1952 and might be recaptured in 1956 with a Catholic vice-presidential nominee (all analyzed in memorandum): New York, New Jersey, Massachusetts, Connecticut, Rhode Island, Pennsylvania, Maryland, Ohio, Illinois, Michigan, Wisconsin, Minnesota, Montana, California—*total electoral votes: 261.*

Southern and Border States which were lost by Stevenson in 1952 and might be recaptured in 1956 with a Southern vice-presidential nominee: Texas, Florida, Virginia, Missouri, Oklahoma, Tennessee (although this is almost certainly Democratic after Dixon-Yates) and Kentucky (which Stevenson carried)—*total electoral votes: 88.*

States with important farm votes, including those listed above, and stretched to include Western mining States, industrial States and livestock States which oppose high grain supports, which were lost by Stevenson in 1952 and might in 1956 be influenced to some degree, however slight, by a farm-belt vice-presidential nominee: Idaho, Iowa, Wyoming, Nevada, Wisconsin, Oregon, Colorado, Montana, Utah, Indiana, Ohio, Michigan, Minnesota, Illinois, Washington, Oklahoma, Texas and Missouri—*total electoral votes: 202.*

2. HOW IMPORTANT IS THE FARM VOTE IN THE FARM BELT ITSELF?

In the "farm revolt" of 1948, only three States of the Midwest can be said to have been swept into the Democratic column by virtue of votes cast by farmers—Iowa, Minnesota and Wisconsin—for a total of only 23 electoral votes. Truman lost Indiana, Kansas, Nebraska, North Dakota and South Dakota. The margin given him by the major urban areas of Illinois and Ohio overcame his deficit in the farm areas of those States; and practically all of his margin in Wisconsin consisted of his margin in Milwaukee, and practically all of his margin in Minnesota consisted of his margin in St. Paul–Minneapolis. Contrast this with the findings of the above memo that the key Catholic city vote was responsible for the Democratic victories of 1940, 1944 and 1948. Even in most farm States, there are more Catholic voters than farm voters, according to official census figures.

Sources

Chapter 1. PRESIDENT

Goldwater quotation: Walter Trohan, "Report from Washington, 'Do You Want This Lousy Job?' " *Chicago Tribune,* Aug. 4, 1961; Nixon remark: private sources; JFK's comments on Presidency: John Steele, "But Also a Man Quietly Planning Next Four Years," *Life,* Dec. 19, 1960; Joseph P. Kennedy (hereafter referred to as JPK) comment on Presidency: Joe Mc-Carthy, *The Remarkable Kennedys,* serialized in *New Haven Register,* Nov. 21, 1960; JFK's first year in office: Chalmers Roberts, *Washington Post,* Feb. 5, and Nov. 12, 1961; *Economist* comment: "Washington's New Mood," Jan. 28, 1961; James Reston letter: Richard M. Nixon, *Six Crises* (Garden City, Doubleday, 1962), p. 397; Murray Kempton observation: "L'Envoi," *N.Y. Post,* Sept. 30, 1960; Westbrook Pegler comment: "Are They Afraid to Really Debate?" *N.Y. Journal-American,* Oct. 7, 1960; Norman Mailer's Sergius O'Shaughnessy reference: "Superman Comes to the Supermart," *Esquire,* Nov. 1960; JPK on JFK's voting appeal: Hugh Sidey, "Joe Kennedy's Feelings About His Son," *Life,* Dec. 19, 1960; Kansas reply: "Those Hayseeds from Kansas," *El Dorado Times* reprinted in *Chicago Tribune,* Jan. 14, 1961; jumpers and screamers in campaign: Philip Deane, "An Intuitive Election," *Globe and Mail,* Oct. 29, 1960; Eric Dwight Pace, "Youth and the Kennedy Effect," *New Leader,* Jan. 30, 1961; *Richmond Times-Dispatch* editorial, "Glamor-Hungry Juveniles Jump and Holler for Jack," Nov. 3, 1960; JFK hired crowd psychologist: Ted Lewis, "Campaign Circus," *N.Y. News,* Oct. 10, 1960; Prime Minister Macmillan on JFK as 18th century man: Marianne

Means, *N.Y. Journal-American,* Jan. 21, 1962; JFK on politics: Irwin Ross, *N.Y. Post* series, July 30–Aug. 1, 1956; JFK on political stimulation: *Time,* Nov. 7, 1960; Norman Thomas on platform: *New America,* Sept. 5, 1960; remark to Nixon on platform: private sources; *Economist* on JFK victory: "Ambiguous Answer," Nov. 12, 1960; Walter Lippmann on JFK victory: "On the Day After," *N.Y. Herald Tribune,* Nov. 10, 1960; Richard Starnes on Lippmann: *N.Y. World-Telegram & Sun,* Nov. 11, 1960; *Wall Street Journal* on victory: Nov. 10, 1960; Schlesinger on significance of narrow victory: "Face the Nation," CBS–TV, Dec. 26, 1960; *N.Y. News* comment on Buckley debate: "Schlesinger Goofs," Feb. 1, 1961; Schlesinger letter to Sen. Mansfield: *Baltimore Sun,* Feb. 14, 1961; JFK dinner party: Theodore White, *The Making of the President 1960* (New York, Atheneum, 1961), p. 349; Helen Fuller, *Year of Trial: Kennedy's Crucial Decisions* (New York, Harcourt, Brace, 1962), p. 36; Walter Lippmann on appointments: *Louisville Times,* Jan. 20, 1961; JFK on appointment of Bobby as AG: William Manchester, "John F. Kennedy, Portrait of a President," *Holiday,* June 1962; Cholly Knickerbocker on JFK inauguration: *N.Y. Journal-American,* Jan. 22, 1961; Suzy comment: *N.Y. Mirror,* Jan. 22, 1961; Fulton Lewis Jr. comment: *Exclusive,* Jan. 25, 1961; Inez Robb on inaugural poetry: *N.Y. World-Telegram & Sun,* Jan. 17, 1961; Hollywood reaction to Rat Pack: *Time,* Dec. 5, 1960; Lady Lawford on JFK: *New York Times,* Dec. 12, 1960, and *Time,* Dec. 5, 1960; Dorothy Kilgallen on omission of Sammy Davis Jr. from inaugural: *N.Y. Journal-American,* Jan. 11, 1961; Don Loper on Sinatra's wardrobe: *Newark Star-Ledger*, Dec. 31, 1960; *Chicago Tribune* editorial on Sinatra: Jan. 13, 1961; JFK tribute to Sinatra: *Variety*, Feb. 15, 1961; Murray Kempton on royal family: *N.Y. Post*, Feb. 7, 1961; Mrs. Shaw on JFK: *Newsweek*, Oct. 9, 1961, p. 33; Marya Mannes on inaugural parties: "Just Looking," *Reporter*, Feb. 16, 1961; Teddy in pool: "The New Frontier After Office Hours," *U.S. News & World Report*, July 10, 1961; Lincoln Kirstein memoir on inaugural: "The New Augustan Age," *Nation*, Feb. 4, 1961; Whittaker Chambers on Walton: *Witness* (New York, Random House, 1952), p. 501–2, 688; pre-inaugural meetings of Ike and JFK: Helen Fuller, *Year of Trial: Kennedy's Crucial Decisions*, p. 192; Nixon on nonrecognition of Red China: *Six Crises*, p. 408; inaugural platform doings: *Time*, Jan. 27, 1961; *Economist* on Frost poem: "Presidential Past and Yet to Come," Dec. 24, 1960; reactions to inaugural address: William Shannon, *N.Y. Post*, Jan. 22, 1961; Walter Trohan, *Chicago Tribune*, Feb. 27, 1961; *Washington Post* editorial, Jan. 21, 1961; *Los Angeles Times* editorial, Jan. 22, 1961; Morrie Ryskind, *Los Angeles Times*, Jan. 25, 1961; Holmes Alexander, *New Haven Register*, Jan. 26, 1961; *Wall Street Journal* editorial, Jan. 23, 1961; James Reston, "President Kennedy's Inaugural, Speech or Policy?" *N.Y. Times*, Jan. 22, 1961; *N.Y. Post* editorial, Jan. 22, 1961.

Chapter 2.   JOE

JPK on no accidents in politics: Ira Henry Freeman, "Joseph Kennedy Is Back on Scene After Seclusion in the Campaign," *N.Y. Times*, Jan. 8, 1961; JFK on family influence: CBS–TV, "Presidential Countdown," Sept. 19, 1960; *The Joint Appearances of Senator John F. Kennedy and Vice President Richard M. Nixon, Presidential Campaign 1960* (Washington, U.S. Government Printing Office, 1961), p. 955; Marquis Childs' remark: "Joe Kennedy's Legend," *N.Y. Post*, Dec. 21, 1961; JPK stroke: "President's Father Is Felled by Stroke," N.Y. *Daily News*, Dec. 20, 1961; JPK on "togetherness": *Time*, Sept. 1, 1961, p. 36; Spalding on JPK: Frank Kluckhohn, *America: Listen!* (Derby, Conn., Monarch, 1962), p. 53; Jackie angry at JPK: William H. A. Carr, *Those Fabulous Kennedy Women* (New York, Wisdom, 1961), pp. 115–116; JPK on being first: Marguerite Higgins, "Jack Will Sur-

mount Problems Dad Says," *Washington Post*, Dec. 13, 1960; Jackie on competitive family: James MacGregor Burns, *John Kennedy: A Political Profile* (New York, Harcourt, Brace, 1960), p. 129; RFK on swinging higher: Joe McCarthy, *The Remarkable Kennedys* (New York, Dial, 1960), p. 29.

JPK on Teddy's problems: Thomas B. Morgan, "Teddy," *Esquire*, April, 1962; Senate like Jaguar to Teddy: Murray Kempton, "The Hat Makers," *N.Y. Post*, June 15, 1962; Teddy on his qualifications: Thomas B. Morgan, *op. cit.*, Richard Starnes on Teddy: "Teddy Wants Own Orbit," *N.Y. World-Telegram & Sun*, Apr. 13, 1962; JPK wanted Teddy to run: Stewart Alsop, "What Made Teddy Run?" *Saturday Evening Post*, Oct. 27, 1962; JPK ambitions for self, then son: William Moore, "Kennedy's Dad Wanted to Be President," *Chicago Tribune*, Nov. 14, 1960; McCarthy, *op. cit.*, pp. 76–78; JPK says he got Jack into politics: Eleanor Harris, "The Senator Is in a Hurry," *McCall's*, August, 1957; Dinneen reference: Joseph F. Dinneen, *The Kennedy Family* (Boston, Little, Brown, 1959), p. 3; Irwin Ross interview with RFK: "Joseph P. Kennedy, The True Story," *N.Y. Post* series, Jan. 13, 1961; Harry Truman's pope-pop remark: Drew Pearson, "Kennedy Wealth Tops Rockefellers'," *Washington Post*, July 6, 1960.

Stevenson on money spent and JFK arrogant: *Newsweek*, Feb. 29, 1960; JPK on U.N. and foreign aid: Burns, *op. cit.*, p. 90; JPK use of ethnic tags: Irwin Ross, *op. cit.*, Jan. 9, 1961; JPK lit Sabbath fires in Jewish homes: *ibid.*, Jan. 12, 1961; JPK member of Jewish golf club: *ibid.*, Jan. 9, 1961; Ziegfeld theater episode: *Newsweek*, Sept. 12, 1960; JPK helped West Point cadets: *ibid.*; *Boston Globe* episode: Irwin Ross, *op. cit.*, Jan. 9, 1961; *Newsweek*, Sept. 12, 1960; JPK tie: (AP) "The Clan Kennedy—Powerful and Bred to the Political Wars," *N.Y. Post*, July 14, 1960; JPK in complete disagreement with son: *ibid.*; J. M. Burns, *op. cit.*, p. 268; Gridiron song: J. M. Burns, *op. cit.*, p. 211; Liberals propose Bobby for President in '68: Victor Riesel, "Kennedy for President in '68— Bobby, That Is," *N.Y. Mirror*, June 19, 1962; Murray Kempton, "The Hat Makers," *N.Y. Post*, June 15, 1962; Eunice on Kennedy-Kennedy ticket in '64: Walter Trohan, "Report from Washington," *Chicago Tribune*, July 28, 1962; JPK remark on Irish-American: Paul F. Healy, "The Senate's Gay Young Bachelor," *Saturday Evening Post*, June 13, 1953; *Newsweek*, Sept. 12, 1960.

JPK's forebears: J. M. Burns, *op. cit.*, pp. 3–14; "Honey Fitz": John Henry Cutler, *"Honey Fitz"* (New York, Bobbs-Merrill, 1962); "lace-curtain" Irish: Joe McCarthy, *op. cit.*, p. 37; Kennedy family quarrel with Curley: James Michael Curley, *I'd Do It Again* (Englewood Cliffs, N.J., Prentice-Hall, 1957); JFK named Presidential yacht "Honey Fitz": David Wise, "Presidential Yacht Is Now Honey Fitz," *N.Y. Herald Tribune*, Mar. 8, 1961; JFK toured wards with Honey Fitz: J. M. Burns, *op. cit.*, p. 23; Honey Fitz speeches and race for Governor, 1922: J. Joseph Huthmacher, *Massachusetts People and Politics* (Cambridge, Harvard Univ. Press, 1959), pp. 72–73; Fitzgerald really Geraldini: see also UPI dispatch on JFK's Columbus Day speech, New York, Oct. 12, 1962; *Chicago Tribune* editorial in 1911: reprinted, "Grandpa Was Lucky," Sept. 18, 1961; Francis Russell on Honey Fitz: "The Kennedys," *National Review*, Feb. 27, 1960; Curley statement on Honey Fitz: J. H. Cutler, *op. cit.*, pp. 215–216; Honey Fitz claimed credit: J. F. Dinneen, *op. cit.*, pp. 7–8; use of Ku Klux Klan in campaign: J. J. Huthmacher, *op. cit.*, p. 62; J. M. Curley, *op. cit.*, JPK at Harvard; J. M. Burns, *op. cit.*, pp. 14–15; Joe McCarthy, *op. cit.*, pp. 32–34; Walter Vincent Carthy, "Kennedy's Father," *This Month*, February, 1962.

Colonial Auto-Sightseeing Company episode: Drew Pearson, "Kennedy Wealth Tops Rockefellers'," *Washington Post*, July 6, 1960; JPK a young banker: J. M. Burns, *op. cit.*, p. 15; J. H. Cutler, *op. cit.*, p. 179; Joe McCarthy, *op. cit.*, p. 34; JPK's courtship and marriage to Rose: J. M. Burns, *op. cit.*, p. 15; J. F. Dinneen, *op. cit.*, pp. 14–15; Joe McCarthy, *op. cit.*, p. 44; *Time*, Dec. 2, 1957; JPK on Boston no place for Catholic children: J. H. Cutler, *op. cit.*, p. 249; Douglass Cater on JFK's way of life: "The Cool Eye of John F. Kennedy," *Reporter*, Dec. 10, 1959; JFK refusal on Furcolo: J. M. Burns, *op. cit.*, pp. 147–148; JFK–Cushing episode: Douglass Cater, *op. cit.*, JPK on JFK can be elected President: Gerald Walker and Donald A. Allan, "Jack Kennedy at Harvard," *Coronet*, May 1961; Dinneen on JPK will spend his last dime: J. F. Dinneen, *op. cit.*, p. 3; *Fortune* 1937 article: "Mr. Kennedy, The

Chairman," September 1937; JPK on *Fortune* article: Irwin Ross, *op. cit.*, Jan. 10, 1961; Rose–JPK exchange on wealth: Maxine Cheshire, "Rose Kennedy Says of Wealth 'We Never Tell,' " *Washington Post*, July 13, 1960; did not talk about money: Marguerite Higgins, "Kennedy Sr. Tells of His Family," *N.Y. Herald Tribune*, Dec. 12, 1960; Ralph Martin and Ed Plaut, *Front Runner, Dark Horse* (Garden City, Doubleday, 1960), p. 124.

JPK contribution to FDR campaign: J. M. Burns, *op. cit.*, p. 17; JPK and Wall Street: Joe McCarthy, *op. cit.*, pp. 45–48; Richard Whelan, "Joseph P. Kennedy, A Portrait of the Founder," *Fortune*, January 1963; JPK and show business: Joe McCarthy, *op. cit.*, pp. 49–52; Marcus Lowe remark and JFK making screen star: *ibid.;* Gloria Swanson: Hedda Hopper, *From Under My Hat* (Garden City, Doubleday, 1952), p. 168; Toots Shor episode: Martin and Plaut, *op. cit.*, pp. 115–116; John Galvin remark: Andrew Tully, "Vigorous Millionaire's Goal Reached Via Wall Street, Hollywood and Scotch," *N.Y. World-Telegram & Sun*, Apr. 8, 1960.

JPK rich in depression: Karl Schriftgiesser, "That Resilient Envoy, Mr. Ambassador Kennedy," *North American Review*, Winter 1938; JPK to Considine on Palm Beach: "The Amazing Kennedys," *N.Y. Journal-American*, series began May 5, 1957; JPK in liquor business: Alva Johnston, "Jimmy's Got It," *Saturday Evening Post*, July 2, 1938; Joe McCarthy, *op. cit.*, pp. 59–60; *Newsweek*, Sept. 12, 1960; JPK reply to Alva Johnston: "Ambassador Kennedy Sails for London with His Sons," *N.Y. Times*, June 30, 1938; speculation on Eleanor Roosevelt's dislike for JFK: Joe McCarthy, *op. cit.*, p. 60; JFK remark on father in campaign: Irv Kupcinet, "Kup's Column," *Chicago Sun-Times*, Oct. 10, 1960; JPK's relations with business associates: Joe McCarthy, *op. cit.*, p. 125; private sources; magazine-editor episode: private sources.

Chapter 3. F.D.R.

JPK's recent reasons for backing FDR: Joe McCarthy, *The Remarkable Kennedys*, *op. cit.*, p. 58; JPK's relations with FDR in 1932: Ralph Martin and Ed Plaut, *Front Runner, Dark Horse*, *op. cit.*, pp. 117–121; Lela Stiles, *The Man Behind Roosevelt: The Story of Louis McHenry Howe* (New

York, World, 1954), pp. 148–149; Raymond Moley, *After Seven Years* (New York, Harper, 1939), p. 288; JFK's remark on businessmen: Wallace Carroll, "Steel, A 72-Hour Drama with an All-Star Cast," *N.Y. Times*, Apr. 23, 1962; Alfred Kazin on JFK: *American Scholar*, Fall 1961, pp. 498–516; JFK on Ike's stag dinners: Tristam Coffin, "The Well-Tempered Politician," *Holiday*, April 1960; *Time* on JFK anti-business: June 22, 1962; JFK wrote father asking about depression: James MacGregor Burns, *John Kennedy: A Political Profile, op. cit.*, p. 25; JPK tried to refuse Maritime job: Henry Denton, "$100,000,000 Pinch Hitter," *American*, November 1937; JPK's Maritime troubles: Karl Schriftgiesser, "That Resilient Envoy, Mr. Ambassador Kennedy," *North American Review*, Winter 1938.

JPK as Ambassador: J. M. Burns, *op. cit.*, pp. 33–47; Cornelius Vanderbilt Jr., *Man of the World* (New York, Crown, 1959), p. 162; Joe McCarthy, *op. cit.*, pp. 68–69; Ickes quotation: *The Secret Diary of Harold L. Ickes*, Vol. II, *The Inside Struggle, 1936–1939* (New York, Simon & Schuster, 1954), p. 340; Westbrook Pegler remark: "Joe Kennedy Loved to Ridicule FDR," *San Diego Union*, Mar. 30, 1960; JPK's first press conference in London: Irwin Ross, "Joseph P. Kennedy, The True Story," *N.Y. Post* series, Jan. 11, 1961; JPK abolished "undemocratic" precedent: *Associated Press Biographical Service*, No. 3090, Dec. 15, 1943; Joseph F. Dinneen, *The Kennedy Family*, pp. 63–64; JPK's Pilgrims speech: *AP Biographical Service, op. cit.;* Ickes quotation: *The Secret Diary of Harold L. Ickes, op. cit.*, p. 370; JPK–FDR relations hurt by talk of JPK as 1940 candidate: "Kennedy's 1940 Ambitions Open Roosevelt Rift," *Chicago Tribune*, June 23, 1938; JPK defense of Chamberlain in Trafalgar Day speech: "Kennedy Urges All Powers to Try for Peace," *N.Y. Herald Tribune*, Oct. 20, 1938; JFK reaction to Trafalgar Day speech: J. M. Burns, *op. cit.*, p. 37; *New York Post* denunciation: Karl Schriftgiesser, *op. cit.;* JPK's disclosure of FDR's message on Munich Pact: Andrew Tully, "3-Time Roosevelt Choice," *N.Y. World-Telegram & Sun*, Apr. 11, 1960.

JPK's plan for Jews: Joe McCarthy, *op. cit.*, p. 80; Ickes conversation with Cudahy: *The Secret Diary of Harold L. Ickes, op. cit.*, p. 685; von Dirksen on JPK:

U.S. State Department, *Documents on German Foreign Policy*, Series D., Vol. 1, p. 713; Vol. 4, p. 633; "Did Kennedy (Sr.) See War Lost in '40?" *N.Y. Herald Tribune*, Apr. 26, 1961; Alistair Cooke, "The Smear Campaign Gathers Force," Manchester *Guardian*, Sept. 2, 1960; JPK remark after Dunkirk: William L. Langer and S. Everett Fleason, *The World Challenge to Isolation 1937–1940* (New York, Harper, 1952), p. 466; JPK cable to FDR on British making incident: "Opinions Were Never Secret," *Daily Telegraph and Morning Post* (London), Apr. 25, 1961; JPK's pessimism: Forrest Davis and Ernest K. Lindley, *How War Came* (New York, Simon & Schuster, 1942), p. 95; "All-Outers Fear Pressure Will Put Kennedy in Job," *PM*, Apr. 21, 1942; "Kennedy Ran with Appeasers," *PM*, Apr. 23, 1942; Ickes on Bullitt episode: *The Secret Diary of Harold L. Ickes*, Vol. III, *The Lowering Clouds, 1939–1941* (New York, Simon & Schuster, 1954), p. 147.

JPK advanced for 1940 nomination: *AP Biographical Service, op. cit.;* JPK returns and endorses FDR for third term: Stewart Alsop, "Kennedy's Magic Formula," *Saturday Evening Post*, Aug. 13, 1960; JPK radio plea for FDR re-election: Joe McCarthy, *op. cit.*, pp. 79–80; FDR speech next night in Boston: J. M. Burns, *op. cit.*, p. 46; *Boston Globe* interview with Louis Lyons: J. F. Dinneen, *op. cit.*, pp. 80–87; Irwin Ross, *op. cit.*, Jan. 9, 1961; Joe McCarthy, *op. cit.*, pp. 87–89; *Newsweek*, Sept. 12, 1960.

Chapter 4. EARLY

Teddy's expulsion from Harvard: John H. Fenton, "Edward Kennedy Admits Ouster by Harvard, Had an Exam Proxy," *N.Y. Times*, Mar. 31, 1962; Walter Trohan, "Report from Washington," *Chicago Tribune*, Apr. 2, 1962; Robert Ruark comment: "Sin, Repent and Profit," *N.Y. World Telegram & Sun*, Apr. 16, 1962; Teddy in Brazil: "Washington Whispers," *U.S. News & World Report*, Aug. 21, 1961; Teddy-McCormack primary: David Wise, "What Makes Teddy Run?" *N.Y. Herald Tribune*, Apr. 9, 1962; Alan L. Otten, "Ted Kennedy Builds Massachusetts Senate Bid Around Brothers," *Wall Street Journal*, June 1, 1962; John L. Saltonstall Jr. on Ted's style: "First Round for Brother Ted," *New Republic*, June 18, 1962; Professor Howe's letter: from text;

Convention delegate on Teddy's arrogance: Paul Driscoll, "Jack Was Asking About You," *New Republic*, June 4, 1962; JFK's oversight in filing: Ralph Martin and Ed Plaut, *Front Runner, Dark Horse*, p. 138.

Joe Jr.: *As We Remember Joe*, privately published memorial volume, 1945, edited by JFK (includes Laski statement); "Joe Is Well Remembered, Kennedy Deeply Influenced by His Brother," *Washington Star*, Jan. 20, 1961; Joe Jr. at 1940 Convention: James A. Farley, *Jim Farley's Story* (New York, McGraw-Hill, 1948), p. 264; JPK on JFK went into politics because Joe Jr. died: Joe McCarthy, *The Remarkable Kennedys*, p. 19; JFK not a robust child: Douglass Cater, "The Cool Eye of John F. Kennedy," *Reporter*, Dec. 10, 1959; parents thought JFK would be writer: Joe McCarthy, *op. cit.*, p. 116; Joy Miller, "Mrs. Rose Kennedy Sees Dream Come True," *Washington Star*, Jan. 15, 1961; Bob Considine interview: "The Amazing Kennedys," *N.Y. Journal American* series, May 10, 1957; Rosemary: Irwin Ross, "Joseph P. Kennedy, The True Story," *N.Y. Post* series, Jan. 9, 1961; *Time*, July 11, 1960; deaths of Joe Jr. and Kathleen: Joe McCarthy, *op. cit.*, pp. 113–114; children emulating Joe Jr. and Kathleen: Harold H. Martin, "The Amazing Kennedys," *Saturday Evening Post*, Sept. 7, 1957; Teddy on family life: Thomas B. Morgan, "Teddy," *Esquire*, April 1962; Eleanor Harris article: "The Senator Is in a Hurry," *McCall's*, August 1957; JPK in New York while Patricia born: Joe McCarthy, *op. cit.*, pp. 47–48.

Making money not important to JPK: Marguerite Higgins, "Jack Will Surmount Problems, Dad Says," *Washington Post*, Dec. 13, 1960; JPK on children could tell him to go to hell: Harold H. Martin, *op. cit.*; JFK on father's speculating: Martin and Plaut, *op. cit.*, p. 121; effect of New Deal on JFK: Douglass Cater, *op. cit.*; JPK–JFK discussions: Martin and Plaut, *op. cit.*, pp. 123–124; JFK on Joe Jr.: *As We Remember Joe*; JPK on wife's courage: Marguerite Higgins, *op. cit.*; Eunice on competitive family: Martin and Plaut, *op. cit.*, p. 121; Jackie on Kennedys: Eleanor Harris, *op. cit.*; Eunice on JFK hates to lose: Martin and Plaut, *op. cit.*, p. 122; "Rules for Visiting the Kennedys": Joseph F. Dinneen, *The Kennedy Family*, pp. 169–171; JPK on Catholic schools: Vincent X. Flaherty, "Tragedy Forged Kennedy Family Bond," *N.Y. Journal-Ameri-*

can, July 20, 1960; Bobby at Protestant school: Marquis Childs, "Bobby and the President," *Good Housekeeping*, May 1962; Kennedy boys at LSE: James MacGregor Burns, *John Kennedy: A Political Profile*, p. 30; John Krueger, "London's 'Stimulating' School of Economics," *Stars and Stripes*, Mar. 11, 1961; Norman Moss, "Revolutionaries and Capitalists Learn at London Economics School," *Louisville Times*, Feb. 3, 1961.

JFK plagued by bad health: Eleanor Harris, *op. cit.*; William Manchester, "John F. Kennedy, Portrait of a President," *N.Y. Post* (serialization), Mar. 26, 1963; JFK at Canterbury and Choate: Bruce Lee, *Boys' Life of John F. Kennedy* (New York, Bold Face, 1961), pp. 24–32; J. M. Burns, *op. cit.*, pp. 25–29; JFK kissed Betty Young: J. M. Burns, *op. cit.*, p. 29; JFK at Princeton: Bruce Lee, *op. cit.*, p. 54; "Kennedy (*ca.* 1935) Models Informal Formal Wear," *N.Y. Times*, Jan. 17, 1961; JFK at Harvard: Mary Perot Nichols, "Geller: The Emergence of a Retiring Firebrand," *Village Voice*, Jan. 18, 1962; Bruce Lee, *op. cit.*, pp. 54–59; Gerald Walker and Donald A. Allan, "Jack Kennedy at Harvard," *Coronet*, May 1961; Bernard Givertzman, "Kennedy as a Student," *Washington Star*, Jan. 20, 1961; Irwin Ross, "Sen. Kennedy," *N.Y. Post* series, July 31, 1956; J. M. Burns, *op. cit.*, pp. 30–32.

Cleveland Amory, Eric Cutler, and Benjamin Smith quotations: Lawrence Lader, "Jack Kennedy at Harvard," *Parade*, June 11, 1961; Dr. Wild's remark: Marguerite Higgins, "Harvard Mentor Recalls Kennedy," *N.Y. Herald Tribune*, Aug. 12, 1960; Harold Ulen remark: Gerald Walker and Donald A. Allan, *op. cit.*; JFK's clubs at Harvard: Douglass Cater, *op. cit.*; Blair Clark remark: Martin and Plaut, *op. cit.*, p. 126; Professor Holcombe comment: Lawrence Lader, *op. cit.*; Mrs. Dee comments: "Mrs. Dee Reminisces," *Washington Star*, Jan. 20, 1961.

JFK had girl friend: Marguerite Higgins, "Rose Fitzgerald Kennedy," *McCall's*, May 1961; Torbert Macdonald's butting in on family affairs: Gerald Walker and Donald A. Allan, *op. cit.*; JFK trip to Western Europe: J. M. Burns, *op. cit.*, p. 32; JFK on Italian Fascism and Franco: J. M. Burns, *ibid.*; JFK trip to Eastern Europe: J. M. Burns, *op. cit.*, pp. 37–38; Gerald Walker and Donald A. Allan, *op. cit.*; JFK's thesis, converted to *Why England Slept*: J. M. Burns, *op. cit.*, pp.

42–44; Martin and Plaut, *op. cit.,* pp. 127–129; George Bilainkin, "President Kennedy, 1940 and 1961," *Contemporary Review,* March 1961; McCarthy, *op. cit.,* p. 84; JPK on status from writing a book: J. M. Burns, *op. cit.,* p. 44.

Chapter 5. POL

Joe Jr.'s death: "Son of J. P. Kennedy Killed in Action," *N.Y. Times,* Aug. 15, 1944; Anthony Leviero, "Kennedy Jr. Died in Air Explosion," *N.Y. Times,* Oct. 25, 1945; Samuel Eliot Morison, "Death of a Kennedy," *Look,* Dec. 27, 1962; Joe McCarthy, *The Remarkable Kennedys,* p. 105; JFK ponders career if Joe Jr. had lived: *The Joint Appearances of Senator John F. Kennedy and Vice President Richard M. Nixon, Presidential Campaign 1960,* pp. 52–53; JFK after Harvard: Joe McCarthy, *op. cit.,* p. 47; JPK's antiwar crusade: James MacGregor Burns, *John Kennedy: A Political Profile, op. cit.,* p. 47; Irwin Ross, "Joseph P. Kennedy, The True Story," *N.Y. Post* series, Jan. 12, 1961; Joseph F. Dinneen, *The Kennedy Family,* pp. 105–106; JPK did not want sons to be killed in foreign war: Irwin Ross, *op. cit.,* Jan. 11, 1961.

JPK and Wheeler: Westbrook Pegler, "Joe Kennedy's Taxes," *Cincinnati Enquirer,* Apr. 4, 1960, and "Elder Kennedy Source of News Concerning Baruch," *Cincinnati Enquirer,* Mar. 31, 1960; Victor Bienstock remarks: text, speech "Report on England," Biltmore Hotel, Jan. 23, 1941; JPK's angry retort: J. F. Dinneen, *op. cit.,* pp. 102–109; JFK lecture on bombs: Fletcher Knebel, "Kennedy's Pals," *Look,* Apr. 25, 1961; JPK pulled strings for JFK reassignment: J. M. Burns, *op. cit.,* pp. 47–48; Frank L. Kluckhohn, *America: Listen! op. cit.,* p. 41.

JFK's PT adventures: Robert J. Donovan, *PT-109* (New York, McGraw-Hill, 1961); Richard Tregaskis, *John F. Kennedy, War Hero* (New York, Dell, 1962); J. F. Dinneen, *op. cit.,* pp. 96–100; John Hersey, "Survival," *Reader's Digest,* August 1944, reprinted from *New Yorker,* June 17, 1944; Robert T. Hartmann comment: "Kennedy Faces Many Problems," *Los Angeles Times,* Feb. 29, 1960; Drew Pearson on MacArthur: *Washington Post,* July 10, 1960.

JFK called "Shafty": R. J. Donovan, *op. cit.,* p. 36; Spalding on JFK's return to Palm Beach: William H. A. Carr, *JFK,*

an Informal Biography (New York, Lancer, 1962), p. 75; JFK's simulated attack on Miami: Chandler Whipple, *Lt. John F. Kennedy, Expendable!* (New York, Envoy, 1962), pp. 152–154; Kathleen's marriage: Joe McCarthy, *op. cit.,* pp. 109–113; *Time,* May 15, 1944; "It Was Another Romeo-Juliet Romance," *N.Y. News,* Sept. 24, 1944; JPK's remark on father-in-law of Masons: *Time,* July 11, 1960; JFK's reply to Harry Hopkins: J. M. Burns, *op. cit.,* p. 55; Selig Harrison, "Kennedy as President," *New Republic,* June 27, 1960; JFK as reporter for Hearst: *N.Y. Journal-American,* Apr. 28, 30, May 2, 3, 4, 5, 7, 9, 10, 14, 16, 18, 19, 21, 23, 28, 1945; also London stories, June 24, July 10, 27, 1945; John Mahanna comment: Martin and Plaut, *op. cit.,* p. 131.

JPK offered services to FDR: J. M. Burns, *op. cit.,* p. 48; JPK's unpublished book: Drew Pearson, "Washington Merry-Go-Round," *N.Y. Mirror,* Jan. 8, 1943; speculation on JPK as Sec'y of Commerce: *N.Y. Times,* Feb. 23, 1944; *PM* attacks: Apr. 21, 23, 1942; JPK's real-estate deals: *Newsweek,* Sept. 12, 1960; Richard Whelan, "Joseph P. Kennedy: A Portrait of the Founder," *Fortune,* January 1963; Lamula disclosures: personal interview; Merchandise Mart purchase: *Newsweek,* Mar. 22, 1948; John Sturdevant, "Money and JFK," *American Weekly,* May 7, 1961; JFK had to carry on politics for Joe Jr.: J. M. Burns, *op. cit.,* pp. 57–62; Joe McCarthy, *op. cit.,* pp. 116–120; J. F. Dinneen, *op. cit.,* pp. 118–127; Rosalie Macrae, " 'You Will Be President, My Son,' " *N.Y. World-Telegram & Sun,* July 31, 1960; JFK's remark on Bobby and Teddy: Joe McCarthy, *op. cit.,* p. 116; JFK's official address: Joe McCarthy, *op. cit.,* pp. 119–120; Fulton Lewis Jr., "Kennedy Home That Isn't," *N.Y. Mirror,* Mar. 13, 1961; 1946 campaign coverage: Martin and Plaut, *op. cit.,* pp. 131–147; Paul F. Healy, "The Senate's Gay Young Bachelor," *Saturday Evening Post,* June 13, 1953; Irwin Ross, "Sen. Kennedy," *N.Y. Post* series, July 30–Aug. 1, 1956; J. M. Burns, *op. cit.,* pp. 60–70; Joe McCarthy, *op. cit.,* pp. 116–123; Radcliffe girl's question: Selig Harrison, "Kennedy as President," *New Republic,* June 27, 1960; Bobby's campaigning: *Time,* Oct. 10, 1960; "Honey Fitz" danced and sang "Sweet Adeline": Fletcher Knebel, *Candidates 1960,* edited by Eric Sevareid (New York, Basic, 1959), p. 196.

Chapter 6. CONGRESS

JFK as a Congressman: Selig Harrison, "Kennedy as President," *New Republic,* June 27, 1960; Ralph Martin and Ed Plaut, *Front Runner, Dark Horse,* pp. 148–155; James MacGregor Burns, *John Kennedy: A Political Profile,* pp. 71–97; JFK's Salem, Mass., speech: *Congressional Record,* Feb. 21, 1949, p. A993; JFK's reference to Dr. Lahey: J. M. Burns, *op. cit.,* p. 89; Westbrook Pegler's disclosure of JFK's frequent sojourns to Lahey Clinic: "McCarthy Incident Dims Kennedy Valor," *San Diego Union,* Mar. 28, 1960; Elizabeth Oldfield's profile of Congressman Kennedy: "Did You Happen to See —John F. Kennedy," *Washington Times Herald,* Feb. 6, 1947; Sam Rayburn on JFK: "Speaker Speaks of Presidents," *N.Y. Times Magazine,* June 4, 1961; Senator Smathers' friendship with JFK: *Time,* May 4, 1962; Smathers' remarks on Pepper: William F. Buckley Jr. and L. Brent Bozell, *McCarthy and His Enemies* (Chicago, Regnery, 1954), p. 304.

Senator Joe McCarthy's friendship with Kennedy family: Martin and Plaut, *op. cit.,* pp. 202–203; Irwin Ross, "Joseph P. Kennedy, The True Story," *N.Y. Post* series, Jan. 9, 1961; Perle Mesta's dinner party: *Perle* (autobiography) (New York, McGraw-Hill, 1960), pp. 129–130; JFK's dressing habits: Irwin Ross, "Sen. Kennedy," *N.Y. Post* series, July 30, 1956; Arthur Schlesinger Jr.'s attack on JPK: *Partisan Review,* May–June, 1947; Richard Starnes, "Schlesinger vs. Kennedy Sr.," *N.Y. World-Telegram & Sun,* Nov. 20, 1961; JFK on Leviathan state: "Shun Gov't Aid, Kennedy Says," *Boston Herald,* Apr. 23, 1950; JFK Notre Dame speech: J. M. Burns, *op. cit.,* p. 242; JFK 1950 support of an across-the-board cut in federal spending: J. M. Burns, *op. cit.,* p. 88; JFK warning against spending for nondefense purposes: *Congressional Record,* May 15, 1951; *Boston Globe,* May 16, 1951.

Newsweek on alleged marriage: reprinted in *Los Angeles Times* ("Rumor on President Found Vicious, False"), Sept. 17, 1962; *N.Y. Times* story on alleged marriage: "Kennedy Rumor Held Unfounded," *N.Y. Times* (city edition), Sept. 18, 1962; McCormack's "Where's Johnny?" remark: J. M. Burns, *op. cit.,* p. 92; JFK on American Legion: *Congressional Record,* Mar. 22, 1949, p. 2950;

Newsweek, Apr. 4, 1959; Martin and Plaut, *op. cit.,* p. 154; JFK remark about Nixon: Joe McCarthy, *The Kennedy Family,* p. 130; Nixon recollection: Richard M. Nixon, *Six Crises* (Garden City, Doubleday, 1962), pp. 298–299; Christoffel case: O. John Rogge, *Our Vanishing Civil Liberties* (New York, Gare, 1949); J. M. Burns, *op. cit.,* p. 133; Healy in *Sign:* "Galahad in the House," *Sign,* July 1950, pp. 9–11; JFK's move to indict Christoffel: *Hearings Before the Committee on Education and Labor, House of Representatives,* 80th Congress, 1st Session (Washington, U.S. Government Printing Office, 1947), Vol. 5, Mar. 8–15, 1947, p. 3616; Buse testimony: *ibid.,* Vol. 4, Mar. 1, 1947, p. 2011; Russ Nixon testimony: *ibid.,* Vol. 5, Mar. 8–15, 1947, pp. 3577–3583.

JFK on Taft-Hartley: Martin and Plaut, *op. cit.,* pp. 151–152; J. M. Burns, *op. cit.,* pp. 76–78; *Congressional Record,* Vol. 93, Apr. 16, 1947, pp. 3512–3513, and Vol. 95, Apr. 27, 1949, pp. 5147–5148; JFK on China: *Congressional Record,* Vol. 95, Part I, Jan. 25, 1949, pp. 532–533; Westbrook Pegler on Baruch episode: "His First Meeting with Joe Kennedy," *N.Y. Journal-American,* Mar. 28, 1960; JFK attacks on Truman policies: J. M. Burns, *op. cit.,* pp. 79–84; JFK on "Meet the Press": transcript, NBC–TV, Dec. 2, 1951; CIO box score: Paul F. Healy, "The Senate's Gay Young Bachelor," *Saturday Evening Post,* June 13, 1953.

JFK on TVA: "Kennedy Attacks TVA Help, Says New England Lax While Aiding Southern Powers," *Boston Post,* Mar. 22, 1952; JFK–Rabaut exchange: *Congressional Record,* Vol. 98, Apr. 1, 1952, p. 3329; *New Republic* article: John P. Mallan, "Massachusetts: Liberal and Corrupt," *New Republic,* Oct. 13, 1952; JFK for aid to Italy: *Congressional Record,* Nov. 20, 1947; Boston Chamber of Commerce speech: reconstructed from newspaper accounts, "Voice of America Policies Futile," *Boston Globe,* Nov. 19, 1951 (includes Hottentot and Uncle Sugar quotes); " 'Tennis, Cocktail' Diplomats of U.S. Scored by Kennedy," *Boston Herald,* Nov. 20, 1951; "Higher Standard Urged in Selecting U.S. Diplomats," *Christian Science Monitor,* Nov. 19, 1951; "Kennedy Asks Change in U.S. East Policies," *Washington Times Herald,* Nov. 20, 1951; "Kennedy Asks Emphasis on Technical Aid," *Washington Post,* Nov. 20, 1951;

"Kennedy Calls for Export of U.S. Know-How to Asia," *N.Y. Herald Tribune,* Nov. 19, 1951; Maxwell Taylor and W. W. Rostow in Saigon: "Washington Behind-the-Scenes," *Richmond Times-Dispatch,* Oct. 29, 1961.

JFK on Marshall Plan: "Shocking Marshall Plan Waste in Europe, Kennedy Asserts, Says Billions in Aid Not 'Getting Down to the People,'" *Boston Globe,* Jan. 20, 1952; JFK and Hoover Commission: J. M. Burns, *op. cit.,* pp. 206–208; JFK on Korea: John P. Mallan, *op. cit.;* JPK's Virginia Law School speech: *Congressional Record,* Dec. 15, 1950, pp. A7723–A7724; "Kennedy Denounces 'Suicidal' U.S. Policies," *N.Y. Times,* Dec. 13, 1950; JFK's radio report on trip to Europe: John O'Connor, "Kennedy Says Reich Vital to Pact Success," *Boston Herald,* Feb. 9, 1951; Kingsbury Smith interview with JPK: "Europe Cool to Rearming," *N.Y. Journal-American,* May 15, 1951; JFK's anti-Truman proposals on troops to Europe: J. M. Burns, *op. cit.,* pp. 82–85; *Hearings Before the Committee on Foreign Relations and Committee on Armed Services, U.S. Senate,* "Assignment of Ground Forces of the United States to Duty in the European Area," Senate Concurrent Resolution 8, February 1951, 82nd Congress, 1st Session, pp. 424–444.

Pravda quoted JPK: "Moscow Gleeful over U.S. 'Crisis,'" *N.Y. Times,* Dec. 31, 1951; JFK's global tour, including Saigon: Selig Harrison, "Kennedy as President," *New Republic,* June 27, 1960; J. M. Burns, *op. cit.,* pp. 83–84; Dewey on Indochina: *Journey to the Far Pacific* (Garden City, Doubleday, 1952), pp. 203–207; JFK on Nehru's views: "Kennedy Calls for Export of U.S. Know-How to Asia," *N.Y. Herald Tribune,* Nov. 19, 1951; JFK remarks on radio–TV after trip: "Cong. Kennedy Returns, Raps U.S. Orient Failure," *N.Y. Journal-American,* Nov. 12, 1951; "Anglo-French Ties Held Costly to U.S.," *Philadelphia Inquirer,* Dec. 3, 1951; JFK remarks to Blagden: Ralph Blagden, "Cabot Lodge's Toughest Fight," *Reporter,* Sept. 30, 1952.

Chapter 7.   LODGE

JFK at Harvard seminar: John P. Mallan, "Massachusetts: Liberal and Corrupt," *New Republic,* Oct. 13, 1952; JFK's contribution to Nixon campaign against Helen Gahagan Douglas: Robert W.

Richards, "Kennedy Gave $1,000 to Aid Nixon," *San Diego Union,* July 20, 1960; Robert Thompson, "Capital Circus," *N.Y. Daily News,* Aug. 26, 1960; JFK's attitude toward aid to education: James MacGregor Burns, *John Kennedy: A Political Profile,* pp. 86–88; Paul Healy, "Galahad in the House," *Sign,* July 1950; private sources; JFK's years-later comment: Irwin Ross, "Sen. Kennedy," *N.Y. Post* series, Aug. 1, 1956; JFK on need for religious education: "Kennedy Backs Bishops' Stand, Bay State Senator-Elect Hits 'Trend' Away from Religious Education," *Providence Journal,* Nov. 17, 1952 (On NBC–TV "Youth Wants to Know"); Professor Holcombe's letter: *New Republic,* Nov. 3, 1952.

Burns and political scientist reaction: J. M. Burns, *op. cit.,* pp. 133–134; Mary McGrory quotation: "Portrait of a President," *N.Y. Post,* Jan. 22, 1961; Joseph C. Harsch on New Dealers: *Reporter,* Sept. 30, 1952; JFK on ADA and AVA: Paul F. Healy, "The Senate's Gay Young Bachelor," *Saturday Evening Post,* June 13, 1953; Burns and indignant lady quoted: J. M. Burns, *op. cit.,* pp. 134, 136; Irwin Ross comment: *op. cit.,* July 30, 1956; JFK on taking a stand: text, NBC–TV, "Meet the Press," Dec. 3, 1951; Blagden on JFK's absenteeism: Ralph Blagden, "Cabot Lodge's Toughest Fight," *Reporter,* Sept. 30, 1952; JFK ineligible for Governorship: W. E. Mullins, "State Constitution Disqualifies Rep. Kennedy as Candidate for Governor in Autumn Election," *Boston Herald,* Feb. 4, 1948.

JFK's 1952 strategy: Eleanor Harris, "The Senator Is in a Hurry," *McCall's,* August 1957; JPK's speech at Chicago Economic Club in 1951: "Kennedy Says U.S. Must Build Own Security," *N.Y. Herald Tribune,* Dec. 18, 1951; Bull's-Eye by J. P. Kennedy," *N.Y. Daily News* editorial, Dec. 30, 1951; "'Suicidal' Foreign Policy," *N.Y. Journal-American* editorial, Dec. 19, 1951; "*Pravda* Says Kennedy Speech Shows Deep U.S. Policy Crisis," *Boston Herald,* Dec. 31, 1951; "Moscow Gleeful over U.S. 'Crisis,' Press Refers to Kennedy's Recent Criticism as Showing Foreign-Policy Conflict," *N.Y. Times,* Dec. 31, 1951; JPK's role in 1952 campaign: Eleanor Harris, *op. cit.,* Paul F. Healy, *Saturday Evening Post, op. cit.;* Ralph Blagden, *op. cit.;* Ralph Martin and Ed Plaut, *Front Runner, Dark Horse,* pp. 175–177; J. M. Burns, *op. cit.,* pp. 104–105; Lodge message to JPK via Krock: Martin and Plaut, *op. cit.*, p. 168; JPK's attack on Gardner Jackson: Irwin Ross, "Joseph P. Kennedy, The True Story," *N.Y. Post* series, Jan. 12, 1961; J. M. Burns, *op. cit.*, pp. 109–110; Martin and Plaut, *op. cit.*, pp. 174–176.

JPK's contribution to Senator Joe McCarthy's 1952 campaign: Joe McCarthy, *The Remarkable Kennedys*, pp. 26–27; Westbrook Pegler rebuttal, "The Correct Version of Gift to McCarthy," *Indianapolis Star*, Dec. 19, 1960; JFK's organization of Jewish Committee: Martin and Plaut, *op. cit.*, pp. 171–173; JFK for cut of economic assistance to Israel: Irwin Ross: "Sen. Kennedy," *N.Y. Post*, Aug. 1, 1956; Martin and Plaut, *op. cit.*, p. 171; JFK for aid to Spain: *Congressional Record*, July 19, 1950; McCormack's aid in 1952 campaign: *Newsweek*, Jan. 15, 1962; campaign leaflets: Martin and Plaut, *op. cit.*, p. 173; Kempton on Truman's Boston speech: *N.Y. Post*, Jan. 24, 1956; JFK memorandum critical of Truman policies: J. M. Burns, *op. cit.*, p. 104.

Selig Harrison, "Kennedy as President," *New Republic*, June 27, 1960; Senator Taft's attitude toward Lodge campaign: William S. White, *The Taft Story* (New York, Harper, 1954), p. 182; JPK's wooing of conservatives: Ralph Blagden, *op. cit.*; J. M. Burns, *op. cit.*, pp. 104–105; *Chicago Tribune* editorial: Nov. 6, 1952; Joseph P. Kennedy's dealings with Fox of *Boston Post*: "Investigation of Regulatory Commissions and Agencies," *Hearings Before Subcommittee on Interstate and Foreign Commerce, House of Representatives*, 85th Congress, 2nd Session, June 27, 1958, pp. 4126–4132; Joe McCarthy, *op. cit.*, pp. 139–140.

Chapter 8. SENATE

JFK on what he could do that Lodge could not: Ralph Blagden, "Cabot Lodge's Toughest Fight," *Reporter*, Sept. 30, 1952; JFK needs money: Paul F. Healy, "The Senate's Gay Young Bachelor," *Saturday Evening Post*, June 13, 1953; Doris Fleeson comment: "Kennedy Has Edge on Lodge," *Washington Star*, Oct. 27, 1952; John Mallan comments: John P. Mallan, "Massachusetts: Liberal and Corrupt," *New Republic*, Oct. 13, 1952; Mary McGrory remarks: "Portrait of the President," *N.Y. Post*, Jan. 22, 1961; Italian government decoration for JFK: "Kennedy's Taking

Italian Award Seen U.S. Violation," *Boston Herald*, Oct. 28, 1952; coffee with Kennedys: Cabell Phillips, "Case History of a Senate Race," *N.Y. Times Magazine*, Oct. 26, 1952; appeal to women: Eleanor Harris, "The Senator Is in a Hurry," *McCall's*, August 1957; Rose Kennedy's campaigning: Cabell Phillips, *op cit.*; Ellen Gibson, "Energetic Mother of Kennedy Aims Appeal at Grandmothers," *Milwaukee Journal*, Mar. 27, 1960.

JFK and Catholic girls: Paul F. Healy, *op. cit.*; Ralph Martin quotation: Ralph Martin and Ed Plaut, *Front Runner, Dark Horse*, pp. 157–186; Bobby's speech and JFK's campaign slogan: Paul F. Healy, *op. cit.*; other background material: James MacGregor Burns, *John Kennedy: A Political Profile*, pp. 98–116; Joe McCarthy, *The Remarkable Kennedys*, pp. 131–140; JFK and sign painters: Hal Clancy, "Non-Union Printing Job Trips Kennedy, AFL-Backed Solon Faces Picketing," *Boston Traveler*, Sept. 15, 1952; JFK pledge to fight Communism: William F. Horner, "Senator-Elect Pledges Fight on Communism," *Boston Herald*, Nov. 6, 1952; "Kennedy in Paris, OK's Ike Trip," *Boston American*, Dec. 4, 1952; Baltimore Democratic dinner (includes "nothing lower" statement): "Kennedy Talks to Democrats," *Baltimore Sun*, Mar. 21, 1953; JFK's turn-down of Truman speech invitation: John Harris, "Young Bay State Senator Too Busy, Too Wedded to Job for Social Whirl," *Boston Globe*, Mar. 1, 1953; JFK's eulogy of Taft: "Sen. Kennedy Asserts Taft 'Credit to U.S.,'" *Boston Herald*, Apr. 13, 1953; "Sen. Taft Nominated as Man of Year," *Los Angeles Times*, Dec. 7, 1953.

Senator Margaret Chase Smith on JFK: letter to author, March 21, 1962; Hoover letter: "Hoover Lauds Sen. Kennedy," *Los Angeles Times*, May 20, 1956; JFK on "Meet the Press" in 1954: "Kennedy Defends Slump Warnings," *N.Y. Times*, Feb. 15, 1954; *Saturday Evening Post* article: Paul F. Healy, *op. cit.*; background on Jacqueline Kennedy: Joe McCarthy, *op. cit.*, pp. 141–155; "Stunning Egghead," *Newsweek*, Feb. 22, 1960; Mini Rhea with Frances Spatz Leighton, *I Was Jacqueline Kennedy's Dressmaker* (New York, Fleet, 1962); Joan Younger, "Jack Kennedy, Democratic Dynamo," *Ladies' Home Journal*, March 1960; *Time*, Dec. 2, 1957.

JFK's illness: J. M. Burns, *op. cit.*, pp. 156–160; Joe McCarthy, *op. cit.*, pp. 150–

151; Eleanor Harris, *op. cit.;* Irwin Ross, "Sen. Kennedy" *N.Y. Post* series, July 31, 1956; Paul Martin on JFK surgery: "How JFK Triumphed over Pain," *Binghamton* (N.Y.) *Sunday Press,* Jan. 29, 1961; JFK's *American Weekly* article: "What My Illness Taught Me," Apr. 29, 1956; background on Sorensen: Irwin Ross, "The Men Around Kennedy," *N.Y. Post* series, Oct. 3, 1960; Martin and Plaut, *op. cit.,* pp. 250–258; Walter Trohan, "Report from Washington," *Chicago Tribune,* Sept. 23, 1961; Donald R. Larabee, "Kennedy Looks to November," *New Bedford Standard-Times,* July 10, 1960; William V. Shannon, "They Knew What They Wanted, or, Two Young Men in a Hurry," *N.Y. Post,* July 13, 1960.

JFK's 3 speeches on New England economy: *Congressional Record,* May 18, 1953, pp. 5054–5070; May 20, 1953, pp. 5227–5240; and May 25, 1953, pp. 5455–5466; Sen. Fulbright's remark on "creeping socialism" and other Southern criticism: *Time,* Jan. 11, 1954; JFK on "Meet the Press": transcript, NBC–TV, Feb. 14, 1954; Arthur G. McDowell's criticism: letter to author, Mar. 27, 1962; JFK's *Atlantic Monthly* article: "New England and the South, The Struggle for Industry," January 1954; manuscript that *Reporter* did not publish: provided by author, Steve Hess; *Time's* description of JFK: Jan. 11, 1954; JFK's personal note to Ike: Sherman Adams, *First Hand Report* (New York, Harper, 1961), p. 454; JFK support of Benson farm policies: John Osborne, "The Economics of the Candidates," *Fortune,* October 1960; JFK's statement on most difficult decision: Robert T. Hartmann, "Kennedy Faces Many Problems," *Los Angeles Times,* Feb. 29, 1960; *Boston Herald* editorial on JFK's "independence": " 'Suicide' Senator," July 5, 1956.

Chapter 9.   VEEP

Rowland Evans Jr. quotation: "The Kennedy Buildup," *N.Y. Herald Tribune,* Aug. 9, 1959; JPK on Catholicism: Andrew Tully, "Senator's Foes See Dad 'Buying' Election," *N.Y. World-Telegram & Sun,* Apr. 7, 1960; Irwin Ross comment: "Sen. Kennedy," *N.Y. Post* series, July 30–Aug. 1, 1956; JFK handsomest member of House: *Newsweek,* July 14, 1952; JFK's broadside for Convention: Douglass Cater, "The Cool Eye of John F. Kennedy," *Reporter,* Dec. 10, 1959; CBS television-

producer comment: Ralph Martin and Ed Plaut, *Front Runner, Dark Horse,* pp. 38–39; Stevenson on JFK as All-American Boy: James MacGregor Burns, *John Kennedy: A Political Profile,* p. 184.

JFK's posthospital return to Senate: *Congressional Record,* May 24, 1955; "Senate Hails Kennedy, Bay Stater, Back After Illness, Greeted by Both Parties," *N.Y. Times,* May 25, 1955; Fletcher Knebel, *Candidates 1960,* edited by Eric Sevareid, *op. cit.,* p. 205; J. M. Burns, *op. cit.,* pp. 169–170; Debs Myers episode: Martin and Plaut, *op. cit.,* p. 27; Colbert in *Boston Post:* Joseph F. Dineen, *The Kennedy Family, op. cit.,* p. 184; JFK visit to Stevenson: "Kennedy, Stevenson Mum on Conversation," *Baltimore Sun,* Dec. 5, 1955; *Des Moines Register* dispatch: Fletcher Knebel, "John Kennedy Discussed as Adlai's Mate," Feb. 26, 1956; Stevenson denial of discussing VP with JFK: Martin and Plaut, *op. cit.,* p. 23; JFK endorsement of Stevenson: "Sen. Kennedy Urges Adlai's Nomination," *Washington Post-Herald,* Mar. 9, 1956.

JFK–Furcolo feud: J. M. Burns, *op. cit.,* pp. 147–148; John H. Fenton, "Kennedy Rebuffs Party Candidate, Refuses to Endorse Furcolo Personally for Senate—Bay State GOP Gleeful," *N.Y. Times,* Oct. 12, 1954; "Sen. Kennedy in TV Snub to Furcolo, Pre-Broadcast Row over Text Change Causes Party Split," *Boston Herald,* Oct. 12, 1954; W. E. Mullins, "Kennedy's Lack of Support for Furcolo May Hurt Him When He Seeks Re-Election," *Boston Herald,* Nov. 7, 1954; JFK refuses to sign Curley petition: Joe McCarthy, *The Remarkable Kennedys,* p. 129; J. M. Burns, *op. cit.,* pp. 92–93; McCormack attitude toward JFK: J. M. Burns, *op. cit.,* pp. 175–180; Martin and Plaut, *op. cit.,* pp. 152–154; C. R. Owens, "Kennedy Viewed as Favorite Son," *Boston Globe,* Nov. 20, 1955.

Struggle for control of delegation to 1956 Convention: J. M. Burns, *op. cit.,* pp. 176–180; Joe McCarthy, *op. cit.,* p. 158; John H. Fenton, "Kennedy Stock Up in the Bay State, Senator Assumes the Titular Leadership of Democrats but Many Scars Remain," *N.Y. Times,* May 13, 1956; Fletcher Knebel remarks: "John Kennedy Discussed as Adlai's Mate," *Des Moines Register,* Feb. 26, 1956; Vice Presidential buildup: J. M. Burns, *op. cit.,* pp. 169–190; Martin and Plaut, *op. cit.,* pp. 17–70.

Bailey Report: reprinted *U.S. News & World Report*, Aug. 1, 1960, pp. 68–72 (see Appendix B); Martin and Plaut, *op. cit.*, pp. 27–28; Doris Fleeson, "Religion Useful in '56," *Charleston Gazette*, Apr. 28, 1960; James Reston, "Party Debate on Kennedy Takes Note of Catholic Vote," *N.Y. Times*, Jan. 3, 1960; David Wise interview: "Kennedy Doesn't Know Answer on Catholic Vote," *N.Y. Herald Tribune*, Aug. 12, 1956; Kefauver recollection of Adlai–JFK closeness: Martin and Plaut, *op. cit.*, p. 27; whispers about JFK's health: Joe McCarthy, *op. cit.*, pp.   153–154; J. M. Burns, *op. cit.*, pp. 183–184; Irwin Ross, "Sen. Kennedy," *N.Y. Post* series, July 30–Aug. 1, 1956; "Kennedy Doing Well, Father Says," *N.Y. Herald Tribune*, Nov. 12, 1954.

Rumors of JFK's contribution to Nixon's 1950 campaign: J. M. Burns, *op. cit.*, p. 184; Kennedy camp analysis of VP possibilities: J. M. Burns, *op. cit.*, pp. 182–183; Ribicoff statement: J. M. Burns, *op. cit.*, pp. 181–182; Leo Egan, "Kennedy Boomed as Vice President, Govs. Ribicoff and Roberts, Supporters of Stevenson, Come Out for Senator," *N.Y. Times*, June 26, 1956; John C. O'Brien, "Kennedy Gets Support for No. 2 Democrat Spot," *Philadelphia Inquirer*, June 26, 1956; Donald Malcolm article: "The Man Who Wants Second Place," *New Republic*, July 30, 1956.

Convention of 1956 proceedings and background: extensive eyewitness accounts; *N.Y. Times, Time,* and *Newsweek;* most important source is Martin and Plaut, *op. cit.* pp. 47–109; extensive use of Fletcher Knebel *Candidates 1960,* pp. 184–185, based on Tom Winship's eyewitness accounts in *Boston Globe;* J. M. Burns, *op. cit.*, pp. 169–190; Joseph R. Slevin, "Kennedy Ties, Then Vote Ebbs," *N.Y. Herald Tribune*, Aug. 18, 1956; Godfrey Sperling Jr., "Kennedy Gains . . ." *Christian Science Monitor*, Aug. 18, 1956; "Kennedy Lost Nomination, but Gained Prestige," *St. Louis Post Dispatch*, Aug. 19, 1956; Newton Minow recollection of JFK remark on fixed convention: Martin and Plaut, *op. cit.*, p. 64; Congressman Smith's statement: Martin and Plaut, *op. cit.*, p. 73; Clare Boothe Luce episode: Betty Beale, " 'Too Bad Jack Didn't Run on GOP Side'—Father," *Washington Star*, Aug. 13, 1960.

Chapter 10. SIGHT

Irwin Ross reference to JFK's aspiration to be America's first Catholic president: "Sen. Kennedy," *N.Y. Post* series, July 30, 1956; Fletcher Knebel quotation: "John Kennedy Discussed as Adlai's Mate," *Des Moines Register*, Feb. 26, 1956; Schlesinger on JFK's call of destiny: *Kennedy or Nixon: Does It Make Any Difference?* (New York, Macmillan, 1960); Bob Considine interview with JFK: "The Amazing Kennedys," *N.Y. Journal-American*, May 5, 1957; Jacqueline's miscarriage: Winzola McLendon, "Sen. Kennedy on Mediterranean Trip Unaware His Wife Has Lost Baby," *Washington Post-Herald*, Aug. 25, 1956; *Time* on gossip story: republished, Frank L. Kluckhohn, *America: Listen!* p. 54; David Barnett story: "Help Is Seen for Kennedy, Child Would Add Zip to His Campaign," *Omaha World-Herald*, July 21, 1957; "Meet the Press" interview: transcript, NBC–TV, Oct. 28, 1956; Ursuline College episode: "Sen. Kennedy Better Than Elvis, Coeds Yell," *Los Angeles Times*, Oct. 5, 1956.

Pittsburgh Knights of Columbus episode: "Kennedy's Tuxedo and Name Misplaced in Comedy of Errors," *St. Louis Post-Dispatch*, Oct. 15, 1956; JFK's strange safari and electioneering remarks: "Kennedy Says Both Parties Exaggerate," *Providence Journal*, Oct. 14, 1956; Boston communion speech: Douglass Cater, "The Cool Eye of John F. Kennedy," *Reporter*, Dec. 10, 1959; Vermont appearance: Vic Maerki, "Truman's 'Hiss Talk' Not Asset—Kennedy," *Burlington* (Vt.) *Free Press*, Sept. 27, 1956; "Kennedy Dissents, Disagrees with Truman's Remarks about Hiss," *Providence Journal*, Sept. 27, 1956; "Meet the Press" appearance: *op. cit.*

JFK named to Foreign Relations Committee: James MacGregor Burns, *John Kennedy: A Political Profile*, pp. 193–194; "Kennedy Given Top Assignment, Picked over Kefauver for Foreign Relations," *Baltimore Sun*, Jan. 9, 1957; "Tradition or Convenience?" *Philadelphia Inquirer* editorial, Jan. 10, 1957; "Mr. Kennedy Moves Up," *Washington Star*, Jan. 13, 1957; "Kennedy Beats Kefauver for Foreign Relations," *N.Y. Herald Tribune*, Jan. 9, 1957; JFK on Democrats losing Negro vote: "Kennedy Sees Democrat Split in Congress," *Washington Star*, Nov. 8, 1956; JFK praise of LBJ: J. A. O'Leary, "Kennedy Urges Unite Behind Party Leaders,"

Washington Star, Dec. 7, 1956; JFK not thinking of 1960: "Senator Kennedy, Man in a Hurry," *Cleveland Plain Dealer,* Nov. 10, 1957; JFK running for 1960: "Man Out Front," *Time,* Dec. 2, 1957; *Saturday Evening Post* article: Harold H. Martin, "The Amazing Kennedys," Sept. 7, 1957; endorsed by Furcolo for 1960: " 'Hand in Hand' in Bay State" *Washington Star* editorial, Nov. 26, 1957.

Dixie's favorite Yankee: Bob Considine, *op. cit.;* Bicknell Eubanks, "Dixie Ponders Kennedy Role," *Christian Science Monitor,* Dec. 3, 1957; Carroll Kilpatrick reference: "Kennedy, the Moderate," *Washington Post,* Oct. 24, 1957; JFK on TV show praises Russell and Talmadge: David Koonce, "Here's the Young Man to Watch for the 1960 Race," *Washington Star,* Aug. 18, 1957; Jackson, Miss., episode: Fletcher Knebel, *Candidates 1960,* p. 207; Joe McCarthy, *The Remarkable Kennedys,* pp. 173–174; J. M. Burns, *op. cit.,* pp. 205–206; Southern Governors Conference: "Deep South Likes Kennedy," *Providence Journal,* Sept. 28, 1958; *Time,* Dec. 2, 1957; David Koonce on JFK's religion a plus: *op. cit.*

JFK subject of magazine articles and TV: Fletcher Knebel, "He's Hottest Runner on the Political Track," *Des Moines Register,* May 6, 1957; *Life* magazine article: "A Democrat Says Party Must Lead, Or Get Left," Mar. 11, 1957; JPK on publicity buildup of JFK: Ralph Martin and Ed Plaut, *Front Runner, Dark Horse,* p. 461; Denver crowds: Del Carnes, "Sen. Kennedy Talks to Crowd of 8,200," *Denver Post,* Feb. 25, 1958; Reston on JFK's effect on women and campaigning in West Virginia: "Kennedy Looks to 1960," *N.Y. Times,* Oct. 10, 1958; JPK compares JFK to movie stars: Martin and Plaut, *op. cit.,* p. 461.

Chapter 11. CHANGE

JFK and American Farm Bureau Federation: John Osborne, "The Economics of the Candidates," *Fortune,* October 1960; JFK's article in *Life:* "A Democrat Says Party Must Lead, Or Get Left," Mar. 11, 1957; Drew Pearson on JFK's growth line: "Kennedy's Record Shows Courage," *Washington Post,* Apr. 8, 1960; quotations from Arthur Schlesinger Jr.: *Kennedy or Nixon: Does It Make Any Difference?;* Joan Younger interview with JFK: "Jack Kennedy, Democratic Dynamo," *Ladies' Home Journal,*

March 1960; Henry Brandon interview with JFK: "Challenger for the White House," *London Sunday Times,* July 3, 1960; Robert Hartmann's interview with JFK: "Kennedy Faces Many Problems," *Los Angeles Times,* Feb. 29, 1960; columnist Thomas O'Neill on JFK's 40th birthday: "Happy Birthday," *Baltimore Sun,* May 29, 1957.

JFK's refusal to be labeled liberal or conservative: *Time,* Dec. 2, 1957; JFK's torrid love affair with Dixie: "Not Our Boy," *Charleston* (S.C.) *News and Courier,* Oct. 21, 1957; Raymond Moley on JFK's ADA record: "A Look into Future of Sen. Kennedy," *Chicago Daily News,* July 18, 1957; Burns on JFK's liberalism: James MacGregor Burns, *John Kennedy: A Political Profile,* p. 267; JFK on his liberalism: Irwin Ross, "Sen. Kennedy," *New York Post* series, July 30, 1956; letter to the editor of *N.Y. Herald Tribune:* "Kennedy's Rising Star," from Robert W. Elbers, Mar. 26, 1957; conservative applause for JFK: Russell Turner, "Senator Kennedy, the Perfect Politician," *American Mercury,* March 1957; Douglass Cater on JFK's review of book: "The Cool Eye of John F. Kennedy," *Reporter,* Dec. 10, 1959; JFK's 1957 visit to Lincoln, Neb.: "Kennedy Visit Could Aid Political Future," *Lincoln Sunday Journal & Star,* May 19, 1957.

Chapter 12. WHY

Fletcher Knebel on "mystery": "He's Hottest Runner on the Political Track," *Des Moines Register,* May 6, 1957; Robert Spivack on JFK's lack of legislative achievements: "Nixon Takes Over, Is This Their Best?" *Nation,* Aug. 6, 1960; Rowland Evans Jr. on JFK rise: "The Kennedy Buildup," *N.Y. Herald Tribune,* Aug. 9, 1959; JFK's "warm image": Harold H. Martin, "The Amazing Kennedys," *Saturday Evening Post,* Sept. 7, 1957; Max Lerner on JFK cold and calculating: "The Cold Fish," *N.Y. Post,* Apr. 13, 1960; Burns on JFK casual as cash register: James MacGregor Burns, *John Kennedy: A Political Profile,* p. 261; *Ladies' Home Journal* quotation: Joan Younger, "Jack Kennedy, Democratic Dynamo," March 1960; Douglass Cater quotation: "The Cool Eye of John F. Kennedy," *Reporter,* Dec. 10, 1959; Burns on JFK unemotional: J. M. Burns, *op. cit.,* p. 263.

JFK on Nixon: Irwin Ross, "Sen. Kennedy," *New York Post* series, Aug. 1, 1956; Reston on JFK's contrived casualness: "Kennedy Looks to 1960," *N.Y. Times,* Oct. 10, 1958; *Newsweek* on streak of vanity: "A Closer Look at Kennedy," July 4, 1960; Martin and Plaut on JFK's age: Ralph Martin and Ed Plaut, *Front Runner, Dark Horse,* p. 471; Wechsler comment on JFK: *Reflections of an Angry Middle-Aged Editor* (New York, Random House, 1959), p. 35; JFK's barber on his haircut: "Cutting the Biggest Crop in Politics," *Newsweek,* June 23, 1958; JFK's reply to youthfulness charge: Charles Bartlett, "Kennedy, A Lack of Years," *Richmond Times-Dispatch,* June 12, 1960; Jacqueline a political asset?: Martin and Plaut, *op. cit.,* p. 471; JFK running early and hard: Alan L. Otten, "Front Runner for Democratic Presidential Nomination Finds He Has Problems Aplenty," *Wall Street Journal,* Sept. 22, 1958; Jacqueline on JFK in hurry: Roger Greene (AP), "Many Favor Kennedy for President," *Providence Journal,* Nov. 10, 1957; Robert Hartmann on Jackie: "Kennedy Faces Many Problems," *Los Angeles Times,* Feb. 29, 1960.

Selig Harrison on JPK: "Kennedy as President," *New Republic,* June 27, 1960; Chalmers Roberts on JPK: "Kennedy's Family Proves a Problem," *Washington Post,* Mar. 13, 1960; James Farley on JPK: *Quadrant* (Australia), Winter 1960; money no problem for JFK: Joan Younger, *op. cit.;* Jack Anderson and Fred Blumenthal, "Washington Brother Act," *Parade,* Apr. 28, 1957; Irwin Ross, *op. cit.,* July 30–Aug. 1, 1956; Eleanor Harris, "The Senator Is in a Hurry," *McCall's,* August 1957; Paul Healy and Tom Allen, "A Lot of Kennedys to Beat," *N.Y. News,* July 10, 1960; court condemnation of JPK real-estate deal: "Kennedy Kin to Get Title I $2.4 Million," *N.Y. World-Telegram & Sun,* Nov. 12, 1959; further background, Gene Gleason, "Kennedy Building Now Condemned by U.S. in Lincoln Square 'Comedy of Errors,'" *N.Y. World-Telegram & Sun,* Aug. 18, 1958.

Drew Pearson's conversation with JFK on JPK: *Newark Star Ledger,* Apr. 6, 1960; Henry Brandon's conversation with JFK on father: "Challenger for the White House," *London Sunday Times,* July 3, 1960; Hartmann: *op. cit.;* Konrad Kellen on JFK as "synthetic" man: "Democratic Party Parade," *New Leader,* Mar. 7, 1960; JFK's honorary degree at Harvard: J.

M. Burns, *op. cit.,* pp. 191–192; Mary Handy, "Scholarly Links to Politics Urged," *Christian Science Monitor,* June 14, 1956; JFK's *Life* article: "A Democrat Says Party Must Lead, Or Get Left," Mar. 11, 1957; *New York Post* criticism: editorial, "The Age of Discretion," Mar. 10, 1957.

Chapter 13.   MAC

Main general sources on Senator Joseph McCarthy: W. F. Buckley Jr. and L. Brent Bozell, *McCarthy and His Enemies* (Chicago, Regnery, 1954); Richard H. Rovere, *Senator Joe McCarthy* (New York, Harcourt, Brace, 1959); James MacGregor Burns, *John Kennedy: A Political Profile,* pp. 131–155; Ralph Martin and Ed Plaut, *Front Runner, Dark Horse,* pp. 202–208; Murray Kempton on JFK's moral failure: "The Keynoter," *N.Y. Post,* Jan. 24, 1956; Schlesinger's denunciation of JFK's critics: letter column, *New Republic,* July 27, 1959; *Kennedy or Nixon: Does It Make Any Difference?;* Robert Bendiner, "News from Our Own Correspondents," *New Statesman,* Apr. 16, 1960; Reston's interview with Schlesinger: *N.Y. Times,* Mar. 11, 1960; account of Nixon's 1950 campaign against Helen Gahagan Douglas: Earl Mazo, *Richard Nixon* (New York, Harper, 1959), pp. 71–83.

JFK's attitude toward Hoffa: Douglass Cater, "The Cool Eye of John F. Kennedy," *Reporter,* Dec. 10, 1959; Nixon phobia: Konrad Kellen, "Democratic Party Parade," *New Leader,* Mar. 7, 1960; liberal appeal for Nixon: Harold G. Tipton, *One Liberal's Answer: Nix on Kennedy* (Seattle, 1960); Pegler on JFK's "McCarthyism": "McCarthy Incident Dims Kennedy Valor," *San Diego Union,* Nov. 28, 1960; Bobby's relations with McCarthy: Robert E. Thompson and Hortense Myers, *Robert F. Kennedy: The Brother Within* (New York, Macmillan, 1962), pp. 98–122; Holmes Alexander, "A Sordid Side of the Cuban Disaster," *New Haven Register,* Mar. 13, 1961; for RFK's continuing "McCarthyism": Gore Vidal, "The Best Man 1968," *Esquire,* March 1963; JPK on Sen. McCarthy: Irwin Ross, "Joseph P. Kennedy, The True Story," *N.Y. Post* series, Jan. 9, 1961; political scientist: J. M. Burns, *op. cit.,* pp. 133–134; JFK on McCarthy: Irwin Ross, "Sen.

Kennedy," *N.Y. Post* series, July 30, 1956; Robert Bendiner, *op. cit.*

Ronald May's quotation: "Liberals Weigh Kennedy Record on McCarthyism," *York* (Pa.) *Gazette and Daily,* Feb. 16, 1960; *Boston Post* editorial: J. M. Burns, *op. cit.,* p. 143; JFK letters to constituents: J. M. Burns, *op. cit.,* pp. 139–140; JFK to newsmen on Congressional investigations: W. E. Mullins, *Boston Herald,* Mar. 19, 1954; JFK's position on Army-McCarthy hearings: AP dispatch from Boise, Idaho, *Boston Herald,* Apr. 4, 1954; liberal legislation outlawing Communist party: *Congressional Record,* Aug. 12, 1954, p. 14210; *Reporter,* Oct. 21, 1954, p. 19; *New Republic* editorial, Aug. 30, 1954; James E. Roper, *Washington Star,* Aug. 26, 1954; C. P. Ives, *Baltimore Sun,* Aug. 23, 1954; *Los Angeles Times* editorial, Aug. 21, 1954; *Labor Action,* Sept. 6, 1954, p. 3; "ACLU Raps Communist Curb," *N.Y. Post,* Nov. 15, 1954; Alistair Cooke, Manchester *Guardian,* Sept. 13, 1954; *Boston Herald* editorial, republished *N.Y. Times,* Aug. 21, 1954.

JFK on Annie Lee Moss case: *Congressional Record,* Aug. 2, 1954, p. 12962; Peter Edson column: *N.Y. World-Telegram & Sun,* Jan. 8, 1960; Gardner Jackson's reply: letter to *Washington Daily News,* Jan. 13, 1960; *Profiles in Courage* ghostwritten?: Martin and Plaut, *op. cit.,* pp. 199–202; JFK at National Book Awards ceremonies: Murray Kempton, *N.Y. Post,* Jan. 24, 1956; JFK interviewed by Chet Huntley: NBC–TV, "The Campaign and the Candidates," Oct. 1, 1960, *The Joint Appearances of Senator John F. Kennedy and Vice President Richard M. Nixon, Presidential Campaign 1960,* p. 122; JFK's "hara-kiri" remark: Irwin Ross, "Sen. Kennedy," *N.Y. Post,* July 30, 1956; Martin Agronsky interview with JFK in November 1957: transcript; Walter Cronkite interview with JFK: CBS–TV, "Presidential Countdown," Sept. 19, 1960, *The Joint Appearances of Senator John F. Kennedy and Vice President Richard M. Nixon, Presidential Campaign 1960,* p. 57; Mrs. Roosevelt's attitude toward JFK: Martin and Plaut, *op. cit.,* pp. 74–75; J. M. Burns, *op. cit.,* p. 153; Eleanor Roosevelt, *On My Own* (New York, Harper, 1958), pp. 163–164; Alfred Steinberg, *Mrs. R: The Life of Eleanor Roosevelt* (New York, Putnam, 1958), p. 343; Joe McCarthy, *The Remarkable Kennedys,* pp. 166–170;

Fletcher Knebel in *Candidates 1960,* pp. 204–205.

JFK's undelivered speech of July 1954: Douglass Cater, *op. cit.;* J. M. Burns, *op. cit.,* pp. 145–147; Martin and Plaut, *op. cit.,* pp. 204–205; Gardner Jackson's retort: *Washington Daily News, op. cit.;* JFK's not being perfect: Martin and Plaut, *op. cit.,* p. 202; JFK's review of Rovere book on McCarthy: *Washington Post,* June 28, 1959, p. E6; critic's letter in *The Tablet,* Aug. 8, 1959; Bazy McCormick Tankersley, *Chicago Tribune,* July 11, 1959; *Boston Globe* episode: Douglass Cater, *op. cit.; Chicago Tribune* editorial: July 2, 1959; Mrs. Roosevelt's 1958 statement: Fletcher Knebel in *Candidates 1960,* p. 204; JFK's leaving hearing room: Joe McCarthy, *op. cit.,* pp. 171–172; JFK's reply to Mrs. Roosevelt on McCarthyism: J. M. Burns, *op. cit.,* p. 154; Selig Harrison comment: "Kennedy as President," *New Republic,* June 27, 1960; Westbrook Pegler on JFK's moral courage: "McCarthy Incident Dims Kennedy Valor," *San Diego Union,* Mar. 28, 1960.

Chapter 14.   COURAGE

Admiral Strauss episode: *Chicago Tribune* editorial, July 2, 1959; JFK at Jewish Theological Seminary dinner: *N.Y. Times,* Nov. 24, 1958; JFK's 1957 views on civil rights: "A Democrat Says the Party Must Lead, or Get Left," *Life,* Mar. 11, 1957; Holmes Alexander, "Senate Civil Rights Vote Record Shows Kennedy Held to Principle," *Los Angeles Times,* Sept. 7, 1960; JFK's later views on civil rights: James MacGregor Burns, *John Kennedy: A Political Profile,* pp. 200–205; Ralph Martin and Ed Plaut, *Front Runner, Dark Horse,* pp. 197–198.

Legislative and parliamentary background of 1957 civil-rights battle: H. E. Shuman, "Senate Rules and the Civil Rights Bill," *American Political Science Review,* December 1957, pp. 955–975; JFK on bypassing Eastland Committee: *Congressional Record,* June 20, 1957, pp. 9793, 9805, 9815; JFK speech endorsing Section 3: *Congressional Record,* July 23, 1957, pp. 12467–12468; vote recorded: *ibid.,* p. 12565; JFK defense of his vote on jury-trial amendment: *Congressional Record,* Aug. 1, 1957, pp. 13305–13307; legislative history of Civil Rights Bill: Douglass Cater, "The Senate Debate on Civil Rights," *Reporter,* Aug. 8, 1957, and "How the Senate Passed the Civil Rights Bill," *Reporter,* Sept. 5, 1957; political implications for JFK: David Lawrence, "The Rights Bill Controversy," *Washington Star,* July 18, 1957; Tom Stokes, "Rights Bill Puts Strain on Presidential Hopefuls," *Newark Evening News,* July 23, 1957; Fletcher Knebel, "Presidency Seen as Rights Forum," *Minneapolis Tribune,* Sept. 27, 1960.

Lawson episode: letter to author by late Louis Lautier, Feb. 6, 1962; *N.Y. Post* editorial criticizing JFK: "The Voices of Caution," Nov. 16, 1958; Governor Patterson's endorsement of JFK: AP dispatch from Birmingham, Ala., *Washington Star,* June 17, 1959; Doris Fleeson, "Southern Support for Kennedy," *Washington Star,* June 19, 1959; Adam Clayton Powell on Patterson endorsement: "Powell Fights Kennedy in '60," *Washington Star,* June 30, 1959; 1960 Southern filibuster: Russell Baker, "Candidates Shun Filibuster Calls, Of 18 Eary Morning Quorum Bells, Kennedy Met None, Others Few, Johnson All," *N.Y. Times,* Mar. 10, 1960; *Time,* Mar. 14, 1960.

Jackie Robinson on JFK: (preference for Humphrey in primary) *N.Y. Post,* Apr. 8, 1960; "Letters to the Editor: Senator Kennedy Replies," *N.Y. Post,* June 3, 1960; Jackie Robinson column, *ibid.;* "Jackie Robinson Supports Nixon," *Indianapolis Star,* Oct. 31, 1960; JFK's secret meeting with Harlem Democrats: Douglas Dales, "Sees Opposition by Negro Voters," *N.Y. Times,* July 14, 1960; Bobby' civil-rights beliefs: Stan Opotowsky, *The Kennedy Government* (New York, Dutton, 1961), p. 59; Murray Kempton's on-the-scene report: "The Uncommitted," *Progressive,* September 1960; incipient revolt of Michigan Negroes: *Time,* July 4, 1960; Philip Potter, "Kennedy Gets a Rights Quiz," *Baltimore Sun,* June 21, 1960; Elie Abel, "Kennedy Seeks Strong Plank on Civil Rights," *Detroit News,* June 21, 1960; P. L. Prattis interview with JFK: "The Courier Questions a Presidential Hopeful, Sen. John Fitzgerald Kennedy," *Pittsburgh Courier,* June 25, 1960; Chuck Stone editorial comments: "Sen. Kennedy's Not a Friend of the Negro," *N.Y. Citizen Call,* June 12, 1960.

Chapter 15. LABOR

Holmes Alexander comment: "Search for Leadership," *St. Louis Globe-Demo-*

crat, Sept. 9, 1960; JFK's absenteeism: Walter Trohan, "Report from Washington," *Chicago Tribune,* Jan. 10, 1962; principal sources: James MacGregor Burns, *John Kennedy: A Political Profile,* pp. 224–229; Fletcher Knebel, *Candidates 1960,* pp. 206–207; Robert F. Kennedy, *The Enemy Within* (New York, Harper, 1960); Robert E. Thompson and Hortense Myers, *Robert F. Kennedy: The Brother Within* (New York, Macmillian, 1962); "Analysis of the Labor-Management Reporting and Disclosure Act of 1959," *Congressional Record,* Sept. 14, 1959, memorandum placed by Senator Barry Goldwater.

JFK's address to Oregon State AFL–CIO convention, text for delivery at Seaside, Ore., Aug. 3, 1959; "The Kennedy Record," *St. Louis Post-Dispatch,* Aug. 17, 1959; "The Low Down on the Kennedy Bill," National Republican Congressional Committee pamphlet, 1959; "Is Reuther 'Immune'?" *Newsweek,* Feb. 22, 1960, p. 27; "A Candidate and a Labor Bill," *Newsweek,* Sept. 7, 1959, p. 31; "That Kennedy 'Bribe,' " *Newsweek,* Mar. 16, 1959; "Labor Rackets—A Senate Feud?" *Newsweek,* July 22, 1957; "Where Bob Kennedy Misled His Hearers," *Chicago Tribune* editorial, July 24, 1959; Robert E. Baskin, "Senator Kennedy, Hoffa Stage Sizzling Clash," *Dallas News,* June 27, 1959; other backgrounders: Wilmot Hercher, "Meany and Kennedy Clash on Union Curbs," *Washington Post,* Mar. 28, 1958; Stanley Levey, "Unionist Attacks 'Friends' of Labor," *N.Y. Times,* Apr. 20, 1958; "Kennedy Looks at Labor Law," *Dallas News* editorial, June 7, 1958; John Van Camp, "What Happened to the Labor-Reform Bill?" *Reporter,* Oct. 2, 1958; Clark Mollenhoff, "What Kennedy Fans . . . ," *Des Moines Register,* Mar. 29, 1959.

Frederic W. Collins, "Timber!! (Presidential)," *Nation,* Apr. 4, 1959; Holmes Alexander, "Labor Influence on Sen. Kennedy Puts Him on Embarrassing Spot," *Los Angeles Times,* Apr. 13, 1959; "Not Slave-Labor," *Baltimore Sun* editorial, Apr. 20, 1959; John Herling, "How Kennedy Triumphed," *Washington News,* Apr. 28, 1959; "Jack Kennedy's Lession," *Indianapolis News* editorial, Aug. 7, 1959; George Minot, "Labor Bill Big Challenge," *Boston Herald,* Aug. 23, 1959; "Sen. Kennedy Polishes the Apple," *Chicago Tribune,* editorial, Oct. 14, 1959; Raymond Moley, "An Assessment of Kennedy,"

Chicago Daily News, Oct. 19, 1959; "Kennedy on All Sides of Labor Law, GOP Says," *Los Angeles Times,* Oct. 22, 1959; "A Johnson Letter Embitters Labor," *N.Y. Times,* Jan. 6, 1960; Alistair Cooke, "Unkindest Cut of All for the Democrats," Manchester *Guardian,* Jan. 21, 1960; J. F. Ter Horst, "GOP Senators See Kennedy, Reuther Pact," *New Hampshire Sunday News,* Jan. 24, 1960.

"Kennedy Defends Brother in Face of GOP Criticism," *Baltimore Sun,* Feb. 17, 1960; Everett S. Allen, "Goldwater Fights Labor 'Bossism,'" *New Bedford Standard Times,* Mar. 17, 1960; Fulton Lewis Jr., "Kennedy Suspected of Committee Report 'Leaks,'" *Cincinnati Enquirer,* Mar. 18, 1960; Antony Mazzolini, "Hoffa Ouster Seen by Robert Kennedy," *Cleveland Press,* Apr. 8, 1960; Westbrook Pegler, "Kennedy Alliance Shames the Nation," *San Diego Union,* Apr. 15, 1960; N. R. Howard, "Kennedy Is Tagged Darling of Unions," *Cleveland Plain Dealer,* July 3, 1960; Victor Riesel, "Hoffa Taunts Kennedy," *N.Y. Mirror,* July 8, 1960; Westbrook Pegler, "Kennedys Spared Reuther, Dubinsky," *N.Y. Journal-American,* July 18, 1960; "Forgotten Man," *Chicago Tribune* editorial, July 20, 1960; Westbrook Pegler, "Did Kennedy Bros. Protect Reuther?" *N.Y. Journal-American,* July 27, 1960; "Kennedy Strives to Pay Union Bosses for Support," *Chicago Daily News* editorial, Aug. 17, 1960; "Jack's Their Boy," *Chicago Tribune* editorial, Aug. 30, 1960; Fletcher Knebel, "The Candidates' Record: Labor Legislation Votes Reflect Kennedy-Nixon Difference," *Minneapolis Tribune,* Sept. 25, 1960; "Kennedy's Labor Record," Republican National Committee, Sept. 30, 1960; George Meany, "Meany, Kennedy Discuss the 1960 Election Issues," *AFL–CIO News,* Oct. 1, 1960; Shaw Livermore, "Goldwater and the Union Boss," *New Republic,* Apr. 17, 1961; Bobby's role: Alexander Bickel, "The Case Against Him for Attorney General," *New Republic,* Jan. 9, 1961.

Chapter 16.   GALL

Galbraith on buildup: *The Liberal Hour* (Boston, Houghton Mifflin, 1960), pp. 114–118; Drew Pearson on JFK buildup: *Washington Post,* Apr. 8, 1960; JFK's "independence" of church in public affairs: Douglass Cater, "The Cool Eye of John F. Kennedy," *Reporter,* Dec. 10, 1959; Liberal party assignment of Niebuhr to question JFK: private source; *New Republic* editorial: "Protestants in Politics," Sept. 19, 1960; "Kennedy for President? A Catholic Priest Says No!" Rev. Juniper B. Carol, *Human Events,* June 2, 1960; religious issue: Fletcher Knebel, "A Catholic in 1960," *Look,* Mar. 3, 1959; John Wicklein, "Catholic Censure of Kennedy Rises," *N.Y. Times,* Mar. 1, 1959; "Cushing Backs Kennedy on Church-State Replies," *N.Y. Herald Tribune,* Mar. 10, 1959; JFK Notre Dame speech in 1950: James MacGregor Burns, *John Kennedy: A Political Profile,* p. 242.

Background on four-chaplains episode: James A. Pike, *A Roman Catholic in the White House* (Garden City, Doubleday, 1960); Dr. Daniel A. Poling, *Mine Eyes Have Seen* (New York, McGraw-Hill, 1959); *U.S. News & World Report,* Dec. 21, 1959, pp. 64–65; "Kennedy Gives Version of Interfaith Incident," *Washington Star,* Jan. 15, 1960; Irwin Ross on JFK and religion: "Sen. Kennedy," *N.Y. Post* series, Aug. 1, 1956; Hoyt article: "Kennedy, Catholicism and the Presidency," *Jubilee,* December 1960; Henry Brandon interview with JFK: "Challenger for the White House," *London Sunday Times,* July 3, 1960; *London Observer* quotation: July 17, 1960; *New Republic* editorial: "Kennedy's Reform," Mar. 2, 1959; JFK's loyalty-oath position: memorandum of National Student Committee for the Loyalty Oath, Feb. 4, 1960; J. M. Burns, *op. cit.,* p. 268; Carl Sandburg quote: Bob Thomas, "Candidates Feel Sting of Sandburg 'Evening,'" *Washington Star,* Mar. 7, 1960; JFK's controversy with head of Bar Association: John Herling, "Kennedy Demand for Action Against Corrupt Lawyers Hit by Bar Head," *Washington Daily News,* Feb. 25, 1958; JFK article, "Union Racketeering: The Responsibility of the Bar," *American Bar Association Journal,* May 1958, reprinted in *Congressional Record,* May 12, 1958, pp. A4324–A4325.

JFK's position on Algeria (1957): J. M. Burns, *op. cit.,* pp. 195–196, 198; John F. Kennedy, *The Strategy of Peace* (New York, Harper, 1960), pp. 65–81, 111, 214; Patrick O'Donovan: reprinted from *London Observer* in *Cincinnati Enquirer,* "Kennedy Seeks Presidency, Capital Denizens Believe," July 16, 1957; Selig Harrison, "Kennedy as President," *New*

Republic, June 27, 1960; Rowland Evans Jr., "Kennedy Bids U.S. Act for Algerian Freedom, Dulles Is Wary, Sees Paris Envoy," *N.Y. Herald Tribune*, July 3, 1957; "Eisenhower Wary on Algeria Policy, U.S. Is Trying to Be Fair and Decent, He Asserts—Paris Reaction Sharp," *N.Y. Times*, July 4, 1957; "Mr. Kennedy on Algeria," *N.Y. Times* editorial, July 3, 1957; "Sen. Kennedy Forgot About Statesmanship," *Providence Journal* editorial, July 5, 1957; Ruth Montgomery, "Kennedy's Speech Has GOP Hopping," *N.Y. Journal-American*, July 5, 1957; "Kennedy on Algeria," *N.Y. World-Telegram & Sun* editorial, July 6, 1957; "Don't Look Now, but Is Kennedy's Hat in Ring?" *San Francisco Chronicle*, July 9, 1957; "Who Could Be Parties to Parley on Algeria?" *Washington Star*, July 18, 1957; "Senator Kennedy's Resolution," *Nation*, July 20, 1957; "Vive La France!" *New Bedford Standard-Times* editorial, July 29, 1957; "Adlai Opposes Algerian Freedom Now," *Washington Post*, July 28, 1957; "No Panacea for Algeria," *Washington Post* editorial, Aug. 1, 1957.

French reaction to JFK's Algeria speech: Volney D. Hurd, "Kennedy Speech Jars Paris," *Christian Science Monitor*, July 3, 1957; Frank Kelley, "Kennedy Talk on Algeria Stirs Protests in France," *Washington Post-Herald*, July 4, 1957; "French Hit at Kennedy on Algeria," *Detroit News*, July 5, 1957; Edmond Taylor, "French Charge That Kennedy Is Adding Fuel to Blaze," *Montreal Star*, July 22, 1957; "Kennedy Eyes Tour of Algeria," *Washington Post-Herald*, July 19, 1957; Robert LaCoste statement: interview by author, December 1957 in Algiers; Homer Bigart, "LaCoste Rejects Algeria Criticism," *N.Y. Times*, July 8, 1957; Frank Kelley, "Kennedy Criticized in Algeria, France's Chief There Hits Back," *N.Y. Herald Tribune*, July 8, 1957; Henry Giniger, "Coty Reaffirms Stand on Algeria, Talk Barring Independence Is Held Reply to Kennedy and Other Critics Abroad," *N.Y. Times*, July 10, 1957; "Kennedy Urged to Visit Algeria to See 'Realities,'" *Washington Star*, July 8, 1957; British correspondent who reminded JFK in June 1960 of his Algerian speech was Henry Brandon: *op. cit.*; account of JFK's telephone conversation with father: *Time*, Dec. 2, 1957; Alistair Cooke remark: "Senator Kennedy Looks Ahead," Manchester *Guardian*, July 7, 1957.

JFK reference to French bomb: J. F. Kennedy, *The Strategy of Peace, op. cit.*,

p. 100; background on Indochina: Selig Harrison, *op. cit.*; John Robinson Beal, *John Foster Dulles: A Biography* (New York, Harper, 1957), pp. 204–218; J. F. Kennedy, *The Strategy of Peace, op. cit.*, pp. 37, 43, 57–61, 72, 184, 194, 211; Earl Mazo, *Richard Nixon, op. cit.*, pp. 255–256; Thomas E. Dewey, *Journey to the Far Pacific*; JFK speeches on Indochina: "The War in Indochina," delivered in U.S. Senate, Apr. 6, 1954, republished *Vital Speeches*, May 1, 1954, pp. 418–424; "The Situation in Indochina," speech before the Executives' Club of Chicago, May 28, 1954, republished *Congressional Record*, June 3, 1954, pp. A4144–A4145; "America's Stake in Vietnam," speech before American Friends of Vietnam, Washington, D.C., June 1, 1956, reprinted *Vital Speeches*, Aug. 1, 1956, pp. 617–619; Bobby's speech on Soviet trip at Notre Dame Alumni Assoc.: "How to Prod Russians to Service," *N.Y. News*, Dec. 12, 1955.

JFK's interest in India: Selig Harrison, *op. cit.*; J. F. Kennedy, *The Strategy of Peace*, pp. 141–158; JFK's *Foreign Affairs* article: "A Democrat Looks at Foreign Policy," October 1957; JFK's relations with Committee of One Million: private sources; John Chamberlin article: "The Chameleon Image of John F. Kennedy," *National Review*, Apr. 23, 1960; JFK's description of self as "vigorous liberal": Murray Seeger, "Kennedy Assumes Mantle of Liberal," *Cleveland Plain Dealer*, July 29, 1959; JFK's joining Democratic Advisory Council: Robert Baskin, "Senators Named to Party Council," *Dallas News*, Nov. 12, 1959; Policy Statement, Democratic Advisory Council Meeting, Dec. 5–7, 1959; William Henry Chamberlain, "Democrats' Dud," *Wall Street Journal*, Dec. 17, 1959; study of JFK's voting record prepared by David S. Broder: *Washington Star*, Apr. 10, 1960.

Life quotation on liberalism: "A President for the '60's," editorial, Oct. 17, 1960; JFK's egghead recruitment: Bill Henry, "Kennedy Drive Well Organized," *Los Angeles Times*, Jan. 5, 1960; "Kennedy Speaks to Broadcasters," *Baltimore Sun*, Mar. 7, 1958; Thomas Winship, "Kennedy Moves to Organize Campus Braintrust," *Boston Globe*, Dec. 13, 1959; Joseph A. Loftus, "Diverse Staffs Assist Kennedy," *N.Y. Times*, Feb. 8, 1960; "Trio of Professors Swings to Kennedy," *Christian Science Monitor*, June 8, 1960;

"Text of Letter to Liberals," *N.Y. Times,* June 17, 1960; Galbraith: Henry Hazlitt letter, *Wall Street Journal,* Nov. 2, 1961; Raymond Moley, "Does Harvard Favor Republicans?" *Chicago Daily News,* Mar. 24, 1960; "Schlesinger, Galbraith Say Harvard Favors GOP on Honorary Degrees," *Washington Post,* Dec. 9, 1959; "If There's Another 'New Deal'—What It's To Be Like," *U.S. News & World Report,* Aug. 8, 1960, pp. 71–73; *Richmond News Leader* editorial, Sept. 6, 1960; Hugh A. Mulligan, "The Harvard Brain-Truster as a Politician," *Washington Star,* Oct. 16, 1960; George Minot, "How the Democrats Hope to Win," *Boston Herald,* Aug. 14, 1960; David McCord Wright, "What Galbraith Says, He Might Do," *National Review,* Aug. 13, 1960; JFK on De Gaulle's rhetoric: William Manchester, "John F. Kennedy, Portrait of a President," *Holiday,* May 1962; Arthur Schlesinger Jr.: Norman Mailer, *Esquire,* Nov. 1960, p. 75; Irwin Ross, "Arthur Schlesinger Jr.," *N.Y. Post* series, Apr. 3–7, 1961; JFK's allergy to dogs: Martin and Plaut, *op. cit.,* p. 164.

Chapter 17. ROAD

General sources on primaries: N.Y. Times, N.Y. Herald Tribune, Time, Newsweek, U.S. News & World Report, N.Y. Journal-American, Milwaukee Journal, London Economist, N.Y. Post, Boston Globe, Baltimore Sun, Washington Star, Washington Post, Los Angeles Times, Charleston Gazette, Capital Times (Madison, Wis.), Christian Science Monitor, Morgantown Post; Martin and Plaut, *op. cit.,* pp. 209–250.

JFK profile: T. H. White on killer instinct and worst damned way: "Perspective/1960," *Saturday Review,* Mar. 26, 1960; London *Economist* profile: Dec. 12, 1959, p. 1067–1068; Max Lerner "cold fish" quotation: *N.Y. Post,* Apr. 13, 1960; Robert Novak piece: "Senator Adds Up to a 'Liberal' Who Is Unemotional, Partisan, Somewhat Ruthless," *Wall Street Journal,* Apr. 7, 1960; Goldwater on Kennedys' gall and money: Westbrook Pegler, *N.Y. Journal-American,* June 10, 1960; JFK's peeve at Ike: "A Closer Look at Kennedy," *Newsweek,* July 4, 1960, p. 20; Rowland Evans Jr. on JFK's reading: *N.Y. Herald Tribune,* Aug. 9, 1959; Norman Mailer interview with JFK: *Esquire,* Nov. 1960; JFK on all those jobs have

to be done by humans: *Newsweek,* June 23, 1958, p. 33; comments on National Press Club speech on Jan. 14, 1960: *Washington Star,* Jan. 15, 1960; *Richmond Times-Dispatch,* Jan. 18, 1960; Reston on JFK in age of television: *N.Y. Times,* Aug. 18, 1958; Gore Vidal on politicians must be actors: "A Liberal Meets Mr. Conservative (Goldwater)," *Life,* June 9, 1961; W. S. White on publicity and send all the bills to daddy: *Des Moines Register,* May 13, 1958.

1958 campaign: Alcorn on JFK: Edward Kernan, "Jack Faces a Beanstalk of Opposition, Alcorn and Mrs. Roosevelt Rap Kennedy," *Cleveland Plain Dealer,* Apr. 13, 1958; Cabell Phillips on JFK: "How to Be a Presidential Candidate," *N.Y. Times Magazine,* July 13, 1958; *Boston Globe's* C. R. Owens quotation: *Washington Post-Herald,* Aug. 18, 1958; Gould Lincoln on conservative support: *Washington Star,* Aug. 10, 1958; backgrounders: Tom Henshaw, AP, Oct. 26, 1958; Robert S. Bird, "Kennedy's Hopes at Stake," *N.Y. Herald Tribune,* Oct. 31, 1958; Walter T. Ridder, "Apathy in Massachusetts," *San Jose Mercury-News,* Oct. 19, 1958.

Eleanor Roosevelt: Eleanor on JFK's charm and money: ABC-TV, "College News Conference," Dec. 7, 1958; Fletcher Knebel, *Candidates 1960,* pp. 204–205; "Mrs. Roosevelt Lauds Humphrey," *N.Y. Times,* Dec. 8, 1958.

Politician: Julius Duscha remarks: "Summitry and the 1960 Hopefuls," *New Leader,* Sept. 21, 1959; *Providence Journal* editorial: Feb. 15, 1960; JPK remark on only issue is can a Catholic be elected: Andrew Tully, *N.Y. World-Telegram & Sun,* Apr. 7, 1960; Bill Henry on spending: *Los Angeles Times,* Jan. 5, 1960.

Organization: JPK on organizations: Martin and Plaut, *op. cit.,* p. 463; organization meeting: T. H. White, *The Making of the President 1960,* pp. 49–58; *Time,* Feb. 15, 1960; open-dated checks: Selig Harrison, *New Republic,* June 27, 1960; money: Douglass Cater, *Reporter,* Aug. 4, 1960; James Reston, *N.Y. Times,* Apr. 8, 1960; Ralph McGill, "Kennedy Reaches Grass Roots," *Washington Star,* May 7, 1960; stewardess Janet des Rosiers: *Washington Post,* Dec. 21, 1960; Martin and Plaut, *op. cit.,* p. 215; Marquis Childs quotation: *N.Y. Post,* Jan. 14, 1960; Wayne Morse on White House not for sale and truth not in JFK: James MacNees, *Balti-*

more Sun, May 29, 1960; Rowland Evans Jr., "The Kennedy Camp" (series), *N.Y. Herald Tribune*, Apr. 7–12, 1960; Jerry Bennett, "Sen. Kennedy's Campaign Flies High in Plush Plane Family Presented to Him," *Harrisburg* (Ill.) *Daily Register*, Mar. 21, 1960; Cecil Holland, "Kennedy Drive Aided by Family and Experts," *Washington Star*, Feb. 23, 1960; Mary McGrory, "The Contenders," *N.Y. Post*, Feb. 16, 1960.

DiSalle and Brown: W. H. Hessler, "How Kennedy Took Ohio," *Reporter*, Mar. 3, 1960; Bruce Biossat, "How Kennedy Did It, DiSalle Declaration Provided Impetus," *Knickerbocker News*, July 20, 1960; Robert G. Spivack, "Kennedy Campaign Shifts into High," *N.Y. Post*, Feb. 9, 1960; James Reston, "400 Votes Counted by Kennedy Camp," *Providence Journal*, Jan. 6, 1960; Richard Wilson, "Ohio Support Is Big Boost for Kennedy," *Des Moines Register*, Jan. 6. 1960; "A Kingmaker's Hedge," *Newsweek*, May 16, 1960; Doris Fleeson, "Kennedy Bows Out of California," *Washington Star*, Mar. 3, 1960; Gould Lincoln, "Kennedy 'Blitz' Causes Resentment," *Washington Star*, Feb. 9, 1960; Drew Pearson, "Kennedy's Record Shows Courage," *Washington Post*, July 12, 1960.

Catholic support: Doris Fleeson, "Religion Useful in '56," *Charleston Gazette*, Apr. 28, 1960; *Time*, May 2, 1960; James Reston, *N.Y. Times*, Apr. 8, 1960.

Tactics: JFK spiritless rootless man: London *Economist*, Dec. 12, 1959; De Sapio on JFK outsmarting foes: Douglass Cater, *Reporter*, Aug. 4, 1960, p. 16; Johnson aide on JFK for VP: *Time*, Apr. 25, 1960; JFK on VP: private sources; Tawes: Charles G. Whiteford, "Kennedy's Whip-Cracking Pleases State's Delegation," *Baltimore Sun*, July 16, 1960; Bobby going to get Humphrey: Douglass Cater, "A Tide in the Affairs of JFK," *Reporter*, Aug. 4, 1960; Bobby's fight with CBS correspondent: Bob Williams, *N.Y. Post*, Dec. 20, 1960, and private sources; *Baltimore Sun* correspondent cut off: private sources; "Jack the Knife" nickname: *Economist*, Mar. 12, 1960, p. 990; Richard L. Strout, "Battle Lines in Wisconsin Drawn for Primary Vote," *Christian Science Monitor*, Mar. 26, 1960.

Wisconsin: polls: James Reston, "Tough State for Kennedy," *N.Y. Times*, Jan. 12, 1960; Nobuo Abiko, "Wisconsin Impact Tests Bay Stater," *Christian Science Monitor*, Jan. 14, 1960; "Brother Thinks Kennedy Should Stay Out of Wisconsin Primary," *N.Y. Post*, Jan. 14, 1960; Gerald Griffin, "Speculation Is Stirred Up by Kennedys," *Baltimore Sun*, Jan. 16, 1960; Joseph Alsop, "Kennedy Play for High Stakes in Wisconsin Primary," *San Diego Union*, Jan. 31, 1960; Gerald Griffin, "Kennedy May Avoid Primary in Wisconsin," *Baltimore Sun*, Jan. 15, 1960; William S. White, "Senator Kennedy Against Pack," *Washington Star*, Feb. 10, 1960; Earl Mazo, "Kennedy Sees Victory as 2 Primaries' Fruit, To Fight Humphrey in Wisconsin and W. Virginia, Poll Favors Him," *N.Y. Herald Tribune*, Mar. 18, 1960; Chalmers M. Roberts, "Bandwagon Psychology Is Being Developed by Kennedy," *Washington Post*, Mar. 16, 1960; Ramond Lahr, "Kennedy Polls Biased, Humphrey Backers Say," *Washington Post*, Mar. 20, 1960; "Magnetic Bandwagon?" *Time*, Mar. 7, 1960; Marquis Childs, "Sen. Humphrey vs. an 'Image,' " *Washington Post*, Mar. 23, 1960; Willard Edwards (*Chicago Tribune*), "Kennedy's Record Is Like Humphrey's," republished in *Human Events*, Mar. 10, 1960; Ron May, "To Buttress Argument, Political Polls Being Used in 'Numbers Game,' " *Madison Capital Times*, Mar. 14, 1960; Ralph Chapman, "'Polls' Use as 'Propaganda' Is Feared by Elmo Roper," *N.Y. Herald Tribune*, May 8, 1960; Marquis Childs, "Efficiency Experts," *N.Y. Post*, Apr. 5, 1960; Senator Young (Ohio) statements, *Congressional Record*, Mar. 16, 1962, p. 3986; "Public's Wisdom Hailed by Gallup," *N.Y. Times*, Feb. 19, 1962; "Politics and Pollsters," *Newsweek*, May 16, 1960; Murray Kempton on Kennedy boys engaging: *N.Y. Post*, Feb. 12, 1960; Bill Stringer on hard-core vote: *Christian Science Monitor:* Apr. 2, 1960; Howard Norton on 30,000 supporters: *Baltimore Sun*, Mar. 25, 1960.

Spending (Wisconsin): "Humphrey Cites Wealth of Kennedy, Says 'Rich Father' Aids Him," *N.Y. Herald Tribune*, Feb. 14, 1960; William R. Bechtel, "Spending for Kennedy Tops Humphrey Total," *Milwaukee Journal*, Mar. 30, 1960; W. R. Bechtel, "Campaign Accounting Stirs Kennedy Anger," *Milwaukee Journal*, Mar. 31, 1960; Walter Lister Jr., "2 Democrats File Expense in Wisconsin," *N.Y. Herald Tribune*, Mar. 31, 1960; Ellen Gibson, "Kennedy Greets 6,000; Foe Hits His Spending," *Milwaukee Journal*, Apr. 2, 1960; "Humphrey Hits Rival as 'Plush,' " *Washington*

Star, Apr. 2, 1960; Paul Martin, "Democrats Pour Money into Wisconsin Primary," *Knickerbocker News,* Apr. 4, 1960; *Milwaukee Journal* editorial, "Pledges to 'Tell All' About Election Costs Not Kept," Apr. 23, 1960.

Hoffa (Wisconsin): Austin C. Wehrwein, "Wisconsin Battle Is Growing Rough," *N.Y. Times,* Feb. 14, 1960; Mitchel Levitas, "Humphrey Denounces Story of Hoffa Link," *N.Y. Post,* Feb. 12, 1960; Robert E. Baskin, "Hectic Campaigns Leave Kennedy, Humphrey at Odds," *Dallas News,* Feb. 15, 1960; Robert D. Novak, "Kennedy and Humphrey, Like-Minded Though They May Be, Are Slugging Hard," *Wall Street Journal,* Mar. 9, 1960.

Glamour candidate: Humphrey on "Meet the Press": NBC–TV, April 3, 1960; Marquis Childs, *Washington Post,* Mar. 23, 1960; Austin C. Wehrwein, "Wisconsin Battle One of Contrasts," *N.Y. Times,* Feb. 21, 1960; James Reston on JFK like Eddie and Liz: *N.Y. Times,* Mar. 4, 1960; "How Humphrey, Kennedy Line Up in Wisconsin 'Beauty Contest,'" *Business Week,* Mar. 26, 1960; Robert D. Novak, "Kennedy the Glamorous Easterner Finds His Foe Is Humphrey the Hometown Boy," *Wall Street Journal,* Mar. 10, 1960.

Family: Rowland Evans Jr., "Friends, Family Run Machine," *N.Y. Herald Tribune,* Apr. 7, 1960; Edward Kernan, "Family-Style Campaign a Romp for Kennedy's High-Flying Crew," *Cleveland Plain Dealer,* Nov. 15, 1959; William S. White, "Family Campaign Strategy for '60," *Washington Star,* Mar. 4, 1960; "Where Campaigning Is a Family Affair," *U.S. News & World Report,* Mar. 14, 1960; Isabelle Shelton, "Seven Kennedys in Act, Mother to Make Eight," *Washington Star,* Feb. 26, 1960.

Bloodletting and smears in Wisconsin: JFK can't bleed like Hubert: *Time,* Feb. 29, 1960; debate: Damon Stetson, "Humphrey Urges Debate on Issues," *N.Y. Times,* Mar. 1, 1960; "Kennedy Refuses to Answer Back as Humphrey Raps Him," *Newark Star-Ledger,* Mar. 30, 1960; JFK public-relations blitz: "Humphrey Says Victory Is 'Sure,'" *N.Y. Times,* Mar. 26, 1960; heart: Ira Kapenstein, "Letter Read by Kennedy," *Milwaukee Journal,* Mar. 29, 1960; Kenneth E. Fry, "Humphrey Discusses Issues Facing US," *Milwaukee Journal,* Apr. 4, 1960; Mary McGrory, "Primary Battle Pits 'Greatness' vs. 'Heart,'" *Washington Star,* Apr. 1, 1960; issue of

issues: Mary McGrory, "Humphrey Welcomes Belated Attention," *Washington Star,* Mar. 26, 1960; Ira Kaperstein, "Humphrey Gain Seen in Vote Record Issue," *Milwaukee Journal,* Mar. 28, 1960; Damon Stetson, "Humphrey Sure Campaign Gains," *N.Y. Times,* Mar. 31, 1960; vote-stealing: Earl Mazo, "Humphrey Is Charged with Vote-Stealing," *N.Y. Herald Tribune,* Feb. 3, 1960; HH questions JFK's liberalism: Carroll Kilpatrick, "Humphrey Questions Kennedy's 'Liberalism,'" *Washington Post,* Feb. 29, 1960; press: Oliver Pilat, "Humphrey Charges Pro-Kennedy Bias in GOP's Press," *N.Y. Post,* Mar. 18, 1960; politics, not love: "Kennedy 'Stole' His Idea, Says Humphrey," *Newark Star-Ledger,* Mar. 22, 1960; JFK to avoid politician image according to Lou Harris: W. H. Lawrence, "Humphrey Scored on His New Tactic," *N.Y. Times,* Mar. 23, 1960; primaries important: Walter Lister Jr., "Kennedy Says Milwaukee Will Make Eye-Wash Famous," *N.Y. Herald Tribune,* Mar. 21, 1960; campaigning style: "The Front Runner," *Newsweek,* Mar. 28, 1960, p. 28; Bill Furlong, "Kennedy Shows Sense of Duty in Wisconsin Trek," *Chicago Daily News,* Mar. 14, 1960; Ira Kapenstein, "Humphrey Rally Sees Victory in the Primary," *Milwaukee Journal,* Mar. 25, 1960; Walter Lippmann, "Primary System Is Not Satisfactory," *Madison Capital Times,* Apr. 8, 1960; Stewart Alsop, "Kennedy vs. Humphrey, The Battle of Wisconsin," *Saturday Evening Post,* Apr. 2, 1960.

Farm: Humphrey pamphlet: "What YOU Have at Stake in Wisconsin's Presidential Primary, April 5"; Austin C. Wehrwein, "Humphrey Pleads for Farmer Vote," *N.Y. Times,* Feb. 16, 1960; John C. McDonald, "Wisconsin Hears Kennedy Explain Farm Prop Stand," *Minneapolis Tribune,* Feb. 17, 1960; *Providence Journal* editorial, "Kennedy Woos Wisconsin Falsely," Feb. 22, 1960; Damon Stetson, "Humphrey Train Without Its Star," *N.Y. Times,* Feb. 28, 1960; Walter Lister Jr., "Humphrey in Open Attack on Kennedy in Wisconsin," *N.Y. Herald Tribune,* Mar. 19, 1960; W. H. Lawrence, "Roosevelt Active in Kennedy Drive," and Donald Janson, "Humphrey Begins Farm-Vote Drive," *N.Y. Times,* Mar. 20, 1960; Loren H. Osman, "Humphrey Puts Foe in Class with GOP," *Milwaukee Journal,* Mar. 20, 1960; Gerald Griffin, "Kennedy Gets Support on Farm Issue," *Baltimore Sun,* Mar. 22, 1960; *Milwaukee Journal* editorial, "Is

Reading the Record Wrong?" Mar. 23, 1960; "Kennedy-Humphrey Farm Records Compared," *Congressional Quarterly,* Mar. 23, 1960; Drew Pearson, "Kennedy Explains His Farm Switch," *Washington Post,* Apr. 6, 1960.

Nixon: Howard Norton, "Kennedy Called 'Soft on Nixon,'" *Baltimore Sun,* Mar. 20, 1960; "J. P. Kennedy Link to Nixon Charged," *N.Y. Times,* Mar. 31, 1960; "Backed Nixon in '50?, Kennedy Sr. Is Silent," *N.Y. Post,* Mar. 31, 1960; "Kennedy Backers Deny His Father Gave Nixon Cash," *Stars and Stripes,* Apr. 2, 1960.

Religion (Wisconsin): Miles McMillin (*Madison Capital Times*), "The Primaries in Wisconsin: Land of the Free-for-All," *N.Y. Post,* Mar. 27, 1960; Robert Ajemian on Catholics for JFK: *Life,* Mar. 28, 1960; Marquis Childs on anti-Catholic literature: *N.Y. Post,* Mar. 28, 1960; *N.Y. Times* on Catholic Republicans crossing over: Donald Janson, "Religion Big Factor in Kennedy Victory," *N.Y. Times,* Apr. 5, 1960; Reston on JFK's benefiting from Catholic feeling of denial of a President: "Kennedy Advantages May Backfire on Him," *Milwaukee Journal,* April 8, 1960; backgrounders: Robert D. Novak, "Big GOP, Catholic Vote to Aid Kennedy in Wisconsin Primary," *Wall Street Journal,* Mar. 4, 1960; John F. Bridge, "The 'Catholic Issue,'" *Wall Street Journal,* Mar. 7, 1960; Richard Hofstadter, "Could a Protestant Have Beaten Hoover in 1928?" *Reporter,* Mar. 17, 1960; Richard L. Strout, "Wisconsin Polls Invite Crossover," *Christian Science Monitor,* Mar. 24, 1960; Don Janson, "Religion Growing as Primary Issue," *N.Y. Times,* Mar. 27, 1960; Ernest K. Lindley, "Kennedy's Big Asset," *Newsweek,* Mar. 21, 1960; "Will Not Accept Dictation, Says Kennedy of Religion," *Baltimore Sun,* Mar. 30, 1960; *Milwaukee Journal* editorial, "The Religious Issue," Mar. 31, 1960; "Religion Ad Sparks Primary Vote Issue," *Milwaukee Journal,* Apr. 1, 1960; "Ad Stirs Up Campaigners," *Baltimore Sun,* Apr. 1, 1960; Gould Lincoln, "Will Religious Issue Stop Kennedy?" *Washington Star,* Apr. 7, 1960; Joseph Alsop, "The Catholic Issue," *Washington Post,* Apr. 1, 1960; Walter Lister Jr., "Catholic Vote a Big Help for Kennedy," *N.Y. Herald Tribune,* Apr. 6, 1960; Lyle C. Wilson, "Stop-Kennedy Drive Is Up to 'Old Pros,'" UPI dispatch, Apr. 7, 1960; Carroll Kilpatrick, "Humphrey Says 1-Day Democrats Brought

Defeat in Wisconsin," *Washington Post,* Apr. 8, 1960.

West Virginia: Lou Harris on West Virginia: Earl Mazo, "Kennedy Sees Victory as 2 Primaries' Fruit," *N.Y. Herald Tribune,* Mar. 18, 1960; Marquis Childs on warm image: *N.Y. Post,* Mar. 28, 1960.

Religion (West Virginia): Douglass Cater quotation: "A Day in West Virginia," *Reporter,* May 12, 1960; Holmes Alexander quotations: "Nixon and Kennedy Have Their Say About Religion," *Morgantown Post,* Apr. 28, 1960; "This Campaign No Joy to West Virginia," *Indianapolis Star,* Apr. 28, 1960; L. T. Anderson, "Nation Misinformed About State," *Charleston Gazette,* May 12, 1960; W. E. Chilton III, "West Virginia and the Primary," *New Leader,* May 23, 1960; Humphrey calls on JFK to repudiate Alsop: Howard Norton, "West Virginians Still Uncertain," *Baltimore Sun,* Apr. 26, 1960; JFK's ASNE speech: full text, *U.S. News & World Report,* May 2, 1960, pp. 90–92; James Reston's comments, *N.Y. Times,* Apr. 22, 1960; *Milwaukee Journal* editorial, Apr. 22, 1960; John Wyngaard, "Kennedy, Critical of Press, Can Blame Himself," reprinted *Congressional Record,* May 9, 1960.

Underdoggery: Harold Lavine in *Newsweek,* May 2, 1960; Joseph Alsop, "Underdoggery," *N.Y. Herald Tribune,* Apr. 8, 1960; Howard Norton, "Speculation," *Baltimore Sun,* May 9, 1960; "Kennedy Role of Underdog Hit by Byrd," *Baltimore Sun,* Apr. 19, 1960; Charles Bartlett, "Democratic Opposition to Kennedy Is Active," *New Bedford Standard-Times,* Apr. 3, 1960; "Humphrey Insists He's an Underdog" (no little black bag and checkbook), *N.Y. Times,* Apr. 27, 1960; "Humphrey, in Coal Fields Tour, Feels Like 'Triumphant Caesar,'" *N.Y. Times,* Apr. 12, 1960; "Humphrey's Plaint Again: Rival's Rich," *N.Y. Herald Tribune,* Apr. 27, 1960.

FDR Jr. on Humphrey: Bob Considine on PT-109 film: *N.Y. Journal-American,* May 5, 1960; W. H. Lawrence, "Roosevelt Spurs Kennedy's Hopes," *N.Y. Times,* Apr. 29, 1960; *Washington Star* editorial, "Very Dirty Politics," Apr. 28, 1960; Rowland Evans Jr., "Roosevelt Jr. Revives Humphrey War Record," *N.Y. Herald Tribune,* May 7, 1960; W. H. Lawrence, "Roosevelt Hits Humphrey," *N.Y. Times,* May 7, 1960; Joseph A. Loftus, "Kennedy Is Firm on Oath of Office". (HH running against son of Joe who was foe of FDR), N.Y. Times, May 9, 1960; Wayne Phillips, "Assails Roosevelt Jr.," N.Y. Times, May 9, 1960; Frank Conniff, "FDR Jr. Slap at Humphrey Has Kennedy Pals Squirming," N.Y. Journal-American, May 7, 1960; Philip Potter, "Kennedy Assails Roosevelt on War Records Discussion," Baltimore Sun, May 7, 1960; Washington Star editorial, "Still Dirty Politics," May 8, 1960; Murray Kempton, "The Kid," N.Y. Post, May 12, 1960; Doris Fleeson, "Kennedy Collects W. Va. Dividends," Chicago Daily News, May 14, 1960; Cecil Holland, "Apology Sent to Humphrey by Roosevelt," Washington Star, June 22, 1960; high and low road: Mary McGrory, "With All Guns Fired, Humphrey Is Bitter," Washington Star, May 8, 1960.

Hoffa (West Virginia): Richard J. H. Johnston, "Invective Traded in West Virginia, Humphrey Answers Robert Kennedy Who Charges Distortion of Record," N.Y. Times, May 1, 1960; "Hube Pans 'Panicky' Jack in W. Va.," N.Y. News, May 1, 1960; Howard Norton, "Kennedy Backed for No. 2 Spot," Baltimore Sun, May 3, 1960; Rowland Evans Jr., "Hoffa Named by Kennedy in W. Virginia, 'Ordered' Teamster Support of Humphrey," N.Y. Herald Tribune, May 6, 1960.

Spending (West Virginia): W. H. Lawrence, "Humphrey Cites Wealth of Foes," N.Y. Times, Apr. 26, 1960; Howard Norton, "Ubiquitous Kennedy Ads Dog Humphrey Campaign," Baltimore Sun, May 6, 1960; teacher's pet and million to win election: Mary McGrory, "Feud in the Hills," N.Y. Post, May 9, 1960; "Kennedy Says Smears Used by Humphrey, Washington Star, Apr. 30, 1960; Schlesinger's letter: Irwin Ross, N.Y. Post, Apr. 3-7, 1961.

West Virginia backgrounders: debate: Frank Conniff, "West Virginia Has Only Underdogs!" N.Y. Journal-American, May 7, 1960, and Mary McGrory, "Kennedy, Humphrey Put on Brother Act," Washington Star, May 5, 1960; radio spots: Philip Potter, "Kennedy Victory Is Seen in W. Va.," Baltimore Sun, May 8, 1960; Hyoobert: Howard Norton, "W. Va. Dinner to Hear Talk by Johnson," Baltimore Sun, May 7, 1960; Smith and $1 bills: Edward F. Woods, "How Much Did Kennedy Spend on His Campaign?" St. Louis Post-Dispatch, Aug. 7, 1960; Bobby buried religious issue in W. Va.: Dorothy McCardle, Washington Post, May 16, 1960; vote buy-

ing: Howard Norton, "West Virginia County Machines Helped Swell Vote for Kennedy in Primary," Baltimore Sun, May 13, 1960, and Time, June 6, 1960; JFK on use of FBI: Newsweek, June 6, 1960; Charles Bartlett, "Scramble Is On to Sink Kennedy," Richmond Times-Dispatch, May 29, 1960; Paul Duke, Wall Street Journal, May 12, 1960; Pearson story on FBI: "Here's Top Banana in Tax Bonanza," Washington Post, Aug. 9, 1960; vote fraud indictments: "Indict 5 More in W. Va. Ballot Probe," Chicago Tribune, Nov. 24, 1960.

Potential Vice Presidents: Powell remark: Alice Dunnigan, "Washington Inside Out," Pittsburgh Courier, July 7, 1960; Mary McGrory, "Ticket Pairing Kennedy and Humphrey Studied, Two Confer at Bostonian's Urging, Roosevelt Apology Seen Significant," Washington Star, June 26, 1960; Hartmann remark, "Kennedy's Chances Given New Boost," Los Angeles Times, May 15, 1960; Andrew Tully, "Humphrey Courts Kennedy," N.Y. World-Telegram & Sun, July 2, 1960; Joseph Alsop, "The North and South of It," Washington Post, July 6, 1960; Time, May 23, 1960; David Wise, "Kennedy's Bid Refused by Meyner," N.Y. Herald Tribune, June 28, 1960, and Time, Dec. 15, 1961; JPK visit to O'Connell: George Dixon, "Kennedys May Ignore This Advice," Washington Post, Mar. 22, 1960, and Human Events, Mar. 31, 1960.

Rat Pack: Dorothy Kilgallen, "A Bow to Kennedy Pere," N.Y. Journal-American, Apr. 11, 1960; Murray Schumach, "Sinatra Defying Writer Blacklist," N.Y. Times, Mar. 21, 1960; ad, "A Statement of Fact from Frank Sinatra," N.Y. Times, Mar. 29, 1960; Dorothy Kilgallen, N.Y. Journal-American, Apr. 13, 1960; Tom Allen, "Kooks, Maybe, But No Clucks in Sinatra 'Clan,'" N.Y. News, Aug. 14, 1960; Richard Gehman, Sinatra and His Rat Pack (New York, Belmont, 1961); Don Dwiggins, Hollywood's Loveable Rogue Frankie (New York, Paperback Library, 1961).

Chapter 18.   CON

General sources: same as previous chapter; author present at Democratic Convention in Los Angeles; Carey McWilliams in Nation: "The Kennedys Take Over," July 23, 1960, pp. 43-45; Bobby on young group: Ralph de Toledano, "Kennedy Prepares for Main Event," July 15, 1960; Lyndon Johnson (LBJ): *Time,* July 18, 1960; *Newsweek,* Mar. 14, 1960; John Chamberlain, "LBJ: Least Popular with the USSR," *National Review,* July 2, 1960; Robert L. Riggs, "The South Could Rise Again," *Candidates 1960,* pp. 280–321; JFK on U-2 episode: *Time,* June 13, 1960; Murray Kempton, "The Team?" *N.Y. Post,* May 26, 1960; *Oregonian* editorial, "How Would Jack Do It?" Sept. 22, 1960; Garroway show: text, NBC-TV, Jan. 7, 1960; Selig Harrison article: "Kennedy as President," *New Republic,* June 27, 1960; LBJ not going to apologize: Earl Mazo, "Johnson Warns Party Against Summit Politics," *Washington Post,* May 28, 1960; *Time,* June 13, 1960; Mary McGrory, "No Regrets," *N.Y. Post,* June 1, 1960; Democratic Advisory Council statement: text, *N.Y. Times,* May 23, 1960; Democratic Convention brochure 1960; Fred Farris, "Pro and Con Continue on Summit Failure," *N.Y. Herald Tribune,* May 23, 1960; *Economist* on JFK communing with polltakers: May 28, 1960, p. 863; Fitchburg speech on federal vs. local: "Kennedy Praises Community Spirit," *Boston Herald,* Oct. 16, 1957; JFK on Khrushchev visit: "Kennedy Raps US A-Policy," *Washington Star,* Aug. 2, 1959; "Khrushchev's Goals Won, Kennedy Says," *Washington Post,* Oct. 16, 1959; "Summit Talk Success Doubted by Kennedy," *Washington Post,* Dec. 3, 1959; Univ. of Rochester speech: John F. Kennedy, *The Strategy of Peace,* pp. 8–14; *Washington Star* editorial: "Attacking with Caution," Oct. 4, 1959; Nixon's "kitchen debate": *The Speeches of Senator John F. Kennedy, Presidential Campaign 1960* (Washington, U.S. Government Printing Office, 1961), pp. 13, 43; Spokane speech: "What Candidates Shouldn't Say," *Life,* Feb. 22, 1960.

Presidential indecision and bipartisanship: text, speech before California Democratic Councils Convention, Fresno, Feb. 12, 1960; West Berlin: Kenneth E. Fry, "Berlin Is Worth Risk of War, Kennedy Says," *Milwaukee Journal,* Aug. 1, 1959; sputnik: "Kennedy Will Fight Tax Hike," *Boston Herald,* Jan. 17, 1958; Calais speech and discussion by Capehart and Symington: *Congressional Record,* Aug. 14, 1958, pp. 16207–16213; our crumbling defenses: text, Roosevelt Birthday Ball, Salt Lake City, Jan. 30, 1960; missile gap: "National Defense," *Congressional Record,* Feb. 29, 1960, pp. 3580–3587; "Kennedy Raps Complacency on U.S. Missiles Program," AP dispatch from Topeka, Kan., Nov. 6, 1959; New Jersey speech on images and bipartisanship: Joseph H. Miller, "Sen. Kennedy Warns Against Delegation of Presidential Powers," *Philadelphia Inquirer,* June 22, 1960; book on U-2: David Wise and Thomas B. Ross, *The U-2 Affair* (New York, Random House, 1962); JFK on Nixon's "kitchen debate": *The Speeches of Senator John F. Kennedy, Presidential Campaign 1960,* p. 43; JFK on disarmament: text, Univ. of Wisconsin speech, Mar. 25, 1960; JFK opposition to Rockefeller call for nuclear testing: Gerald Griffin, "Kennedy Hits Rockefeller on His Nuclear Stand," *Baltimore Sun,* Nov. 3, 1959; Chalmers Roberts, "Kennedy Takes Rockefeller to Task for Backing of Underground A-Tests," *Washington Post,* Nov. 3, 1959; images: *Time,* July 11, 1960, p. 18; Bowles appointed foreign-policy adviser: "Scratch My Back," *Washington Post* editorial, Jan. 27, 1960; William V. Shannon, "No Sale," *N.Y. Post,* Feb. 11, 1960; Earl Mazo, "Boomlet for Bowles in California," *N.Y. Herald Tribune,* Feb. 17, 1960; Drew Pearson, *Washington Post,* Apr. 6, 1960.

Stevenson-Kennedy ticket: *N.Y. Post* editorial, June 29, 1960; Eleanor Roosevelt: June 13, 1960, reprinted *Congressional Record,* June 16, 1960, pp. A5118–A5119; Mrs. Roosevelt, "Bosses Ruled," *Spokesman Review,* July 15, 1960; May Craig, "Mrs. Roosevelt Got Right to the Point," *Portland Press Herald,* June 22, 1960; Goldberg: Victor Riesel, "Kennedy Woos Liberal Party," *Knickerbocker News,* June 24, 1960; N.Y. Liberal Party and JFK relations with South: Leo Egan, "Kennedy Assures Liberals He Seeks No Help in South," *N.Y. Times,* June 24, 1960; Frank van der Linden: "Kennedy May Be Writing Off South in His Nomination Bid," *Richmond Times-Dispatch,* June 26, 1960; Kennedy letter to Southern delegates: "Letters from Kennedy Seek Support from Southern States' Delegates," *Washington Post,* June 28, 1960; Oscar Chapman statement: Walter C. Hornaday, "Johnson's Camp Ired at Kennedy," *Dallas News,* June 25, 1960; Bobby's meeting with Sanford: Drew Pearson, "Kennedy Forces Made Deals Early," *Washington Post,* July 13, 1960; Frank van der Linden, "Kennedy Opens Southern Vote Drive," *Richmond Times-Dispatch,* June 19, 1960; Philip Potter, "Kennedy," *Baltimore Sun,* July 9, 1960; *Atlanta Constitution* editorial: "Kennedy's Comment Is Rather Disappointing," June 25, 1960; Governors' conference uproar: W. H. Lawrence, "Kennedy Appeals to South to Support His Nomination," *N.Y. Times,* June 28, 1960; *Wall Street Journal* on Ribicoff's statement: "Below the Potomac, East of the Hudson," June 29, 1960; Johnson distribution of Scott letter: Robert D. Novak, "Key Theme of Johnson Presidential Drive: 'Kennedy Can't Win,' " *Wall Street Journal,* July 1, 1960; Senator Hugh Scott's "Dear Jack" letter: " 'If You Have Time, Drop In.' A Senator Invites Kennedy," *N.Y. Herald Tribune,* June 20, 1960; June 29 Senate exchanges on JFK absences: "Senate Disputes Kennedy Absence," *San Diego Union,* June 30, 1960; Johnson announcement: text, *N.Y. Times,* July 6, 1960; "Senator Johnson in Race as 'Working' Leader," *Chicago Tribune,* July 6, 1960; Joan Younger quotation: "Jack Kennedy, Democratic Dynamo," *Ladies' Home Journal,* March 1960; Arvey on JFK had country laid out like switchboard: *Time,* July 4, 1960; NANA correspondent on expense accounts: "How Kennedy Organized for 1960," *San Francisco Chronicle,* July 14, 1960.

Truman "Are you ready?" press conference: *Newsweek,* July 11, 1960, pp. 23–24; "The Monkey Wrench," *Chicago Tribune* editorial, July 3, 1960; Reston comment on Truman: "The Tragedy and Consequences of Harry's 'Last Hurrah,' " *N.Y. Times,* July 3, 1960; complaints about Butler: Robert G. Spivack, "Humphrey Demands Butler Resign," *N.Y. Post,* Mar. 16, 1960; "Convention Not Rigged Says Butler, Renews Truman Invitation," *Washington Post,*. July 1, 1960; *Washington Star* editorial, "Other Complaints," July 1, 1960; "Mrs. Edwards Cites Butler Staff Memo," *N.Y. Times,* July 2, 1960; "Johnson Assails Chairman Butler," *Baltimore Sun,* July 4, 1960; "Smathers Calls It Butler's 'Get-Even,' " AP dispatch, July 4, 1960; Robert G. Spivack, "Adlai Aides Charge Sniping by Butler," *N.Y. Post,* July 6, 1960; JFK rebuttal to Truman: text, Statement of Sen. John F. Kennedy, TV-Radio-News Conference, July 4, 1960, Hotel Roosevelt, New York; *N.Y. Herald Tribune* editorial: "It Depends on Who Does the Rigging," July 6, 1960; *Wall Street Journal* editorial: "The Ages of Man," July 6, 1960.

John Connally and India Edwards on JFK's health: Philip Potter, "Reference to Addison's Disease Made, Senator Challenged to Prove Condition Is Better than Texan's," *Baltimore Sun,* July 5, 1960; Bobby's reaction: W. H. Lawrence, "Johnson Backers Urge Health Test," *N.Y. Times,* July 5, 1960; Charles G. Whiteford, "Kennedy Health Held 'Excellent,' " *Baltimore Sun,* July 5, 1960; Philip Potter, "Health Issue Seen Quieted," *Baltimore Sun,* July 6, 1960; Cecil Holland, "Kennedy Backers Blast Issue About His Health," *Washington Star,* July 5, 1960; "Candidates' Health? Let's Check Them," *Newark Star-Ledger,* July 6, 1960; *Time* statement on Addison's disease: July 18, 1960, p. 12; James MacGregor Burns reference: Burns, *op. cit.,* p. 159; Symington supporter comment: David Wise, "Now It Seems Democrat Race Is to the Healthiest," *N.Y. Herald Tribune,* July 6, 1960; Dr. Travell's post-Vienna meeting statement: "Excerpts from News Conference by President's Physician," *N.Y. Times,* June 23, 1961; "More on the State of Kennedy's Health," *U.S. News & World Report,* July 24, 1961, pp. 60–61; Judd statement: press release, Nov. 5, 1960.

Johnson and Rayburn announce recess: Chalmers Roberts, "Kennedy Faces Two Big Problems: August Session and Sen. Johnson," *Washington Post,* July 11, 1960; *Newsweek,* July 11, 1960; "Johnson Charges Smear Campaign, Tells Senate of Innuendoes and McCarthyism," *Baltimore Sun,* July 1, 1960; Forest Davis, "Latest Parlor Game: Recessmanship," *Cincinnati Enquirer,* July 5, 1960; Johnson moving westward: Gerald Griffin, "Texan Calls 2d Place on Ticket Good Spot for Front Candidate," *Baltimore Sun,* July 9, 1960; "Johnson Echoes Hints of Rigging," *N.Y. Times,* July 8, 1960; Adam Clayton Powell statement: "Harlem Leader Talks to Kennedy," *N.Y. Times,* July 8, 1960; Anthony Lewis, "Kennedy Pledges to Stand Firm in Support of Negroes' Rights," *N.Y. Times,* July 2, 1960; Doris Fleeson on Johnson: "Kennedy-Johnson Tilt Fails to Alter Picture," *Los Angeles Examiner,* July 14, 1960; Johnson vs. ADA: "Transcript of Johnson's News Conference on His Presidential Candidacy," *N.Y. Times,* July 6, 1960; "Johnson Charges Smear Campaign," *Baltimore Sun,* July 1, 1960; Johnson arrival: "Johnson Fights Kennedy Tide," *Cincinnati Enquirer,* July 11, 1960; Rowland Evans Jr., "Kennedy Camp Attacks 'Vicious' Says Johnson," *N.Y. Herald Tribune,* July 9, 1960; Mort Sahl on candidates arriving: Irv Kupcinet, "Kup's Column," *Chicago Sun-Times,* July 13, 1960; Edward T. Folliard on Machiavelli strategy: "Kennedy Team Shifts with Tide," *Washington Post,* July 7, 1960; Dixie handled by Troutman: Drew Pearson, "Kennedy System, A New Deal in Politics," *Miami Herald,* July 13, 1960; Sen. Eastland on JFK: private sources; John C. O'Brien on JFK's operation: "Kennedy 'Snows' Delegates with Free Service, Favors," *Philadelphia Inquirer,* July 12, 1960; Art Hoppe on coffee machine: "Smooth Kennedy Machine Rolls On," *San Francisco Chronicle,* July 9, 1960; Gladwin Hill on money's-no-object: "Notes from Convention Land: Badges Are Offered in All Sizes," *N.Y. Times,* July 8, 1960; Bobby directing operation: Charles Cleveland, "How Kennedy Won the Nod," *Chicago Daily News,* July 14, 1960; "Kennedy in the Saddle," *Economist,* July 23, 1960; *Newsweek,* July 18, 1960; *Time,* July 18, 1960; Bobby on Connally amendment: Morrie Ryskind, "The Rover Boys in Los Angeles," *National Review,* July 30, 1960; delegate file box: Rowland Evans Jr., "Kennedy Organization Was Decisive Weapon," *N.Y. Herald Tribune,* July 20, 1960; Bobby as "Raul": Holmes Alexander, "Can Kennedy Rise to Greatness Despite His Mediocre Record?" *Los Angeles Times,* Sept. 9, 1960; *Newsweek,* Nov. 21, 1960, p. 33; Bobby as Sioux: Joseph Alsop, "Kennedy Clan Tough Fighters," *San Diego Union,* July 19, 1960; Joseph Alsop, "The Young Pros," *N.Y. Herald Tribune,* July 11, 1960; Bobby likes to win: Stewart Alsop, "Kennedy's Magic Formula," *Saturday Evening Post,* Aug. 13, 1960; Jim Bishop on Bobby and his serfs: "Irritating Man Named Bobby," *Longview Daily News,* Oct. 25, 1960; Bobby dressed down staff: private sources, and Irwin Ross interview with Bobby, *N.Y. Post,* Oct. 4, 1960.

Kennedy arrival and gray-hair statement: *Time,* July 18, 1960; JFK visit to Lawrence: *Time,* July 18, 1960; Convention activities: Murray Kempton, "Jack Kennedy's Long Day," *N.Y. Post,* July 11, 1960; *Time,* July 25, 1960; James Reston, "Democrats in Doubt," *N.Y. Times,* July 12, 1960; *Dallas News* on farm weakness: "John F. Kennedy, Democrat," July 15, 1960; Hawaiians call on JFK, discuss McCarthy: Jim Bishop, "The Day Kennedy Was Nominated," *Los Angeles Examiner,* July 14, 1960; JPK at Marion Davies mansion: J. F. Ter Horst, " 'Joe' Kennedy Is Out of Sight, Not Mind," *Washington Star,* July 12, 1960; Edward B. Simmons, "Eloquent Silence Kept by Joseph P. Ken-

nedy," *New Bedford Standard-Times,* July 15, 1960; Ruth Montgomery, "His Papa Joe Knew Best," *N.Y. Journal-American,* July 13, 1960; Rayburn on JPK in bushes: "Kennedy Sr. Gets Mention," *N.Y. News,* July 17, 1960; JFK's secret apartment: Robert K. Walsh, "Kennedy Drive Is Pushed in Final Day," *Washington Star,* July 15, 1960; Sidney Skolsky, "Then, Darkness," *N.Y. Post,* July 17, 1960; "Penthouse Is Close to Hollywood," *Baltimore Sun,* July 14, 1960; JFK not exuding confidence: *Time,* July 25, 1960, p. 15; Janet Leigh on JFK's dancing: "Movie Star Says Jack Is 'Wonderful Dancer,' " UPI, July 11, 1960; Sinatra: Drew Pearson, "Vice Presidential Hassle Under Way," *Los Angeles Mirror News,* July 14, 1960; *Time,* July 25, 1960; Sammy Davis booed: "Sammy Near Tears over Demo Boos," *Long Beach Independent,* July 12, 1960; "Delegates Boo Negro," *N.Y. Times,* July 12, 1960; Sen. Church's speech: Alistair Cooke, "Democratic Convention Comes to Life," *Manchester Guardian,* July 13, 1960; William V. Shannon, "The Orator," *N.Y. Post,* July 11, 1960; "Keynoter Is Wide of Mark in Piling Blame on GOP," *Chicago Daily News* editorial, July 12, 1960; Gore Vidal's party: Andrew Tully, "Democrats Had a Grand Old Party with Stars in Dizzyland," *N.Y. World Telegram & Sun,* July 16, 1960; Robert Bendiner, "Personal Impressions," *Reporter,* Aug. 4, 1960.

Schlesinger agonizing: Irwin Ross series, *N.Y. Post,* Apr. 3–7, 1961; Galbraith effective worker: Drew Pearson, "Washington Merry-Go-Round," *Newark Star-Ledger,* July 20, 1960; Bobby on Stevenson's "beatnik" supporters: private sources; Bobby called "brash young man" by *N.Y. Times:* editorial, "Still Smoke Filled," July 9, 1960; Minnesota's traditional emotional outpouring: William Broom, "Brown Misses Kennedy Boat," *Long Beach Independent,* July 12, 1960; "Humphrey . . . Calls His Choice Best Qualified," *N.Y. Times,* July 14, 1960; Drew Pearson, "Labor Had Role in Kennedy Choice," *Washington Post,* July 19, 1960; JFK remark about Humphrey after HH announced for Adlai: Philip Potter, "Kennedy," *Baltimore Sun,* July 14, 1960; Bobby on Stevenson's indecisiveness: *ibid.;* Hollings called JFK to go down to debate LBJ: *Time,* July 25, 1960; debate: "Excerpts from Debate by Johnson and Kennedy Before Texas Delegation," *N.Y. Times,* July 13, 1960; Murray Kempton, "Big Daddy," *N.Y. Post,* July 13, 1960;

Time, July 25, 1960; Alexander F. Jones, *Syracuse Herald-Journal* on delegate apathy: "Johnson Sharp, Kennedy Smooth But Debate Changed No Votes," July 13, 1960; Price Day on JFK machine: "Just Before the Battle," *Baltimore Sun,* July 11, 1960.

William S. White on cold fixed order: "Convention Lacks Drama," *N.Y. Journal-American,* July 13, 1960; DiSalle on Stevenson's appearance: "Stevenson Wins Double Triumph," *N.Y. Times,* July 13, 1960; Mrs. Roosevelt's comments: Eugene Patterson, "Kennedy Power Is Cracking, Foes Say in Last Minute Push," *Atlanta Constitution,* July 14, 1960; Eleanor Roosevelt, "Active in '56, '60 Campaigns Despite Vows to Stay Out," *N.Y. World-Telegram & Sun,* Nov. 30, 1961; Lawrence E. Davies, "Mrs. Roosevelt Notes Issue of Religion," *N.Y. Times,* July 12, 1960; Johnson's attacks on JFK: John D. Morris, "Johnson's Attacks on Kennedy Range from McCarthy to Hitler," *N.Y. Times,* July 14, 1960; Marvin Sleeper, "Johnson Says N.Y. 'Stacked Cards,' " *N.Y. Journal-American,* July 12, 1960; Henry L. Trewhitt, "Texan Levels Criticism at His Chief Foe, Hits Wealth, Voting Record and Father's Views," *Baltimore Sun,* July 14, 1960; Frank Hughes, "Lyndon Rips Kennedy for Arrogance," *Chicago Tribune,* July 8, 1960; Kennedy setup at Convention hall: Charles Cleveland, "Bobby Keeps Tab on Jack's Victory," *Chicago Daily News,* July 14, 1960; *Chicago Tribune's* George Tagge on Butler message to Daley: "Spy-Proof Net of Phones Has a Victory Role," *Chicago Tribune,* July 15, 1960; Lehman's fight for standard: "Lehman, 82, Has to Fight to Get Standard in Parade," *N.Y. Herald Tribune,* July 14, 1960; "Lehman Wins Banner Tug-of-War," *N.Y. Post,* July 14, 1960; Bobby's call to JFK—"We're in": *Time,* July 25, 1960; JFK's afternoon with father: Earl Wilson, *Los Angeles Mirror-News,* July 15, 1960; JFK visits William Gargan: James Bacon, "Kennedy Mystery Flight Before Voting Unsolved," *Washington Post,* July 19, 1960; Sidney Skolsky, "Then, Darkness," *N.Y. Post,* July 17, 1960.

Sen. Olin Johnston's effort to correct record: "Which Leadership?" (Columbia, S.C.) *State* editorial, Oct. 29, 1960; more on Olin: Harry Ashmore, "Johnson Just Wouldn't Believe the Evidence," *N.Y. Herald Tribune,* July 12, 1960; Stevenson suite: William V. Shannon, "Vigil in Room 620," *N.Y. Post,* July 14, 1960; Johnson

reaction: Allen Duckworth, "Johnson Pledges Support," *Dallas News,* July 14, 1960; Truman reaction: "Truman Has No Comment on Kennedy," *Los Angeles Times,* July 15, 1960; Bobby called father: *Time,* July 25, 1960; James Marlow (AP) on little emotion: "The Modern Touch," *N.Y. Post,* July 14, 1960; Doris Fleeson on "hand, not heart": "Kennedy-Johnson Tilt Fails to Alter Picture," *Los Angeles Examiner,* July 14, 1960; *Washington Post* on triumph of organization: July 15, 1960; *Economist* questions JFK's ability to conduct foreign policy: "Ritual at Los Angeles," July 16, 1960; Lehman remark to Buckley on "greatest calamity": Tom O'Hara, "Offbeat N.Y. Politics," *N.Y. Herald Tribune,* June 18, 1961; Rose Kennedy on every mother thinks of baby as President: Ruth Montgomery, "Jack's Mother: 'My Son Was Born to Be President,' " *San Francisco Examiner,* July 12, 1960.

JFK angry with Stevenson: Howard Norton, "No Answer on Request Irks Nominee," *Baltimore Sun,* July 15, 1960; Farley's reaction to LBJ for VP: *Newsweek,* July 25, 1960; "Soapy" assured Michigan it would not be LBJ: Earl Mazo, " 'Dear Jack' Wire Gained Second Spot for Johnson," *N.Y. Herald Tribune,* July 16, 1960; California lady to McCormack: *Time,* July 25, 1960, p. 18; "I'm sick"— Schlesinger: *Newsweek,* July 25, 1960; "I'm shocked"—Nathan of ADA: Claude Sitton, "Johnson Choice Hailed by South," *N.Y. Times,* July 15, 1960; Burns—"Blurs the picture": Mary McGrory, "Johnson Opponents United in Dismay," *Washington Star,* July 15, 1960; Mrs. Soapy Williams turned in her buttons: *Time,* July 25, 1960, p. 18; Dixie delegates wore "All the way with LBJ" buttons: Alan L. Otten, "Democrats Must Pacify Unions, Negroes, Avoid Alienating the South," *Wall Street Journal,* July 18, 1960; platform: Stan Opotowsky, "Kennedy, Johnson Say They'll Stick to the Liberal Platform," *N.Y. Post,* July 17, 1960; *Life* editorial, "The New Democrats," July 25, 1960; Norman Thomas on "utopian" platform: "Candidates and Issues," *New America,* Sept. 5, 1960; platform perfect setup for JFK: Vermont Royster, "The New Radicalism," *Wall Street Journal,* July 15, 1960; JFK's two views on platform: "Battle Gives Kennedy View on Platform," *Washington Star,* July 14, 1960.

JPK had long wanted JFK-LBJ ticket: Rowland Evans Jr., "In '58 Johnson Rejected the Ticket," *N.Y. Herald Tribune,* July 15, 1960; Earl Mazo, " 'Dear Jack' Wire Gained Second Spot for Johnson," *N.Y. Herald Tribune,* July 16, 1960; Allen-Scott, "Story Behind Johnson Decision," *San Diego Union,* July 21, 1960; JFK offered LBJ second spot: Sam Rayburn, "Speaker Speaks of Presidents," *N.Y. Times Magazine,* June 4, 1961; William McGaffin and Charles Cleveland, "Why Kennedy Picked Johnson for Ticket," *Chicago Daily News,* July 15, 1960; Robert Thompson and Paul Healy, "Kennedy to Plug at One Big Issue: Its Name Is Nixon," *N.Y. News,* July 17, 1960; Philip Potter, "Party Chief Bid to Texan Irks Rayburn," *Baltimore Sun,* July 15, 1960; Max Lerner's reaction: "The Angle," *N.Y. Post,* July 15, 1960; *New York Post* editorial: July 15, 1960; *St. Louis Post-Dispatch* reaction: July 15, 1960; George Meany passed Harriman at hotel: Alan L. Otten, "Democrats Must Pacify Unions, Negroes, Avoid Alienating the South," *Wall Street Journal,* July 18, 1960; Rev. John Wesley (Negro) on choice: Claude Sitton, "Johnson Choice Hailed by South," *N.Y. Times,* July 15, 1960; Harold Tipton reaction: *One Liberal's Answer, Nix on Kennedy* (Seattle, 1960); Lt. Gov. Phileo Nash of Minnesota: Mary McGrory, "Johnson Opponents United in Dismay," *Washington Star,* July 15, 1960; Bobby unhappy: "Kennedy Picks Johnson to Woo South and West," *Wall Street Journal,* July 15, 1960; Joe Rauh on TV: Murray Kempton, "The Morning After," *N.Y. Post,* July 15, 1960; Robert Spivack in *Nation:* "Nixon Takes Over, Is This Their Best?" *Nation,* Aug. 6, 1960; *Nashville Banner* on Bowles statement: "Mr. Bowles' 'Explanation' Doesn't Explain," July 19, 1960; David Lawrence quote of Johnson supporter: "Report Johnson Accepted to Ride Herd on Kennedy," *N.Y. Herald Tribune,* July 20, 1960.

Johnson nominated by "acclamation": Robert Bendiner, "Personal Impressions," *Reporter,* Aug. 4, 1960; Soapy Williams and Joe Rauh yell NO: Peter Lisagor, "Demo Gulp, Then Swallow Kennedy-Johnson Ticket," *Chicago Daily News,* July 15, 1960; Grace Bassett, "Angry District Delegates Protest Johnson Choice for Party Ticket," *Washington Star,* July 15, 1960; *Time* (also photo), July 25, 1960, p. 16; *Christian Science Monitor* reaction to acceptance speech and platform: July 18,

1960; *Economist* on speech: Sept. 17, 1960, p. 1079; Nixon's reaction: private sources; JPK in NY with Luce: "Kennedy's Father Explains Absence," *N.Y. Journal-American,* Aug. 3, 1960; "All Kennedys Present Except Senator's Father," *Washington Star,* July 16, 1960; Randolph Churchill's remark: "British View of U.S. Politics," Hearst Headline Service, July 20, 1960; Murray Kempton remark: "A New Leader of the Clan," *N.Y. Post,* July 17, 1960; Mort Sahl telegram: UPI dispatch, July 16, 1960.

Chapter 19. CAMP

James Reston on doubt in every mind: quoted by Richard F. Pourade, "Where, Oh Where Has He Gone," *San Diego Union,* Aug. 28, 1960; Edward R. Murrow on JFK: "Ed Murrow's Size-Up of Candidate Kennedy," *U.S. News & World Report,* Aug. 1, 1960, p. 10; Joseph Barry on year no one would vote: "GOP-Dixiecrat Alliance Thwarts Liberal Hopes," *New America,* Sept. 5, 1960; Liberals disgruntled: Oliver Pilat, "Kennedy Keys Drive to Liberalism," *N.Y. Post,* Sept. 15, 1960; Jackie Robinson on "loathsome" ticket: "GOP-Dixiecrat Alliance Thwarts Liberal Hopes," *New America,* Sept. 5, 1960; Stewart Alsop on liberals like Victorian lady: "Kennedy's Magic Formula," *Saturday Evening Post,* Aug. 13, 1960; James Jackson Kilpatrick on LBJ a "counterfeit confederate": *Human Events,* Aug. 25, 1960.

Gov. Vandiver on LBJ makes it palatable: *Newsweek,* Aug. 25, 1960; other Southern comment: "Southern Governors Debate Johnson Role," *Washington Star,* Sept. 26, 1960; Earl Mazo, "S.C. Governor Finds Latins for Kennedy," *N.Y. Herald Tribune,* Sept. 27, 1960; Johnson to see Leader at Hyannis: *Time,* Aug. 8, 1960, p. 17; *Newsweek,* Aug. 15, 1960; Frank Falacci, "All Roads Lead to Hyannis Port for Nation's Democratic VIP's," *Boston Globe,* Aug. 7, 1960; J. F. Ter Horst, "Boston Gets Look at Lodge, Johnson," *Detroit News,* Sept. 9, 1960; Reuther visit to Hyannis: W. H. Lawrence, "Reuther Praises Kennedy Ticket," *N.Y. Times,* Aug. 4, 1960; Murray Kempton, "Season in the Sun," *N.Y. Post,* Aug. 4, 1960; Soapy's visit to Hyannis: *National Review Bulletin,* Aug. 20, 1960; eggheads on Marlin: *Time,* Aug. 15, 1960; Kennedy staffer on eggheads: Robert D. Novak, "Kennedy's Braintrust, More Professors Enlist but They Play Limited Policy-Making Role," *Wall Street Journal,* Aug. 4, 1960; *Time* on why JFK had eggheads around: Aug. 15, 1960; Galbraith on eggheads: Grace and Fred M. Hechinger, "Election Cry 'Win with Harvard,'" *N.Y. Times Magazine,* Oct. 9, 1960; William French, "Galbraith, Influence," *Toronto Globe Magazine,* Nov. 5, 1960; brain-truster's wife on eggheads: Robert D. Novak, *op. cit.,* Aug. 4, 1960.

JFK to Nixon on relying on Sorensen: Richard M. Nixon, *Six Crises* (Garden City, Doubleday, 1962), p. 407; *Wall Street Journal* story on "Operation Academic": Robert D. Novak, *op. cit.,* Aug. 4, 1960; Dr. Beer and *Cleveland Plain Dealer* comment: guest editorial, *Chicago Tribune,* May 30, 1960; Dr. Beer said ADA for JFK: "Kennedy Endorsed in ADA's Appeal," *N.Y. Times,* Sept. 19, 1960; "ADA for Kennedy, Silent on Johnson," *N.Y. Times,* Aug. 28, 1960; Mrs. Roosevelt visited by JFK: Eleanor Roosevelt, "My Day, The Candidate's Visit," *N.Y. Post,* Aug. 17, 1960; "Kennedy Gains Mrs. Roosevelt's Aid," *N.Y. Post,* Aug. 15, 1960; "Mrs. Roosevelt Backs Tabling of Rights Bill," AP dispatch, New York, Aug. 18, 1960.

JFK visit to Truman: Press Conference, Independence (Mo.), Truman Library, *The Speeches of Senator John F. Kennedy, Presidential Campaign 1960* (Washington, U.S. Government Printing Office, 1961), p. 24; Betty Beale, "Politics Served . . . Well Seasoned," *Newark Star-Ledger,* Aug. 28, 1960; Philip Potter, "Kennedy," *Baltimore Sun,* Aug. 3, 1960; John G. McCullough, "Truman and Humphrey Sing Kennedy's Praises," *Philadelphia Bulletin,* Oct. 3, 1960; JFK to give Nixon hell, like Truman did Dewey: Richard F. Pourade, "A Rough Campaigner and His Pupil," *San Diego Union,* Sept. 4, 1960; JFK visit to Senator Byrd: *Charleston* (S.C.) *News and Courier,* Oct. 29, 1960; TRB on JFK left of Adlai: *New Republic,* Aug. 29, 1960; *N.Y. Post* waiting for August session: July 17, 1960.

Cincinnati Enquirer on hopes for bobtail session: Sept. 2, 1960; JFK and civil rights: "Big Day for Mr. Dirksen, Bad Day for Democrats," *N.Y. Post,* Aug. 10, 1960; *Chicago Tribune* on filibuster: "Broken Faith on Civil Rights," Aug. 10, 1960; Robert Novak on JFK inept: "Kennedy Letdown, After His Decisive Con-

vention Leadership, He Flounders in Senate over Civil Rights," *Wall Street Journal,* Aug. 19, 1960; N.Y. *Daily News* on reaction of Negroes: "Clever Trick, Or Was It?" Aug. 11, 1960; Mary McGrory on JFK's irritation: "Frets in Special Session, Kennedy Has Yen to Open Campaign," *Chicago Daily News,* Aug. 25, 1960; *Newsweek* on LBJ lolling: Aug. 22, 1960, p, 18; Robert D. Novak, "Failure of the Johnson Magic in the Senate Short Session Marks End of an Era," *Wall Street Journal,* Sept. 7, 1960.

Javits on JFK's behavior on medicare bill: Mary McGrory, "Finished Business," *N.Y. Post,* Aug. 24, 1960; *Time,* Sept. 5, 1960, p. 12; Jacob K. Javits, "Needed—A New Bipartisanship," *New Republic,* Jan. 23, 1961; *Time* on JFK's leadership: Sept. 5, 1960; JFK on bobtail session: "Top Labor Leaders Back Kennedy-Johnson Ticket," *N.Y. Times,* Aug. 27, 1960; Senators Scott and Keating exchange poems: *Congressional Record,* Aug. 31, 1960, pp. 17317–17319; *St. Louis Globe-Democrat* on JFK's leadership: "Disaster for Kennedy," Sept. 4, 1960; *St. Louis Post-Dispatch* defends JFK: "Who Won in Congress?" Sept. 2, 1960; *New America* on platform promises: "GOP-Dixiecrat Alliance Thwarts Liberal Hopes," Sept. 5, 1960; *Chicago Sun-Times* on JFK: "Carry What Fight to the Country?" Sept. 1, 1960; *Economist* on dangling carrots: "Congress Falls Flat," Sept. 10, 1960.

JFK's Labor Day speech on veto: *The Speeches of Senator John F. Kennedy, Presidential Campaign 1960,* p. 111; William H. Stringer on Nixon and Congress: "State of the Nations, Divided Government," Sept. 1, 1960; David Lawrence on conservatives: "Divided Government," *U.S. News & World Report,* Sept. 12, 1960; *Cleveland Plain Dealer* on JFK's leadership: "Kennedy's 'Leadership,'" Nov. 4, 1960; "People Machine": Thomas B. Morgan, "The People Machine," *Harper's,* January 1961, pp. 53–57; Roscoe Drummond, "People Predictor Revealed as Kennedy Secret Weapon," *N.Y. Herald Tribune,* Dec. 19, 1960; "Top Aides Deny It, 'Brain' Assist Seen in Kennedy Campaign," *Los Angeles Times,* Dec. 19, 1960; *Cincinnati Enquirer* editorial, "Politics' Ultimate Weapon," Dec. 22, 1960; Roscoe Drummond, "Why Not a President-Predictor?" *N.Y. Herald Tribune,* Dec. 25, 1960; *N.Y. Herald Tribune* editorial, "It's What Candidate Does That Counts," Dec.

30, 1960; "The People Machine," *Newsweek*, Apr. 2, 1962; Leonard Rubin, "A Construction That Is the Real Political You," *Village Voice*, July 19, 1962; Raymond Moley, "Kennedy's People Machine Has Been Tried Out Before and Failed," *Los Angeles Times*, Jan. 11, 1961. David H. Beetle on JFK discussing religion: " 'Let Washington Do It' Conflicts with Kennedy Call for Pioneer Spirit," *Knickerbocker News*, July 16, 1960; Bobby and religion: Philip Potter, "Democrats Forming Unit on Religion, Robert Kennedy Tells of Plan to Deal with Issue in Campaign," *Baltimore Sun*, Aug. 18, 1960; Bobby in Cincinnati on religion: Earl Mazo, "Who's Ahead in the Home Stretch?" *N.Y. Herald Tribune*, Sept. 25, 1960; "Faith and Tears," *N.Y. Post*, Sept. 4, 1960; LBJ on Kennedys and Hoffa: Rowland Evans Jr., "Kennedy Camp Attacks 'Vicious,' Says Johnson," *N.Y. Herald Tribune*, July 9, 1960; Bobby in Catskills: "Catskills Toured by Robert Kennedy," *N.Y. Times*, Sept. 18, 1960; Drew Pearson's column on JPK at Convention: "The Mystery of Joe Kennedy," *Newsweek*, Sept. 12, 1960; JPK in France will speak up later: *ibid.*; *N.Y. World-Telegram & Sun* on JPK in New York: "Heard Around City Hall, Kennedy's Father Lets Nixon Take Only Virginia," Sept. 23, 1960; Bobby's statement to New York Reform Democrats: *Time*, Aug. 8, 1960, pp. 17–18, and Oct. 10, 1960, p. 22.

Walton: Douglass Cater, "A Tide in the Affairs of John F. Kennedy," *Reporter*, Aug. 4, 1960; Ralph de Toledano on Bobby should vacation: "Nixon's Secret Weapon," King Features, Aug. 5, 1960; Nixon on family in campaign: *Six Crises*, p. 421; Bobby in New York radio interview: transcript, Barry Gray Show, WMCA, New York, Aug. 24, 1960; "Bobby Rips into Fight," *Des Moines Register*, Aug. 30, 1960; Jackie Robinson's reply: *N.Y. Post*, Aug. 26, 1960; Roulhac Hamilton on JFK apology for Bobby: "Apology to South Made by Kennedy," *Charleston* (S.C.) *News and Courier*, Sept. 4, 1960; William S. White on Smathers' plan: "Democrats Plan Soft-Sell in South," *Washington Star*, Aug. 29, 1960; Smathers on Nixon-NAACP: Dick Shelton, "Smathers, Ellington Fire Salvos at Democrat Rally," *Shelby* (N.C.) *Daily Star*, Oct. 11, 1960; Powell on Nixon–Ku Klux Klan: "Memo from Our Harlem

Correspondent," *National Review*, Nov. 5, 1960.

Jack Bell story: "Johnson Silent Partner as Jack Campaigns in Oregon," *Oregonian*, Sept. 8, 1960; Schlesinger on LBJ: "Johnson Role Minor, Schlesinger Asserts," *Los Angeles Times*, Sept. 27, 1960; LBJ on spending: Ernest B. Furgurson, "GOP Handling of West Hit by Johnson," *Baltimore Sun*, Sept. 16, 1960; LBJ on Rockefeller rewriting platform: *The Joint Appearances of Senator John F. Kennedy and Vice President Richard M. Nixon, Presidential Campaign 1960*, p. 130; John D. Morris, "Johnson Sticking to Liberal Theme," *N.Y. Times*, Sept. 16, 1960; LBJ's dual candidacy: "Attack Dual Candidacy of Sen. Johnson," AP dispatch, Dallas, Sept. 13, 1960; LBJ on Goldwater: Peter Lisagor, "LBJ Draws Rebel Yells in Dixie Swing," *Newark Star-Ledger*, Oct. 16, 1960; LBJ's platforms: Arthur Krock, "In Texas the Democratic Platform is Different," *N.Y. Times*, Sept. 22, 1960; Earl Mazo, "On Which Platform Does Johnson Stand?" *N.Y. Herald Tribune*, Oct. 11, 1960; *N.Y. World-Telegram & Sun* story on LBJ-Liberal: "He Had to Do It," Oct. 7, 1960; Johnson on TV interview on oil: *The Joint Appearances of Senator John F. Kennedy and Vice President Richard M. Nixon, Presidential Campaign 1960*, p. 131; *N.Y. Post* on LBJ: Oct. 3, 1960; Marianne Means story: *N.Y. Journal-American*.

Frank Conniff on Quemoy-Matsu: "Policy That Works Hurt by TV Debates," *N.Y. Journal-American*, Oct. 15, 1960; JFK on unwise place to draw line: *The Joint Appearances of Senator John F. Kennedy and Vice President Richard M. Nixon, Presidential Campaign 1960*, p. 120; JFK in Oct. 7 debate: *ibid.*, pp. 162–164; JFK three days later: *The Speeches of Senator John F. Kennedy, Presidential Campaign 1960*, p. 1107; JFK calls Nixon trigger-happy over "indefensible islands": *ibid.*, p. 574; *The Joint Appearances of Senator John F. Kennedy and Vice President Richard M. Nixon, Presidential Campaign 1960*, pp. 204–205; Admiral Yarnell quoted by JFK: *ibid.*, p. 207; "The Stampede Technique," *Cincinnati Enquirer*, Nov. 6, 1960; JFK quotes of Admiral Spruance: *The Joint Appearances of Senator John F. Kennedy and Vice President Richard M. Nixon, Presidential Campaign 1960*, p. 163; Spruance reply: "Adm. Spruance Says West Mustn't Quit Quemoy Now," *Philadelphia Bulletin*, Oct. 19,

1960; Oct. 13 debate, JFK on Ike letter to Green: *The Joint Appearances of Senator John F. Kennedy and Vice President Richard M. Nixon, Presidential Campaign 1960,* p. 206; Ike issued full text of letter: "President's 1958 Letter on Quemoy," *Philadelphia Bulletin,* Oct. 16, 1960; vanden Heuvel telegram to Herter: Sanford E. Stanton, "Kennedy Has Big Day Here," *N.Y. Journal-American,* Oct. 12, 1960.

Senator Lausche position: Jay G. Hayden, *Detroit News,* Oct. 14, 1960; Truman position: George E. Sokolsky, "Kennedy's Puzzling Stand on Quemoy," *N.Y. Journal-American,* Oct. 22, 1960; *N.Y. Times* report from Hong Kong: "Kennedy's Stand Outrages Taiwan," Oct. 15, 1960; Lubell on Quemoy-Matsu issue: Jerry Greene, "Let's Drop Quemoy as Issue, Says Jack," *N.Y. News,* Oct. 17, 1962.

JFK in Tulsa in 1959 on national unity: John F. Kennedy, *The Strategy of Peace,* p. 104; Lindley comment: "On 'Hitting Harder,'" *Newsweek,* Oct. 31, 1960; JFK on "Meet the Press" on Oct. 16: *The Joint Appearances of Senator John F. Kennedy and Vice President Richard M. Nixon, Presidential Campaign 1960,* pp. 244–247; *Los Angeles Times* comment: "Sen. Kennedy and the Islands," Oct. 18, 1960; *Chicago Daily News* comment: "Nixon Pushes Advantage in Quemoy-Matsu Debate," Oct. 19, 1960; Nixon quotation from *Six Crises:* p. 348; William S. White on LBJ began Cuban issue: "Castro Election Sleeper," *N.Y. Journal-American,* Sept. 14, 1960; JFK in Jacksonville, Fla.: Jerry Greene, "Campaign Circus," *N.Y. News,* Oct. 20, 1960; JFK in Evansville, Ind.: *The Speeches of Senator John F. Kennedy, Presidential Campaign 1960,* p. 477; JFK's Cuba speech in Cincinnati: *ibid.,* pp. 510–516; JFK visits to Smith: *The Joint Appearances of Senator John F. Kennedy and Vice President Richard M. Nixon, Presidential Campaign 1960,* p. 263; JFK on "Face the Nation": transcript, CBS-TV, Apr. 3, 1960; *Strategy of Peace* quotation: p. 132; *Washington Star* editorial: "Fooled by Castro," Oct. 9, 1960; Ambassador Smith testimony: *Subcommittee to Investigate the Administration of the Internal Security Act and Other Internal Security Laws, Hearings,* Part 9, Aug. 27, 30, 1960, p. 683; JFK on not interfering in L.A. internal affairs: J. F. Kennedy, *The Strategy of Peace,* p. 137; *Chicago Daily News* comment: "Kennedy Talks Nonsense in Blaming Ike for Cuba,"

Oct. 8, 1960; FDR's SOB remark: Stewart Alsop, "The Fruits of Castro's Plotting," republished *Congressional Record,* Mar. 25, 1963, pp. 4562–4564.

Trujillo's station supported JFK: FBIS report, Oct. 12, 1960; Nixon on his 1959 memo: *Six Crises,* pp. 351–352; Szulc-Meyer book, *The Cuban Invasion:* p. 65; Nixon quarantine speech: *The Speeches of Vice President Richard M. Nixon, Presidential Campaign 1960,* pp. 655–662; KENNEDY ADVOCATES U.S. INTERVENTION IN CUBA headline: R. M. Nixon, *Six Crises,* p. 353; JFK statement: *The Speeches of Senator John F. Kennedy, Presidential Campaign 1960,* pp. 679–681; JFK-CIA briefing: Ted Lewis, "Capital Circus," *N.Y. News,* Mar. 22, 1962; Joseph A. Loftus, "Kennedy Is Given a Secret Briefing by Dulles of CIA, World Situation Discussed for 2½ Hours, Emphasis Put on Cuba and Africa," *N.Y. Times,* July 23, 1960; Nixon's account: *Six Crises,* pp. 353–357; Larry G. Newman in *New Bedford Standard-Times:* "Kennedy, CIA Chief to Meet," July 19, 1960; Salinger denial 1962: William Knighton Jr., "Nixon's Cuba Charge Denied by Kennedy," *Baltimore Sun,* Mar. 21, 1962; David Wise, "Latest Nixon Cuban Blast Draws Only Silence in White House," *N.Y. Herald Tribune,* Mar. 23, 1962; CIA press release: Foster Hailey, "Nixon Adds a Note on Kennedy in Book," *N.Y. Times,* Mar. 29, 1962; Seaton quotation to *N.Y. Times* 1962: "Nixon Supported on Cuba Charge," *N.Y. Times,* Mar. 25, 1962; Raymond Moley quotation: "Nixon, Kennedy and Castro," *N.Y. Herald Tribune,* Apr. 15, 1962.

Fourth debate, Nixon calls JFK "irresponsible" and JFK rebuttal: *The Joint Appearances of Senator John F. Kennedy and Vice President Richard M. Nixon, Presidential Campaign 1960,* pp. 265–266; Murray Kempton comment: "Knees and Elbows," *N.Y. Post,* Oct. 7, 1960; Norman Thomas statement: "Norman Thomas Raps U.S. Cuba Policy," *New Haven Register,* Apr. 25, 1961; Senator Chavez statement: "Cuba Settlement Seen in Kennedy Victory," *San Diego Union,* Oct. 29, 1960; Corliss Lamont comment: Daniel Roberts, "Kennedy Saws Off Lamont," *Militant,* Oct. 31, 1960; "Still for Kennedy," *Militant,* Nov. 7, 1960, p. 4.

Curran on Khrushchev: "The Kremlin," *N.Y. News* editorial, Aug. 13, 1960; Lippmann on JFK and Nixon: *Time,* Nov. 7,

1960; Lippmann on FDR, 1932: David Elliott Weingast, *Walter Lippmann, A Study in Personal Journalism* (New Brunswick, Rutgers Univ. Press, 1949), p. 48; Eastland and other Southern support for JFK: Jay G. Hayden, "Eastland Talk Shows Why South Won't Bolt," *Washington Star*, Oct. 9, 1960; Warren Weaver Jr., "GOP Fund Charge Angers Kennedy," *N.Y. Times*, Aug. 19, 1960; Arthur Edson, "Texans Give Sen. Kennedy Big Turnout," *St. Louis Globe-Democrat*, Sept. 14, 1960; "Patterson to Make Plea," *Washington Post*, Aug. 13, 1960; Earl Mazo, "Troutman, Long a Kennedy Man," *N.Y. Herald Tribune*, Apr. 6, 1962; "Meriwether Has Grade A Record as Administrator, Campaigner," *South*, Feb. 20, 1961, reprinted *Congressional Record*, Feb. 23, 1961, pp. A1183–A1184; "Kennedy Agreed to 'No Troops,' Vandiver Claims," *Baltimore Sun*, May 10, 1961; Mrs. Meyer on Nixon and JFK: "Mrs. Eugene Meyer Tells Why She Quit Republicans," *N.Y. Herald Tribune*, Sept. 27, 1960; LBJ on JFK conservative: "Johnson Says Kennedy Is Conservative," *Los Angeles Times*, Sept. 19, 1960; LBJ on Ike sitting in rocking chair: "Johnson Shortens Talk in Brooklyn for Series," *Washington Post*, Oct. 6, 1960.

Tallulah Bankhead introduces JFK: *The Joint Appearances of Senator John F. Kennedy and Vice President Richard M. Nixon, Presidential Campaign 1960*, p. 343; Eunice Shriver statement: Louise Hutchinson, "Mrs. Robert Shriver Is Impatient for Campaign Swing," *Chicago Tribune*, Sept. 11, 1960; Princess Grace to help: "Aid to Kennedy Denied," *N.Y. Times*, Sept. 24, 1960; *Congressional Quarterly* count of promises: "220 Specific Promises Were Made by Kennedy," *Congressional Quarterly* release, Jan. 11, 1961; Republican National Committee list of 500: "500 Kennedy Campaign Pledges, Promises and Programs, Indexed," Research Division, Republican National Committee, January 1961; James Reston on promises: "Nixon and Kennedy Held Escaping Hard Analysis," *Louisville Courier-Journal*, Oct. 2, 1960.

Second debate, question on sacrifice: *The Joint Appearances of Senator John F. Kennedy and Vice President Richard M. Nixon, Presidential Campaign 1960*, p. 160; JFK speech in Kentucky: *The Speeches of Senator John F. Kennedy, Presidential Campaign 1960*, p. 1093; *Nashville Banner* on JFK-TVA: Sept. 22,

1960; Henry Wallace on JFK farm program: Allan Keller, "Wallace Sees 50% Food Cost Hike in Kennedy's Farm Program," *N.Y. World-Telegram & Sun*, Oct. 24, 1960; JFK remark to RN on farm program: *Six Crises*, p. 407; JFK on Herbert Hoover: *The Speeches of Senator John F. Kennedy, Presidential Campaign 1960*, pp. 885, 889; JFK against McKinley, Landon, and Dewey: *The Joint Appearances of Senator John F. Kennedy and Vice President Richard M. Nixon, Presidential Campaign 1960* pp. 165, 249, 345; JFK on 17 million go to bed hungry: "Kennedy Says 17 Million Go to Bed Hungry Every Night," *Washington Post*, Apr. 18, 1960; "How Many Hungry," *Minneapolis Tribune* editorial, Oct. 2, 1960; *N.Y. Daily News* reaction: "Was You There, Jack?" Apr. 9, 1960; Agriculture Dept. report: *Time*, Jan. 13, 1961; Hodges appointed for businessmen: Cecil Holland, "Hodges Will Direct Kennedy Businessmen": *Washington Star*, Aug. 14, 1960; W. M. Barbee on Hodges: Stan Opotowsky, *The Kennedy Government* (New York, Popular Library, 1961), p. 94.

JFK on his economic advisers: "Senator John F. Kennedy's Views on Business Problems," Democratic National Committee release, Oct. 10, 1960; JFK at Assoc. Business Pub. Conference: *The Speeches of Senator John F. Kennedy, Presidential Campaign 1960*, pp. 557–562; *Chicago Tribune* comments on JFK's new economic line: "Kennedy vs. Kennedy," Oct. 19, 1960; JFK in 1st debate: *The Joint Appearances of Senator John F. Kennedy and Vice President Richard M. Nixon, Presidential Campaign 1960*, p. 74; JFK on Africa: *The Speeches of Senator John F. Kennedy, Presidential Campaign 1960*, pp. 311–314; Rockefeller on JFK-disarmament absenteeism: "Kennedy Held Inactive as Senator," *San Diego Union*, Oct. 28, 1960; Nixonpedia: *Time*, Oct. 10, 1960, p. 27; Pocatello press conference: *The Speeches of Senator John F. Kennedy, Presidential Campaign 1960*, pp. 122–123; JFK boast on slogans: *ibid.*, pp. 280–281, 303–304; 342, 362, 369, 600, 616, 709, 768, 778, 1015.

JFK on Hoffa free: *The Joint Appearances of Senator John F. Kennedy and Vice President Richard M. Nixon, Presidential Campaign 1960*, p. 74; JFK on Dept. of Justice vs. Hoffa: *The Speeches of Senator John F. Kennedy, Presidential Campaign 1960*, pp. 273, 351, 475; *The*

Joint Appearances of Senator John F. Kennedy and Vice President Richard M. Nixon, Presidential Campaign 1960, p. 117; Hoffa on JFK: "Jimmy Hoffa Returns Mr. Kennedy's Fire," *Detroit Free Press,* reprinted *Chicago Tribune,* Oct. 7, 1960; JFK on Hoffa and Bridges not supporting him: *Washington Star* editorial, "Unwanted Support," Aug. 11, 1960; Gladwin Hill, "Brother Relates 'Slip' by Kennedy, Says He Intended to Reject Teamster and Longshore Leaders, Not Members," *N.Y. Times,* Aug. 22, 1960.

Communist party on JFK the lesser evil: *People's World* (West Coast Communist weekly), Sept. 10, 1960; medicare film: "Let's Talk About It Now!" *Cincinnati Enquirer* editorial, May 27, 1962; *Subcommittee on Freedom of Communications of Senate Commerce Committee, Hearings,* Mar. 27–29, 1961, pp. 605–608; Exhibits 58A–58D; prestige issue: John G. McCullough, "Kennedy Says He'll Restore Prestige Lost by the U.S.," *Philadelphia Bulletin,* Sept. 28, 1960; Michael Padev, "Kennedy's Prestige Issue Is Foolishness," *Indianapolis Star,* Oct. 30, 1960; *Chicago Tribune* editorial, "The Prestige Issue," Oct. 27, 1960; De Sapio on prestige: *Reporter,* Apr. 13, 1961, p. 30; JFK review of Larson book: "If the World's to Know Us," *N.Y. Times Book Review,* Feb. 8, 1959 (review of Arthur Larson, *What We Are For* (New York: Harper, 1959); *N.Y. Times* prints USIA polls: Oct. 25, 1960; *London Daily Telegraph* comments: "Prestige and Politics," Oct. 28, 1960.

JFK invokes FDR name: *The Speeches of Senator John F. Kennedy, Presidential Campaign 1960,* pp. 112, 172, 284, 292, 306, 374, 396, 402, 408, 427, 469, 487, 543, 591, 643, 656, 657, 708, 717, 769, 770, 781, 798, 821, 852, 913, 972, 1005, 1084, 1104, 1138, 1147, 1151, 1159, 1163, 1168, 1184, 1249; Manchester *Guardian's* Alistair Cooke on JFK visit to aircraft factory: "Unemployment in U.S., Sen. Kennedy Confirmed," Dec. 8, 1960; JFK on growth (Oct. 12): *The Speeches of Senator John F. Kennedy, Presidential Campaign 1960,* p. 558; Nixon on growth: *The Joint Appearances of Senator John F. Kennedy and Vice President Richard M. Nixon, Presidential Campaign 1960,* p. 90; *Chicago Daily News* comment: "Kennedy's Plea to Move Based on a Phony Promise," Nov. 4, 1960; Labor Day statement: *The Speeches of Senator John F. Kennedy, Presidential Campaign 1960,* pp. 112–113;

Holmes Alexander's reaction: "Kennedy Plays Phony Numbers Game," *New Haven Register,* Oct. 15, 1960; Nixon estimate on cost of JFK programs: *The Joint Appearances of Senator John F. Kennedy and Vice President Richard M. Nixon, Presidential Campaign 1960,* p. 77; LBJ's reaction: *ibid.,* pp. 184–186; *Washington Post* comment on LBJ: "Coming and Going," Oct. 11, 1960.

JFK on 90 days: Anthony Lewis, "Kennedy Pledges to Outdo Soviet in 'First 90 Days,'" *N.Y. Times,* Sept. 21, 1960; Henry Brandon on JFK's Churchill warning: "Ike v. Winston for President," *London Sunday Times,* Nov. 6, 1960; JFK on Republican gaps: *The Speeches of Senator John F. Kennedy, Presidential Campaign 1960,* p. 427; *N.Y. World-Telegram & Sun* on trick coin: "Jack, the Giant-Heckler," Oct. 24, 1960; JFK pledge on stable dollar: *The Speeches of Senator John F. Kennedy, Presidential Campaign 1960,* p. 825; Lucius Beebe comment: "The Democratic Road to Ruin," *San Francisco Chronicle,* Oct. 31, 1960; Ralph McGill comment: "Kennedy's Keen Edge Lost," *Washington Star,* Sept. 13, 1960; Mazo and Finch views on importance of TV debates: *"Great Debates" Symposium,* Center for the Study of Democratic Institutions of the Fund for the Republic, Santa Barbara, Calif.; Ed Folliard statement: "How Kennedy Views Nation's Mood," *Nation's Business,* December 1960, pp. 27–28; T. H. White comment: *The Making of the President 1960,* p. 289; Harvey Wheeler quotation: *"Great Debates" Symposium;* Lawrence Laurent on Madison Avenue sell: "TV's Election Role Polled," *Washington Post,* Jan. 22, 1961; JFK preparation for TV debates: David S. Broder, "Kennedy Did His Homework," *Washington Star,* Nov. 13, 1960; JFK man followed Nixon: Arthur Hoppe, "Mr. Richard Tuck, Loyal to the End," *San Francisco Chronicle,* Oct. 2, 1962; Sandor Vanocur in 1st debate: *The Joint Appearances of Senator John F. Kennedy and Vice President Richard M. Nixon, Presidential Campaign 1960,* p. 81.

Nixon on Ike's chagrin: *Six Crises,* p. 339; T. H. White on JFK not "debating": *The Making of the President 1960,* pp. 287–288; JFK gibberish on price line: *The Joint Appearances of Senator John F. Kennedy and Vice President Richard M. Nixon, Presidential Campaign 1960,* p. 79; JFK on oil-depletion allowances: *ibid.,* pp. 217–219; Henry Steele Commager and Earl Mazo on debates: *"Great Debates" Symposium;* Ralph McGill on radio reaction: *Chicago Daily News* editorial, "TV Electioneering," Oct. 7, 1960; *Richmond News Leader* on JFK's footwork: "Two Weeks to Go," Oct. 25, 1960; other comments on debates: *"Great Debates" Symposium;* JFK on 1964 debates: text, second Presidential press conference, *N.Y. Times,* Feb. 2, 1961.

Richard Scammon comment on religion in election: "Foreign Policy, Prestige Not a Big Election Factor," *Washington Post,* Dec. 15, 1960; *Commonweal* comment: July 22, 1960; Cushing nomination of Nixon as Good Will Man: R. M. Nixon, *Six Crises,* p. 421; JFK reluctance on Cardinal Spellman's dinner: T. H. White, *The Making of the President 1960,* p. 298; JFK's speech at Spellman dinner: *The Speeches of Senator John F. Kennedy, Presidential Campaign 1960,* pp. 666–669; JFK remarks to Nixon afterward: R. M. Nixon, *op. cit.,* p. 353; *Chicago Tribune* on Nixon's efforts: "Who Keeps Religion in the Campaign," Sept. 13, 1960; Gov. Almond's remarks: *Newsweek,* Sept. 12, 1960, p. 61; "Recommended Reading for a Governor," *Richmond News Leader* editorial, Sept. 1, 1960; "Religion, Whose Issue?" *Cincinnati Enquirer* editorial, Sept. 6, 1960; Gov. Faubus' remarks: Bo Byers, "Daniel Censures Ticket-Switchers," *Houston Chronicle,* Sept. 26, 1960; *Richmond News Leader* on JFK efforts to keep religious issue alive: "Two Weeks to Go," Oct. 25, 1960; James W. Wine in charge of Protestants: *Newsweek,* Sept. 12, 1960, p. 61; Dean Duncan, "Anti-Catholic Sentiments Held Acute in Kentucky, Kennedy Aide Says Religion No. 1 Issue," *Louisville Courier-Journal,* Sept. 11, 1960; Hodges on Catholic-Quaker tickets: R. M. Nixon, *op. cit.,* p. 366; Adlai's and Bobby's remarks in Libertyville: "Who Keeps Religion in the Campaign?" *Chicago Tribune* editorial, Sept. 13, 1960.

JFK on Truman's remark: *The Speeches of Senator John F. Kennedy, Presidential Campaign 1960,* p. 123; *The Joint Appearances of Senator John F. Kennedy and Vice President Richard M. Nixon, Presidential Campaign 1960,* p. 210; 3rd debate remarks by JFK and RN: *ibid.,* pp. 212–213; JFK with Powell in Harlem: *The Speeches of Senator John F. Kennedy, Presidential Campaign 1960,* pp. 580–583; "Memo from Our Harlem Correspondent,"

National Review, Nov. 5, 1960; Lehman at ILGWU rally on bigotry: "Smash Bigotry Forever Nov. 8, Ex-Gov. Lehman Asks ILGWU," *AFL-CIO News,* Sept. 24, 1960; Elie Abel on "Meet the Press": "Text of FEPC's Statement," *Detroit News,* Oct. 17, 1960; *The Joint Appearances of Senator John F. Kennedy and Vice President Richard M. Nixon, Presidential Campaign 1960,* pp. 247–248; Tallulah Bankhead on ILGWU program: *ibid.,* pp. 343–345; Ralph de Toledano comment: *Indianapolis News,* Oct. 3; 1960; *National Review* comment on Dr. Peale's statement: "A Little Positive Thought for Norman Peale," Sept. 24, 1960; William Walton's comment: Clayton Knowles, "Kennedy Backers See Upsurge Here," *N.Y. Times,* Sept. 14, 1960.

Sorensen on win or lose election in Houston: T. H. White, *The Making of the President 1960,* p. 260; Houston meeting: Robert S. Bird, "Houston Tension Rises over Kennedy, Clerics," *N.Y. Herald-Tribune,* Sept. 12, 1960; *The Speeches of Senator John F. Kennedy, Presidential Campaign 1960,* pp. 206–218; cut-off date on religion: "It's Time for a Cut-Off," *Minneapolis Tribune,* Sept. 16, 1960; Doris Fleeson on Peale reaction in N.Y.: "The Big Prize," *N.Y. Post,* Oct. 17, 1960; "Comeback of the Native," *N.Y. Post,* Oct. 16, 1960; *N.Y. Times* on effect on Jewish groups: Clayton Knowles, "Kennedy Backers See Upsurge Here," *N.Y. Times,* Sept. 14, 1960; "Different Kinds of Bigotry," *N.Y. Times* editorial, Oct. 20, 1960.

Time on JFK polls and Houston film showings: Oct. 10, 1960, p. 26; *Commonweal* comment on film showings: editorial, July 22, 1960; David Lawrence comment: "Is Democratic Committee Fanning Religious Issue?" *N.Y. Herald Tribune,* Oct. 12, 1960; Bobby's accusation of GOP: Merriman Smith, "Nixon Calls on Kennedy to Spike Brother's Lies," *N.Y. World-Telegram & Sun,* Oct. 24, 1960; Campaign Fair Practices Committee comment: *Report, Fair Campaign Practices Committee,* February 1962; *Greenville* (S.C.) *News* on literature: "That Anti-Roman Literature," Sept. 27, 1960; Sam Lubell statement: partial transcript; Louis Bean comment: Anti-Defamation League press release, Jan. 14, 1961; Gallup figures: "Catholics' Vote Analyzed, a 62% Switch to Kennedy," *N.Y. Herald Tribune,* Dec. 6, 1960; Roper comment: "Polling Post-Mortem," *Satur-*

day Review, Nov. 26, 1960; *N.Y. Times* on Negro vote: Laymond Robinson, "Negro Vote Gave Kennedy Big Push," Nov. 11, 1960; Eisenhower on Negro vote: Felix Belair Jr., "President Rueful on the Negro Vote," *N.Y. Times,* Dec. 14, 1960; Nixon statement to Simeon Booker: "What Republicans Must Do to Regain the Negro Vote," *Ebony,* April 1962; "Negro Vote Beat Him, Nixon Says," *N.Y. Herald Tribune,* Mar. 27, 1962.

Bobby's comments on how JFK won: David Sentner, "A Couple of Bobs Get All Tangled Up on Protocol South of the Border," *N.Y. Journal-American,* Nov. 26, 1960; *N.Y. Daily News* on reporting: "And Now a Word to Some Newspapers," Nov. 14, 1960; Fletcher Knebel on RN on reporting: "Nixon Believes Reporting Bias Cost Election," *Minneapolis Tribune,* Jan. 1, 1961; official tabulation: *1962 World Almanac,* p. 417; Sinatra phoned RN: Ruth Montgomery, "Rat Pack in White House?" *N.Y. Journal-American,* Dec. 13, 1960; *Time,* Dec. 5, 1960; *N.Y. Times* reflection: "The Presidential Election," Nov. 10, 1960; *N.Y. Times* endorsement of JFK and Morrie Ryskind's comment: "N.Y. Seems to Go for Kennedy, So Get to the Polls—or the Hills," *Los Angeles Times,* Nov. 2, 1960; "The Choice of a Candidate," *N.Y. Times,* Oct. 29, 1960; Bobby on election frauds: James McCartney, "Recount No Worry to Bobby," *Chicago Daily News,* Dec. 2, 1960.

Backgrounders on election frauds: Richard Wilson, "How to Steal an Election," *Look,* Feb. 14, 1961; *Hearing Before the Subcommittee on Privileges and Elections of the Committee on Rules and Administration, U.S. Senate,* 87th Congress, 1st Session, July 13, 1961; vote frauds in Chicago: Earl Mazo, "Chicago Poll Bares Old Political Tricks," *N.Y. Herald Tribune,* Dec. 6, 1960; *Chicago Tribune* editorial, "The Lesson of the Stolen Votes," Dec. 15, 1960; *Chicago Daily News* editorial, "Kennedy Has State's Vote but Election Riddles Stay," Dec. 16, 1960; "3 Get Jail in Vote Thefts!" *Chicago Tribune,* Mar. 7, 1962; *Chicago Tribune* editorial, "Surprise! Vote Fraud Is Punished," Mar. 7, 1962; *Chicago Tribune* comment: "Once an Election Is Stolen," Dec. 11, 1960.

Texas vote frauds: Raymond Moley, "Texas Needs Change in Election System," *Los Angeles Times,* Dec. 3, 1960; Earl Mazo, "Texas Vote Injunction Sought,"

N.Y. Herald Tribune, Dec. 5, 1960; Barry Goldwater, "Election 'Errors' in Texas," *Los Angeles Times,* Feb. 16, 1961; *Washington Post* editorial: "Flirting with Uncertainty," Dec. 14, 1960; Nixon decision: *Six Crises,* p. 413; JFK-Nixon post-election meeting: R. M. Nixon, *Six Crises,* pp. 406–410; Paul Martin, "What Jack Told Dick: He'll Ignore More. Radical Planks in Party's Platform," *Elmira Star-Gazette,* Jan. 5, 1961; *Time* description of Kennedys: July 11, 1960; JPK on appearing in public with JFK: Ira Henry Freeman, "Joseph Kennedy Is Back on Scene After Seclusion in the Campaign," *N.Y. Times,* Jan. 8, 1961.

Chapter 20. BEGIN

JFK-Ike meeting: Helen Fuller, *Year of Trial, Kennedy's Crucial Decisions,* p. 192; Fletcher Knebel on settling down: "Potomac Fever," *Washington Star,* Jan. 23, 1961; *Economist* on great expectations: "Great Expectations," Jan 21, 1961; TRB and Reston comments: quoted by Frank S. Meyer, "Principles and Heresies, Which Way for JFK?" *National Review,* Feb. 11, 1961; Frank Meyer prediction: *ibid.;* Shannon on JFK: *N.Y. Post,* Jan. 21, 1961; Hatcher statement: "The Word Is Out," *San Diego Union,* Sept. 22, 1962; Paul Martin on JFK's elite corps of newsmen: Gannett News Service, Feb. 18, 1961; Tom Wicker review: "Biographer's Hero," *N.Y. Times Book Review,* Sept. 30, 1962; Mauldin visit: reprinted from *Chicago Sun* in *San Francisco Chronicle,* Sept. 30, 1962; Vidal parody: *Newsweek,* Nov. 13, 1961.

JFK a golfer: William Knighton Jr., "Gilpatric To Be Defense Aide," *Baltimore Sun,* Dec. 22, 1960; "The Kennedy Vacations, Lots of Sports, Travel," *U.S. News & World Report,* Dec. 26, 1960; Ted Lewis, "Capital Circus," *N.Y. News,* Dec. 30, 1960; "The 'Presidential' Game," *Newsweek,* Jan. 16, 1961, p. 78; "Rule Barring Kennedy Golf Photos Eased," *N.Y. Herald Tribune,* Apr. 4, 1961; Fay on JFK's fear of golfing disclosure: William Manchester, "John F. Kennedy, Portrait of a President," *Holiday* series, May 1962; golf layout present: "White House Denies Kennedy Golf Tale," *N.Y. Times,* May 24, 1961; AP poll on Ike or JFK: Dillon Graham, "Could Kennedy Beat Eisenhower in Golf?" *Washington Star,* Apr. 10, 1961; Douglass Cater article: "Mr. Kennedy's Open Door Policy," *Reporter*, Apr. 27, 1961; Jacques Lowe on photos: "Picture-Conscious President," *Editor & Publisher*, Dec. 10, 1960; Burns in *New Republic:* "John Kennedy and His Spectators," *New Republic*, Apr. 3, 1961.

TV shows: David Lawrence, "Propriety of Sponsored TV for Kennedy Is Questioned," *N.Y. Herald Tribune*, Apr. 13, 1961; R. J. Donovan, "Kennedy's Way with Press," *N.Y. Herald Tribune*, Nov. 12, 1961; Douglass Cater, *op. cit.;* missile gap: *Time*, Feb. 17, 1961; JFK press conference: text, *N.Y. Times*, Feb. 9, 1961; "Missing Gap," *Chicago Daily News*, Feb. 10, 1961; Fulton Lewis Jr. comment: *Exclusive*, Feb. 15, 1961; J. F. ter Horst comment: "Political Missile Gap Held Closed," *Washington Star*, Nov. 4, 1961; prestige: "Escape Literature," *Reporter*, Mar. 28, 1963; Forrest Davis, "Is JFK De-Feathering the American Eagle?" *Cincinnati Enquirer*, June 2, 1961; JFK press conferences: texts, *Wall Street Journal*, Feb. 15 and Feb. 22, 1963; European reaction: Drew Middleton, "What Europe Thinks of Us Now," *Saturday Evening Post*, Aug. 19, 1961.

Theodore Draper on perfect failure: Tad Szulc and Karl E. Meyer, *The Cuban Invasion* (New York, Ballantine, 1962), p. 146; JFK remark on surrounding himself with best brains: Sidney Hyman, "The Testing of Kennedy," *New Republic*, Oct. 2, 1961; JFK at 2nd press conference: text, *N.Y. Times*, Feb. 2, 1961, question 24; JFK's Cuban invasion: Tad Szulc and Karl E. Meyer, *op. cit.;* Charles J. V. Murphy, "Cuba: The Record Set Straight," *Fortune*, September 1961; Stewart Alsop, "The Lessons of the Cuban Disaster," *Saturday Evening Post*, June 24, 1961; Hans J. Morgenthau, "The Trouble with Kennedy," *Commentary*, January 1962, pp. 51–55; Crosby S. Noyes, "Watching the World," *Washington Star*, Oct. 6, 1961; Hanson W. Baldwin, "The Cuban Invasion," *N.Y. Times*, July 31 and Aug. 1, 1961; James Daniel and John G. Hubbell, *Strike in the West: The Complete Story of the Cuban Crisis* (New York, Holt, Rinehart, 1963).

Fulbright was JFK choice for State: Harrison E. Salisbury, "Kennedy Mapping 100 Days of Action," *N.Y. Times*, Nov. 9, 1960; JFK campaign remark: *The Speeches of John F. Kennedy, Presidential Campaign 1960*, pp. 515, 609; Roa on invasion: Tad Szulc and Karl E. Meyer, *op. cit.,*

p. 122; Roa on Schlesinger's White Paper: *ibid.*, pp. 108–110; Stevenson reply in U.N.: *ibid.*, pp. 123–124, 134; party at White House: "A Real Nice Clambake at the Kennedys'," *N.Y. Post*, Apr. 19, 1961; Nehru: Ted Lewis, "Capital Circus," *N.Y. News*, Apr. 24, 1961; JFK on victory: transcript of press conference, *N.Y. Times*, Apr. 22, 1961; Marquis Childs on Bobby: "Bobby and The President," *Good Housekeeping*, May 1962; Bobby and Bowles: *Time*, Feb. 16, 1962; Lippmann on responsibility: "Post-Mortem on Cuba," *N.Y. Herald Tribune*, May 2, 1961; JFK confers with Republicans: "President Seeks Unity on Cuba," *World Almanac, 1962*, p. 100.

Bobby heads CIA investigation: *Time*, Jan. 5, 1962; Ike on Cuban invasion: "Sen. Scott Quotes Ike's Cuba Invasion Criticism," *N.Y. Herald Tribune*, Mar. 26, 1962; Udall blames Ike: "Udall Et Al.," *Baltimore Sun*, Apr. 26, 1961; Ted Lewis, "Capital Circus," *N.Y. News*, Apr. 24, 1961; *N.Y. Herald Tribune* comment: "Behaving Like a Statesman," May 3, 1961; Doris Fleeson comment: "The High Road," *N.Y. Post*, May 2, 1961; Sen. Clark on Ike's plan: William Anderson, "Charges Ike with Foolish Plan for Cuba Invasion," *Chicago Tribune*, May 15, 1961; James Burnham comment: "What Lesson, What Profit?" *National Review*, May 6, 1961; Reston in *N.Y. Times:* "The President and the Press, The Old Dilemma," May 10, 1961; ANPA speech on press: "Here is Text of Kennedy's Talk to Press, Asks Voluntary Curb to Guard Secrets," *Chicago Tribune*, Apr. 28, 1961; *St. Louis Post-Dispatch* comment: "Cold War and the Press," Apr. 30, 1961; *Los Angeles Times* comment: "The President and the Press," May 12, 1961; JFK meeting with editors: *Time*, May 19, 1961; *Newsweek*, May 22, 1961; David Wise, "Publishers See Kennedy, Turn Down Voluntary Censorship," *N.Y. Herald Tribune*, May 10, 1961; "Newspaper Leaders Reject Kennedy's Bid for Curb on Stories," *Wall Street Journal*, May 10, 1961; "Censorship Plan Avoided in Talk with President," *Editor & Publisher*, May 13, 1961; *Baltimore Sun* on meeting: "Still Baffled," May 10, 1961; Reston in *N.Y. Times:* "The President and the Press, The Old Dilemma," *N.Y. Times*, May 10, 1961; *N.Y. Times* editorial: May 10, 1961; JFK sent Taylor to complain: Hanson W. Baldwin, "Managed News: Our Peacetime Censorship," *Atlantic*, April 1963.

Reston on image: "Administration Grows Sensitive to Criticism," *Los Angeles Times,* July 17, 1961; Dealey-Bartlett episode: author, "Bartlett's Unfamiliar Quotations," *Human Events,* Jan. 13, 1962; republished *Congressional Record,* Mar. 27, 1962, p. A2396; *Time,* Nov. 17, 1961, p. 39; "A Man on Horseback," *N.Y. Times* editorial, Nov. 12, 1961; "Kennedy's Reply to Texan Related," *N.Y. Times,* Nov. 5, 1961; Bobby on criticism: Paul Martin, "Unfair Barbs Rankle President, Brother Says," *Washington Star,* Nov. 10, 1961; Merriman Smith comment: "The Kennedy Image: How It's Built," *U.S. News & World Report,* Apr. 9, 1962.

Bobby's numerous complaints: Fletcher Knebel, "Kennedy vs. The Press," *Look,* Aug. 28, 1962; Bobby sent ships to Dominican Republic: *Time,* Feb. 16, 1962; JFK wanted Bobby in Berlin crisis: *ibid.;* Schlesinger on Bobby: Dan Wakefield, "Bob," *Esquire,* April 1962; Max Lerner comment: "The Victors," *N.Y. Post,* Apr. 16, 1962; Robert Ruark comment: "Jack Kennedy, Young Caesar," *N.Y. World-Telegram & Sun,* Dec. 21, 1960; Bobby hates like father: Jack Anderson and Fred Blumenthal, "Washington Brother Act," *Parade,* Apr. 28, 1957; JPK to Considine on Bobby: "The Amazing Kennedys," *N.Y. Journal-American,* series began May 5, 1957; Marquis Childs on Bobby-Jackie episode: "Bobby and the President," *Good Housekeeping,* May 1962; JFK on nepotism: "Kennedy and Nixon Discuss Press Conferences, Nepotism," *N.Y. World-Telegram & Sun,* Oct. 18, 1960; Marquis Childs on JPK requests: "Joe Kennedy's Legend," *N.Y. Post,* Dec. 21, 1960; JFK on precedent: "Opportunity, or Trouble, for President's Brother?" *U.S. News & World Report,* Jan. 9, 1961; *Parade* 1957 story: Jack Anderson and Fred Blumenthal, *op. cit.;* night after 1960 election: Irwin Ross, "Joseph P. Kennedy, The True Story," *N.Y. Post* series, Jan. 13, 1961; Marianne Means on head of clan: "JFK Has Ascended to Power But He's Still His 'Father's Son,' " *N.Y. Journal-American,* Dec. 20, 1961; JPK arranged JFK-RN post-election meeting: Richard M. Nixon, *Six Crises,* pp. 403–405.

Meriwether appointment: *Newsweek,* Feb. 20, 1961; JFK on JPK: Irwin Ross, "Sen. Kennedy," *N.Y. Post* series, July 31, 1956; Sinatra visits: Marianne Means, "Why Ribicoff Quits JFK to Run for Senate," *N.Y. Journal-American,* Apr. 8, 1962;

"The Hollywood Set and the Kennedy Family," *U.S. News & World Report,* Oct. 16, 1961; Rubirosa before grand jury: Henry Lee, "Rubi Too Grand to Talk to Jury," *N.Y. News,* Jan. 10, 1962; JFK friend of Franco's p.r. man: "The Persuasive and Enduring Lobbyist," *Holiday,* April 1962, p. 155; Romagna firing: Roberta Hornig, "Stenographer of 4 Presidents Loses His Job to Machines," *Washington Star,* June 2, 1962.

N.Y. Herald Tribune canceled: Merriman Smith, "Washington's Pavements Bubble with the Heat, So Do Tempers," *Nation's Business,* July 1962; Robert Spivack comment: "Liberal's View—'Creeping Censorship,' " *N.Y. Herald Tribune,* June 10, 1962; Schlesinger-Taylor story: Frank L. Kluckhohn, *America: Listen!* pp. 165–166.

Galbraith confession: text, "Perils of Responsibility," Mysore University, Nov. 25, 1961; Bartlett on Galbraith: "Washington Behind-the-Scenes," *Richmond Times-Dispatch,* Aug. 19, 1962; Mansfield remark: *Time,* Aug. 24, 1962; Arthur Krock comment: "A Big Christmas at Palm Desert, Calif.," *N.Y. Times,* Dec. 26, 1961; U.S. planes in Katanga: "Transcript of Kennedy's Press Conference on Foreign and Domestic Affairs," *N.Y. Times,* Feb. 8, 1962, question 12; 1962 State-of-the-Union: text, *N.Y. Times,* Jan. 12, 1962; *Chicago Tribune* on Castro's trial: "They Stand Alone," Apr. 3, 1962; Joan Braden interview of Jackie: "An Intimate Chat with Jackie Kennedy" (*Saturday Evening Post*), republished N.Y. Post, Aug. 28, 1962.

Events leading to Cuban missile showdown: James Daniel and John G. Hubbell, *Strike in the West;* Max Lerner comment: "Cuba Policy," *N.Y. Post,* Sept. 14, 1962; Charles Keely comment: "The Door Is Open for Intervention," *San Diego Union,* Sept. 15, 1962; polls on Cuban issue: Joseph Alsop, "President Makes No Bones About It, He Likes the Pork-Chop Issues," *N.Y. Herald Tribune,* Oct. 4, 1962; RN on quarantine: Bill Becker, "Cuba Quarantine Is Urged by Nixon," *N.Y. Times,* Sept. 19, 1962; JFK and LBJ reactions: James Daniel and John G. Hubbell, *op. cit.,* p. 90; Ralph McGill on ignorant and contemptible: "Politics and Cuba," *N.Y. Herald Tribune,* Sept. 30, 1962; Joe Alsop's election post-mortem: "Matter of Fact," *N.Y. Herald Tribune,* Nov. 11, 1962; stated policy of managing news:

"People of the Week: Official Spokesman for 'Managed News,' " *U.S. News & World Report*, Apr. 1, 1963; Sylvester denial: *Chicago Tribune*, Mar. 27, 1963; Hanson W. Baldwin article: "Managed News: Our Peacetime Censorship," *Atlantic*, April 1963; Agronsky episode: James Daniel and John G. Hubbell, *Strike in the West*, pp. 7–8; Ted Lewis comment: "Capital Circus," *N.Y. News*, Sept. 5, 1962.

McNamara's TV show: text, Defense Dept.; Warren Rogers Jr. article: "Reflections on the Bob and John Show," *New Republic*, Feb. 23, 1963; *Chicago Tribune* editorial: Mar. 7, 1963; JFK's grand design: Stewart Alsop, "The Collapse of Kennedy's Grand Design," *Saturday Evening Post*, Apr. 6, 1963; Canadian row: Michael Gillan, "Premier Takes Canada Out of 'New Frontier,' " *Philadelphia Inquirer*, Feb. 2, 1963; West German official: private sources; JFK background briefing and European reaction: *Newsweek*, Jan. 14, 1963; Walter Trohan, "Report from Washington," *Chicago Tribune*, Jan. 14, 1963; Nixon on salesmanship: author, "Nixon Thinks Kennedy Can Be Beaten in 1964," *Washington Star*, Mar. 5, 1963; William Shannon on liberal disenchantment: *N.Y. Post*, Mar. 21, 1963; Gore Vidal on Bobby: "The Best Man 1968," *Esquire*, March 1963; Mort Sahl quotation: Vernon Scott, "Life on the Grim New Frontier: Mort Sahl Wants His License Renewed," *Washington News*, Mar. 6, 1963; Father Coughlin interview: Harold Schachern, "Fr. Coughlin's 1st Interview in 20 Years," *Detroit News*, Dec. 16, 1962; Joseph Barry on Herb Gold: *N.Y. Post*, June 1, 1962; JFK's Seattle speech: Chalmers M. Roberts, "Text for the Future," *Washington Post*, Nov. 18, 1961; "A Plea for Maturity," *Washington Post* editorial, Nov. 18, 1961; "Pressured President," *Washington Star* editorial, Nov. 18, 1961; *Time*, Jan. 5, 1962, p. 9; JFK on what to do?: William Manchester, "John F. Kennedy, Portrait of a President," *Holiday*, April 1962; Ben B. Seligman comment: "Courage and Economics in Washington," *Dissent*, Winter 1962, pp. 23–28; William Shannon comment: "Curtain Time," *N.Y. Post*, Feb. 12, 1961.

JFK remark on businessmen: Wallace Carroll, "Steel, A 72-Hour Drama with an All-Star Cast," *N.Y. Times*, Apr. 23, 1962; JFK on tax legislation: *Time*, Aug. 24, 1962; *London Times* comment: "New Administration Losing Momentum," June 23, 1961; William Shannon comment: "The Kennedy Administration, The Early Months," *American Scholar*, pp. 481–488; Joe Alsop on polls on Birchites: "Nixon's Quasi-Victory," *N.Y. Herald Tribune*, June 8, 1962; *N.Y. Herald Tribune* on polls on Berlin: political notes by staff, July 19, 1961; Joe Alsop on polls on Cuban issue: "President Makes No Bones About It, He Likes the Pork-Chop Issues," *Los Angeles Times*, Oct. 4, 1962.

Roscoe Drummond comment: "His Tactics on Urban Bill Believed Harming Kennedy," *N.Y. Herald Tribune*, Mar. 2, 1962; JFK on Urban Dept. in '60: *The Speeches of Senator John F. Kennedy, Presidential Campaign 1960*, pp. 551–554; JFK on Republicans on Rules Committee and Executive Order: Russell Baker, "House Rules Unit Kills Urban Bill, President to Act," *N.Y. Times*, Jan. 25, 1962; Republican support for Weaver: "Proposed Department of Urban Affairs," *Congressional Record*, Jan. 29, 1962, p. 913; Thomas O'Neill comment: "Young Old Master," *Baltimore Sun*, Jan. 26, 1962; Reston comment: "President Squares Off," Jan. 25, 1962; *New Republic* comment: "Urban Affairs," Feb. 5, 1962; JFK on Lodge's remark in '60: *The Speeches of Senator John F. Kennedy, Presidential Campaign 1960*, p. 1151; *Cincinnati Enquirer* comment: "RIP: Urban Affairs," Feb. 24, 1962; Humphrey-Wilkins telegram: *Newsweek*, Feb. 5, 1962; *Newsday* comment: reprinted, *Congressional Record*, Feb. 27, 1962, pp. A1467–A1468; JFK strategy: "Kennedy's Strategy for Winning Elections—How It Works," *U.S. News & World Report*, Feb. 12, 1962.

JFK note to Khrushchev: Ted Lewis, "Capital Circus," *N.Y. News*, Mar. 24, 1961; *Time*, Mar. 31, 1961; Karl Meyer comment: "Waiting for Kennedy," *Progressive*, September 1961, pp. 12–15; JFK on Laos: transcript of press conference, *N.Y. Times*, Mar. 24, 1961; Gromyko in rose garden: Mary McGrory, "No Sure Answers Now," *Washington Star*, Oct. 12, 1961; Ayub Khan remark: *Newsweek*, June 26, 1961, p. 15; Jean Daniel comment: "Kennedy and De Gaulle," *New Republic*, Apr. 20, 1961; Holmes Alexander, "France Gives U.S. Some Lessons in Good Diplomacy," *Richmond News Leader*, Oct. 26, 1961; JFK called in Nixon after Bay of Pigs: *World Almanac 1962*, p. 100; JFK speech at Coliseum: *The*

Speeches of Senator John F. Kennedy, Presidential Campaign 1960, p. 909; JFK-Khrushchev met in '59: "U.S., Russian Chieftains Met Before, Didn't Talk," *New Haven Register*, May 28, 1961; John F. Kennedy, *The Strategy of Peace*, pp. 8–14; Vienna trip comment by *Richmond News Leader:* "Silver Screen vs. Iron Curtain," June 6, 1961; JFK on "cold winter": *Newsweek*, Dec. 25, 1961, p. 44; Khrushchev boast: Marguerite Higgins, "At the Brink," *N.Y. Herald Tribune*, Aug. 27, 1962; *Time* on JFK's return trip: Jan. 5, 1962, p. 11; JFK outlook somber: Henry Brandon, "Reflections on Vienna," *London Sunday Times*, June 11, 1961.

JFK's Berlin speech: text, *U.S. News & World Report*, Aug. 7, 1961; JFK's UN speech: text, *Wall Street Journal*, Sept. 26, 1961; Fay on shelters: William Manchester, "John F. Kennedy, Portrait of a President," *Holiday*, April 1962, p. 167; Marquis Childs comment: "Nehru's Visit," *N.Y. Post*, Oct. 26, 1961; Nixon should have won: *Time*, Feb. 10, 1961; JFK can't quit: William Manchester, "John F. Kennedy, Portrait of a President," *Holiday*, May 1962; DiSalle quotation: Arthur Edson, "Kennedy at 44, Has He Changed Much?" *Newark Star-Ledger*, May 28, 1961; State-of-the-Union 1961: text, *N.Y. Times*, Jan. 30, 1961; *Wall Street Journal* comment: "One View of the Nation," Jan. 31, 1961; Joe Alsop comment: "The Dialogue Begins," *N.Y. Herald Tribune*, Feb. 1, 1961.

JFK's can of worms: William Manchester, "John F. Kennedy, Portrait of a President," *Holiday*, April 1962; Irving Kristol comment: "The Drift of Things," *Encounter*, January 1962, pp. 108–112; David Lawrence comment: "Future U.S. Prestige Seen Not Up to Kennedy Alone,"

N.Y. Herald Tribune, Jan. 17, 1961; JFK can't do everything: "Kennedy's Next Three Years," *Life* editorial, Jan. 5, 1962; "Operation Counterattack": author, "Everything Is Coming up Roses—And Thorns —on the New Frontier," *Los Angeles Times*, Mar. 18, 1963; JFK at Fresno: text, speech before California Democratic Councils Convention, Feb. 12, 1960; Carroll Kilpatrick remark: "JFK Leadership Image Dulls in Washington," *Washington Post*, Mar. 18, 1963; Mar. 6, 1963, press conference on winter of discontent: text, *Wall Street Journal*, Mar. 7, 1963; Reston comment: "Kennedy's Philosophy Seen in Adversity," *Richmond Times-Dispatch*, Mar. 8, 1963; Doris Fleeson and *Time* quotations: *Time*, Mar. 15, 1963.

Thomas Hart Benton on cultural activities: Austin C. Wehrwein, " 'Dilettante' View Laid to Kennedys, Approach to Culture Decried by Thomas Hart Benton," *N.Y. Times*, May 13, 1962; Walter Trohan on Frost: reprinted from *Chicago Tribune* in *Human Events*, Apr. 6, 1963; Malcolm Muggeridge report: "Malcolm Muggeridge's American Diary," Bell-McClure Syndicate; Murray Kempton on JFK like Duke of Edinburgh: "Style and Substance," *N.Y. Post*, Jan. 30, 1962; Art Hoppe on JFK's swim at Santa Monica: "Mr. Kennedy's Big Navel Engagement," *San Francisco Chronicle*, Aug. 22, 1962; Peter Lawford's *McCall's* article: January 1963; Mrs. Javits on White House party: "A Guest's-Eye View of White House Party," *N.Y. Post*, Apr. 11, 1962.

APPENDIX B

Bailey Report, reprinted from *U.S. News & World Report*, Aug. 1, 1960.

Index

ABC, "Adventures on the New Frontier," 509
Abel, Elie, and JFK, 488
Abelson, Robert, 428
Acheson, Dean, 127, 129, 355, 557; on JFK and Algeria, 286
Adenauer, Konrad, 292; and JFK, 507
The Affluent Society (Galbraith), 298–299, 300
The Age of Jackson (Schlesinger), 302
The Age of Roosevelt (Schlesinger), 302
Agronsky, Martin, 553; and JFK, 239; on 1956 Chicago Convention, 189
Aiken, George, 196
Ajemian, Robert, on JFK and Catholicism, 336
Alcorn, Meade, 203; on JFK, 315
Alexander, Holmes, 343; on Eisenhower, JFK, and Cuba, 529; on Inaugural Address, 22–23; on JFK, 167, 259, 260; on JFK and religion, 340; on JFK's politics, 567
Algeria, JFK on, 283–286
All My Sons (Miller), 18
Allen, Frederick Lewis, 36
Allen, Robert S., 329, 536; on Kennedy Sr., 403
Almond, James L., on Nixon and religion, 484
Alsop, Joseph, 123, 329; and JFK, 3, 12; on JFK after Vienna, 571–572; on JFK State of Union Message, 575; on Kennedy Sr., 57; on polls, 562; on West Virginia primary, 341
Alsop, Stewart, 123, 517, 552; JFK, 276; on JFK's Catholicism, 481; on Kennedy Sr., 58; quoted, 412; on Robert Kennedy, 383
Ambrose, Margaret, 103
America, on JFK and Catholicism, 278, 279; on TEW bill, 109
American Bar Association, and JFK, 283
American Civil Liberties Union, and Schlesinger, 303
American Committee for Cultural Freedom, and Schlesinger, 303
Americans for Constitutional Action, rates JFK, 294; voting index of, 381
Americans for Democratic Action, 9, 140, 183, 249, 271,

277, 293, 415, 420; formed, 134, 135, 137; on JFK-Johnson ticket, 412; on L. B. Johnson, 379; rates JFK, 212, 294; Schlesinger a founder of, 303; voting index of, 381
AFL–CIO, 367; Committee on Political Education (COPE), 261, 488; on JFK-Johnson ticket, 404
American Freedom and Catholic Power (Blanshard), 488–489
American Medical Association, Archives of Surgery, Vol. 71, JFK case in, 162; case Number 3, 377
American Mercury, on JFK, 215
American Scholar, on "Irish Mafia," 562; on JFK, 49–50
American Society of Newspaper Editors, JFK speaks on Cuba to, 530–531; JFK's speech to, 341–342
American Veterans Committee, and JFK, 253
American Weekly, JFK article in, 162–163
Amory, Cleveland, on JFK, 72–73
Anderson, Clinton, 183; and JFK, 246, 351
Anderson, Eugene, at Chicago Convention, 189; on JFK, 408
Anderson, L. T., on JFK and religious issue, 340
Arnold, William, 130
Aronsohn, J. William, 108
Arvey, Jake, 371
Asbury, Herbert, on JFK, 278
Ascali, Max, on JFK appointments, 10
Association of Blauvelt Descendants, East Orange, N.J., genealogy of, 107–109
Atlanta Constitution, on JFK, 201, 368; on radio and TV debates, 479
Atlantic Monthly, JFK speeches in, 166, 167; Baldwin article in, 551
Auchincloss, Hugh D., 557; weds Janet Bouvier, 159
Auden, W. H., 16

Bacall, Lauren, 389
Bailey, John, 179–180, 181, 319
"Bailey Report," 179–180, 182, 326, 490, 492; text of, 587–598
Baldwin, Hanson W., 551–553

Baldwin, Stanley, 78
Baltimore Sun, on Democratic National Convention, 393; on JFK, 211, 266, 343, 532, 564; on JFK's political skill, 564; on JFK's Presidential campaign, 328, 331; on JFK in West Virginia primaries, 347–348; on James Wine, 485
Bancroft, Elizabeth, 301
Bankhead, Tallulah, on JFK, 457, 488
Barbee, W. Millard, 460
Barber, Samuel, 16
Barden, Graham A., 131–132
Bardot, Brigitte, and Sinatra, 352
Barnett, David, 195–263
Bartlett, Charles, 158, 332–333, 552; on JFK, 220; on JFK campaign organization, 324; on JFK-Dealey encounter, 534–535; on West Virginia primaries, 349
Baruch, Bernard, Truman letter to, 118
Bates, George J., 583
Batista, Fulgencio, 447, 448
Bay of Pigs, 2, 9, 506, 556, 570, 577. *See also* Cuba
Bayh, Birch, 549
Bean, Louis, on Catholic vote, 492; on JFK, 181
Beck, Dave, 204, 262, 263, 264, 273
Beebe, Lucius, on JFK, 473
Beer, Samuel H., 379, 415
Beetle, David H., on JFK's religion, 430
Bell, Jack, on JFK at Chicago Convention, 189; on L. B. Johnson, 435–436
Benchley, Robert, 36
Bennett, John C., on Catholicism, 277
Benson, Ezra Taft, 170, 315
Benton, T. H., 579
Bergman, Ingmar, 161
Berkshire Evening Eagle, on John F. Fitzgerald, 33
Berkshire Evening News, on JFK, 88
Berle, Adolf A. Jr., and Cuba, 518, 525
Bersbach, F. John, 107
Bickel, Alexander, on Robert Kennedy, 270
Big Business, and JFK, 460–462, 537–538
"The Big Decision" (Schlesinger), 304–305
Billings, Lemoyne, 71, 72, 76; and JFK, 92